Changes in Exchange Rates in Rapidly Developing Countries

NBER–East Asia Seminar on Economics
Volume 7

National Bureau of Economic Research
Tokyo Center for Economic Research
Korea Development Institute
Chung-Hua Institution for Economic Research
Hong Kong University of Science and Technology
National University of Singapore

Changes in Exchange Rates in Rapidly Developing Countries

Theory, Practice, and Policy Issues

Edited by   Takatoshi Ito and
Anne O. Krueger

The University of Chicago Press

Chicago and London

TAKATOSHI ITO is professor in the Institute of Economic Research at Hitotsubashi University, Tokyo, and a research associate of the National Bureau of Economic Research. ANNE O. KRUEGER is the Herald L. and Caroline L. Ritch Professor of Economics, senior fellow of the Hoover Institution, and director of the Center for Research on Economic Development and Policy Reform at Stanford University, and a research associate of the National Bureau of Economic Research.

The University of Chicago Press, Chicago 60637
The University of Chicago Press, Ltd., London
© 1999 by the National Bureau of Economic Research
All rights reserved. Published 1999
Printed in the United States of America
08 07 06 05 04 03 02 01 00 99   1 2 3 4 5
ISBN: 0-226-38673-2 (cloth)

Library of Congress Cataloging-in-Publication Data

Changes in exchange rates in rapidly developing countries : theory, practice, and policy issues / edited by Takatoshi Ito and Anne O. Krueger.
     p.   cm.—(NBER–East Asia seminar on economics ; v. 7)
    Includes bibliographical references and index.
    ISBN 0-226-38673-2 (alk. paper)
    1. Foreign exchange—Government policy—East Asia—Congresses.   2. Foreign exchange—Government policy—Developing countries—Congresses.   3. Foreign exchange rates—East Asia—Congresses.   4. Foreign exchange rates—Developing countries—Congresses.
I. Itō, Takatoshi, 1950– . II. Krueger, Anne O. III. Series: NBER–East Asia seminar on economics (Series) ; v. 7.
HG3873.E18C48 1999
338.4′56′091724—dc21   98-33860
                                        CIP

Contents

Acknowledgments

This volume contains edited versions of papers presented at the NBER–East Asia Seminar on Economics' seventh annual conference, held in Hong Kong, China, on 19–22 June 1996.

We are indebted to members of the program committee who organized the conference, and to Chung-Hua Institution, Taipei; Korea Development Institute, Seoul; Tokyo Center for Economic Research; the National University of Singapore; and the Hong Kong University of Science and Technology for their sponsorship of the conference and of the ongoing seminar series.

Professor Francis Lui and his colleagues in the Economics Department of the Hong Kong University of Science and Technology were the local hosts. All participants are grateful to them for the excellent organization and hospitality they provided.

The National Bureau of Economic Research provided logistical support, as well as support for the North American–based conference participants. We are greatly indebted to the NBER, as well as to the Asian institutions which support the research and conferences.

Introduction

Takatoshi Ito and Anne O. Krueger

Choice of exchange rate regime is a key policy variable for all countries. The exchange rate is the crucial variable linking the domestic economy to the international economy. An exchange rate that made exporting relatively attractive was clearly a key component of East Asian countries' rapid economic growth over the past several decades.

Yet recognition of the importance of the exchange rate regime is not sufficient to guide policymakers in their choice of regime. Policymakers can and do decide, at least in the short run, on the determinants of the nominal exchange rate. They can fix that rate in terms of a single currency or a basket of currencies, they can let the exchange rate float and let the market determine the exchange rate, they can determine a rule by which they will adjust the nominal exchange rate (when, e.g., the domestic rate of inflation exceeds the international rate), or they can follow some combination of these policies.

But other policies—monetary and fiscal policy which determine the rate of inflation, the degree of capital controls which affects the supply and demand for foreign exchange, and protection and the height of tariffs—all affect the way the exchange rate operates and influence the "real exchange rate." While in the short run, authorities might set a fixed nominal exchange rate despite rapid inflation, in the longer run, such an exchange rate cannot be maintained unless either the inflation rate is sharply reduced or exchange controls are imposed. Market determination of the price level ensures that the real exchange rate cannot over the longer term be determined solely by choice of a nominal exchange rate at the existing price level.

Takatoshi Ito is professor in the Institute of Economic Research at Hitotsubashi University, Tokyo, and a research associate of the National Bureau of Economic Research. Anne O. Krueger is the Herald L. and Caroline L. Ritch Professor of Economics, senior fellow of the Hoover Institution, and director of the Center for Research on Economic Development and Policy Reform at Stanford University, and a research associate of the National Bureau of Economic Research.

Broadly speaking, in the longer run, there are three alternatives. Under the first alternative, the nominal exchange rate can be fixed and monetary and fiscal policy can then be tightened or eased as the balance-of-payments position of the country deteriorates or improves. In that case, the domestic price level is adjusted (through monetary and fiscal policy) to achieve the real exchange rate appropriate to the country's international position.

Under the second alternative, the nominal exchange rate can float and monetary and fiscal policy can be used to achieve domestic economic objectives. If domestic price stability were achieved, of course, the nominal exchange rate could remain fairly constant, unless significant external shocks warranted a change in the real exchange rate.

Under the third alternative, exchange controls are used to contain demand for foreign exchange to available supply. In this policy regime, the nominal exchange rate loses much of its function as a signal for resource allocation; overvaluation of the real exchange rate (relative to the rate that would clear the foreign exchange market without exchange control) tends to discourage exports and to lead to increasingly protectionist measures.

Until recent years, most developing countries—except those in East Asia—chose the third alternative and attempted to grow through "import substitution," which entailed heavy protection for domestic industries. East Asian countries instead chose various nominal exchange regimes that maintained a real exchange rate for exports that resulted in rapid growth. In Korea, for example, the exchange rate was floating during the latter half of the 1960s and frequently adjusted to account for inflation differentials until the mid-1980s. Only when inflation was reduced to a rate similar to that of internationally traded goods was the nominal exchange rate maintained at a relatively constant level.

While it became evident that the third alternative—exchange controls and heavy domestic protection—was inconsistent with good growth performance, experience also demonstrated that inflation itself had costs for economic growth. As that was recognized, some countries began using the fixity of the nominal exchange rate as a policy device to bring down the domestic rate of inflation. That policy, too, has its costs, and it has raised significant questions, especially since Mexico was forced, at the end of 1994, to abandon the policy and undergo a massive devaluation.

While questions have arisen about the linkages between exchange rate regimes, growth, and inflation, East Asian and other countries are liberalizing their capital accounts and removing remaining tariffs and other barriers to trade. Issues arise as to appropriate exchange rate policy in these circumstances. Moreover, for East Asian countries other than Japan, important issues arise with regard to their choice of peg or currency basket, given the importance of both yen and dollar transactions.

At the seventh annual NBER–East Asia Seminar on Economics, questions regarding nominal and real exchange rate behavior, inflation, and economic growth were considered. This volume contains the papers presented at that conference, as well as discussants' comments on them.

The first group of papers examines the cross-country behavior of exchange rates, capital flows, and financial crises. The paper by Sebastian Edwards contains an analysis of the reasons why the authorities choose alternative exchange rate regimes. Edwards uses a model in which there is a trade-off between inflation and unemployment targets and the authorities are choosing the exchange rate regime to minimize their losses given the relative costs they associate with inflation and unemployment. A flexible exchange rate regime results in higher inflation rates but smaller unemployment (or growth) losses, whereas a fixed exchange rate reduces inflation but at the cost of more unemployment. Edwards also modifies the analysis to take into account regimes in which the exchange rate is fixed but is then altered when growth-unemployment costs of the fixed exchange rate regime mount to unacceptable levels. In that instance, the authorities incur political costs in altering the exchange rate.

Edwards then implements his model empirically. He shows that the choice of exchange rate regime depends on the history of political instability: more unstable countries have, all else given, a lower probability of selecting a pegged exchange rate regime. Capital controls also seem to accompany pegged exchange rate regimes.

The second paper, by Eichengreen and Rose, uses panel data over a 30-year period from the OECD countries to test the extent to which financial crises are contagious across countries. Financial crises are defined as large changes in exchange rates, interest rates, or foreign exchange reserves. Even after the effects of macroeconomic fundamentals have been controlled, a crisis in one country is shown to increase the probability of a crisis in another country. The paper attempts to specify different channels of contagion through the strength of trade linkages and macroeconomic similarity. Contagion appears to spread more easily to countries that are closely linked through trade than to countries with similar macroeconomic circumstances.

Milesi-Ferretti and Razin present a paper that addresses some key questions for policymakers: What determines a country's susceptibility to a sharp reversal of capital flows? Is the composition of capital flows important in determining sustainable current account balances? And, finally, what factors have contributed to the vulnerability of developing countries to capital flow reversals? Here the authors consider such factors as the goodness of macroeconomic policy and the level of real interest rates. They start by developing a model of intertemporal solvency, defining a theoretically sustainable current account situation. They then consider episodes in particular countries in Latin America (Chile, Colombia, Mexico) and in East Asia (Korea, Malaysia, Thailand) in the 1980s and 1990s. Based on their findings across countries and in the two decades, they conclude that a large number of macroeconomic and structural factors contribute to the likelihood of an external crisis and believe that there is no single factor that can be cited as dominant.

The second group of papers examines the behavior of real exchange rates for various countries. The behavior of the real exchange rate, of course, depends on the domestic price level as well as the nominal exchange rate. But in the longer term, economists believe, the equilibrium real exchange rate will prevail. One of the best known empirical hypotheses in the literature is that of Balassa and Samuelson: they noted that as countries' per capita incomes rise, purchasing power in domestic currency tends to fall. That is, a dollar's worth of a currency from a poor country will buy more in that country than a dollar's worth of a rich country's currency will buy in that country.

The paper by Ito, Isard, and Symansky tests the Balassa-Samuelson hypothesis, interpreted in a growth context. Ito et al. note that since rapid economic growth implies rising real incomes, there should be more real exchange rate appreciation in richer countries because of the differential in productivity growth between traded and nontradable sectors. Ito et al. use data for the APEC countries for the period 1973–92. They find that Japan, Korea, and Taiwan all experienced real exchange rate appreciation, in accordance with the Balassa-Samuelson hypothesis. However, Hong Kong and Singapore experienced only very moderate real exchange rate appreciation despite their rapid growth, while other rapidly growing countries—Thailand, Indonesia, and Malaysia—did not experience real appreciation. In the cases of Hong Kong and Singapore, rapid growth in the service sector may account for the failure of exchange rates to appreciate more than they did. However, closer examination of the components of the real exchange rate leads Ito et al. to conclude that there is no uniform pattern for the movement of nontradable prices relative to tradables, and that tradable prices, at least for most of the APEC countries, do not show international arbitrage.

In his paper, Jeffrey Sachs sets forth and tests the hypothesis that differences in Asian and Latin American experiences with real exchange rates are related to differences in their resource endowments. The labor-abundant developing countries of East Asia have tended to export manufactures, while land- and resource-abundant Latin American countries have tended to export agricultural and mining products. Theory suggests that resource abundance will result in a high price of nontradable goods, thus leaving a more appreciated real exchange rate and squeezing out manufacturing production. That, in turn, will lead to slow growth. In the longer run, real depreciation will stimulate more rapid growth of labor-intensive, manufacturing, industries. Sachs finds confirmation of his hypothesis in the data.

The Lin paper examines real exchange rate movements from the demand side. Lin first develops several alternative models with three goods (exportables, importables, and nontradables) and suggests several possible reasons why purchasing power parity might not hold. For each reason, the testable implication for real exchange rate behavior is developed. One particular hypothesis of interest is that the currency of the country with more rapid consumption growth will experience real appreciation. Empirical estimates, using his models, are formulated in the context of time-series data. Exchange rates of Korea relative to Japan and of Taiwan vis-à-vis the United States are tested for cointegration. Lin found among other things that the exchange rate did not stay stationary, mainly due to the trend behavior of the yen. A hypothesis of convergence of real consumption among these countries was also rejected.

The next group of papers considers particular issues of relevance to East Asia. In his paper, Takagi examines the behavior of exchange rates of Asian developing countries over the period 1980–95 in an effort to ascertain how different East Asian countries resolve the dilemma over the weights given to the dollar and to the yen. He finds that the weight of the yen has increased in the determination of the nominal exchange rates of Korea, Singapore, and Malaysia. The real exchange rates of the Thai baht and the Indonesian rupiah vis-à-vis the yen seem to be stable. For Korea and Malaysia, the authorities seem to react asymmetrically to yen appreciation and depreciation relative to the dollar: when the yen depreciates they appear to be anxious to maintain their relationship with the yen, while when there is yen appreciation they tend to stay with the dollar. This would suggest that they are very sensitive to the competitive position of their products relative to Japanese substitutes.

One of the key issues in analysis of exchange rates is the extent to which changes in exchange rates and foreign prices are "passed through" to domestic prices. Wang and Wu study this issue in their paper by examining behavior in the Taiwanese petrochemical industries during the period of currency appreciation from 1987 to 1992. They find that pass-through pricing was not evident in those industries despite the sharp appreciation of the New Taiwan dollar. This result would tend to suggest that, at least in the short run, exchange rate changes may not be reflected in domestic prices.

The final set of papers focuses on macroeconomic aspects of exchange rates in individual East Asian countries. Three examine aspects of Korea's exchange rate behavior. The first paper, by Sang-Woo Nam and Se-Jong Kim, examines Korean exchange rate policy in the past and the movements of the real exchange rate. When the Korean won moves with the U.S. dollar, Korean export industries benefit or suffer depending on whether the dollar-yen exchange rate is depreciating or appreciating. Nam and Kim also conduct a counterfactual simulation analysis of what would have happened under two alternative exchange rate regimes: in the first, a nominal peg to the U.S. dollar is maintained; in the second, the real exchange rate is maintained constant with respect to a basket of currencies. Nam and Kim conclude that exports and investment might have improved their performance if the policy of pegging to a real basket (with weights derived from the relative elasticities of demand) had been followed.

In his paper, Stanley Black considers the major factors influencing Korean policy with respect to the exchange rate. Of particular importance for Korea, with its history of inflation, was the extent to which monetary policy should be targeted at the external sector or at the domestic rate of inflation. However, as Korea undergoes financial liberalization, that may significantly influence the demand and supply for foreign goods and assets in real terms, and it is difficult to anticipate the net effect on the real exchange rate. Although the Korean won has appreciated fairly steadily, Black argues that further real appreciation is probably not warranted because further appreciation would accelerate the shift of Korean firms' production to other Asian countries, which in turn would increase Korean purchases of Japanese machinery.

The third paper, by Cho and Koh, attempts to assess the likely effects of liberalizing capital flows on the Korean economy and evaluates the desirable time path of liberalization in that light. Cho and Koh first show how capital market liberalization has proceeded to date in Korea, examine the behavior of capital flows and interest rate differentials, and analyze how the exchange rate has responded. They then proceed to simulate the time path of key variables under alternative capital account liberalization scenarios: sudden ("big bang") liberalization and gradual liberalization.

Two papers examine exchange rate behavior in Japan. In their paper, Okazaki and Korenaga describe and analyze the Japanese foreign exchange "allotment policy," a quota system of foreign exchange that was used during the early years of Japanese reconstruction and development. The yen was overvalued, but the exchange rate was fixed, and the quota system used administrative means to allocate scarce foreign exchange. Okazaki and Korenaga show that being allotted foreign exchange was equivalent to winning a "prize" for successful exporting in a MITI-sponsored "contest."

The McKinnon, Ohno, and Shirono paper examines the factors that contributed to the long-run appreciation of the yen against the U.S. dollar. Trade tensions placed pressure on Japan to permit its currency to appreciate. However, deflationary policies of the Bank of Japan were also a contributing factor. There was then a vicious circle: there were large current account surpluses, which in turn led to pressures on the yen to appreciate but also increased trade tensions. But McKinnon et al. note that it was investment-savings balances, independent of the yen-dollar rate, that were fundamentally at work in affecting the Japanese current account balance.

For Taiwan, Wu examines the determinants of the real exchange rate. She first demonstrates that purchasing power parity did not hold. She then uses time-series analysis to show that shocks in the exchange rate, in domestic prices, and in foreign prices all resulted in permanent rather than temporary changes. Differential productivity growth in the nontraded and traded sectors in Taiwan (relative to the United States) also led to permanent changes in the real exchange rate.

In their paper, Kwan and Lui consider the experience of Hong Kong's currency board. They discuss the historical background of Hong Kong's currency board and then attempt to identify the structure of responses under the flexible exchange rate that was in effect from 1974 to 1983 and under the currency board system during which there was a "linked exchange rate," in effect since

1983. They associate temporary shocks with demand shocks and permanent shocks with supply shocks (such as productivity or oil price increases). They show that much of the difference in performance during the two exchange rate regime periods was attributable to differences in the structure of shocks, although they give the currency board credit for relatively good performance. They believe that output growth was reduced somewhat, but inflation was also significantly reduced. They attribute much of Hong Kong's good macroeconomic performance to government fiscal constraint, which was relatively constant across the two periods.

1　The Choice of Exchange Rate Regime in Developing and Middle Income Countries

Sebastian Edwards

1.1　Introduction

In most developing and transitional economies, exchange rate issues have tended to dominate macroeconomic policy discussions during the past few years. In particular, attention has focused on two broad problems: first, defining, measuring, detecting, and correcting situations of *real* exchange rate misalignment and overvaluation and, second, understanding the relationship between *nominal* exchange rates and macroeconomic stability. Issues related to real exchange rate misalignment have been central, for example, in debates that preceded the devaluation of African currencies participating in the Communauté Financière Africaine franc zone in 1994, in post mortems of the Mexican crisis of December 1994, and in recent analyses of the Argentine stabilization program of 1991.

Regarding the relationship between exchange rates and macroeconomic stability, four specific questions have attracted the attention of analysts and policymakers: (a) Why have some countries adopted rigid, including fixed, exchange rate regimes, while others have opted for more flexible systems? (b) Do fixed exchange rate regimes impose an effective constraint on monetary behavior and thus result in lower inflation rates over the long run? (c) Are exchange-rate-based stabilization programs superior to money-based stabilization programs? (d) How should exchange-rate-based stabilization programs actually be designed?

Sebastian Edwards is the Henry Ford II Professor of International Business Economics at UCLA's Anderson Graduate School of Management and a research associate of the National Bureau of Economic Research.

This is a revised version of a paper titled "The Determinants of the Choice between Fixed and Flexible Exchange Rate Regimes." The author is indebted to Anne O. Krueger, Andy Rose, and a reviewer for comments. He is grateful to Fernando Losada and Daniel Lederman for their invaluable research assistance. He also benefited from discussions with Miguel Savastano.

The first two issues deal with the long run, while the third is related to the short-run, transitional consequences of stabilization programs.[1] All four issues, however, have important implications for a country's macroeconomic performance and growth. Moreover, most of these questions are intimately related to political economy and institutional considerations.

This paper deals with the first question from a political economy perspective. I ask why some countries (e.g., Argentina) have fixed exchange rate regimes while other countries (e.g., Chile) opt for significantly more flexible systems. The more general question is why, approximately 25 years after the abandonment of the Bretton Woods system, 84 countries (out of 167 reported in the IMF's *International Financial Statistics*) continue to peg their currencies to a major currency or a currency composite (these are data for December 1994). The theoretical discussion, presented in section 1.2, emphasizes the role of credibility, politics, and institutions. In the empirical analysis (section 1.3) I use a large cross-country panel data set for developing and middle-income countries to analyze empirically the determinants of the choice of regime.

1.2   The Political Economy of Exchange Rate Regimes

In this section I develop a simple theoretical framework for analyzing the selection of an exchange rate regime. The analysis relies on the existence of a trade-off between "credibility" and "flexibility" and assumes that a pegged exchange rate system allows the authorities to resolve, at least partially, the time inconsistency problem. I assume that policymakers minimize a loss function defined over a monetary variable (inflation) and a real variable (say, unemployment). In order to simplify the discussion I initially assume that the two alternative regimes are a flexible exchange rate system and a permanently fixed exchange rate system. I then extend the analysis to the case where the two options are a flexible regime and a pegged-but-adjustable regime. In this case I assume that the abandonment of the pegged exchange rate entails important political costs.

1.2.1   Fixed or Flexible? A Simple Framework

Assume, for simplicity, that the monetary authorities must choose between two nominal exchange rate regimes: (permanently) fixed or flexible. Assume that the authorities take into account the expected value of a loss function under the two alternative systems. Consider the case where the loss function is quadratic and depends on inflation (π) squared and on squared deviations of unemployment (u) from a target value (u^*). This type of approach has been adopted, with some variants, by a number of authors (see, e.g., Persson and Tabellini 1990; Devarajan and Rodrik 1992; Frankel 1995). The model is given by equations (1) through (5):

---

1. See Sachs (1996). On the selection of exchange rate regimes, see Corden (1994), Edison and Melvin (1990), Tornell and Velasco (1995), and Isard (1995).

(1) $$L = E[\pi^2 + \mu(u - u^*)^2], \quad \mu > 0;$$

(2) $$u = u' - \theta(\pi - \omega) + \psi(x - x'), \quad E(x) = x', \quad V(x) = \sigma^2;$$

(3) $$u^* < u';$$

(4) $$\omega = E(\pi) + \alpha E(x - x');$$

(5) $$\pi = \beta d + (1 - \beta)\omega.$$

Equation (1) is the loss function. Equation (2) states that the observed rate of unemployment (u) will be below the natural rate (u') if inflation exceeds wage increases ($\pi - \omega > 0$) and if external shocks (x) are below their mean (x'). Variable x can be interpreted as a composite of terms of trade and world interest rate shocks. It is assumed to have a variance equal to σ^2. Equation (3) establishes that the target rate of unemployment u^* is below the natural rate u'. Equation (4) implies that agents are rational in setting wage increases ($\alpha < 0$), and equation (5) defines inflation as a weighted average of the rate of devaluation (d) and the rate of wage increases (ω). Under fixed rates d is by definition equal to zero, while under flexible rates the authorities set d according to an optimal devaluation rule. A limitation of this approach is that it assumes fixed rates are unchangeable. The case of a pegged-but-adjustable regime can be handled assuming that the fixed rule has escape clauses (see Flood and Isard 1989).

The model's solution depends on the sequence in which decisions are made. Assume that workers determine ω before they observe x, d, or π. The government, on the other hand, sets its exchange rate policy after both ω and x are observed. The government's objective is to set its exchange rate policy so as to minimize the value of the loss function (1). The solution in the case of fixed exchange rates is

(6a) $$\pi = 0,$$

(6b) $$u = u' + \psi(x - x').$$

These results assume that the fixed exchange rate system allows the government to solve its credibility problem by providing a precommitment technology.

The solution is slightly more complicated under flexible exchange rates. In this case the authorities have to determine the optimal exchange rate adjustment rule. The final solution for d, π, and u under flexible exchange rates is given by

(7a) $$d = -\Delta[\beta^2(1 + \theta^2\mu)\theta\mu(u^* - u') - \mu\theta\beta\psi(x - x')],$$

(7b) $$\pi^{flex} = \pi^{fixed} - \theta\mu(u^* - u') + \beta^2\mu\theta\psi\Delta(x - x'),$$

(7c) $$u^{flex} = u^{fixed} - \beta^3\psi\Delta(x - x'),$$

where

$$\Delta = [\beta^2(1 + \mu\,\theta^2) - \beta]^{-1},$$

which under most plausible conditions is greater than zero. Equation (7b) establishes that due to the unemployment objective, inflation under flexible rates will tend to exceed its equilibrium level under fixed rates. That is, if the unemployment objective is important in the loss function, the authorities will be tempted to "overinflate." On the other hand, unemployment under flexible rates will be higher (lower) than under fixed rates if there are negative (positive) external shocks.

In selecting the exchange rate regime, the authorities will compare the expected value of the loss function under both regimes:

(8) $K = E(L^{\text{flex}} - L^{\text{fixed}}).$

If $K > 0$, a fixed exchange rate regime will be adopted. It is easy to see that K is given by

(9) $K = E[(\pi^{\text{flex}})^2 + \mu(u^{\text{flex}} - u^*)^2 - \mu(u^{\text{fixed}} - u^*)^2].$

This expression is intuitively appealing. It states that the selection of the exchange rate regime will depend on the square of inflation under flexible rates—remember that expected inflation is zero in the fixed rate regime—and on the difference between the squared deviations of unemployment from their respective targets. After some manipulation equation (9) can be rewritten as

(10) $K = (\theta\mu)^2(u^* - u')^2 - \gamma\sigma^2,$

where γ is a positive function of Δ, β, μ, θ, and ψ. For K to be positive, and thus for fixed rates to be preferred, the country's "employment ambition"—measured by $u^* - u'$—has to be "large enough." More specifically, it has to exceed the variance of the external shocks. On the other hand, if σ^2 is high enough, K can be negative, indicating that flexible rates are preferred. This would allow the authorities to reduce the deviation from their unemployment target. An important question in the empirical evaluation of this (and related) models is how to *measure* the degree of "ambition" of the authorities' unemployment target, $u^* - u'$. I take up this issue in section 1.3.

1.2.2   Flexible versus Pegged-but-Adjustable Exchange Rate Regimes

The preceding analysis assumed that under a fixed regime the nominal exchange rate would never be altered. This is, of course, a major simplification. In reality, under fixed exchange rates, governments always have the choice of abandoning the peg. This possibility can be captured formally by assuming that the authorities follow a rule with some kind of escape clause. In other words, the nominal exchange rate will be maintained at its original level under certain circumstances. However, if these circumstances change markedly, the peg will be abandoned. This means that at any moment in time there is a positive probability that the pegged rate will be altered. This type of arrangement formed the basis of the original Bretton Woods system that ruled the international monetary system from 1948 to 1973. According to the original International Monetary Fund (IMF) Articles of Agreement, a country could alter its peg if it was facing a "fundamental disequilibrium." In this subsection I sketch the analytics of this case.

Assume that ex ante a country can choose between two possible regimes: flexible nominal rates (F) or pegged but adjustable rates (P). Also consider a two-period economy, where under a pegged regime there is a positive probability that the peg will be abandoned at the end of the first (or beginning of the second) period. The probability of abandoning the peg is denoted by q, and the discount factor by β. As in the preceding analysis, assume that the authorities have a distaste for both inflation and for deviations of unemployment from a target level.

Assume further that the authorities will incur a political cost equal to C if the peg is indeed abandoned. This assumption captures the stylized fact, first noted by Cooper (1971), that stepwise devaluations have usually resulted in serious political upheavals and, in many cases, in the fall of the government. Cooper reports that more than two-thirds of the finance ministers that engineered the devaluations lost their jobs within two months of the devaluation (see also Edwards 1994). The magnitude of this cost will, in turn, depend on the political and institutional characteristics of the country, including the degree of political instability. In politically unstable countries a major economic disturbance, such as the abandonment of a parity that the authorities have promised to defend, will tend to have major political consequences. For example, this can explain why the vast majority of stepwise devaluations take place during the early years of an administration, when its degree of political popularity is higher. The degree of political instability will also affect the government's discount factor. In more unstable countries the authorities will tend to be more impatient, discounting the future more heavily. This means that, denoting the degree of political instability by ρ, we can write

(11) $C = C(\rho)$,   with $C' > 0$;

(12) $\beta = \beta(\rho)$,   with $\beta' < 0$.

In this two-period economy, the loss function under flexible rates is (where the notation is consistent with that used in the previous section)

(13) $L^{\text{flex}} = \xi(\pi^F)^2 + \mu(u^F - u^*)^2 + \beta(\xi(\pi^F)^2_{t+1} + \mu[(u^F)_{t+1} - u^*]^2)$,

where ξ is a parameter that captures the degree of distaste for inflation. The loss function under a pegged rate regime is

(14) $L^{\text{pegged}} = \xi(\pi^P)^2 + \mu(u^P - u^*)^2 + \beta\{(1 - q)(\xi(\pi^P)^2_{t+1}$

$+ \mu[(u^P)_{t+1} - u^*]^2) + q(\xi(\pi^D)^2_{t+1} + \mu[(u^D)_{t+1} - u^*]^2) + qC\}$, where the superscript D refers to the value of a specific variable in the second period under the devaluation scenario. If the escape clause is exercised and the peg abandoned, we assume that the country moves into a flexible regime. That is, once the peg is abandoned, inflation and unemployment in the second period will be determined as under a flexible system. The rate of inflation will be higher under the pegged-but-adjustable regime than under the (unrealistic) "forever" fixed system considered in section 1.2.1. This is because under a pegged regime the public's expected rate of inflation (in period 2) will explicitly take into account the probability that the peg will be abandoned:

$$E(\pi^P)_{t+1} = q(\pi^D)_{t+1} + (1 - q)(\pi^P)_{t+1}$$

(see Edwards 1996).

In order to simplify the discussion and concentrate on the selection of the exchange rate regime, I do not specify explicitly the process governing the decision to use the escape clause. As in equation (8) in the preceding section, the regime decision rule will be based on an ex ante comparison between both loss functions:

(15) $$K = E(L^{\text{flex}} - L^{\text{pegged}}).$$

If $K > 0$, then the pegged-but-adjustable regime is preferred. Some simple manipulation yields

(16) $$K = \xi(\pi^F)^2 + \mu[(\kappa^F)^2 - (\kappa^P)^2] + \beta(1 - q)\xi(\pi^F)_{t+1}^2$$
$$+ \beta(1 - q)\mu[(\kappa^F)_{t+1}^2 - (\kappa^P)_{t+1}^2] - q\beta C,$$

where $(\kappa^F)^2 = (u^F - u^*)^2$ and $(\kappa^P)^2 = (U^P - u^*)^2$. From the analysis in the previous section it follows that $(\kappa^F)^2 - (\kappa^P)^2 < 0$ and that $(\kappa^F)_{t+1}^2 - (\kappa^P)_{t+1}^2 < 0$. From equation (16) it is possible to derive a number of hypotheses regarding the likelihood of a country's choosing a pegged-but-adjustable exchange rate regime. A higher rate of inflation under flexible rates (in either period) will increase the likelihood of a pegged regime's being chosen. Moreover, with other things given, a higher weight for inflation in the loss function—that is, a higher ξ—will also increase the probability of choosing a pegged exchange rate. On the other hand, an increase in unemployment volatility under pegged rates, generated by a higher variance in the foreign shock—a higher σ^2, from the previous section—will increase the likelihood that a flexible system will be selected. A greater distaste for unemployment deviations—that is, a higher μ—will reduce the likelihood of selecting a pegged rate. Likewise, a higher cost of abandoning the peg—a higher C—will reduce the ex ante probability of selecting a pegged rate. Interestingly enough, a higher probability of abandoning the peg—a higher q—will have an ambiguous effect on the ex ante likelihood of choosing a pegged regime. This follows from the expression

(17) $$K_q = -\beta\gamma(\pi^F)_{t+1}^2 - \beta\mu[(\kappa^F)_{t+1}^2 - (\kappa^P)_{t+1}^2] - \beta C.$$

Notice that the presence of political costs of abandoning the peg (C) increases the likelihood that this expression will be negative, making it more likely that a flexible regime will be selected.

An important question relates to the relationship between political instability and the selection of exchange rate regime. In principle there will be two offsetting forces. First, a higher degree of political instability will increase the cost of abandoning the peg—recall equation (11)—and thus will reduce the ex ante probability that a pegged regime will be chosen. Second, a higher degree of instability will increase the authorities' discount rate—equation (12)—reducing the importance of "the future" in their decision-making process. Formally,

$$(18) \qquad K_\rho = -\beta q C' + K_\beta \beta'.$$

While the first term is negative, the second can be either positive or negative, because the sign of K_β is indeterminate. This means that the way in which instability will affect the selection of an exchange rate system is an empirical question. I tackle this issue in the following section, where I present the results of a number of probit regressions on panel data for 49 developing and middle-income countries during 1980–92.

1.3   Empirical Results

In this section I use a cross-country, unbalanced panel data set for 49 developing and middle-income countries during 1980–92 to analyze why some countries have adopted pegged exchange rate regimes while others have opted for more flexible systems; see the appendix for a list of the countries included in the analysis. I estimate a number of probit equations to investigate whether, when controlling for other factors, a country's political and economic structure, including its degree of political instability, helps explain the selection of an exchange rate regime. Two classes of independent variables were used in the analysis: the first attempts to capture long-term structural characteristics—both political and economic—of these countries, which are assumed to change very slowly over time. In the empirical analysis these variables are defined as averages for the decade prior to the one included in the analysis. The second class of independent variables tries to capture, for each country, the evolution of some key macroeconomic time series.

Probit equations of the following type were estimated:

$$(19) \qquad \mathrm{peg}_{it} = \rho' P_i + \lambda' Q_{it} + \phi' R_{it-1} + E_{it},$$

where subindexes i and t refer to country i in year t; peg is an exchange rate regime index defined below; and ρ, λ, and ϕ are parameter vectors. P represents variables specifying national political and economic characteristics. In order to avoid simultaneity problems these variables were defined, in most cases, as averages for the previous decade, 1970–80 (see the discussion below for details). Q and R are variables (economic and structural) for which panel data are available; while the Qs are timed at period t, the Rs are lagged one (or more) periods. This is done mostly to reduce the pitfalls of simultaneity problems.

1.3.1   Data

The empirical analysis poses some difficult data challenges. Chief among them are (a) classifying the broad variety of exchange rate systems observed in the real world into two broad categories, pegged and flexible, (b) measuring political instability, and (c) defining measures of the authorities' incentives to "tie their own hands."

Defining Exchange Rate Regimes

The IMF's *International Financial Statistics* (*IFS*) classifies countries according to their exchange rate systems in three broad groups:

1. Countries whose currencies are pegged either to a single currency or to a currency composite.
2. Countries whose exchange rate systems have limited flexibility "in terms of a single currency or group of currencies." This group includes a rather small number of countries that have adopted narrow bands, including those in the European Exchange Rate Mechanism. In June 1991, for example, only 11 countries were listed in this group.
3. Countries with "more flexible" exchange rate systems. This group includes countries where the exchange rate is adjusted frequently according to a set of indicators, countries that float independently, and countries with "other managed floating" regimes.

In the empirical analysis presented in this paper, a country is classified according to its exchange rate regime in a binary fashion as "pegged" or "flexible." A difficulty with this approach, however, is that it is not entirely clear how the middle group—that is, nations that according to the IMF have "limited flexibility"—should be classified. In order to deal with this issue I have used two alternative classifications. The first considers as having a pegged exchange rate system only those countries classified by *IFS* as such. Thus a variable peg1 that takes a value of one for those countries and zero for countries with "limited flexibility" and "more flexible" regimes was defined. The second classification considers as having a pegged regime those countries classified as such by *IFS*, plus those with flexibility limited "in terms of a single currency or group of currencies." Variable peg2, then, takes a value of one for "pegged" and "limited flexibility" countries and zero for those nations with "more flexible" regimes.

Measuring Political Instability

Most empirically based political economy studies have used rather crude measures of political instability, including the number of politically motivated assassinations and attacks (Barro 1991). Other studies have used the frequency—either actual or estimated—of government change as a measure of political turnover and instability (Cukierman, Edwards, and Tabellini 1992). A limitation of this type of measure, however, is that it treats *every* change in the head of state as an indication of political instability, without inquiring whether the new leadership belongs to the same party as the departing leader or to the opposing party. In that sense, for example, the replacement of a prime minister by another from the same party is considered to have the same meaning as a change in the ruling party (Cukierman 1992).

In this paper I use a new index of political instability (POLTRAN) that focuses on instances when there has been a *transfer of power* from a party or group in office to a party of group formerly in the opposition, between 1972 and 1980; the merits of this type of index were first discussed in Edwards and Tabellini (1994). This index measures the instability of the political system by capturing changes in the political leadership from the governing party (or group, in the case of a nondemocratic regime) to an opposition party. In constructing this index, a transfer of power is defined as a situation where there is a break in the governing political party's (or dictator's) control of executive power. More specifically, under a presidential system a transfer of power would occur if a new government headed by a party previously in the opposition takes over the executive. Under a parliamentarian regime a transfer of power is recorded when a new government headed by a party previously in the opposition takes over, or when there are major changes in the coalition so as to force the leading party into the opposition. However, when the governing coalition remains basically unaltered, even if the new prime minister belongs to a party different from that of the outgoing prime minister, a transfer of power is not recorded. Finally, in the case of single-party systems, dictatorships, or monarchies, a transfer of power only takes place if there is a forced change of the head of state. The appointment of a successor by an outgoing dictator (as in Brazil during the 1970s) is not recorded as a transfer of power. This variable has a single value for each country, corresponding to the period 1971–80. By concentrating on the period immediately preceding the period used in the probit analysis, potential endogeneity problems are reduced.

In addition to the POLTRAN index of political instability, three indicators were used as proxies for the extent of weakness of the government in office. The first refers to whether the party or coalition of parties in office has an absolute majority of seats in the lower house of parliament. In any given year this indicator, called MAJ, takes a value of zero if the party (coalition) does not have a majority, a value of one if it has a majority, and a value of two if the system is a dictatorship. A higher value of MAJ, then, reflects a stronger government. In the cross-country regression the average of MAJ over 1971–80 was used.

The second indicator of political weakness is the number of political parties in the governing coalition (NPC). This index takes a value of zero for monarchical or dictatorial systems and the number of parties participating in a ruling coalition under a democratic regime (e.g., if there is a single-party government, NPC will take the value of one). It is expected that the higher the number of parties in that coalition, the higher the probability of conflict of interest across ministries and thus the higher the reliance on the inflation tax.

The third indicator of government weakness is whether the government is a coalition government or a single-party government (COAL). This index takes a value of zero for dictatorships, a value of one for single-party governments, and a value of two for coalition governments. As with MAJ, NPC and COAL were defined as averages for 1971–80.

Other Data

According to the model presented in section 1.2, in addition to the political factors discussed above, other variables that capture structural characteristics of the economy are important in the process of selecting an exchange rate system.

External shocks. Two alternative indexes were used to measure the extent of external shock variability. A coefficient of variation of real export growth for 1970–82 (CVEX) was constructed with raw data obtained from *IFS*. A coefficient of variation of real bilateral exchange rate changes for 1970–82 (EXVAR) was constructed from data obtained from *IFS*. The use of these variables in the regression analysis presents a potential endogeneity problem. In order to minimize this danger in the probit reported below, lagged values (for 1970–82) of these indexes were used. It is expected that the coefficients of these variables in the probit regressions will be negative, indicating that, as reflected in equation (10), countries with more volatile external sectors will tend to select more flexible regimes.

In principle, the actual importance of external shocks should also depend on the degree of openness of the economy—more open countries are more "vulnerable" to external disturbances. In order to consider this effect I added an interactive term (VAR_OPEN) between external variability and the degree of openness. The latter was defined as the ratio of imports plus exports to GNP and was constructed from data obtained from *IFS*. This variable was defined as the average for 1971–80.

Degree of "ambition" of the real target. A cornerstone of the model developed above—and of most Barro-Gordon types of model—is the idea that countries with very "ambitious" real objectives will have an incentive to "tie their own hands" in order to solve their credibility problems. That is, with other things given, they will have a greater incentive to select pegged exchange rate systems. It is not easy, however, to measure empirically this degree of "ambition." In particular, only a handful of middle-income and developing countries have reliable data on unemployment. For this reason I have used deviations of average real rates of growth of GDP from the group's average (for 1970–80) as a proxy for the countries' incentives to tie their own hands. In using this variable I assume that, with other things given, countries with historically low rates of growth will be more tempted to "overinflate" as a way to accelerate growth, even in the short run. If this is the case, low-growth countries will have an incentive to tie their own hands as a way to avoid falling into this temptation. It is expected that the coefficient of GROWTH will be negative in the probit regressions. Naturally, the use of growth as a regressor raises the possibility of endogeneity. It is indeed possible that the exchange rate regime will, per se, affect economic performance, including growth. In order to avoid this problem I use lagged averages (by one decade) of growth rates in the estimation of the probit model (19). To the extent that this variable tries to capture the historical and structural incentives faced by a country to tie its authorities' hands, the use of lagged averages is, indeed, appropriate.

Probability of abandoning the peg (or ability to maintain it). As discussed in the preceding section, a higher probability of abandoning the peg—a higher q—can, in principle, affect the likelihood of selecting a pegged rate either positively or negatively. Since it is not possible to observe q directly, three variables that capture the probability of having a devaluation were considered in the empirical analysis: LOGINF is the (logarithm of the) historical rate of inflation. A country with a history of rapid inflation will tend to have a greater propensity to devalue. This variable is defined as the average for 1970–80. RESMONEY is the yearly lagged ratio of international reserves to high-powered money. Higher reserves reduce, with other things given, the probability of abandoning the peg. This variable was defined, for each country and each year, as the one-year lagged ratio of central bank reserves to monetary base. CREGRO is the rate of growth of domestic credit. A country with a higher rate of growth of domestic liquidity will have a lower ability to sustain the peg. This variable was constructed from data obtained from the IMF and was defined as a five-year moving average. Notice that according to equation (17), in spite of the theoretical ambiguity of the effect of a higher q on the selection of exchange regime, in a country with a high political cost of devaluing, a higher q will reduce the likelihood that a pegged regime will be adopted.

In addition to the variables of political instability, external shocks, and probability of devaluing, the logarithm of per capita income (PCGDP) measured in 1989 dollars was included in the analysis. This variable was taken from the World Bank's *World Development Report.* More advanced countries tend to have a greater degree of intolerance for inflation. Also, it has often been claimed that less advanced countries do not have the institutional and administrative ability to implement a flexible exchange rate regime. On both counts, the coefficient of PCGDP should be positive.[2]

2. See Aghevli, Khan, and Montiel (1991). For a critical view, see Collins (1994).

1.3.2   Results

Table 1.1 contains the main results from the probit analysis for both the peg1 and peg2 measures of exchange rate regime. Overall these results are very satisfactory and provide broad support for the model developed in the preceding section. Surprisingly, perhaps, there are few differences in the estimates obtained when the alternative definitions of dependent variables were used.

The estimates obtained strongly suggest that the structural degree of political instability plays an important role in the selection of exchange rate regime—more unstable countries have, with other things given, a lower probability of selecting a pegged exchange rate system. The consistent negative coefficient of this variable indicates that empirically the direct effect of a higher political cost of devaluing offsets the effect via a higher discount rate on the authorities' decision-making process. Two indexes of the degree of weakness of the political system (NPC and COAL) are not significant; MAJ, on the other hand, is marginally positive, suggesting that a stronger government will have a greater tendency to select a pegged system. The intuition here is quite simple: a stronger government will be in a better position to withstand the political costs of a (possible) currency crisis and thus will be more willing to accept them.

The coefficients associated with the (lagged) indexes of external volatility—EXVAR and CVEX—are also negative, as expected, and in the case of EXVAR significantly so. What is particularly interesting is that the coefficients of the interactive term between external variability and openness (VAR_OPEN) are positive, and significantly so in four of the five regressions. This suggests—somewhat puzzlingly—that as countries become more open, the importance of external disturbances in the selection of exchange rate regime declines.

The estimated coefficients of the variables that capture the ability to maintain the peg have the expected signs and are also significant at conventional levels. The coefficient of lagged inflation is significantly negative, suggesting that countries with histories of inflation will have a lower probability of maintaining a peg and will thus tend to favor the adoption of more flexible systems. Along similar lines, the coefficients of lagged credit creation are also negative. The lagged coefficient of the ratio of central bank international reserves to base money (RESMONEY) is positive in all regressions, indicating that countries with lower holdings of international reserves will have a lower probability of adopting a pegged exchange rate regime. There is, however, a potential endogeneity problem: it is possible that a country that has decided to adopt a flexible rate regime will "need" a lower stock of reserves. The use of one-year lagged values of the reserves ratio reduces, however, the extent of this problem.

The estimated coefficient of the historical rate of deviations of GDP growth is significantly negative indicating that, with other things given, countries with lower growth rates than the average will tend to prefer more rigid exchange rate regimes. To the extent that historical growth deviations are a good proxy for the "temptation to inflate," this result can be interpreted as providing evi-

Table 1.1 **Determinants of Exchange Rate Regimes: Probit Regression Results for Developing Countries**

Variable	peg 1			peg 2	
	A	B	C	A	B
Constant	2.677	0.897	2.177	2.366	1.030
	(9.194)	(0.818)	(2.391)	(8.373)	(0.972)
POLTRAN	−1.761	−2.514	−2.099	−1.185	−1.930
	(−3.614)	(−4.856)	(−4.220)	(−2.486)	(−3.782)
NPC		−0.393	−0.150		−0.567
		(−1.616)	(−0.650)		(−2.361)
COAL		0.569	0.138		0.578
		(0.972)	(0.271)		(1.022)
MAJ		1.171	0.737		0.873
		(2.217)	(1.663)		(1.733)
EXVAR	−0.256	−0.288		−0.274	−0.031
	(−4.581)	(−5.087)		(−4.319)	(−4.872)
CVEX			−0.007		
			(−0.402)		
VAR_OPEN	0.039	0.049	0.004	0.047	0.061
	(1.949)	(2.104)	(0.129)	(2.317)	(2.597)
CREGRO	−0.102	−0.084	−0.128	−0.113	−0.114
	(−1.184)	(−1.017)	(−2.000)	(−1.362)	(−1.401)
LOGINF	−0.919	−0.899	−1.232	−0.819	−0.760
	(−6.795)	(−5.833)	(−8.884)	(−6.287)	(−5.173)
RESMONEY	0.171	0.099	0.239	0.140	0.088
	(1.822)	(1.222)	(2.565)	(1.669)	(1.141)
GROWTH	−0.117	−0.126	−0.138	−0.095	−0.100
	(−3.976)	(−4.035)	(−4.162)	(−3.284)	(−3.361)
PCGDP	0.394	0.771	0.560	0.343	0.645
	(3.851)	(5.263)	(5.094)	(3.371)	(4.647)
N	566	566	593	552	552
χ^2	182.6	213.7	186.5	160.1	188.21

Note: Dependent variables are peg 1 and peg 2. Numbers in parentheses are *t*-values.

dence in favor of the "tying their own hands" hypothesis. Countries with poorer performance—measured, in this case, by the *historical* rate of growth deviations—will have a greater incentive to renege on their low inflation promises and thus will benefit from adopting more rigid exchange rate systems. In order to analyze the robustness of these results I used the yearly difference between the rate of unemployment and its long-term historical average (1970–90) as an alternative measure of the temptation to inflate. Within the context of the credibility view it would be expected that the estimated coefficient of this variable will be positive. A limitation of this measure, however, is that very few countries have data on unemployment. For this reason, the results obtained from these estimates should be interpreted with caution.

Finally, the coefficient of log of per capita income is significantly positive, indicating that contrary to basic intuition, more advanced countries will tend to adopt pegged exchange rate regimes. These results, in fact, contrast with those obtained in Edwards (1996) for a group of countries that included the advanced nations. The results reported in table 1.1 are in part explained by the fact that the poorer countries in the sample suffered from significant external crises during the period under analysis and had no alternative but to adopt more flexible exchange rate regimes.

1.4 Conclusions

This paper has dealt with the issue of exchange rate regime selection. In particular, I ask: why do some countries select a flexible exchange rate regime while others choose a pegged regime? I argue that the answer to this question is largely related to the political structure of the country in question. In this paper I develop a formal political economy model to analyze this issue. The model assumes that a fixed exchange rate regime is more credible than a flexible regime. However, if the pegged regime is abandoned—that is, if the authorities decide (or are forced) to devalue—the authorities suffer a significant political cost. The empirical results reported here indicate that for a sample of developing and middle-income countries, countries with more unstable political regimes will tend to select more flexible exchange rate regimes.

Appendix
Countries in the Sample (Listed by IFS Code)

South Africa	Sri Lanka	Kenya
Bolivia	India	Lesotho
Brazil	Indonesia	Mauritius
Chile	Pakistan	Morocco
Colombia	Philippines	Nigeria
Dominican Republic	Thailand	Zimbabwe
Ecuador	Botswana	Rwanda
El Salvador	Burundi	Sierra Leone
Honduras	Cameroon	Somalia
Mexico	Central African Republic	Sudan
Nicaragua	Chad	Tanzania
Paraguay	Congo	Togo
Peru	Zaire	Tunisia
Venezuela	Ethiopia	Uganda
Jamaica	Gabon	Zambia
Trinidad Tobago	Ghana	
Iran	Côte d'Ivoire	

References

Aghevli, Bijan, Mohsin Khan, and Peter Montiel. 1991. Exchange rate policy in developing countries: Some analytical issues. IMF Occasional Paper no. 78.

Barro, Robert. 1991. Economic growth in a cross-section of countries. *Quarterly Journal of Economics* 106, no. 2 (May): 407–43.

Collins, Susan. 1994. On becoming more flexible: Exchange-rate regimes in Latin America and the Caribbean. Paper presented at the seventh IASE/NBER meetings, Mexico City, November.

Cooper, Richard. 1971. Currency devaluation in developing countries. Princeton Essays in International Finance, no. 86. Princeton, N. J.: Princeton University.

Corden, W. Max. 1994. *Economic policy, exchange rates, and the international system.* Chicago: University of Chicago Press.

Cukierman, Alex. 1992. *Central bank strategy, credibility, and independence.* Cambridge, Mass.: MIT Press.

Cukierman, Alex, Sebastian Edwards, and Guido Tabellini. 1992. Seignorage and political instability. *American Economic Review* 82 (June): 537–55.

Devarajan, Shantanayan, and Dani Rodrik. 1992. Do the benefits of fixed exchange rates outweigh their costs? The CFA Zone in Africa. In *Open economies: Structural adjustment and agriculture,* ed. Ian Goldin and Alan Winters. Cambridge: Cambridge University Press.

Edison, H., and M. Melvin. 1990. The determinants and the implications of the choice of an exchange rate system. In *Monetary policy for a volatile economy,* ed. W. S. Haraf and T. D. Willet. Washington, D.C.: AEI Press.

Edwards, Sebastian. 1994. The political economy of inflation and stabilization in developing countries. *Economic Development and Cultural Change* 42, no. 2 (January): 235–66.

———. 1996. The determinants of the choice between fixed and flexible exchange rate regimes. NBER Working Paper no. 5756. Cambridge, Mass.: National Bureau of Economic Research, October.

Edwards, Sebastian, and Guido Tabellini. 1994. Political instability, political weakness and inflation. In *Advances in econometrics,* ed. Chris Sims. New York: Cambridge University Press.

Flood, Robert, and Peter Isard. 1989. Monetary policy strategies. *IMF Staff Papers* 36 (3): 612–32.

Frankel, Jeffrey. 1995. Monetary regime choices for a semi-open country. In *Capital controls, exchange rates and monetary policy in the world economy,* ed. Sebastian Edwards. New York: Cambridge University Press.

Isard, Peter. 1995. *Exchange rate economics.* Cambridge: Cambridge University Press.

Persson, Torsten, and Guido Tabellini. 1990. *Macroeconomic policy, credibility and politics.* New York: Harwood.

Sachs, Jeffrey. 1996. Economic transition and the exchange rate regime. *American Economic Review* 86 (2): 147–52.

Tornell, Aaron, and Andres Velasco. 1995. Fixed versus flexible exchange Rates: Which provides more fiscal discipline? NBER Working Paper no. 5108. Cambridge, Mass.: National Bureau of Economic Research.

Comment   Anne O. Krueger

In this paper, Sebastian Edwards considers an important question: what determines what exchange rate regime governments choose? His paper is positive rather than normative, as he posits a trade-off for governments between inflation and unemployment. In his (Barro-Gordon) framework, when countries have high credibility as to their macroeconomic policies, they can afford to choose a flexible exchange rate regime; on the other hand, if credibility is limited, the inflation costs of a flexible exchange rate regime will be much higher.

On the basis of the model he develops, he tests the determinants of exchange rate regimes for 49 countries, finding that political instability, the probability of abandoning pegged rates, and variables reflecting the importance attached to unemployment and growth targets are the most significant determinants of the choice of exchange rate regime.

I have four comments regarding the paper. The first is a political economy question: is the choice of exchange rate regime a "rational choice" or the consequence of a learning experience? In the 1950s and 1960s, after Milton Friedman wrote his classic paper, much of the rejection of the idea of flexible exchange rates was based on emotional grounds: defense of national pride, belief in the sanctity of the gold standard, and so on. These same ideas permeated thinking in many developing countries: in Turkey, at the beginning of independent economic policy in 1931, one of the first measures was a law requiring the maintenance of a fixed exchange rate. The national currency was, especially in newly independent countries, a symbol of national sovereignty, and its fixity had considerable emotional appeal, whatever the realities of the trade-off between inflation and unemployment may have been. It should also be recalled that early development thought stressed the irrelevance of monetary incentives: primary commodity exports were thought by many to be in highly inelastic demand as exemplified by their exogeneity in the Chenery-Strout (1966) two-gap model. While there were some dissenters even in early days, the thinking continued, especially among policymakers, for a long time.

A second question relates to the assumption of a trade-off. Here, I have several misgivings. In the model, when an exchange rate is fixed there is zero inflation and unemployment costs can be higher than under a flexible exchange rate regime, where unemployment can be lower because of inflation. In reality, most of the developing countries that have chosen fixed exchange rates have not altered their domestic monetary and fiscal policies sufficiently to insure against inflation—how else could we have the specter of Ghana in 1984 with a black market premium on the exchange rate of over 900 percent? Indeed, in most countries where nominal anchor exchange rate policies have been cho-

Anne O. Krueger is the Herald L. and Caroline L. Ritch Professor of Economics, senior fellow of the Hoover Institution, and director of the Center for Research on Economic Development and Policy Reform at Stanford University, and a research associate of the National Bureau of Economic Research.

sen—even when the nominal anchor was a rate of exchange rate adjustment less than the domestic rate of inflation—the continuing inflationary process has undermined the nominal anchor regime.

Perhaps even more fundamental, fiscal deficits in developing countries are seldom incurred because of Keynesian-type considerations. Instead, they are largely the outcome of governments' inability to enforce fiscal discipline because of political weakness. Pressures to spend in order to gain political support and resistances to raising revenues are simply too strong in those circumstances.

Finally, many policymakers in developing countries are now rejecting inflation because it hurts growth. Certainly, in countries such as Argentina and Chile, policymakers do not view inflation as being consistent with more employment and growth; on the contrary, one reason for their commitment to achieving a stable price level has been their belief that inflation harms the real economy. To the extent that that belief is pervasive, the basis of the model is undermined: believers in the inefficacy of inflation for achieving real goals would believe there is a positive relationship between low or zero inflation and the real variables they seek, and not a trade-off.

Yet a third consideration has to do with the growth-rate–exchange-rate linkage. When high rates of inflation have been prevalent and policymakers have nonetheless adhered to a fixed exchange rate, there is an a priori basis to believe that low growth will result. One wonders how much of Edwards's results are picking up the low-growth–poor-policy relationship, rather than trade-offs between objectives on the part of rational decision makers.

Finally, I have misgivings about the use of similar time periods for all countries. After all, countries did alter their exchange and payments regimes at different times, and the use of common time periods obscures that fact. The Korean real appreciation of the latter half of the 1970s, for example, is seen by all analysts as having been a significant policy mistake; yet Edwards's choice of time periods would take that to have been the underlying exchange rate policy. If, instead, one picked "stable policy periods," such as Ghana pre- and post-1984, Turkey pre- and post-1980, and Chile pre- and post-1985 (or 1975?), the results might be significantly different. It would be interesting to see how the results would turn out if Edwards tested, within each country, for the periods when there were changes in policy regimes and then used the periods so delineated as his units of observation. Certainly the exchange rate regime would generally be far clearer than it is when the same chronological time periods are used for all countries independent of changes in their policy regimes.

Reference

Chenery, Hollis, and Allan Strout. 1966. Foreign assistance and economic development. *American Economic Review* 56 (4): 679–733.

Comment   Andrew K. Rose

Sebastian Edwards's paper deals with an important question that remains at the heart of open economy macroeconomics, namely: what determines the choice of exchange rate regime? His paper provides a rigorous theoretical framework, in which he derives the choice as an optimal response to the magnitude and sources of different shocks striking the economy. He does this in a familiar Barro-Gordon–style setting that includes the government's preferences over inflation and unemployment. He sensibly differentiates between two types of fixed exchange rate regimes: an adjustable peg and a permanent fix (which is really more akin to a currency union).

Edwards also takes the extra step of going to the data. Using a panel of 12 years of annual data for 49 developing and middle-income countries, Edwards estimates a probit model using both political and economic regressors to explain actual exchange rate choices. His most striking finding is that political stability is associated with fixed exchange rates. He also shows that growth is associated with flexible exchange rates. But he finds a number of other sensible (if more straightforward) results: lower real exchange rate variability, lower inflation, greater reserves, and capital controls are also associated with fixed exchange rates. All in all, this is clearly interesting and potentially important work.

I view this paper more as an intriguing taste of what is to come than as the sort of work that marks the end of a long-term project. Thus I encourage the author to continue the research program begun with this paper. A number of both technical and methodological improvements could make work like this more definitive, and I am sure that Edwards plans to pursue them (and many others) in future work. More research is very much warranted by the scope and importance of the task Edwards sets for himself.

There is a potentially nontrivial problem of reverse causality associated with many of the regressors, especially exchange rate volatility and inflation. After all, countries *choose* their exchange rate regimes, as the theoretical model implies. Thus an expected change in the nature of the economy (e.g., in the sources or sizes of shocks or in the government's preferences) should lead to a deliberate change in the exchange rate regime. In such circumstances, using historical data would be inappropriate, and using lagged data would provide an even less reasonable test of the model. In any case, the standard Lucas critique applies to work like this. The exchange rate regime should be expected to change the structure of the economy, even if the switch is inadvertent. This is yet another reason to treat the historical data carefully in cross-regime estimation.

Andrew K. Rose is the B. T. Rocca Professor of Economic Analysis and Policy in the Haas School of Business at the University of California, Berkeley; acting director of the International Finance and Macroeconomics Program at the National Bureau of Economic Research; and a research fellow of the Centre for Economic Policy Research.

For all these reasons, I urge Edwards to consider estimation with instrumental variables, using his theoretical framework to derive the appropriate first-stage regressors. One of the great advantages of having an explicit structural model is the ability to derive reasonable instrumental variables. More generally, it would also be useful have more clear and well-defined linkages between the theory and the data.

While it is reasonable to use the IMF's exchange rate regime classifications as a starting point, the variable is suspect. For instance, Canada (the country I know best) is classified as a floating exchange rate country in this classification, and there is no distinction between the tight Dutch and loose Italian fixes in the European Monetary System. I urge Edwards to compare the IMF's categories with actual exchange rate volatility, as a simple robustness check. A propos, multinomial logit could be used to handle the "intermediate cases"; indeed, this is the way to test the appropriateness of a two-way (as opposed to a three-way) regime classification.

Edwards uses annual data, which is certainly reasonable from many perspectives (including handling the all-important data availability issue). Nevertheless, this frequency may be inappropriate in this context. Perhaps the right unit is "an exchange rate cycle" (just as some researchers believe that data should be "phase averaged" for business cycle investigations). An explicit test of "time deformation" would be a useful addition to the literature.

2   Contagious Currency Crises: Channels of Conveyance

Barry Eichengreen and Andrew K. Rose

I have studied foreign exchange crises,
their technique and their history, too.
And even—alas—their theory,
With ardent labour through and through.
Yet here I stand, as wise, poor fool,
As when I first went to school.
—Einzig (1968)

2.1   Introduction

Currency crises cluster in time. Figure 2.1, constructed from quarterly data for 20 industrial countries, is dominated by a few spikes indicating clusters of speculative attacks in particular quarters, separated by long periods of tranquillity. (Crises are episodes when the exchange rate depreciates, interest rates are raised to defend it, or reserves are expended to fend off speculative pressure and maintain the currency peg. We discuss the construction of the data underlying this figure in section 2.3 below.) Why crises should be distributed in this way has become a matter of some concern in the wake of the turbulence in the European Monetary System (EMS) in 1992–93 and the "tequila effect" associated with the Mexican meltdown in 1994–95.

A popular explanation for the pattern is that crises spread contagiously across countries. An attack on one currency, the argument runs, increases the probability of an attack on another. Even after controlling for the effects of movements in economic fundamentals like money supplies, output, and the current account of the balance of payments, an attack on one currency is believed to increase the

Barry Eichengreen is professor of political science and the Simpson Professor of Economics at the University of California, Berkeley; a research associate of the National Bureau of Economic Research; and a research fellow of the Centre for Economic Policy Research. Andrew K. Rose is the B. T. Rocca Professor of Economic Analysis and Policy in the Haas School of Business at the University of California, Berkeley; acting director of the International Finance and Macroeconomics Program at the National Bureau of Economic Research; and a research fellow of the Centre for Economic Policy Research.

The authors are grateful to Shirish Gupta for research assistance; the National Science Foundation for financial support; Takatoshi Ito, Ronald McKinnon, Gian Maria Milesi-Ferretti, and seminar participants at the 1996 East Asia Seminar on Economics, the U.S. Department of the Treasury, the University of Pennsylvania, Harvard University, the Centre for Economic Policy Research, and the Bank of Israel for comments; and Charles Wyplosz for collaboration on the project of which this paper is a part. In particular, the present manuscript draws liberally on Eichengreen, Rose, and Wyplosz (1996).

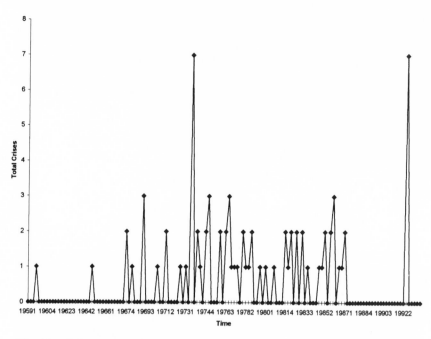

Fig. 2.1   Crises per quarter

probability of an attack on another in the same or immediately subsequent period.

One can think of a number of channels through which instability in foreign exchange markets might be transmitted across countries. One is the impact of a speculative attack on the current and prospective international competitiveness of the countries concerned and hence on their current accounts. Thus the attack on the United Kingdom in September 1992 and sterling's subsequent depreciation are said to have damaged the international competitiveness of the Republic of Ireland, for which the United Kingdom is the single most important export market, and to have provoked the attack on the punt at the beginning of 1993. Finland's devaluation in September 1992 was widely regarded as having had negative repercussions for Sweden, not so much because of direct trade between the two countries as because their exporters competed in the same third markets. Attacks on Spain in 1992–93 and the depreciation of the peseta are said to have damaged the international competitiveness of Portugal, which relies heavily on the Spanish export market, and to have provoked an attack on the escudo despite the virtual absence of imbalances in domestic fundamentals.

Trade links may not be the only channel of transmission, of course. It is difficult to argue, for example, that the tequila effect—the pressure applied to currencies in Latin America and East Asia following the crash of the Mexican peso in 1994—stemmed from strong trade links between Mexico and the other countries concerned. Argentina and Brazil may have traded extensively with Mexico, but the same was not true of Hong Kong, Malaysia, and Thailand. Rather than focusing on trade links, commentators pointed to similarities across countries in macroeconomic policies and conditions (see, e.g., Sachs, Tornell, and Velasco 1996).

Thus one can imagine a second model focusing on comovements in macroeconomic policies and conditions in the countries subject to attack. Evidence that certain market participants are skeptical about the stability of a currency may lead their colleagues to suspect that they are also skeptical about the prospects for the currencies of other countries in a similar macroeconomic position. Difficulties in one country pursuing a program of exchange-rate-based stabilization, for example, might lead currency traders to revise their assessment of the likelihood that other countries pursuing this macroeconomic strategy will carry it off. An attack on one currency and the issuing government's response to the pressure may thus provide new information relevant for expectations of how other governments will respond if placed in a similar position. For example, evidence that a country with an unusually high unemployment rate succumbed to a speculative attack and abandoned its currency peg out of reluctance to raise interest rates if that meant further aggravating unemployment might lead investors to revise their expectations of the likelihood that other countries in similar positions would be prepared to do so.

These two interpretations emphasizing different channels of international transmission of currency crises have different empirical implications. The interpretation emphasizing trade links suggests that currency crises will spread contagiously among countries that trade disproportionately with one another. The interpretation emphasizing economic and political commonalities suggests that instability will instead infect countries in broadly similar economic and political positions.

An entirely different view is that currency crises do not spread contagiously; rather, the clustering in figure 2.1 reflects the independent impact on different currencies of national economic factors that move together over time (perhaps because they emanate from a country at the center of international financial activity). Global macroeconomic conditions can cause national unemployment rates to rise and fall in tandem; if high unemployment weakens the resolve with which governments are prepared to defend their currency pegs, for example, one will see clusters of speculative attacks in periods of global slowdown. In this view, several currencies are attacked simultaneously because the countries in question are all experiencing unemployment that leaves their governments reluctant to adopt the restrictive policies needed to defend the exchange rate. But while crises cluster in time, there is no causal connection between their occurrence in one country and another, and no contagion, strictly speaking. Rather, the coincidence of currency crises reflects common environmental factors conducive to instability in all the countries concerned. This explanation has featured prominently in official post mortems of the 1992–93 crises in the EMS (Commission of the European Communities 1993; Committee of Governors of the Central Banks 1993a, 1993b), crises that coincided with a pan-European recession. It resonates with the literature on the tequila effect that emphasizes the role played by rising U.S. interest rates (a common environmental factor) in the balance-of-payments difficulties of the various Latin American and East Asian countries (see, e.g., Dooley, Fernandez-Arias, and Kletzer 1996; Sachs et al. 1996).

In principle, one can test this explanation by controlling for environmental factors when analyzing the impact of speculative attacks in neighboring countries. If environmental factors account for the clustering of attacks, then the incidence of crises in neighboring countries—a proxy for contagion—should have no additional effect when environmental controls are included in the analysis. In collaboration with Charles Wyplosz, we have taken this approach in previous papers (Eichengreen, Rose, and Wyplosz 1995, 1996). Employing a panel data set for 20 countries spanning a third of a century, we found that a crisis elsewhere in the world increased the probability of a crisis in the subject country by 8 percentage points, even after controlling for observable economic fundamentals. Our contagion proxy was constructed in the simplest possible way, as a binary indicator that equals unity if there is a currency crisis elsewhere in the world in the same period, and zero otherwise. Thus this approach disregards both the number of countries experiencing speculative attacks at a point in time and their economic proximity to one another. In effect, we treat an attack on the Finnish markka as of equal relevance for the Swedish krona, the French franc, and the Japanese yen.

This assumption is unlikely to be strictly correct, and even if it were there would remain the practical problem of controlling adequately for common environmental factors. There is always the possibility that the significance of the coefficient on the contagion proxy reflects a common omitted influence affecting both the subject country and its neighbors, which may be unobservable and will in any case be difficult to control for convincingly. This situation is familiar to epidemiologists who seek to determine whether the incidence of infection in a population reflects the contagious nature of the virus bearing the disease or the disease-conducive nature of the environment in which that population resides.

The obvious treatment is to impose additional structure on the problem by modeling the channels of transmission. We take this approach in the present paper. We again ask whether the likelihood of a crisis rises significantly when there is also a crisis elsewhere, after controlling for economic fundamentals in the countries concerned. But we weight crises elsewhere in the world by country characteristics intended to capture the extent to which contagion is transmitted through specific channels. We compare two different weighting schemes. First, on the assumption that countries that trade disproportionately with one another are prone to contagion operating through the competitiveness effects of crisis-induced exchange rate changes, we weight crises in neighboring countries by the importance of trade with those countries. Second, on the assumption that crises and governments' reactions to them lead investors to revise their expectations of officials' resolve in similar ways with respect to countries in broadly similar macroeconomic positions, we weight crises by the similarity of macroeconomic policies and outcomes.

The results support the hypothesis that speculative attacks in foreign exchange markets spread contagiously across countries. Our trade-weighted measure of crises elsewhere in the world is important economically as well as being significant statistically at high levels of confidence; it is robust to a variety of sensitivity tests. Our macro-weighted measure of crises does not display the same level of significance. Although it is always possible that our empirical measures of macroeconomic contagion are not capturing these phenomena adequately, we are inclined to interpret these results as suggesting that trade, rather than revisions of expectations based on macroeconomic factors, has been the dominant channel of transmission for contagious currency crises for the bulk of the sample period.

Importantly, however, the trade- and macro-weighted specifications both outperform the naive model of contagion estimated in our previous paper when they are included one at a time in alternative specifications. This supports the interpretation of our results in terms of contagion rather than omitted environmental variables. It is nevertheless appropriate to err on the side of caution: inevitably, there remains the possibility that the size and significance of the coefficient on our contagion variable reflect an unmeasured shock to fundamentals that strikes several countries simultaneously.

The rest of the paper is organized as follows. Section 2.2 summarizes what the literature has to say about contagion. Section 2.3 describes our data and methodology. Section 2.4 presents results and sensitivity analysis. Section 2.5 summarizes the findings and sets out the agenda for research.

2.2 Speculative Attacks and Contagion

The classic Krugman (1979) model of speculative attacks on pegged exchange rates, from which the subsequent literature derives, provides no obvious mechanisms for the contagious spread of currency crises. Domestic prices are given by purchasing power parity; it is not possible for relative prices to move and the currency to become undervalued subsequent to a successful attack and to thereby create competitive difficulties for a country's trading partners. There is no uncertainty in the Krugman model; with full information, the timing of the attack is determined by the relationship between the pegged exchange rate and the shadow rate (that which would prevail if official intervention in the foreign exchange market were abandoned); thus it is not possible for a speculative attack abroad to affect the timing of an attack on the subject country by resolving uncertainty about governments' preferences and options.

Subsequent work extended the Krugman model in ways that make it easier to accommodate the possibility of contagious speculative attacks. Willman (1988) and Goldberg (1994) endogenized relative prices, allowing events abroad to influence the real exchange rate and domestic competitiveness. Flood and Garber (1984) and Claessens (1991) introduced uncertainty about the domestic policy process. Flood and Garber, followed by Obstfeld (1986), added the idea of a contingent policy process, in which one-time events could lead the authorities to substitute one policy for another, thereby introducing the possibility of self-fulfilling speculative attacks.

While these extensions introduced channels through which currency crises can arise as a result of events in neighboring countries, as a result of extraneous events, and even as a result of speculative pressure itself, none of them was explicitly concerned with contagion. Work explicitly concerned with contagious currency crises was then stimulated by the EMS crises of 1992–93 and the Mexican crisis of 1994–95. Gerlach and Smets (1994) considered a model of two countries linked by trade in merchandise and financial assets. In their setup, a successful attack on one exchange rate leads to its real depreciation, which enhances the competitiveness of the country's merchandise exports. This produces a trade deficit in the second country, a gradual decline in the reserves of its central bank, and ultimately an attack on its currency. A second channel for contagious transmission is the impact of crisis and depreciation in the first country on the import prices and the overall price level in the second. Postcrisis real depreciation in the first country depresses import prices in the second. In turn, this reduces its consumer price index and the demand for money by its residents. Their efforts to swap domestic currency for foreign exchange then deplete the reserves of the central bank, conceivably culminating in an attack.

A second class of models developed the idea that there can exist multiple equilibria in foreign exchange markets (e.g., Flood and Garber 1984; Obstfeld 1986). If traders expect a currency to be devalued and act accordingly, they may so increase the cost of defending the peg that the authorities will choose to abandon it instead and shift to a more expansionary policy; under these circumstances, speculative attacks can be self-fulfilling. Thus, if a successful attack on one currency leads financial market participants to revise their expectations about the intentions of other governments and resolves uncertainty about whether those other governments will have the wherewithal to defend their currencies, instability can spread contagiously across markets.[1]

Subsequent work has identified still other potential channels for the contagious spread of currency crises.[2] But these two classes of analysis, focusing on

1. This approach has much in common with the literature in closed economy finance on information cascades and wisdom after the fact, in which a large movement in the price of one financial asset can lead traders to revise their expectations about the prices of others (see Caplin and Leahy 1994).
2. One such paper providing an analysis of contagious currency crises is Goldfajn and Valdés (1995). They focus on the role of illiquidity in financial markets. A key feature of their model is the introduction of financial intermediaries. These authors show how, in the presence of such intermediaries, small disturbances can provoke large-scale runs on a currency. Intermediaries supply liquid assets to foreigners unwilling to commit to long-term investments; i.e., they provide

trade and informational effects, are at the center of the literature. To this point, however, theory has run ahead of empirics. The remainder of this paper makes a modest attempt to rectify this imbalance.

2.3   Data and Methodology

We analyze a panel of quarterly macroeconomic and political data covering 20 industrial countries from 1959 through 1993 (a total of 2,800 observations). We pose the following question: is the incidence of a currency crisis in a particular country at a given point in time (e.g., France in the third quarter of 1992) correlated with the incidence of a currency crisis in a different country (e.g., the United Kingdom) at the same point in time, even after taking into account the effects of current and lagged domestic macroeconomic and political influences? While the finding of a positive partial correlation is consistent with the existence of contagion, since it implies that speculative attacks are temporally correlated even after conditioning on domestic factors, we are reluctant to interpret this as proof of contagion, since it may reflect an unmeasured common shock to economic fundamentals that strikes several countries simultaneously (or an unmeasured shock to Germany, our center country) rather than spillovers from one country to another.[3]

2.3.1   Measuring Currency Crises

The first issue that must be confronted is how to determine when a speculative attack has occurred. Having addressed this issue in a number of previous papers (Eichengreen et al. 1995, 1996), we provide only a summary of our thinking here.

Currency crises cannot be identified with actual devaluations, revaluations, and instances in which the currency is floated, for two reasons.[4] First, not all speculative attacks are successful. The currency may be supported through the expenditure of reserves by the central bank or by foreign central banks and governments.[5] The authorities may repel attacks by raising interest rates and adopting other policies of austerity. Further, many realignments are taken deliberately in tranquil periods, possibly to preclude future attacks.

Ideally, an index of speculative pressure would be obtained by employing a

---

maturity transformation services. By offering attractive terms on liquid deposits, their presence augments the volume of capital inflows. But when, for exogenous reasons, foreign investors withdraw their deposits, intermediaries unable to costlessly liquidate their assets face the risk of failure. Hence, a bank run can produce a self-fulfilling banking crisis (Diamond and Dybvig 1983), in the same way that a run on the currency can provoke a self-fulfilling exchange rate crisis. Moreover, the run on intermediaries can spill over into a run on the currency as foreign investors withdraw their deposits and convert them into foreign exchange. These crises can spread contagiously to other countries when international investors encountering liquidity difficulties as a result of the banking crisis in one country respond by liquidating their positions in other national markets.

3. We return to this point below.

4. We refer to actual changes in exchange rates and in exchange arrangements as "events" to distinguish them from the "crises" that are the focus of our analysis.

5. And occasionally by the actual or threatened imposition of capital controls.

structural model of exchange rate determination, from which one would derive the excess demand for foreign exchange. In practice, however, empirical models linking macroeconomic variables to the exchange rate have little explanatory power at short and intermediate horizons.[6] In the absence of an empirically valid macromodel, we resort to an ad hoc approach, the intuition for which is derived from the well-known model of exchange market pressure due to Girton and Roper (1977). The idea is that an excess demand for foreign exchange can be met through several (not mutually exclusive) channels. If the attack is successful, depreciation or devaluation occurs. But the authorities may instead accommodate the pressure by running down their international reserves or deter the attack by raising interest rates. As a measure of speculative pressure, we therefore construct a weighted average of exchange rate changes, reserve changes, and interest rate changes, measuring all variables relative to those prevailing in Germany, the reference country. The index of exchange market pressure then becomes

$$\text{EMP}_{i,t} \equiv \{(\alpha\%\Delta e_{i,t}) + [\beta\Delta(i_{i,t} - i_{G,t})] - [\gamma(\%\Delta r_{i,t} - \%\Delta r_{G,t})]\},$$

where $e_{i,t}$ denotes the price of a deutsche mark in i's currency at time t; i_G denotes the short German interest; r denotes the ratio of international reserves;[7] and α, β, and γ are weights.

We define crises as extreme values of this index:

$$\text{Crisis}_{i,t} = 1 \quad \text{if EMP}_{i,t} > 1.5\sigma_{\text{EMP}} + \mu_{\text{EMP}},$$

$$= 0 \quad \text{otherwise},$$

where μ_{EMP} and σ_{EMP} are the sample mean and standard deviation of EMP, respectively.

A critical step is weighting the three components of the index. One obvious option is an unweighted average, which has the advantage of simplicity. But since the volatilities of reserves, exchange rates, and interest differentials are very different, we instead weight the components so as to equalize the volatilities of the three components, preventing any one of them from dominating the index. We then check the sensitivity of our results to this scheme (subsection 2.4.5).

We identify quarters in which our index of speculative pressure is at least 1.5 standard deviations above the sample mean as instances of speculative attack (although we again test for sensitivity with respect to this arbitrarily chosen threshold). To avoid counting the same crisis more than once, we exclude the later observation(s) when two (or more) crises occur in successive quarters (though it would be interesting for future researchers to examine long-lived crises explicitly). Thus our "exclusion window" is one quarter (though again

---

6. Frankel and Rose (1995) provide a recent survey.
7. Following Girton and Roper, r is actually the ratio of reserves to narrow money (M1).

we vary this parameter). We refer to our noncrisis observations as "tranquil" periods and use these as the control group.[8]

Our choice of a one-quarter exclusion window (so that each country contributes no more than two observations annually) and a 1.5 standard deviation outlier threshold produces a sample of 77 crises and 1,179 periods of tranquillity.[9]

The crisis observations are not randomly distributed. There are clusters of speculative attacks in 1973 (at the time of the breakup of the Bretton Woods system) and in 1992 (at the time of the European currency crises), as displayed in figure 2.1 above.

2.3.2 Data

Most of the financial and macroeconomic variables that we utilize are taken from the CD-ROM version of the International Monetary Fund's (IMF's) *International Financial Statistics* (*IFS*). The data set is quarterly, spanning 1959–93 for 20 industrial countries.[10] It has been checked for transcription and other errors and corrected. Most of the variables are transformed into differential percentage changes by taking differences between domestic and German annualized fourth-differences of natural logarithms and multiplying by 100.

We employ the following variables: total nongold international reserves (*IFS* line 11d); period-average exchange rates (line rf); short-term interest rates (money market rates [line 60b] where possible, discount rates otherwise [line 60]); exports and imports (both measured in dollars, lines 70d and 71d, respectively); the current account (line 77a.d, converted to domestic currency) and the central government budget position (line 80), both measured as percentages of nominal GDP (frequently line 99a); long-term government bond yields (line 61); a nominal stock market index (line 62, which sets 1990 = 100); domestic credit (line 32); M1 (line 34); M2 (line 35 + M1); the CPI (line 64); and real GDP (usually line 99a.r). We use the real effective exchange rate as a measure of competitiveness (line reu, which uses normalized relative unit labor costs), though this variable is only available from 1975.

We also utilize a number of labor market indicators not included in *IFS*. Data on total employment, the unemployment rate, and the business sector wage rate were drawn from the Organization for Economic Cooperation and Development's *Main Economic Indicators*. To capture political conditions we

---

8. Just as we do not allow crises in successive quarters to count as independent observations by excluding the later observations, we also do not allow two successive periods of tranquillity to count as independent observations. We do this by applying our exclusion window to periods of both crisis and tranquillity. Our exclusion window should also reduce potential problems with serial correlation that might occur if EMP is close to our 1.5σ threshold.

9. However, missing data will preclude use of some of these observations.

10. The countries in our sample are (in order of IMF country number): the United States, the United Kingdom, Austria, Belgium, Denmark, France, Italy, the Netherlands, Norway, Sweden, Switzerland, Canada, Japan, Finland, Greece, Ireland, Portugal, Spain, and Australia, along with our center country, Germany.

construct indicators of governmental electoral victories and defeats, using Keesing's *Record of World Events* and Banks's *Political Handbook of the World*.

Finally, we use a list of exchange market "events" (devaluations, flotations, changes in exchange rate bandwidths, etc.). These are gleaned from the IMF's annual report *Exchange Arrangements and Exchange Restrictions*. These volumes also provide us the basis for constructing dummy variables indicating the presence of capital controls.

The available data on international reserves are less than ideal for a number of well-known reasons. Off-balance sheet transactions, third-party intervention, standby credits, and foreign liabilities, all of which are relevant for foreign exchange intervention, tend to be omitted or incompletely reported. Short-duration attacks (especially unsuccessful ones) may not be evident in quarterly data. Finally, subtle changes in actual or anticipated capital controls, while difficult to measure, may in fact be quite important, especially when countries are mounting defenses against speculative attacks.

2.3.3   Testing for Contagion

We test the null hypothesis that the incidence of currency crises elsewhere in the world at the same point in time does not affect the probability of a speculative attack on the domestic currency. While our model attempts to control for the influence of a wide range of current and lagged macroeconomic variables, it is nonstructural. This is one reason to view our evidence (which turns out to be inconsistent with the null at standard confidence levels) as consistent with but not definitive proof of contagion.

We estimate a binary probit model, linking our dependent variable (an indicator variable that takes on a value of unity for a speculative attack and zero otherwise) to our controls with maximum likelihood, including additional regressors to capture the effects of macroeconomic and political influences that affect crisis incidence. We cast our net as widely as possible, including (1) presence of capital controls; (2) electoral victory or defeat of the government; (3) growth of domestic credit; (4) inflation; (5) output growth; (6) employment growth; (7) unemployment rate; (8) central government budget surplus (+) or deficit (−), expressed as a percentage of GDP; and (9) current account surplus or deficit, again, as a percentage of GDP.

Since the literature on currency crises does not provide much guidance about the time horizon for these influences, we consider a range of plausible alternatives. At the short end of the spectrum, we allow only contemporary influences to affect the probability of a crisis. We then allow for explanatory variables lagged up to two quarters, one year, and two years. We allow these lagged influences to operate jointly with the contemporaneous variables or by themselves (as would be appropriate if lags in data collection or processing preclude the consideration of contemporaneous developments). To conserve degrees of freedom, we model the lags using moving averages. Rather than including the first and second lags of inflation separately, for example, we include only a single term that is the average inflation differential in the two preceding quarters.

This leads us to estimate the following model:

$$\text{Crisis}_{i,t} = \omega \sum_j w_{ij,t}(\text{Crisis}_{j,t}) + \lambda I(L)_{i,t} + \varepsilon_{i,t},$$

$$W_{ij,t}(\text{Crisis}_{j,t}) = w_{ij,t} \quad \text{if Crisis}_{j,t} = 1 \text{ for any } j \neq 1,$$

$$= 0 \quad \text{otherwise},$$

where $w_{ij,t}$ is a weight that corresponds to the "relevance" at time t of country j for country i; $I(L)_{i,t}$ is an information set of 10 contemporaneous and/or lagged control regressors; λ is the corresponding vector of nuisance coefficients; and ε is a normally distributed disturbance representing a host of omitted influences that affect the probability of a currency crisis. Under the null hypothesis of no common shocks and no contagion, this equation can be estimated with standard least squares techniques. The null hypothesis of interest to us is $H0: \omega = 0$. We interpret evidence against the null as being consistent with the existence of a contagion effect.[11]

Our first weighting scheme quantifies the ties between countries i and j using trade data. We use the weights that the IMF has computed in the course of constructing its real multilateral effective exchange rates.[12] The IMF's methodology derives the weight for j in country i's effective exchange rate as a convex combination of bilateral import weights and double export weights, using trade in manufacturing. The weights use unit labor costs, which are widely considered to be reliable indicators of international competitiveness. The weights are time invariant. They have been computed for our 20 industrial countries by the IMF and were created in October 1994.

Thus our trade-weighting scheme is

$$w_{ij,t} = \text{EER}_{ij} \quad \text{for any } j \neq i,$$

where EER_{ij} is the weight for country j in country i's IMF effective exchange rate index.

Our second weighting scheme is intended to capture macroeconomic similarities whose existence is a potential channel for contagion. We think of two countries as being "similar" if they display similar macroeconomic conditions—for example, if they have similar rates of growth of domestic credit. We then test the hypothesis that an attack on the currency of country j affects the probability of an attack on the currency of country i.

In practice, implementing this notion depends on being able to measure "similarity." We concentrate on seven "focus variables" that appear to be the

11. By way of contrast, Sachs et al. (1996) do not control for fundamentals when testing for contagion.
12. Documentation and references regarding these weights are to be found in *IFS*.

subject of considerable attention among participants in foreign exchange markets: (1) domestic credit growth (as always, relative to Germany); (2) money growth; (3) CPI inflation; (4) output growth; (5) the unemployment rate; (6) the current account (as always, in nominal GDP percentage points); and (7) the government budget deficit.[13] We multiply the rate of GDP growth, the current account, and the government budget by -1 in order to allow for easier comparison with the other four variables; this means that higher values are associated with greater risk. We standardize the variables by subtracting sample means and dividing the result by the sample standard deviation. In practice, we standardize in two ways: we take a country-specific approach in which a country is compared only with itself (so that, e.g., the average rate of growth of French domestic credit is subtracted from the raw series and then divided by the sample French credit growth standard deviation); alternatively, we take a time-specific approach in which the observations at one point in time are compared with observations for all 20 countries at that same point in time. The first approach is appropriate if currency speculators compare credit growth in a country in a quarter to that country's own past credit growth; the second is relevant if speculators compare the country's credit growth to that typical of other countries in the same quarter.

Having standardized the variables, we compute the macro weights as follows for the "country-specific" and "time-specific" standardizations, respectively:

$$w_{ij,t} = \sum_j (1 - \{\Phi[(x_{jt} - \mu_i)/\sigma_i] - \Phi[(x_{it} - \mu_i)/\sigma_i]\}) \quad \text{for any } j \neq i,$$

$$w_{ij,t} = \sum_j (1 - \{\Phi[(x_{jt} - \mu_t)/\sigma_t] - \Phi[(x_{it} - \mu_t)/\sigma_t]\}) \quad \text{for any } j \neq i,$$

where $\Phi(\cdot)$ is the cumulative distribution function of the standardized normal function, $\mu_i(\mu_t)$ is the country-specific (time-specific) sample average of variable x, $\sigma_i(\sigma_t)$ is the country-specific (time-specific) standard deviation of variable x, and the x's are the seven macroeconomic focus variables.

This specification implies that if country j is attacked at time t and it is similar to country i in the sense of having similar standardized growth rates of relevant macroeconomic variables, then it receives a high weight on the contagion variable. If j and i have identical (standardized) domestic credit growth rates, the weight is unity; the more dissimilar are the growth rates (in the sense of being distant in terms of the cumulative distribution), the lower is the weight. If i's credit growth is at the extreme lower end of i's cumulative distribution while j's is at its upper end, then the weight is zero.

Since we have two standardizing techniques (country and time specific) and seven focus variables, we obtain 14 sets of macroeconomic contagion weights.

---

13. One could imagine adding focus variables. The presence of capital controls and the total stock of external debt would be interesting, especially in the case of developing countries. However, such variables tend to move slowly. In addition, our seven focus variables turn out to be extremely collinear in any case.

2.4 Results

We begin with the simplest test for contagion. We test whether a crisis in country i at time t is affected by an attack in the same quarter anywhere else in the world, after controlling for a variety of political and economic variables. This is an "unweighted" approach to contagion. The indicator variable is unity if there is at least one attack elsewhere in the world during the quarter, and zero otherwise. Hence, both the number of attacks and their relevance for the country in question are ignored.[14]

2.4.1 Unweighted Contagion Indicators

These results are presented in table 2.1. Its five columns correspond to five assumptions about the appropriate time horizon for the regressors. Since probit coefficients are not easily interpretable, we report the effects of one-unit (percentage point) changes in the regressors on the probability of speculative attack (again expressed in percentage points), evaluated at the mean of the data. We also tabulate the associated z-statistics, which test the null hypothesis of no effect. Statistics that are inconsistent with the null hypothesis of no effect at the 5 percent significance level are printed in boldface. Diagnostics appear at the bottom of the table, including an omnibus test for the joint significance of all coefficients.

The results are consistent with the existence of a contagion effect (i.e., an estimate of ω) that is economically important and statistically significant. A speculative attack elsewhere in the world increases the probability of a currency crisis by around 8 percentage points. However, though this finding is consistent with a contagion effect, it is not definitive for at least two reasons. First, it may simply reflect a common shock (e.g., a shock to our center country, Germany, that is not captured by our control regressors). Second, the impact of the control regressors is not what one would like. Indeed, the lack of strong sensible partial correlations between crisis incidence and traditional economic fundamentals makes us cautious of over interpreting the results.

In Eichengreen et al. (1996) we provide details for a number of sensitivity analyses that we conducted. None disturbs the basic thrust of the findings. We think of these results as *consistent* with the evidence of contagion per se. However, they do not shed light on its source. We turn next to that task.

2.4.2 Trade Weights

Table 2.2 substitutes our first set of weights—those based on the IMF's REER weights and intended to capture bilateral trade linkages—for the un-

---

14. This simplest test for contagion is the focus of Eichengreen et al. (1996). We reproduce those results here to provide a point of reference and departure for the present analysis. Our estimation technique does not ensure "model coherence"; we condition our crisis measure on the incidence of crises elsewhere without taking into account the resulting expected conditional probabilities of the regressand.

Table 2.1   Probit Results with Unweighted Contagion Variable

Variable	Contemporaneous	Moving Average of Contemporaneous + 2 Lags	Moving Average of 2 Lags	Moving Average of Contemporaneous + 4 Lags	Moving Average of Contemporaneous + 8 Lags
Crisis elsewhere	**7.45 (3.8)**	**8.33 (4.0)**	**8.14 (4.3)**	**8.72 (4.0)**	**8.83 (3.8)**
Capital controls	−1.66 (.7)	.22 (.1)	.66 (.3)	.48 (.2)	1.24 (.4)
Government victory	−4.24 (1.0)	−1.71 (.3)	−.60 (.2)	5.30 (1.6)	−.45 (.2)
Government loss	−3.45 (.9)	−7.44 (1.3)	−3.34 (1.2)	2.49 (.8)	−.63 (.2)
Credit growth	.19 (1.8)	.11 (.8)	.10 (1.2)	−.00 (.0)	−.09 (.4)
Inflation rate	**.75 (3.5)**	**.57 (2.4)**	.40 (1.9)	**.59 (2.1)**	.64 (1.8)
Output growth	.21 (.6)	−.39 (.9)	−.50 (1.4)	−.74 (1.3)	−.36 (.4)
Employment growth	.37 (.7)	.86 (1.5)	.78 (1.5)	1.08 (1.6)	1.30 (1.6)
Unemployment rate	**.86 (3.0)**	**.96 (3.2)**	**.92 (3.5)**	**1.04 (3.3)**	**1.19 (3.4)**
Budget position/GDP	.47 (1.9)	.41 (1.6)	.35 (1.5)	.46 (1.6)	.57 (1.8)
Current account/GDP	−.23 (.8)	−.36 (1.1)	−.51 (1.9)	−.42 (1.2)	−.34 (.8)
N	645	626	703	608	572
McFadden's R^2	.15	.12	.13	.12	.10
Joint test for slopes χ^2 (11)	**55**	**46**	**53**	**43**	**36**

Notes: Table reports probit slope derivatives ($\times$ 100, to convert into percentages) and, in parentheses, associated z-statistics (for hypothesis of no effect). Model is estimated with a constant, by maximum likelihood. Slopes significantly different from zero at the .05 value are in boldface.

Table 2.2   Probit Results with Contagion Variable Weighted by International Trade

Variable	Contemporaneous	Moving Average of Contemporaneous + 2 Lags	Moving Average of 2 Lags	Moving Average of Contemporaneous + 4 Lags	Moving Average of Contemporaneous + 8 Lags
Crisis elsewhere	**.44 (5.0)**	**.66 (5.1)**	**.61 (5.3)**	**.72 (5.2)**	**.74 (5.2)**
Capital controls	−1.8 (.8)	−.77 (.3)	−.06 (.0)	−.76 (.3)	.16 (.1)
Government victory	−3.9 (.9)	.59 (.1)	.39 (.1)	3.7 (1.1)	−2.0 (.7)
Government loss	−2.0 (.5)	−6.9 (1.1)	−3.5 (1.2)	3.0 (.9)	.43 (.2)
Credit growth	.17 (1.6)	.05 (.3)	.09 (1.1)	−.09 (.5)	−.10 (.5)
Inflation rate	**.82 (3.8)**	**.73 (3.0)**	**.53 (2.6)**	**.81 (2.8)**	**.79 (2.3)**
Output growth	.10 (.3)	−.39 (.8)	−.48 (1.3)	−.49 (.8)	−.21 (.3)
Employment growth	.44 (.8)	.99 (1.6)	.95 (1.8)	1.12 (1.7)	1.4 (1.6)
Unemployment rate	**.71 (2.3)**	**.78 (2.5)**	**.76 (2.8)**	**.85 (2.5)**	**.97 (2.7)**
Budget position/GDP	**.52 (2.1)**	.49 (1.8)	.40 (1.6)	**.58 (2.0)**	**.71 (2.2)**
Current account/GDP	−.28 (1.0)	−.24 (.8)	−.31 (1.1)	−.33 (.9)	−.21 (.5)
N	645	626	703	608	572
McFadden's R^2	.18	.19	.19	.19	.18
Joint test for slopes χ^2 (11)	70	70	76	67	63

Notes: Table reports probit slope derivatives ($\times$ 100, to convert into percentages) and, in parentheses, associated z-statistics (for hypothesis of no effect). Model is estimated with a constant, by maximum likelihood. Slopes significantly different from zero at the .05 value are in boldface.

weighted contagion variable. Trade weighting the contagion variable improves the fit of the equation. In contrast to the unweighted results in table 2.1, however, it is not easy to interpret the size of the contagion variable, since it is no longer an indicator variable but is instead the product of a dummy and a trade weight. Nevertheless, the positive sign of the coefficient on the contagion variable indicates that an attack elsewhere in the world still increases the probability of an attack by a statistically significantly amount. The level of statistical significance for the contagion effect is higher than in table 2.1.

We interpret this evidence as supporting the hypothesis that currency crises are transmitted, at least in part, via bilateral trade ties. It leads us to the belief that there is contagion, rather than simply a shock to an unmeasured fundamental common to a number of countries.

2.4.3   Macro Weights

In table 2.3 we present results using the macro weights. We substitute all seven macro-weighted contagion variables for the trade-weighted measure. The macro-weighted contagion proxies are generally insignificant at conventional statistical levels when considered individually.[15] However, the seven variables are jointly significant at high confidence levels (the relevant chi-square test statistic, labeled "contagion test," is reported at the foot of the table). This suggests collinearity among the seven contagion variables, as one would expect.

Table 2.4 provides direct evidence on the extent of this collinearity. It reports coefficients on the macro-contagion variables when the latter are included in the equation one by one. (The coefficient estimates for the political and macroeconomic fundamentals are not reported for ease of presentation.) As expected, the estimated coefficients are positive, indicating that a currency crisis in a country that is similar, in the relevant macroeconomic sense, raises the probability of an attack on the domestic currency. The coefficients are statistically significant at standard confidence levels and do not vary much across macroeconomic focus variables, conditioning set, or standardization technique.

We interpret this evidence as consistent with the existence of macroeconomic contagion. But it answers only a subset of the relevant economic questions. For example, is contagion spread through both trade and macroeconomic links? Or does one channel dominate the other? We now proceed to these issues.

2.4.4   Comparing the Trade and Macro Channels

We are interested in testing the explanatory power of the different measures of contagion against each other. This requires dealing with the collinearity

---

15. This result does not depend on the conditioning set—specifically, on whether the traditional political and macroeconomic fundamentals are entered only contemporaneously or with moving average lags as well. It is also insensitive to whether the macro weights are computed with variables standardized by country or time period.

Table 2.3   Probit Results with Contagion Variable Weighted by Macro Similarity: All Seven Contagion Variables Included Simultaneously

Variable	Country-Specific Averages			Time-Specific Averages		
	Contemporaneous	Moving Average of 2 Lags	Moving Average of Contemporaneous + 8 Lags	Contemporaneous	Moving Average of 2 Lags	Moving Average of Contemporaneous + 8 Lags
Crisis*Credit similarity	−.10 (.0)	1.68 (.7)	2.72 (.9)	−2.44 (.9)	−.10 (.0)	.01 (.0)
Crisis*Money similarity	−.32 (.1)	1.06 (.4)	−.38 (.1)	.41 (.2)	.61 (.3)	12 (.0)
Crisis*Inflation similarity	2.54 (.8)	4.12 (1.4)	5.24 (1.5)	3.06 (1.1)	4.02 (1.5)	5.93 (1.9)
Crisis*GDP similarity	−1.97 (.8)	−3.48 (1.5)	−3.42 (1.3)	−1.06 (.6)	−2.57 (1.6)	−2.77 (1.4)
Crisis*Unemployment similarity	−.60 (.3)	−.93 (.6)	−1.08 (.5)	3.35 (1.5)	3.66 (1.8)	3.55 (1.4)
Crisis*Current account similarity	2.10 (.7)	1.19 (.4)	1.72 (.5)	4.25 (1.7)	3.07 (1.4)	3.59 (1.3)
Crisis*Budget similarity	1.80 (.8)	.16 (.1)	−.39 (.2)	−4.19 (1.5)	−4.86 (1.9)	−5.99 (2.0)
Capital controls	−2.56 (1.1)	−.43 (.2)	−.49 (.2)	−2.68 (1.1)	−.64 (.3)	−.84 (.3)
Government victory	−3.81 (.9)	−.05 (.0)	−1.87 (.7)	−3.52 (.8)	−.36 (.1)	−2.02 (.7)
Government loss	−2.62 (.6)	−3.74 (1.4)	−1.03 (.4)	−2.88 (.7)	−3.99 (1.4)	−.99 (.4)
Credit growth	.20 (1.7)	.09 (1.1)	−.16 (.7)	.22 (1.9)	.10 (1.2)	−.18 (.7)
Inflation rate	**.80 (3.6)**	**.48 (2.3)**	**.81 (2.3)**	**.71 (3.1)**	**.42 (2.0)**	**.75 (2.1)**
Growth	.10 (.3)	−.58 (1.6)	−.46 (.6)	.15 (.4)	−.58 (1.6)	−.38 (.5)
Employment growth	.24 (.5)	.57 (1.1)	1.08 (1.3)	.20 (.4)	.67 (1.3)	1.24 (1.5)
Unemployment rate	**.86 (2.9)**	**.92 (2.4)**	**1.16 (3.2)**	**.65 (2.0)**	**.69 (2.4)**	**.91 (2.4)**
Budget position/GDP	**.57 (2.2)**	.37 (1.5)	.62 (1.9)	.33 (1.1)	.20 (.8)	.40 (1.1)
Current account/GDP	−.23 (.8)	−.46 (1.7)	−.37 (.9)	−.08 (.3)	−.29 (1.1)	−.13 (.3)
N	645	703	572	645	703	572
McFadden's R^2	.16	.16	.14	.17	.17	.15
Slopes test χ^2 (17)	**63**	**64**	**49**	**65**	**67**	**53**
Contagion test χ^2 (7)	**20**	**27**	**25**	**21**	**28**	**27**

Notes: Table reports probit slope derivatives ($\times$ 100, to convert into percentages) and, in parentheses, associated z-statistics (for hypothesis of no effect). Model is estimated with a constant, by maximum likelihood. Slopes significantly different from zero at the .05 value are in boldface.

Table 2.4   Probit Results with Contagion Variable Weighted by Macro Similarity: Contagion Variables Included One by One

Variable	Country-Specific Averages			Time-Specific Averages		
	Contemporaneous	Moving Average of 2 Lags	Moving Average of Contemporaneous + 8 Lags	Contemporaneous	Moving Average of 2 Lags	Moving Average of Contemporaneous + 8 Lags
Crisis*Credit similarity	6.67 (3.7)	7.46 (4.4)	8.82 (4.1)	4.73 (2.7)	5.68 (3.4)	6.60 (3.2)
Crisis*Money similarity	6.23 (3.8)	7.05 (4.4)	7.81 (3.8)	5.41 (3.3)	6.44 (4.0)	7.33 (3.7)
Crisis*Inflation similarity	7.17 (4.1)	7.79 (4.7)	9.21 (4.4)	7.23 (4.2)	8.12 (4.9)	9.81 (4.8)
Crisis*GDP similarity	6.03 (3.7)	5.74 (3.8)	6.84 (3.6)	5.41 (3.5)	4.81 (3.4)	5.90 (3.3)
Crisis*Unemployment similarity	5.10 (3.4)	5.25 (3.6)	5.82 (3.2)	6.66 (4.3)	7.00 (4.8)	8.02 (4.5)
Crisis*Current account similarity	7.35 (4.3)	7.53 (4.7)	8.91 (4.4)	7.40 (4.1)	7.26 (4.5)	9.05 (4.3)
Crisis*Budget similarity	6.15 (3.7)	5.78 (3.8)	6.13 (3.1)	5.13 (3.2)	5.40 (3.6)	5.87 (3.1)

Notes: Table reports probit slope derivatives ($\times$ 100, to convert into percentages) and, in parentheses, associated z-statistics (for hypothesis of no effect). Each model is estimated by maximum likelihood with a constant and seven political and macroeconomic controls. All reported slopes differ significantly from zero at the .01 value.

among our seven macro-contagion variables, for which purpose we employ factor analysis.

Factor analysis both verifies the existence of multicollinearity and provides a convenient method of rank reduction. We estimated a single-factor model for the seven macro-contagion variables using the method of principal factors. The single-factor model works well for both the country-specific and time-specific standardizations.[16] We use the resulting factor—a linear combination of the seven macroeconomic variables—in place of the vector of standardized variables.[17]

Table 2.5 reports estimates of the probit model when the effects of the different classes of contagion variables are estimated simultaneously. The three variables correspond to those used in tables 2.1, 2.2, and 2.3: they are unweighted, trade weighted, and weighted by the macro factor, respectively. As always, the full set of political and macroeconomic controls is included.

Again there is overwhelming evidence consistent with contagion; a joint test of the hypothesis that all three contagion variables are significant, which appears at the foot of the table, is wildly inconsistent with the null of no contagion. The weighted measure designed to capture trade linkages remains positive and highly significant, consistent with contagion via the trade channel. The unweighted measure is also positive and moderately significant at standard confidence levels, perhaps indicating that there is still evidence of a shock to unmeasured common fundamentals. But now the macro factor is negative and insignificant for all three conditioning sets and both standardization techniques.

Thus our results suggest that contagious currency crises tend to spread across countries mainly as a function of international trade links. In contrast, the influence of macroeconomic similarities disappears when the various classes of contagion measures are included simultaneously. The continuing significance of the unweighted measure of contagion, even when the trade- and macro-weighted measures are included simultaneously, suggests that contagion may also spread through other channels than those that we have emphasized.

2.4.5   Sensitivity Analysis

We have performed a number of robustness checks to investigate the sensitivity of our finding that trade linkages are more important than macroeconomic similarities. For instance, we split our sample into two parts (at, e.g.,

---

16. E.g., the first eigenvalue is substantially higher than the second (for both the country-specific and time-specific factors, the first eigenvalue is almost 6 while the second is less than 0.2). In addition, the first factor explains a high proportion of the data variance (close to 100 percent); the individual factor uniquenesses are low (never more than 30 percent). Finally, all the scoring coefficients are positive, as expected.

17. Of course, there are two factors, one for each of the two standardizations (country and time specific).

Table 2.5   Probit Results with Three Different Measures of Contagion

Variable	Country-Specific Averages			Time-Specific Averages		
	Contemporaneous	Moving Average of 2 Lags	Moving Average of Contemporaneous + 8 Lags	Contemporaneous	Moving Average of 2 Lags	Moving Average of Contemporaneous + 8 Lags
Crisis elsewhere: unweighted	**4.66 (2.0)**	**5.18 (2.3)**	4.80 (1.7)	**4.74 (2.0)**	**4.97 (2.2)**	4.44 (1.6)
Crisis elsewhere: international trade weights	**.39 (3.6)**	**.58 (4.3)**	**.75 (4.3)**	**.40 (3.7)**	**.58 (4.2)**	**.73 (4.1)**
Crisis elsewhere: macro-factor weights	-.85 (.6)	-1.87 (1.3)	-2.18 (1.2)	-.94 (.7)	-1.64 (1.2)	-1.68 (1.0)
Capital controls	-1.62 (.7)	.25 (.1)	.32 (.1)	-1.55 (.7)	.27 (.1)	.29 (.1)
Government victory	-3.70 (.9)	.29 (.1)	-1.60 (.6)	-3.70 (.9)	.32 (.1)	-1.57 (.6)
Government loss	-2.24 (.6)	-3.32 (1.1)	.44 (.2)	-2.23 (.5)	-3.31 (1.2)	.43 (.2)
Credit growth	.17 (1.6)	.08 (1.0)	-.09 (.4)	.17 (1.7)	.09 (1.0)	-.09 (.4)
Inflation rate	**.77 (3.7)**	**.47 (2.3)**	**.72 (2.1)**	**.77 (3.7)**	**.48 (2.4)**	**.74 (2.1)**
Output growth	.09 (.3)	-.53 (1.5)	-.35 (.4)	.09 (.3)	-.52 (1.5)	-.34 (.4)
Employment growth	.39 (.8)	.93 (1.8)	1.29 (1.6)	.40 (.8)	.89 (1.8)	1.25 (1.5)
Unemployment rate	**.69 (2.4)**	**.76 (2.9)**	**.96 (2.7)**	**.70 (2.4)**	**.78 (2.9)**	**.98 (2.7)**
Budget position/GDP	**.48 (2.0)**	.37 (1.6)	**.68 (2.1)**	**.47 (2.0)**	.37 (1.6)	**.67 (2.1)**
Current account/GDP	-.23 (.9)	-.33 (1.3)	-.26 (.6)	-.24 (.9)	-.36 (1.4)	-.29 (.7)
N	645	703	572	645	703	572
McFadden's R^2	.20	.20	.19	.20	.20	.19
Slopes test χ^2 (13)	**75**	**81**	**66**	**74**	**81**	**66**
Contagion test χ^2 (3)	**31**	**38**	**34**	**31**	**37**	**33**

Notes: Table reports probit slope derivatives ($\times$ 100, to convert into percentages) and, in parentheses, associated z-statistics (for hypothesis of no effect). Model is estimated with a constant, by maximum likelihood. Slopes significantly different from zero at the .05 value are in boldface.

1974 and 1979) to check whether different models of contagion dominate different parts of the sample. We have split our sample into observations in which capital controls are present and absent. We have added additional macroeconomic fundamentals and compared macroeconomic and trade contagion channels without our unweighted variable. None of these checks disturbs our basic finding that trade links are the more important conduit for the infectious spread of currency crises.

2.5 Conclusions and Implications

We have sought to test for contagion in foreign exchange markets using a framework that distinguishes two channels of international transmission of speculative attacks. The first channel is trade links, and the hypothesis is that attacks spill over contagiously to other countries with which the subject country trades. The second channel is macroeconomic similarities, and the hypothesis is that attacks spread to other countries where economic policies and conditions are broadly similar. The first approach emphasizes the implications for competitiveness of an attack elsewhere in the world. The second focuses on the information content of an attack (where the assumption is that an attack on one country reveals information about market sentiment regarding the viability of a particular economic strategy).

Using data for 20 industrial countries spanning more than three decades, we have tested these alternatives against the null of no contagion. The null is decisively rejected: we find consistent, robust, and statistically significant evidence of contagious speculative attacks. This result poses a fundamental challenge to those who would dismiss contagion out of hand. The simplest test, using an unweighted contagion proxy, suggests that an attack elsewhere in the world raises the probability of an attack on the domestic currency by 8 percentage points, even after controlling for a substantial number of macroeconomic and political fundamentals. Strikingly, however, both the trade-weighted contagion proxy, designed to capture the first story sketched in the preceding paragraph, and the macro-weighted proxy, intended to capture the second, outperform the naive unweighted contagion measure when they are included one at a time. We take this as confirmation that what our tests are picking up is contagion per se, and not only the effects of omitted environmental factors common to the countries in question (although the latter are still present).

The effect of contagion operating through trade is stronger than that of contagion spreading as a result of macroeconomic similarities. When measures of both mechanisms are included in the specification, trade-related contagion dominates the macro effect. Admittedly, similarities in macroeconomic policies and performance across countries are more difficult to capture in a weighting scheme than is the intensity of bilateral trade; the stronger showing of trade-related contagion may simply reflect our greater success in proxying for this effect. At the same time, considerable experimentation with alternative measures of macro-related contagion, all of which points to the same conclusion, lends some support to our favored interpretation that it is trade links rather than macroeconomic similarities that have been the dominant channel for the contagious transmission in the sample period.

In the 1960s, toward the beginning of our sample, the debate over contagion centered on the industrial countries. The fear was that a currency crisis in one industrial country might destabilize the exchange rate pegs of the other advanced industrial nations. The fallout from the 1967 devaluation of sterling provides some retrospective justification for these fears (see Eichengreen 1996). Today the debate over contagion increasingly focuses on emerging markets, in Latin America, Asia, and elsewhere (e.g., Sachs et al. 1996). The nature of the data makes systematic cross-country analyses of the sort we undertake here more difficult for emerging markets. But it is clear that this should be a high priority for future research.

References

Banks, Arthur S. Various years. *Political handbook of the world.* Binghamton, N.Y.: CSA Publications.

Caplin, Andrew, and John Leahy. 1994. Business as usual, market crashes, and wisdom after the fact. *American Economic Review* 84:548–65.

Claessens, Stijn. 1991. Balance of payments crises in an optimal portfolio model. *European Economic Review* 35:81–101.

Commission of the European Communities. Directorate-General for Economic and Financial Affairs. 1993. The ERM in 1992. *European Economy* 54:141–57.

Committee of Governors of the Central Banks of the Member States of the European Economic Community. 1993a. *Annual report 1992.* Basle: Committee of Governors.

———. 1993b. The implications and lessons to be drawn from the recent exchange rate crisis—Report of the Committee of Governors. Basle: Committee of Governors. 21 April. Processed.

Diamond, Douglas, and Phillip Dybvig. 1983. Bank runs, deposit insurance, and liquidity. *Journal of Political Economy* 91:401–19.

Dooley, Michael, Eduardo Fernandez-Arias, and Kenneth Kletzer. 1996. Is the debt crisis history? Recent private capital inflows to developing countries. *World Bank Economic Review* 10:27–50.

Eichengreen, Barry. 1996. *Globalizing capital: A history of the international monetary system.* Princeton, N.J.: Princeton University Press.

Eichengreen, Barry, Andrew K. Rose, and Charles Wyplosz. 1995. Exchange market mayhem: The antecedents and aftermath of speculative attacks. *Economic Policy* 21: 249–312.

———. 1996. Contagious currency crises: First tests. *Scandinavian Journal of Economics* 98:1–22.

Einzig, Paul. 1968. *Foreign exchange crises.* London: Macmillan.

Flood, Robert, and Peter Garber. 1984. Gold monetization and gold discipline. *Journal of Political Economy* 92:90–107.

Frankel, Jeffrey A., and Andrew K. Rose. 1995. An empirical characterization of nominal exchange rates. In *Handbook of international economics,* vol. 3, ed. Gene Grossman and Kenneth Rogoff, 1689–1729. Amsterdam: North Holland.

Gerlach, Stefan, and Frank Smets. 1994. Contagious speculative attacks. CEPR Discussion Paper no. 1055. London: Centre for Economic Policy Research, November.

Girton, Lance, and Don Roper. 1977. A monetary model of exchange market pressure applied to postwar Canadian experience. *American Economic Review* 67:537–48.

Goldberg, Linda. 1994. Predicting exchange rate crises: Mexico revisited. *Journal of International Economics* 36:340–66.

Goldfajn, Ilan, and Rodrigo Valdés. 1995. Balance of payments crises and capital flows: The role of liquidity. Cambridge: Massachusetts Institute of Technology. Unpublished manuscript.

Keesing's Contemporary Archives. Various years. *Record of world events.* Cambridge: Longman.

Krugman, Paul. 1979. A model of balance of payments crises. *Journal of Money, Credit and Banking* 11:311–25.

Obstfeld, Maurice. 1986. Rational and self-fulfilling balance-of-payments crises. *American Economic Review Papers and Proceedings* 76:72–81.

Sachs, Jeffrey, Aaron Tornell, and Andrés Velasco. 1996. Financial crises in emerging markets: The lessons from 1995. NBER Working Paper no. 5576. Cambridge, Mass.: National Bureau of Economic Research.

Willman, Alpo. 1988. The collapse of the fixed exchange rate regime with sticky wages and imperfect substitutability between domestic and foreign bonds. *European Economic Review* 32:1817–38.

Comment   Takatoshi Ito

This paper is detective work by two doctors fighting an epidemic of financial crises. Determining whether the disease (financial crisis) is contagious, caused by a virus, or noncontagious but caused by an environmental change like a heat wave is the problem.

The paper asks an interesting question: why do financial crises cluster in time? As the European Exchange Rate Mechanism (ERM) crisis in 1992–93 and the Mexican crisis and its aftermath vividly show, attacks on currencies appear to spread from one currency to another. Eichengreen and Rose construct a crisis indicator, EMP, as a weighted average of three variables: devaluation, interest hikes, and loss of foreign reserves—all in relation to Germany. When EMP deviates by more than 1.5 standard deviations, it is a crisis. A probit model is constructed to measure a contagion effect from another crisis controlling for an environmental change. When a contagion effect is confirmed, a further effort is made to identify a transmission process, whether through trade linkage or macroeconomic similarities.

Takatoshi Ito is professor in the Institute of Economic Research at Hitotsubashi University, Tokyo, and a research associate of the National Bureau of Economic Research.

I comment on three aspects of this line of investigation: (1) on the definition of financial crises, (2) on the effectiveness of controlling for an environmental change, and (3) on the coverage of countries and the frequencies of data.

First of all I would like to comment on the correspondence between financial crises picked up by the EMP variable in this paper and situations that we commonly think of as crises. Are there cases in which EMP flags a crisis but it is not what we commonly regard as a crisis (the first type of error)? Are there cases that we think of as a crisis that are not identified as such by EMP (the second type of error)? All three components of EMP are measured against Germany. So, if for some reason a speculation that the deutsche mark will appreciate develops in the market, it would show up as widespread financial crises among other currencies. Although it is a German problem, it appears as contagious crises among other countries. A large depreciation or devaluation is often a much-needed "correction" of a misalignment (overvalued currency), and not necessarily a "crisis." The sharp depreciation of the U.S. dollar (vis-à-vis the deutsche mark) in 1985–86, partly engineered by the Plaza Accord, was hardly a crisis, but rather an adjustment of the U.S. dollar from an overvalued level to more or less an equilibrium level. If the U.S. dollar in 1985–86 is flagged by EMP as being in crisis, it may be an error of the first type. In general, the EMP variable does not differentiate a depreciation of a disturbing nature (causing misalignment) from a corrective depreciation (restoring equilibrium).

We typically think of a financial crisis as an acute attack by speculators. Speculative pressures on a currency may be short-lived or long-lasting. For example, the "contagious" tequila effect on East Asian currencies, which was indeed caused by speculators according to market participants, did not last long. The duration of pressure (evidenced by depreciation, interest hike, or loss of reserves) ranged from one day for Hong Kong, to a few weeks for Thailand and the Philippines. Since most Asian countries restored their precrisis levels of exchange rate, interest rate, and reserves within the quarter (the frequency used in this investigation), none of the Asian currency crises in the wake of the Mexican crisis would have been picked up by EMP, had the paper covered these currencies. This episode is an example of an error of the second type.

In order to control for noncontagious environmental changes, the probit model of crisis is regressed on, not only the crisis indicator of other countries, but also environmental changes. Since these variables are included simply to control for possible linkage from fundamentals to a crisis probability, it appears enough to "cast a net" as widely as possible. The statistical significance or magnitude of the coefficients on these variables is not of interest in itself. However, if such a variable has a statistically significant coefficient, that result needs to be interpreted. Table 2.3 shows that only two variables have statistically significant coefficients: the inflation rate and the unemployment rate. These should be interpreted by explaining how they would lead to a financial crisis. One might question a linear specification on the grounds that a crisis is often a nonlinear process, in that deviation of a macro variable, such as the inflation rate or the unemployment rate, would not become a concern until it went beyond the usual band of business cycles. This kind of criticism of a linear specification is "unfair" in usual discussions of empirical work. However, in this work, the problem is more serious, as one of the possible transmission channels of contagion, "macroeconomic similarity," is tested. Several variables measuring macroeconomic similarity, "focus variables," also appear among the control variables. The contagion weight of macroeconomic similarity shows up only when the other country is attacked. It is likely that the nonlinear effect of the macroeconomic variables on causing a crisis independently in several countries is picked up in this term. For this reason, I am more convinced by trade linkage than by macroeconomic similarities as a contagion transmission mechanism.

Estimating the power of contagion is an attempt to isolate the "carrier" of the transmission virus. Suppose that a financial crisis in country j triggers a change in investors' expectations about the variability of country i. The usual market talk is that investors-cum-speculators look for countries under similar conditions to attack after a success in attacking one country. Obviously, expectations about the probability of success in an attack suddenly change. Any econometric attempt to specify trade links and macroeconomic similarities can be regarded as an attempt to read the minds of speculators.

Last, I would like to encourage the authors to apply their technique to developing countries. Although the paper's introduction cites the Mexican crisis and the tequila effect as motivation, no Latin American countries are in the sample. Currently, only the OECD countries are used, so that the financial crises studied in the paper have more or less been cases of misalignment among major currencies. Also the counts of crises indicate that crisis cases are dominated by two periods, the demise of Bretton Woods and the first oil crisis, in 1971–73, and the ERM crisis, in 1992. Again these are very much German problems or, more broadly speaking, European problems. Naturally, the trade link variable works. A true test of contagion would be to apply the technique to emerging market crises, like the ones in 1982 and 1995.

The choice of quarterly data may miss a temporary, unsuccessful crisis. At the height of the ERM crisis the Swedish overnight interest rate was raised to 500 percent for a few days in an attempt to fend off speculators, but the result was depreciation (so counted as a crisis from the point of view of depreciation but not interest rate hikes). Several Asian countries employed various measures, including higher interest rates and intervention in January 1995, to fend off the tequila effect. The defense was successful and capital flows came back by March. Hence, the Asian countries in the first quarter of 1995 would not show signs of stress. From the finance viewpoint, attacks come and go quickly, especially those of a contagious nature, and the quarterly frequency is too coarse to catch them.

Comment   Ronald I. McKinnon

This ingenious paper addresses a very important issue: to what extent do currency crises show contagion? Everyone agrees that currency crises come in clusters, whether at the end of the fixed-rate dollar standard in 1971–73, the great debt crisis among less developed countries in 1981–82, the breakdowns of the ERM in 1992–93, or—beginning with Mexico in late 1994—the tequila speculative attacks on the currencies of similar emerging market countries in early 1995. However, because of data limitations, Eichengreen and Rose's formal statistical analysis covers just 20 industrialized countries from the OECD.

The authors define a speculative attack on any one country to be an unusual quarterly movement in the weighted average of changes in its exchange rate, interest rate, and exchange reserves relative to its German counterpart. (Germany is the center country in their analysis—and something more than just a numéraire as I discuss below.) Beyond identifying the clustering of these speculative attacks, however, the authors go one difficult econometric step further. They try to distinguish "pure" contagion, based on psychological or trade links with countries that themselves suffer speculative attacks, from some common global economic factor that tends to affect most countries simultaneously. Using a probit regression model, they estimate the probability of a speculative attack on any one country where a crisis elsewhere is one explanatory variable. But to control for common factors other than a speculative crisis somewhere else, numerous macroeconomic variables—domestic credit expansion, level of unemployment, current account surplus, and so on, as shown in their table 2.1—are also right-hand-side explanatory variables.

The conceptual problem then becomes whether these macroeconomic control variables successfully proxy common economic factors roiling the world economy that each country faces simultaneously. If not, the authors' regression method gives too much weight to "crises elsewhere." That is, pure contagion will be overweighted. And this would also be true when the authors trade-weight the importance of crises elsewhere (table 2.2), as always using considerable ingenuity.

Unfortunately, this method of control is not strong enough. It founders on the fact that the macroeconomic control variables simultaneously represent two kinds of disturbances that could foment currency crises: (1) disturbances that are peculiar to each country itself and (2) general disturbances in the world economy. Inability to distinguish between the two would not matter if either kind of shock registered unambiguously (i.e., in the same direction) the probability of a currency crisis. However, the effects of the two kinds of shocks on the macroeconomic control variables often offset each other. Thus the impact of general disturbances in the world economy are not fully factored out.

Let me illustrate this offsetting effect with a leading example of a "general"

Ronald I. McKinnon is professor of economics at Stanford University.

disturbance, that is, one emanating from the center country in the world economy. Consider the enormous fiscal expansion–cum–tight money in Germany in the early 1990s, leading the German current account to swing from a large annual surplus to a substantial deficit—a $70 billion swing from 1990 to 1992. Everyone now agrees that this major shock contributed to numerous speculative attacks on European currencies in 1992–93. But how would this shock show up in the right-hand-side variables of the regression model? Would it be consistent with the expected signs of Eichengreen and Rose's macroeconomic control variables?

Not for some of them. In response to very tight money sucking in foreign financial capital and an emerging current account deficit in Germany, peripheral countries were all forced to contract their domestic credit, disinflate, and allow their current account surpluses to increase in the course of defending (perhaps unsuccessfully) their exchange rates. So given the prior expectations of the regression model based on idiosyncratic shocks, these three variables each move the "wrong" way in response to the German fiscal expansion. For example, just before a speculative attack on the currencies of other ERM countries, domestic credit in each of them would be contracting—rather than expanding as the model would have it. (Similarly, in response to this common international shock, domestic inflation and the current account would move in the "wrong" directions and not accurately reflect the fact that the currency in question was under attack because of the German fiscal expansion.)

Alternatively, if domestic credit suddenly expanded because, say, of some domestic political breakdown, then a currency crisis–cum–devaluation would likely follow. The sign of the domestic credit variable would then be "right," that is, positive. The problem is that the regression model juxtaposes both domestic and international shocks in the control variables—with domestic credit rising in the former case and falling in the latter just prior to devaluation. This offsetting effect then weakens, and possibly largely negates, domestic credit as a control variable—along with domestic inflation and the current account surplus as control variables.

In summary, I think that common factors are still largely responsible for the clustering of currency crises. But my heart is with the authors in believing that pure contagion is important in some circumstances. Nevertheless, their regression model seems to overstate the strength of the pure contagion effect.

3 Current Account Deficits and Capital Flows in East Asia and Latin America: Are the Early Nineties Different from the Early Eighties?

Gian Maria Milesi-Ferretti and Assaf Razin

3.1 Introduction

A number of East Asian and Latin American countries have been the recipients of a large portion of total international capital flows to developing countries, both in the late seventies to early eighties and in the early nineties. These inflows have financed persistent current account imbalances, as well as the accumulation of foreign exchange reserves. The Mexican crisis and the recent Asian crisis have shown, however, that abrupt reversals in international capital flows can cause severe problems for economies with large external imbalances and have spurred renewed interest in the question of current account sustainability. A number of recent studies have focused on potential early warning indicators in predicting exchange rate, financial, and balance-of-payments crises.[1] This chapter contributes to this literature by examining the sustainability of current account deficits in three East Asian countries (Korea, Malaysia, and Thailand) and three Latin American countries (Chile, Colombia, and Mexico) in the early eighties and in the early nineties. Having been originally written

Gian Maria Milesi-Ferretti is an economist in the research department of the International Monetary Fund and a research fellow of the Centre for Economic Policy Research. Assaf Razin is the Mario Henrique Simonsen Professor of Public Economics at Tel Aviv University, a research associate of the National Bureau of Economic Research, and a research fellow of the Centre for Economic Policy Research.

The authors are grateful to Patricia Reynolds and to conference participants, particularly discussants Koichi Hamada and Andy Rose, for useful comments and suggestions. Claire Adams and Manzoor Gill provided excellent research assistance. A companion paper was circulated as NBER Working Paper no. 5791 (October 1996), under the title "Current Account Sustainability: Selected East Asian and Latin American Experiences." The views expressed are those of the authors and do not necessarily reflect those of the International Monetary Fund.

1. See, e.g., Eichengreen, Rose, and Wyplosz (1995) on speculative attacks, Frankel and Rose (1996) on exchange rate collapses, Kaminsky and Reinhart (1996) on banking and balance-of-payments crises, Goldstein (1996) on financial crises, and Milesi-Ferretti and Razin (1996) on current account sustainability.

in early 1996, it does not include the 1997–98 Asian crisis, but it nevertheless provides some links between these events and the paper's findings. The methodology builds on Milesi-Ferretti and Razin (1996); this study emphasizes in particular regional aspects and stresses the differences between the experiences of the early eighties and those of the early nineties.

A remarkable feature of the experience of highly indebted East Asian countries in the early eighties was that (with the exception of the Philippines) they avoided the debt crisis that instead affected a large number of Latin American countries. Sachs (1985) argued that differences in external conditions could not account for the differences in outcomes across the two regions and emphasized instead the importance of differences in exchange rate policy and trade openness. A decade later, some of the countries that experienced severe external imbalances in the early eighties have been running large current account deficits again. Given the differences in the macroeconomic policy stance and in the type of financing of these deficits, as well as the similarities in the exchange rate regime, it is interesting to compare these more recent episodes with those of the early eighties in order to draw inferences about what factors make a country that runs persistent external imbalances vulnerable to a crisis.

Given the growth record of the East Asian countries we consider over the past 25 years, a natural question to ask is whether their macroeconomic and structural features make them less likely to experience a reversal in international capital flows. In our sample, East Asian countries are characterized by a higher degree of openness and by higher levels of savings and investment than Latin American countries. In our analysis we provide arguments as to why these macroeconomic and structural features can (but need not) enhance the ability of an economy to sustain protracted current account imbalances, and we highlight the importance of other factors, such as the degree of exchange rate flexibility and domestic financial fragility.

Another important question that we address in this chapter is whether the composition of capital inflows plays an important role in determining the sustainability of external imbalances. There is a significant difference in the composition of capital flows between the late seventies to early eighties and the early nineties. In the earlier period, during which most of the countries we consider had relatively closed capital accounts, capital flows to developing countries took mainly the form of official lending and commercial bank loans, while in the latter period, characterized by increased capital account openness, portfolio flows and foreign direct investment played a major role (see, e.g., Fernández-Arias and Montiel 1996 for an overview and Calvo, Leiderman, and Reinhart 1994 and Corbo and Hernández 1996 for a comparison between the experiences of East Asia and Latin America).

Finally, we examine the implications of differences across decades in the domestic macroeconomic policy stance and the external environment (in particular, terms of trade and world interest rates) for the sustainability of current account deficits. There is an ongoing debate on whether the resumption of large capital flows to several developing countries (among which those in our sample) in the early nineties has been driven mainly by "pull" factors, such structural reforms and improved macroeconomic policy management, or by "push" factors, such as the low level of real interest rates and weak economic activity in OECD countries in the early nineties (see, e.g., Calvo et al. 1993; Chuhan, Claessens, and Mamingi 1993; Fernández-Arias 1996).

The rest of the chapter is organized as follows. Section 3.2 discusses solvency and sustainability of current account deficits in the context of standard intertemporal models of current account determination, in which the supply of foreign funds is infinitely elastic at the world interest rate. Section 3.3 examines key determinants of the supply of foreign funds in the presence of capital market imperfections, in particular asymmetric information. Section 3.4 describes the country episodes. Section 3.5 presents a cross-country comparison of potential sustainability indicators, related to macroeconomic and structural features of the countries, as well as to the composition of external liabilities and the magnitude of external shocks. Section 3.6 concludes.

3.2   Intertemporal Solvency

The current account balance, CA, is the change in the net foreign asset position of a country. In an accounting framework, it is defined as follows:

$$(1) \qquad CA_t \equiv F_t - F_{t-1} = Y_t + rF_{t-1} - C_t - I_t - G_t$$

$$= S_{pt} + S_{gt} - I_t,$$

where F is the stock of net foreign assets, Y is GDP, r is the world interest rate (assumed for simplicity to be constant), C is private consumption, G is government current expenditure, I is total investment (private and public), S_p is private savings, and S_g is public savings. As the second equality in equation (1) shows, the current account balance is also equal to the difference between the economy's total savings and its total investment. Current account imbalances are a vehicle for the intertemporal allocation of resources.[2]

We assume in this section that capital mobility is perfect, so that the net supply of foreign funds is infinitely elastic at the world interest rate level, postponing the discussion of imperfections in international capital markets to section 3.3. We define intertemporal solvency as a situation in which the country as a whole and each economic unit within the country, including the government, obey their respective intertemporal budget constraints. The basic sol-

---

2. This section draws on Milesi-Ferretti and Razin (1996). For a more complete discussion of the intertemporal approach to the current account, see, e.g., Obstfeld and Rogoff (1995, 1996) and Razin (1995).

vency requirement can be expressed by iterating forward the difference equation (1) and imposing the standard transversality condition that the present value of net indebtedness in the indefinite future has to tend to zero:

$$(2) \qquad -(1 + r)F_{t-1} = \sum_{t}^{\infty} \frac{1}{(1 + r)^{s-t}} (Y_s - C_s - I_s - G_s).$$

The right-hand side of equation (2) is simply the present discounted value of future trade surpluses (deficits), which must be equal to the present level of foreign debt (assets) in order for the country to be solvent.

Solvency, a long-run concept, clearly depends on the evolution of the macro-economic aggregates on the right-hand side of equation (2). This equation, while valid in an accounting sense, has limited operational use because it does not incorporate any behavioral assumption and thus does not impose any structure on future events or policy decisions. Indeed, if future trade surpluses are sufficiently large, solvency is always ensured. Therefore, researchers have attempted to define a baseline for private agents' behavior and for future policy actions. With regard to private agents' behavior, it is typically assumed that they aim at smoothing their consumption stream, consistently with maximization of a concave utility function. With regard to future policy actions, in the case of public sector solvency the baseline has typically been established by postulating a continuation into the indefinite future of the current policy stance *and* no change in the relevant features of the macroeconomic environment (see, e.g., Corsetti and Roubini 1991). This gives rise to the notion of "sustainability"—the current policy stance is sustainable if its continuation in the indefinite future does not violate solvency (budget) constraints. The definition of sustainability based on solvency considerations is simpler for fiscal imbalances, given that these can be associated (at least to some degree) with direct policy decisions about taxation and government expenditure. Defining sustainability is more complex in the case of current account imbalances, given that these reflect the interaction between savings and investment decisions of the government and domestic private agents, as well as the lending decisions of foreign investors. While government decisions can, to a first approximation, be taken as given, private sector decisions are going to depend on investors' expectations about future government actions. Furthermore, a key relative price—the exchange rate—is a forward-looking variable that by definition depends on the future evolution of policy variables.

The question of whether current account imbalances are sustainable can be reformulated as follows. Is a continuation of the current policy stance and/or of the present private sector behavior going to entail the need for a "drastic" policy shift (such as, e.g., a sudden policy tightening causing a large recession) or to lead to a "crisis" (such as an exchange rate collapse leading to an inability to service external obligations)? If the answer is yes, we have a case of unsustainability. This drastic change in policy or crisis situation can be triggered by a domestic or an external shock that causes a shift in domestic and foreign investors' confidence and a reversal of international capital flows.[3] Note that the shift in foreign investors' confidence may relate to their perception of a country's *inability* or *unwillingness* to meet its external obligations.

What are the implications of the solvency condition for the long-run level of income and absorption? It is possible to impose some more "structure" on the condition for solvency by considering that for an economy to remain solvent, the ratio of external indebtedness to output cannot grow without bound. Assume that the domestic economy grows at a given rate $\gamma < r$,[4] and let lower-case letters indicate ratios of variables to GDP. Abstracting from changes in the real exchange rate, equation (1) can then be expressed as follows:

$$(3) \qquad f_{t+1} - f_t = \frac{1}{1 + \gamma_t}[\text{tb}_t + f_t(r^* - \gamma_t)],$$

where tb is the trade balance. This expression simply says that changes in the ratio of foreign assets to GDP are driven by trade imbalances and by a "debt dynamics" term proportional to $f(r^* - \gamma)$. This latter term rises with the world rate of interest and falls with the rate of growth of the domestic economy. Consider now an economy in steady state, in which consumption, investment, and public expenditure are constant as a fraction of GDP. The long-run net resource transfer (trade surplus) that an indebted country must undertake in order to keep the ratio of debt to output constant is determined by

$$(4) \qquad \text{tb} = 1 - i - c - g = -f(r^* - \gamma).$$

In the presence of economic growth a country can sustain permanent current account deficits while remaining solvent even when the growth rate is below the world interest rate, provided these deficits are accompanied by sufficiently large trade surpluses. Clearly, if the long-run growth rate of the economy is zero, the current account must be balanced in order for the ratio of foreign liabilities (assets) to GDP to be constant. In this case, a country that is a debtor in the long run will have to run a trade surplus, equal to $-rf$, to pay the interest on its external liabilities. The size of the net resource transfer implied by condition (4) has been used as a simple measure of solvency in a number of studies. For example, Cohen (1996) considers the Mexican resource transfers (as a fraction of GDP) after the 1982 debt crisis as an "upper bound" on the feasible

---

3. In the presence of uncertainty, definitions of solvency and sustainability rely on expected values, implying that in some states of the world insolvency will occur. Under these circumstances, the issue becomes how likely the occurrence of a "bad" scenario is and how vulnerable a country is to external shocks.

4. Otherwise, a country could play "Ponzi games" indefinitely—i.e., borrow to repay interest on its outstanding debt, without violating solvency conditions, as long as total indebtedness rises at a rate below the economy's growth rate. This possibility, which can arise in a Samuelson-type overlapping generations model (see Gale 1973), implies that the economy follows a dynamically inefficient growth path.

resource transfers for heavily indebted countries, and he compares this magnitude with each high-debt country's resource transfer as defined by equation (4), in order to assess its solvency prospects (see also Cohen 1992).

Two main approaches to the empirical implementation of intertemporal models of the current account have been used. The first approach emphasizes the consumption-smoothing role of the current account. Consider a small open economy under perfect capital mobility that takes the world interest rate as given. In the absence of adjustment costs, investment will be undertaken so as to equate the marginal product of capital to the world interest rate in every period, regardless of the consumption profile. The latter will be determined by utility maximization considerations, subject to an intertemporal budget constraint. Assume for simplicity that the consumption function takes a quadratic form and that the discount rate equals the real interest rate.[5] In this case, it is easy to show that even in the presence of uncertainty the expected level of consumption will be fixed along the optimal path and will be a function of the expected present discounted value of future net output. It can thus be shown that current account deficits will reflect expected increases in future net output, $Y - I - G$ (see, e.g., Ghosh and Ostry 1995).

This relation between the current account and expected changes in net future output has been used as the basis for tests of current account behavior by Sheffrin and Woo (1990), Otto (1992), and Ghosh (1995) for a sample of industrial countries and by Ghosh and Ostry (1995) for developing countries. The basic idea is an application of Campbell's (1987) methodology for testing the permanent income theory of consumption and consists in the estimation of a vector autoregression model linking the (detrended) current account and changes in net output to past values of the same variables. The current account needs to be detrended in order to control for the presence of long-run trends in foreign savings (see n. 5 below). The model implies that the current account should incorporate all available information for predicting future changes in net output, and therefore, the coefficient on past net output changes in the equation determining current net output changes should be zero. The simple model sketched above allows one to construct a predicted current account path that can be compared with the actual one in order to gauge whether, according to the model, actual current account balances have been "excessive."

An alternative method of estimating an intertemporal model of current account determination has been used by Glick and Rogoff (1995) and Leiderman and Razin (1991). The methodology consists in the determination from an intertemporal model with investment adjustment costs and perfect capital mobility of the predicted responses of the investment and the current account to productivity shocks (global and country specific, temporary and permanent), as well as to other shocks, and in the subsequent estimation of the model.

5. The latter assumption is not innocuous: it implies the absence of a "consumption-tilting" term that would lead to an increasing or a decreasing consumption path.

While the presence of investment adjustment costs and stochastic productivity lends more realism to the model, the data requirements for this type of estimation have so far limited its application to industrial countries only.

What is the relation between external solvency, current account sustainability, and "excessive" current account deficits? The concepts of solvency and sustainability discussed earlier in this section are binary—a country is either solvent or insolvent, and a current account deficit either sustainable or unsustainable—and imply an increasing order of restrictiveness. The first concept, based on the intertemporal budget constraint, can accommodate a variety of future behavior patterns. The second is based on a continuation of the current policy stance and therefore imposes more structure on future behavior.[6] The notion of excessive current account deficits provides instead a quantitative metric based on deviations from an optimal benchmark (structurally derived from a model under the assumption of perfect capital mobility and efficient financial markets). One problem in using this metric as a basis for evaluating how close to unsustainability is a given path of current account imbalances is that its benchmark relies on the absence of capital market imperfections; consequently, deviations from the benchmark can simply reflect the existence of liquidity constraints or other financial market imperfections. We discuss how these imperfections can affect the supply of external funds in section 3.3; we do not, however, attempt to incorporate imperfect capital markets in an encompassing intertemporal model. Instead, we rely on the insights of the theoretical discussion to examine the issue of sustainability of protracted current account imbalances following a nonstructural approach. We can thus incorporate a broader set of theoretical considerations than those that can be accommodated in a structural approach using the state-of-the-art equilibrium models, at the cost of lacking the ability to provide a quantitative analysis of sustainability.

3.3 Supply of External Funds and Debt Flows

So far we have considered a world in which market imperfections such as asymmetric information, moral hazard, and absence of bankruptcy arrangements do not play a role in shaping international borrowing and lending. These problems, however, are relevant, in particular for developing countries, typically characterized by shallower financial markets and higher vulnerability to external shocks, such as changes in the terms of trade. A vast literature, mostly spawned by the debt crisis experiences of 1982,[7] has used imperfect capital market models to study how the equilibrium level of international lending depends on the form of creditor sanctions (including loss of reputation), the ability of the borrower to make credible commitments (e.g., through investment),

---

6. Within the notion of sustainability, we can also include cases in which a timely reversal of the current policy stance is sufficient to prevent a "hard landing."

7. For an early analysis of sovereign borrowing in private financial markets predating the debt crisis, see Eaton and Gersovitz (1981).

the relative bargaining power in debt renegotiations, and so forth (see Eaton and Fernández 1995 for a recent theoretical survey on sovereign debt, and see Cline 1995 for a retrospective on the debt crisis).

In this section we first present a simple illustrative framework that emphasizes the factors that determine international investors' willingness to lend to a given country and their interaction with factors affecting the country's willingness to meet its external obligations. We turn next to the issue of asymmetric information between borrowers and lenders and its relation to the composition of capital flows.

3.3.1   Willingness to Lend: Portfolio Diversification

Consider a simple (static) model of international portfolio diversification. An international investor has to decide its optimal portfolio allocation by choosing investment projects across $J + 1$ countries, indexed by j. The rate of return in the home country ($j = H$) expressed in foreign currency follows an i.i.d. process with mean ρ_H and variance σ_H^2. The remaining J countries (the rest of the world) are symmetric and have rates of return r^j, which follow a random i.i.d. process with mean ρ and variance σ^2.

Assume that the international investor has a portfolio of size W, and denote by θ the share of the investor's portfolio allocated to the home country. Her or his portfolio's expected return is given by

$$(5) \qquad W[\theta\rho_H + (1 - \theta)\rho], \qquad \rho_H = i_H - \dot{s}/s,$$

and the variance is given by

$$(6) \qquad W^2\left[\theta^2\sigma_H^2 + \frac{(1 - \theta)^2}{J}\sigma^2\right],$$

where i_H is the rate of return in the home country's currency, s is the exchange rate between the home country and the rest of the world, and a dot indicates a time derivative. The variance of the rate of return, σ_H^2, represents the combined effect of exchange rate and domestic interest rate risk. Clearly, both ρ_H and σ_H^2 are endogenous, since they depend on the government's policy choices, but this is not made explicit here. The international investor is assumed to have constant absolute risk aversion γ; thus expected utility U is given by

$$(7) \qquad U = W[\theta\rho_H + (1 - \theta)\rho] - \frac{\gamma W^2}{2}\left[\theta^2\sigma_H^2 + \frac{(1 - \theta)^2}{J}\sigma^2\right].$$

Maximizing expected utility with respect to θ and denoting the foreign currency value of the home country's indebtedness θW by B_H we obtain

$$(8) \qquad B_H = \left(\sigma_H^2 + \frac{\sigma^2}{J}\right)^{-1}\left(\frac{i_H - \dot{s}/s - \rho}{\gamma} + W\frac{\sigma^2}{J}\right).$$

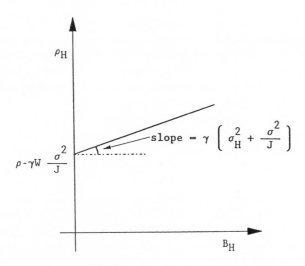

Fig. 3.1   Supply of external funds

Figure 3.1 depicts the supply of external finance B_H as a function of the mean rate of return in the home country ρ_H, which will be identified as the cost of foreign borrowing. From equations (5) and (8) one can verify that the supply schedule is upward sloping; that is, the country has to raise the rate of interest (adjusted for expected exchange rate changes) in order to elicit more capital from abroad. Furthermore, the supply schedule shifts upward as (i) the opportunities for international diversification (J) rise (as in the case of "emerging markets"), (ii) the country's credit and exchange rate risk (σ_H^2) increases, and (iii) the rate of interest in the rest of the world (ρ) increases. It shifts downward as (iv) the riskiness of the rest of the world's investment projects (σ) rises and (v) the size of the world's portfolio (W) increases.

As highlighted in figure 3.1, at the given level of external liabilities B_H, in order to elicit external funding a country must pay the rate of interest ρ_H, which is determined as the intersection between the supply-of-external-funds schedule and the vertical line originating at B_H. If a negative shock that shifts the supply schedule upward occurs, there will be an increase in the country's cost of external borrowing ρ_H. This increase may force the country to change its policy stance in order to generate the additional flow of resources necessary to service external liabilities.[8] For example, Calvo (1997) shows how small "news" about the mean return of the investment project in the home country

8. The risk premium is exogenous in this model, and the home country's share of the world portfolio adjusts so as to ensure that eq. (8) holds. A more complete model would endogenize the domestic rate of return and its variance, the rate of depreciation, and hence the risk premium. Dornbusch (1990) emphasizes the importance of the option value of waiting on the part of international investors (or domestic residents holding funds abroad) in determining the required risk premium for investing in the country.

can have a large effect on the share of world portfolio allocated to the home country when the portfolio is well diversified (J is large). In a similar setup, Calvo and Mendoza (1996b) find that in the presence of costly learning about country-specific information, multiple portfolio allocation equilibria characterized by investors' herding behavior can occur. Furthermore, the range of possible allocations widens when J increases.

How would structural and policy factors impinge on the variables that determine willingness to lend in the stylized portfolio model presented above? The domestic rate of return can be linked with the economy's productivity growth prospects and with fiscal policy (directly in the form of current tax rates and indirectly through expected future taxation needed to repay the public debt). It will also be affected by the efficiency with which domestic financial markets intermediate foreign funds. The variance of domestic returns is linked, for example, to the overall degree of macroeconomic stability and in particular to the vulnerability of the domestic economy to shocks such as fluctuations in the terms of trade. In that context, the variance is reduced when the diversification of the production and export structure increases.

3.3.2 Asymmetric Information and Composition of External Flows

In addition to risk aversion considerations, asymmetric information and enforcement problems can also play a pervasive role in international borrowing and lending, in particular for countries with less developed capital markets. The composition of the supply of external funds can have important implications for the intensity of asymmetric information problems in the context of international capital flows. Foreign investors can lack the same kind of information with respect to domestic agents and would thus require a positive spread between domestic and international rates of return. Razin, Sadka, and Yuen (1998) formalize the idea that these problems can be more severe in the case of portfolio debt and equity than in the case of foreign direct investment, insofar as the latter is a "tie-in" activity, involving an inflow of both capital and managerial inputs. This combination of inputs can give foreign investors the same kind of "home court" advantage (with respect to, say, business information) that domestic investors have, but foreign portfolio (debt and equity) investors lack.[9]

One general aspect of asymmetric information is that the rate of interest a bank charges may itself affect the riskiness of loans by affecting either (i) the action of borrowers (moral hazard or incentive effect) or (ii) their characteristics (sorting or adverse selection effect). As shown in Stiglitz and Weiss (1981) this type of asymmetric information problem can lead to credit rationing (see also Folkerts-Landau 1985 for an open economy application). The existence of implicit or explicit bailout clauses can worsen moral hazard problems, in an

---

9. For empirical studies of the link between foreign direct investment and macroeconomic performance, see Fry (1993) and Borensztein, De Gregorio, and Lee (1998) among others.

analogous fashion to a decline in collateral. In practice, the international financial community may be unwilling to let a country default on its debt obligations because of the trade and capital markets disruptions this could induce or for protection of foreign investors.[10] Moral hazard problems may also be exacerbated by implicit or explicit bailout clauses *within* a debtor country: for example, excessive borrowing by the banking sector can be induced by expectations of a government bailout should the sector run into financial difficulties.

In international borrowing and lending, problems of moral hazard can arise whenever the borrower can take "hidden actions" that affect output and hence its ability or willingness to meet external obligations. Gertler and Rogoff (1990) emphasize this point in a model in which the borrower cannot commit to using funds for investment, rather than for "disguised consumption" or capital flight. This argument links the intensity of moral hazard problems—and hence the level of lending—with the level of investment or (inversely) with capital flight; it also underscores how foreign direct investment may be a way for foreign investors to ensure that the final use of their funds is "appropriate."

What other macroeconomic and structural features of a borrower can affect willingness to pay and willingness to lend? In principle, variables that increase the cost of default on foreign obligations (by raising, e.g., the impact on the domestic economy of sanctions or isolation from international capital markets) strengthen willingness to pay and therefore make a sudden reversal in capital flows less likely. If default is associated with trade disruptions, its cost will be higher for more open economies. If the "punishment" for default consists in the inability to borrow and lend on international capital markets (at least for some time), its cost would be higher for countries with higher output variability, because of the inability to smooth consumption.

In sum, informational asymmetries, enforcement problems, and other forms of capital market imperfections can cause the supply of external funds to be less than perfectly elastic, and to be subject to shifts under a number of domestic and external shocks. Structural factors as well as the macroeconomic policy stance determine the vulnerability of the economy to shocks, as the theoretical discussion has highlighted.

3.4   Country Episodes

We now turn to a description of the experience of a selected group of countries with persistent current account imbalances. We attempt to characterize these different experiences in terms of macroeconomic policy stance, structural characteristics of the economy, composition of external liabilities, and balance-of-payments shocks. Figures 3.2 through 3.8 illustrate the behavior of the current account balance, the level of savings and investment, the real ex-

---

10. On the effect of this type of moral hazard on the behavior of commercial banks lending to developing countries, see, e.g., Dooley (1995).

change rate, the degree of openness, and the level of external liabilities. We do not discuss developments in Chile and Korea during the nineties, because in the period under examination (1990–95) these countries did not experience sustained current account imbalances.

3.4.1 Latin America and the Early Eighties

Chile, 1977–82

The first half of the seventies was a turbulent period for Chile, both politically and economically. The coup in 1973 ousted Allende's socialist government and installed a military regime with radically different economic policies. After a period during which the role of government in the economy had steadily increased, the new regime strived for a balanced budget, privatization, and financial and trade liberalization. In the aftermath of the coup the economy endured a severe recession (1974–75), resulting from a combination of external shocks (fall in the price of copper and increase in the price of oil) and domestic policy tightening. (See figs. 3.2 and 3.3.)

By 1978, yearly inflation was reduced from over 400 percent in 1973 to 30 percent, the public sector budget was in surplus (1.5 percent of GDP), and the economy was growing at 8 percent. However, the pickup in investment and the low level of private savings implied a large current account deficit (5 percent of GDP). Furthermore, the unemployment rate stood above 14 percent. After having adopted a schedule of preannounced devaluations of the nominal exchange rate (the *tablita*) for a year and a half, the government decided to use the exchange rate as a full-fledged nominal anchor in the disinflation process and fixed the rate vis-à-vis the dollar in June 1979. The following years were characterized by a continuation of strong recovery. Inflation, however, declined slowly, with full backward-looking indexation providing inertial momentum (Edwards and Cox-Edwards 1987). This inflationary process was sustained by monetary growth due to large capital inflows, reflecting private sector external borrowing to finance investment in the wake of financial liberalization.[11] Consequently, the real exchange rate appreciated rapidly and the current account balance deteriorated, with the ratio of the deficit to GDP reaching double digits in 1981.

By late 1981 wholesale prices were falling, but the magnitude of the cumulative real appreciation caused expectations of a devaluation and therefore a widening of interest rate spreads between peso- and dollar-denominated assets. Output began to decline and unemployment increased. In 1982 a sequence of external events—a sharp decline in the terms of trade, the large increase in world interest rates, and a drying up of external sources of financing following

---

11. As pointed out by Edwards and Cox-Edwards (1987) among others, private foreign borrowing did not carry government guarantees. A large fraction of foreign borrowing was carried out by the so-called *grupos*—large conglomerates that included industrial firms as well as banks. They had been major buyers of privatized firms, and their banks extended most of their lending to firms of the same conglomerate, circumventing lax regulations.

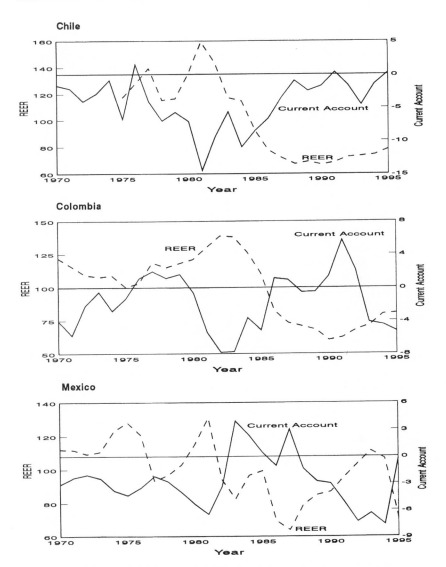

Fig. 3.2   Current account and real effective exchange rate: Chile, Colombia, and Mexico, 1970–95

Sources: IMF, *International Financial Statistics* (Washington, D.C., various issues); IMF, *World Economic Outlook* (Washington, D.C., various years).

the Mexican debt crisis—forced the government to abandon its exchange rate peg. In June 1982, the exchange rate was devalued by 18 percent and the wage indexation scheme was abandoned. This, however, was not sufficient. As in Mexico in 1994, speculation against the peso increased and reserves declined rapidly. Toward the end of 1982, in the shadow of an impending financial crisis the government imposed capital controls and import surcharges. By June 1983,

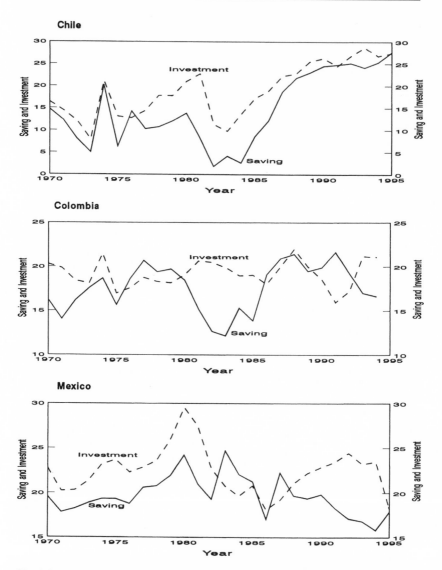

Fig. 3.3   Saving and investment: Chile, Colombia, and Mexico, 1970–95
Sources: See fig. 3.2.

the peso had been devalued in nominal terms by close to 100 percent with respect to its June 1982 level.

The crisis caused widespread bankruptcies in the private sector, and the government was forced to liquidate banks but also to bail out several other financial and nonfinancial institutions. In particular, the central bank intervened in support of the banking system, giving rise to a large quasi-fiscal deficit. The absence of government guarantees on private foreign borrowing notwithstanding, the government assumed responsibility for a large fraction of the private sector's foreign liabilities. The crisis was extremely severe: output fell by 14 percent in 1983 alone and unemployment rose dramatically to close to 20 percent (Corbo and Fischer 1994). Inflation rebounded to its "historical" level of 27 percent, and the management of the crisis caused an initial policy reversal with respect to exchange rate policy, wage indexation, current and capital account openness, and privatization. Starting in 1984, however, the government resumed its policy of trade liberalization, privatization, and deregulation, and the adjustment of the Chilean economy, although painful, was relatively rapid. Growth resumed in 1984 and has averaged over 6 percent over the past 10 years.

It should be noted that not all indicators pointed to a likely crisis. The economy was experiencing fast economic growth. The fiscal balance was in surplus throughout this period; indeed, the government had been reducing its external liabilities. Investment was growing rapidly, albeit from a low base, and so were exports (until 1981). Which factors can then explain the Chilean 1982 crisis? Five factors are most commonly mentioned:

1. Size of external debt. External indebtedness was close to 50 percent of GDP in 1981, with interest payments totaling 5.5 percent of GDP.

2. Overvalued real exchange rate. Inflation failed to converge rapidly to world levels due to the effects of lagged wage indexation, as well as to increased demand for nontradables fueled by foreign borrowing. Investment was stimulated by the reduced price of imported capital goods, as well as by the possibility of getting financing on world markets at the world rate of interest, given the pegged exchange rate.

3. Low level of savings. National savings averaged only around 10 percent of GDP during the period 1978–81. Their decline was particularly significant in 1981, possibly reflecting intertemporal substitution effects.

4. Weak financial system and overborrowing. "Overborrowing" by the private sector was fueled by the availability of foreign credit (following the recycling of oil exporters' surpluses) and facilitated by weak supervision of the banking sector, which encouraged risk-taking behavior (see Diaz-Alejandro 1985; Velasco 1991). In this context, de la Cuadra and Valdes-Prieto (1992) stress the negative role played by the government's extension to the private sector of exchange rate and interest rate risk guarantees.

5. Severe external shocks. The large increase in world interest rates, the drying up of foreign financing, and a decline in the terms of trade, the intensity of which was compounded by the narrow commodity specialization of exports, dominated by copper, all contributed to precipitating the external crisis.

Colombia I, 1980–88

Colombia is one of the few Latin American economies that did not experience an external debt crisis during the early eighties, notwithstanding severe external shocks. The success of Colombia has been attributed to a conservative macroeconomic policy stance that avoided large fiscal imbalances and swings in the real exchange rate (see, e.g., Ocampo 1989; Cline 1995; Clavijo 1995). After a period of rapid economic growth during the second half of the seventies, characterized by a "coffee boom," the economic situation deteriorated in the period 1981–84. Economic growth slowed considerably, the current account turned to a large deficit (close to 8 percent of GDP in 1982 and 1983), and net capital inflows fell, causing foreign exchange reserve losses. The deterioration in the current account reflected both weaker export performance because of the world recession and fast growth in imports. Fiscal accounts deteriorated, both because of the impact of slower growth on revenues and because of an increase in current expenditure. Investment expenditure was reduced after 1982 because of difficulties in obtaining external financing. During 1981 and 1982 the real exchange rate appreciated, leading the authorities to increase the monthly rate of depreciation. This succeeded in reversing the appreciation. Notwithstanding an improvement in the trade balance, the current account was negatively affected by higher interest payments and all external debt indicators worsened.

A fiscal adjustment plan was adopted at the end of 1984 and resulted in a rapid reduction of the fiscal deficit in the following two years (by around 7 percentage points). The fiscal adjustment plan was accompanied by a large depreciation in the real effective exchange rate and opened the door to a series of large loans from commercial banks, which allowed a refinancing of principal coming due without the need for rescheduling. Favorable terms-of-trade developments (an increase in the price of coffee), as well as coal and oil discoveries, led to a current account surplus and an acceleration of economic growth to 5 percent in 1986. The reduction in current account imbalances, reflecting an increase in both public and private sector savings, together with the increase in growth, allowed Colombia to reverse the increasing trend of the ratio of external debt to GDP.

Mexico I, 1977–82

After a short period of fiscal adjustment following a balance-of-payments crisis in 1976, the policy stance was relaxed as a result of the increase in the amount of proven oil reserves from 6.4 billion barrels in 1975 to 16 billion barrels in 1977. Constraints on foreign borrowing were lifted as foreign banks started to compete to lend to Mexico on very attractive terms. On the domestic policy front, public expenditure increased substantially from 29 percent of GDP in 1977 to 41 percent in 1981, with state-owned enterprises taking an important role in public investment. During 1978–81 public and private investment rose rapidly, and growth was above 8 percent. While private savings increased, public sector savings experienced a significant decline; this, together with the investment boom, was reflected in large current account deficits (over 6 percent of GDP in 1981). As a result, external debt almost doubled in dollar terms between 1979 and 1981.

Although domestic inflation exceeded 20 percent, the nominal exchange rate was being devalued at a slower rate, resulting in a large real appreciation. During 1981 it became clear that the earlier assumptions regarding the rate of increase of oil export revenues were unrealistic. This fueled speculation that the peso would be devalued, causing massive capital flight. To stem the drain of foreign exchange reserves, the government increased its external borrowing by over $20 billion; the terms of the debt, however, began to worsen with an increase in the spreads over the London Interbank Offer Rate (LIBOR; at a time when the LIBOR was increasing) and a shortening of maturity.

The crisis worsened in 1982, as a result of external shocks (such as the increase in world real interest rates and the world recession) and increasing fiscal imbalances. A 40 percent devaluation of the peso in February stemmed capital flight only briefly, and the government had to borrow an additional $5.7 billion in medium-term, syndicated loans. In August a dual exchange rate system was established. Shortly thereafter, dollar deposits at Mexican commercial banks were converted into pesos at an unfavorable exchange rate, and on 1 September the banking system was nationalized. During the last four months of the year, there was a de facto moratorium on foreign debt service, until a December agreement with foreign commercial banks to reschedule $23 billion of debt amortization was reached. In 1983, the new de la Madrid administration implemented a drastic adjustment plan, characterized by a fiscal contraction, a lifting of previously adopted trade restrictions, and a reduction in real wages. The turnaround in the current account was immediate—it registered a surplus, although this came at a heavy price. Output contracted by over 5 percent in 1983, with public and private investment falling drastically.

Aside from external shocks and the high level of external indebtedness, what were the key aspects of the 1982 Mexican crisis? Four factors are often mentioned in the literature:[12]

1. Real exchange rate appreciation. Between 1977 and 1981, Mexico's exchange rate appreciated by over 30 percent in real terms vis-à-vis the dollar (Buffie 1989). This appreciation stimulated a boom in imports, which increased much faster than oil exports. The perceived unsustainability of the exchange rate led to large capital flight during the years preceding the crisis, as well as in the following years.

2. Large fiscal imbalances. Unlike in Chile, in Mexico most of the debt accumulation reflected public sector external borrowing. The increase in public expenditure during the late seventies and early eighties was extremely large, and it came on top of another large increase in the early seventies. Further-

---

12. Some observers (Diaz-Alejandro 1984) attributed the debt crisis mainly to external factors and underlined that several distinguished commentators (and the commercial banks themselves) argued that there was nothing to worry about because the current account deficits were financing higher public and private investment. Indeed, the macroeconomic performance between 1978 and 1981 was very good, with high growth and rapid increases in public and private investment.

more, it financed not only increased public investment but also growing public consumption. Notwithstanding the large revenue increase coming from oil, total revenues failed to keep up with expenditures, causing large fiscal deficits to emerge. The government's external position was worsened by the fact that public sector external borrowing went to finance not only fiscal imbalances but also private capital flight, as foreign exchange reserves were rapidly depleted.

3. Misperceptions regarding oil wealth. Policy design in Mexico was based on an overoptimistic assessment of future oil prices; when the expected price increases failed to materialize, the government did not introduce alternative measures to limit fiscal imbalances.

4. Weakness of the financial system. The Mexican system was characterized by financial repression, with high reserve requirements that had the main purpose of facilitating the financing of public sector deficits. The sharp deterioration in macroeconomic conditions in 1982 worsened banks' and firms' balance sheets, which were further hit by the effects of the exchange rate depreciation on their dollar exposure.

3.4.2   East Asia in the Early Eighties

Korea, 1978–86

Korea experienced fast growth rates during the 1960s and the 1970s, driven by investment and exports.[13] Foreign indebtedness, after rising sharply at the time of the first oil crisis, remained stable as a fraction of GDP at around 32 percent in the latter part of the seventies, notwithstanding persistent current account deficits, thanks to the high growth rate and low or negative real interest rates. The second oil shock, however, hit the Korean economy at a particularly delicate juncture. It was preceded by a period of real exchange rate appreciation, due to high domestic inflation coupled with a fixed nominal exchange rate vis-à-vis the U.S. dollar, and coincided with a period of political instability, following the assassination of President Park in October 1979, and with a bad harvest. As a result, the economy experienced a deep recession in 1980; the current account deficit rose to over 8 percent of GDP as savings declined sharply, and the ratio of foreign debt to GDP increased to 44 percent. (See figs. 3.4 and 3.5.)

The policy response to the recession consisted of a devaluation of the exchange rate, a tightening of macroeconomic policy, and the adoption of structural reforms, such as trade and financial liberalization. Economic growth resumed in 1981, and the fiscal stance was relaxed. During this adjustment period, Korea was able to continue to borrow on international markets and finance large current account deficits: the ratio of foreign debt to GDP reached 52 percent in 1982. With strong growth under way and a recovery in external

---

13. For analyses of the Korean experience, see, e.g., Collins and Park (1989), SaKong (1993), Soon (1993), and Haggard et al. (1994).

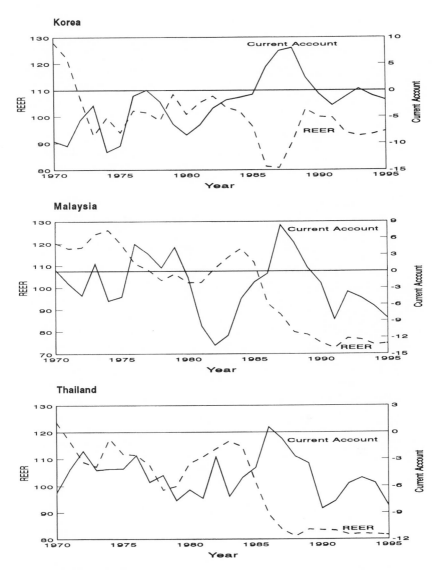

Fig. 3.4   Current account and real effective exchange rate: Korea, Malaysia, and Thailand, 1970–95
Sources: See fig. 3.2.

demand, Korea turned to the objective of reducing the ratio of foreign debt to GDP: it tightened monetary and fiscal policy in 1983–84, let the exchange rate depreciate in real terms, and accelerated the pace of structural reform. By 1984, the objectives of inflation reduction and fiscal stabilization were met, and the current account deficit was reduced to less than 2 percent of GDP.

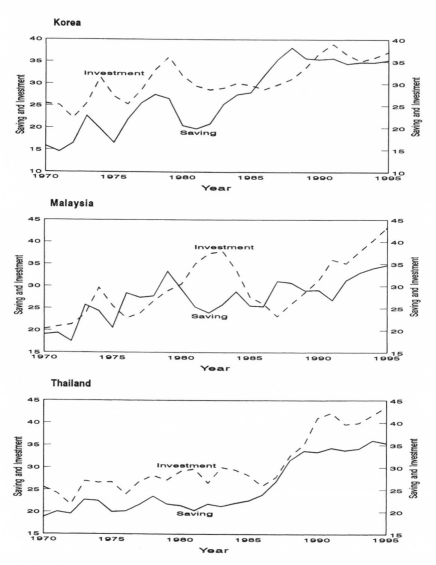

Fig. 3.5   Saving and investment: Korea, Malaysia, and Thailand, 1970–95
Sources: See fig. 3.2.

During this period, investment and economic growth remained strong, unlike in other highly indebted countries after the debt crisis, and savings increased, thanks to a rebound in household saving.

The second half of the eighties was characterized by more favorable external developments, such as the fall in the price of oil and the depreciation of the dollar, and by a more flexible exchange rate policy, characterized by a large real depreciation until 1986. The current account turned to large surpluses, allowing the government to prepay a large portion of the external debt. By 1988, the ratio of foreign debt to GDP was only 20 percent.

What lessons can be drawn from the Korean experience? Notwithstanding rapid growth (driven by investment and exports) before the second oil shock, the situation in 1979–80 was difficult. The policies pursued in the wake of the first oil shock had led to a loosening of monetary policy and to an overvalued real exchange rate, and the second oil price shock and a bout of political turmoil posed a threat to macroeconomic stability. However, Korea experienced a rapid recovery following the recession of 1980. This was facilitated by the continuation of Korea's access to international capital markets, which allowed the country to borrow until growth was solidly under way again; indeed, the debt-GDP ratio continued to rise until 1982. With inflation under control and a more stable macroeconomic environment, a second stage of the adjustment process was undertaken, characterized by monetary and fiscal tightening and a gradual real depreciation of the exchange rate. This was very successful: external imbalances were rapidly reduced and economic growth remained strong.

Malaysia I, 1979–86

At the end of the seventies, Malaysia's macroeconomic situation was stable.[14] The country had grown at an average rate of over 6 percent during the seventies; it had low inflation, fast export growth, low external debt, and hefty current account surpluses. The country had diversified substantially its production and export structure away from primary commodities toward manufactured goods and textiles. Nevertheless, primary commodities still accounted for over 70 percent of Malaysia's total exports in 1980.

The oil shock of 1979–80 implied a sharp terms-of-trade improvement. Around the same time, there was a shift in the government's macroeconomic policy stance. Namely, the government pushed forward a heavy industry drive, similar to the one pursued by the Korean authorities a few years earlier. This drive was pursued through large investment projects undertaken both directly and through state-owned enterprises, which led to a rapid increase in the share of public investment in GDP and a widening of the federal budget deficit to over 17 percent of GDP in 1982. Around 40 percent of the deficit was financed through external borrowing. The deterioration in the fiscal accounts was mirrored in external developments: the deficit on the current account reached 13 percent of GDP in 1982, resulting in a sharp increase in external debt. This deficit also reflected unfavorable external conditions—the slowdown in the world economy, the increase in world real interest rates, and a progressive deterioration in the terms of trade, as well as a real exchange rate appreciation.

Worries about the rapid rise in domestic and external imbalances prompted

14. See, e.g., Demery and Demery (1992) for an account of the Malaysian experience during the 1979–86 period.

the Malaysian government to undertake a fiscal consolidation program, characterized by a curtailment of public sector investment—"development expenditure" was reduced in nominal terms by 30 percent in the period 1983–84. The federal deficit was reduced to 7 percent of GDP and the current account deficit to 6 percent of GDP by 1984. The macroeconomic effects of fiscal adjustment were in part cushioned by a temporary reversal in the terms-of-trade deterioration in 1984, a recovery in world demand, and a sustained expansion in the manufacturing and construction sectors; as a result, the economy continued to grow at a rapid pace.

However, economic activity experienced a sharp downturn in 1985 and 1986, reflecting a marked deterioration of external conditions (a substantial worsening in the terms of trade and weak external demand), further fiscal tightening, and a drastic slowdown in construction activity. Public investment was scaled back further; at the same time, monetary policy was loosened, interest rates were allowed to decline, and the exchange rate depreciated substantially. The slowdown was accompanied by severe problems in the financial system, triggered by the collapse in the real estate market. The combined effect of the large real exchange rate depreciation and of fiscal contraction led to a reduction in absorption and expenditure switching; imports declined substantially and export growth picked up. Although weak economic activity limited the size of the deficit adjustment, a sharp fall in private consumption and private investment implied a virtual balancing of the current account in 1986. Starting in 1987, economic activity recovered, and for the rest of the decade the current account balance recorded large surpluses, reflecting a large increase in the savings rate. This allowed Malaysia to substantially reduce its external debt.

What are the salient features of the Malaysian experience? The rapid buildup in domestic and external debt of the early eighties required a drastic policy shift to ensure fiscal and external sustainability. This shift involved not only fiscal consolidation but also structural measures to encourage private sector investment. The prolonged period of fiscal adjustment took its toll on economic activity in 1985–86, as domestic and external conditions deteriorated. Nevertheless, the downturn was reversed rapidly, as the sharp real exchange rate depreciation and the more favorable environment for private sector investment allowed for a resumption in growth, driven by exports and private investment.

Thailand I, 1979–90

After a period of rapid growth and persistent current account deficits in the late seventies, the second oil shock hit the economy at the same time as a decline in services receipts due to the closure of American bases. As had been the case after the first oil shock, savings declined and the current account deficit widened to over 7 percent of GDP in 1979. The following period was characterized by repeated standby arrangements with the International Monetary Fund (IMF) and Structural Adjustment Loans from the World Bank; while progress was made in the area of structural reform and in reducing the inflation rate, external imbalances and budget deficits persisted in the following years, in part because of unfavorable external developments (the worldwide recession, the increase in real interest rates, and a further decline in the terms of trade), as well as because of a consistent pattern of revenue overestimation (see Robinson, Byeon, and Teja 1991). As a result, the ratio of external debt to GDP continued to increase.[15] The exchange rate was devalued by 9 percent at the end of 1981 but continued to appreciate in real effective terms thereafter, being pegged to the dollar in a period of dollar appreciation. The slowdown in economic activity exacerbated weaknesses in the financial system, and a crisis occurred in 1983, when the authorities had to intervene in several finance and security companies, as well as five commercial banks (Johnston 1991).

A policy shift occurred at the end of 1984. It consisted of a 15 percent nominal exchange rate depreciation, accompanied by a drastic tightening in the fiscal policy stance. This time the baht depreciated significantly in real effective terms, as domestic inflation did not erode the competitiveness gains and the dollar (which the baht continued to shadow) started to depreciate. The combined effect of the fiscal adjustment, real depreciation, and the more favorable external environment were impressive: the current account deficit was eliminated in 1986, as manufacturing exports increased rapidly, the budget was balanced in 1987, and the ratio of external debt to GDP, after peaking in 1985 at 45 percent, began to decline. Growth accelerated to over 11 percent in 1987–90, driven by exports and by a boom in private investment, while fiscal policy generated increasing budget surpluses. Export growth resulted in an increase in the share of exports in GDP to 35 percent by 1989 (against 22 percent in 1985); the share of private investment in GDP more than doubled between 1986 and 1990, with the investment boom sustained by inflows of foreign direct investment from Japan and other Asian newly industrialized economies. The increase in private investment more than compensated for the decline in public investment caused by the fiscal retrenchment, and the large increase in public savings was not accompanied by a decline in private savings. As a result, during this period both investment and savings continued to rise as a fraction of GDP.

3.4.3   Latin America in the First Half of the Nineties

Colombia II, 1992–95

At the beginning of the decade, Colombia was characterized by a depreciated level of the real exchange rate, which reflected in part unfavorable terms-of-trade developments in the period 1987–89. Tight fiscal policy and the competitiveness of the exchange rate resulted in a small current account surplus. The Colombian economy experienced a surge in capital inflows starting in

---

15. State-owned enterprises accounted for around 70 percent of total public investment and about two-thirds of external debt by the mideighties.

1991. These inflows were initially attracted by high domestic interest rates, reflecting the monetary authorities' tight policy stance, by the trade and financial liberalization undertaken in 1990, and by a tax amnesty to holders of domestic assets abroad granted at the end of 1990. The inflows were initially met with an aggressive sterilization policy on the part of the central bank, both directly through open market operations and indirectly through increases in reserve requirements. Capital controls, taxes on capital inflows, and a liberalization of capital outflows were also used to reduce net inflows (see Schadler et al. 1993). By the end of the year, the exchange rate had appreciated by 11 percent in real effective terms and foreign exchange reserves had risen considerably, reflecting also a large current account surplus.[16] However, quasi-fiscal losses were substantial (0.8 percent of GDP in 1991), because of the large interest differentials between domestic and foreign assets.

The sterilization policy was significantly modified in 1992; money growth accelerated and interest rates were substantially reduced. At the same time, the crawling peg exchange rate regime was replaced with a managed float within a band vis-à-vis the dollar; an immediate consequence of the increase in exchange rate flexibility was a real appreciation (see Carrasquilla 1995 for a discussion). After a slowdown in 1991, economic activity recovered and the growth rate averaged 5 percent a year over the next four years, stimulated by new oil discoveries and higher coffee prices in 1994. During this period external accounts worsened, as imports of consumption and capital goods grew rapidly, responding to the trade liberalization and the real appreciation of the peso, while private transfer receipts fell. Nontraditional exports grew rapidly as well. Capital inflows continued throughout the period, mostly in the form of foreign direct investment and long-term borrowing, and foreign exchange reserves continued to increase. To stem the inflows the Colombian authorities imposed restrictions on foreign borrowing during 1993 and 1994. The current account deficit widened in 1995 as public finances worsened, but capital inflows have continued, albeit at a slower pace than in 1994, with no significant effect of the Mexican crisis.

Mexico II, 1990–95

The Mexican economy experienced large structural changes in the late eighties and early nineties: a change in monetary and fiscal policy stance was followed by restructuring of the external debt, privatization of public enterprises and of nationalized banks, and trade liberalization. In the aftermath of the debt-restructuring agreement, Mexico regained access to international capital markets: net capital inflows increased dramatically in the period 1990–93,

---

16. For Colombia part of the surge in capital inflows was effectively recorded in the current account as increased transfers; therefore, the capital account balance understates the amount of inflows.

totaling over $90 billion (an average of 6 percent of GDP per year), or roughly one-fifth of all net inflows to developing countries. Net foreign direct investment during this period was about $17 billion, while inflows of over $60 billion occurred in the form of portfolio investment (IMF 1995a).

Notwithstanding a large increase in government savings, national savings fell sharply, and the current account deficit reached almost 7 percent of GDP in 1992. The capital account surplus, however, was more than sufficient to finance the deficit and allow for rapid reserve accumulation. After a slowdown in 1993, with output growth falling below 1 percent, the economy recovered the following year, with output growing at 3.5 percent, sustained by rapid export growth (over 14 percent in dollar terms). Imports, however, continued to grow even more rapidly, and the current account deficit widened to 8 percent of GDP.

Financial market developments in 1994, however, turned unfavorable. A series of domestic and external shocks (the peasant revolt in Chiapas in January, the assassination of presidential candidate Colosio in March, and the increase in U.S. interest rates in the early part of the year) as well as a change in the policy stance in the run-up to the August 1994 presidential election caused loss of confidence in international financial markets and a reversal in capital flows. The real exchange rate was allowed to depreciate within its band, and the central bank sterilized the impact of the loss of reserves on money supply. Subsequently, reserves remained fairly stable until October, as capital inflows resumed somewhat during the third quarter. Between March and October, the authorities reacted to an increase in the interest differential between peso- and dollar-denominated short-term public debt (Cetes and Tesobonos, respectively) by increasing the share of dollar-denominated Tesobonos in total government debt outstanding from 6 percent at the end of February to 50 percent at the end of November.

The crisis unfolded very quickly. At the end of November tensions resurfaced on foreign exchange markets, and the Bank of Mexico lost reserves again. The fluctuation band of the peso was widened by 15 percent on 19 December in an attempt to stem foreign exchange pressures. This was, however, insufficient. The peso reached the new edge of the bank within two days, and reserves were drained trying to maintain the exchange rate at the band's edge. On 22 December it was announced that the peso would be allowed to float against the U.S. dollar. The Mexican currency plummeted, as doubts surfaced about the ability of Mexico to service its short-term liabilities. Notwithstanding an international rescue package put together at the end of January, 1995 was a very difficult year for the Mexican economy, with widespread bankruptcies, generalized financial distress, and a sharp decline in economic activity.

There are several, to some degree complementary, explanations of the Mexican crisis (see IMF 1995b for an early assessment). Dornbusch, Goldfajn, and Valdes (1995) argue that the use of the peso as a nominal anchor in the disinflation process had led, in the presence of sticky prices, to overvaluation and large current account deficits, which were ultimately unsustainable. According to this view, an exchange rate correction was overdue (see Dornbusch and Werner 1994 for a precrisis analysis along these lines). The domestic political shocks and the external shocks simply exposed the vulnerability of the Mexican economy.[17]

An alternative, but possibly complementary view, stresses policy inconsistencies that emerged in 1994: in particular, the monetary policy stance and the management of the public debt, as well as a shift in investors' sentiment. Once capital inflows stopped in the second quarter of 1994 because of the increase in U.S. interest rates and political events in Mexico, reserves started to drop because of the current account deficit. The sterilization of reserve losses by the Bank of Mexico, however, prevented interest rates from exerting an impact on the direction of capital flows and, through a dampening of economic activity, on the current account balance.[18] Furthermore, the large conversion of short-term peso-denominated public debt into short-term dollar-denominated public debt implied an increasing stock of short-term liabilities denominated in foreign exchange that could be "redeemed" at the central bank in exchange for reserves (see, e.g., Sachs, Tornell, and Velasco 1996; Calvo and Mendoza 1996a).

How does the Mexican experience relate to the sustainability indicators discussed in the theoretical section? The ratios of foreign debt to GDP and of debt to exports (34.7 and 184 percent, respectively) were not excessively high by historical standards and also in comparison with other heavily indebted middle-income developing countries. Fiscal policy, a clear culprit in the previous two Mexican crises, had been restrained for the past four years. Exports, although still low as a fraction of GDP,[19] were going strong in 1994. On the other side, the banking system was weak, with a large fraction of bad loans and a mismatch between the maturity structures of assets and liabilities; the national savings rate had declined to very low levels; and the real exchange rate was overvalued, at least to some degree (although there is disagreement on what would have been the appropriate way to "unwind" the overvaluation). Finally, the impending election made it more difficult to undertake policy ad-

---

17. Dornbusch et al. (1995) recognize that the current account deficit and the real exchange rate appreciation were, to some degree, the logical consequence of the productivity increases facilitated by the implementation of large market-oriented reforms, the access to the North American Free Trade Area, the reduction of inflation, and the size of the public sector. In this context, the increase in permanent income would lead private agents to raise their consumption level, while the increase in output would take some more time to surface because of the lags associated with investment and the intersectoral reallocation of resources induced by trade liberalization and changes in relative prices. The issue is to what degree the real appreciation reflected a misalignment.

18. The reluctance of the monetary authorities to raise domestic interest rates was allegedly driven by the fragile situation of the banking system. However, a drastic increase in interest rates was later forced on the authorities by the currency crisis.

19. The ratio of exports to GDP in Mexico differs depending on whether it is calculated using national income accounts or balance-of-payments statistics (as reported in the IMF's *International Financial Statistics*). Using the former, the ratio of exports of goods and services to GDP was 12.4 percent in 1993. Using the latter, it was 17 percent. The number reported in table 3.2 corresponds to the balance-of-payments definition.

justments in response to the series of domestic and external shocks that hit the economy during 1994.

3.4.4   East Asia in the First Half of the Nineties

Malaysia II, 1991–95

The second episode of large current account deficits in the nineties is characterized by a different macroeconomic environment than in the early eighties, with high growth driven by booming private investment and exports (helped by fast growth among East Asian trading partners) and large surpluses in the capital account. The share of investment in GDP reached 38 percent in 1994, with private investment accounting for two-thirds of the total. A rising fraction of this investment reflected inflows in the form of foreign direct investment, in particular from Japan and Asian newly industrialized countries. Exports (82 percent of GDP by 1994) grew rapidly, in particular exports of manufactures, accounting for close to 80 percent of total exports. The private investment boom encouraged fast import growth, in particular of intermediate and capital goods, causing a narrowing of the trade surplus. The economic policy stance was different from the one adopted during the early eighties: fiscal policy was much more restrained, with the ratio of public debt to GDP steadily declining, and monetary policy aimed at maintaining control over monetary aggregates in the face of substantial capital inflows while resisting a sharp appreciation of the exchange rate.

Large capital inflows began in 1990 and increased significantly in the following years—in 1993 alone the capital account surplus was over 20 percent of GDP. Long-term flows remained relatively stable during 1992–94, but the importance of short-term capital inflows (mainly changes in the net foreign asset position of financial institutions, as well as portfolio investment) increased significantly in 1992 and 1993. The monetary authorities reacted by trying to sterilize the inflows; as a result, between 1991 and 1993 their total accumulation of foreign exchange reserves was $17 billion, or 16 percent of GDP per annum. The size of the capital inflows, and in particular the large short-term component, prompted the authorities to adopt a series of measures in early 1994 directed at discouraging short-term flows. As a result, there was a large outflow of short-term capital in 1994, but long-term flows, including foreign direct investment, were basically unaffected. The real effective exchange rate depreciated slightly, after having appreciated during the period 1991–93. In 1995 a continuation of fast growth and booming investment widened current account imbalances further, to over 8 percent of GDP.

Notwithstanding its large and protracted current account deficits, Malaysia has avoided a rapid accumulation of external debt, thanks to large non-debt-creating inflows; the debt burden measured by interest payments as a fraction of GDP, has steadily declined. Relatively to the previous episode, there are no large fiscal imbalances, private investment plays a more prominent role, the real exchange rate is more competitive, and the more diversified export structure reduces the vulnerability to shifts in commodity prices. As to the end of 1995, the risks seemed to be on the side of "overheating," with bottlenecks developing in labor markets.

Thailand II, 1990–95

During the early nineties, the Thai economy continued to grow at a rate close to 9 percent, driven by rapid export growth and growth of domestic demand. Imports grew even faster than exports, and as a result the trade balance worsened and the current account deficit widened to an average of close to 7 percent of GDP during 1990–95. Thanks to a continuation of large capital inflows, however, the balance of payments remained in surplus (an average of close to 4 percent of GDP in 1990–95) and reserves accumulated.

The response to capital inflows changed during the period. At the beginning of the inflow episode (1988) the authorities relied on a tightening of fiscal policy and on sterilization operations. Furthermore, reserve requirements were extended to nonresident deposits. Toward the end of 1990 trade liberalization measures were undertaken, and in early 1991 restrictions on capital outflows were eased. During this period the process of financial liberalization continued. The monetary policy stance was relaxed by 1993, and interest rates were lowered. The composition of inflows changed as well: during 1994 there was an increase in short-term inflows, in particular to the banking sector.[20] During this period, the authorities took steps to enhance prudential supervision of banks and other financial institutions (Khan and Reinhart 1995; Koenig 1996).

After a drastic fiscal contraction in the second half of the eighties, which led to a budget surplus of over 5 percent of GDP, fiscal policy turned more expansionary during the nineties, in order to meet infrastructural bottlenecks, but the overall budget balance remained in surplus. At the beginning of 1995, the fallout from the Mexican crisis briefly affected capital markets in Thailand; equity prices slumped in January, and there was a surge in capital outflows. The episode, however, was short-lived.

At the end of 1995, the fundamentals of the Thai economy appeared mostly robust: economic growth was still rapid; the large current account deficits reflected high levels of investment; exports, a large fraction of GDP, were growing rapidly; foreign exchange reserves were high; and the exchange rate was not appreciated relative to its historical average. Given the persistently large current account deficits, sources of concern were the level of external indebtedness, the large share of short-term debt, and the weakness of the banking system, which made the Thai economy vulnerable to shifts in foreign investors' sentiment. More recently, Thailand has been mired in a banking crisis, originat-

---

20. There are, however, classification problems for capital inflows in Thailand. As a consequence of the establishment of an offshore banking center in 1994, an important fraction of foreign direct investment flows are now channeled through the domestic banking system and are therefore registered as short-term flows. See Koenig (1996).

ing mainly from a fall in real estate prices, and export growth has slowed down. As a result, the baht has repeatedly come under pressure.

3.5   A Comparative Analysis

Before discussing in more detail different indicators identified in the theoretical analysis, it is useful to briefly highlight some common features of the different country experiences, starting with the eighties. First, all the countries in our sample experienced a substantial worsening in external conditions during this period, with large terms-of-trade shocks, a substantial increase in world interest rates, and the demand effects of the world recession of 1981–82. Second, each country in our sample experienced a sustained real exchange rate appreciation during the period of high current account imbalances (a partial exception being Korea). As a result, the exchange rate at the time of the crisis or policy shift was appreciated with respect to historical averages. Third, in Malaysia, Thailand, Colombia, and Mexico persistent current account deficits during the late seventies or early eighties were associated with large fiscal imbalances. Therefore, the policy adjustment (preemptive or forced by an external crisis) involved both a fiscal and an external dimension and took the form of a large fiscal consolidation together with a nominal depreciation of the exchange rate. The latter resulted in a substantial real depreciation that, together with an output slowdown at the beginning of the adjustment period, temporarily raised the ratio of external debt to GDP. However, in the countries that avoided a crisis the real depreciation also spurred export growth and therefore reduced current account imbalances; as a result, the ratio of external debt to GDP after the initial increase started to decline.

The experience with protracted current account deficits during the 1990s has different characteristics, both on the external side and on the macroeconomic policy side. With regard to external conditions, short-term interest rates were low and economic activity in industrial countries weak. These conditions, together with the change in domestic conditions in a number of developing countries that implemented market-oriented reforms and undertook macroeconomic stabilization policies, played an important role in the new wave of capital inflows from industrial to developing countries, a significant fraction of which took the form of portfolio and foreign direct investment.[21] Also, the volatility of terms of trade has been less severe than in the eighties. Macroeconomic conditions were in general more stable; none of the countries we consider experienced sustained fiscal imbalances, and current account imbalances mainly

21. Calvo et al. (1993) find that external factors account for a significant fraction of the variance in real exchange rates and foreign exchange reserves in a sample of Latin American countries; Chuhan et al. (1993) find that external variables "explain" around half of bond and equity flows from the United States to Latin American countries; Fernandez-Arias (1996) finds that the decline in world interest rates in the early 1990s improved the creditworthiness of debtor countries and that "push" factors were dominant in the renewal of capital flows.

reflected a gap between private savings and private investment. Only Mexico, which used the exchange rate as a nominal anchor in a disinflation process, experienced a sustained real exchange rate appreciation comparable to those of the previous decade.

A number of features distinguish the Latin American and East Asian countries in our sample. During both the eighties and the nineties the East Asian countries had higher levels of savings, investment, and growth and a higher degree of trade openness (as measured by the ratio of exports of goods and services to GDP). Since there was no significant difference in debt levels as a fraction of GDP during the eighties, this implied that the ratio of debt to exports was considerably lower in East Asian countries. Openness increased for every country we consider between the 1980s and the 1990s; the East Asian countries and Chile stand out for their large increase of national savings and domestic investment between the two decades.

We turn now to a more detailed examination of factors related to current account sustainability, based on the theoretical analysis of sections 3.2 and 3.3. Clearly, the evaluation of indicators for the 1990s may be subject to a "peso problem"; that is, an indicator may be considered poor simply because it signals a crisis that has not yet occurred but may do so in the near future.

Table 3.1 shows the behavior of the average real interest rate on external debt.[22] It highlights the very large increases in the period 1979–82. The overall impact of these interest rate increases was compounded by the dynamics of tradable goods prices, measured in dollar terms: these implied very large increases in real interest rates, in particular for Mexico, Chile, Korea, and Thailand in 1982. The overall impact of the real interest rate increase depends on the debt-GDP ratio: among the countries in our sample, Chile, Korea, and Malaysia had a higher ratio of external debt to GDP than Colombia, Thailand, and Mexico around the time of the debt crisis (see table 3.3). In the mideighties— at the time Colombia, Malaysia, and Thailand implemented policy shifts— external conditions (in terms of interest rates) were more favorable.

Table 3.2 presents the evolution of the terms of trade. All countries experienced large shocks during the late seventies and the eighties, but with different timing. Mexico had a dramatic terms-of-trade improvement in the period 1979–81, reflecting the oil price boom, but a large subsequent deterioration, which brought its terms of trade back to their level of the late seventies. Korea was hit heavily by the oil shock, with a large terms-of-trade deterioration in 1980. Chile's terms of trade worsened considerably from 1980 onward, while Malaysia's adjustment period in 1985–86 also coincided with a large negative terms-of-trade shock. Thailand had a significant terms-of-trade deterioration between 1978 and 1982, while Colombia experienced large swings. Overall, terms-of-trade volatility was higher in the three Latin American countries dur-

---

22. The real interest rate is defined as the average nominal interest rate on external debt, in dollar terms, deflated by a three-year moving average index of domestic tradables prices measured in dollars. Domestic tradables prices are proxied by a weighted average of the country's export unit values and industrial countries' export prices. The methodology draws from Sachs (1985).

Table 3.1   **Real Interest Rates on External Debt**

Year	Chile	Colombia	Mexico	Korea	Malaysia	Thailand
1975	−4.6	−14.5	−5.9	−5.9	−4.3	−4.3
1976	3.1	−14.3	−8.4	−0.1	3.3	−0.3
1977	−1.3	−12.2	−9.6	−3.6	−0.4	2.4
1978	−7.1	−6.8	−9.3	−7.1	−5.6	−2.3
1979	−7.9	−0.1	−16.4	−6.2	−4.0	0.3
1980	3.3	7.3	−0.2	3.9	1.4	4.1
1981	17.6	10.2	−0.5	11.6	8.0	14.3
1982	22.3	16.3	15.5	15.2	13.1	15.2
1983	14.8	12.8	15.0	12.3	11.0	14.2
1984	16.6	7.1	13.8	11.9	10.3	11.0
1985	10.4	1.3	14.1	7.9	9.9	7.5
1986	3.3	−1.1	5.1	2.5	4.9	2.2
1987	−2.9	0.7	4.4	−2.4	2.9	−2.1
1988	−2.6	6.9	0.3	0.5	1.8	1.3
1989	3.2	6.2	4.4	3.4	4.2	2.9
1990	9.0	7.7	3.4	6.4	5.7	5.9
1991	7.5	8.2	3.7	6.4	3.5	6.4
1992	10.5	10.1	5.9	7.6	4.4	7.2
1993	5.9	6.4	3.3	6.4	2.6	6.0
1994	0.6	3.2	2.3	4.3	1.7	4.3

Sources: World Bank, *World Debt Tables* (Washington, D.C., various years); IMF, *World Economic Outlook* (Washington, D.C., various years).

Note: Table reports average dollar nominal interest rate on external debt deflated by a three-year moving average of domestic tradables price inflation. Tradables price inflation is the average of changes in domestic export unit values and of industrial countries' export prices.

ing the eighties; however, the impact of terms-of-trade shocks on the domestic economy is also a function of the degree of openness, which was much larger in the East Asian countries. During the nineties, the variability of terms of trade has been much more modest, in part because of increased export diversification toward manufactured goods.

A number of macroeconomic and structural indicators for the various country episodes are summarized in table 3.3, while table 3.4 presents external financial indicators. The first set of indicators of external sustainability relate to the level and interest burden of external debt in relation to GDP. Table 3.3 presents a gross measure of external indebtedness, and table 3.4 a net measure that subtracts foreign exchange reserves. Overall, ratios of debt to GDP tended to be higher in the eighties than in the nineties, reflecting among other things the increased importance of non-debt-creating capital flows in recent years (see discussion below). In our limited sample, this ratio does not allow us to clearly discriminate between crisis and noncrisis episodes—ratios of external debt to GDP were much higher in Korea and Malaysia I than in Mexico I and II.[23] The interest burden of external debt "singles out" the experiences of the eighties,

23. Among the countries in our sample affected by the Asian crisis, Malaysia stands out as having a low ratio of net external debt to GDP.

Table 3.2   **Terms of Trade (period average = 100)**

Year	Chile	Colombia	Mexico	Korea	Malaysia	Thailand
1970	186.7	76.7	95.8	108.3	127.0	113.4
1971	176.2	73.0	101.7	105.3	110.1	108.8
1972	173.0	74.8	102.1	105.0	99.7	108.4
1973	188.9	79.4	95.6	101.1	111.9	117.7
1974	157.2	84.0	85.2	93.4	110.9	121.7
1975	84.6	77.7	80.7	86.3	88.5	114.7
1976	92.4	102.9	93.4	98.2	95.9	95.0
1977	85.2	132.1	110.9	103.4	105.5	117.0
1978	84.2	105.1	107.4	106.9	106.9	117.6
1979	93.8	96.0	104.8	104.6	112.6	107.7
1980	92.5	95.1	153.8	92.9	108.5	100.3
1981	83.5	110.1	166.5	91.9	103.9	101.6
1982	78.3	114.8	107.0	97.7	99.5	87.2
1983	79.7	117.0	102.8	93.6	99.2	91.3
1984	74.3	117.5	100.0	95.1	105.9	93.4
1985	69.0	106.9	94.0	91.5	97.0	87.9
1986	69.0	133.4	70.6	97.0	82.2	97.3
1987	75.8	109.4	94.9	100.1	89.3	95.9
1988	86.9	104.1	85.8	101.1	91.7	94.7
1989	85.5	103.4	86.7	105.5	92.8	92.5
1990	78.1	101.1	95.8	104.0	90.9	89.4
1991	78.4	99.1	91.1	103.6	91.2	90.2
1992	78.9	93.3	92.9	103.1	93.5	88.4
1993	73.8	92.5	94.4	104.0	93.2	88.1
1994	82.0	98.7	94.8	104.5	95.2	89.8
1995	92.1	102.0	91.4	101.9	97.0	89.9

Source: IMF, *World Economic Outlook* (Washington, D.C., various years).

and in particular Chile and Korea, while for the experiences of the nineties, the interest burden is quite similar across countries. The "operational solvency condition" (eq. [4]), augmented so as to include the effects of real exchange rate changes, implies that the perpetual resource transfer needed to keep the ratio of external debt to GDP from increasing is determined by the interest burden adjusted for growth and real exchange rate appreciation or depreciation. In Chile and Mexico I all three components that had been favorable during the late 1970s turned unfavorable in the run-up to the crisis: interest rates increased, high growth came to a halt, and the real exchange rate started to depreciate. In Colombia, Korea, Thailand, and Malaysia the adjustment period also involved a large up-front depreciation; however, the growth slowdown was short-lived. In the case of Mexico II, the crisis was preceded by a relatively modest increase in interest burden but followed by a large real depreciation and a deep recession. Based on our sample, it appears therefore that the resource transfer, while clearly a measure of the cost of external adjustment, is not an unambiguous predictor ex ante. Overall, the interest burden and the

Table 3.3   Macroeconomic Indicators

Indicator	Chile 1979–81 (1982–83)	Colombia I 1980–84 (1985–88)	Mexico I 1977–81 (1982–83)	Colombia II 1992–95	Mexico II 1991–94 (1995)	Korea 1977–82 (1983–88)	Malaysia I 1979–84 (1985–86)	Thailand I 1979–84 (1985–86)	Malaysia II 1991–95	Thailand II 1991–95
Current account balance[a]	−9.1 (−7.6)	−5.1 (0.5)	−5.0 (0.3)	−3.4	−6.7 (−0.3)	−5.4 (2.6)	−8.2 (−1.1)	−6.1 (−1.7)	−6.4	−6.8
Savings[a]	11.4 (3.0)	14.6 (20.5)	18.7 (22.0)	16.4	15.7 (17.9)	25.6 (31.6)	26.6 (25.7)	22.5 (26.9)	32.1	33.9
Investment[a]	20.5 (10.6)	19.7 (20.0)	23.7 (21.8)	19.8	22.4 (18.2)	31.0 (29.0)	34.8 (26.8)	28.7 (28.6)	38.5	40.6
Exports[a]	19.7 (21.3)	12.6 (18.1)	10.6 (17.2)	18.3	12.7 (24.0)	32.5 (36.9)	53.2 (55.6)	23.0 (27.8)	85.0	36.6
Real effective exchange rate[b]	124.1 (118.5)	135.5 (80.2)	126.4 (103.5)	77.6	113.9 (76.0)	103.6 (92.2)	117.9 (111.8)	115.5 (95.0)	83.5	88.5
Fiscal balance[a]	2.1 (−3.3)	−3.5 (−1.0)	−8.0 (−11.2)	−0.8	0.4 (0.0)	−2.8 (0.0)	−14.5 (−8.9)	−4.3 (−2.8)	−1.5	3.2
Growth[b]	7.2 (−7.4)	2.6 (5.1)	7.5 (−2.4)	5.0	2.6 (−6.9)	5.8 (10.7)	6.9 (0.0)	5.4 (8.2)	8.4	8.9
Interest payments[c]	5.5 (8.6)	3.5 (3.5)	3.9 (6.7)	1.8	2.4 (4.5)	5.6 (1.7)	4.4 (5.4)	2.9 (2.5)	1.8	2.6
External debt[c]	48.2 (89.5)	40.8 (43.3)	31.4 (62.7)	28.9	35.5 (65.1)	50.0 (19.6)	55.2 (78.9)	37.1 (66.3)	39.3	50.8

Sources: IMF, *International Financial Statistics* (Washington, D.C., various issues); World Bank, *World Debt Tables* (Washington, D.C., various years); national sources.

[a]Current account balance, savings, investment, exports, and fiscal balance are average ratios to GDP during the period.

[b]Real effective exchange rate and growth rate are period averages (real effective exchange rate: average 1970–95 = 100).

[c]Interest payments and gross external debt are ratios to GDP and refer to the last year of the period.

Table 3.4   **Financial Indicators**

Indicator	Chile 1979–81 (1982–83)	Colombia I 1980–84 (1985–88)	Mexico I 1977–81 (1982–83)	Colombia II 1992–95	Mexico II 1991–94 (1995)	Korea 1977–82 (1983–88)	Malaysia I 1979–84 (1985–86)	Thailand I 1979–84 (1985–88)	Malaysia II 1991–95	Thailand II 1990–95
Net external debt[a,b]	36.2 (88.8)	34.5 (33.9)	29.5 (59.5)	15.5	35.4 (59.5)	44.5 (12.8)	42.1 (53.8)	29.5 (23.6)	11.1	28.6
Cumulative current account deficits[a,c]	44.2 (83.7)	38.0 (32.6)	26.0 (42.3)	23.0	41.5 (62.9)	33.9 (0.5)	31.3 (43.5)	39.2 (31.9)	33.3	43.7
Short-term debt[d]	19.3 (14.5)	21.8 (9.5)	32.0 (11.0)	25.4	28.1 (22.5)	33.2 (30.0)	13.5 (13.2)	23.7 (22.1)	21.2	49.5
Foreign exchange reserves[d]	24.8 (14.6)	15.4 (21.8)	6.4 (5.2)	39.5	4.6 (10.3)	7.9 (34.9)	23.7 (31.7)	17.9 (32.8)	71.9	43.7
Net FDI flows[e]	0.9 (1.3)	1.2 (1.0)	0.9 (0.7)	2.0	1.8 (2.8)	0.1 (0.3)	4.1 (2.1)	0.7 (0.8)	7.5	1.5
Net portfolio flows[e]	0.0 (0.0)	−0.0 (0.1)	0.0 (0.0)	0.6	4.9 (−4.3)	0.0 (0.1)	0.0 (0.0)	0.3 (0.9)	2.2	1.4

Sources: IMF, *International Financial Statistics* (Washington, D.C., various issues); IMF, *World Economic Outlook* (Washington, D.C., various years); World Bank, *World Debt Tables* (Washington, D.C., various years).

[a]Net external debt and cumulative current account deficits are ratios to GDP for last year of the period.

[b]External debt minus nongold foreign exchange reserves.

[c]Initial net external debt plus cumulative value of current account deficits, as a ratio to last period's GDP.

[d]Short-term debt and foreign exchange reserves are ratios to total debt for last year of the period.

[e]Net FDI flows and net portfolio flows are average ratios to GDP during the period.

level of external debt appear to be better indicators of sustainability when expressed as ratios to exports, rather than to GDP.

A second set of indicators comprises the real exchange rate and exports (see figs. 3.2, 3.4, and 3.6). A persistent real exchange rate appreciation can be driven by "fundamental" factors, such as high productivity growth in the traded goods sector, or favorable terms-of-trade shocks. However, in the context of a fixed or managed exchange rate system, it could also reflect a fundamental inconsistency between the monetary policy stance and exchange rate policy or the effects of inflation inertia or imperfect credibility in the context of an exchange-rate-based inflation stabilization plan (see Calvo 1986). An "overvaluation" would encourage a decline in savings as domestic residents intertemporally substitute present for future consumption, thus contributing to a widening of current account imbalances and loss of foreign exchange reserves, reinforced by expectations of a future devaluation.

It is difficult to make the definition of real exchange rate overvaluation operational in the absence of a well-established theoretical framework explaining real exchange rate behavior (see Edwards 1989). In developing countries that have undertaken structural reforms, large capital inflows and a real exchange rate appreciation may reflect an increase in productivity and in the return to capital; if current account deficits also emerge because of the underlying increase in permanent income, they would not be an indicator of unsustainability. The difficulty lies in evaluating to what degree a real appreciation reflects improved fundamentals.

Table 3.3 also reports the level of the real effective exchange rate (measured in terms of relative consumer price indexes) relative to historical averages. The three crisis episodes we consider—Mexico I and II and Chile—are all characterized by a sustained real exchange rate appreciation in the period preceding the crisis, leading to an appreciated level of the real exchange rate. Colombia, Malaysia, and Thailand also experienced a sustained real appreciation during the late seventies and early eighties, and an exchange rate devaluation was a key component of their adjustment process. In the crisis episodes, an exchange rate depreciation was indeed undertaken before the full onset of the crisis but failed to prevent it. Our sample evidence thus suggests that large current account imbalances are more likely to result in a crisis when they are accompanied by a relatively appreciated level of the exchange rate.[24]

In order to service and reduce external indebtedness, a country needs to rely on traded goods production as a source of foreign exchange. Clearly, countries with large export sectors can service external debts more easily, because debt service will absorb a lower fraction of their total export proceeds. In order to generate the foreign exchange necessary to service external debt in case of

24. The real effective exchange rate appreciated in Thailand and Malaysia between the end of our sample period (1995) and the onset of the Asian crisis, following the appreciation of the U.S. dollar, to which these currencies were de facto pegged. The magnitude of the appreciation (around 10 percent) was, however, modest and the real exchange rate was still depreciated relative to historical averages.

Chile, Colombia and Mexico

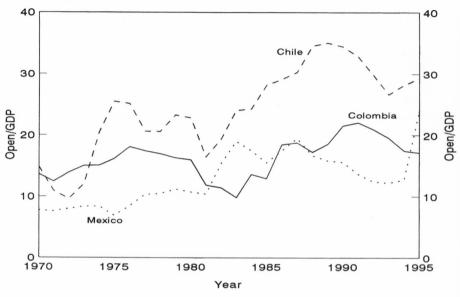

Korea, Malaysia and Thailand

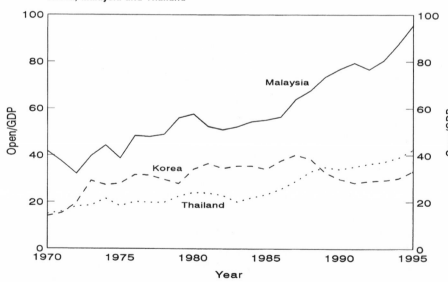

Fig. 3.6   Degree of openness, 1970–95
Sources: See fig. 3.2.

an interruption in capital flows, a country needs to engineer a resource shift toward the export sector. Since this shift cannot occur instantly, sharp import compression may become necessary, with adverse consequences on domestic industries relying on imported inputs (Sachs 1985; Sachs and Warner 1995). This import compression may be more costly in a relatively closed economy, because it is more likely to entail cuts of "essential" imported inputs (Williamson 1985). The size of the export sector can also be related to willingness-to-lend and willingness-to-pay considerations. Insofar as debt default is associated with trade disruptions (such as difficulties in obtaining export credits) it may be more costly for an open economy. Furthermore, the constituency against actions that would entail trade disruptions is also likely to be stronger, the larger the size of the export sector. According to the theory of international borrowing sketched in section 3.3, higher costs of default would reduce the likelihood of sudden reversals of capital inflows, because foreign investors will perceive the country—ceteris paribus—as less risky.

On the other side, a more open economy is, ceteris paribus, more vulnerable to external shocks such as fluctuations in the terms of trade or foreign demand shocks. In this regard, vulnerability is reduced by a well-diversified commodity composition of trade. Fluctuations in commodity prices have a larger impact on the terms of trade for countries with narrow export bases, and those particularly dependent on raw materials for their imports, thus weakening their ability to sustain current account deficits.[25] In addition, open economies with strong trade ties within a region may be more vulnerable to common regional shocks and contagion effects through the effects of exchange rate devaluation in neighboring countries on competitiveness.

Among the countries in our sample, the East Asian ones that successfully adjusted after experiencing large current account imbalances during the eighties (Korea, Malaysia, and Thailand) had large export shares and managed to increase exports significantly during the adjustment period. By contrast, the export-GDP ratio was lower in Mexico (especially in 1982) and in Chile, although it should be pointed out that exports were rising rapidly prior to all three crisis episodes considered (Mexico I and II and Chile). In Colombia, which had a low export share in the early eighties, both the export share and the degree of export diversification increased substantially. These findings are in line with results presented by Sachs (1985), who compared East Asian and Latin American countries at the time of the debt crisis. The episodes we considered thus suggest that large current account imbalances are less likely to lead to external crises when the economy has a large export base.[26]

---

25. Ghosh and Ostry (1994) found support for the view that large current account deficits are more likely to be unsustainable in countries with less diversified export bases in the context of a model based on precautionary savings. Mendoza (1997) presents evidence that the *volatility* of terms of trade is associated with lower economic growth in a wide sample of countries.

26. Export growth declined significantly in East Asian countries in 1996, after the end of our sample period. E.g., export growth in U.S. dollars turned slightly negative in Thailand in 1996, after close to 20 percent growth over the previous period.

A third set of factors comprises national savings and investment (figs. 3.3 and 3.5). For a given current account balance, the levels of savings and investment can have implications for the sustainability of the external position. To the extent that investment is allocated efficiently to high-return activities, high levels of investment imply—ceteris paribus—higher future growth through the buildup of a larger productive capacity and therefore enhance intertemporal solvency (see eq. [3]). High savings and investment ratios can also act as a signal of creditworthiness to international investors, because they act as a form of commitment to higher future output and thus raise the perceived ability to service and reduce external debt. However, investment projects may be chosen inefficiently, because of financial market distortions or because they are driven by political priorities. For example, relative price distortions may skew investment toward the nontraded goods sector, therefore failing to enhance a country's ability to generate future trade surpluses. Under these circumstances, high levels of investment may not enhance sustainability.[27] Among the episodes we consider, savings were extremely low in Chile in the run-up to the crisis. At the other extreme, Korea, Malaysia, and Thailand had high savings and investment rates. Savings were also low in Mexico in the early nineties. It is interesting to observe that in both Chile and Mexico II, the low savings rates were not attributable to public sector imbalances, but rather to low private savings. In summary, all three crisis episodes are characterized by low savings, especially by middle-income developing country standards.[28]

A fourth factor is the fiscal balance. In a pure debt neutrality case (Barro 1974) the current account is independent of the time profile of taxation, and therefore of the public sector deficit. Imperfect substitutability between private and public savings caused by, for example, distortionary taxes and liquidity constraints, implies a positive correlation between budget deficits and current account deficits. The strength of this correlation may depend on the degree of development of domestic financial markets; in countries with underdeveloped or highly regulated financial markets we would expect to find stronger links between the fiscal stance and the current account balance, and therefore between government budget solvency and current account sustainability.[29]

27. The Asian crisis has brought to the fore the importance of the mechanisms allocating savings to investment through financial intermediaries. See Krugman (1998) for a model in which moral hazard generated by implicit or explicit government guarantees lead to overinvestment and to a crisis.

28. In Colombia the level of national savings was low until 1984 but was raised considerably over the following period, thanks in particular to a large increase in public savings. In recent years savings have declined following financial liberalization, but current account imbalances are not as large as, say, in the case of Mexico. For recent cross-sectional studies of determinants of savings, see Masson, Bayoumi, and Samiei (1995) and Edwards (1995).

29. The degree of private sector saving offset by a given increase in public sector saving may also depend on the level of public debt (Sutherland 1995). With low public debt the current generation could view a future debt stabilization policy (via fiscal surpluses) as remote; thus the future tax liabilities are perceived to be small, and fiscal adjustments affect aggregate demand and savings. In contrast, with high public debt the future debt stabilization looks imminent and debt neutrality

The evidence provided by our sample suggests that the absence of large fiscal imbalances ex ante does not imply that current account deficits will prove sustainable, as exemplified by the cases of Chile and Mexico II. Implicit or explicit government guarantees can lead to excessive external exposure on the part of the private sector, and eventually to a crisis. Ex post, the government is faced with large fiscal costs in the form of bailouts of banks and firms, as well as the shouldering by the budget of private external debt.[30] Clearly, large fiscal imbalances, which were present in Mexico I, Malaysia I, Colombia I, and Thailand I, raise fiscal sustainability issues and did therefore require a policy shift. Indeed, the main element of the policy reversal in the latter three cases consisted in a substantial reduction of the fiscal deficit; for all these countries, the increase in public savings raised the overall savings rate and contributed to the reduction of external imbalances.

Drastic changes in the composition of capital flows took place between the late seventies to early eighties and the early nineties. During the late seventies and early eighties all the countries in our sample relied heavily on commercial bank borrowing in the form of syndicated loans, as well as on borrowing from official creditors. In contrast, the experience of the nineties is characterized by large private capital inflows, a sizable fraction of which took the form of foreign direct investment and portfolio investment. Economic theory suggests that the degree of risk sharing, as well as the intensity of asymmetric information and enforcement problems are related to the composition of external liabilities (see the discussion in section 3.3). Table 3.4 reports some summary statistics on the level and composition of external liabilities and capital flows (see also figs. 3.7 and 3.8).

Among these statistics, the cumulative value of current account imbalances as a fraction of GDP can be taken as an approximate measure of net external liabilities. This measure shows that the lower level of net external indebtedness during the nineties with respect to the eighties is mostly due to the relative importance of non-debt-creating capital inflows, such as foreign direct investment, in recent years. This is particularly striking in the case of Malaysia, but is also evident from the cases of Mexico, Thailand, and (to a lesser degree) Colombia during the nineties.[31] A corollary of these developments is that interest payments on external debt constitute a declining fraction of net resource transfers associated with existing external liabilities, while profit repatriation takes a more important role.

---

is at full force. The link between the twin deficits may therefore be stronger, the lower the level of public debt. Another implication of this line of reasoning is that the effects of fiscal stabilization on aggregate demand are weaker, the higher the public debt burden.

30. The Asian crisis provides further evidence on this issue; the effective level of government debt increased substantially because of the high cost of restructuring a financial system saddled with bad loans, and the fiscal deficit is increased by the amount of the debt service, as well as by the output effects of the crisis.

31. For Mexico I the net external liabilities measure is well below external debt (especially after 1981), signaling the presence of capital flight.

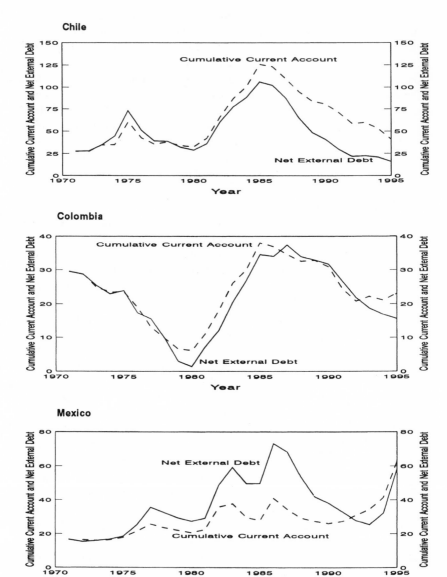

Fig. 3.7 Cumulative current account and net external debt: Chile, Colombia, and Mexico, 1970–95

Sources: IMF, *International Financial Statistics* (Washington, D.C., various issues); IMF, *World Economic Outlook* (Washington, D.C., various years); World Bank, *World Debt Tables* (Washington, D.C., various years).

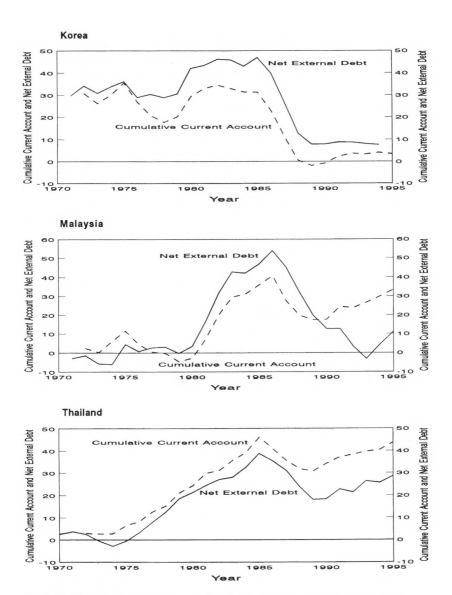

Fig. 3.8 Cumulative current account and net external debt: Korea, Malaysia, and Thailand, 1970–95

Sources: See fig. 3.7.

Table 3.4 also reports other debt composition factors, such as the fraction of short-term debt in total debt and the size of portfolio flows, which potentially play a role in determining the sustainability of external imbalances. There is a notion that vulnerability to external shocks and capital flow reversals is enhanced when portfolio investment and short-term inflows account for most of capital inflows, as these are perceived to be potentially more volatile than long-term flows or foreign direct investment.[32] The ability of a country to withstand a reversal in short-term flows is in principle linked to the size of foreign exchange reserves. In our limited sample, reserves were low with respect to short-term debt in both of Mexico's episodes, as well as in Korea in the eighties. In the nineties, short-term debt is particularly high in Thailand, although reserves are high as well.[33] In a study of currency collapses, Frankel and Rose (1996) find a weak correlation between debt composition variables and the probability of exchange rate crashes, but a significant negative correlation between the proportion of external liabilities accounted for by foreign direct investment and crash incidence.

The lesson we draw from the individual country studies and from existing empirical evidence is that the composition of external liabilities may affect the vulnerability of a country to an external crisis but more data is needed to establish a clear link between sources of external financing and current account sustainability. For this purpose, the composition of external liabilities should not be considered in isolation, but rather together with the other macroeconomic, structural, and external factors highlighted in this section.

3.6 Conclusions and Extensions

Our interpretation of the evidence presented in this limited sample of country episodes is that the likelihood of external crises has to be related to a composite set of macroeconomic and structural factors, rather than relying on the robustness of individual indicators (such as exchange rate overvaluation). Specifically, the degree of openness, the level and flexibility of the exchange rate, and the intensity of external shocks interact with the servicing burden of external obligations and the composition of external liabilities in determining whether protracted current account balances are likely to result in external crises. Clearly, the case study approach we adopted has limitations, such as poten-

32. For theoretical arguments about the effects of short-term debt on the likelihood of balance-of-payments crises, see, e.g., Calvo (1997) and Cole and Kehoe (1996). With regard to capital flow volatility, however, Claessens, Dooley, and Warner (1995) find that in a sample of industrial and developing countries the statistical labels "short term" and "long term" in most cases do not provide information regarding the persistence and volatility of flows.
33. After the end of our sample period short-term debt in Thailand increased further in relation to foreign exchange reserves. The refusal of foreign banks to roll over large short-term debt exposures has been a defining feature of the Asian crisis.

tial selectivity bias and collinearity between indicators, that formal statistical analysis on a larger sample of countries could address. The fact that we focus on current episodes also adds inference problems because of the potential for "peso problems" in the evaluation of indicators.

In the analysis of section 3.5 we did not explicitly discuss two related capital market factors that are more difficult to quantify: the degree of capital account openness and the health of the financial system. For all countries we have considered, the capital account is more open in the nineties than it was a decade earlier, although the degree of liberalization differs across countries. Remaining controls on international capital movements are mainly designed to limit the size of capital inflows, as opposed to controls on capital outflows that were preponderant during the seventies and eighties (see Grilli and Milesi-Ferretti 1995 for an empirical analysis of determinants and effects of capital controls during this earlier period). In part, the more limited reliance on capital controls can be explained by the increased difficulty of enforcing effective limitations on international capital mobility. Furthermore, there is increased awareness of the distortions that capital controls cause by imposing a wedge between rates of return on capital in the domestic economy and abroad.[34] An open capital account should improve resource allocation and can also provide a disciplining device, since a policy inconsistency between, say, an expansionary monetary policy and a pegged exchange rate would result in the collapse of the peg. Furthermore, an open capital account could serve as a signal of a country's commitment to the pursuit of "sustainable" policies and thereby raise foreign investors' perception of the country's creditworthiness (see, e.g., Bartolini and Drazen 1997). On the other side, when the capital account is very open, de jure or de facto, a country is more vulnerable to sudden reversals in the direction of capital flows. This reversal may concern not only foreign capital but also domestic capital.[35] Furthermore, economic research and practical experience have also highlighted the potential dangers associated with poor financial supervision and a weak banking system when the capital account is open (see, e.g., Diaz-Alejandro 1985). Indeed, considerations pertaining to the health of the financial system play an even more important role during the nineties because a larger fraction of external funds are intermediated by the domestic financial system with respect to the previous decade, when a large fraction of external borrowing was undertaken by the public sector.

34. The degree of de facto opening of the capital account is endogenous and depends in particular on the strength of the incentives to export capital (risk-adjusted rate of return differentials due to domestic policy misalignments, political instability, etc.).

35. This is exemplified by the experience of several Latin American countries (such as Argentina, Mexico, Peru, and Venezuela) in the run-up to the debt crisis (see, e.g., Diaz-Alejandro 1985; Sachs 1985). For those countries, the level of "official" foreign debt at the time of the debt crisis was much higher than the cumulative value of past current account imbalances, indicating that the accumulation of debt had financed not only excess of imports over exports but also private capital outflows.

The degree of fragility of the financial system has played an important role in all the crises we have considered.[36] Weaknesses in banking system supervision, distortions in the incentive structure of banks, the practice of directed bank lending, and lack of competition within the banking sector and from nonbank financial institutions can imply inefficiencies in the intermediation of external funds associated with large current account deficits. For a given size of current account imbalance, these inefficiencies make the economy more vulnerable to changes in foreign investors' sentiment or other shocks. As underscored by Goldstein (1996), a weak banking system is more vulnerable to a sudden reversal in capital flows when the exchange rate regime is not flexible.[37] Under these circumstances, monetary policy is "tied to the mast" because of the need to defend the exchange rate peg, thus limiting the ability of the central bank to exercise its role as a lender of last resort. The stability of the financial system remains an essential prerequisite for ensuring an appropriate macroeconomic response to potentially volatile capital flows.

References

Barro, Robert J. 1974. Are government bonds net wealth? *Journal of Political Economy* 82 (November): 1095–1117.

Bartolini, Leonardo, and Allan Drazen. 1997. Capital controls as a signal. *American Economic Review* 87 (March): 138–54.

Borensztein, Eduardo, José De Gregorio, and Jong-Wha Lee. 1998. How does foreign direct investment affect economic growth? *Journal of International Economics* 45 (June): 115–35.

Buffie, Edward F. 1989. Economic policy and foreign debt in Mexico. In *Developing country debt and economic performance* vol. 2, ed. Jeffrey Sachs. Chicago: University of Chicago Press.

Calvo, Guillermo A. 1986. Temporary stabilization: Predetermined exchange rates. *Journal of Political Economy* 94:1319–29.

———. 1997. Varieties of capital market crises. In ed. G. A. Calvo and Mervyn King. *The debt burden and its consequences for monetary policy,* London: St. Martin's.

Calvo, Guillermo A., Leonardo Leiderman, and Carmen M. Reinhart. 1993. Capital inflows and real exchange rate appreciation in Latin America: The role of external factors. *IMF Staff Papers* 40 (March): 108–51.

———. 1994. The capital inflow problem: Concepts and issues. *Contemporary Economic Policy* 12 (July): 54–66.

Calvo, Guillermo A., and Enrique G. Mendoza. 1996a. Mexico's balance-of-payments crisis: A chronicle of a death foretold. *Journal of International Economics* 41 (November): 235–64.

36. For a recent attempt to relate balance-of-payments and banking crises, see Kaminsky and Reinhart (1996). Goldstein (1996) provides a discussion of potential indicators of financial crises that shares many features with ours.

37. The importance of this point is further underscored by the nature of the recent Asian crisis. As in Mexico, the weakness of financial intermediaries and their external exposure affected the authorities' willingness to adjust the exchange rate in response to the initial reversal in capital flows.

————. 1996b. Rational herd behavior and the globalization of securities' markets. College Park: University of Maryland; Washington, D.C.: Federal Reserve Board. Mimeograph.

Campbell, John. 1987. Does savings anticipate declining labor income? An alternative test of the permanent income hypothesis. *Econometrica* 55:1249–73.

Carrasquilla, Alberto. 1995. Exchange rate bands and shifts in the stabilization policy regime: Issues suggested by the experience of Colombia. IMF Working Paper no. 95/42. Washington, D.C.: International Monetary Fund, April.

Chuhan, Punam, Stijn Claessens, and Nlandu Mamingi. 1993. Equity and bond flows to Latin America and Asia: The role of external and domestic factors. PRE Working Paper no. 1160. Washington, D.C.: World Bank.

Claessens, Stijn, Michael Dooley, and Andrew Warner. 1995. Portfolio flows: Hot or cold? *World Bank Economic Review* 9 (1): 153–74.

Clavijo, Sergio. 1995. A survey of economic policies and macroeconomic performance in Chile and Colombia, 1970–95. IMF Working Paper no. 95/139. Washington, D.C.: International Monetary Fund, December.

Cline, William R. 1995. *International debt reexamined.* Washington, D.C.: Institute for International Economics.

Cohen, Daniel. 1992. The debt crisis: A postmortem. In *NBER Macroeconomics Annual,* ed. Olivier Blanchard and Stanley Fischer, 65–105. Cambridge, Mass.: MIT Press.

————. 1996. The sustainability of African debt. World Bank Policy Research Paper no. 1621. Washington, D.C.: World Bank.

Cole, Harold L., and Timothy J. Kehoe. 1996. A self-fulfilling model of Mexico's 1994–5 debt crisis. *Journal of International Economics* 41 (November): 309–30.

Collins, Susan M., and Won-Am Park. 1989. External debt and macroeconomic performance in South Korea. In *Developing country debt and economic performance,* vol. 3, ed. Jeffrey Sachs, 153–369. Chicago: University of Chicago Press.

Corbo, Vittorio, and Stanley Fischer. 1994. Lessons from the Chilean stabilization and recovery. In *The Chilean economy: Policy lessons and challenges,* ed. B. Bosworth, R. Dornbusch, and R. Labán, 29–80. Washington, D.C.: Brookings.

Corbo, Vittorio, and Leonardo Hernández. 1996. Macroeconomic adjustment to capital inflows: Lessons from recent Latin American and East Asian experience. *World Bank Research Observer* 11 (February): 61–86.

Corsetti, Giancarlo, and Nouriel Roubini. 1991. Fiscal deficits, public debt and government solvency: Evidence from OECD countries. *Journal of the Japanese and International Economies* 5:354–80.

De la Cuadra, Sergio, and Salvador Valdes-Prieto. 1992. Myths and facts about financial liberalization in Chile: 1974–83. In *If Texas were Chile: A primer on banking reform,* ed. Philip Brock. San Francisco: ICS Press.

Demery, David, and Lionel Demery. 1992. *Adjustment and equity in Malaysia.* Paris: Organization for Economic Cooperation and Development.

Diaz-Alejandro, Carlos F. 1984. Latin American debt: I don't think we are in Kansas anymore. *Brookings Papers on Economic Activity,* no. 1:335–89.

————. 1985. Goodbye financial repression, hello financial crash. *Journal of Development Economics* 19:1–24.

Dooley, Michael P. 1995. A retrospective on the debt crisis. In *Understanding interdependence: The macroeconomics of the open economy,* ed. Peter B. Kenen, 262–88. Princeton, N.J.: Princeton University Press.

Dornbusch, Rudiger. 1990. The new classical macroeconomics and stabilization policy. *American Economic Review Papers and Proceedings* 80 (May): 143–47.

Dornbusch, Rudiger, Ilan Goldfajn, and Rodrigo Valdes. 1995. Currency crises and collapses. *Brookings Papers on Economic Activity,* no. 2: 219–93.

Dornbusch, Rudiger, and Alejandro Werner. 1994. Mexico: Stabilization, reform and no growth. *Brookings Papers on Economic Activity,* no. 1: 253–315.

Eaton, Jonathan, and Raquel Fernández. 1995. Sovereign debt. in *Handbook of international economics,* vol. 3, ed. Gene M. Grossman and Kenneth S. Rogoff, 2031–77. Amsterdam: North Holland.

Eaton, Jonathan, and Mark Gersovitz. 1981. Poor-country borrowing in private financial markets and the repudiation issues. Princeton Studies in International Finance no. 47. Princeton, N.J.: Princeton University, June.

Edwards, Sebastian. 1989. *Real exchange rates, devaluation and adjustment.* Cambridge, Mass.: MIT Press.

———. 1995. Why are savings rates so different across countries? An international comparative analysis. NBER Working Paper no. 5097. Cambridge, Mass.: National Bureau of Economic Research, April.

Edwards, Sebastian, and Alejandra Cox-Edwards. 1987. *Monetarism and liberalization: The Chilean experiment.* Cambridge, Mass.: MIT Press.

Eichengreen, Barry, Andrew K. Rose, and Charles Wyplosz. 1995. Exchange market mayhem: The antecedents and aftermath of speculative attacks. *Economic Policy* 21 (October): 249–312.

Fernández-Arias, Eduardo. 1996. The new wave of private capital inflows: Push or pull? *Journal of Development Economics* 48:389–418.

Fernández-Arias, Eduardo, and Peter Montiel. 1996. The surge in capital inflows to developing countries: An analytical overview. *World Bank Economic Review* 10 (January): 51–77.

Folkerts-Landau, David. 1985. The changing role of international bank lending in development finance. *IMF Staff Papers* 32 (June): 317–63.

Frankel, Jeffrey A., and Andrew K. Rose. 1996. Currency crashes in emerging markets: Empirical indicators. *Journal of International Economics* 41 (November): 351–66.

Fry, Maxwell. 1993. Foreign direct investment in a macroeconomic framework: Finance, efficiency, incentives and distortions. International Economics Department Policy Working Paper no. 1141. Washington, D.C.: World Bank, May.

Gale, David. 1973. Pure exchange equilibrium of dynamic models. *Journal of Economic Theory* 6:12–36.

Gertler, Mark, and Kenneth S. Rogoff. 1990. North-South lending and endogenous domestic capital market inefficiencies. *Journal of Monetary Economics* 26 (October): 245–66.

Ghosh, Atish. 1995. International capital mobility amongst the major industrialized countries: Too little or too much. *Economic Journal* 128 (January): 107–28.

Ghosh, Atish R., and Jonathan D. Ostry. 1994. Export instability and the external balance in developing countries. *IMF Staff Papers* 41 (June): 214–35.

———. 1995. The current account in developing countries: A perspective from the consumption smoothing approach. *World Bank Economic Review* 9 (2):305–33.

Glick, Reuven, and Kenneth S. Rogoff. 1995. Global versus country-specific productivity shocks and the current account. *Journal of Monetary Economics* 35 (April): 159–92.

Goldstein, Morris. 1996. Presumptive indicators/early warning signals of vulnerability to financial crises in emerging-market economies. Washington, D.C.: Institute for International Economics, January. Mimeograph.

Grilli, Vittorio, and Gian Maria Milesi-Ferretti. 1995. Economic effects and structural determinants of capital controls. *IMF Staff Papers* 42 (September): 517–51.

Haggard, Stephen, Richard Cooper, Susan M. Collins, Chongsoo Kim, and Sung-Tael Ro. 1994. *Macroeconomic policy and adjustment in Korea, 1970–1990.* Cambridge, Mass.: Harvard Institute for International Development.

International Monetary Fund (IMF). 1995a. *International capital markets: Developments, prospects and policy issues.* Washington, D.C.: International Monetary Fund.
————. 1995b. *World economic outlook.* Washington, D.C.: International Monetary Fund, May.

Johnston, R. Barry. 1991. Distressed financial institutions in Thailand: Structural weaknesses, support operations, and economic consequences. In *Banking crises: Cases and issues,* ed. V. Sundararajan and Tomás J. T. Baliño. Washington, D.C.: International Monetary Fund.

Kaminsky, Graciela, and Carmen M. Reinhart. 1996. The twin crises: The causes of banking and balance-of-payments problems. FRB International Finance Discussion Paper no. 544. Washington, D.C.: Federal Reserve Board, March.

Khan, Mohsin S., and Carmen M. Reinhart. 1995. Capital flows in the APEC region. IMF Occasional Paper no. 122. Washington, D.C.: International Monetary Fund, March.

Koenig, Linda M. 1996. Capital inflows and policy responses in the ASEAN region. IMF Working Paper no. 96/25. Washington, D.C.: International Monetary Fund, April.

Krugman, Paul. 1998. What happened to Asia. Internet website http://web.mit.edu/krugman/www.disinter.html, January.

Leiderman, Leonardo, and Assaf Razin. 1991. Determinants of external imbalances: The role of taxes, government spending, and productivity. *Journal of the Japanese and International Economies* 5:421–50.

Masson, Paul R., Tamim Bayoumi, and Hossein S. Samiei. 1995. International evidence on the determinants of private savings. In *Staff studies for the world economic outlook.* Washington, D.C.: International Monetary Fund.

Mendoza, Enrique G. 1997. Terms of trade uncertainty and economic growth: Are risk indicators significant in growth regressions? *Journal of Development Economics* 54 (December): 323–56.

Milesi-Ferretti, Gian Maria, and Assaf Razin. 1996. Current account sustainability. Princeton Studies in International Finance no. 81. Princeton, N.J.: Princeton University, October.

Obstfeld, Maurice, and Kenneth S. Rogoff. 1995. The intertemporal approach to the current account. In *Handbook of international economics,* vol. 3, ed. Gene M. Grossman and Kenneth S. Rogoff. Amsterdam: North Holland.
————. 1996. *Foundations of international macroeconomics.* Cambridge, Mass.: MIT Press.

Ocampo, José Antonio. 1989. Colombia and the Latin American debt crisis. In *Debt, adjustment and recovery: Latin America's prospects,* ed. Sebastian Edwards and Felipe Larraín, 241–66. Oxford: Blackwell.

Otto, Glenn. 1992. Testing a present-value model of the current account: Evidence from U.S. and Canadian time series. *Journal of International Money and Finance* 11 (October): 414–30.

Razin, Assaf. 1995. The dynamic-optimizing approach to the current account: Theory and evidence. In *Understanding interdependence: The macroeconomics of the open economy,* ed. Peter B. Kenen, 169–98. Princeton, N.J.: Princeton University Press.

Razin, Assaf, Efraim Sadka, and Chi-Wa Yuen. 1998. A pecking order theory of capital inflows and international tax principles. *Journal of International Economics* 44 (February): 45–68.

Robinson, David, Yangho Byeon, and Ranjit Teja with Wanda Tseng. 1991. Thailand: Adjusting to success—current policy issues. IMF Occasional Paper no. 85. Washington, D.C.: International Monetary Fund, August.

Sachs, Jeffrey. 1985. External debt and macroeconomic performance in Latin America and East Asia. *Brookings Papers on Economic Activity,* no. 1:523–64.

Sachs, Jeffrey, Aaron Tornell, and Andrés Velasco. 1996. The collapse of the Mexican peso: What have we learned? *Economic Policy* 22 (October): 15–56.

Sachs, Jeffrey, and Andrew Warner. 1995. Economic reform and the process of global integration. *Brookings Papers on Economic Activity,* no. 1:1–95.

SaKong, Il. 1993. *Korea in the world economy.* Washington, D.C.: Institute for International Economics.

Schadler, Susan, Maria Carkovic, Adam Bennett, and Robert Kahn. 1993. Recent experiences with surges in capital inflows. IMF Occasional Paper no. 108. Washington, D.C.: International Monetary Fund, December.

Sheffrin, Steven, and Wing Thye Woo. 1990. Present value tests of an intertemporal model of the current account. *Journal of International Economics* 29 (November): 237–53.

Soon, Cho. 1993. The dynamics of Korean economic development. Washington, D.C.: Institute for International Economics.

Stiglitz, Joseph, and Andrew Weiss. 1981. Credit rationing in models with imperfect information. *American Economic Review* 71 (June): 393–410.

Sutherland, Alan. 1995. Fiscal crises and demand: Can high public debt reverse the effects of fiscal policy? CEPR Discussion Paper no. 1246. London: Centre for Economic Policy Research, September.

Velasco, Andrés. 1991. Liberalization, crisis, intervention: The Chilean financial system, 1975–85. In *Banking crises: Cases and issues,* ed. V. Sundararajan and Tomás J. T. Baliño. Washington, D.C.: International Monetary Fund.

Williamson, John. 1985. Comments on Sachs. *Brookings Papers on Economic Activity,* no. 1:565–70.

Comment   Koichi Hamada

This ambitious paper by Milesi-Ferretti and Razin addresses questions that are important from the standpoints of both theory and policy. How can a country continue to sustain its current account? What are the criteria for a sustainable growth path with international indebtedness? The paper devotes a substantial number of pages to these questions, but because these issues are intrinsically so difficult the authors solve only part of the problem.

The authors discuss the basic tools for answering these questions: the permanent income approach, the portfolio selection approach, and the asymmetric information approach. All of them are well explained. What I would like to ask for, in addition to the careful explanation given for each component, is a perspective that integrates all three approaches. Since the economic universe is the same, all of the approaches should be mutually consistent in an integrated model and could be adapted to each other. I am probably setting the authors a difficult task, a task that can hardly be achieved in one conference

Koichi Hamada is professor of economics at Yale University.

paper. But I ask for it because an integrated perspective would give a clear understanding of each partial approach.

The authors update the somewhat old-fashioned indicators of sustainability in terms of simple ratios, such as the debt service ratios and debt-income ratios used frequently in the practice of the Bretton Woods institutions. In my view, the optimal dynamic pattern of borrowing and lending of a nation can be analyzed in an open growth model. Usually a country starts as a debtor, becomes a creditor, and then finally evolves into a mature creditor that runs a trade deficit but a current account *surplus* because of sufficient investment income from abroad. The process generates various changes in indicators of external viability.

The difficulty of finding a proper indicator of interest payments ahead lies in the difficulty of finding a proper indicator of external viability, because we know the past and the present but do not know the future except for scheduled interest payments ahead. The test of the equality of the marginal rate of inter-temporal substitution between home and abroad is easily done, but the test of transversality conditions assuring the non-Ponzi condition is difficult. This kind of global condition can now only be tested by a unit root test, which gives only a weak sufficient condition for a non-Ponzi path.

For more practical purposes, we have ratios of debt service to GNP, debt to exports, debt to GDP, and so forth. But most of the indexes are static because they are related to levels. We should get to the changes-of-indebtedness indexes developed by Obstfeld and Rogoff and Cohen. Cohen's index captures the speed with which the debt-export (GDP) ratio is changing and gives at least a cinematographic picture of the debt situation.

As for the country section, I welcome the authors' efforts to obtain and sort out relevant figures for Latin American and Asian countries. They are all instructive. Since it is often difficult to obtain homogenous standardized data across countries, we should appreciate the authors' efforts even more. My only criticism is that the explanations of these tables are hardly accompanied by direct reference to the theoretical framework or by explanations of economic mechanisms (rather than chronological explanations).

I do not agree with the authors' statement that indicators that use exports as the denominator are better than those that use GDP as the denominator. If the government could stop imports and the nation could still export the same way, then the export-denominated indexes would be meaningful. This is unrealistic. The same argument applies as well to indicators with government revenue in the denominator. Could the government immediately stop making public expenditures and repay the debt? Even the trade-related model developed by Razin would indicate that national indebtedness relative to income or GNP is a more appropriate index for external viability than what is defined relative to exports. Comparing Côte d'Ivoire, which is very open, with Uganda, which is less open, will illustrate my point. Uganda would appear very precarious for external viability and Côte d'Ivoire would appear—contrary to reality. I quite agree that the financial health of a country is an important characteristic used to assess the sustainability of debt.[1]

Comment   Andrew K. Rose

Gian Maria Milesi-Ferretti and Assaf Razin have provided us with a valuable and illuminating paper. Not only have they provided a reasonable theoretical framework with which to understand current account swings; but they have gone the extra step to interpret the actual data. In particular, they survey a number of countries in Latin America and Southeast Asia in two different time periods. Their particular focus is the macroeconomic and financial characteristics that could account for the actual swings in current accounts. They are to be commended for tackling an ambitious topic in a comprehensive fashion.

Though Milesi-Ferretti and Razin have blazed the trail, much work remains to be done (as the authors readily acknowledge). I see a number of ways forward.

First, it would be useful to establish closer ties between the theoretical framework set forth by the authors and the data. For instance, it would be nice to assess the importance of asymmetric information in a *quantitative* way. Of course this is likely to be very difficult to do in practice, not least because market participants have incentives to try to minimize such problems. This may be one reason why foreign direct investment is used to such a high degree in Southeast Asia, and perhaps also why Asian countries tend to have been more open historically (since openness raises the importance of trade sanctions). How important are the issues associated with portfolio diversification? Is there any reason to be concerned that global capital market flows might diminish as the well-known "home market bias" disappears?

Next, I feel it would be extremely useful for the literature to establish the value (or lack thereof) of *accessible* measures of current account solvency and sustainability that can actually be implemented. These concepts are extremely useful theoretically, but it would be nice to be able to assess their empirical merit (even in the context of the case study approach).

The case study methodology employed by Milesi-Ferretti and Razin has a number of merits, primarily in terms of flexibility. The case study approach allows the authors to look at many indicators and aspects without a narrow

1. As an afterthought, this point has become especially valid with the recent financial fiascos among the Asian countries, including some of those studied by the authors.

Andrew K. Rose is the B. T. Rocca Professor of Economic Analysis and Policy in the Haas School of Business at the University of California, Berkeley; acting director of the International Finance and Macroeconomics Program at the National Bureau of Economic Research; and a research fellow of the Centre for Economic Policy Research.

scope. It is easy to focus on interesting events and issues. Here we focus on 10 cases, eight macroeconomic variables, and extra financial variables. Nevertheless, this flexibility does not come without a price. I think of statistical work as being more restrictive but more disciplined than case studies. It is often difficult for the reader to absorb all the material in the case studies. As a result, we tend to look for common themes or threads (as do the authors). But testing the importance of common themes across observations is exactly what statistical analysis does, although the latter is more formal. Further, the case study methodology allows one to ignore cases and variables that do not fit, resulting potentially in selection bias, collinearity, and specification error. Also, I sometimes find it hard to think about raw data without a comparison set of benchmark countries. For instance, is a 6 percent current account deficit "large"? Large compared to what?

In the final analysis, I think of the case study empirics such as those in the paper as being useful as a first step toward more disciplined statistical and theoretical analysis guided by empirics. Since that is precisely what the authors have in mind, I applaud their choice of technique, while urging future authors to be more cautious.

A number of questions are raised by this work. Among them, I would include the following.

1. What is the role played by capital controls in current account determination? Should they be used if they work? Do they work?

2. Is there a bottom line on the role of the exchange rate regime for countries with potential current account difficulties? Do fixed rates allow for the appreciation needed to draw in capital during development more easily than floating rates?

3. Is there a consensus on the (ir)relevance of the "Lawson thesis," namely, that current account deficits are irrelevant and sustainable if accompanied by fiscal balance?

4. Is there a special "Asia effect"? Is the typical precariousness of large Latin current accounts simply because they are usually associated with inflation stabilization? Or is it a thing of the past?

5. Why are large current account deficits in developing countries different from those in the OECD? Many industrialized countries experience persistent large current account deficits; but crises do not appear. Is it good luck? Good policy? Or good capital markets? If the latter, why does financial liberalization often lead to trouble?

I look forward to the views of the authors (and others) on these topics in the future.

4   Economic Growth and Real Exchange Rate: An Overview of the Balassa-Samuelson Hypothesis in Asia

Takatoshi Ito, Peter Isard, and Steven Symansky

4.1   Introduction

The relationship between the exchange rate and economic development is certainly an important subject, from both a positive (descriptive) and a normative (policy prescription) perspective. Several developing countries that have implicitly or explicitly fixed their exchange rates to the currency of another country (say, the U.S. dollar) and whose inflation rates are higher than that of the foreign country (the United States) often experience persistent current account deficits and eventual devaluations of their currencies. Devaluation often invites a recession and inflation and thus pushes the economy into an inflation-devaluation spiral, causing a serious setback in economic development. Other developing countries grow exceptionally fast and often face the opposite pressure on their currencies. A high economic growth rate is most likely accompanied by a high investment rate, and high export growth as well. Successful exports produce current account surpluses, resulting in *nominal* appreciation pressure on the currency unless the central bank intervenes in the foreign exchange market and accumulates foreign reserves. Even if the intervention maintains the fixed exchange rate, unsterilized intervention results in inflation, and the *real* exchange rate appreciates anyway. In the world of free capital mobility, another channel for appreciation exists. Fast growth often invites in-

Takatoshi Ito is professor in the Institute of Economic Research at Hitotsubashi University, Tokyo, and a research associate of the National Bureau of Economic Research. Peter Isard is division chief in the research department of the International Monetary Fund. Steven Symansky is deputy division chief in the fiscal affairs department of the International Monetary Fund.

Comments from Anne Krueger, Kenichi Ohno, and other conference participants were very helpful in revising the paper. Help in obtaining data by Kenneth Lin and Baekin Cha is appreciated. This paper was written when the first author was senior advisor in the research department of the International Monetary Fund. Research assistance by Susanna Mursula is also appreciated. The views and opinions expressed in this paper do not necessarily represent those of the International Monetary Fund or the National Bureau of Economic Research.

flows of foreign capital. Some investors in industrial countries pursue high returns (even with high risk) as part of a diversified portfolio. Capital inflows put pressure on the (nominal) exchange rate to appreciate. For example, demand for the currency of an emerging market will rise when foreign investors plan to purchase bonds and stocks, because the local currency has to be obtained first. Put simply, successful economic development results in a currency appreciation with improvement in the standard of living, while failure in economic development often results in a sharp currency depreciation.

One of the most popular hypotheses with respect to long-term real exchange rate movements is the so-called Balassa-Samuelson hypothesis, which conjectures that productivity increases in the tradable sector tend to be higher than those in the nontradable sector, so that the conventionally constructed real exchange rate (using a price index that includes both tradable and nontradable prices, such as the CPI or GDP deflator) will move in a manner that reflects cross-country differences in the relative speed of productivity increases between the tradable and nontradable sectors.[1] Since the differences in productivity increases are expected to be larger in high-growth countries, the Balassa-Samuelson prediction should be most visible among rapidly growing countries. It is well known in the literature that the postwar Japanese record has been a prime example of the Balassa-Samuelson hypothesis. However, one country does not prove the case. Hence, the Asian emerging markets with high growth rates seem to offer a good testing ground. A few additional thoughts and regressions are also shown and interpreted.

Although the Balassa-Samuelson hypothesis makes a prediction about the movement of the real exchange rate based on the common pattern (tradable sector productivity growth is higher than nontradable) among high-growth countries, the original mechanism for high growth is not explained. The present paper examines why some countries grow faster and whether the mechanism for high growth makes a difference in proving or refuting the Balassa-Samuelson hypothesis.

Japan and other high-growth countries in East Asia have completed, or have been experiencing, a transformation from agricultural, stagnant economies to manufacturing, export-oriented, growing economies. Their success is based on a change in industrial structure, gradually moving up a technological ladder. In many countries, economic development changed the structure from low-value-added goods sectors, such as primary goods and textiles, to high-value-added goods sectors, such as manufacturing and machinery. Moreover, each sector changes its trade status from net importer, to domestically self-sufficient, to net exporter. The important element of economic development in Asia seems to be a constant upgrading (higher quality and more sophisticated

---

1. The original articles are Balassa (1964) and Samuelson (1964). For recent studies, see Asea and Mendoza (1994), De Gregorio and Wolf (1994), De Gregorio, Giovannini, and Wolf (1994), Marston (1990). See also Corden (1960). This paper draws heavily on Ito et al. (1996) but has a different emphasis and updated data.

products) of the industrial structure and exporting goods. This observation is sometimes nicknamed the "flying geese pattern" of economic development.[2] Its original meaning was that a particular manufacturing sector, such as the steel industry in Japan, experiences stages from an import surge, to a domestic production surge replacing imports, to an export surge; then the same pattern is repeated in the next industry up the sophistication ladder, say the automobile industry. The more recent, popularized version of the flying geese pattern is that the different Asian countries experience the same pattern of industrial development but with time lags. At a particular point in time, Japan is a leader followed by Singapore and Hong Kong, which are followed by Korea and Taiwan, and then by Thailand and Indonesia, and so forth. We will make observations about the relationship between the Balassa-Samuelson hypothesis and the flying geese hypothesis below.

The rest of the paper is organized as follows. In section 4.2, the relationship between changes in real exchange rates and growth rates among East Asian countries is reviewed. Section 4.3 examines the relationship between machinery exports and growth. Section 4.4 examines a relationship between export characteristics and growth, and another between export characteristics and real exchange rate changes. Section 4.5 examines the link between the Balassa-Samuelson hypothesis and stages of economic development. The link between productivity growth and relative price changes, one of the important links in the Balassa-Samuelson hypothesis, is examined in section 4.6 using sectoral data for Japan and the United States during 1960–92.

4.2   Stylized Facts about the Balassa-Samuelson in APEC

For testing the Balassa-Samuelson hypothesis, the relationship between the growth rate and changes in the real exchange rate is examined. The Asia-Pacific Economic Cooperation Council (APEC) countries and economies are taken as examples here. Since economic development stages differ widely among APEC countries, the examination will be a good test of how universally the Balassa-Samuelson hypothesis may apply.

The growth rate and real exchange rate change are defined as follows. The growth rate, denoted by $dG(j, t + k)$, is the average per capita GDP growth rate of country j between t and $t + k$:

$$Y(j, t + k) = [1 + dG(j, t + k)]^k Y(j, t),$$

where $Y(j,t)$ is per capita GDP of country j in year t. The growth rate relative to the United States is the difference between $dG(j)$ and $dG(US)$. Let us denote by $S(j,t)$ the nominal exchange rate of country j in year t, in the unit of the value of country j's currency in terms of the U.S. dollar, for example, dollars

2. See Ito (1995) for this hypothesis. For traditional economic development theory, see, e.g., Kuznets (1959, 1971).

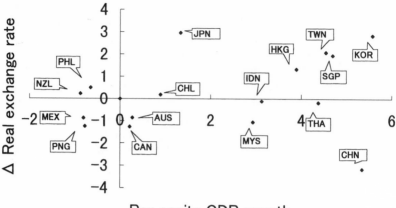

Per capita GDP growth

Fig. 4.1   Growth versus real exchange rate changes: relative to the United States, 1973–95
Source: See appendix.
Note: Sample period for Chile is 1975–95.

per yen for Japan; $P(j,t)$ is the GDP deflator of country t, and $P(US,t)$ is the GDP deflator of the United States.

The (average compound) change in the real exchange rate Q of country j, $dQ(j,t + k)$, for k years, is defined in the equation

$$Q(j, t + k) = [1 + dQ(j, t + k)]^k Q(j, t),$$

where $Q(j,t) = S(j,t)P(j,t)/P(US,t)$. If $dQ(\cdot)$ is positive, the currency of country j is appreciating in the real exchange rate.

Figure 4.1 shows the relationship between the economic growth rate and changes in the real exchange rate for the APEC countries for the period 1973–95 (except for Chile, where the sample period is 1975–95).[3] The positive relationship between economic growth and real appreciation that is a hallmark of the Balassa-Samuelson hypothesis is found in Japan; among the four "tigers," or newly industrialized economies (NIEs); and, to a much lesser extent, in Chile. One can also point out that the positive correlation was found in two other countries, Mexico and Papua New Guinea (PNG), in terms of negative growth (again relative to the United States) and depreciation (negative appreciation). However, not all APEC countries experienced positive correlation between growth and real appreciation. Australia, Canada, New Zealand, and the Philippines experienced growth rates similar to that of the United States

3. For data sources, see Ito et al. (1996). For this paper, the data are updated to 1995. In our earlier work, the magnitude of real appreciation in Hong Kong and Singapore was smaller. Some possible reasons for the result were discussed. The real appreciation in the updating years made them comparable to Taiwan. Although Young (1992) emphasizes the difference in the investment and growth pattern between the two city-states, they look very similar in real exchange rate performance in the framework of the Balassa-Samuelson hypothesis.

Table 4.1   **Balassa-Samuelson Effect**

	Coefficients		
Sample	a	b	$\bar{R}^2$
Total sample	−0.167	0.181	.01
	(−0.322)	(1.070)	
All but China	−0.236	0.357	.29
	(0.357)	(2.664)	

Note: Numbers in parentheses are t-statistics.
Equation: $dQ(j, t + k) = a + b\, dG(j, t + k)$.

(within 1 percentage point) with little depreciation or appreciation. Indonesia, Thailand, and Malaysia experienced high growth with real depreciation, although the magnitude of depreciation was small.

China, another high-growth country, experienced a large depreciation, thus appearing to violate the Balassa-Samuelson prediction. China's depreciation can be understood as an "outlier," in that the country rapidly transformed from a closed, planned economy to an open economy in the last half of the sample period. The opening also meant correction of the overvalued exchange rate. In a sense, depreciation was necessary in order to compete in global markets. In a sense, large depreciation preceded high growth rates, but both are included in the sample period. This kind of drastic economic reform is not considered in the Balassa-Samuelson theory.

As shown in table 4.1, a simple regression produces an insignificant coefficient for the growth rate, while a regression excluding China yields a growth coefficient significant at the 2 percent level. A possible justification for excluding China from the sample, as suggested above, is that China had maintained strict trade and exchange controls in the 1970s and the 1980s. Although the sample used in the regression is too small to justify a general statement, it can be said that the Balassa-Samuelson hypothesis is in most cases supported by the APEC findings.

In summary, figure 4.1 and table 4.1 indicate that the high-growth economies in East Asia generally experienced high growth and real appreciation in the period 1973–95. This finding is consistent with the Balassa-Samuelson hypothesis. Although it is difficult to generalize the finding to other APEC members, the gross violation of the hypothesis is limited to China, which made the unusual economic transformation from a planned economy to a market economy during the period.

4.3 Export-Led Growth

In the theoretical Balassa-Samuelson framework, growth is exogenously given to the economy. How the tradable and nontradable sectors differ in productivity growth is not explained in the model. However, the theory hypothesizes and predicts how they collectively contribute to the overall growth and change of relative prices, given growth in different sectors.

The Balassa-Samuelson theory also differs from the often-heard advice that in order to promote growth, depreciation must be induced. If that were a predominant mechanism for promotion of high economic growth, we would have found a negative correlation between growth and real appreciation for many countries (not just for China).

In order to shed some light on where growth comes from, our next task is to investigate the source of growth and its relationship to real exchange rate behavior. Many works, for example World Bank (1993), emphasize the importance of exports in achieving sustained growth. In addition, a hypothesis that is often emphasized in development economics is that a country's industrial and export structures have to change in order to make fast growth possible for a sustained period. As the economy grows, there is a limit to how much of a single kind of product, say textiles, can be exported to the global market, even if the economy becomes better at producing the product. Sooner or later, the comparative advantage of the industry is eroded either by political resistance to rapidly increasing imports in destination countries or by wage hikes at home. With improved skills and work ethics among workers, the next-level industry, say machinery, would be ready to take off. Change in the structure of exports is one of the important aspects of economic development and a high rate of economic growth. A proxy variable for development of high-value-added manufactured goods is needed for quantitative examinations. Here, the ratio of machine exports (value) to total exports (value), denoted by $M(j, t)$, is chosen as an indicator of structural change. Its change from 1973 to 1992, denoted by $dM(j,t + k)$, is defined as

$$dM(j, t + k) = M(j, t + k) - M(j, t).$$

The growth rate, as defined above, dG, is expected to be closely related to export structure change. Figure 4.2 shows the relationship between the per capita growth rate and changes in the machine export ratio from 1973 to 1992 (the last year that data for export ratios were available). A rise in the manufacturing sector in output and exports is one condition for a spurt in growth. Figure 4.2 shows a positive relationship between the increase in machine exports and the growth rate. Korea, Taiwan, Singapore, Malaysia, Thailand, and Japan show a strong correlation between the machine export ratio and growth. For this group of countries, exports are often called an engine of growth.

Hong Kong and Indonesia experienced only a mild increase in the machine export ratio. China achieved high economic growth without a visible change in machine exports. The Western Hemisphere countries also show a positive relationship between a moderate increase in the machine export ratio and moderate growth. Advanced countries such as the United States and Japan have already achieved high *levels* of machine export ratio, so it would not be possible to produce a high increase in the ratio.

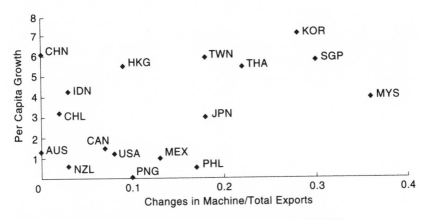

Fig. 4.2   Changes in machine export ratio versus growth, 1973–92
Source: See appendix.

Table 4.2   Machine Exports' Effect on Growth

	Coefficients		
Sample	*a*	*b*	$\bar{R}^2$
Total sample	2.234	8.431	.098
	(2.59)	(1.657)	

Note: Numbers in parentheses are *t*-statistics. Sample period is 1973–92.
Equation: $dG(j, t + k) = a + b \, dM(j, t + k)$.

The regression analysis reported in table 4.2 supports, although with weak statistical significance, the casual observation of the positive relationship noted in figure 4.2. More machine exports have been important in achieving high economic growth in many East Asian countries. This is consistent with the conventional wisdom (in the literature explaining Asian growth) that for high-speed growth, the shift in export items is to high-value-added, manufactured goods.

The coefficient implies that a 10 percentage point rise in the ratio of machine exports to total exports increases the growth rate by 0.8 percentage points over the "natural" growth rate of 2.23 percent. Although the regression is very simple, it accords with a popular belief in the importance of structural changes in boosting the growth rate "temporarily" (for a decade or two) before it comes down. The machine export ratio is bounded by unity, so exceptional growth cannot continue.

Suppose that a trade structure change, either policy driven or market driven, is the exogenous engine that pushes the economy to grow fast. The increasing share of machines in exports can be interpreted as faster productivity growth

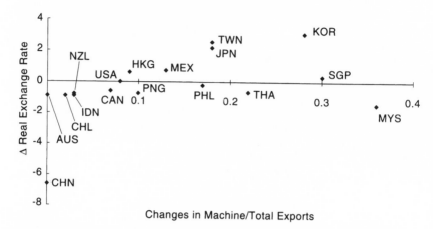

Fig. 4.3   **Changes in machine export ratio versus real exchange rate changes, 1973–92**
Source: See appendix.

in the tradable sector, one of the assumptions of the Balassa-Samuelson mechanism. In this interpretation, both per capita growth and real exchange appreciation are the results of fundamental structural change. According to this interpretation, in explaining real exchange rate change, it would be more appropriate to regress it on the increase in the machine export ratio rather than on economic growth.

Figure 4.3 shows the relationship between the machine export ratio and real exchange rate changes from 1973 to 1992, the relationship between a pair of variables from figures 4.1 and 4.2, respectively. Among the Asian high-growth countries, Korea, Taiwan, and Japan show strong gains in machine export ratio and real exchange rate. Hong Kong is now in line with Korea and Taiwan in the sense that it has only moderate gains in machine export ratio and real exchange rate. Singapore and Malaysia remain a puzzle to believers in the flying geese and Balassa-Samuelson hypotheses: despite large gains in machine export ratio, their real exchange rates have not appreciated. Thailand and the Philippines also advanced in machine export ratio without real appreciation. China and Chile again are outliers with large real exchange rate depreciation.

Table 4.3 shows that when the real exchange rate change is regressed on the change in machine export ratio, the coefficient is positive and significant (at the 10 percent significance level).

In summary, figures 4.2 and 4.3 show that trade structure changes influence both the growth rate and the real exchange rate. The evidence in these figures is consistent with the hypothesis that an economic transformation to high-value-added industries is a key to economic growth with real exchange rate appreciation. Advances in productivities and competitiveness in the high-value-added tradable sectors (here proxied by the machine export ratio) are consistent with

Table 4.3   Machine Exports' Effect on the Real Exchange Rate

| | Coefficients | | |
Sample	a	b	$\overline{R}^2$
Total sample	-1.373	0.752	.139
	(-1.827)	(1.892)	

Note: Numbers in parentheses are t-statistics.
Equation: $dQ(j, t + k) = a + b\, dM(j, t + k)$.

both a positive correlation between growth rates and real appreciation and the basic premise of economic development with industrial transformation.

4.4   Examination of the Balassa-Samuelson Hypothesis

In this section, some of the basic assumptions of the Balassa-Samuelson hypothesis are examined to confirm how it works for Japan and the NIEs and how it does not necessarily work for other countries (especially Association of South East Asian Nations countries).[4]

In the Balassa-Samuelson hypothesis, high economic growth is made possible by high productivity growth, with differential sectoral growth rates that cause inflation differentials among different sectors. The relative price of nontradable (N) goods to tradable (T) goods is expected to rise faster in countries with faster growth, since the differential in inflation rates must widen in order to make the overall growth rate higher. Combining this with the assumption that the prices of tradable goods are equalized across countries, the real currency appreciation of countries with high growth is derived. In a schematic way, the Balassa-Samuelson hypothesis can be decomposed into four steps:

A1. The differential in productivity growth rates between the tradable and nontradable sectors causes relative price changes.

A2. The ratio of nontradable prices to tradable prices is higher in a faster growing economy.

A3. The ratio of tradable prices across countries remains constant (or in the special case when tradable prices are equalized across countries).

A4. A combination of A2 and A3 causes real exchange rate appreciation.

In the rest of this section, we investigate whether the relationship between growth and relative prices holds and whether tradable price equality holds. In order to do this, the decomposition of real appreciation is helpful. Let us denote the broad price index of country j by $P(j)$. The price index could be the GDP deflator or the CPI index. The price index is composed of nontradable prices, P_N, and tradable prices, P_T. The weight of nontradable goods is n.

4. This section is largely based on Isard (1995) and Ito, Isard, and Bayoumi (1996).

Therefore,

(1) $$P(j) = n(j)P_N(j) + [1 - n(j)]P_T(j).$$

Similarly for world prices (denoted by an asterisk):

(2) $$P^* = n^* P_N^* + (1 - n^*)P_T^*.$$

Here "world prices" means prices in the United States, the benchmark country. Let us denote the ratio of common currency prices of tradables by b, which, according to A3, is supposed to stay constant:

$$b(j) = S(j)P_T(j)/P_T^*.$$

Then

(3) $$Q(j) = S(j)P(j)/P^* = b(j)\{[1 - n(j)] + n(j)[P_N(j)/P_T(j)]\} /$$

$$[(1 - n^*) + n^*(P_N^*/P_T^*)].$$

This equation decomposes the real exchange rate into four primary components:

$b(j)$ — the ratio of common currency prices of tradables,
$P_N(j)/P_T(j)$ — the relative nontradable price of country j,
P_N^*/P_T^* — the relative nontradable price of the benchmark country, and
n and n^* — the weights of the nontradable sector in the overall price indexes.

As mentioned above, the Balassa-Samuelson hypothesis assumes that b stays constant, or the law of one price for tradables. Then for countries other than the benchmark country (the United States, for which P_N^*/P_T^* is given), the higher the relative price of nontradable goods, $P_N(j)/P_T(j)$, the higher the real exchange rate becomes.

The first issue in estimating the relative nontradable price is to identify the sectors that can be regarded as "nontradable" and "tradable." Here, manufacturing is assumed to be "tradable" and services "nontradable." The prices are recovered as unit values from nominal and real series of these sectors.[5]

Figure 4.4 shows the relationship between relative per capita GDP growth (as in fig. 4.1) and changes in the nontradable-tradable price ratio. Both variables are measured relative to the benchmark values of the United States. The sample periods vary slightly for different countries, depending on the availability of relative price data. If differential productivity growth rates between the nontradable and tradable sectors are the source of both high income growth

5. For developing countries, the data set used in this analysis is the World Bank's Economic and Social Database, while for industrial countries, the data set is from the Organization for Economic Cooperation and Development (OECD).

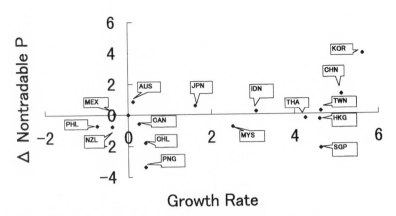

Fig. 4.4   **Growth versus changes in nontradable prices, 1973–93**
Source: See appendix.
Note: Data restrictions limit the sample periods of the following countries as noted: Australia, 1974–93; Canada, 1973–92; Chile, 1975–88; Korea, 1973–92; Malaysia, 1974–93; New Zealand, 1977–92; Papua New Guinea, 1980–93; Hong Kong, 1975–93.

and inflation differentials between the two sectors, there should exist a positive correlation between change in the nontradable-tradable price ratio and income growth. However, figure 4.4 does not show such a correlation. Although some difficulties exist in passing from theory to data, such as making a precise differentiation between tradable and nontradable sectors in the data, the evidence in this figure does not support the logic of the Balassa-Samuelson hypothesis.

Figure 4.4 also shows that several fast-growing Asian countries, namely, Thailand, Hong Kong, Malaysia, and Singapore, have not experienced rises in the relative price of nontradables (relative to the United States), while other countries—Korea, China, Taiwan, Indonesia, and Japan—show positive correlations between growth and change in the nontradable-tradable price ratio (both relative to the United States). Other, slow-growth countries do not show any patterns on this relationship. As long as the United States is taken as a benchmark, a causality link from growth to relative nontradable prices is not confirmed.

Figure 4.5 shows the relationship between changes in the ratio of common currency tradable prices and the real exchange rate. The vertical axis is the same as in figure 4.1, change in the real exchange rate (vis-à-vis the United States, using the GDP deflator). The horizontal axis is change in tradable prices (vis-à-vis those of the United States). This is an investigation into whether assumption A3 holds. Assumption A3 states that the ratio of tradable prices across countries remains the same (in other words, "relative" purchasing power parity [PPP] in tradables holds), implying that $b(j)$ should be constant for all time periods, so that all countries should cluster around the vertical line at zero. However, evidence shows that many countries experienced a sustained

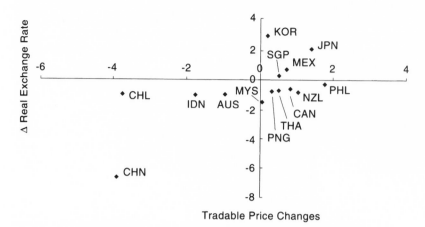

Fig. 4.5   Changes in common currency tradable prices versus real exchange rate changes, 1973–92
Source: See appendix.

change in tradable prices vis-à-vis U.S. tradable prices, or a deviation from the vertical axis when the tradable price change equals zero.

In many countries (see the southeast quadrant of the figure), the movement of tradable prices (increase) is opposite to real exchange rate changes, in contrast to the partial correlation suggested by equation (3). In other countries (Korea, Japan, Mexico, Singapore, Australia, and Indonesia), the overall correlation has the same sign as the partial correlation. Both Korea and Japan experienced high real exchange rate appreciation. However, Korea seems to be consistent with the Balassa-Samuelson hypothesis (it lies near the vertical axis; i.e., relative PPP in tradables holds), while Japan seems to have experienced a deviation from it. Again, the evidence in figure 4.5 does not generally support one of the basic assumptions of the Balassa-Samuelson hypothesis.

In order to quantify the contribution of the different components of real exchange rate changes as depicted in equation (3), a decomposition of the changes is shown in table 4.4. The proximate determinants of the real exchange rate are calculated. The table quantifies what we have learned from the series of figures. In table 4.4, the real exchange rate is calculated based on the GDP deflator, but as if the GDP consisted only of the output of the manufacturing and service sectors. The table shows that proximate causes of real exchange rate change are quite different from country to country. Among high-growth Asian countries, only Japan, Korea, and Singapore had real exchange rate appreciation (with Hong Kong and Taiwan omitted due to unavailability of data). In Singapore relative nontradable prices changed in the wrong direction (from the Balassa-Samuelson point of view). Some typology emerges from the above observations. Section 4.5 summarizes the applicability of the Balassa-Samuelson effect on each country in the Asian region and, if the effect is not

Table 4.4   **Changes in Real Exchange Rates and Proximate Determinants, 1973–92**

Country	Q	b	n	P_N/P_T
Australia	−20.9	−18.7	2.9	−4.8
Canada	−0.6	16.2	7.0	−20.4
Chile	−32.7	−13.8	0.1	−29.0
China	−74.5	−77.7	−27.6	46.0
Indonesia	−35.9	−35.3	−23.8	−4.3
Japan	36.8	27.8	−7.7	17.0
Korea	62.9	3.8	−27.0	86.0
Malaysia	−16.4	1.1	−6.4	−23.6
Mexico	11.0	15.5	−7.7	−6.3
New Zealand	23.3	21.6	−1.8	1.5
Papua New Guinea	−22.7	6.6	−0.7	−34.3
Philippines	15.8	36.0	6.2	−20.6
Singapore	8.6	59.4	−1.5	−41.8
Thailand	−1.8	11.3	−17.9	−15.2

Source: Ito et al. (1996).

Notes: Determinants n and P_N/P_T are measured as ratios to U.S. levels. Sample periods are different for the following countries: Canada, 1971–90; Chile, 1975–88; New Zealand, 1977–90; Papua New Guinea, 1980–92; and Malaysia, 1973–83.

applicable, reasons for the deviation. (All the comparative statements are vis-à-vis the United States.)

In summary, we have two ways to interpret the rather disappointing findings in figures 4.4 and 4.5 and to reconcile them with the more positive findings in figure 4.1. One interpretation is that because the assumptions that make up the Balassa-Samuelson hypothesis are not verified, the validity of the hypothesis itself is in question. The other interpretation is that the Balassa-Samuelson hypothesis is basically confirmed, as shown in figure 4.1, but examination of each component of the hypothesis is not practicable because, for example, differentiation between the tradable and nontradable sectors is hardly possible in the available data.

4.5   Balassa-Samuelson Effects with Stages of Economic Development

Japan is known in the literature to be a country that conforms with the Balassa-Samuelson prediction, namely, the positive correlation between economic growth and real exchange rate appreciation. Figure 4.1 showed that Korea and Taiwan, and to a lesser extent Hong Kong and Singapore, also experienced strong real appreciation with growth. However, examining closely how assumptions for the Balassa-Samuelson prediction hold up in the data, careful statements are needed. In the Korean case, tradable prices did not rise but nontradable prices rose sharply, consistent with the Balassa-Samuelson assumptions; Japan experienced rises in both tradable and nontradable prices vis-à-vis the United States, with nontradable prices rising much more than tradable prices. Machine exports rose for Korea, suggesting that high-value-added exports have been the engine of rapid growth. In Singapore, although tradable prices rose only slightly, nontradable prices rose less than tradable prices. Both Hong Kong and Singapore thrive on entrepôt trade and financial services (nontradables). At this point, our data are so coarsely aggregated that it is difficult to make a judgment, but it is possible that the service sector experienced productivity increases as fast as tradables did, so that relative prices between the two sectors did not follow the traditional logic of the Balassa-Samuelson hypothesis. There is a group of countries that contradicts the Balassa-Samuelson hypothesis; namely, the real exchange rate depreciated rather than appreciated while economic growth took place. The Balassa-Samuelson hypothesis does not explain the real exchange rate behavior of Thailand and Malaysia, either. The real exchange rates of these countries were relatively stable. Nontradable prices (relative to tradable prices) did not change much, or even slightly declined, in contradiction to assumption A2. The fact that Thailand, Malaysia, and Indonesia managed to keep their real exchange rates more or less constant as their economies grew rapidly is not well explained. All three countries have traditionally had strong primary goods exports: Thailand, food; Malaysia, primary goods such as palm oil and rubber; Indonesia, oil. Industrialization has changed their export structures quickly, especially in Thailand and Malaysia. In both Thailand and Malaysia, the machine export ratio rose at a moderate pace. Although these countries are also prime examples of how growth can be achieved by transforming the export structure to more high-value-added products, it is somewhat puzzling why nontradable prices are not rising in these countries.

The Philippines provides an even stronger contradiction of assumption A2 in which the tradable prices rose relative to nontradable goods. The Philippines was one country that did not share in the high growth of the region. The growth rate remained low. The nominal exchange rate depreciated as general inflation was higher than in the United States, and the real exchange rate was kept more or less constant. However, with tradables prices rising relative to nontradables prices, the price advantage in exports has been lost.

China experienced the largest real depreciation in our samples, while economic growth was respectably high. The primary reason for the real depreciation was the large nominal exchange rate depreciation after 1979. We should note that both trade and capital account restrictions were rather tight in China during most of the sample period. At the initial point of our sample (1973) China's exchange rate was probably overvalued, but large current account deficits did not occur only because of high tariffs and trade restrictions. The change in policy in the late 1980s allowed a decrease in dollar-value tradable prices and a depreciation in the nominal exchange rate, both of which promoted exports and growth. The foreign exchange restrictions on current account transactions remained imposed in China for the entire period of our sample, while other developing countries in our sample lifted restrictions sometime in the 1980s.[6]

It is quite likely that a country that moves from a closed economy policy to an open, growth-oriented policy must depreciate its currency before opening the economy. In this case, the real depreciation is not the result of economic growth but a precondition for trade-oriented growth. The findings above support the view that China (in 1973–92) is a successful case. According to this view, China depreciated its currency (toward equilibrium) to promote exports, which resulted in growth. Since the machine export ratio did not rise (fig. 4.2), the export increase came mostly from price competitiveness, and not from a trade compositional shift to high-value-added products. Indonesia may be similar to China, in that the nominal exchange rate depreciated as the economy grew. Both dollar-value tradable and nontradable prices had declined (thus promoting exports and growth). Since Indonesia's machine export ratio did not rise (fig. 4.2), the export increase came mostly from price competitiveness, and not from a trade compositional shift to high-value-added products.

The above examinations suggest that there are at least three ways that Balassa-Samuelson's basic assumptions can be violated. First, relative tradable prices across countries may not stay constant. When industrial and export structures are changing fast, not only relative prices but also the composition among tradables are changing. Tradable prices may appear to rise when the composition of domestic products and exports changes to high-value-added goods. Assumption A2 still holds if nontradable prices increase much faster than tradable prices. Second, the ratio of nontradable prices to tradable prices may not behave as Balassa and Samuelson postulated. In some economies, nontradable sectors, especially financial services, increased productivity. Third, trade restrictions and foreign exchange rate restrictions may prevent both economic growth and the adjustment of prices and exchange rates to reflect the competitiveness of industries. Economic reform often produces large depreciation to kick start growth. High growth follows large depreciation, apparently violating the Balassa-Samuelson hypothesis.

The following summary based on development stages is consistent with the apparently conflicting pieces of evidence presented above. When the economy first opens up (to market mechanisms and to trade), it often needs real depreciation in order to eliminate import barriers and promote exports. If reforms are successful, the data would show that the economy experiences both growth and real depreciation. In the initial stage of industrialization, both nontradable and tradable prices may stay relatively stable, since the labor shift from surplus sectors (often agriculture) to booming sectors cancels out any inflation pressure. However, as the economy moves into a stage of producing sophisticated goods with a limited supply of labor, relative price movements reflect produc-

---

6. China liberalized foreign exchange controls on the current account transactions and accepted IMF Article 8 in December 1996.

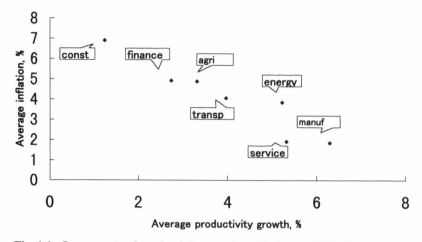

Fig. 4.6   Japan: sectoral productivity growth and inflation, 1961–92
Source: OECD (various issues).
Note: Const = construction; agri = agriculture; transp = transportation; manuf = manufacturing.

tivity differentials among different sectors. Increasing sophistication of the economy, for example proxied by the machine export ratio, can be correlated with growth and real appreciation. As there are diverse economies in the APEC group, the picture we obtain from APEC (e.g., fig. 4.1) is a mix of different combinations of growth and real exchange rate changes.

4.6   Productivity Increases and Relative Price Changes

The key observation of the Balassa-Samuelson hypothesis is that productivities grow at different rates among different sectors and countries. As technological progress tends to occur in manufacturing sectors and other tradable goods sectors, a country can achieve higher overall economic growth by increasing the difference between the productivities of tradable sectors and those of nontradable sectors. The productivity differentials result in relative price changes. The link between productivities and relative price changes was not tested in this paper because it is often difficult to obtain reliable data on sectoral productivities in developing countries. In this section, as an example, sectoral (labor) productivities and sectoral (GDP) deflators are examined for Japan and the United States using OECD sectoral output data for 1961–92.

Figures 4.6 and 4.7 show the correlation between changes in labor productivities and relative price changes of different sectors in Japan and the United States, respectively.[7] The figures clearly show the negative correlation between

---

7. The data come from OECD (various issues). The tables that correspond to these figures are also shown in Ito (1996, table 2).

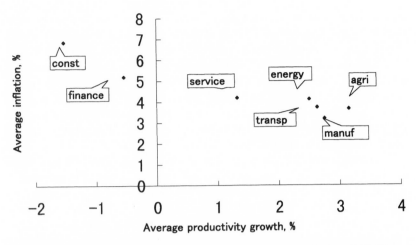

Fig. 4.7   United States: sectoral productivity growth and inflation, 1961–92
Source: OECD (various issues).
Note: Const = construction; agri = agriculture; transp = transportation; manuf = manufacturing.

productivity increase and price inflation among different sectors in both countries. In each country, the manufacturing sector has achieved the highest (or a close second in the United States) productivity increase and the lowest inflation. The agriculture industry, as well as the energy and transport industries, is better than average in both countries. Typical nontradable industries, such as construction, achieved only low productivity increases (or negative in the United States) and very high inflation. Hence, the link between productivity increase and sectoral inflation is clearly shown.

Comparing Japan and the United States, tradable sectors in Japan had much faster productivity growth, thus raising the overall growth rate, than the United States. Low inflation in the manufacturing sector also contributed to low price increases among tradables in Japan relative to the United States. Figures 4.6 and 4.7 clearly show that assumption A1—the larger the productivity difference between the tradable and nontradable sectors, the larger the inflation differential—was a reasonable one at least in Japan and the United States, and also in the comparison between the two countries. The differential in inflation rates among the tradable and nontradable sectors explains the real exchange rate appreciation of the yen vis-à-vis the U.S. dollar.

4.7   Concluding Remarks

The typology and evidence in the previous sections showed some evidence of the applicability of the Balassa-Samuelson hypothesis to high-growth countries in Asia, although violations were also evident. The Balassa-Samuelson effect is found to be most prominent in Japan, Korea, and Taiwan, resourceless economies that transformed from agricultural states, to light industrial goods (e.g., textile) exporters, to heavy industrial goods exporters. As trade was promoted, nontradable goods became relatively expensive. Subsequent analysis showed that there are at least three ways to violate the logic of the hypothesis: nontradable prices relative to tradable prices may not rise as the economy grows; tradable prices, measured in U.S. dollars, may deviate from tradable prices in the United States; and economic reforms may cause negative correlation between growth and real appreciation.

The paper suggests that applicability of the Balassa-Samuelson hypothesis to a particular economy depends on the development stage of the economy. It is especially applicable when a resourceless open economy is growing fast by changing industrial structure and export composition. Even if the economy is growing fast, Balassa-Samuelson may not be applicable if the economy has just come out of the primary goods exporter or planned economy phase. It is possible, however, that for these countries, further development of the economy will result in real appreciation in the future.

Appendix

APEC Economies Membership List and Acronyms Used in the Figures

Asian Countries

JPN	Japan
KOR	Republic of Korea
TWN	Taiwan (Taiwan Province of China according to the IMF convention; Chinese Taipei in the APEC membership list)
HKG	Hong Kong
SGP	Singapore
CHN	People's Republic of China
IDN	Indonesia
MYS	Malaysia
PHL	Philippines
THA	Thailand
BRU	Brunei Darussalam

Western Hemisphere

USA	United States of America
CAN	Canada
MEX	Mexico
CHL	Chile

Oceania

AUS   Australia
NZL   New Zealand
PNG   Papua New Guinea

Data Description

GDP per capita growth rate. Real GDP is divided by population. Average change (growth rate) is defined as a compound rate for a specified period. *Source:* IMF, *International Financial Statistics* (*IFS;* Washington, D.C., various issues).

Nominal exchange rate and real exchange rate. Nominal exchange rate is defined as the local currency value in terms of the U.S. dollar. Real exchange rate is defined as the bilateral exchange rate vis-à-vis the United States, adjusted to the difference between the GDP deflators of the country and the United States. Average change for a period is defined as a compound rate for the period. *Source: IFS.*

Machine export ratio. Machine exports (value) divided by total exports (value). *Source:* World Bank, World*Data database.

Nontradable-tradable price ratio and tradable prices. Tradable price (P_T) index is the GDP deflator for the manufacturing sector, and nontradable price (P_N) index is the weighted average of GDP deflators for other sectors. Relative P_N/P_T ratio for country j vis-à-vis the United States was calculated as

$$P(j) = [P_N(j)/P_T(j)]/[P_N(US)/P_T(US)].$$

Source: For industrial countries, OECD (various issues, detailed tables). For developing countries, World Bank, NA data bank.

Exceptions are as follows: (i) Data for Hong Kong are not reported in the above sources. The P_N/P_T ratio for Hong Kong is constructed by Baekin Cha from the Hong Kong disaggregated consumer index, CPI (A) series. Nontradable categories are housing, transport, and miscellaneous services. Tradable categories are all others, including clothing and footwear, durable goods, food, fuel and light, miscellaneous goods, alcoholic drinks, and tobacco. The index is constructed for 1975–95. (ii) Data for Taiwan are not reported in the above sources. The P_N/P_T ratio for Taiwan is constructed by Kenneth Lin from Taiwan National Income Accounts. Tradable prices are a weighted average of GDP deflators for agriculture and fishing, quarrying, and manufacturing. Nontradable prices are a weighted average of GDP deflators for utilities, construction, commerce, transport and communications, financial and business services, and other services.

References

Asea, Patrick, and Enrique G. Mendoza. 1994. The Balassa-Samuelson model: A general-equilibrium appraisal. *Review of International Economics* 2:244–67.

Balassa, Bela. 1964. The purchasing power parity doctrine: A reappraisal. *Journal of Political Economy* 72:584–96.

Corden, W. Max. 1960. The geometric representation of policies to attain internal and external balance. *Review of Economic Studies* 28 (October): 1–22.

De Gregorio, Jose, Alberto Giovannini, and Holger Wolf. 1994. International evidence on tradables and nontradables inflation. *European Economic Review* 38:1225–44.

De Gregorio, Jose, and Holger Wolf. 1994. Terms of trade, productivity, and the real exchange rate. NBER Working Paper no. 4807. Cambridge, Mass.: National Bureau of Economic Research.

Isard, Peter. 1995. *Exchange rate economics.* Cambridge: Cambridge University Press.

Ito, Takatoshi. 1995. Japanese economic development: Idiosyncratic or universal? Paper presented at International Economic Association world congress, Tunis, December.

———. 1996. Japan and the Asian economies: A "miracle" in transition. *Brookings Papers on Economic Activity,* no. 2: 205–72.

Ito, Takatoshi, Peter Isard, Steven Symansky, and Tamim Bayoumi. 1996. *Exchange rate movements and their impact on trade and investment in the APEC region.* IMF Occasional Paper no. 145. Washington, D.C.: International Monetary Fund, December.

Kuznets, Simon. 1959. *Six lectures on economic growth.* Glencoe, Ill.: Free Press.

———. 1971. *The economic growth of nations.* Cambridge, Mass.: Harvard University Press.

Marston, Richard. 1990. Systematic movements in real exchange rates in the G-5: Evidence on the integration of internal and external markets. *Journal of Banking and Finance* 14 (5): 1023–44.

Organization for Economic Cooperation and Development (OECD). Various issues. *National accounts,* vol. 2. Paris: Organization for Economic Cooperation and Development.

Samuelson, Paul A. 1964. Theoretical notes on trade problems. *Review of Economics and Statistics* 46 (May): 145–54.

World Bank. 1993. *East Asian miracle: Economic growth and public policy.* Oxford: Oxford University Press.

Young, Alwyn. 1992. A tale of two cities: Factor accumulation and technical change in Hong Kong and Singapore. In *NBER macroeconomics annual 1992,* ed. Olivier J. Blanchard and Stanley Fischer. Cambridge, Mass.: MIT Press.

Comment   Kenichi Ohno

This paper by Ito, Isard, and Symansky provides us with good material for thinking seriously about the Balassa-Samuelson effect in the fast-growing Asian economies. Using comparable data from a fairly large number of coun-

Kenichi Ohno is professor of economics at the National Graduate Institute for Policy Studies, Japan.

tries, the authors discover that the experiences of Japan, Taiwan, and Korea—the first geese in the Asian dynamic growth chain—are generally consistent with the implications of the Balassa-Samuelson hypothesis. This alone is an important finding. However, the authors place greater emphasis on the fact that when the scope of the study is enlarged to include all APEC countries, one does not find apparent conformity to the hypothesis. The authors then suggest possible reasons for this failure.

As thought-provoking, introductory research, this paper raises more questions than it answers. Economists who wish to pursue this line of research must tackle the puzzles that Ito et al. uncover, collect necessary data and use appropriate statistical techniques, and identify the reasons why the Balassa-Samuelson hypothesis fails in many of these countries. This is not done adequately in the present paper. The cross-country data set used here, with no particular concern for the different economic structures or exchange rate policies of the different countries (see below), is a bit too crude for these purposes.

As the authors correctly recognize, the Balassa-Samuelson hypothesis is based on two separate propositions that are each statistically verifiable. The first proposition is that productivity growth in the tradable sector is faster than in the nontradable sector—a structural and sectoral phenomenon. The second is PPP in tradable goods—a macroeconomic, exchange rate phenomenon. When these conditions hold simultaneously, the home currency is observed to appreciate over time in real terms when a broad basket including both tradable and nontradable commodities is used to calculate the real exchange rate. These two underlying propositions are good starting points for asking why real appreciation—defined in this way—does not seem to occur in many Asia Pacific countries.

As to the first proposition (sectoral productivity gap), there are a few empirical issues to be checked. First, we must identify the pattern of productivity growth across different sectors of each economy using perhaps two-digit or three-digit industrial data. Measurement of productivity is not a trivial exercise, especially for those countries with less than reliable data, and this unavoidably leads to a margin of error. Second, again for each economy, we must distinguish "tradable" industries with significant international price arbitrage from "nontradable" industries without such arbitrage. The paper adopts a simplifying assumption that manufactured products are tradable and services are nontradable in all countries, but this may not be true—especially for Hong Kong and Singapore, where many services (finance, leasing, entertainment, insurance, computer software, and even construction) are highly tradable. In Japan, wholesale prices have been more representative of tradable goods than consumer prices, but this presumption may not hold in other countries. There is no common list of tradable goods for all countries. After these questions are adequately answered, we can finally ask: are high-productivity-growth industries concentrated in the tradable sector?

The second proposition (PPP in tradables) is even more tenuous—as is well known from the existing literature on PPP. In fact, even PPP in actually traded goods generally does not hold. The violation occurs for two distinct reasons. First, the exchange rate as an asset price is sensitive to news and prone to short-term volatility and medium-term misalignment. Given this instability, the observed degree of "overvaluation" depends critically on the particular sample period chosen. Even though there may be a long-term trend toward overvaluation reflecting sectoral real change, short-term noise may simply be too great. Second, deviation from PPP may be the result of a deliberate policy—either of the home country or of a foreign country. The government may wish to keep the currency depreciated in order to bolster exports. Conversely, surplus countries are often pressured into appreciating their currencies. Thus market forces as well as intentional policies seriously undermine PPP in tradable goods, which is one of the two key ingredients of the Balassa-Samuelson hypothesis.

Then there is the intractable problem of systemic change. China is an outlier in the present paper partly because it had a large nominal devaluation in 1994. But the devaluation was accompanied by the unification of two exchange rates and other reforms. The question is: how can we correctly measure the real exchange rate when the foreign exchange market—and the economy as a whole—is making a transition from plan to market? Simply deflating the official exchange rate by the official price index may seriously bias the result.

The Balassa-Samuelson hypothesis is easy to demonstrate in a simple two-sector model, but its empirical application may not be so straightforward because of all the complications mentioned above. Researchers must control for different economic and trade structures, policy bias, temporary exchange rate overvaluation, systemic change, and so forth. After all these "other factors" have been controlled, my conjecture—but only a conjecture—is that the Balassa-Samuelson effect might be more applicable to the dynamic Asian economies than the present paper finds.

Comment   Anne O. Krueger

This is a valuable paper. It has long been recognized that "real" exchange rates tend to appreciate as living standards rise. That is, if one estimates PPP exchange rates, one finds that countries with low per capita incomes tend to have exchange rates that permit a unit of foreign currency to command more purchasing power than countries with higher per capita income.

Anne O. Krueger is the Herald L. and Caroline L. Ritch Professor of Economics, senior fellow of the Hoover Institution, and director of the Center for Research on Economic Development and Policy Reform at Stanford University, and a research associate of the National Bureau of Economic Research.

In examining the PPP relation, Balassa and Samuelson each pointed to the observed real appreciation with rising per capita incomes as an empirical phenomenon. Independently, a Swedish economist, Aukrust, developed a model that might explain the phenomenon. In Aukrust's view, productivity tends to increase more rapidly in traded goods sectors than in nontraded goods sectors; as a result, real wages must rise in nontraded goods as well as traded goods. Since, he thought, nontraded goods were labor intensive, the higher real wage would raise their relative prices, thus giving the result.

In testing the Balassa-Samuelson hypothesis, Ito, Isard, and Symansky simply accept the hypothesis, without any underlying analytical framework, and yet seem puzzled by their results. In my comments, I want first to sketch out an analytical framework that can, at least broadly, predict Ito et al.'s findings. After that, I raise some questions about the value of the machinery indicator.

Ito et al. report on tests of the Balassa-Samuelson hypothesis for East Asian countries. They do so by assuming that the real exchange rate reflects the relative price of tradables in terms of home goods.

This procedure spurs the starting point for my first comment: what is the real exchange rate under examination? If, for example, there is factor price equalization across traded goods, and home goods are produced with the same production functions and the same factors of production as traded goods, one would observe home goods price equalization. Even if Aukrust was right, as long as productivity in tradables grew at the same rate across countries and factor price equalization continued to hold, there would still be no Balassa-Samuelson effect: all countries would experience the same rate of increase in real wages. This result would continue to hold even if a time unit of labor had different efficiencies in different countries.

If the price of nontraded goods does differ across countries, the question is: what generates that difference? One possible answer arises in the context of an Arthur Lewis–type model, in which the real wage is set in the rural sector during the early stages of development: growth of other economic activities can take place at a constant real wage (or a real wage rising in line with increases in the marginal product of labor in agriculture, presumably very slowly) until labor can no longer be released from agriculture without an increase in its marginal product. At that point, the real wage would start rising throughout the economy.

If one were to blend the Lewis model of labor supply to a trade model, the prediction would be that countries with higher labor productivity in agriculture would have higher real incomes and their exchange rates would conform to the Balassa-Samuelson hypothesis. In the post-Lewis phase, growth of labor productivity would drive the appreciating real exchange rate.

All of the above assumes no trade restrictions. It is well known that a highly protected economy will have, at equilibrium (given whatever tariffs and quantitative restrictions are in place), a more appreciated real exchange rate than it would at free trade.

This simple framework can go a long way to explaining, or at least providing one explanation of, Ito et al.'s results. China liberalized and hence has had a real depreciation despite rapid growth. Korea, Japan, and Taiwan have passed the Lewis phase, so their real wages have been rising rapidly, and with it their real exchange rate relative to PPP. Countries in Southeast Asia, however, probably have large enough populations in rural areas that the behavior of the real wage is driven at least partly by Lewis-type effects from the countryside, and one would not observe the Balassa-Samuelson effect to the same degree. There has also been some liberalization of the trade regime in Southeast Asia, which might also account for some part of the observed exchange rate behavior.

Let me now turn to the use of the machinery-to-total-export ratio. I think that it is highly dangerous, especially if policymakers view the link as a causal one. First of all, I am not sure why Ito et al. think that high-value-added activities are important. Moreover, they do not specify what they mean by high value added: as a percentage of sales price? Per worker? Diamond cutting is a highly skilled job, yet value added as a percentage of sales price is low. It is not the percentage value added of final product that matters, but rather the marginal product of the domestic factors of production (especially labor).

In addition, it may well be that East Asia's comparative advantage lies at least in part in abundance of factors (skilled labor?) that are employed intensively in the production of machines. That does not prove that more machines exported lead to more growth. It might instead simply reflect the underlying realities of economic efficiency: those Asian countries with realistic exchange rates also had rapid rates of growth of machinery exports. For other countries, the appropriate commodity composition of trade might be significantly different, and machinery might continue to be a major import item.

Nonetheless, if there were better estimates of the appropriate real exchange rate, policymakers would be able to make their decisions with less uncertainty than is currently the case. Ito et al.'s paper makes an important contribution to increasing understanding of what is appropriate.

Moreover, if one were to take Ito et al.'s results literally, one could increase world GDP without limit by having countries import machinery in order to re-export it. A machine could go from country to country adding value as it was reexported. Ito et al. assume that the percentage of exports constituting machinery and equipment is bounded above by 100, but that need not be the case.

5 Resource Endowments and the Real Exchange Rate: A Comparison of Latin America and East Asia

Jeffrey D. Sachs

5.1 Introduction

One of the most important puzzles of economic development is the postwar failure of Latin American economic growth in comparison with the dramatic growth in East Asia. Table 5.1 shows the per capita growth performance of several key countries in each region for the extended period from 1870 to 1990. The table highlights a striking fact: the relative growth performance of the two regions in the most recent period, 1960–90, is the *reverse* of the relative growth performance in the preceding period, 1870–1960. Even the recent Asian financial crisis is unlikely to reverse the long-term difference in growth since 1960. The reversal in relative growth performance over the course of a century should caution us immediately against simplistic theories ascribing Asia's successes, or Latin America's failures, to ostensibly stable social characteristics such as family structure, attitudes toward education, social trust, religion, or attitudes toward authority, which are frequently invoked to explain the differential growth performance of the two regions (though less so since Asia's financial crisis exploded in 1997!).

There is little doubt that much of the explanation of differential long-term performance lies in differing economic policies in the two regions, especially policies regarding international trade (see Sachs and Warner 1995a for a brief historical overview of trade policies, and Bulmer-Thomas 1994 for a comprehensive survey of Latin America). In the period 1870–1910, most of Latin America operated under a liberal trade regime that aimed to foster export-led growth of primary products. Argentina benefited enormously from export-led growth in grains and meat products; Chile enjoyed a boom in nitrates and cop-

Jeffrey D. Sachs is director of the Harvard Institute for International Development, the Galen L. Stone Professor of International Trade at Harvard University, and a research associate of the National Bureau of Economic Research.

Table 5.1   Annual GDP Growth Per Capita, 1870–1990: Regions and
            Selected Countries

	1870–1910	1910–60	1960–90
Latin America	1.5	1.7	1.5
Argentina	2.7	0.7	0.6
Brazil	0.2	2.2	2.4
Mexico	0.9	1.3	2.0
Asia	0.6	0.7	3.6
China[a]	0.6	0.5	3.8
Indonesia	0.6	0.6	2.7
Thailand[a]	0.4	0.4	4.8

Source: Maddison (1995, app. D).
[a]1913 rather than 1910.

per; Bolivia grew on the basis of tin and silver; Brazil exported coffee and
rubber; and so on. Northeast Asian countries such as Korea and Taiwan had
few natural resources to support a comparable export boom. In the recent period, by contrast, much of Asia pursued open trade policies and export-led
growth based on labor-intensive manufactures, while most of Latin America
pursued relatively closed trade policies, with attempts at import-substituting
industrialization.[1] In the postwar era, much of Latin America began to open to
international trade only in the 1980s, after the failure of the import substitution
strategy. *Thus we can say that in both periods, rapid GDP growth was favored
by open trade and export-led growth.* The failures of Asian economies that
were closed to trade in the recent period (North Korea, Vietnam until 1989,
Myanmar, India until 1991) underscore the basic fact that growth has depended
not merely on geography but on the trade (and other) policies pursued by the
individual countries. Similarly, Chile was the first Latin American country to
liberalize trade in the recent period, and its recent growth success demonstrates
the possibility of export-led growth in Latin America.

It is easy, nonetheless, to fall into the trap of ascribing all of the difference
in economic performance to economic policies. The purpose of this paper is
to consider again the role that economic *structure* has also played in the relative
growth performance of the two regions. In the late nineteenth century, abundant natural resources were the key to rapid growth in peripheral countries.
Primary commodity export-led growth in countries such as Argentina was aug-

1. The precise nature of the trade regimes in East Asia remains a matter of dispute. Some economies, such as Hong Kong and Singapore, were almost completely free trade economies. Others,
particularly several Southeast Asian countries, including Indonesia, Malaysia, and Thailand, were
moderately protective for final consumer goods, but nearly free trade for both capital goods and
inputs used by exporters (e.g., through mechanisms such as export-processing zones). The northeast Asian economies of Korea and Taiwan were probably even more protective, on average, of
final goods markets but similarly provided a regime of "(nearly) free trade for exporters" through
duty drawbacks, tax exemptions, tax holidays, export-processing zones, and other related mechanisms.

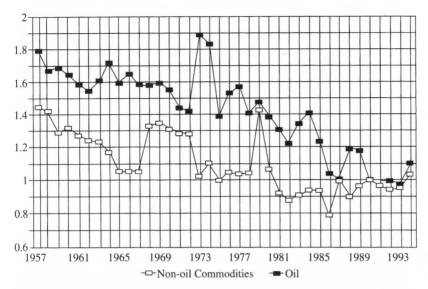

Fig. 5.1   Commodity price index versus industrial country export unit value, 1957–94
Source: International Monetary Fund, *International Financial Statistics* (Washington, D.C., various issues).

mented by rapid capital inflows from the advanced economies to build railways and other infrastructure in support of the export sector (see Bulmer-Thomas 1994, 102–8, for data on foreign direct investment and railway construction). In the past three decades, it has been the export of labor-intensive manufactures—especially apparel and electronics—rather than primary commodities that has played the key role in spurring developing country growth.[2] On one important issue Raul Prebisch seems to have been mostly right: primary commodities were not an effective base for sustained, long-term high growth in the postwar era (see his famous analysis of Latin American development, published as United Nations 1950). There appear to be two main reasons. First, the terms of trade have indeed tended to move against primary commodities over the postwar period, as Prebisch forecasted. Figure 5.1 shows the prices of nonoil commodities and petroleum relative to the unit export values of the industrial countries. The relative prices of both nonoil commodities and oil fell sharply between 1957 and 1994, by around 40 percent in the case of nonoil commodities and 24 percent in the case of oil. Second, productivity increases in manufacturing have outstripped productivity increases in primary produc-

2. The electronics sector in East Asia began with assembly operations (e.g., semiconductor assembly), using low-skilled labor and often in export-processing zones. As a result of increased investments, learning, technology transfer, and upgraded skills in East Asian economies, production shifted from assembly to high-technology operations (e.g., wafer fabrication) and production of more sophisticated consumer appliances.

tion and in services. This is shown, for example, in Chenery, Robinson, and Syrquin (1986), and in Young (1995) in the case of East Asia. Prebisch's serious miscalculations were twofold: first, his belief that manufacturing sector growth could be sustained on the basis of *internal* demand via import substitution and, second, his neglect of the possibility that developing countries could achieve export-led growth in manufactures. The recent path to success has in fact been to hitch growth to the *export* of labor-intensive manufactures, rather than to the substitution of capital-intensive manufacturing imports.

Note that the two factors—the terms-of-trade decline of primary commodities and relatively low productivity growth in the primary sector—are probably the reverse of the pattern at the end of the nineteenth century. In the earlier period, enormous advances in railways, ocean transport, refrigeration, and packaging, as well as the rapid industrialization underway in Europe and the United States, gave a boost to the international terms of trade of primary producers, albeit one punctuated by periodic short-term crises. Moreover, there were rapid technological advances possible through the introduction of new agricultural and mining techniques. We might also note in passing that in the future, technological changes in information processing and communications might once again alter the basis for the economic integration of developing countries into the world economy. Rather than export-led growth in primary commodities or labor-intensive manufactures, the next phase of development might favor export-led growth in the service sectors of the economy.

The theme of this paper is that economic structure, in addition to economic policy, has affected the capacity of countries to enjoy manufacturing export-led growth in the past 30 years, and even to avoid the kind of short-run macroeconomic crises that have plagued much of Latin America. In particular, East Asia's disadvantage at the end of the nineteenth century—the (relative) absence of land and natural resources—has been its *advantage* in the recent phase of the world economy. The striking difference in resource endowments in the two regions is shown in figure 5.2, where we show the population densities for eight East Asian and six Latin American countries. The Asian countries are all more densely populated than their Latin counterparts, typically by a very wide margin. Of course, land endowment is just one aspect of the differences between the regions: Latin America is also mineral rich, while much of East Asia (particularly northeast Asia) is mineral poor.

Broadly speaking, trade patterns match the resource endowments: the labor-abundant developing economies of East Asia have tended to export manufactures, while the land- and resource-abundant developing economies of Latin America have tended to export agricultural and mining products. Some striking evidence in support of this proposition is found in figure 5.3, adapted from Wood and Berge (1997). On the x-axis is a measure of relative factor endowments, years of schooling divided by land area, and on the y-axis is the ratio of manufactures exports to primary exports. The plot confirms that countries tend to export goods that are intensive in their abundant factors of production. In

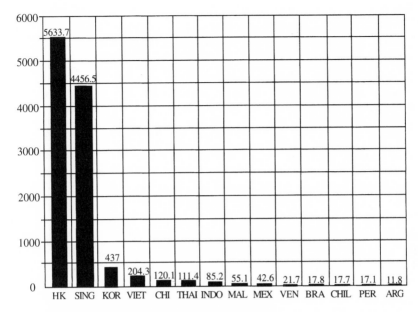

Fig. 5.2 Population density (per square kilometer)
Source: World Bank, World*Data.

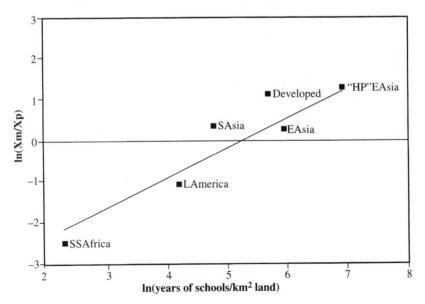

Fig. 5.3 Resource endowments and trade
Source: Wood and Berge (1997).

Table 5.2   Structure of Exports by Main Category (percent of total)

Region	1970		1992	
	Primary[a]	Manufactures[b]	Primary[a]	Manufactures[b]
Americas	89.4	10.6	64.2	35.8
Chile	95.7	4.3	83.5[c]	16.5[c]
South and Southeast				
Asia	56.6	43.5	19.5	80.5
China	52.5	47.5	19.4	80.6

Source: United Nations (1995).
[a]Primary products include all food items, agricultural raw materials, fuels, ores, and metals.
[b]Manufactured products include SITC categories 5–8, except for 68.
[c]1993.

particular, labor-abundant economies tend to export manufactures, while land-abundant economies (Latin America and sub-Saharan Africa) tend to export natural resources. Table 5.2 shows that Latin American exports remain heavily based in natural resources, while Asia is predominantly a manufacturing exporter.

It is very likely that Latin America's low share of manufactured exports is a function not only of resource endowments but also of restricted trade practices. Manufacturing exports require, in general, access to imported primary and intermediate inputs and capital machinery at, or close to, world prices. Latin America's import substitution policies until the past decade certainly limited the scope for manufactured exports. For example, Morawetz's (1981) excellent study of Colombian apparel exports showed that Colombian manufacturers were severely hampered by the lack of access to necessary inputs, especially textiles, at world prices, because of a protective trade regime and inefficient administrative support for would-be exporters. On top of that, however, Morawetz shows that Colombia's coffee boom in the late 1970s also contributed to a real appreciation of the currency and a resulting profit squeeze in the fledgling textile and apparel export sector—the kind of phenomenon stressed in this paper. It is notable that Chile, after almost 20 years of open trade, is still predominantly a resource-based exporter rather than a manufacturing exporter. In 1993, the share of manufactures in total merchandise exports came to only 16.5 percent, as seen in table 5.2. Our focus in this paper is on the role of resource endowments, rather than trade policy, though a complete theoretical and empirical treatment will require the incorporation of both considerations.

The World Bank (1996a) has recently produced calculations on national wealth that underscore the differences in resource endowments by region. On the World Bank's methodology, national wealth is divided among human resources (human capital), produced assets (plant, equipment, structures, and inventories), and natural capital (land, minerals, etc.). As seen in table 5.3, the Asian regions (India and China, East Asia and Pacific) have very high propor-

Table 5.3   **Economic Growth and Sources of Wealth**

	Per Capita GDP Growth, 1985–94 (annual)	Per Capita GDP, 1994 (U.S.$)	Share in Total Wealth		
Region			Human Resources	Produced Assets	Natural Capital
Sub-Saharan Africa	−1.2	460	31	17	52
India and China	5.7	439	73	18	9
East Asia and Pacific (except China)	4.9	860	75	13	12
Latin America and Caribbean	0.6	3,340	50	15	35
Middle East and North Africa	−0.4	1,580	39	29	32

Sources: Annual growth rates and per capita GDP are from World Bank (1996b, table 1, basic indicators). Note that regional GDP growth rates and levels are based on population weights. Sources of wealth are from World Bank (1996a).

tions of wealth in human resources and low proportions of wealth in natural capital (below 15 percent). Sub-Saharan Africa, Latin America and the Caribbean, and Middle East and North Africa, by contrast, have much higher proportions of wealth (over 30 percent) in natural capital. We also see, once again, that resource endowments are at least loosely correlated with growth performance: the regions with a high share of natural capital endowment are also the regions with a low or negative rate of per capita GDP growth during 1985–94.

To summarize the argument of the paper, it seems that the Dutch disease is a disease after all, both with regard to long-term growth rates and short-term macroeconomic crises. As shown in a sample of more than 90 developing countries in Sachs and Warner (1995b), natural-resource-abundant economies tended to grow less rapidly than natural-resource-scarce economies in the period since 1970. Many factors probably contribute to this pattern, including political as well as economic factors. This paper discusses one major channel: the linkages from natural resources via the real exchange rate to long-term growth. Resource-rich and resource-poor economies differ markedly in the patterns of real exchange rate levels and changes, as well as in the linkages of the real exchange rate to income distribution and growth. The differing links of the real exchange rate to income distribution affect short-run macroeconomic management in the two regions.

Section 5.2 introduces an extremely simple baseline model of an economy with three sectors: natural resources, manufacturing tradables, and nontraded goods. Using this simple model, we trace the effects of four variables on the real exchange rate, income distribution, and growth: capital accumulation, capital inflows, currency devaluation, and skill accumulation. Resource-rich and resource-poor economies differ markedly in their adjustment patterns, and it is easy to illustrate how resource-abundant economies can get stuck in a no-growth trap while resource-poor economies achieve rapid growth. In section 5.3 we then turn our attention to an empirical comparison of East Asia and Latin America, to assess the relevance of resource endowments versus alternative factors in recent economic performance.

5.2 A Basic Theoretical Model

Let us introduce an extremely simple framework to highlight the forces at play.[3] Suppose that there are just three goods: a natural resource R whose output is exogenous at R_0; a labor-intensive traded manufacturing good M, with production linear in labor input L_M; and a capital-intensive, nontraded output N, which uses labor L_N, a sector-specific capital K_N, and an internationally tradable input T_N in a constant-returns-to-scale production technology. (It would be straightforward to introduce more general neoclassical production functions without altering the main themes of the paper.) We assume that the domestic resource sector uses no domestic inputs (and we define the output R as net of any tradable inputs). Thus:

$$R = R_0,$$

(1) $$M = \theta L_M,$$

$$N = N(L_N,\ K_N,\ T_N).$$

For simplicity, we assume that L_N and K_N are combined according to Cobb-Douglas technology to produce value added V_N, which is then combined with the intermediate input in fixed proportions to produce gross output. In particular,

(2) $$N = \min[(L_N)^\alpha (K_N)^{1-\alpha},\ T/\lambda].$$

This implies that the price of output in sector N can be written as a weighted sum of the value-added deflator P_V^N and the price of tradables, which we take to be numéraire:

---

3. Of course, many theoretical treatments are available that highlight some of the phenomena at play. The important paper by Anne Krueger (1977) models an economy with a natural resource sector (using land and labor) and a multiindustry manufacturing sector, in which each of the manufacturing industries uses capital and labor in a neoclassical production function, but with varying degrees of capital intensity. A large natural resource sector leaves less labor for the manufacturing sector, and thus a higher capital-labor ratio in the sector. As a result, a natural-resource-abundant economy is more likely to produce capital-intensive manufactures (if it produces manufactures at all) and less likely to produce labor-intensive manufactures. The small size or absence of labor-intensive manufacturing industries is the major theme of the Dutch disease literature, and of this paper. Alan Deardorff (1984) extends the Krueger model to consider the role of trade protection. Edward Leamer (1987) offers a graphical account of a three-factor (capital, land, labor), multisector Heckscher-Ohlin model to show how resource abundance affects the sectoral allocation of productive factors and the economy-wide pattern of trade. Neither the Krueger nor Leamer model includes nontradable goods production.

$$(3) \qquad\qquad P_N = P_V^N + \lambda.$$

All consumers have identical tastes, which for simplicity we take to be Cobb-Douglas. A constant fraction β of income is spent on tradable goods, which we take as numéraire, and the remainder is spent on nontradable goods $(1 - \beta)$.

$$(4) \qquad\qquad \begin{aligned} C_M &= \beta, \\ P_N C_N &= 1 - \beta. \end{aligned}$$

Note that the consumer price index is simply

$$(5) \qquad\qquad P_C = P_M^\beta P_N^{1-\beta} = P_N^{1-\beta}$$

since the price of tradables is one.

The trade deficit equals final consumption of tradables, C_T, minus total production of tradables net of intermediate inputs of tradables. The trade deficit equals the net resource transfer NRT, which we take to be exogenous and generally set equal to zero:

$$(6) \qquad\qquad \text{NRT} = C_T - (R + M - T).$$

In addition, nontraded consumption must equal nontraded production:

$$(7) \qquad\qquad C_N = N.$$

Finally, full employment requires

$$(8) \qquad\qquad 1 = L_M + L_N.$$

The labor supply is normalized to equal one, so that L_M and L_N signify the *shares* of labor allocated to each sector. We assume that the labor force is competitive, so that workers are paid their marginal value products. The marginal value product in nontradables is $P_N^V(\partial N/\partial L_N)$, so that the wage is given by

$$(9) \qquad\qquad W = P_N^V(\partial N / \partial L_N).$$

The marginal value product of workers in manufacturing is simply θ. If $W > \theta$, then wages are too high for the country to be competitive in manufacturing (barring trade barriers), and $L_M = 0$. Alternatively, if $W = \theta$, then both L_N and L_M are positive. The wage can never be less than θ since manufacturing firms have an unlimited demand for workers at the wage θ.

When R is large enough, L_M will equal zero. The economy relies entirely on its natural resource exports to cover its consumption demand for tradables as well as the derived demand for traded intermediate inputs into nontradable production. As stylized descriptions, we refer to the case of specialization in production ($M = 0$) as the "Latin American case" and the case of no specialization as the "East Asian case." We will discuss the empirical realism of these descriptions in section 5.3. Let us underscore here, however, that these designations are obviously a caricature. Some Latin American economies, such as Brazil, are highly competitive in manufacturing exports, while some East Asian economies, such as Indonesia and Malaysia, have significant natural resource endowments. Nonetheless, the labeling has broad analytical and empirical merit.

High R eliminates the tradable manufacturing sector through the usual Dutch disease mechanism. High R leads to high demand in the economy, and in particular for nontraded goods. This high demand causes P_N to rise (compared with the case of low R), and labor flows into the nontraded sector. Assuming that P_N is high enough, the entire labor force flows into nontradables, with the marginal value product of labor in nontradables remaining above the marginal value product of labor in manufacturing. Specifically, for the Latin American case to obtain we must have $P_N^V(\partial N/\partial L_N|_{L=1}) > \theta$. Note that the relative price of tradable goods to nontradable goods—that is, the real exchange rate—is simply $1/P_N$. Therefore, a rise in P_N is a real exchange rate appreciation, and a fall in P_N is a real exchange rate depreciation. The most common way to describe the Latin American case is that the large natural resource sector causes the real exchange rate to become so appreciated that labor-intensive manufactures are not profitable.

A key point of the analysis is that real wages tend to respond oppositely to changes in P_N in the Latin American and East Asian cases. In the Latin American case, the nontraded sector is the labor-intensive sector: a rise in P_N therefore raises the real wage. In the East Asian case, by contrast, the manufacturing sector is the labor-intensive sector: a rise in P_N therefore lowers the real wage. As a result of this crucial distinction, real wages—and much else in the economy—respond differently to exogenous shocks in Latin America and East Asia. As a result, the political economy of trade and monetary policy is also different. Patterns of endogenous growth may also be very different.

Consider a numerical illustration based on the following parameter values:

$$\alpha = 0.75,$$

$$\lambda = 0.25,$$

$$\theta = 1.0,$$

(10)

$$K_N = 1.0,$$

$$\beta = 0.5,$$

$$\text{NRT} = 0.$$

In this case, the East Asian case obtains for $P_N \leq 0.58$, while the Latin American case obtains for $P_N > 0.58$. As shown in figure 5.4, in the interval (0.25, 0.58), W/P_C is a declining function of P_N, while in the range (0.58, ∞), W/P_C is a rising function of P_N. (Note that P_N must be greater than or equal to 0.25, so that $P_N^V \geq 0.$)

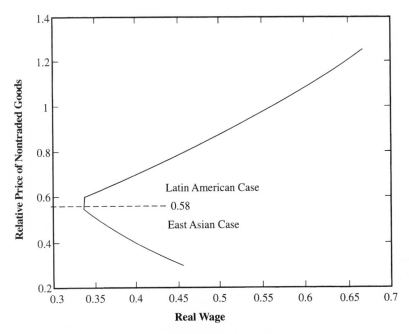

Fig. 5.4   Real wages and the relative price of nontradables

Events that tend to raise P_N have opposite effects on real wages in East Asia and Latin America. For example, a natural resource discovery can actually *lower* real wages in East Asia by bidding up the price of nontradable goods that are purchased by manufacturing sector workers. By contrast, in Latin America, a natural resource boom will tend to *raise* the real wage by pushing up P_N and thereby reducing the relative price that service sector workers pay for tradable commodities. To put it another way, imports look cheap to Latin urban workers during a resource boom. By contrast, housing costs look high to Asian manufacturing workers during a similar boom. The result is depicted in figure 5.5, which shows the relationship between R and W/P_C. As R rises from low levels, the real wage decreases. Eventually (at the point where $L_M = 0$), higher R starts to cause the real wage to increase.

Capital accumulation in the nontradable sector presents a special problem in the Latin American case. Suppose that K_N increases in Latin America. What happens to the real wage? Surprisingly, as shown in figure 5.6, the real wage *may decline,* even though the marginal physical product of labor expands. There are two main effects. On the one hand, W/P_N^V rises, because of the capital deepening in the nontradable sector. This of course tends to push up the real wage. On the other hand, the increase in nontradable production leads to a decline in P_N (relative to the numéraire good, tradable manufactures). This leads to a more than proportionate decline in P_N^V, which is equal to $P_N - \lambda$

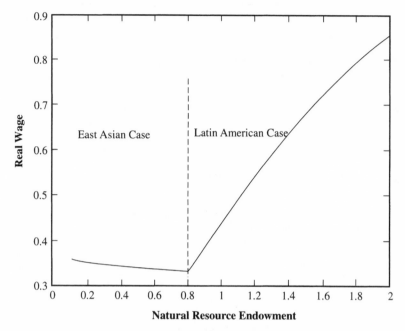

Fig. 5.5 Real wages and natural resource endowment

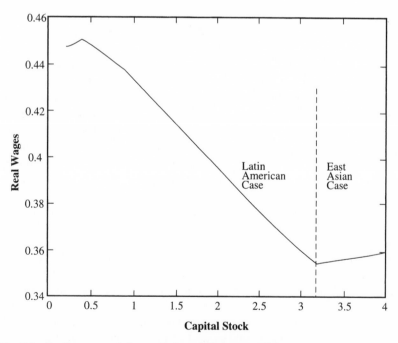

Fig. 5.6 Real wages and the capital stock in nontradables

(note that the proportionate decline in P_N^V is larger the larger is λ). The decline in P_N^V lowers the marginal value product of labor in nontradables and thus tends to *reduce* the real wage. While the overall effect is ambiguous, it is certainly possible that capital accumulation lowers, rather than raises, the real wage. In fact, the real wage might continue to decline with capital accumulation in nontradables until the wage is so low that the country becomes competitive in tradable manufactures. At that point, the country shifts from the Latin American to the East Asian case.

Consider a country like Venezuela, for example, which lives off a fixed flow of oil export earnings and has virtually no other exports. An improvement in nontradable infrastructure (e.g., financed by the government out of oil revenues) could actually lower real wages by forcing a real depreciation of the exchange rate. The problem would be interpreted by the general public as a balance-of-payments problem: higher nontraded production leads to increased demand for imports, against a backdrop of constant export supply. The real exchange rate therefore tends to depreciate (abstracting from short-run foreign borrowing). The real exchange rate depreciation, in turn, pushes up import costs and can lower the real wage (especially if the import component in nontradable production, λ, is large).

Notice what would happen as growth continues in the nontraded goods sector, pushing P_N and W/P_C still lower. Eventually the real exchange rate depreciates enough that the nominal wage falls to the level θ. It finally becomes profitable to produce labor-intensive exports in the country, and the economy enters the "East Asian region," with positive production of labor-intensive manufactured goods. For a country like Venezuela, with a large but fairly fixed stock of natural resources, the time path of the real wage may therefore be U-shaped. High oil revenues at the start give a high level of the real wage. Over time, as capital accumulates in the nontraded sector, the real wage declines. Finally, the bottom is hit as the country takes on the new vocation of manufacturing exporter. *This basic observation may help to account for the long-term stagnation or even decline in real wages in much of Latin America in the past 20 years. Stagnant primary exports have led to a prolonged slide in real wages, until these economies finally achieve competitiveness in manufacturing exports.*

If accumulation of K_N can lower the real wage in the Latin American case, does accumulation of capital in tradables tend to lower the real wage in the East Asian case?[4] The answer is no: the cases are not perfectly symmetrical. Latin America cannot easily raise export production since R is fixed, while East Asia *can* readily raise nontradable production through increased employment and capital in the sector. Therefore, a rise in capital in the tradable sector in Asia does *not* tend to lead to a sharp rise in the relative price of nontradables,

---

4. Note that we do not formally model capital accumulation in the manufacturing sector. This deficiency can easily be removed in an extension to the model in the paper.

as long as nontradable production can expand. The rise in productivity of labor due to higher K therefore tends to outweigh any adverse effects on the real wage due to a rise in P_N.

It is easy to see that a nominal exchange rate devaluation will tend to have different impacts on the real wage in the two cases. Suppose that overall demand is determined, in part, by real money balances M/P_C. A nominal exchange rate depreciation will tend to reduce real money balances (and raise domestic interest rates, in the case of capital controls that isolate the home financial market from the rest of the world). The demand for nontradables will tend to fall, pushing down P_N. In East Asia, the result will be higher real wages (experienced as increased demand for labor in manufactures as a result of the devaluation). In Latin America, the result will be lower real wages (experienced as higher prices for imported manufactures). We can also note that foreign borrowing will tend to raise real wages in Latin America in the short run (by supporting an *appreciated* real exchange rate), while lowering real wages in East Asia. Of course, debts eventually come due and typically require a real exchange rate depreciation in order to pay them off. In Latin America, debt servicing therefore tends to require a sharp fall in real wages, while in East Asia, debt servicing may well be accompanied by an *increase* in real wages.

If we put these pieces together—a long-term slide in real wages of a commodity-rich economy, with short-run real wage movements depending on the nominal exchange rate and foreign borrowing—we can see the outlines of a political economy interpretation of macroeconomic crises in Latin America. For countries like Venezuela that are experiencing a long-term decline in real wages, overvalued nominal exchange rates and heavy foreign borrowing give a way to halt the slide of the real wage temporarily. Of course these are destructive palliatives in the longer term, but palliatives nonetheless. The deeper underlying problem is that export-led growth is blocked by an initially overstrong exchange rate, which undermines the competitiveness of manufacturing exports.

Perhaps the most interesting differences in economic performance relate to long-term growth. We have already referred to evidence in Sachs and Warner (1995b) indicating that resource-poor countries have fared better than resource-rich countries in economic growth over the period 1970–89, after controlling for other variables typically associated with growth, such as initial per capita income, trade policy, and national saving rate. Matsuyama (1992) offered a small endogenous growth model that could account for this pattern. In Matsuyama's model, the manufacturing sector is characterized by learning by doing that is external to the enterprise but internal to the sector as a whole. The resource-rich country specializes in the resource sector and never benefits from the learning by doing, while the resource-poor country specializes in manufacturing and begins automatically to enjoy productivity growth in that sector. The productivity growth, in turn, widens the comparative advantage of the resource-poor country in the production of manufactures, thus reinforcing the initial trade patterns. The resource-abundant economy is more firmly locked into the export of natural resources and the import of manufactures, all with a stagnant economy, while the resource-poor country enjoys long-term growth based on learning by doing in manufactures.

The following (sketch of a) model extends Matsuyama's framework to allow for a nontraded goods sector, while relaxing the assumption of learning by doing that is external to the firm. The latter extension is worthwhile since recent empirical evidence (e.g., Young 1995) casts some doubt on the role of pure technical change in Asia's rapid growth in the past 30 years. Empirical evidence suggests that productivity growth is indeed most rapid in manufacturing, but that the productivity growth is based on higher capital intensity and higher skills of workers, rather than on dynamic external economies of scale or learning by doing. We therefore suggest a simple model that is compatible with these observations.

Suppose that there are overlapping generations of workers, with each generation a constant population size equal to one. Individuals live for two periods. Total population at any time is therefore two, with half old and half young. All workers are born unskilled and work as unskilled laborers in the first period. Workers in the first period may acquire education in order to become skilled workers in the second generation (thus being "educated" and being "skilled" are synonymous in this model). For simplicity, we assume that education is pursued in addition to first-period work (e.g., in night school). The skills obtained in education augment the productivity of workers in the production of traded manufactures M, but not in the production of nontraded final goods N. Young workers choose whether or not to pursue an education depending on the monetary returns to being educated in the second period. There are four sectors in the economy: natural resources, traded manufactures, education, and nontraded final goods.

The education process uses an input of $\sigma < 1$ units of an older skilled worker to convert one unskilled worker into a skilled worker. The level of skill of the worker can be measured by the productivity of the worker in the production of manufactures. An unskilled worker has a constant marginal productivity equal to θ^U, while a skilled worker in period t has productivity equal to $\theta_t^S > \theta^U$. Skilled workers are divided between work in manufacturing L_M and work in teaching L_T. At the maximum, the demand for teachers is given by $L_T = \sigma < 1$, in the case where the entire younger generation enrolls in schooling. In the equilibria that we examine, all younger workers either enroll in education or all forgo education. Therefore, in equilibria in which education is pursued, the entire older generation is composed of skilled workers, $\sigma < 1$ percent of the old workers are teachers, and $1 - \sigma > 0$ percent are manufacturing workers. Since the wage of manufacturing workers is equal to θ_t^S, competitive labor markets will ensure that the wage of teachers is also θ_t^S.

The next assumption is critical. We assume that the future productivity of students enrolled at time t depends on the productivity of their teachers at time *t*. Specifically, with θ^S_{t+1} the future productivity of today's students and θ^S_t the productivity of today's teachers, we posit

$$(11) \qquad \theta^S_{t+1} = (1 + \mu)\theta^S_t.$$

In this way, each generation is better trained than the previous generation, resulting in sustained, endogenous growth.[5] Consider, now, the choice of a young worker as to whether to pursue an education. Since education makes sense only to join the manufacturing labor force (since nontraded goods do not use skilled labor), the young worker must look to the future skilled wage in manufacturing. The future wage with an education is therefore θ^S_{t+1}. Denote the future unskilled wage as W^U_{t+1}. Workers choose an education if the discounted wage advantage of being educated exceeds the direct costs of an education:

$$(12) \qquad \text{If } (\theta^S_{t+1} - W^U_{t+1})/(1 + \delta) > \sigma\theta^S_t, \text{ then choose education;}$$

$$\text{if } (\theta^S_{t+1} - W^U_{t+1})/(1 + \delta) < \sigma\theta^S_t, \text{ then choose no education.}$$

Now, let us consider the differing dynamics of Latin American–type and East Asian–type economies. Suppose that both economies begin with a young generation of unskilled workers and an older generation of skilled workers with initial skills θ^S_1. Consider first the Latin American case. As usual, the Latin American–type economy has a large constant flow of earnings of R, which pushes up the unskilled wage in services. Indeed, it can easily be the case that $W_N > (1 + \mu)\theta^S_1 > \theta^S_1$, so that *unskilled* workers in services today earn more money than both *skilled* manufacturing workers today, θ^S_1, and *even more skilled* workers tomorrow, $(1 + \mu)\theta^S_1$. In this case, today's skilled workers will work in the service sector rather than in manufacturing or teaching, and *today's young have no market incentive to pursue an education,* since they know that they will earn more as unskilled workers in services than as skilled workers in manufacturing in the next period. As a result, the economy specializes in nontraded final goods, with no manufactures or education. The economy remains stagnant over time.

Now consider the East Asian case. With R small or zero, W_N is less than the wage of skilled workers in manufacturing. The older skilled workers therefore all work in manufacturing or education. Young unskilled workers may be divided between manufactures and the nontraded final goods sector, or they may work entirely in the nontraded sector, depending on parameter values of the economy. As long as the first condition in equation (12) holds, all young unskilled workers choose to become educated, and the skill level of the skilled workers rises in the next generation. Equation (12) continues to hold each period, so that in each period the young generation becomes educated and yet

<hr>

5. Notice that in a growth-accounting framework, the endogenous growth would not show up as rapid growth in *total factor productivity* in manufacturing, but rather as a rapid improvement in the skill level of the labor force, which has been observed in the East Asian economies.

more skilled, since each new generation is trained by more skilled teachers than the previous generation. Sooner or later, all unskilled workers work in the nontraded goods sector. The volume and world market value of traded manufacturing production grows at the rate μ, while the value of nontraded sector production, $P_N N$, remains a fixed fraction of the traded goods sector and thus also grows at the same rate (though employment and physical production remain unchanged in the nontraded goods sector).

Why do the two economies diverge after they have reached identical levels of per capita GDP? This divergence results from the *composition* of GDP. In East Asia, GDP is composed heavily of human capital, rather than natural resources, and the returns to the continued accumulation of human capital are high. In the Latin American–type economy, human capital is low, and the returns to human capital accumulation are also low. Schooling is not very effective, partly because the quality of teaching is also low. The Latin American–type economy ends in a low-level-income trap. One way out of the trap is clear. If Latin America could generate a sufficient accumulation of human capital—for example, through a temporary subsidization of education for one or more generations—then skilled workers would work in manufacturing rather than in nontraded production, and the incentive for further investment in manufacturing skills would also be enhanced. The intergenerational equity and efficiency properties of alternative subsidization schemes are yet to be investigated.

The next step of the theoretical argument should be to expand the model to allow for capital accumulation, including foreign-financed capital, in the tradable manufacturing sector. Arguments analogous to the case of education can be established: the strong real exchange rate of resource-abundant economies will tend to crowd out capital accumulation in labor-intensive manufactures. Resource scarcity, on the other hand, will favor rapid capital accumulation and the inflow of capital from abroad. An additional important step would be to consider the interaction between resource abundance and trade policy. For a resource-rich economy, even moderate levels of protection could be sufficient to eliminate the profitability of manufacturing exports, while for a resource-poor economy, manufacturing exports might remain profitable even in the face of moderate import protection. It is at least suggestive that when resource-rich Malaysia embarked on manufacturing exports in the early 1970s, it relied on free trade for exporters (i.e., access to all imported inputs and capital goods free of tariffs) through the introduction of special export-processing zones, especially for the electronics sector. Even moderate protection might have been enough to frustrate the start-up of manufacturing exports.

5.3 Empirical Evidence

As shown in Sachs and Warner (1995b), a standard growth equation, including initial income and other standard variables in cross-country growth models, confirms the role of structural variables in helping to account for differential growth patterns. Whether we proxy the resource base by population density, the ratio of manufactures exports to total exports, or the ratio of resource-based exports to GDP, we find that resource-abundant economies have tended to grow less rapidly than resource-scarce economies. Of course, other variables also played a role in determining cross-country growth, especially initial incomes, trade policies, and fiscal policies. What is especially notable in examining the high growth performance in East Asia is the crucial role of manufacturing exports, especially textiles and apparel in the early stage of export-led growth and electronics at a later stage. Only two countries in the world with populations in excess of one million have sustained rapid growth during the past decade without a heavy reliance on the growth of manufacturing exports.[6]

Interestingly, growth patterns *within* East Asia also support the general view that structural factors have contributed to long-term growth performance. The fastest growing countries (annual per capita GDP growth) in the region during 1970–89—South Korea (6.8), Taiwan (6.6), Hong Kong (6.1), and Singapore (6.8)—are also the countries with the smallest per capita endowments of land and natural resources. The resource-abundant economies—Indonesia (4.9), Malaysia (4.1), and Thailand (4.0)—have had slower, though still very high, long-term economic growth. Moreover, it appears that for the resource-abundant countries, very rapid sustained growth emerged in the mid-1980s, approximately one decade after the first group, and only when the latter countries embarked on a boom in labor-intensive manufacturing exports.

Table 5.3 provides some further support for the real exchange channel linking resource endowments to growth. For the year 1970, around the start of the rapid growth phase in East Asia, we calculate the ratio of a country's nominal GDP in U.S. dollars (measured at the market exchange rate) to its GDP in U.S. dollars at purchasing power parity, $GDP^{\$US}/GDP^{\$US,PPP}$, and denote this ratio as Π_i for country i. When Π_i is high, domestic prices in the country, converted to U.S. dollars, are above world dollar price levels. If tradable goods prices are approximately equal across countries, and if overall prices are a weighted average of tradable and nontradable prices, then a high ratio will indicate a high relative price of nontradable goods. The theoretical observations of section 5.2 suggest that resource-rich economies should have a high relative price of nontradable goods, and thus a high value of Π_i. Considering a sample of East Asian and Latin American countries, we indeed find that the labor-abundant economies tended to have lower domestic price levels than the resource-abundant economies. This is true not only between East Asia and Latin

6. World Bank (1996b, 188–89, table 1) lists 11 countries with per capita GDP growth during 1985–94 in excess of 5 percent per annum: Botswana, Chile, China, Hong Kong, Indonesia, Ireland, Korea, Malaysia, Mauritius, Singapore, and Thailand. Botswana and Chile remain substantially primary commodity exporters, while the other nine have all had very rapid growth of manufacturing exports.

America but also within East Asia (comparing resource-abundant Indonesia, Malaysia, and Thailand with the labor-abundant economies).

We mention, in conclusion, that two important findings of the World Bank's (1993) *East Asian Miracle* are also consistent with the viewpoint taken here. First, at the start of the fast-growth phase, the East Asian economies had much higher primary enrollment rates than other developing countries at the same per capita income levels (World Bank 1993, 45, fig. 1.8). This is consistent with the view expressed earlier that the returns to education have been higher in the resource-scarce economies, since unskilled wages are not bid up by Dutch disease effects. It remains to check whether, on a cross-country basis, enrollment rates can indeed be linked to the natural resource base, with resource-abundant economies having *lower* enrollment rates at given levels of per capita income. Second, the East Asian economies, not surprisingly, have tended to have a *higher* share of GDP originating in manufacturing than would be predicted by a simple cross-sectional regression of sectoral production shares on per capita GDP and population (World Bank 1993, 306, table 6.15). Once again, it remains to verify on a cross-country basis that the share of GDP in manufacturing is negatively related to resource abundance.

5.4   Conclusions and Extensions

Comparisons of economic performance across countries or regions should be based on three pillars, comparisons of economic policies, economic structure, and initial (historical) conditions. Economic performance differs according to the policies that are pursued; the underlying economic and social structures (including factor endowments, climate, topography, geography, cultural patterns); and specific historical conditions. The earliest comparative analyses of country performance, such as by Montesquieu, tended to put great stress on economic and social structures, but at least since Adam Smith, economists have rightly pointed to economic policies as the centerpiece of comparative analysis. What should be clear, however, is that all three factors are crucial to an adequate comparative analysis of economic performance.

This paper returns to a classic theme of Latin American historiography: the special dependence of the region on natural resource sectors. A century ago, resource-based development was at the center of economic growth; in recent decades, resource dependence has probably contributed to underlying crises and stagnation. If it is true that rapid productivity growth in recent years has come mainly in manufactures, then countries endowed with labor and human capital rather than natural resources might indeed have a structural advantage in reaping the benefits of open trade. (The evidence also suggests, however, that even for resource-based economies, open trade significantly outperforms strategies built on closed trade, viz. Chile). The theoretical models in this paper highlight some of the problems that confront countries with large but relatively static resource-based sectors. Nonetheless, this work remains very sketchy and preliminary. A number of empirical hypotheses have been introduced but are as yet untested. For example, the specific proposition that the returns to schooling have been higher in resource-scarce economies is testable. Even the basic linkages between resource endowments and high relative prices of nontradables have, as yet, only been examined superficially. On the theoretical side, it is important to extend the analysis to include a richer production structure in the resource sector (e.g., explicitly modeling agriculture), capital accumulation and international capital movements, and various aspects of trade policy.

It is also worth stressing, in conclusion, that the bases for long-term comparative advantage will change along with changes in technology and global resource endowments. Just as Latin America's commodity-based growth of the end of the nineteenth century could not be sustained in the middle of the twentieth century, it may be true that the highly labor-intensive manufacturing growth of the second half of the twentieth century will give way to new kinds of export-led growth (e.g., of labor-intensive services via high-capacity international data transmission). The study of long-term comparative advantage of developing countries seeking to integrate into the world economy remains a high priority of applied research in international economics.

References

Bulmer-Thomas, Victor. 1994. *The economic history of Latin America since independence.* Cambridge: Cambridge University Press.
Chenery, Hollis B., S. Robinson, and M. Syrquin. 1986. *Industrialization and growth: A comparative study.* London: Oxford University Press.
Deardorff, Alan. 1984. An exposition and exploration of Krueger's trade model. *Canadian Journal of Economics* 17 (4): 731–46.
Krueger, Anne. 1977. Growth, distortions, and the pattern of trade among many countries. Princeton Studies in International Finance no. 40. Princeton, N.J.: Princeton University.
Leamer, Edward E. 1987. Paths of development in the three-factor N-good general equilibrium model. *Journal of Political Economy* 95:961–99.
Maddison, Angus. 1995. *Monitoring the world economy, 1820–1992.* Paris: Organization for Economic Cooperation and Development.
Matsuyama, Kiminori. 1992. Agricultural productivity, comparative advantage, and economic growth. *Journal of Economic Theory* 58:317–34.
Morawetz, David. 1981. *Why the emperor's new clothes are not made in Colombia.* New York: Oxford University Press.
Sachs, Jeffrey, and Andrew Warner. 1995a. Economic reform and the process of global integration. *Brookings Papers on Economic Activity,* no. 1: 1–118.
———. 1995b. Natural resource abundance and economic growth. NBER Working Paper no. 5398. Cambridge, Mass.: National Bureau of Economic Research, December.
United Nations. 1950. Economic Commission on Latin America. *The economic devel-*

opment of Latin America and its principal problems. Report prepared by Raul Prebisch. Lake Success, N.Y.: United Nations Department of Economic Affairs.
————. 1995. *Handbook of international trade and development statistics, 1994.* New York: United Nations.
Wood, Adrian, and Kersti Berge. 1997. Exporting manufactures: Human resources, natural resources, or trade policy? *Journal of Development Studies* 34 (1): 35–59.
World Bank. 1993. *The East Asian miracle.* Oxford: Oxford University Press.
————. 1996a. Sustainability and the wealth of nations: First steps in an ongoing journey. Environmentally Sustainable Development Studies and Monographs Series, no. 5. Washington, D.C.: World Bank.
————. 1996b. *World development report.* Washington, D.C.: World Bank.
Young, Alwyn. 1995. The tyranny of numbers: Confronting the statistical realities of the East Asian growth experience. *Quarterly Journal of Economics* 110 (3): 641–80.

Comment   Kazuo Ueda

In this interesting paper, Sachs discusses the relationship between the structure of an economy, as defined by resource endowments, and its potential for growth led by productivity improvements in the manufacturing sector. He also seems to open the way to potentially fruitful areas of research, such as the role of economic structure for the determination of the effectiveness of trade policies as a strategy for growth.

The main discussion has three parts (presented in sections 5.2 and 5.3). In the first part a static general equilibrium model of a small open economy is constructed and used to analyze a version of the Dutch disease problem. Specifically, a larger endowment of natural resources, by raising income and the demand for nontraded goods, results in a higher relative price of nontraded goods and thus in a smaller share of the manufacturing sector. Beyond a certain point the economy enters a "Latin American region" where there is no manufacturing sector at all.

The second part of the paper appends to the model an endogenous growth story whereby investment in human capital in the manufacturing sector creates the possibility of sustained growth. Such growth may not occur in an economy with a large nontraded goods sector. In such an economy real wages in the nontraded goods industry are too high to create an incentive for human capital investment for workers. Thus the Dutch disease becomes a chronic disease.

The third component of the paper (section 5.3) is the confrontation of the implications of the theoretical analysis with the data. Sachs argues that the model explains very well the divergent growth behaviors of Latin American and East Asian economies.

Let me make some comments on each of the three aspects of the paper. In the first part, some special assumptions are made to derive the strong implica-

Kazuo Ueda is a member of the policy board of the Bank of Japan.

tions of the model. For example, the manufacturing (= traded goods) sector is assumed to be more labor intensive than the nontraded goods sector. Moreover, it is assumed that the manufacturing sector uses only labor in the production process.

A reversal of the factor intensity assumption will change some of the comparative statics results. For example, it would change the relationship between the relative price of nontraded goods and real wages. This is serious because many of the results of the paper turn on real wages being relatively higher in Latin America.

The relaxation of the manufacturing sector production function to include capital as a factor of production in the usual way makes Latin America less likely to specialize in nontraded goods (and resources). Under no-specialization, real wages will be equalized between the nontraded and manufacturing sectors. This would make it difficult for the author to argue in the second part that endogenous growth will not occur due to high wages in the nontraded goods sector.

The endogenous growth story based on investment in human capital in the manufacturing sector is neat but does not make clear why Latin America could not grow based on a different mechanism.

The growth story in the paper corresponds to that of Balassa-Samuelson. That is, productivity growth in the traded goods sector, by increasing income and, in turn, demand for nontraded goods, results in real exchange rate appreciation. The empirical evidence on this relationship between growth and the real exchange rate as reported by Ito, Isard, and Symansky (chap. 4 in this volume) is at best mixed. Japan, Taiwan, and Korea conform to the pattern. But the pattern does not seem to hold as clearly for other countries.

To summarize, the paper provides a neat and intuitively appealing story about why resource-poor countries performed well in the age of export-led growth in manufacturing. We are left with the feeling, however, that there could be and will be other types of sustained growth and that explaining changes in the pattern of growth will be a much harder task.

6   Private Consumption, Nontraded Goods, and Real Exchange Rate: Evidence from South Korea and Taiwan

Kenneth S. Lin

6.1   Introduction

There is little empirical evidence from the production perspective that any known fundamentals have reliable effects on real exchange rates.[1] According to Balassa (1964) and Samuelson (1964), real exchange rate movements reflect cross-country differences in the productivity differential between the traded and nontraded sectors. If higher productivity growth is expected to occur in the traded sector, there is a positive relation between real exchange rates and cross-country disparities in productivity growth.[2] Even though productivity differentials can account for long-run real exchange rate movements, a much higher productivity growth rate in the traded sector is required to justify the long-run movement.

This paper presents an empirical study of long-run real exchange rate movements from the consumption perspective. In most industrial countries, private consumption and the real exchange rate both have clear trends but exhibit different fluctuations. If the real exchange rate (or the relative price of nontraded goods) varies over time, aggregate consumption will respond to those price changes. Here I emphasize the role of risk aversion for nontraded goods consumption in accounting for long-run real exchange rate movements. When risk

Kenneth S. Lin is professor of economics at National Taiwan University.
This work is part of the NBER's project on International Capital Flows, which receives support from the Center for International Political Economy. The author thanks Ching-Sheng Mao and conference participants for helpful discussions on an earlier draft. He also thanks Takatoshi Ito and Gian Maria Milesi-Ferretti, whose comments led to an improvement of the paper, and Chia-Wei Hong for excellent research assistance.

1. Examples include Adler and Lehmann (1983), Hsieh (1982), Huizinga (1987), Ito, Isard, and Symansky (chap. 4 in this volume), Kravis and Lipsey (1987), and Strauss (1996).
2. The real exchange rate has been a natural indicator of export competitiveness. Establishing the positive relation and underlying growth mechanism has become a central research topic in economic development (e.g., Ito et al., chap. 4 in this volume).

aversion is the inverse of intertemporal elasticity of substitution, the lower risk aversion is, the easier it is for private agents, in terms of utility, to forgo current consumption for future consumption, and thus the higher the consumption growth rate is. On the other hand, lower risk aversion decreases the value of diversification. Suppose that agents are more risk averse for nontraded goods than for traded goods. Even in a perfect international credit market, agents cannot fully diversify away preference and productivity shocks to nontraded goods through consumption smoothing. Those shocks could induce changes in real exchange rate movements. As a result, relatively higher risk aversion for nontraded goods implies a tighter relationship in trend properties between nontraded goods consumption and the real exchange rate.

Volatile and persistent movements of real exchange rates and small cross-country correlations of private consumption have been separate research topics in international macroeconomics.[3] However, few researchers have attempted to account for the comovement between private consumption and the real exchange rate. One exception is Backus and Smith (1993). They studied a dynamic exchange economy with one traded good, one nontraded good for each country, and an arbitrary number of countries. A main theoretical finding is that the private consumption ratio between the foreign country and the home country and the real exchange rate have similar fluctuations and are positively correlated over time. However, they found little evidence for the positive correlation in eight OECD countries. There are two possibilities for the discrepancy between theory and evidence. First, preference shocks are not admitted in their model. When endowment shock is the sole external shock, it can only generate positive correlation between changes in the consumption ratio and changes in the real exchange rate. Second, agents have identical preferences across countries.

In this paper, I adopt Ogaki and Park's (1989) cointegration-Euler equation approach. Given the assumption of stationary preference shocks, my model implies that the real exchange rate and private consumption in different countries have similar trend properties in the sense that they are cointegrated. Here preference shocks not only induce negative correlation between the real exchange rate and consumption in different countries but also provide an identifying assumption. Preference parameters and weights assigned to nontraded goods in the construction of a price index determine the similarity. Heterogeneous preferences across countries induce dissimilarity. For example, when agents' preferences and weights used in the construction of a price index are

3. Stulz (1987) analyzed the effect of nontraded goods on international portfolio allocation. Devereux, Gregory, and Smith (1992) used a different model assuming separable leisure that generates lower cross-country consumption correlations. Stockman and Tesar (1995) used the nonseparable utility function with respect to nontraded goods consumption to generate a low cross-country correlation of aggregate consumption growth rates. Lewis (1996) found that both nonseparabilities and certain capital market restrictions are necessary to explain international consumption comovements.

identical across two countries, the real exchange rate becomes positively related to the cross-country consumption disparity in traded goods, but negatively related to the cross-country consumption disparity in nontraded goods.[4] The cointegration-Euler equation approach has two advantages: (1) The regression relationship is not affected by the specification of an intertemporal budget constraint. (2) The consistency and asymptotic properties of coefficient estimates are unaffected by the presence of arbitrary stationary measurement error.

The remainder of the paper is organized as follows. In section 6.2, I derive the stationarity restriction on the trend properties of real exchange rates and private consumption from the Euler equation for the agent's optimization problem. These restrictions are the foundation for the cointegration-Euler equation approach. In section 6.3, I describe the econometric specifications concerning the trend property of individual series and their implications for the stationarity restriction. Section 6.4 explains the data and reports empirical results. The countries under consideration are Japan, South Korea, Taiwan, and the United States. Two sets of bilateral relations are examined, with South Korea and Taiwan each serving as the home country. The focus is on the role of private consumption of nontraded goods in accounting for long-run real exchange rate movements in South Korea and Taiwan. Recently, Froot and Rogoff (1991) found that the cross-country difference in government spending accounts for real exchange rate movements. When government consumption is concentrated in the purchase of nontraded goods, my model predicts real exchange rate appreciation in the country with a high growth rate of government consumption. I also investigate this alternative explanation. Section 6.5 contains concluding remarks.

6.2 A Cointegration-Euler Equation Approach

Consider two countries in a world economy. Imagine that each economy is populated with an infinitely lived representative household. The household in the home country in period t is endowed with X_t^* units of exportable goods, Y_t^* units of importable goods, and Z_t^* units of nontraded goods. Goods X_t and Y_t are costlessly traded in the world markets, while Z_t is only traded domestically.

The household ranks its consumption stream $\{(X_t, Y_t, Z_t)', t \geq 0\}$ according to its lifetime utility function

$$E_0 \left[\sum_{t=0}^{\infty} \beta^t U(X_t, \ Y_t, \ Z_t) \right],$$

4. Lucas (1982) also studied a two-country model in which the representative agent ranks the exportable good and the importable good according to its preferences and must use currency to purchase the goods. The relative price between these two goods (terms of trade) is determined by the cross-country difference in the endowments of these two goods.

in which β is a constant discount factor with $0 < \beta < 1$ and E_t denotes the mathematical expectation conditioning on the information set available at the beginning of time t, Ω_t. The intraperiod utility is assumed to be the addilog utility function

$$U(X_t,\ Y_t,\ Z_t) \equiv \sigma_{xt}\frac{X_t^{1-\alpha_x} - 1}{1 - \alpha_x} + \sigma_{yt}\frac{Y_t^{1-\alpha_y} - 1}{1 - \alpha_y} + \sigma_{zt}\frac{Z_t^{1-\alpha_z} - 1}{1 - \alpha_z},$$

in which preferences take the constant relative risk aversion form for each good and $\alpha_i > 0$, for $i = x, y, z$. When $\alpha_x = \alpha_y = \alpha_z$, preferences are homothetic in the three consumption categories. Finally, preference shocks are allowed to influence the household utility via the stationary processes $\{\sigma_{xt}, \sigma_{yt}, \sigma_{zt}, t \geq 0\}$.

Let P_{xt}, P_{yt}, and P_{zt} be the prices of exportable goods, importable goods, and nontraded goods, respectively, in period t measured in units of domestic currency. Let $b_t + _1$ be the real value of international assets carried from period t to period $t + 1$ measured in units of exportables, and let r_t be the real interest rate measured in units of exportables. Without borrowing and lending restrictions in the international capital market, the household's budget constraint at time t is

$$b_{t+1} = \frac{P_{zt}}{P_{xt}}(Z_t^* - Z_t) + \frac{P_{yt}}{P_{xt}}(Y_t^* - Y_t) + (X_t^* - X_t) + (1 + r_{t-1})b_t.$$

The representative agent's intertemporal optimization problem is to maximize the lifetime utility function subject to the budget constraint, and the necessary first-order conditions for this problem are

$$\frac{\partial U}{\partial Y_t} = \frac{P_{yt}}{P_{xt}}\frac{\partial U}{\partial X_t},$$

$$\frac{\partial U}{\partial Z_t} = \frac{P_{zt}}{P_{xt}}\frac{\partial U}{\partial X_t},$$

$$E_t\left[\beta\frac{\partial U}{\partial X_{t+1}}(1 + r_t) - \frac{\partial U}{\partial X_t}\right] = 0,$$

and the budget constraint holds. Under my specification of the intraperiod utility function, Euler equations in the first-order conditions can be expressed as

$$\frac{\sigma_{xt}X_t^{-\alpha_x}}{\sigma_{yt}Y_t^{-\alpha_y}} = \frac{P_{xt}}{P_{yt}},$$

$$\frac{\sigma_{zt}Z_t^{-\alpha_z}}{\sigma_{xt}X_t^{-\alpha_x}} = \frac{P_{zt}}{P_{xt}}.$$

Taking the natural logarithm on both sides of the above equations yields

(1) $$p_{xt} - p_{yt} + \alpha_x x_t - \alpha_y y_t = u_{yt},$$

(2) $$p_{xt} - p_{zt} + \alpha_x x_t - \alpha_z z_t = u_{zt},$$

where $x_t \equiv \log X_t$, $y_t \equiv \log Y_t$, $z_t \equiv \log Z_t$, $p_{it} \equiv \log P_{it}$, for $i = x, y, z$, and $u_{it} = \log \sigma_{xt} - \log \sigma_{it}$, for $i = y, z$. In equilibrium, prices and consumption must satisfy equations (1) and (2).

If u_{it} is stationary for $i = y, z$, then equations (1) and (2) imply the stationarity of $p_{xt} - p_{yt} + \alpha_x x_t - \alpha_y y_t$ and $p_{xt} - p_{zt} + \alpha_x x_t - \alpha_z z_t$. This implication allows for different trend properties of consumption of various goods, depending on preference parameters. For example, when $\alpha_i > \alpha_x$, the restriction allows good i consumption to grow at a lower rate than good X consumption for any given path of relative price and preference shocks and $i = y, z$. This is because a given change in $p_{it} - p_{xt}$ induces a greater response of good i consumption.

Suppose that the general price index in the home country can be described by

$$p_t = \theta_x p_{xt} + \theta_y p_{yt} + \theta_z p_{zt} + u_{pt},$$

in which p_t is the logarithm of the domestic price index at time t and θ_i is the weight given to good i in the index with $\theta_i > 0$, for $i = x, y, z$, and $\theta_x + \theta_y + \theta_z = 1$. The error term, u_{pt}, captures the third-country effect and is assumed to be uncorrelated with p_{it}, for $i = x, y, z$. I use this definition to eliminate p_{zt} in equation (2):

(3) $$p_t = (\theta_x + \theta_z)p_{xt} + \theta_y p_{yt} + \alpha_x \theta_z x_t - \alpha_z \theta_z z_t - v_{zt},$$

in which $v_{zt} \equiv \theta_z u_{zt} - u_{pt}$. The foreign-country counterpart of equation (3) is

$$\hat{p}_t = (\hat{\theta}_x + \hat{\theta}_z)\hat{p}_{xt} + \hat{\theta}_y \hat{p}_{yt} + \hat{\alpha}_x \hat{\theta}_z \hat{x}_t - \hat{\alpha}_z \hat{\theta}_z \hat{z}_t - \hat{v}_{zt},$$

in which $\hat{v}_{zt} \equiv \hat{\theta}_z \hat{u}_{zt} - \hat{u}_{pt}$. Here and from now on, all variables and parameters pertaining to the foreign country are designated by a hat.

For my purpose, the real exchange rate at time t, denoted q_t, is defined as

(4) $$q_t = p_t - s_t - \hat{p}_t,$$

in which s_t is the logarithm of the nominal bilateral exchange rate. A decrease in s_t means an appreciation of the domestic currency. The purchasing power parity (PPP) doctrine states that the nominal exchange rate equals the ratio between domestic and foreign prices. Therefore, real exchange rate movements indicate deviations from PPP for p_t. To sharpen the focus on the role of nontraded goods, I assume that the law of one price holds for the goods that are traded between the two countries.[5] This is captured by the following relationship:

---

5. The law of one price obtains if (1) markets are competitive, (2) there are no transportation costs, and (3) there are no barriers to trade, such as tariffs or quotas. Hsieh (1982), Fisher and Park (1991), and Strauss (1996), among others, also adopted this assumption for traded goods.

$$p_{it} = s_t + \hat{p}_{it},$$

for $i = x, y$. The above assumption may not be as restrictive as it appears; we can easily abandon it by allowing movements in $p_{it} - s_t - \hat{p}_{it}$. If these deviations contain a trend component, that is, if PPP for either p_{xt} or p_{yt} does not hold in the long run, v_{zt} in equation (3) will contain a trend component. Hence, checking if the estimated residual in equation (3) is stationary provides a diagnostic analysis for possible misspecifications.

Substituting equation (3) and its foreign-country counterpart into equation (4) for p_t and $\hat{p}_t$, respectively, yields

$$(5) \quad q_t = (\hat{\theta}_y - \theta_y)(p_{xt} - p_{yt}) + \alpha_x \theta_z x_t - \hat{\alpha}_x \hat{\theta}_z \hat{x}_t - \alpha_z \theta_z z_t + \hat{\alpha}_z \hat{\theta}_z \hat{z}_t + v_t,$$

in which $v_t \equiv -v_{zt} + \hat{v}_{zt}$. It is clear from equation (5) that trade between two countries imposes an equilibrium relationship among the real exchange rate, the terms of trade, and private consumption in the two countries.[6] If v_t is stationary, equation (5) imposes the restriction regulating the comovement of q_t, $p_{xt} - p_{yt}, x_t, \hat{x}_t, z_t,$ and $\hat{z}_t$ that

$$q_t - (\theta_y - \hat{\theta}_y)(p_{xt} - p_{yt}) - \alpha_x \theta_z x_t + \hat{\alpha}_x \hat{\theta}_z \hat{x}_t + \alpha_z \theta_z z_t - \hat{\alpha}_z \hat{\theta}_z \hat{z}_t$$

be stationary. I call this restriction the stationarity restriction, which is the foundation of the cointegration-Euler equation approach. The derivation of this restriction does not require any use of budget constraint or first-order conditions relating to the intertemporal choice of consumption. Hence, the cointegration-Euler equation approach allows for the existence of liquidity constraints or other market imperfections.

The stationarity restriction has different long-run implications for the comovement of individual variables in equation (5), depending on the trend properties of those variables. For example, if PPP for p_t holds in the long run (i.e., q_t is stationary), then the stationarity restriction requires that $p_{xt} - p_{yt}, x_t, \hat{x}_t, z_t,$ and $\hat{z}_t$ be cointegrated with the cointegrating vector $(\hat{\theta}_y - \theta_y, \Pi')'$, in which $\Pi' = (\alpha_x \theta_z, -\hat{\alpha}_x \hat{\theta}_z, -\alpha_z \theta_z, \hat{\alpha}_z \hat{\theta}_z)$.[7] Suppose there is a change in the nominal exchange rate caused by nominal factors. Both traded and nontraded goods consumption in the two countries have significant influence on the general price index in each country. As a result, changes in consumption in both countries must manage to maintain the long-run relationship between price ratios in the two countries and the nominal exchange rate, and the nominal factors have effects only on the short-run movements of consumption. On the other hand, if q_t contains a trend component and $p_{xt} - p_{yt}, x_t, \hat{x}_t, z_t,$ and $\hat{z}_t$ are cointe-

6. Helpman and Razin (1982) also include export goods, import goods, and nontraded goods in their model, but they limit the discussion to a nonstochastic model.
7. Here I adopt the definition of cointegration given in Campbell and Perron (1991, 164). An $n \times 1$ vector of variables, S_t, is said to be cointegrated if there exists at least one nonzero n-element vector β such that $\beta'S_t$ is trend stationary. This definition does not require that each of the individual series in S_t contain a unit root; some or all series can be trend stationary.

grated with the cointegrating vector $(\hat{\theta}_y - \theta_y, \Pi')'$, then the stationarity restriction implies that private consumption in equation (5) cannot be a driving force for the trend component of q_t.

As argued in Hsieh (1982), different weights (θ_i) used in the construction of the price index can cause the movement of q_t. To see this, assume that the law of one price holds for both goods X and Y and that there are no nontraded goods in the world economy $(\theta_z = \hat{\theta}_z = 0)$. Then equation (5) becomes

$$q_t = (\hat{\theta}_y - \theta_y)(p_{xt} - p_{yt}) + v_t.$$

Clearly, it is private consumption of nontraded goods that creates a link between the real exchange rate and private consumption in the model. It is trade between the two countries that creates a link between the terms of trade and the real exchange rate. When $\hat{\theta}_y \neq \theta_y$ and $v_t = 0$, the terms of trade and the real exchange rate have similar dynamics. It is preference shocks that make the correlation between the real exchange rate and the terms of trade imperfect. If there is only one good, say good Y, in the world economy, then $\theta_y = \hat{\theta}_y = 1$ and equation (5) becomes $q_t = v_t$. That is, unlike the result obtained in Backus and Smith (1993), PPP for p_t does not necessarily hold exactly, due to the presence of preference shocks.

Even though the terms of trade can account for a significant fraction of real exchange rate movements, the real exchange rate (q_t) does not necessarily have positive correlation with the terms of trade. The sign of correlation is determined by that of $\hat{\theta}_y - \theta_y$. To see this, consider an increase in the terms of trade caused by a lower importables price. If consumption of importable goods is more important in the home country than in the foreign country in the sense that $\theta_y > \hat{\theta}_y$, then the value of a unit of domestic currency (in terms of a basket of goods) must rise relative to that of the equivalent units of foreign currency. When the real exchange rate appreciates, it is optimal for private agents to increase their consumption of importables. For this case, the terms of trade and the real exchange rate are negatively correlated.

To identify other sources for the movement of q_t, assume that households in the two countries have identical preferences $(\alpha_i = \hat{\alpha}_i,$ for $i = x, y, z)$ and that the weights used in the construction of the price index are the same for the two countries. Given those assumptions, equation (5) can be reduced to

$$q_t = \alpha_x \theta_z (x_t - \hat{x}_t) - \alpha_z \theta_z (z_t - \hat{z}_t) + v_t.$$

It is obvious that the cross-country consumption disparities for traded and nontraded goods account for the movement of q_t: q_t increases with the cross-country consumption disparity in traded goods but decreases with the cross-country consumption disparity in nontraded goods. A country that experiences real appreciation of its currency enjoys either more rapid growth in private consumption of traded goods or less rapid growth in private consumption of nontraded goods. Since nontraded goods will be relatively more expensive in a fast-growing economy, that country's currency will experience real appreciation.

Without preference shocks and the third-country effect on the demand side, I cannot derive the long-run restriction from equation (1). However, for productivity differential models, productivity shocks do not play such a role. For example, in Hsieh's (1982) model, the supply of labor is fixed but is mobile between the tradable goods, and labor is the only input factor in production. Then the real exchange rate is a deterministic function of the following variables: productivity differentials between the tradable and nontradable sectors in both countries and the cross-country disparity in unit labor costs of the traded goods.

6.3   Econometric Specifications

The stationarity restriction summarizes the long-run equilibrium restrictions from the consumer's perspective. In a closed exchange economy, consumption equals production, and preference parameters can be identified from the stationarity restriction if the supply side exhibits much more volatility in the long run than the demand side. Ogaki (1992) and Ogaki and Park (1989) achieved the identification by assuming that productivity shocks have a stochastic trend.

Instead of modeling the production technology on the supply side, I consider an open exchange economy in the world markets. Trading opportunities imply that the consumption of goods X and Y in each country may not equal domestic production in equilibrium. For an open economy, the trend properties of private consumption of both exportable goods and importable goods are unlikely to be closely related to their domestic production. To achieve the identification of preference parameters, it is not sufficient to assume that the productivity shocks have a stochastic trend. However, preference parameters can be identified if the trend properties of export and import activities do not offset those of the corresponding production. Productivity shock is the dominant driving force in the long run.

In empirical investigation, it is difficult to obtain data on the consumption of exportables and importables. My focus will be on the two-good case: a traded good and a nontraded good. Let X_t denote the traded good. Since $p_{xt} = p_{yt}$ in the two-good case, equation (5) can be reduced to

$$(6) \qquad q_t = \alpha_x \theta_z x_t - \hat{\alpha}_x \hat{\theta}_z \hat{x}_t - \alpha_z \theta_z z_t + \hat{\alpha}_z \hat{\theta}_z \hat{z}_t + v_t.$$

According to Campbell and Perron's (1991) definition of cointegration, the stationarity restriction does not require difference stationarity of all individual series. The stationarity restriction simply states that there exists at least a 5×1 vector $(1, -\Pi')$ for q_t, x_t, $\hat{x}_t$, z_t, and $\hat{z}_t$ such that v_t is trend stationary. If all individual variables are trend stationary, then they are trivially cointegrated.

To assess the empirical significance of a heterogeneous utility function across countries, I follow the tradition in international trade and assume $\alpha_i = \hat{\alpha}_i$ for $i = x, z$ and $\theta_z = \hat{\theta}_z$. Then equation (6) can be further simplified to

(7) $$q_t = \alpha_x \theta_z (x_t - \hat{x}_t) - \alpha_z \theta_z (z_t - \hat{z}_t) + v_t.$$

If both the real exchange rate and the cross-country consumption disparities, $x_t - \hat{x}_t$ and $z_t - \hat{z}_t$, contain different trend components, then the stationarity restriction implies that q_t, $x_t - \hat{x}_t$, and $z_t - \hat{z}_t$ are cointegrated. However, when q_t is stationary, the stationarity restriction does not necessarily imply the stationarity of $y_t - \hat{y}_t$ and $z_t - \hat{z}_t$. The disparities $y_t - \hat{y}_t$ and $z_t - \hat{z}_t$ can be cointegrated with the cointegrating vector $(\alpha_x \theta_z, -\alpha_z \theta_z)$ so that $\alpha_x \theta_z (x_t - \hat{x}_t) - \alpha_z \theta_z (z_t - \hat{z}_t)$ is stationary. For this case, if good X has a lower income elasticity than good Z ($\alpha_x > \alpha_z$), then the stationarity of q_t forces $z_t - \hat{z}_t$ to grow at a faster rate than $x_t - \hat{x}_t$, but private consumption does not have long-run effects on q_t. Finally, the estimates of α_x/α_z and $\hat{\alpha}_x/\hat{\alpha}_z$ can be identified here.

6.4   Data and Empirical Results

As displayed in figures 6.1 and 6.2, the consumption of both traded and nontraded goods and the bilateral real exchange rate all exhibit clear trends. I first present statistical tests for the trend properties of individual series and then estimate various cointegrating regressions under the two specifications of preference parameters and the weights given in the construction of p_t.

6.4.1   Data

The countries involved are Japan, South Korea, Taiwan, and the United States. Two sets of bilateral relations are examined, with South Korea and Taiwan each serving as the home country. Data on the exchange rates of the New Taiwan (NT) dollar against the U.S. dollar and the Japanese yen were taken from *Monthly Financial Statistics,* while the exchange rates of the Korean won against the two foreign currencies were taken from *International Financial Statistics (IFS).* To study the sensitivity of empirical results with respect to the use of the price index as a measure of general price level, the two selections of p_t are the consumer price index (CPI) and the wholesale price index (WPI; or producer price index, PPI). Japanese, South Korean, and U.S. price series were taken from *IFS,* and Taiwanese price series were taken from *National Income Accounts.* Let q_t^c denote the real exchange rate when the CPI is the measure of price index, and let q_t^w denote the real exchange rate when the WPI is the measure.

Following Kakkar and Ogaki (1993), real consumption expenditure on durables, semidurables, and nondurables is defined as the consumption of traded goods, while real consumption expenditure on services is defined as the consumption of nontraded goods. South Korean data on x_t and z_t were taken from *National Accounts,* published by the Bank of Korea, while Taiwanese series were taken from *National Income Accounts.* Japanese series for $\hat{x}_t$ and $\hat{z}_t$ were

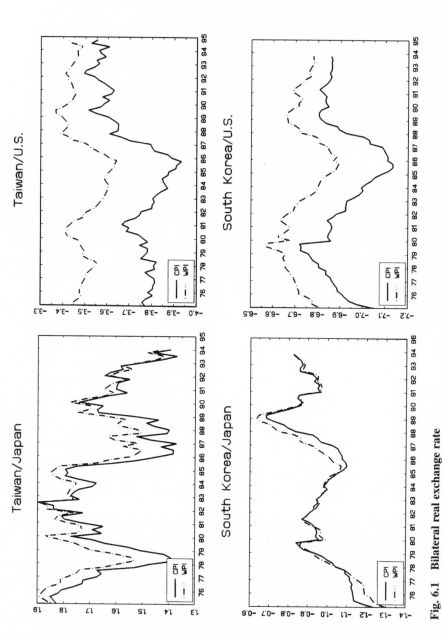

Fig. 6.1 Bilateral real exchange rate

Sources: Taiwan, *Financial Statistics Monthly* (Taipei: Central Bank of China, various issues); Japan, South Korea, and United States, *International Financial Statistics* (Washington, D.C.: International Monetary Fund, various issues).

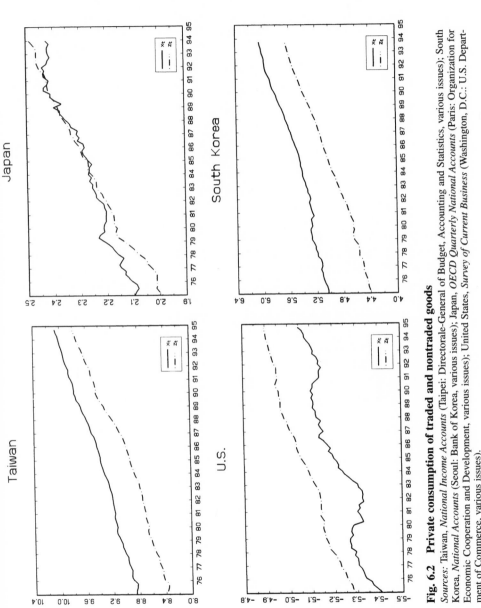

Fig. 6.2 Private consumption of traded and nontraded goods

Sources: Taiwan, *National Income Accounts* (Taipei: Directorate-General of Budget, Accounting and Statistics, various issues); South Korea, *National Accounts* (Seoul: Bank of Korea, various issues); Japan, *OECD Quarterly National Accounts* (Paris: Organization for Economic Cooperation and Development, various issues); United States, *Survey of Current Business* (Washington, D.C.: U.S. Department of Commerce, various issues).

taken from *OECD Quarterly National Accounts*, and U.S. series were taken from the *Survey of Current Business*, published by the Department of Commerce. Per capita real consumption of goods and services is constructed as follows. I deflate nominal consumption expenditure by the appropriate price index and then divide the resulting number by total population. All data are quarterly series. The sample period is 1975:1–1994:4 for Taiwan and the United States, and 1975:1–1993:4 for Japan and South Korea.

6.4.2   Evidence from Time-Series Data

Real bilateral exchange rates are displayed in figure 6.1, plots of x_t, z_t, $\hat{x}_t$, and $\hat{z}_t$ in figure 6.2, and those of $x_t - \hat{x}_t$ and $z_t - \hat{z}_t$ in figure 6.3. Two points are worth mentioning. First, Taiwan generally experienced a real appreciation of its currency against U.S. dollars during the sample period. The nominal depreciation of NT dollars against U.S. dollars caused a real depreciation of Taiwan's currency from 1981 to 1986, and then the real value of NT dollars was pushed up under pressure from the United States when Taiwan had a sizable current account surplus in the 1986–89 period. The bilateral exchange rate of Korean won against U.S. dollars exhibits a less clear upward trend. The real depreciation of the Korean won in 1980 and in 1982–86 was caused by the continuing nominal depreciation of Korean won against U.S. dollars. When South Korea began to enjoy a sizable current account surplus in 1986, the Korean won also came under pressure from the United States to have an unprecedented appreciation against the U.S. dollar through 1989. After 1989, a mild real depreciation of the won against the U.S. dollar was mainly due to two factors: the deterioration of South Korea's international payment position and the appreciation of the Japanese yen against the U.S. dollar since 1991. As a result, the real value of Korean won against U.S. dollars fell to the level of the late 1970s in 1993–94. The bilateral real exchange rate between South Korea and Japan exhibits a similar clear upward trend in the 1975–94 period. However, the real exchange rate between Taiwan and Japan exhibits a downward trend with volatile fluctuations.

Second, real per capita private consumption expenditures on traded goods and nontraded goods contain different trend components in the four countries. As a result, the cross-country disparities in private consumption of traded goods and nontraded goods exhibit upward trends for the four pairs of countries. The cross-country evidence in figure 6.2 indicates higher growth in the per capita real consumption of services in the course of economic development.

6.4.3   Testing for the Purchasing Power Parity Doctrine

I first test the trend property of the bilateral real exchange rate between the home country and the foreign country. If the real exchange rate does not contain a trend component, then the PPP doctrine for p_t holds in the long run. Otherwise, it does not hold in the long run. Therefore, testing the trend

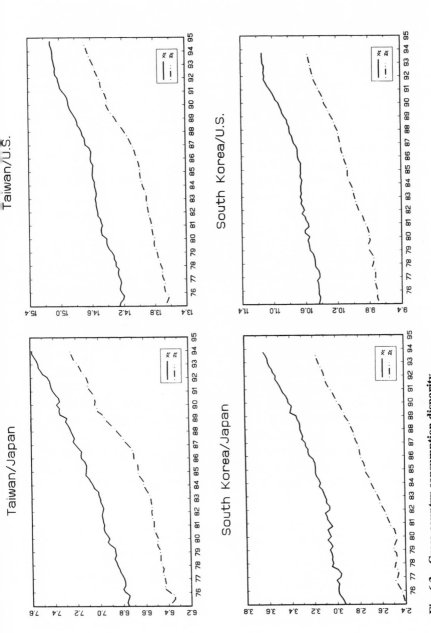

Fig. 6.3   Cross-country consumption disparity
Sources: See fig. 6.2.

property of the real exchange rate is equivalent to testing the PPP doctrine. Here, I use Park and Choi's (1988) $J(p, q)$ and $G(p,q)$ tests. I reject the null of difference stationary around a linear time trend when the $J(1,q)$ statistic is smaller than the critical values tabulated in Park and Choi (1988)[8] and reject the null of trend stationarity when the $G(1,q)$ statistic is larger than the critical values.[9]

Table 6.1 displays test results for the trend property of bilateral real exchange rates. For q_t^c and q_t^w between Taiwan and the United States, the $J(1,q)$ tests with $q = 2,3,4$ cannot reject the null of difference stationarity around a linear time trend at the 10 percent significance level. There is evidence against the trend stationarity of q_t^c at the 5 percent significance level in terms of the $G(1,2)$ and $G(1,4)$ tests. On the other hand, the $G(1,q)$ tests with $q = 2,3,4$ yield weaker evidence against the trend stationarity of q_t^w.

For q_t^c between Taiwan and Japan, the $J(1,q)$ tests all reject the null of difference stationary. The $J(1,3)$ and $J(1,4)$ tests even reject it at the 1 percent significance level. When the WPI is the measure of P_t, there is slightly improved evidence for the difference stationarity of q_t^w. The $J(1,3)$ and $J(1,4)$ tests still reject the null, and only $J(1,2)$ fails to reject it at the 10 percent significance level. On the other hand, I did not find significant evidence against the null of trend stationarity for both q_t^c and q_t^w in terms of the $G(1,q)$ tests.[10]

There is conflicting evidence for the trend property of q_t^c between South Korea and Japan. I found that the $J(1,2)$ and $J(1,4)$ tests cannot reject the null of difference stationarity. But results of the $G(1,q)$ tests with $q = 2,3,4$ support the null of trend stationarity. On the other hand, there is more consistent evidence for the difference stationarity of q_t^w. The $J(1,q)$ tests with $q = 2,3,4$ all fail to reject the null of difference stationarity for q_t^w at the 10 percent significance level. Only the $G(1,3)$ test fails to reject the null of trend stationarity for q_t^w at the 10 percent significance level. Finally, for q_t^c between South Korea and the United States, both $J(1,q)$ and $G(1,q)$ tests with $q = 2,3,4$ provided significant evidence for the null of difference stationarity. However, there is slightly weaker evidence for the difference stationarity of q_t^w in terms of the $J(1,q)$ tests. Only the $G(1,2)$ and $G(1,3)$ tests fail to reject the null of trend stationarity.

The above findings can be summarized as follows. First, the bilateral ex-

8. The $J(p, q)$ test does not require the estimation of the long-run variance and has an advantage over Phillips and Perron's Z_α (Z_t) test and the augmented Dickey-Fuller (ADF) test in that neither the bandwidth parameter nor the order of autoregression needs to be chosen. Monte Carlo experiments also show that the $J(p, q)$ test has a stable size and is not dominated by the ADF test in small samples in terms of powers.

9. Kahn and Ogaki (1992) recommend small q when the sample size is small, according to their Monte Carlo simulations. Here I chose $q = 2$, 3, and 4. For estimation of the long-run variance, I use Andrews's (1991) quadratic spectral kernel with the automatic bandwidth parameter estimator based on AR(1).

10. I report the ADF test in table 6.3 because it was widely used in the literature. None of the ADF tests reject the null of difference stationary for both q_t^c and q_t^w in the Taiwan/Japan and Taiwan/U.S. cases. In the following discussion, I only present the $J(p, q)$ and $G(p, q)$ test results when there is no conflicting evidence between these tests and the ADF test.

Table 6.1   **Tests for Trend Property of Real Exchange Rates**

Null and Statistic[a]	Taiwan/ Japan	Taiwan/ U.S.	South Korea/ Japan	South Korea/ U.S.
	Price Index: CPI			
Difference stationarity				
$J(1, 2)$	0.007*	0.397	0.026	0.257
$J(1, 3)$	0.008***	0.414	0.098*	0.484
$J(1, 4)$	0.048***	1.144	0.341	3.194
Difference stationarity				
ADF(1)	−2.352	−1.798	−2.204	−1.295
ADF(2)	−2.628	−1.936	−2.571	−1.583
ADF(3)	−2.683	−1.895	−2.554	−1.770
Trend stationarity				
$G(1, 2)$	0.135	5.586**	0.487	3.628*
$G(1, 3)$	0.171	5.750*	1.710	5.794*
$G(1, 4)$	0.951	10.483**	4.869	13.520***
	Price Index: WPI			
Difference stationarity				
$J(1, 2)$	0.053	0.168	0.193	0.028
$J(1, 3)$	0.073*	0.248	0.226	0.164
$J(1, 4)$	0.096**	0.622	0.500	1.648
Difference stationarity				
ADF(1)	−2.612	−1.894	−2.331	−1.822
ADF(2)	−2.429	−2.274	−2.537	−1.775
ADF(3)	−2.673	−2.469	−2.694	−1.885
Trend stationarity				
$G(1, 2)$	1.128	2.806*	3.098*	0.511
$G(1, 3)$	1.509	3.871	3.538	2.598
$G(1, 4)$	1.947	7.463*	6.395*	11.487***

[a]$J(p, q)$ and $G(p, q)$ denote Park and Choi's (1988) tests with a time polynomial of order p in the null hypothesis and a time polynomial of order q in the fitted regression. ADF(p) denotes Dickey and Fuller's (1984) test with a time polynomial of order 1 in the null hypothesis and p lagged first-difference terms in the fitted regression.
*Significant at the 10 percent level.
**Significant at the 5 percent level.
***Significant at the 1 percent level.

change rates contain a unit root and linear time trend in the South Korea/Japan, South Korea/U.S., and Taiwan/U.S. cases. And q_t^c and q_t^w between Taiwan and Japan are stationary around a linear time trend. Second, the measure of p_t chosen in testing the trend property of the real exchange rate does not matter for the long-run deviation of PPP for q_t. Recently, based on data in other countries, Kim (1990) and Kakkar and Ogaki (1993) found more favorable evidence for long-run PPP when the WPI is used as the measure of p_t than when the CPI is used. They argued that the large weight given to nontraded goods in the CPI could be the reason the long-run PPP doctrine based on the CPI did not receive much empirical support.

6.4.4   Testing for the Trend Property of Private Consumption

Given the trend property of the real exchange rate, private consumption in different countries must exhibit trends in order to account for long-run real exchange rate movements under the stationarity restriction. Table 6.2 presents test results for the trend property of x_t, z_t, $\hat{x}_t$, and $\hat{z}_t$.

First, for both x_t and z_t in Taiwan, the null of difference stationarity around a linear time trend cannot be rejected at the 10 percent significance level in terms of the $J(1,q)$ tests with $q = 2,3,4$. The $G(1,q)$ tests with $q = 2,3,4$ significantly reject the null of trend stationarity in favor of difference stationarity at the 1 percent significance level. Second, the null of difference stationarity for both x_t and z_t in South Korea received strong support from the $J(1,q)$ tests. But the $G(1,q)$ tests yield significant evidence against trend stationarity for these two series. In light of the above results, I assume that both x_t and z_t in South Korea and Taiwan contain a unit root around a linear time trend.

For the U.S. series of $\hat{x}_t$, I found weaker evidence for the null of difference stationarity around a linear trend. Even though the $G(1,q)$ tests with $q = 2,3,4$ reject the null of trend stationarity at the 10 percent significance level, both the $J(1,2)$ and $J(1,4)$ tests reject the null of difference stationarity at the 10 percent significance level. On the other hand, there is significant evidence for the null of difference stationarity for the U.S. series of $\hat{z}_t$. These results are confirmed by results of the $G(1,q)$ tests. For $\hat{x}_t$ and $\hat{z}_t$ in Japan, there is mixed evidence for difference stationarity. First, both the $J(1,2)$ and $J(1,3)$ tests reject the null of difference stationarity for $\hat{x}_t$ at the 10 percent significance level. Second, the $J(1,q)$ tests with $q = 2,3,4$ cannot reject the null of difference stationarity for $\hat{z}_t$ at the 10 percent significance level. They are consistent with the results of the $G(1,q)$ tests in table 6.2. Since the $G(p,q)$ test tends to overreject the null when the autoregressive root is close to one, the above findings can be viewed as conclusive evidence for the trend stationarity of $\hat{x}_t$ in Japan and the United States. And I assume that $\hat{z}_t$ in Japan and the United States contains a unit root and linear time trend.

Recently, Ogaki and Park (1989) have found significant evidence for the null of difference stationarity for the U.S. data on $\hat{z}_t$ and evidence against the trend stationarity of $\hat{z}_t$. They use seasonally adjusted monthly data on durables, nondurables, and services in the National Income and Product Accounts. The sample period is from January 1959 to December 1986. When a shorter sample period is used (February 1968 to December 1986), the null of trend stationarity for $\hat{z}_t$ cannot be rejected. Given the mixed evidence on the null of difference stationarity for the consumption of durables and nondurables, their findings are generally consistent with my results.

6.4.5   Testing for Cross-Country Consumption Disparity

If preference parameters and weights used in the construction of p_t are identical across the home country and the foreign country, the cross-country con-

Table 6.2   Tests for Trend Property of Private Consumption

Consumption[a]	Null: Difference Stationarity						Null: Trend Stationarity		
	$J(1, 2)$	$J(1, 3)$	$J(1, 4)$	ADF(1)	ADF(2)	ADF(3)	$G(1, 2)$	$G(1, 3)$	$G(1, 4)$
				Japan					
$\hat{x}_t$	0.008*	0.025**	1.573	−1.993	−2.156	−2.206	0.175	0.530	13.184***
$\hat{z}_t$	1.063	1.153	1.323	−1.760	−2.296	−2.066	10.105***	10.502***	11.165**
				South Korea					
x_t	2.331	2.346	9.972	−1.041	−1.126	−1.438	12.407***	12.432***	16.115***
z_t	1.986	3.135	3.175	−2.487	−2.357	−2.241	12.829***	14.622***	14.668***
				Taiwan					
x_t	1.065	1.072	3.601	−1.590	−0.925	−1.276	9.980***	10.013***	15.144***
z_t	2.131	2.179	6.300	−1.106	−0.769	−1.446	12.723***	12.814***	16.132***
				United States					
$\hat{x}_t$	0.000***	0.164	0.172*	−1.563	−1.922	−2.106	0.000	2.730	2.843
$\hat{z}_t$	0.427	0.550	0.831	−1.744	−1.639	−1.957	5.951**	7.048**	9.021**

[a]x_t and z_t denote per capita real consumption on traded and nontraded goods, respectively.

*Significant at the 10 percent level.

**Significant at the 5 percent level.

***Significant at the 1 percent level.

sumption disparity must be nonstationary in order to account for long-run real exchange rate movements. For this purpose, I test for cointegration between private consumption in different countries. If domestic consumption and foreign consumption of traded goods (nontraded goods) are not cointegrated with the normalized cointegrating vector $(1, -1)$, then the cross-country consumption disparity for traded goods (nontraded goods) contains a trend component.

Here I use Park's (1992) $H(p,q)$ statistics in testing the cointegrating relationship.[11] In particular, the $H(0,1)$ statistic can be used to test the deterministic cointegrating restriction. According to the $H(p,q)$ statistics in table 6.3, I found much evidence against cointegration between x_t and $\hat{x}_t$ (and between z_t and $\hat{z}_t$) for all possible pairs of home and foreign countries: the deterministic cointegration restriction was rejected by the $H(0,1)$ test, while the stochastic cointegration restriction was rejected by the $H(1,q)$ tests with $q = 2,3,4$ at the 1 percent significance level. These results are consistent with visual impressions obtained from figure 6.3. Both test results and visual impressions clearly indicate that the cross-country consumption disparities for traded and nontraded goods contain a trend component.

6.4.6 Testing for the Stationarity Restriction

Given the difference stationarity of q_t, the stationarity restriction simply implies that private consumption series in different countries are not cointegrated with the cointegrating vector Π'. It is still possible that private consumption series in different countries are cointegrated with other cointegrating vectors. The hypothesis-testing strategy is to conduct cointegration tests for private consumption in different countries with and without the real exchange rate included. Suppose that the test results reject the null of cointegration for the set of variables excluding q_t but fail to reject the null for the set of variables including q_t. Then the long-run movements of q_t are driven by private consumption in different countries.

Table 6.3 reports the $H(0,q)$ and $H(1,q)$ tests for the null of cointegration for the four private consumption series. When Taiwan (the United States) is designated as the home (foreign) country, the $H(0,1)$ test fails to reject the null of deterministic cointegration for x_t, $\hat{x}_t$, z_t, and $\hat{z}_t$, and the $H(1,q)$ tests with $q = 2,3,4$ also provide strong evidence for the null of stochastic cointegration restriction. When Japan is the foreign country, the $H(0,1)$ test rejects the null of deterministic cointegration for x_t, $\hat{x}_t$, z_t, and $\hat{z}_t$ at the 10 percent significance level. However, the $H(1,q)$ tests with $q = 2,3,4$, strongly favor the stochastic cointegration restriction.

I found much evidence against the null of cointegration for x_t, $\hat{x}_t$, z_t, and $\hat{z}_t$ in the South Korea/Japan and South Korea/U.S. cases. Only the deterministic cointegration restriction in the South Korea/Japan case cannot be rejected by

---

11. Park (1992) showed that the $H(p, q)$ statistic converges in distribution to a $\chi^2(p - q)$ random variable under the null of cointegration.

Table 6.3 **Tests for Cointegration**

	Null: Cointegration				
Variable[a]	$H(0, 1)$	$H(0, 2)$	$H(1, 2)$	$H(1, 3)$	$H(1, 4)$
South Korea/Japan					
$(x_t, \hat{x}_t)$	3.154*	19.104***	15.529***	15.538***	16.676***
$(z_t, \hat{z}_t)$	14.361***	16.584***	6.900***	10.029***	10.356**
$(x_t, \hat{x}_t, z_t, \hat{z}_t)$	1.231	10.621***	11.737***	11.761***	17.770***
$(x_t - \hat{x}_t, z_t - \hat{z}_t)$	0.862	12.060***	14.586***	14.690***	14.004***
$(q_t^c, x_t, \hat{x}_t, z_t, \hat{z}_t)$	1.136	5.078*	3.325*	3.339	3.491
$(q_t^w, x_t, \hat{x}_t, z_t, \hat{z}_t)$	2.872*	5.232*	1.834	2.085	2.367
$(q_t^c, x_t - \hat{x}_t, z_t - \hat{z}_t)$	4.671**	4.833*	0.552	0.973	4.234
$(q_t^w, x_t - \hat{x}_t, z_t - \hat{z}_t)$	7.275***	7.326**	0.019	1.695	4.309
South Korea/United States					
$(x_t, \hat{x}_t)$	14.152***	17.612***	14.819***	14.932***	16.226***
$(z_t, \hat{z}_t)$	14.189***	16.994***	12.207***	14.243***	14.632***
$(x_t, \hat{x}_t, z_t, \hat{z}_t)$	4.117**	9.964***	7.764***	9.424***	12.677***
$(x_t - \hat{x}_t, z_t - \hat{z}_t)$	1.136	5.629*	4.003**	8.967**	11.601***
$(q_t^c, x_t, \hat{x}_t, z_t, \hat{z}_t)$	0.637	0.688	0.009	0.225	2.287
$(q_t^w, x_t, \hat{x}_t, z_t, \hat{z}_t)$	0.639	0.642	0.000	0.279	2.396
$(q_t^c, x_t - \hat{x}_t, z_t - \hat{z}_t)$	0.030	1.936	1.281	1.291	4.383
$(q_t^w, x_t - \hat{x}_t, z_t - \hat{z}_t)$	3.747*	4.253	0.597	0.961	3.491
Taiwan/Japan					
$(x_t, \hat{x}_t)$	12.466***	20.772***	14.266***	14.357***	15.436***
$(z_t, \hat{z}_t)$	9.408***	16.151***	11.388***	11.396***	15.564***
$(x_t, \hat{x}_t, z_t, \hat{z}_t)$	2.842*	3.004	0.108	0.130	5.350
$(x_t - \hat{x}_t, z_t - \hat{z}_t)$	13.770***	14.074***	4.987**	7.893**	8.720**
$(q_t^c, x_t, \hat{x}_t, z_t, \hat{z}_t)$	0.397	1.320	0.493	0.651	1.438
$(q_t^w, x_t, \hat{x}_t, z_t, \hat{z}_t)$	0.818	1.811	0.527	1.071	2.671
$(q_t^c, x_t - \hat{x}_t, z_t - \hat{z}_t)$	0.069	0.133	0.019	0.083	2.839
$(q_t^w, x_t - \hat{x}_t, z_t - \hat{z}_t)$	0.320	0.752	0.068	0.371	2.978
Taiwan/United States					
$(x_t, \hat{x}_t)$	16.968***	17.812***	13.980***	13.980***	15.998***
$(z_t, \hat{z}_t)$	9.136***	17.143***	13.803***	13.843***	15.588***
$(x_t, \hat{x}_t, z_t, \hat{z}_t)$	1.608	2.056	0.744	1.494	1.764
$(x_t - \hat{x}_t, z_t - \hat{z}_t)$	6.534**	9.456***	3.393*	5.130*	5.132
$(q_t^c, x_t, \hat{x}_t, z_t, \hat{z}_t)$	1.316	2.159	0.360	0.720	0.723
$(q_t^w, x_t, \hat{x}_t, z_t, \hat{z}_t)$	1.306	2.808	0.798	1.848	2.594
$(q_t^c, x_t - \hat{x}_t, z_t - \hat{z}_t)$	6.756***	6.914**	0.488	1.666	1.828
$(q_t^w, x_t - \hat{x}_t, z_t - \hat{z}_t)$	2.953*	2.966	0.054	2.153	2.170

[a] q_t denotes real exchange rate; x_t and z_t denote per capita real consumption on traded and nontraded goods, respectively.

*Significant at the 10 percent level.

**Significant at the 5 percent level.

***Significant at the 1 percent level.

the $H(0,1)$ test. There is more than a single source of nonstationarity in generating the long-run movements of x_t, $\hat{x}_t$, z_t, and $\hat{z}_t$ here.

Next, I apply the $H(p,q)$ tests to q_t, x_t, $\hat{x}_t$, z_t, and $\hat{z}_t$; the results are also given in table 6.3. Using both measures of p_t, I found little evidence against the stationarity restriction in the Taiwan/Japan and Taiwan/U.S. cases: the deterministic cointegration restriction was not rejected by the $H(0,1)$ test, nor was the stochastic cointegration restriction rejected by the $H(1,q)$ tests with $q = 2,3,4$. Even if the four individual private consumption series are cointegrated, the above finding clearly suggests that private consumption in different countries can account for long-run movements of the real exchange rate. And the private consumption series are cointegrated with a cointegrating vector other than Π'. In previous subsections, I found evidence for the trend stationarity of q_t between Taiwan and Japan and of $\hat{x}_t$ in Japan and the United States. These results apparently did not affect the test results for the stationarity restriction.

There is mixed evidence for the stationarity restriction in the South Korea/ Japan case. When the CPI is the measure of p_t, the $H(0,1)$ test fails to reject deterministic cointegration for q_t, x_t, $\hat{x}_t$, z_t, and $\hat{z}_t$. On the other hand, the stochastic cointegration restriction was rejected by the $H(1,2)$ test at the 10 percent significance level. When the WPI is the measure of p_t, the stationarity restriction was rejected by the $H(0,1)$ test but cannot be rejected by the $H(1,q)$ tests with $q = 2,3,4$. For the South Korea/U.S. case, I found little evidence against the stationarity restriction. The difference stationarity of q_t and the stationarity restriction together imply that private consumption accounts for the long-run movement of the real exchange rate.

When I assumed that preference parameters and weights used in the construction of p_t are identical across the home country and the foreign country, I found significant evidence for the stationarity restriction in the Taiwan/Japan case, and weaker evidence for the stationarity restriction in the Taiwan/U.S. case. The stochastic cointegration restriction cannot be rejected by the $H(1,q)$ tests with $q = 2,3,4$ in the South Korea/Japan and South Korea/U.S. cases.

6.4.7 Cointegrating Regression Results

In addition to the stationarity restriction, our model imposes restrictions on the signs of coefficients in the cointegrating regressions. In this subsection, I investigate the signs of coefficient estimates as a way to evaluate the economic significance of the model. Table 6.4 reports the cointegrating regression results using Park's (1992) canonical cointegrating regression (CCR) procedure and Phillips and Hansen's (1990) fully modified (FM) estimation procedure. When heterogeneous utility functions are assumed in estimation, coefficient estimates are generally inconsistent with the predictions of the model. These results make at least two points clear. First, private consumption can account for the long-run movement of the real exchange rate. Second, if we take the restrictions on the signs of coefficients imposed by the model seriously, it is necessary to refine the specifications of preferences so that private consumption will have consistent effects on the real exchange rate.

ble 6.4　　　　　　**Cointegrating Regressions of Real Exchange Rates on Private Consumption**

ce Index Equation	$\alpha_x\theta_z$	$\hat{\alpha}_x\hat{\theta}_z$	$\alpha_z\theta_z$	$\hat{\alpha}_z\hat{\theta}_z$
		South Korea/Japan		
I				
Eq. (6)	1.502*/1.462*	−0.686/−0.804	2.778*/2.775*	1.159/1.057
Eq. (7)	1.669*/1.628*		2.488*/2.452*	
PI				
Eq. (6)	1.341*/1.267*	−0.591/−0.786	3.546*/3.543*	1.298/1.113
Eq. (7)	1.241*/1.209*		2.756*/2.728*	
		South Korea/United States		
'I				
Eq. (6)	2.657*/2.653*	1.477*/1.503*	1.864*/1.826*	2.662*/2.767*
Eq. (7)	2.061*/2.057*		1.625*/1.601*	
PI				
Eq. (6)	1.686*/1.682*	1.233*/1.236*	1.728*/1.707*	2.425*/2.439*
Eq. (7)	1.427*/1.424*		1.721*/1.700*	
		Taiwan/Japan		
'I				
Eq. (6)	−8.731*/−8.476*	0.032/−0.073	−5.225*/−5.087*	3.770*/3.749*
Eq. (7)	−1.222/−1.232		−0.342/−0.331	
PI				
Eq. (6)	−5.414*/−5.331*	−0.476/−0.498	−3.114*/−3.068*	2.923*/2.964*
Eq. (7)	−1.364/−1.343		−0.270/−0.255	
		Taiwan/United States		
ʔI				
Eq. (6)	−0.791/−0.943	1.462*/1.475*	−1.841*/−1.945*	2.784*/2.824*
Eq. (7)	0.657*/0.646*		−0.673*/−0.700*	
PI				
Eq. (6)	0.149/−0.064	0.698*/0.741*	−0.815/−0.961	2.078*/2.213*
Eq. (7)	0.226/0.215		−0.487*/−0.512*	

ote: In each entry A/B, A denotes Park's (1992) CCR estimate, and B denotes Phillips and Hansen's 990) FM estimate.

significant at the 5 percent level.

When utility functions are identical across two countries, I found that estimates of $\alpha_x\theta_z$ and $\alpha_z\theta_z$ have theoretically correct signs in the South Korea/Japan and South Korea/U.S. cases. Note that α_x/α_z measures the ratio of income elasticities of z_t and x_t in South Korea. The implied value of α_x/α_z is less (greater) than one in the South Korea/Japan (South Korea/U.S.) case. The unstable ratio across the two cases indicates that the model does not perform well in this respect. As revealed in figures 6.1 and 6.3, South Korea experienced mild real appreciation against both the U.S. dollar and the Japanese yen, and $x_t - \hat{x}_t$ and $z_t - \hat{z}_t$ both exhibit clear upward trends in these cases. To account for the more significant upward trend in real exchange rate, the risk aversion for nontraded good consumption must be higher in the South Korea/Japan case.

For the Taiwan/Japan case, I had theoretically wrong signs for the estimates of $\alpha_x\theta_z$ and $\alpha_z\theta_z$. The bilateral real exchange rate between Taiwan and Japan exhibits a downward trend, which reflects the depreciation of NT dollars against Japanese yen in the sample period. Since Taiwan experienced relatively more rapid growth in x_t and z_t, as displayed in figure 6.3, coefficient estimates for $x_t - \hat{x}_t$ and $x_t - \hat{z}_t$ must switch sign to account for the declining pattern of the real exchange rate. Facing continuing real appreciation of the Japanese yen in the two-country world economy, private agents in Japan are expected to increase their consumption of traded goods by increasing imports from Taiwan, while those in Taiwan are expected to substitute relatively cheaper nontraded goods for more expensive traded goods. Since Taiwan had increasing trade deficits with Japan in the sample period, the substitution effects in the two-country world economy cannot be a crucial element in the determination of real exchange rate movements. Finally, I found that the coefficient estimates of $\alpha_z \theta_z$ have wrong signs in the Taiwan/U.S. case. When Taiwan experienced a significant real appreciation against the U.S. dollar, my model predicts that private agents in Taiwan enjoyed less rapid growth in the consumption of nontraded goods. When the upward trend in cross-country disparity in traded good consumption is not significant enough in accounting for the real appreciation, it forces the sign of the $\alpha_z \theta_z$ estimate to change.

6.4.8   Private Consumption versus Government Consumption

An alternative explanation of the long-run movement of the real exchange rate was recently proposed by Froot and Rogoff (1991). The channel linking government consumption expenditure and the real exchange rate can be described as follows. When a larger fraction of government consumption falls on nontraded goods than does private consumption, an increase in government consumption increases the real appreciation of domestic currency against foreign currency. Those countries that experienced real appreciation against foreign currency enjoyed relatively more rapid growth in government consumption expenditure.

Table 6.5 shows the results of cointegrating regressions of the real exchange rate on private consumption and government consumption:

$$(8) \qquad q_t = \alpha_x \theta_z x_t - \hat{\alpha}_x \hat{\theta}_z \hat{x}_t - \alpha_z \theta_z z_t + \hat{\alpha}_z \hat{\theta}_z \hat{z}_t + \gamma g_t - \hat{\gamma} \hat{g}_t + v_t',$$

in which g_t and $\hat{g}_t$ are per capita real government consumption expenditure in the home country and foreign country, respectively. If government consumption expenditure is assumed to fall totally on nontraded goods, then the movement of private consumption of nontraded goods completely reflects that of government consumption spending. Hence, we expect that the coefficient estimates of γ and $\hat{\gamma}$ are insignificantly different from zero once private consumption of traded and nontraded goods is a regressor in the cointegrating regressions. In general, we expect that $\gamma > 0$ and $\hat{\gamma} > 0$. The evidence in table 6.5 indicates that the empirical relationships between the real exchange rate and private consumption are not significantly affected by the presence of government consumption expenditure in the cointegrating regressions. The data show

Table 6.5   Cointegrating Regressions of Real Exchange Rates on Private Consumption and Government Consumption

Price Index and Equation	$\alpha_x\theta_z$	$\hat{\alpha}_x\hat{\theta}_z$	$\alpha_z\theta_z$	$\alpha_z\hat{\theta}_z$	γ	$\hat{\gamma}$
South Korea/Japan						
CPI						
Eq. (8)	1.671*/1.655*	−0.774/−0.832	2.886*/2.743*	1.011/0.834	−0.076/−0.067	−0.235/−0.468
Eq. (9)	1.214*/1.272*		2.335*/2.348*		0.227/0.182	
WPI						
Eq. (8)	1.564*/1.513*	−0.629/−0.746	3.513*/3.285*	0.948/0.665	−0.067/−0.051	−0.586/−0.934
Eq. (9)	0.785/0.839*		2.644*/2.658*		0.233/0.192	
South Korea/United States						
CPI						
Eq. (8)	2.304*/2.327*	1.367*/1.306*	1.110*/1.171*	3.749*/3.585*	0.005/0.003	0.912*/0.910*
Eq. (9)	1.611*/1.666*		1.292*/1.343*		0.299*/0.260*	
WPI						
Eq. (8)	1.536*/1.562*	1.311*/1.241*	1.437*/1.513*	3.091*/2.894*	−0.001/−0.002	0.239/0.240
Eq. (9)	1.279*/1.295*		1.677*/1.685*		0.104*/0.091*	
Taiwan/Japan						
CPI						
Eq. (8)	−9.457*/−9.333*	3.070*/2.803*	−5.555*/−5.495*	4.775*/4.690*	1.694*/1.588*	0.542/0.515
Eq. (9)	0.440/0.286		0.838/0.785		1.066/1.029	
WPI						
Eq. (8)	−5.715*/−5.635*	1.534*/1.365*	−3.316*/−3.255*	3.591*/3.471*	0.818*/0.794*	0.362/0.347
Eq. (9)	0.148/0.051		0.619/0.584		0.633/0.621	
Taiwan/United States						
CPI						
Eq. (8)	−0.451/−0.569	2.111*/2.114*	−1.645*/−1.755*	3.653*/3.716*	−0.163/−0.231	−0.672*/−0.611*
Eq. (9)	0.912*/0.908*		−0.620/−0.635*		−0.260/−0.257	
WPI						
Eq. (8)	0.693/0.604	1.847*/1.830*	−0.644/−0.708	3.561*/3.565*	−0.406*/−0.426*	−1.029*/−0.992*
Eq. (9)	0.783/0.775*		−0.352/−0.370		−0.557*/−0.529*	

Note: In each entry A/B, A denotes Park's (1992) CCR estimate, and B denotes Phillips and Hansen's (1990) FM estimate. Sample period is 1975:1–1993:4.

*Significant at the 5 percent level.

no evidence of government consumption effects on real exchange rates. Some of the coefficients on government consumption in the home country and foreign country are not statistically different from zero and are even of the wrong sign. The inclusion of government consumption regressors in equation (8) has little effect on the estimates of $\alpha_x \theta_x$, $\hat{\alpha}_x \hat{\theta}_z$, $\alpha_z \theta_z$, and $\hat{\alpha}_z \hat{\alpha}_z$. These remain as statistically significant as before, with the signs for coefficient estimates unchanged.

To access the empirical significance of the cross-country disparity in real government consumption, $g_t - \hat{g}_t$, in the cointegrating regression of equation (7), table 6.5 also presents the results of the following cointegrating regression:

$$(9) \qquad q_t = \alpha_x \theta_z (x_t - \hat{x}_t) - \alpha_z \theta_z (z_t - \hat{z}_t) + \gamma (g_t - \hat{g}_t) + v_t''.$$

I obtain results for the effect of the cross-country disparity in government consumption on the real exchange rate similar to those above. The coefficients on domestic and foreign private consumption become larger and even more statistically significant when $g_t - \hat{g}_t$ is included. But the wrong signs for the estimates of $x_t - \hat{x}_t$ and $z_t - \hat{z}_t$ remain quite severe. Thus accounting for government consumption does not seem to overturn the result that private consumption affects the long-run movement of the real exchange rate.

6.5 Concluding Remarks

The empirical evidence suggests that private consumption in home and foreign countries provides a significant component of the explanation of long-run movements in the real exchange rate in South Korea and Taiwan. Based on the signs of coefficient estimates in the cointegrating regressions, it seems that private consumption may not be a reliable fundamental that has reliable effects on the real exchange rate.

It is useful to incorporate supply-side elements such as productivity differentials in a general equilibrium model of real exchange rate determination and explore the trend and cyclical implications from equilibrium relationships obtained in the model. Since fluctuations in the relative price of traded goods account for a significant fraction of real exchange rate movements, another interesting topic for future research is to estimate equation (5).

References

Adler, Michael, and B. Lehmann. 1983. Deviations from purchasing power parity in the long run. *Journal of Finance* 38:1471–87.
Andrews, Donald W. K. 1991. Heteroskedasticity and autocorrelation consistent covariance matrix estimation. *Econometrica* 59:817–58.
Backus, David K., and G. W. Smith. 1993. Consumption and real exchange rates in dynamic economies with non-traded goods. *Journal of International Economics* 35: 297–316.

Balassa, Bela. 1964. The purchasing-power parity: A reappraisal. *Journal of Political Economy* 72:584–96.

Campbell, J. Y., and P. Perron. 1991. Pitfalls and opportunities: What macroeconomists should know about unit roots. In *NBER macroeconomics annual 1991,* ed. O. Blanchard and S. Fischer, 141–201. Cambridge, Mass.: MIT Press.

Devereux, M. B., A. W. Gregory, and G. W. Smith. 1992. Realistic cross-country consumption correlations in a two-country, equilibrium, business cycle model. *Journal of International Money and Finance* 11:3–16.

Fisher, Eric O., and J. Y. Park. 1991. Testing purchasing power parity under the null hypothesis of co-integration. *Economic Journal* 101:1476–84.

Froot, K. A., and K. Rogoff. 1991. The EMS, the EMU, and the transition to a common currency. In *NBER macroeconomics annual 1991,* ed. O. Blanchard and S. Fischer, 269–371. Cambridge, Mass.: MIT Press.

Helpman, Elhanan, and Assaf Razin. 1982. A comparison of exchange rate regimes in the presence of imperfect capital markets. *International Economic Review* 23: 365–88.

Hsieh, David A. 1982. The determination of the real exchange rate: The productivity approach. *Journal of International Economics* 12:355–62.

Huizinga, John. 1987. An empirical investigation of the long run behavior of real exchange rate. *Carnegie-Rochester Conference Series on Public Policy* 27:149–214.

Kahn, James A., and M. Ogaki. 1992. A consistent test for the null of stationarity against the alternative of a unit root. *Economics Letters* 39:7–11.

Kakkar, Vikas, and M. Ogaki. 1993. Real exchange rates and nontradables. Rochester, N.Y.: University of Rochester. Manuscript.

Kim, Yoonbai. 1990. Purchasing power parity: Another look at the long-run data. *Economics Letters* 32:339–44.

Kravis, Irving B., and R. E. Lipsey. 1987. The assessment of national price levels. In *Real and financial linkages among open economies,* ed. S. W. Arndt and J. D. Richardson, 97–134. Cambridge, Mass.: MIT Press.

Lewis, Karen K. 1996. What can explain the apparent lack of international consumption risk sharing? *Journal of Political Economy* 104:267–97.

Lucas, Robert E., Jr. 1982. Interest rates and currency prices in a two-country world. *Journal of Monetary Economics* 10:335–60.

Ogaki, Masao. 1992. Engel's law and cointegration. *Journal of Political Economy* 100: 1027–46.

Ogaki, Masao, and Y. Y. Park. 1989. A cointegration approach to estimating preference parameters. Rochester, N.Y.: University of Rochester. Manuscript.

Park, Joon Y. 1992. Canonical cointegrating regressions. *Econometrica* 60:119–43.

Park, Joon Y., and B. Choi. 1988. A new approach to testing for a unit root. Ithaca, N.Y.: Cornell University. Mimeograph.

Phillips, P. C. B., and B. E. Hansen. 1990. Statistical inference in instrumental variables regression with $I(1)$ processes. *Review of Economic Studies* 57:99–125.

Samuelson, Paul. 1964. Theoretical note on trade problems. *Review of Economics and Statistics* 46:145–54.

Stockman, Alan C., and L. L. Tesar. 1995. Tastes and technology in a two-country model of the business cycle: Explaining international comovements. *American Economic Review* 85:168–85.

Strauss, Jack. 1996. The cointegrating relationship between productivity, real exchange rates and purchasing power parity. *Journal of Macroeconomics* 18:299–313.

Stulz, Rene M. 1987. An equilibrium model of exchange rate determination and asset pricing with non-traded goods and imperfect information. *Journal of Political Economy* 95:1024–40.

Comment   Yun-Wing Sung

This paper is interesting because it approaches the long-run behavior of real exchange rates from the demand side instead of the more usual supply side. The paper also contains a vast amount of empirical tests and statistical results.

In the empirical tests, four different sets of stationarity assumptions were used for identification. Each assumption was tested for four different cases of real exchange rate movements between (i) South Korea and Japan, (ii) South Korea and the United States, (iii) Taiwan and Japan, and (iv) Taiwan and the United States. For each of these cases, two measures of the real exchange rate were used: one by the CPI and the other by the WPI. There were thus a total of 32 cases (4 × 4 × 2).

The empirical results were disappointing. In quite a lot of cases, the stationarity assumptions required for identification were not satisfied. In the cases where the stationarity assumptions were satisfied, the regression coefficients were often the wrong signs or were insignificant. Among the 32 cases, only two cases (the real exchange rate between South Korea and the United States measured by the CPI and by the WPI under one set of assumptions) gave good results, that is, significant regression coefficients with the right signs.

While a researcher always hopes for good empirical results, he or she may not find them, and the fault may not be with the researcher. Maybe the real world is too complicated for even the best methodology, or maybe the data are deficient. A paper should not be judged merely by its empirical results.

In terms of exposition, the paper could certainly be improved. The paper is rich in technical details and statistical tests but short on economics and interpretation of results. For instance, the author did not give the motivation for the demand-side approach. Though I am not familiar with this approach, I think it may be superior to the more traditional supply-side approach of Balassa and Samuelson in several ways. In the supply-side approach, the behavior of the real exchange rate hinges on differential changes in productivity between tradables and nontradables, and productivity change in nontradables (services) is notoriously difficult to measure. In the demand-side approach, the real exchange rate is positively (negatively) related to the ratio of consumption of traded (nontraded) goods in the two countries, and the consumption of traded and nontraded goods is much easier to measure than productivity change in these goods, especially in nontraded goods.

Some assumptions of the demand-side approach are less stringent than those of the supply-side approach, and this can be an important advantage. The demand-side approach requires the equalization of the marginal rates of substitution in consumption across countries. Under free trade, this is generally true except when there are quantitative restrictions on consumption, which is rare.

Yun-Wing Sung is professor in and chairman of the economics department at the Chinese University of Hong Kong.

In general, it can be claimed that market imperfections on the demand side are much less likely than those on the supply side. However, the demand-side approach requires an additive utility function, and the author did not make clear what limitations this would imply.

The author summarized the results of his cointegrating regressions in about one page, and very little economic interpretation was given for any of the results. The paper would benefit from more discussion of the pros and cons of the demand-side approach, the economics behind the assumptions used in identification, and careful interpretations of the economics of the results.

Comment   Gian Maria Milesi-Ferretti

In recent years a number of theoretical and empirical studies have examined the determinants of real exchange rates (see the excellent survey by Froot and Rogoff 1995). Most of these studies have focused on supply-side factors, such as differences in productivity growth rates within a country (between the traded and the nontraded goods sectors) and across countries. This paper focuses instead on demand-side determinants of the real exchange rate and tests the implications of a simple theoretical model on bilateral real exchange rate data between Taiwan and Korea, on the one side, and Japan and the United States, on the other side.

The theoretical analysis links real exchange rate changes to the dynamics of the terms of trade and of relative consumption growth and shows in particular that the real exchange rate should appreciate (depreciate) when traded (nontraded) goods consumption growth in the home country increases relative to consumption growth in the foreign country.

The link between the real exchange rate, the terms of trade, and cross-country consumption ratios of traded and nontraded goods can be easily understood in the following simplified setting. Assume that preferences and the weights of traded and nontraded goods in the price index are the same across countries and that the utility function is separable in the two goods and exhibits constant intertemporal elasticity of substitution. In this case the relative price of nontraded goods in terms of traded goods is equal to the ratio of marginal utilities, which in turn is inversely proportional to the consumption ratio of nontraded and traded goods:

$$(1) \qquad \frac{P_N}{P_T} = \frac{C_N^{-\alpha_N}}{C_T^{-\alpha_T}},$$

Gian Maria Milesi-Ferretti is an economist in the research department of the International Monetary Fund and a research fellow of the Centre for Economic Policy Research.

where the α terms are the inverse of the intertemporal elasticities of substitution. An analogous expression obtains for the foreign country. The (logarithm of the) real exchange rate q is defined as

(2) $q = (p_T - s - p_T^*) + \theta_N[(p_N - p_T) - (p_N^* - p_T^*)],$

where lowercase variables indicate logs, an asterisk indicates "foreign" variables, s is the nominal exchange rate between the domestic and the foreign currency, and θ_N is the weight of nontraded goods in the price index of both countries. Taking logs of equation (1) and inserting it into equation (2) we obtain the result that the real exchange rate is a function of the relative price of traded goods across countries (itself a function of the terms of trade) and of the relative consumption of nontraded and traded goods across countries:

(3) $q = (p_T - s - p_T^*) + \theta_N[\alpha_T(c_T - c_T^*) - \alpha_N(c_N - c_N^*)].$

The paper derives more general forms of equation (3), considering the case in which there are two traded goods, and tests the theoretically implied restrictions on the time-series properties of the real exchange rate and consumption series. The author uses an impressive array of state-of-the-art tests to characterize these time-series properties. I have nothing useful to say about the tests, other than ritually recalling their limited power when the time series is short. I feel, however, that the paper could be improved by (i) providing better links between its different parts and (ii) integrating this demand-side approach with supply-side considerations.

With regard to the first point, the econometric specification section should rely more clearly on the results of the univariate time-series analysis of the real exchange rate and consumption series. For example, if unit root tests provide evidence of level stationarity for a series (e.g., consumption of tradables in Japan or the United States), then it seems inappropriate to run cointegrating regressions that treat that same variable as a difference-stationary one. Also, some economic interpretation of the empirical results would help to improve the link between theoretical and quantitative analysis and would provide the reader with a feel for the performance of the model. Finally, since we know the composition of the CPI and WPI, it seems logical and straightforward to use the results of the empirical analysis to draw inferences about the underlying preference parameters.

With regard to the second point, it should not be difficult in future work to incorporate supply-side considerations into this paper's basic theoretical structure and empirical analysis. For example, theoretically it is sufficient to extend the endowment model to allow for production and productivity growth. Indeed, a number of authors have studied theoretically and empirically both demand- and supply-side determinants of real exchange rates (see, e.g., Froot and Rogoff 1991; De Gregorio, Giovannini, and Krueger 1994), although they did not rely on the time-series properties of consumption series.

On a more general note, a nice aspect of this paper's approach is that it establishes links between the real exchange rate and consumption variables, which are in general more readily available than productivity data. The issue, of course, is how far one can get in explaining real exchange rate behavior relying solely on these variables. In the empirical analysis carried out in the paper, terms-of-trade fluctuations are not explicitly considered, and the focus is on variables explaining the relative price of nontraded goods in terms of traded goods within countries, under the assumption that the law of one price holds for traded goods. A general problem plaguing real exchange rate analysis based on the supply-side, Balassa-Samuelson approach is that intersectoral productivity differentials are good predictors of the relative price of nontraded goods in terms of traded goods but poor predictors of real exchange rate behavior (see, e.g., Asea and Mendoza 1994). This empirical result reflects the widely documented fact that fluctuations in the relative price of traded goods account for a significant fraction of real exchange rate changes. It seems therefore that future research in this area cannot abstract from the examination of determinants of the terms of trade. This paper's theoretical analysis is a step in this direction; the task is now to make it empirically implementable.

References

Asea, Patrick K., and Enrique G. Mendoza. 1994. The Balassa-Samuelson model: An Euler equation approach. *Review of International Economics* 2:244–67.
De Gregorio, José, Alberto Giovannini, and Thomas Krueger. 1994. The behavior of non-tradable prices in Europe: Evidence and interpretation. *Review of International Economics* 2 (October): 284–305.
Froot, Kenneth, and Kenneth Rogoff. 1991. The EMS, the EMU, and the transition to a common currency. In *NBER macroeconomics annual,* ed. Olivier Blanchard and Stanley Fischer, 269–317. Cambridge, Mass.: MIT Press.
———. 1995. Perspectives on PPP and long-run real exchange rates. In *Handbook of international economics,* vol. 3, ed. Gene M. Grossman and Kenneth Rogoff. Amsterdam: Elsevier.

7   The Yen and Its East Asian Neighbors, 1980–1995: Cooperation or Competition?

Shinji Takagi

7.1   Introduction

There has recently been a marked increase in real economic integration among the Asian countries. For example, the share of intraregional trade in the total exports of Asia (which excludes Japan) rose from 30.9 percent in 1986 to 45.7 percent in 1994, while the share of exports to the United States declined from 34.0 to 24.5 percent during the same period (Kwan 1995). In the rapidly industrializing economies of Asia, the share of Japan is now considerably larger than that of the United States in imports, although not in exports (table 7.1). Japan is at least equal in importance to the United States as a trading partner of most Asian countries.

Despite the increasing pace of intraregional integration, the declining share of the United States in international trade, and the significant status of Japan as a trading partner, the exchange rate policies of most East Asian countries remain that of limiting fluctuations in the nominal values of their currencies relative to the U.S. dollar in one form or another. Most empirical studies as well as casual observation seem to suggest that the U.S. dollar remains strong, and the Japanese yen remains marginal, as the anchor of exchange rate policies in the region.

Against this background, the paper will examine the role of the Japanese yen in the exchange rate policies of selected Asian countries,[1] namely, Korea, Singapore, Malaysia, Indonesia, the Philippines, and Thailand. This is not a

Shinji Takagi is professor of economics at the University of Osaka.

The author thanks Takatoshi Ito, K. C. Fung, Tetsuji Okazaki, Andrew Rose, and an anonymous reader for useful comments. Needless to say, the author alone is responsible for any remaining errors.

1. In discussing the role of the yen in Asia, there is also the separate question of how widely the yen is used in intraregional transactions. The emphasis of the paper, however, is strictly on the importance of the yen in the determination of the nominal values of East Asian currencies.

Table 7.1   Import and Export Shares of the United States, Japan, and European Union
in Selected Asian Countries, 1994 (percent of total)

Country	Imports			Exports			Total Trade		
	U.S.	Japan	EU	U.S.	Japan	EU	U.S.	Japan	EU
Korea	21.6	25.4	13.0	21.4	14.1	10.6	21.2	19.6	11.
Singapore	15.3	22.0	12.1	18.8	7.0	13.0	17.0	14.7	12.
Malaysia	16.6	26.7	13.5	21.2	11.9	13.9	18.9	19.4	13.
Indonesia	10.1	27.6	18.5	16.8	30.9	16.7	13.8	29.4	17.
Philippines	18.5	24.2	10.3	38.5	15.0	17.1	26.0	20.8	12.
Thailand	11.3	30.4	14.4	23.2	18.0	15.7	16.5	25.0	15.

Source: IMF, *Direction of Trade Statistics Yearbook* (Washington, D.C., 1995).

new topic. The widely cited study by Frankel and Wei (1994), for example, has examined this very issue by econometrically estimating the implicit weights of the U.S. dollar and the Japanese yen in the determination of the nominal values of major Asian currencies. The present study is meant to complement the empirical findings obtained from the econometric approach by taking the alternative approach of observing currency movements when the Japanese yen fluctuates sharply in one direction against the U.S. dollar.

To be sure, the monetary authorities of Asian countries must assign different weights to variables that may enter the objective functions of their exchange rate policies, such as price stability, stability of nominal effective exchange rate indexes, stability of real effective exchange rate indexes, encouragement or discouragement of capital flows, accumulation of foreign exchange reserves, and export promotion. Thus the role of the yen in the exchange rate policy of a given country cannot be independent of the domestic and international environments within which the authorities are forced to operate. In this context, it is important to bear in mind that during the past 15 years or so, the yen significantly appreciated against the U.S. dollar in both nominal and real terms (table 7.2). In this environment, the decision to minimize fluctuations against the yen would have meant that the authorities must accept some appreciation of their currency against the U.S. dollar and other Asian currencies.

If a large weight is given to export promotion in the objective function of the authorities, they may have been reluctant to tie their currency too closely to the appreciating yen, to the extent that nominal currency appreciation may work to reduce the growth of exports in the short run. Thus, ex post, the currency in question must have moved closely with the U.S. dollar and depreciated against the yen, such that its relationship with the yen may be characterized as "competitive" in that, relative to the yen, exchange rate stability was willingly sacrificed in favor of depreciation to preserve competitiveness.

On the other hand, if a large weight is given to price stability, the authorities may have been less willing to tolerate nominal depreciation and hence higher domestic inflation, by tying the currency too closely to the U.S. dollar. This

Table 7.2   **Nominal and Real Exchange Rates of the Japanese Yen against the U.S. Dollar and Selected Asian Currencies, 1980–95 (annual averages, 1990 = 100)**

Year	United States Nominal	United States Real	Korea Nominal	Korea Real	Singapore Nominal	Singapore Real	Malaysia Nominal	Malaysia Real	Indonesia Nominal	Indonesia Real	Philippines Nominal	Philippines Real	Thailand Nominal	Thailand Real
1980	63.9	91.5	54.8	83.8	75.4	72.8	51.4	n.a.	21.7	63.0	19.7	94.2	73.3	109.6
1981	65.7	87.5	63.2	81.3	76.5	72.1	55.9	n.a.	22.5	60.2	21.3	90.1	78.3	108.4
1982	58.1	77.3	60.0	75.2	68.6	68.7	50.2	n.a.	20.9	52.5	20.4	79.5	66.4	92.8
1983	61.0	78.3	66.8	81.6	71.1	72.2	52.3	n.a.	30.1	61.8	27.9	91.4	67.1	89.8
1984	61.0	76.3	69.4	84.0	71.7	73.2	52.8	63.1	33.9	61.5	41.9	82.0	66.7	91.9
1985	60.7	75.5	74.6	88.5	73.7	76.0	55.7	67.2	36.6	62.8	46.5	76.0	64.9	88.4
1986	85.9	99.9	107.0	116.9	103.2	113.9	82.0	95.8	59.8	86.0	72.0	108.9	78.0	97.0
1987	101.1	109.3	116.3	121.9	116.3	115.0	93.2	101.1	89.3	107.4	84.7	113.0	97.7	110.4
1988	113.0	117.3	116.8	117.9	125.4	125.1	109.4	109.4	103.4	111.5	98.0	114.2	108.2	111.9
1989	105.0	106.5	99.6	101.6	112.9	112.6	105.1	103.9	100.8	104.5	93.8	101.3	103.2	104.6
1990	100.0	100.0	100.0	100.0	100.0	100.0	100.0	100.0	100.0	100.0	100.0	100.0	100.0	100.0
1991	107.5	107.5	111.4	106.6	102.4	107.0	109.3	105.3	113.8	106.1	121.5	107.3	103.1	96.7
1992	114.3	112.0	126.1	116.3	102.7	110.6	107.7	101.0	125.9	109.1	120.0	99.8	104.8	96.7
1993	130.2	120.9	147.7	129.2	116.1	125.7	123.9	110.3	147.5	114.9	145.3	117.6	114.2	101.8
1994	141.7	127.2	160.8	134.0	119.4	127.2	137.4	114.2	166.1	114.8	153.9	112.8	123.7	103.8
1995	153.9	132.3	167.7	132.4	120.4	127.0	142.5	111.3	187.8	112.7	162.8	114.6	134.5	103.5

Source: IMF, *International Financial Statistics* (Washington, D.C., various issues); author's estimates.

Note: Bilateral real exchange rate indexes are based on wholesale prices; an increase in the index means an appreciation of the yen against the currency of the country concerned.

may be a particularly pertinent consideration, given the significant share of Japanese goods in total imports. In this case, ex post, the currency in question must have moved with the yen and appreciated against the U.S. dollar to a greater extent, and its relationship with the yen may be regarded as "cooperative," in that such behavior has tended to contribute to monetary cooperation in Asia by promoting greater exchange rate stability in the environment of secular yen appreciation.

Occasionally, however, the yen did depreciate against the U.S. dollar on a sustained basis. On such occasions, the considerations of export promotion and price stability would have created exactly the opposite kind of reaction to the yen's fluctuation on the part of the monetary authorities. With greater emphasis on export promotion, the authorities would have been more willing to allow the currency concerned to depreciate along with the yen against the U.S. dollar. With more emphasis on price stability, they would have been more unwilling to allow the currency to depreciate along with the yen. Thus, in the case of yen depreciation, export promotion would have encouraged greater exchange rate stability within Asia. However, throughout this paper, emphasis on price stability is regarded as "cooperative" behavior because, for the period taken as a whole, it has contributed more to promoting exchange rate stability within Asia.

The rest of the paper is organized as follows. Section 7.2 reviews the exchange rate arrangements of the six Asian countries, with some comments on the nominal and real exchange rate movements. Section 7.3 summarizes the econometric estimates of the implicit weights of the U.S. dollar and the Japanese yen in the determination of the nominal values of the currencies of the six Asian countries, as reported by Frankel and Wei (1994) and the more recent study of Kwan (1995). Section 7.4 provides additional insight into the relative weights of the U.S. dollar and the Japanese yen in the determination of the values of the six Asian currencies by looking at how they move when the yen fluctuates sharply against the dollar. Sections 7.5 and 7.6 take a look at the daily movements of the six Asian currencies during the periods of sharp yen appreciation and depreciation in the late 1980s and in 1995, respectively, in order to assess the response of the monetary authorities when the yen fluctuates sharply against the U.S. dollar. Section 7.7 presents concluding remarks.

7.2   An Overview of Exchange Rate Arrangements and Movements of Selected Asian Countries

At the outset, it may be useful to review briefly the exchange rate arrangements of the six individual countries. According to official statements, Korea, Singapore, Malaysia, and Indonesia are classified as maintaining "other managed floating" rates, while Thailand maintains a peg to a currency composite, or a currency basket (International Monetary Fund [IMF] 1994). Of the six countries, only the Philippines is classified as maintaining a floating exchange rate system. In practice, however, Indonesia and the Philippines are similar in that the rupiah and the peso are both managed tightly in terms of their U.S. dollar exchange rates over a short time horizon, while they have shown significant trend depreciation over a longer horizon (table 7.2); their exchange rate systems may more appropriately be classified as crawling pegs to the dollar.

Consistent with the crawling peg arrangement, both the Indonesian rupiah and the Philippine peso depreciated significantly against the U.S. dollar in nominal terms over the period 1980–95: the rupiah depreciated from 627 to 2,249 units per U.S. dollar, and the peso moved from 7.51 to 25.71 units per U.S. dollar, both on an annual average basis. In contrast, the other currencies showed relative stability against the U.S. dollar over this period. The Korean won first depreciated from 607.43 to 881.45 units per U.S. dollar between 1980 and 1986 but then appreciated to 671.46 units per U.S. dollar in 1989. The Singapore dollar showed a fairly steady appreciation against the U.S. dollar, rising from 2.14 to 1.42 units per U.S. dollar between 1980 and 1995. The Malaysian ringgit and the Thai baht depreciated at a modest pace against the U.S. dollar, with the ringgit falling from 2.18 to 2.50 units per U.S. dollar and the baht from 20.48 to 24.80 units per U.S. dollar over the period.

In real bilateral terms (on a wholesale price basis), the Korean won, the Singapore dollar, the Malaysian ringgit, and the Indonesian rupiah generally depreciated against both the U.S. dollar and the Japanese yen over the period, although they became much more stable during the latter part of the period (table 7.2). The Philippine peso, in contrast, appreciated in real terms against the U.S. dollar, although it depreciated against the Japanese yen over the period. Reflecting the higher rate of inflation, it even appreciated against the Japanese yen from 1988 to 1990 despite the significant nominal depreciation. Finally, the Thai baht appreciated against both the U.S. dollar and the Japanese yen over the period.

7.2.1   Korea

From February 1980 to March 1990, the won was officially linked to a basket of currencies, although it was effectively pegged to the U.S. dollar. On 2 March 1990, however, the Korean authorities adopted the "market average rate" (MAR) system, by which the dollar exchange rate is in principle determined by supply and demand conditions in the market, subject to a type of daily price limit. The Bank of Korea sets the won-dollar rate on the basis of a weighted average of interbank rates for spot transactions of the previous day. On each business day, the won-dollar exchange rate in the interbank market is allowed to fluctuate within fixed margins (currently, 1 percent on either side) against the MAR of the previous day.

The real exchange rates of the Korean won against the U.S. dollar and the Japanese yen closely followed the nominal exchange rates because the rate of inflation only slightly exceeded those in the United States and Japan. Over the period 1980–95, the Korean won depreciated against both the U.S. dollar and the Japanese yen, naturally with the extent of depreciation against the yen being much more significant. From 1990 to 1994, although the won remained relatively stable against the dollar, it depreciated by as much as 34 percent against the yen. From 1994 to 1995, however, it marginally appreciated against the yen.

7.2.2   Singapore

The Monetary Authority of Singapore (MAS) "monitors the external value of the Singapore dollar against a trade-weighted basket of currencies, with the objective of promoting noninflationary sustainable economic growth" (IMF 1994). In Singapore, the central bank functions are performed by the Board of Commissioners of Currency (currency board) and the MAS. The currency board issues and redeems currency notes and coins, as demanded and backed by foreign assets. The MAS intervenes in the foreign exchange market whenever the exchange rate is out of line with the undisclosed target, which may well be changed from time to time. Given the openness and the small size of the economy, price stability is paramount as an objective of exchange rate policy (Toh 1996).[2]

In real terms, the Singapore dollar depreciated against both the U.S. dollar and the Japanese yen over the entire period 1980–95. From 1986 to 1990, however, the Singapore dollar appreciated against both currencies. From 1990 to 1994, it depreciated against the yen by almost 30 percent, while it remained stable against the U.S. dollar; from 1994 to 1995, it marginally appreciated against the yen. Judging from the behavior of the real exchange rate, it appears that, from about 1986, price stability became a particularly important objective of Singapore's exchange rate policy.

7.2.3   Malaysia

From September 1975, the value of the ringgit has been determined by supply and demand conditions in the foreign exchange market by Bank Nagara Malaysia with reference to the value determined by a basket of currencies of the country's major trading partners (Ong 1996). According to the IMF (1994), the central bank is said to intervene "only to maintain orderly market conditions and to avoid excessive fluctuations in the value of the ringgit."

In real terms, the ringgit depreciated against both the U.S. dollar and the Japanese yen over the entire sample period. The depreciation was particularly substantial against the yen. From 1990, however, the ringgit began to appreciate moderately against the U.S. dollar, in line with its nominal appreciation. However, it continued to depreciate against the yen until 1994, at which time it began to appreciate somewhat.

---

2. The term "low and stable domestic inflation" appeared as the official objective of Singapore's exchange rate policy for the first time in the 1989 issue of the IMF's annual report *Exchange Arrangements and Exchange Restrictions.*

7.2.4 Indonesia

With the devaluation of the rupiah in November 1978, the link with the U.S. dollar was discontinued, and the middle rate of the rupiah began to be determined by the value of a basket of currencies and other considerations, subject to periodic devaluations. Following the 45 percent devaluation of September 1986, however, Bank Indonesia launched the exchange rate policy of maintaining the real effective exchange rate at a stable level in order to maintain Indonesia's competitiveness in the light of higher domestic inflation relative to its major trading partners (Goelton 1996). From 1986 to 1994, the rupiah thus depreciated at a rate of roughly 5 percent against the U.S. dollar per year in nominal terms.

Bank Indonesia continues to set the middle or reference rate of the rupiah in terms of the U.S. dollar by taking into account the behavior of a basket of currencies of Indonesia's major trading partners. In September 1994, however, Bank Indonesia ceased to announce the middle rate and at the same time began to widen the intervention band around the middle rate in order to increase the risk of speculation in the rupiah. Currently, the intervention band is approximately 3 percent on either side of the now undisclosed reference rate against the U.S. dollar.

Although the Indonesian rupiah depreciated against both the U.S. dollar and the Japanese yen over the entire period in real terms, it remained much more stable after 1986, in line with the stated objective of the exchange rate policy. In fact, it appreciated in real terms against the U.S. dollar by about 20 percent from 1990 to 1995, while it depreciated against the yen by about 13 percent, indicating that the Indonesian authorities are concerned about the stability of the real effective exchange rate of the rupiah, in which the yen must have significant weight.

7.2.5 Philippines

Prior to October 1984, the central bank had intervened to keep the peso-dollar exchange rate within a certain target range. Since then, the value of the peso has in principle been determined freely in the foreign exchange market, though it is apparent that the central bank controls short-run fluctuations in the exchange rate. With the major liberalization of the foreign exchange market in 1992, there is presumably a greater role of market forces in the determination of the exchange rate (Cororaton 1996).

Reflecting the much higher and variable rate of inflation in the Philippines as well as the frequency of changes in the target dollar exchange rate, the real exchange rate of the Philippine peso fluctuated greatly against the U.S. dollar and the Japanese yen. From 1990 to 1995, the peso depreciated against the yen by over 14 percent, while it appreciated against the U.S. dollar by nearly 18 percent in real terms. It is possible that, to the extent that the Philippine authorities have allowed the peso to appreciate substantially against the U.S. dollar in real terms, they are paying some attention to the real *effective* exchange rate, in which the yen has significant weight.

7.2.6   Thailand

The Thai baht was de facto pegged to the U.S. dollar from 1981 to November 1984, when it was devalued by 14.7 percent. The baht was subsequently pegged to a weighted basket of currencies of Thailand's major trading partners. The basket is not disclosed, nor is the frequency with which the basket is changed. It is believed, however, that the weight of the U.S. dollar was raised from about 50 percent to over 80 percent when the U.S. dollar began to depreciate sharply against major currencies from late 1985 (Leeahtam 1991).

In the morning of every business day, the Bank of Thailand announces the central rates of major currencies against the baht. For the U.S. dollar, the buying and selling rates are two satang below and above the central rate. In a recent meeting of the Exchange Equalization Fund, however, the governor of the Bank of Thailand is reported to have announced the possibility of widening the band from the current two satang to four satang on either side of the central rate, in order to discourage short-term speculative capital inflows by increasing the cost of investing in the baht (Phatra Research Institute 1996).

In real terms, the Thai baht remained fairly stable against the U.S. dollar from 1980 to 1985, but it began to appreciate sharply from 1985, when the yen began to appreciate against the U.S. dollar. In contrast, while the baht appreciated against the yen during the earlier period in real terms (reflective of the fact that it was pegged to the appreciating dollar), it remained fairly stable against the yen in real terms from 1986 to 1995. As a result, from 1990 to 1995, the baht appreciated against the U.S. dollar by nearly 30 percent.

7.3   Implicit Weights of the U.S. Dollar and the Japanese Yen: A Review of Frankel and Wei (1994) and Kwan (1995)

The widely cited study by Frankel and Wei (1994) was the first to estimate econometrically the implicit weights of the U.S. dollar and the Japanese yen in the determination of the nominal values of major Asian currencies during the period 1979–92. This study was replicated by Kwan (1995) on the basis of more recent data. Their major findings, summarized in table 7.3, seem to show that the dominant weight is given to the U.S. dollar in the determination of all six Asian currencies studied here.[3]

According to Frankel and Wei, however, the weight of the yen, although small, was significant in the Singapore dollar and became larger in the Malaysian ringgit and the Thai baht during the latest subperiod of 1991–92 (not reported in the table). The recently increased weight of the yen is reported by

---

3. The reported weights do not necessarily add up to unity because there may be other currencies or variables included in the estimation equations, sometimes with negative weights.

Table 7.3 Implicit Weights of the U.S. Dollar and Japanese Yen in Nominal Values of Selected Asian Currencies

| | Frankel and Wei January 1979–May 1992 (weekly) | | Kwan | | | |
| | | | January 1991–May 1995 (monthly) | | January–August 1995 (weekly) | |
Currency	U.S. Dollar	Japanese Yen	U.S. Dollar	Japanese Yen	U.S. Dollar	Japanese Yen
Korean won	0.96	−0.01	0.9435	0.0623	0.8374	0.1737
Singapore dollar	0.75	0.13	0.6897	0.1052	0.7459	0.1835
Malaysian ringgit	0.78	0.07	0.8411	0.0431	0.8728	0.1561
Indonesian rupiah	0.95	0.16	0.9896	−0.0005	0.9682	0.0102
Philippine peso	1.07	−0.01	1.1464	−0.2359	1.0672	0.0252
Thai baht	0.91	0.05	0.8202	0.1051	0.8593	0.0883

Sources: Frankel and Wei (1994) and Kwan (1995).

Kwan for the Korean won, the Singapore dollar, the Malaysian ringgit, and the Thai baht.

7.3.1 Korea

According to the estimates of Frankel and Wei based on weekly data for the period January 1979–May 1992, the share of the U.S. dollar in the determination of the Korean won was 0.96 while the share of the Japanese yen was practically zero. In fact, they show that the Korean won remained linked more or less to the U.S. dollar even after the introduction of the MAR system in March 1990. This finding is confirmed for the later period of January 1991–May 1995 by Kwan on the basis of monthly data. However, Kwan reports that for the most recent subperiod of January–August 1995, the weight of the dollar declined to 0.8374, while that of the yen increased to 0.1737.

7.3.2 Singapore

According to Frankel and Wei, the Singapore dollar was the only Asian currency that consistently assigned weight to the yen throughout the entire period 1979–92. The weight of the dollar was 0.75, while that of the yen was 0.13, when the weights were calculated for the entire sample. They also show that the weight of the yen doubled in the 1980s from around 5 percent to 10 percent, or from 10 percent to 20 percent, depending on the method of estimation (not reported in the table). For the most recent period, Kwan reports that the weight of the U.S. dollar was 0.7459, while that of the yen was 0.1835.

7.3.3 Malaysia

According to Frankel and Wei, the weight of the yen in the Malaysian ringgit was extremely small in the early 1980s, and even disappeared during the rest of the 1980s, but increased to about 14 percent in the early 1990s (not reported in the table). For the entire period, the weight of the yen was 0.07, while that of the dollar was 0.78. For the later subperiod January 1991–May 1995, however, Kwan assigns virtually zero weight to the yen (0.0431), while greater weight is given to the U.S. dollar (0.8411). For the most recent subperiod January–August 1995, the yen's weight rose to 0.1561, while the share of the U.S. dollar was 0.8728.

7.3.4 Indonesia

Frankel and Wei report that although the Indonesian rupiah remained tightly pegged to the U.S. dollar until 1982, the dollar peg became looser in 1983. In 1985, the yen received significant weight, so much so that the weight exceeded that of the U.S. dollar for the period 1985–86 (not reported in the table). Subsequently, however, the weight of the yen declined, disappearing altogether during the latest subperiod 1991–92 (not reported in the table). For the entire sample period, the weights of the U.S. dollar and the Japanese yen were estimated to be 0.95 and 0.16, respectively. The insignificant weight of the yen in more recent years is confirmed by Kwan for the subperiod January 1991–May 1995 as well as for the subperiod January–August 1995.

7.3.5 Philippines

Although the peso depreciated significantly against the U.S. dollar throughout the period in nominal terms, the estimated weight of the U.S. dollar (about unity) indicates that the peso was closely linked to the U.S. dollar. This suggests that although the peso was devalued from time to time, its fluctuations against the U.S. dollar were strictly managed over shorter intervals.

7.3.6 Thailand

Until 1984, the Thai baht was de facto linked to the U.S. dollar, so that the yen received no weight prior to that year. When the baht was delinked from the dollar, however, the yen began to receive some weight: according to Frankel and Wei, in the neighborhood of 10 percent during 1985–86 when the nominal value of the U.S. dollar was at its peak (not reported in the table). The weight of the yen became smaller during 1987–90 but rose again to 12 percent during the latest subperiod 1991–92 (not reported in the table). For the entire sample, the weights of the U.S. dollar and the Japanese yen were 0.91 and 0.05, respectively. For the more recent subperiod January 1991–May 1995, Kwan reports 0.8202 and 0.1051 as the weights of the U.S. dollar and the yen, respectively.

7.4   Movements of Asian Currencies When the Yen Fluctuates Sharply against the U.S. Dollar

While econometric estimation of the implicit weights of the U.S. dollar and the Japanese yen is useful in revealing the relative covariances of the currency in question with the U.S. dollar and the Japanese yen during a particular sample period, it can yield misleading interpretations unless proper caution is exercised. Most important, it must be borne in mind that the econometric approach stresses the covariances between the currency in question and the currencies included in the currency basket without much regard to the magnitude of the underlying changes in currency values. This point is important even if the currency in question is strictly pegged to a currency basket (Thailand) and the composition of the basket remains unchanged, as long as a fluctuation margin is provided around the central rate (Takagi 1988). Naturally, the problem becomes greater in the case of a managed float of more discretionary nature (Korea, Singapore, and Malaysia).

To understand this point, assume, for example, that the authorities of a country care deeply about the nominal stability of the currency against the Japanese yen and hence assign a weight of 10 percent to the yen in the currency basket. If the yen is relatively stable against the U.S. dollar, however, stability against the yen can be secured by simply pegging the currency to the U.S. dollar, presumably the intervention currency, as long as the market rate remains within the prescribed margins around the theoretical rate. Thus the estimated weight of the yen may turn out to be zero.

On the other hand, if the yen sharply fluctuates against the U.S. dollar in one direction, the policy of pegging the currency to the dollar will result in a sharp movement of the currency against the Japanese yen and may lead to a situation where the market rate goes out of the prescribed margins unless the market rate is changed in line with the weight of the yen in the country's exchange rate policy. The authorities will likely change the dollar rate so as to offset part of the fluctuation of the currency against the yen. In this case, the estimated weight of the yen may approach the theoretical value of 10 percent, or even higher if the maximum margin on both sides is utilized.

Thus, in order to assess the role of the Japanese yen in the exchange rate policies of the Asian countries, it is important not only to look at the econometric estimates of the weights of the dollar and the yen over some sample period but also to examine how the currencies move vis-à-vis the dollar and the yen when the yen fluctuates sharply in one direction against the U.S. dollar. For this purpose, we will next consider twelve episodes of large yen appreciation or depreciation (of at least 5 percent) against the U.S. dollar. There were eight episodes of yen appreciation and four episodes of yen depreciation. Table 7.4 shows how much the Japanese yen and the other Asian currencies appreciated (when the figures are positive) or depreciated (when negative) against the U.S. dollar during each of these twelve episodes.

The numbers in parentheses indicate the direction of change of each Asian currency as a percentage of the movement of the Japanese yen, which can be roughly interpreted as the weight of the yen during that episode.[4] For example, a negative number in parentheses means that the movement of the yen and the movement of the currency in question go in opposite directions relative to the U.S. dollar; a figure of 20, for example, means that the magnitude of the movement of the currency in question is 20 percent of the movement of the yen against the U.S. dollar.

7.4.1   Korea

When the episodes of yen appreciation or depreciation during 1982–95 are individually examined, we find that when the yen depreciated, the won depreciated against the U.S. dollar three out of four times. In these cases of yen depreciation, the weight of the yen ranged between 6 and 43 percent. On the other hand, when the yen appreciated against the U.S. dollar, there were times when the won even depreciated against the U.S. dollar. During the appreciation of

---

4. Admittedly, this is a crude measure of the weight of the yen because there can be other currencies whose movements are being considered by the authorities. This measure is simply to be taken as a rough indication of how closely the currency in question moved with the yen ex post, relative to the U.S. dollar. As another qualification, it should also be noted that this measure may underestimate the "weight" of the yen if the currency in question moves with the yen with a longer lag (Cho 1996).

Table 7.4   Movements of Selected Asian Currencies against the U.S. Dollar during Periods of Sharp Yen-Dollar Exchange Rate Change

Period	Japanese Yen	Korean Won	Singapore Dollar	Malaysian Ringgit	Indonesian Rupiah	Philippine Peso	Thai Baht
1. October 1982 to March 1984	21.0	-6.1 (-29)	5.7 (27)	2.7 (13)	-38.4 (-183)	-46.1 (-219)	0.0 (0)
2. March 1984 to February 1985	-14.4	-6.2 (43)	-8.0 (55)	-11.9 (83)	-8.8 (61)	-27.1 (188)	-19.9 (138)
3. August 1985 to September 1986	43.5	1.1 (2.6)	4.5 (10)	-5.6 (-13)	-37.8 (-87)	-9.5 (-22)	3.0 (6.8)
4. November 1986 to April 1987	15.2	3.6 (24)	3.5 (23)	4.9 (32)	0.6 (3.6)	-0.2 (-1.5)	2.6 (17)
5. September 1989 to April 1990	-13.5	-5.4 (40)	4.4 (-32)	-1.1 (8.0)	-2.6 (19)	-3.8 (29)	-0.9 (6.3)
6. June 1990 to October 1990	16.7	0.3 (1.8)	7.6 (46)	0.4 (2.2)	-1.5 (-9.0)	-10.1 (-61)	2.8 (16)
7. September 1991 to December 1991	5.9	-2.6 (-43)	3.6 (60)	0.7 (11)	-0.5 (-7.7)	1.3 (22)	-0.2 (-2.7)
8. April 1992 to September 1992	11.3	-1.0 (-8.8)	3.9 (34)	1.2 (11)	-0.8 (-7.0)	2.7 (24)	2.1 (19)
9. December 1992 to August 1993	18.0	-2.5 (-14)	2.4 (13)	2.5 (14)	-1.9 (-11)	-11.1 (-62)	1.4 (7.7)
10. August 1993 to December 1993	-7.1	0.04 (-0.5)	-0.1 (2.0)	-5.8 (82)	-0.4 (5.4)	1.2 (-17)	-1.5 (21)
11. December 1993 to May 1995	29.6	6.1 (21)	12.5 (42)	9.1 (31)	-5.8 (-20)	7.1 (24)	3.6 (12)
12. May 1995 to September 1995	-16.7	-1.1 (6.5)	-0.1 (0.6)	-1.7 (10)	-1.7 (10)	1.0 (-6.2)	-1.8 (11)

Source: IMF, *International Financial Statistics* (Washington, D.C., various issues).

Note: On the basis of end-of-month data; a positive number means an appreciation of the currency in question against the U.S. dollar. Numbers in parentheses indicate the direction of change of each currency as a percentage of the movement of the Japanese yen.

the yen in December 1993–May 1995, however, the won also appreciated against the U.S. dollar, with the implicit weight of the yen in the determination of the won corresponding to 21 percent.

7.4.2 Singapore

When the currency value of the yen changed sharply against the U.S. dollar, the weight of the yen in the determination of the Singapore dollar was consistently significant throughout the period, with the weight ranging between 10 and 55 percent. However, there were two exceptions: the Singapore dollar appreciated against the U.S. dollar by 4 percent during September 1989–April 1990, when the yen depreciated by 13 percent; and it remained stable against the U.S. dollar during May–September 1995, when the yen depreciated by almost 17 percent.

7.4.3 Malaysia

In terms of individual episodes, the weight of the yen in the determination of the ringgit became consistently significant after the episode of November 1986–April 1987. The weight ranged between 8 and 32 percent.

7.4.4 Indonesia

The yen even had a negative weight during August 1985–September 1986, meaning that the rupiah depreciated against the U.S. dollar when the yen significantly appreciated against the U.S. dollar. The rupiah generally depreciated against the U.S. dollar whenever the yen depreciated against the U.S. dollar. The weight of the yen for the most recent episode (May–September 1995) was about 10 percent, but this may simply reflect the fact that the yen depreciated against the U.S. dollar when there was a trend depreciation of the rupiah.

7.4.5 Philippines

Consistent with the fact that the peso depreciated against the U.S. dollar in nominal terms during this period, the yen and the peso generally moved in the same direction only when the yen depreciated against the U.S. dollar. The implicit weight of the yen becomes larger when the magnitude of the yen's movement against the U.S. dollar is small. On the other hand, the implicit weight becomes small (or negative) when the yen's movement against the dollar is large, indicating that the yen plays little role in the peso's nominal exchange rate determination.

7.4.6 Thailand

When the individual episodes are considered, it becomes clear that the weight of the yen in the determination of the baht was between 7 and 19 percent during 1985–95. The order of magnitude of these implied weights is similar to the econometrically estimated weights. Together with the fact that the weight of the yen was apparently symmetrical with respect to appreciation and depreciation, this seems to suggest that the Thai baht is pegged fairly strictly to a basket of currencies, in which the weight of the yen is stable.

7.5 Daily Movements of Asian Currencies during Periods of Sharp Yen Appreciation and Depreciation in the 1980s

In the first half of the 1980s, the yen-dollar exchange rate fluctuated in the range of 200–270 yen per dollar, with the yen showing general weakening against the dollar from the middle of 1984 through the early part of 1985. Following the Plaza Agreement of 22 September 1985, however, the yen began to appreciate sharply from the pre-Plaza level of around 240 to reach the level of almost 200 yen per dollar in two months. The appreciation of the yen, from 19 September to 25 November, amounted to almost 20 percent. The yen continued its trend appreciation throughout the rest of the 1980s, except for one notable period of substantial reversal from the latter part of 1988 through the first part of 1989. Somewhat more gradually than on other occasions, the yen depreciated from the high of 120.9 yen per dollar on 24 November 1988 to the low of 149.6 yen per dollar on 15 June 1989, a depreciation of almost 20 percent.

This section will take a detailed look at the daily movements of the Japanese yen and the Asian currencies against the U.S. dollar during the period immediately following the Plaza Agreement of 1985 (fig. 7.1) and a portion of the latter period of yen depreciation, namely, from 3 January to 14 June 1989 (fig. 7.2).[5]

7.5.1   Korea

During the first period when the yen was appreciating against the U.S. dollar, the Korean won remained virtually pegged to the dollar. During the second period of sharp yen depreciation, the won moderately appreciated against the dollar. In neither period is there evidence to suggest that the Korean authorities were paying much attention to the movement of the won against the yen.

7.5.2   Singapore

During the first period of sharp yen appreciation, the Singaporean authorities allowed the Singapore dollar to appreciate along with the yen against the U.S. dollar. The cumulative appreciation of the Singapore dollar over this period was almost 5 percent, as opposed to almost 20 percent for the yen. In contrast, when the yen depreciated in the early part of 1989, the Singapore dollar remained stable against the U.S. dollar, underscoring the importance the Singaporean authorities attach to price stability.

---

5. Daily exchange rate data were obtained from the *Asian Wall Street Journal*. Exchange rates for 1985 are mid rates at 5 P.M. in Hong Kong, while those for 1989 are selling rates at 3 P.M. in New York.

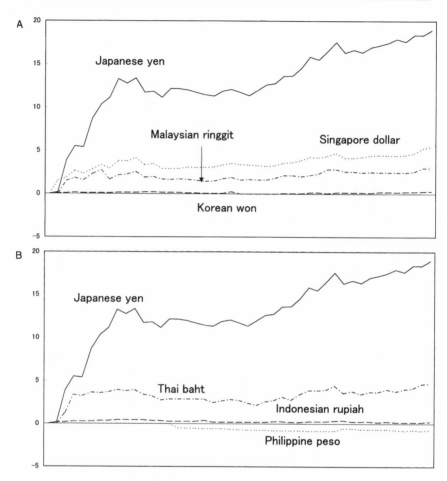

Fig. 7.1   Daily movements of selected Asian currencies against the U.S. dollar during the period of sharp yen appreciation 19 September to 25 November 1985
Note: A, Korean won, Singapore dollar, and Malaysian ringgit. B, Indonesian rupiah, Philippine peso, and Thai baht. Logarithmic change in basis points.

7.5.3   Malaysia

During the period of yen appreciation, the Malaysian authorities allowed the ringgit to appreciate moderately along with the yen against the U.S. dollar. In contrast, during the time of yen depreciation, the ringgit initially depreciated somewhat but subsequently appreciated marginally. On both occasions, the movement of the ringgit was similar to that of the Singapore dollar.

7.5.4   Indonesia

On the first occasion of yen appreciation, the Indonesian rupiah remained stable against the U.S. dollar, indicating that the rupiah was effectively pegged

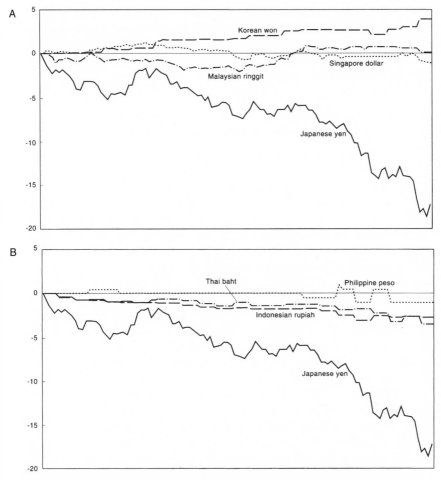

Fig. 7.2   Daily movements of selected Asian currencies against the U.S. dollar during the period of sharp yen depreciation 3 January to 14 June 1989
Note: A, Korean won, Singapore dollar, and Malaysian ringgit. *B,* Indonesian rupiah, Philippine peso, and Thai baht. Logarithmic change in basis points.

to the U.S. dollar over this interval. When the yen depreciated in 1989, how-ever, the rupiah moderately depreciated.

7.5.5   Philippines

On both occasions, the Philippine peso was virtually pegged to the U.S. dollar.

7.5.6   Thailand

When the yen appreciated, the Thai authorities allowed the baht to appreci-ate moderately along with the yen against the U.S. dollar; when the yen depreciated, they depreciated the baht slightly along with the yen against the U.S. dollar. From these two episodes, it appears that the Thai authorities strictly adhered to a basket peg and that the weight of the yen in the currency basket was reduced somewhat somewhere between 1985 and 1987, presumably in the light of the appreciating trend of the yen.

7.6 Daily Movements of Asian Currencies during Periods of Sharp Yen Appreciation and Depreciation in 1995

In 1995, the Japanese yen moved sharply against the U.S. dollar on two occasions. On the first of these occasions, from 1 March to 19 April, the yen appreciated against the U.S. dollar by over 15 percent, rising from 96.75 to 81.08 yen per U.S. dollar (fig. 7.3). On the second occasion, from 1 August to 19 September, the yen reversed its position against the U.S. dollar by depreciating by more than 15 percent, declining from 88.29 to 104.20 yen per U.S. dollar (fig. 7.4).[6] These two periods may be instructive in revealing not only the reactions of the monetary authorities but also how they might have changed since the 1980s.

7.6.1 Korea

When the yen fluctuated sharply against the U.S. dollar in either direction, the Korean authorities initially kept the won-dollar exchange rate stable. It appears that a substantial adjustment of the won-dollar exchange rate takes place only after it is determined that the movement of the yen against the dollar is significant and more or less permanent. It is interesting to note that when the yen sharply depreciated against the dollar from 14 to 17 August (by as much as 5 percent in three days), the Korean authorities immediately reacted by depreciating the won (from 761.75 won per U.S. dollar on 15 August to 787.65 won on 18 August), indicating the greater weight they assign to a depreciating yen. It is clear that the depreciation of the Korean won in August 1995 was deliberate as the balance of foreign exchange reserves was increasing during this period.

7.6.2 Singapore

When the yen appreciated, the Singaporean authorities allowed the Singapore dollar to appreciate moderately along with the yen against the U.S. dollar. When the yen depreciated, however, the authorities kept the nominal value of the Singapore dollar virtually constant against the U.S. dollar for two full business weeks before allowing the Singapore dollar to depreciate moderately in response to a further depreciation of the yen. This may reflect the importance

---

6. Daily exchange rate data, except for the Indonesian rupiah, were obtained from the *Financial Times.* The exchange rates are closing mid rates in London. Daily data for the rupiah were obtained from the *Wall Street Journal.* The exchange rates are selling rates at 3 P.M. in New York.

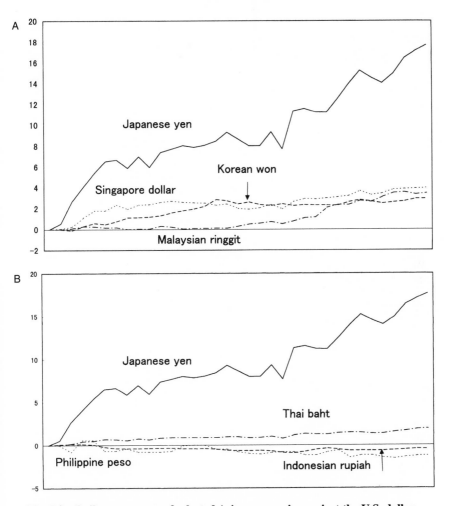

Fig. 7.3   Daily movements of selected Asian currencies against the U.S. dollar during the period of sharp yen appreciation 1 March to 19 April 1995
Note: A, Korean won, Singapore dollar, and Malaysian ringgit. *B,* Indonesian rupiah, Philippine peso, and Thai baht. Logarithmic change in basis points.

of price stability in Singapore's exchange rate policy, hence the greater resistance to exchange rate depreciation and the greater propensity to accommodate the yen's exchange rate appreciation.

7.6.3   Malaysia

On a daily basis, Malaysia's policy response was quite asymmetric with respect to the yen's depreciation and appreciation. When the yen appreciated in March 1995, the nominal value of the ringgit remained extremely stable for

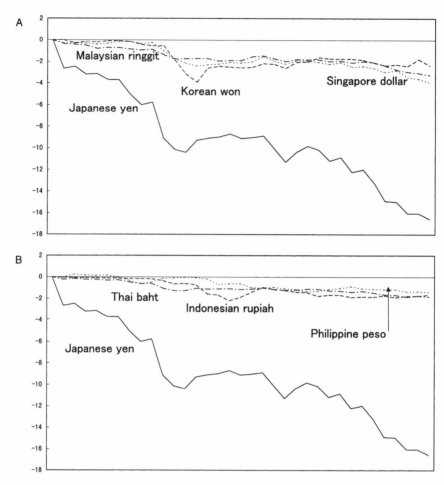

Fig. 7.4   Daily movements of selected Asian currencies against the U.S. dollar during the period of sharp yen depreciation 1 August to 19 September 1995
Note: A, Korean won, Singapore dollar, and Malaysian ringgit. B, Indonesian rupiah, Philippine peso, and Thai baht. Logarithmic change in basis points.

most of the period, although it began to appreciate moderately against the U.S. dollar during the very last part of the yen's appreciation phase. When the yen depreciated in August, however, the ringgit depreciated immediately against the U.S. dollar so as to offset a portion of its appreciation against the yen.

7.6.4   Indonesia

The nominal value of the Indonesian rupiah remained fairly constant against the U.S. dollar on both occasions. In fact, it continued to depreciate against the

U.S. dollar at a moderate pace regardless of the movement of the yen against the dollar.

7.6.5 Philippines

The behavior of the Philippine peso was similar to that of the Indonesian rupiah. Regardless of how the yen moved against the U.S. dollar, the peso remained on a moderately depreciating trend against the dollar.

7.6.6 Thailand

The Thai baht's movement was symmetrical with respect to the yen's appreciation and depreciation. In both cases, the baht moved so as to offset a portion of its movement against the yen, indicative of the policy of the Thai authorities to peg the baht fairly strictly to a currency basket, of which the yen is a component. Judging from the movement of foreign exchange reserves (not reported here), it is most likely that the Thai authorities sold foreign exchange in the market during the period of yen appreciation (so as to appreciate the baht), while they purchased foreign exchange during the period of yen depreciation (so as to depreciate the baht).

7.7 Conclusion

By looking at how six East Asian currencies moved when the yen fluctuated sharply against the U.S. dollar during 1980–95, we have found that the reaction was sometimes much more significant than would be suggested by the econometric estimates of the yen's weight in the determination of their nominal values. When the individual episodes of sharp yen fluctuation were examined, the "weight" of the yen often appeared larger than most of the econometric estimates taken from a longer sample period. The exceptions were the Indonesian rupiah and the Philippine peso, both of which showed secular depreciation against the U.S. dollar over the period. Clearly, the paramount objective of the Indonesian and Philippine exchange rate policies was to prevent a real appreciation of their currencies in the light of higher domestic inflation by consistently depreciating their currencies in nominal terms. In these countries, little attention was paid to the movement of the yen, although it is evident that the yen is prominently included in the real effective exchange rate indexes.

Except for Thailand, which strictly adheres to a basket peg, the other countries have more recently shown asymmetric responses to the yen's depreciation and appreciation. The Singapore dollar has tended to move more closely with an appreciating yen, underscoring the importance the authorities attach to price stability in their exchange rate policy. On the other hand, the Korean won and the Malaysian ringgit have tended to move more closely with a depreciating yen, suggesting an emphasis on export promotion. In this sense, the yen is perceived in Korea and Malaysia as the currency of a competitor country in the export market.[7]

In contrast to Korea, which has demonstratively become Japan's competitor in the world market for manufactures, the case for Malaysia as a competitor of Japan may sound a little farfetched. To be sure, Malaysia's manufacturing exports are not as voluminous as Korean exports, nor do they compete as directly with Japanese exports. In terms of growth in recent years, however, Malaysia has considerably raised its status as an exporter of manufactured goods. For example, from 1989 to 1994, Malaysia's export of Sections 6 and 7 manufactured goods (as classified by the Organization for Economic Cooperation and Development [OECD]) to the United States increased fourfold from $3 billion to $12 billion, while Japan only marginally increased its export of similar goods from $91 billion to $112 billion during the same period (OECD 1994). It is thus possible that in tying the currency more to a depreciating yen, the Malaysian authorities were protecting the gains being made in manufacturing exports.

Emphasis on export promotion produces more convergent movement with a depreciating yen and more divergent movement with an appreciating yen. Conversely, emphasis on price stability produces more convergent movement with an appreciating yen and more divergent movement with a depreciating yen. As things have turned out, because the yen showed sustained and significant appreciation against the U.S. dollar for the sample period as a whole, an exchange rate policy targeted at price stability has contributed more to monetary cooperation in Asia, by promoting intraregional exchange rate stability, than a more competitive exchange rate policy targeted at export promotion.

References

Cho, Dongchul. 1996. Korea's exchange rate movements in the 1990s: Evaluation and policy implications. Seoul: Korea Development Institute, March.

Cororaton, Caesar B. 1996. Exchange rate movements in the Philippines. Manila: Philippine Institute for Development Studies, March.

Frankel, Jeffrey A., and Shang-Jin Wei. 1994. Yen bloc or dollar bloc? Exchange rate policies of the East Asian economies. In *Macroeconomic linkage: Savings, exchange rates, and capital flows,* ed. Takatoshi Ito and Anne Krueger. Chicago: University of Chicago Press.

Goelton, Miranda S. 1996. Exchange rate fluctuations and macroeconomic management: The case of Indonesia, 1980–1996. Jakarta: University of Indonesia, March.

International Monetary Fund (IMF). Various years. *Exchange arrangements and exchange restrictions* (annual report). Washington, D.C.: International Monetary Fund.

---

7. Although it is likely that the industrial composition of Korean exports is similar to that of Japanese exports, it is not clear to what extent Malaysian exports compete with Japanese exports. The characterization of the behavior of the Malaysian ringgit as "competitive" relative to the yen remains only tentative.

Kwan, C. H. 1995. *Enken no keizaigaku* (The economics of the yen bloc). Tokyo: Nihon Keizai Shinbunsha.
Leeahtam, Pisit. 1991. *From crisis to double digit growth.* Bangkok: Dokya Publishing House.
Ong, Hong Cheong. 1996. Exchange rate fluctuations and macroeconomic management, 1980–1994: Malaysia's experience. Kuala Lumpur: Institute of Strategic and International Studies, March.
Organization for Economic Cooperation and Development (OECD). 1994. *Foreign trade by commodities,* vol. 5. Paris: Organization for Economic Cooperation and Development.
Phatra Research Institute. 1996. Commentary. Bangkok: Phatra Research Institute, 25 April.
Takagi, Shinji. 1988. A basket peg policy: Operational issues for developing countries. *World Development* 16:271–79.
Toh Mun-Heng. 1996. Exchange rate policy in Singapore. Singapore: National University of Singapore, March.

Comment   Tetsuji Okazaki

Since Frankel and Wei's pioneering paper of 1994, currency blocs have come to be a subject of quantitative research. Takagi's paper joins this line of research and makes a new contribution. He pays attention to the movements of the exchange rates of selected Asian countries in cases when the yen fluctuated sharply against the U.S. dollar. He takes up twelve cases of large yen fluctuation against the dollar from 1982 to 1995, of which eight were yen appreciation and four were yen depreciation. The main finding of the paper is that the exchange rates of some countries responded to sharp yen fluctuations asymmetrically between the cases of depreciation and appreciation. That is, the exchange rates of the Korean won and the Malaysian ringgit moved more in line with the yen against the U.S. dollar when the yen depreciated than when it appreciated. On the other hand, the exchange rate of the Singapore dollar moved more in line with the yen against the U.S. dollar when the yen appreciated than when it depreciated. Takagi interprets this asymmetry as reflecting the policy of each currency authority. The Korean and Malaysian authorities regard the yen as the currency of a competitor country, while the authority of Singapore makes much of stability of prices. The asymmetrical responses of the exchange rates are phenomena that have not been given much attention in the research since the Frankel and Wei paper, and this finding is a substantial contribution.

However, there remains some room for consideration in the author's interpretation of the asymmetry, because we can derive another implication from table 7.4 in the paper. In table 7.4 he takes the U.S. dollar as numéraire. If we take the yen as numéraire in this table, we can say that the exchange rates of

Tetsuji Okazaki is associate professor of economics at the University of Tokyo.

the Korean won and Malaysian ringgit moved more in line with the U.S. dollar against the yen when the U.S. dollar depreciated than when it appreciated. Also we can say that the exchange rate of the Singapore dollar moved more in line with the U.S. dollar against the yen when the U.S. dollar appreciated than when it depreciated. In sum, the Korean and Malaysian authorities are inclined to depreciate their currencies in both the case of yen depreciation against the U.S. dollar and the case of U.S. dollar depreciation against the yen. And the Singapore authority is reluctant to depreciate its currency in both the case of yen depreciation against the U.S. dollar and the case of U.S. dollar depreciation against the yen. Therefore, it is true that the Singapore authority places more importance on price stability. On the other hand, the Korean and Malaysian authorities' responses shown in table 7.4 might not be due to their perception of Japan as a competitor country but might reflect a more general policy of export orientation.

Takagi further interprets the asymmetrical responses as revealing different roles of the yen with respect to each currency, that is, competition and cooperation, which is the subtitle of his paper. Aside from the above-mentioned problem, the asymmetry can be interpreted as reflecting the relationship between the industries of Japan and those of each Asian country. For example, the leading industries of Korea and Japan are substitutive, while those of Singapore and Japan are complementary. However, there is some distance between the relationship of the industries of the two countries and the relationship of their currencies.

Comment   K. C. Fung

I find this paper very interesting. It takes another look at how much currencies of some Asian countries (South Korea, Singapore, Malaysia, Indonesia, the Philippines, and Thailand) respond to changes in the Japanese yen and the U.S. dollar. The contribution of the paper is its focus on the reactions of these currencies during episodes when the yen moved sharply against the U.S. dollar. The paper also examines movements of the Asian currencies *both* when the yen depreciates and when the yen appreciates against the U.S. dollar.

I think one important motivation for focusing on episodes of large exchange rate changes is that large fluctuations of the yen can have persistent effects on these Asian economies (Baldwin and Krugman 1986). Confronted by possible long-term effects, the central banks of these countries may feel that they have no choice but to reveal, clarify, and pursue their objectives through their ex-

K. C. Fung is professor of economics at the University of California, Santa Cruz; associate director of the Hong Kong Centre for Economic Research, University of Hong Kong; and a visiting scholar in the Asia/Pacific Research Center at Stanford University.

change rate policies. The paper shows that some currencies (such as the South Korean won) behaved quite differently when the yen appreciated as compared to when the yen depreciated. This *asymmetric* behavior gives us additional insight into the goals of the exchange rate policies of these countries.

By and large, I interpret the results of the paper to be consistent with earlier studies that show that currencies of East Asian countries (other than Japan) are pegged de facto to the U.S. dollar and with few exceptions place little weight on the role of the Japanese yen. In addition to the work by Frankel and Wei (1994) cited in the paper, Ito (1994), for example, found evidence that while countries in Asia are gradually expanding their use of the yen as an invoice currency, most still rely mainly on the U.S. dollar. In fact, it was pointed out that in invoicing import and export transactions, other developed countries use their own national currencies far more than Japan uses the yen.

The de facto pegging of the Asian currencies to the U.S. dollar may reflect the underlying choices that these governments and their central banks had to make. Since 1985, two events put pressure on real exchange rates to appreciate in Asia. First, between 1985 and 1987, the U.S. dollar sharply depreciated against major currencies, including the Japanese yen and the German deutsche mark. This improved the export competitiveness of these Asian economies, which led to large increases in their trade balances. Second, U.S. interest rates declined between 1989 and 1993. This encouraged capital to flow to regions like Asia.

Faced with these conditions, governments could have allowed their nominal exchange rates to appreciate, which would have reduced exports, or they could have taken measures to maintain their nominal exchange rates, which would have led to more inflation. Basically, most of the Asian governments chose to pay attention to their export competitiveness. Because their major export market is the United States, these governments took steps to avoid sharp appreciation of their nominal exchange rates against the U.S. dollar. The choice between export competitiveness and inflation facing these economies is illustrated by the different strategies pursued by the Hong Kong and Singaporean governments. Hong Kong apparently is more interested in its export competitiveness. The Hong Kong dollar has been pegged to the U.S. dollar, and since 1985 it has had cumulative inflation of more than 50 percent relative to that in the United States. In contrast, Singapore seems to be more concerned with inflation. The government of Singapore allowed its nominal exchange rate to go up by about 50 percent against the U.S. dollar. Since 1985, cumulative inflation has been 20 percent lower than in the United States (Glick and Moreno 1995).

The paper also highlights an interesting micro question about the use of currency in international trade. The question is: as East Asia conducts more trade with Japan, why do we not see any significant increase in the use of the Japanese yen? Part of the answer may lie in the nature and the character of trade rather than just the total volume of trade. In an earlier NBER–East Asia

Seminar study, Urata (1993) documented that a significant fraction of East Asia–Japan trade is intrafirm trade and that Japanese affiliates in East Asia tend to export a large share of their final goods to the U.S. market. Since it has been documented that Japanese firms continue to conduct their international trade in U.S. dollars (Ito 1994), it should not be surprising that even as the volume of trade with Japan increases, the use of the Japanese yen in East Asia does not proportionally expand.

References

Baldwin, R., and P. Krugman. 1986. Persistent trade effects of large exchange rate shocks. NBER Working Paper no. 2017. Cambridge, Mass.: National Bureau of Economic Research.
Frankel, J., and S. J. Wei. 1994. Yen bloc or dollar bloc? Exchange rate policies of the East Asian economies. In *Macroeconomic linkages: Savings, exchange rates, and capital flows,* ed. T. Ito and A. O. Krueger. Chicago: University of Chicago Press.
Glick, R., and R. Moreno. 1995. Is pegging the exchange rate a cure for inflation? East Asian experiences. FRBSF Weekly Letter no. 95-37. San Francisco: Federal Reserve Bank of San Francisco.
Ito, T. 1994. On the possibility of a yen bloc. In *Exchange rate policy and interdependence: Perspectives from the Pacific Basin,* ed. R. Glick and M. Hutchison. Cambridge: Cambridge University Press.
Urata, S. 1993. Japanese foreign direct investment and its effects on foreign trade in Asia. In *Trade and protectionism,* ed. T. Ito and A. O. Krueger. Chicago: University of Chicago Press.

8   Exchange Rate Pass-through and Industry Characteristics: The Case of Taiwan's Exports of Midstream Petrochemical Products

Kuo-Liang Wang and Chung-Shu Wu

8.1 Introduction

In the 1980s there were many significant structural changes in Taiwan's economy. One of them was the drastic appreciation of the New Taiwan (NT) dollar. It can be seen from table 8.1 that though the export price index had been decreasing along with the appreciation of NT dollars during this period, the magnitude of the export price index's decline did not match that of the NT dollar appreciation.[1] Furthermore, the trade imbalance kept growing. Does this imply that there exists incomplete exchange rate "pass-through" in Taiwan's export price index, or do Taiwan's domestic firms display "pricing-to-market" behavior?[2]

Most recent empirical studies show that firms in newly industrializing countries tend to have pricing-to-market behavior in response to changes in real exchange rates (Hooper and Mann 1989; Athukorala 1991; Liu 1994).[3] However, Marston (1990), Knetter (1993), and Athukorala and Menon (1994) find

Kuo-Liang Wang is professor of economics at National Cheng-Chi University, Mucha, Taipei, Taiwan. Chung-Shu Wu is a research fellow of the Institute of Economics, Academia Sinica, Nankang, Taipei, Taiwan.

The authors have benefited from the comments of Takatoshi Ito, Anne Krueger, Koichi Hamada, and conference participants. They are also indebted to two discussants, Kenichi Ohno and Y. C. Jao, and two anonymous referees for valuable comments and suggestions. All remaining errors are the authors'.

1. It can be seen from table 8.1 that the average NT dollar–U.S. dollar exchange rate had been decreasing from 36.84 in 1981 to 26.41 in 1989, which is over a 38.31 percent appreciation. However, during the same period the export price index dropped from 111.68 to 97.40, only 12.79 percent.

2. Incomplete exchange rate pass-through is often mentioned as one of the main reasons for sluggish adjustment in trade imbalances among countries.

3. For the case of Japan and other countries, see Athukorala and Menon (1994), Froot and Klemperer (1989), Knetter (1993), Marston (1990), Menon (1995), and Ohno (1989).

Table 8.1   **Main Economic Indicators for Taiwan External Sectors**

Indicator	1980	1981	1982	1983	1984	1985	1986	1987	1988	1989	1990	1991	1992	1993	1994	1995
Export price index	103.93	111.68	113.01	112.85	113.15	112.43	108.44	102.06	100.29	97.40	99.64	100.00	96.39	100.94	103.60	110.07
Import price index	116.03	126.00	124.20	122.72	122.02	120.07	109.46	101.93	101.03	98.09	100.39	100.00	95.27	99.33	103.85	113.23
Exchange rate (NT/U.S.$)	36.00	36.84	39.12	40.07	39.60	39.83	37.84	31.74	28.59	26.41	26.89	26.81	25.16	26.39	26.46	26.48
Exports of goods and services (million U.S.$)	21,758	24,998	24,347	27,809	33,270	33,674	43,836	58,456	66,694	73,959	74,896	85,062	92,038	98,477	106,305	127,437
Imports of goods and services (million U.S.$)	22,251	24,015	21,847	23,281	26,643	25,101	28,900	40,768	53,743	62,777	66,914	76,929	87,592	94,274	101,730	121,441
Trade surplus (million U.S.$)	−493	983	2,500	4,528	6,628	8,574	14,937	17,689	13,221	11,183	7,981	8,132	4,445	4,204	4,576	5,996
GDP growth rate	7.30	6.16	3.55	8.45	10.60	4.95	11.64	12.74	7.84	8.23	5.39	7.55	6.76	6.32	6.54	6.06

Source: Directorate-General of Budget, Accounting and Statistics, Executive Yuan, *National Income, Taiwan Area, R.O.C.* (Taipei, 1996).

that different industries even in the same country may not have identical behavior toward pricing to market. Therefore, if we want to investigate the exchange rate pass-through pattern, it is more appropriate to explain pricing to market on the basis of observable industry characteristics. Similarly, Krugman (1987), Dornbusch (1987), Feenstra (1987), Fisher (1989), Knetter (1989), and Shinjo (1993) also show that the elements of market structure are very important in determining the degree of exchange rate pass-through.

There do exist a few studies that investigate exchange rate pass-through effects in Taiwan (Hooper and Mann 1989; Liu 1994; Wu 1995). However, most of them are based on aggregate data. As mentioned before, if we study the pass-through effect by examining general aggregate price indexes, we might obtain misleading results because market structure elements are neglected. In order to avoid the aggregation problem, in this paper we use survey data on the exports of 22 Taiwanese petrochemical industries during 1986–92 to investigate the exchange rate pass-through effect. Moreover, in addition to production cost and capacity utilization, special attention has been paid to the Herfindahl index and price elasticities of demand in order to emphasize the importance of market structure and industry characteristics to the study of exchange rate pass-through effects.[4]

A number of important features should be noted when discussing exchange rate pass-through effects for Taiwan's petrochemical industry. First, though it is a large-scale industry in Taiwan, it only exports a relatively small portion of its total output.[5] Second, it is a highly concentrated industry; that is, it has relatively strong monopoly power. Therefore, we expect this kind of industry to have a lower incentive to adjust its markup ratio in response to exchange rate changes except for the purpose of holding foreign market share (Froot and Klemperer 1989). By studying these particular industries' exchange rate pass-through effects, we can not only examine whether all industries in Taiwan have manipulated the exchange rate for the purpose of gaining an unfair competitive advantage in the international market but also obtain more information about industry-specific pricing behavior.

The rest of the paper is organized as follows. Section 8.2 sets up the analytical framework for our empirical analysis of exchange rate pass-through and builds the empirical equations used in this study. Section 8.3 illustrates the characteristics of Taiwan's petrochemical industries and gives a data description. Section 8.4 presents and analyzes econometric estimates of exchange rate pass-through effects. Section 8.5 summarizes some of the main findings of this paper.

---

4. The Herfindahl index is a measure of market concentration or fewness and is equal to the sum of squares of the market shares of the firms in the market.
5. It can be seen in table 8.2 that 12 out of 22 industries had average shares of exports in domestic production of less than 10 percent during the period 1986–92.

8.2   Analytical Framework

As mentioned by Hooper and Mann (1989), exchange rate pass-through can be broadly defined as the extent to which a change in the nominal exchange rate induces a change in the import price. Since our analysis is focused on the export price index, it is natural to define the exchange rate pass-through effect as the partial derivative of the export price index with respect to the exchange rate minus one. In addition, following previous empirical research (e.g., Hooper and Mann 1989; Marston 1990; Kim 1990; Athukorala 1991; Athukorala and Menon 1994), we adopt a variant of markup models of price determination. In this kind of framework, we can discuss the strategic interaction between domestic and foreign firms operating through variations in the markup.

Under the assumption of imperfect competition, domestic firms more or less have the capability to control their prices of output and set home currency export prices (PEX) at a markup (MK) over the level of normal unit production cost (MC):

(1) $$PEX = (1 + MK)MC.$$

According to the existing literature, many factors may have an impact on the markup ratio, for example, demand pressures in all markets combined, competitive pressures in foreign markets, desire to maintain foreign market share, and market structure. In this study, the demand pressures in all markets are proxied by the capacity utilization rate (CU). As the capacity utilization rate goes up, it implies that total demand in all markets is increasing. It is then easier for domestic firms to raise domestic and export prices above marginal and average costs. Competitive pressures in foreign markets are represented by price elasticities of demand with respect to domestic firms in foreign markets (EL) and the weighted exchange rate (RX). Pricing theory tells us that, other things being equal, markup ratios are inversely related to elasticities of demand. Therefore, the higher the price elasticities of demand with respect to domestic firms in foreign markets, the less possible it is for domestic firms to raise export prices above marginal costs. As for the exchange rate, it partly reflects the pressure of the foreign competitive price and partly reflects domestic firms' pricing strategy toward foreign market share (Mann 1986; Froot and Klemperer (1989). On the other hand, market structure is captured by domestic market concentration (H). It has been shown in oligopoly theory that the higher the level of domestic market concentration, the more likely it is that domestic firms will be able to raise domestic prices and then export prices above marginal and average cost (Khalizadeh-Shirazi 1974). As a result the markup ratio function can be expressed as follows:

(2) $$MK = MK(\overset{(+)}{CU},\ \overset{(-)}{EL},\ \overset{(+)}{RX},\ \overset{(+)}{H}).$$

Substituting equation (2) into equation (1), the export price equation can be written as

(3)
$$\text{pex}_t^i = \alpha_0 + \alpha_1 \text{rx}_t^i + \alpha_2 \text{mc}_t^i + \alpha_3 \text{CU}_t^i + \alpha_4 \text{H}_t^i + \alpha_5 \text{EL}_t^i + \varepsilon_{1t};$$
$$0 \leq \alpha_1 \leq 1; \quad \alpha_2, \ \alpha_3, \ \alpha_4 \geq 0; \quad \alpha_5 \leq 0; \quad i = 1, \dots, 22;$$

where lowercase letters represent logarithmic values of variables, superscript i denotes the ith petrochemical product, and subscript t denotes the time period.

Not all of the export prices of petrochemical products are based on f.o.b. terms, some of them are based on c&f or c.i.f. terms. When the distance between the home and destination countries increases, the transportation cost and the probability of an accident occurring during shipping will go up, and domestic firms will tend to raise export prices. Therefore, we add a transportation cost variable (TC) to equation (3) to yield

(4)
$$\text{pex}_t^i = \alpha_0 + \alpha_1 \text{rx}_t^i + \alpha_2 \text{mc}_t^i + \alpha_3 \text{CU}_t^i + \alpha_4 \text{H}_t^i + \alpha_5 \text{EL}_t^i + \alpha_6 \text{tc}_t^i + \varepsilon_{2t};$$
$$0 \leq \alpha_1 \leq 1; \quad \alpha_2, \ \alpha_3, \ \alpha_4, \ \alpha_6 \geq 0; \quad \alpha_5 \leq 0.$$

The partial derivative of pex with respect to rx, α_1, measures the responsiveness of the domestic currency export price to a change in the weighted exchange rate. The pass-through coefficient or pricing-to-market coefficient (PTM) is then $\alpha_1 - 1$, which measures the effect of a changing exchange rate on the foreign currency price. At one extreme, if domestic firms are price takers, then $\alpha_1 = 1$, and exchange rate changes are reflected entirely in domestic currency prices through a markup adjustment leaving foreign currency prices unchanged while PTM will be zero. At the opposite extreme, where domestic firms have market or monopoly power in foreign markets, changes in the exchange rate are passed through completely and the markup is left unchanged; that is, $\alpha_1 = 0$ and PTM $= -1$. Between these two extremes, we have the case of incomplete pass-through or pricing to market, where $-1 \leq \alpha_1 - 1 \leq 0$.

Rewriting equation (1) and substituting the related explanatory variables into the equation, we can get a variant of the empirical model of the markup ratio equation as follows:

(5)
$$\text{MK}_t^i = \beta_0 + \beta_1 \text{rx}_t^i + \beta_2 \text{CU}_t^i + \beta_3 \text{H}_t^i + \beta_4 \text{tc}_t^i + \beta_5 \text{EL}_t^i + \varepsilon_{3t};$$
$$0 \leq \beta_1 \leq 1; \quad \beta_2, \ \beta_3, \ \beta_4 \geq 0; \quad \beta_5 \leq 0;$$

where MK $=$ (PEX $-$ MC)/MC.

Equation (5) can directly measure the effects of factors influencing a change in the markup ratio, and its estimation results are supposed to be consistent with those in equation (4).

Furthermore, we can discuss the pricing behavior of the exporting firms through price-cost margin (PCM). Assuming that the PCM function has the same explanatory variables as MK or pex, the PCM equation can be expressed as

$$PCM_t^i = \gamma_0 + \gamma_1 rx_t^i + \gamma_2 CU_t^i + \gamma_3 H_t^i + \gamma_4 tc_t^i + \gamma_5 EL_t^i + \varepsilon_{4t};$$

(6)

$$0 \leq \gamma_1 \leq 1; \quad \gamma_2, \gamma_3, \gamma_4 \geq 0; \quad \gamma_5 \leq 0;$$

where $PCM = (PEX - MC)/PEX$.

However, the effect of exchange rate fluctuations on PCM is not as clear as the above equations. Nevertheless, appendix A shows that under some reasonable assumptions, the exchange rate still has a positive effect on PCM.

8.3 Data Descriptions and Features of Taiwanese Petrochemical Industries

The data used in this study are based on annual survey data of 22 midstream petrochemical industries in Taiwan for the period 1986–92. Though there are more than 30 different products in the midstream petrochemical industries, data on some of these products are not complete. Therefore, we take samples from only 22 products. Moreover, because data for some related explanatory variables are missing before 1986, we have to limit our sampling period to start from 1986. Detailed information about the 22 petrochemical products, computations of the Herfindahl index, price elasticities, weighted exchange rate, and weighted transportation cost, and related data sources are given in appendix B.

Before we begin our empirical analysis, it is worth describing the features of Taiwanese petrochemical industries. Table 8.2 reports some characteristics of those 22 petrochemical industries. First, in column (7) we see that 10 out of 22 industries had Herfindahl indexes equal to one during the period; that is, they had strong monopoly power in the domestic market. Second, from columns (3), (4), and (5) we find that only 5 of 22 industries had average ratios of exports to domestic production higher than 30 percent during the period. However, most industries' ratios of exports to domestic production were increasing during the period. This implies that foreign countries' market shares became more and more important for Taiwan's petrochemical industries. Third, in the early stages of the petrochemical industries' development, their focus was on the domestic market; not until the mid-1980s did they start to export their products. Moreover, most of the export destination countries were small countries in which domestic firms usually produced a small amount of those outputs. It can be seen from table 8.3 that only a few products' export destination countries are developed countries.

8.4 Estimation Results

Since each of equations (4), (5), and (6) in section 8.2 has different economic implications, in this section we will estimate the above-mentioned equations and examine whether the empirical results are consistent or not. Table 8.4 reports empirical results of the export price (pex), markup ratio (MK),

ble 8.2   **Important Characteristics for 22 Midstream Petrochemical Industries (average for 1987–92)**

			EX/PRO (%)				
dustry[a]	PRO (1)	EX (2)	1987–89 (3)	1990–92 (4)	1987–92 (5)	CU (%) (6)	H (7)
ЗS	373,437.50	229,783.70	53.28	65.44	59.36	66.08	0.60
Ν	134,428.50	2,876.50	3.57	6.62	2.10	97.55	1.00
R	41,687.17	21,742.67	59.80	45.35	52.58	104.05	1.00
ΡL	104,830.17	896.67	0.36	1.34	0.85	103.13	1.00
)P	191,212.33	7,144.33	3.86	3.71	3.78	61.88	0.55
;	189,398.00	9,407.67	6.66	2.84	4.75	73.97	0.52
)PE	162,913.17	50,362.00	26.18	36.67	31.42	79.28	0.54
)PE	197,460.50	38,800.67	10.90	28.40	19.65	81.73	0.50
Ε	11,338.50	2,537.00	25.19	19.62	22.40	97.32	1.00
ιL	26,331.83	3,620.50	9.13	54.66	27.34	23.98	1.00
ΜA	27,465.83	2,575.50	0.82	18.22	9.52	69.95	1.00
↓	66,728.17	1,575.33	63.16	1.58	2.37	91.92	1.00
•	224,162.33	13,228.33	2.57	9.01	5.79	80.00	0.51
'G	20,938.33	3,138.17	8.45	21.56	15.01	81.98	1.00
;	336,417.00	119,572.50	22.88	40.98	31.93	70.52	0.34
ΓA	780,547.17	13,199.67	0.00	2.10	1.05	87.17	0.90
∕A	40,798.67	30,578.83	79.13	71.69	75.41	82.25	1.00
∕C	888,982.67	29,244.83	1.21	5.01	3.11	80.23	0.78
ЗR	140,195.50	21,627.83	10.94	28.57	19.76	56.97	0.88
∕Ι	333,008.83	15,600.33	8.32	1.37	4.85	85.52	0.51
ΛM	78,779.00	4,953.67	7.15	5.48	6.32	78.93	1.00
CM	661,603.67	0.00	0.00	0.00	0.00	75.47	0.91

ote: PRO, domestic production; EX, exports; CU, capacity utilization rate; H, Herfindahl index.
or a key to industry abbreviations, see appendix table 8B.1.

and price-cost margin (PCM) equations for Taiwan's petrochemical industries. Since all we have is seven years of annual survey data for 22 petrochemical industries, we adopt the pooling regression procedure to estimate the three equations. The explanatory variables consist of unit production cost (mc), weighted exchange rate (rx), capacity utilization rate (CU), Herfindahl index (H), demand elasticity (EL), and transportation cost (tc). The production cost, weighted exchange rate, and transportation cost are in logarithmic form. Because not all variables have significant estimates, we report several variants of estimates. In addition to the coefficient for each variable, the table also reports the adjusted R^2 and root mean square error.

The estimation results for the export price equations show that, except for demand elasticity, all the explanatory variables have the expected signs. Among them, most coefficients of unit production cost, weighted exchange rate, capacity utilization rate, and transportation cost are significantly different from zero. Though the effect of the exchange rate on export prices is signifi-

Table 8.3   **Major Export Destination Countries for Taiwanese Petrochemical Products in 1992 (percent of product exports)**

ABS		HDPE		PA	
Hong Kong	78.01	Hong Kong	87.18	Hong Kong	27.51
Malaysia	3.52	Malaysia	4.35	Korea	27.51
United States	3.22	Thailand	3.09	Indonesia	23.21
Japan	1.58	Japan	2.81	Japan	9.08
Thailand	1.25	Philippines	0.94	Singapore	7.95
Netherlands	1.16	Jordan	0.91	Philippines	1.93
Belgium	1.14	Indonesia	0.73	Australia	1.83
United Kingdom	1.03	LDPE		South Africa	0.97
Philippines	0.86	Hong Kong	69.36	PP	
Singapore	0.86	Thailand	6.72	Hong Kong	59.04
AN		Japan	5.85	Indonesia	25.40
Indonesia	98.82	Australia	5.11	Thailand	6.75
Hong Kong	0.94	Malaysia	3.12	Malaysia	5.07
Bahrain	0.24	Philippines	2.49	Italy	1.20
BR		Singapore	2.41	South Africa	0.31
Hong Kong	22.38	India	1.82	Philippines	0.30
Japan	13.62	Indonesia	1.33	Vietnam	0.28
Malaysia	10.03	Vietnam	0.80	Venezuela	0.28
Thailand	7.89	ME		United States	0.26
Philippines	7.82	Japan	69.52	PPG	
Germany	7.76	Indonesia	18.75	Hong Kong	86.68
United Kingdom	6.33	Malaysia	8.84	Singapore	7.63
Korea	3.90	Thailand	1.54	Thailand	2.90
Australia	3.13	United States	0.35	Australia	1.18
United States	2.86	Israel	0.35	Indonesia	0.69
CPL		Iran	0.31	Pakistan	0.42
Hong Kong	83.88	Singapore	0.28	Malaysia	0.40
Thailand	16.12	Belgium	0.06	India	0.10
DOP		ML		PS	
Hong Kong	58.80	Hong Kong	96.14	Hong Kong	85.02
Vietnam	12.28	Pakistan	3.69	Japan	3.30
Australia	9.84	Malaysia	0.06	Thailand	2.59
Korea	8.55	Macao	0.06	Malaysia	2.06
Philippines	3.66	Korea	0.03	Korea	1.48
Thailand	1.93	Vietnam	0.03	Singapore	0.99
Libya	1.60	MMA		South Africa	0.77
Indonesia	1.57	Thailand	25.50	Philippines	0.66
Japan	0.52	Philippines	14.83	India	0.61
United States	0.52	Hong Kong	13.44	Vietnam	0.54
EG		South Africa	9.02	PTA	
Hong Kong	56.51	Korea	7.78	Thailand	78.02
Singapore	18.71	Australia	7.66	Indonesia	9.07
Philippines	8.67	Japan	6.27	Hong Kong	8.12
Malaysia	6.67	New Zealand	5.19	Singapore	1.62
South Africa	2.89	Indonesia	4.97	Philippines	1.35
Indonesia	2.65	Malaysia	3.04	Iceland	0.68
Australia	1.97			Pakistan	0.68
New Zealand	1.16			Japan	0.32
Japan	0.72			Australia	0.11
Sri Lanka	0.04			Spain	0.03

Table 8.3 (continued)

PVA		SBR		VAM	
United States	55.84	Hong Kong	46.86	Hong Kong	49.28
Germany	12.61	Korea	21.15	Nigeria	18.97
Indonesia	7.05	Indonesia	14.43	Indonesia	13.09
Thailand	3.86	Philippines	10.58	Sri Lanka	11.76
Malaysia	3.82	Thailand	2.82	Thailand	5.31
Mexico	2.45	Pakistan	2.82	New Zealand	0.76
Singapore	1.99	Mexico	0.80	India	0.38
Korea	1.86	Singapore	0.53	Malaysia	0.38
Pakistan	1.85	India	0.00	Japan	0.08
Hong Kong	1.19	SM		VCM	
PVC		Hong Kong	59.62	Hong Kong	100.00
Hong Kong	32.50	Indonesia	11.89		
Thailand	30.81	Malaysia	11.31		
Philippines	22.34	Australia	4.99		
Japan	4.80	United Arab	4.11		
Singapore	3.30	Emirates			
Malaysia	3.06	Egypt	4.11		
Indonesia	1.90	Pakistan	2.06		
Vietnam	0.68	Thailand	0.73		
South Africa	0.19	Nigeria	0.44		
United States	0.15	Saudi Arabia	0.44		

Table 8.4   Estimates of Export Price, Markup Ratio, and Price-Cost Margin, 1986–92

Dependent Variable	Constant	mc	rx	CU	tc	H	EL	Adjusted R^2	Root Mean Square Error
				Independent Variables					
pex	4.293	0.341	0.073	0.835	0.196	0.0006	0.0002	.094	.297
	(−1.470)	(1.357)	(2.008)**	(1.997)*	(1.632)	(1.411)	(0.155)		
pex	3.008	0.481	0.077	1.118	0.156	0.0006		.279	.287
	(1.261)	(2.379)**	(2.357)**	(3.563)***	(1.454)	(1.503)			
pex	2.972	0.512	0.054	0.897	0.170			.280	.284
	(1.672)*	(3.336)***	(2.070)**	(3.167)***	(1.819)*				
MK	−4.260		0.156	2.183	0.373	0.001	−0.0004	.425	.431
	(−3.447)***		(3.072)***	(3.854)***	(2.188)**	(1.706)*	(−0.272)		
MK	−4.217		0.138	2.137	0.334	0.001		.448	.417
	(−3.402)***		(2.913)***	(4.731)***	(2.224)**	(1.779)*			
PCM	−2.270		0.067	0.751	0.219	0.0005	−0.0004	.196	.281
	(−2.594)***		(2.027)**	(2.031)**	(1.972)*	(1.131)	(−0.428)		
PCM	−2.064		0.063	0.796	0.190	0.0005		.233	.265
	(−2.619)		(2.095)**	(2.771)***	(1.993)**	(1.239)			

Note: Numbers in parentheses are *t*-statistics.

*Significant at the 10 percent level.

**Significant at the 5 percent level.

***Significant at the 1 percent level.

cantly different from zero, the magnitude is rather small, around 0.07. This implies that, on average, Taiwanese petrochemical firms absorb only about 7 percent of a given exchange rate change in their export prices; that is, the exchange rate pass-through effect is as high as 93 percent. This is contrary to the general perception that most exporters in developing countries have pricing-to-market behaviors.

The results for the markup ratio function are very similar to those for the export price equations. Weighted exchange rate, capacity utilization rate, transportation cost, and market concentration rate all have significant positive effects on the markup ratio. Though demand price elasticity has the right sign, it is insignificantly different from zero. Since the markup ratio is not expressed in logarithmic form, we cannot interpret the coefficient of the weighted exchange rate as an elasticity. However, we can approximate it through dividing the coefficient by the sample mean of MK. In this way, we get an elasticity of the markup ratio with respect to the weighted exchange rate of around 0.19.[6] The results for the price-cost margin equations are also very similar to those for the export price and markup ratio equations. The computed elasticity of PCM with respect to the weighted exchange rate is also around 0.19, which is very close to the findings for the markup equations.[7] Moreover, by reference to equation (A12) in appendix A, the positive sign of the coefficient of the exchange rate in the PCM equation implies that firms in Taiwanese petrochemical industries and export destination countries are in a competitive situation.

The empirical results for the export price, markup, and price-cost margin equations all show that the impact of the exchange rate on the export price is relatively small, in the range of 7 to 19 percent. These results are quite different from economists' general impression. Actually, in some existing empirical studies, exporters in developing countries such as Korea and Taiwan have been found to show pricing-to-market behavior (Athukorala 1991; Liu 1994). However, why do the exporting firms of petrochemical products in Taiwan enjoy more than an 80 percent pass-through effect? The possible reasons are as follows. First, it is a general feature of the petrochemical industry that the volatility of profitability is very large. Therefore, firms are unwilling to change their markups when the exchange rate fluctuates. Second, table 8.2 showed that the petrochemical industries in Taiwan are highly concentrated. They have strong monopoly power and a large domestic market share. Moreover, as we showed in section 8.3, the share of exports in domestic production is relatively small. Petrochemical industries do not rely on foreign markets to maintain production efficiency. Third, most of the markets to which Taiwan's petrochemical products are being exported are small-scale markets in which the domestic firms usually do not produce or only produce a small amount of related products. Therefore, Taiwanese petrochemical firms can take a strong position toward

---

6. The sample mean of the markup ratio during the period 1987–92 is 0.737.
7. The sample mean of the price-cost margin for the sampling period is 0.333.

those countries. This can also be justified by all the estimated coefficients of demand elasticity in the variant equations being insignificantly different from zero.

It can be noted from table 8.1 that the NT dollar–U.S. dollar exchange rate has been stabilizing since 1989. It is interesting to ask whether the exchange rate pass-through effect for Taiwan's petrochemical industries has undergone structural changes or not (Kim 1990). However, our data period is too short to analyze the time-varying properties of exchange rate pass-through parameters. Nevertheless, we can discuss the issue by dividing our sample period into two separate periods. Our estimation results are presented in tables 8.5 and 8.6.

Comparing the exchange rate parameters between these two tables, we find that when the coefficients are significant, the exchange rate parameters in the second period are all almost twice as large as those in the first period. The exchange rate elasticity of MK or PCM in the first period was around 13 percent; in the second period it was about 30 percent.[8] In table 8.7 we also present a rolling estimation for every four years of each equation. It can be seen from the table that exchange rate elasticities of the estimated parameters do have the tendency to increase through time. By reference to equation (A12) in appendix A, this implies that when the elasticity of collusion (β) is negative and the absolute value of β is increasing, the impact of exchange rate change on price-cost margin will be positive and increasing. That is, Taiwan's petrochemical export firms have been pricing to market more and more in recent years. This implication may be justified by the fact that while petrochemical firms in most countries have continued expanding their capacities since 1986, the degree of competition in world petrochemical markets has increased. In addition, Taiwanese petrochemical firms have not been so well protected as before in holding their market shares in domestic markets since the government lifted all restrictions on the import of petrochemical products and lowered related import tariffs in 1986. They have gradually realized that proper pricing behavior in response to exchange rate changes is very important if they are to penetrate the world market, to reach minimum efficient scale, and to attain production efficiency. On the other hand, the increasing degree of pricing to market may also be explained by the acquisition of modern management and marketing knowledge among entrepreneurs in Taiwan's petrochemical industries. Therefore, they are increasingly aware of the importance of holding world market share in order to maintain a long-run business (Froot and Klemperer 1989).[9]

8. The sample means of the markup ratio and price-cost margin are respectively 0.769 and 0.359 for the first period and 0.706 and 0.307 for the second period.

9. Since 1985, accompanied by the recovery of the world economy, petrochemical industries worldwide have vigorously expanded their production capacities, which increases competitiveness among world petrochemical exporters.

Table 8.5   Estimates of Export Price, Markup Ratio, and Price-Cost Margin, 1986–89

Dependent Variable	Constant	mc	rx	CU	tc	H	EL	Adjusted R^2	Root Mean Square Error
pex	-3.004 (-0.715)	1.183 (3.283)***	0.071 (2.321)**	2.120 (3.368)***	-0.038 (-0.270)	0.0005 (1.799)*	-0.0008 (-0.565)	.576	.178
pex	-2.021 (-0.598)	1.082 (3.784)***	0.065 (2.318)**	1.496 (4.040)***	0.033 (0.309)	0.0005 (1.730)		.639	.178
pex	3.756 (1.986)*	0.639 (4.097)***	0.033 (1.326)	1.247 (3.939)***	-0.108 (-1.145)			.553	.192
MK	-1.895 (-1.665)		0.108 (2.642)**	3.502 (3.959)***	-0.094 (-0.551)	0.0009 (2.105)*	-0.0009 (-0.520)	.605	.251
MK	-2.706 (-1.923)*		0.102 (2.668)**	2.742 (5.503)***	0.016 (0.125)	0.0009 (2.136)**		.659	.248
PCM	-0.454 (-0.752)		0.044 (2.024)*	1.331 (2.833)**	-0.058 (-0.634)	0.0003 (1.439)	-0.0003 (-0.287)	.387	.133
PCM	-0.594 (-1.031)		0.043 (2.085)*	0.838 (3.152)***	0.015 (0.228)	0.0003 (1.385)		.382	.132

The column group "Independent Variables" spans Constant, mc, rx, CU, tc, H, EL.

Note: Numbers in parentheses are *t*-statistics.

*Significant at the 10 percent level.

**Significant at the 5 percent level.

***Significant at the 1 percent level.

Table 8.6   Estimates of Export Price, Markup Ratio, and Price-Cost Margin, 1990–92

Dependent Variable	Independent Variables							Adjusted R^2	Root Mean Square Error
	Constant	mc	rx	CU	tc	H	EL		
pex	7.903 (2.218)**	-0.170 (-0.556)	0.054 (0.848)	0.251 (0.500)	0.406 (2.307)**	0.0032 (0.675)	0.0005 (0.421)	.121	.294
pex	5.149 (1.764)*	0.164 (0.672)	0.106 (1.943)*	0.588 (1.306)	0.344 (2.174)**	-0.0021 (-0.751)		.257	.298
pex	4.314 (1.839)*	0.205 (0.961)	0.116 (2.517)**	0.726 (1.971)*	0.355 (2.783)***			.349	.280
MK	-7.149 (-2.461)**		0.211 (1.901)*	1.872 (2.193)**	0.712 (2.219)**	0.0012 (0.139)	0.0007 (0.284)	.375	.539
MK	-6.074 (-2.805)***		0.167 (1.793)*	1.551 (2.038)*	0.644 (2.417)**	-0.0004 (-0.081)		.385	.510
PCM	-3.200 (-1.638)		0.095 (1.269)	0.543 (0.946)	0.375 (1.738)*	-0.0019 (-0.340)	-0.0003 (-0.215)	.131	.362
PCM	-3.023 (-2.149)**		0.089 (1.472)	0.470 (0.950)	0.365 (2.108)**	-0.0021 (-0.672)		.211	.332

Note: Numbers in parentheses are *t*-statistics.

*Significant at the 10 percent level.

**Significant at the 5 percent level.

***Significant at the 1 percent level.

Table 8.7   **Estimated Exchange Rate Elasticities for Different Periods**

Dependent Variable	1987–89	1988–90	1989–91	1990–92
pex	0.065	0.066	0.074	0.106
MK	0.102	0.114	0.122	0.167
	(0.133)	(0.152)	(0.179)	(0.237)
PCM	0.043	0.048	0.054	0.089
	(0.120)	(0.137)	(0.172)	(0.290)

Note: Since the estimates of demand elasticity in all equations are insignificantly different from zero, in this table we present regression results that contain mc, rx, CU, tc, and H as explanatory variables. The numbers in parentheses are elasticities.

8.5 Conclusion

In the existing literature, there is a general perception that newly industrializing countries like Korea and Taiwan have little control over the prices at which they sell and that therefore exchange rate changes may not have a significant impact on their foreign-currency-denominated export prices in international markets. In this paper we investigate a special industry, petrochemicals, which has a high degree of monopoly power and faces weak competition in export destination countries, in order to demonstrate that not all industries in Taiwan's export sectors display a strong pricing-to-market pattern. The empirical results show that Taiwanese petrochemical export firms absorb only about 7 percent of a given weighted exchange rate change in their export prices, and we find a 19 percent impact of a 1 percent exchange rate change on the markup ratio or price-cost margin. This implies that Taiwan's petrochemical industries have had a weak pricing-to-market pattern during the period 1987–92. The empirical results may be explained by the great volatility of profitability, high market concentration, and small share of exports in domestic production. These empirical results further support the argument, pointed out by Knetter (1993), that the range of parameter estimates across industries within each source country is very wide and there exist few differences in behavior within common industries of different source countries. We also show that though the influence of the exchange rate on export prices, markup ratios, and price-cost margins is relatively weak in Taiwan's petrochemical industries, the impact has tended to increase over time. This might be attributed to increasing competition in the world market or the realization of the importance of world market shares for Taiwanese petrochemical export firms. Finally, our results are very preliminary due to the short sampling period and insufficient data for foreign countries. If we could obtain the prices of petrochemical products in every Taiwan export destination country, we would have more reasonable proxies for demand pressures. In addition, more rigorous analyses of the causes of structural change in pricing-to-market behavior and the cyclical nature of pass-through effects are worthy of future research.

Appendix A
Derivation of the Impact of the Exchange Rate on PCM

Following Cowling and Waterson (1976), Brander and Krugman (1983), and Dei (1990), we envisage two open economies, a home and a foreign country. Assume that there is a monopolist producing a homogeneous product with the same cost condition in each country. Suppose that marginal costs are constant at c for both monopolists, and the inverse market demand functions in both countries are as follows:[10]

$$(A1) \qquad P^d = P^d(X^h + X^m), \quad P^{d\prime} < 0,$$

$$(A2) \qquad P^w = P^w(X^e + X^f), \quad X^w = X^e + X^f, \quad P^{w\prime} < 0;$$

where P^d and P^w represent prices at home and in the foreign country, respectively; X^h and X^e quantities produced by the domestic firm and sold at home and in the foreign country, respectively; X^m and X^f quantities produced by the foreign firm and sold at home and in the foreign country, respectively; and X^w total quantity demanded in the foreign country. Let $P^e = r \cdot P^w$, where P^e represents the home currency export price and r is the exchange rate. Then the domestic firm's and the foreign firm's profits can be formulated as follows:

$$(A3) \qquad \pi^d = (P^d - C)X^h + (P^e - C)X^e - F^d,$$

$$(A4) \qquad \pi^w = (rP^w - C)X^f + (P^d - C)X^m - F^w,$$

where π^d and π^w represent the domestic firm's and the foreign firm's profits, respectively; and F^d and F^w the domestic firm's and the foreign firm's fixed costs, respectively.

Assuming profit-maximizing behavior and Cournot zero conjectural variation, the first-order conditions for a maximum can be derived as follows:

$$(A5) \qquad \frac{\partial \pi^d}{\partial X^e} = P^e + rX^e P^{w\prime} - C = 0,$$

$$(A6) \qquad \frac{\partial \pi^w}{\partial X^f} = rP^w + rX^f P^{w\prime} - C = 0.$$

By total differentiation of equations (A5) and (A6), and rearrangement and manipulation, we obtain

$$(A7) \qquad \begin{bmatrix} 2rP^{w\prime} & rP^{w\prime} \\ rP^{w\prime} & 2rP^{w\prime} \end{bmatrix} \begin{bmatrix} dX^e \\ dX^f \end{bmatrix} = \begin{bmatrix} -(P^w + P^{w\prime}X^e)dr + dC \\ -(P^w + P^{w\prime}X^f)dr + dC \end{bmatrix}.$$

---

10. For computational convenience, the notation in this appendix differs from that in the text.

Assuming that the costs of production remain constant (i.e., $dC = 0$), we can obtain by Cramer's rule

(A8)
$$\frac{\partial X^e}{\partial r} = \frac{rP^{w\prime}[(P^{w\prime}X^f - 2X^e) - P^w]}{3(rP^{w\prime})^2},$$

$$> 0 \quad \text{if } X^f > 2X^e,$$

$$? \quad \text{otherwise}.$$

(A9)
$$\frac{\partial X^f}{\partial r} = \frac{rP^{w\prime}[P^{w\prime}(X^e - 2X^f) - P^w]}{3(rP^{w\prime})^2},$$

$$> 0 \quad \text{if } X^e > 2X^f,$$

$$< 0 \quad \text{if } X^f > 2X^e,$$

$$? \quad \text{otherwise},$$

where the absolute value of $-3X^eP^{w\prime}$ is assumed to be greater than that of P^w.

In order to allow possible collusion between the domestic and foreign firms, we relax the assumption that the domestic firm expects no response from the foreign firm to its output change. Therefore, equation (A5) becomes

(A10)
$$rX^eP^{w\prime}\left(1 + \frac{\partial X^f}{\partial X^e}\right) + rP^w - C = 0.$$

By rearranging and manipulating equation (A10), we can obtain

(A11)
$$\text{PCM} \equiv \frac{P^e - C}{P^e} = \left(1 + \frac{X^f}{X^e}\beta\right)\frac{1}{\varepsilon^p_{w,h}},$$

where PCM represents the exporting price-cost margin of the domestic firm, β the elasticity of collusion between the domestic and foreign firms, and $\varepsilon^p_{w,h}$ the domestic firm's price elasticity of demand in the foreign country. Finally, by partial differentiation of equation (A11) with respect to r and referring to equations (A8) and (A9), we can obtain

(A12)
$$\frac{\partial \text{PCM}}{\partial r} = \frac{\beta}{\varepsilon^p_{w,h}} \cdot \frac{X^e(\partial X^f / \partial r) - X^f(\partial X^e / \partial r)}{(X^e)^2},$$

$$> 0 \quad \text{if } \beta < 0 \text{ and } X^f > 2X^e,$$

$$< 0 \quad \text{if } \beta > 0 \text{ and } X^f > 2X^e,$$

where $\beta = 1$ stands for perfect collusion, $\beta = -1$ is perfect competition, $0 < \beta < 1$ is imperfect collusion, and $-1 < \beta < 0$ is imperfect competition (Clarke and Davies 1982; Cubbin 1983).

Appendix B
Computation of Related Variables and Data Sources

Computation of Related Variables

MK   *markup ratio* = (PEX − MC)/MC

PCM   *price-cost margin* = (PEX − MC)/PEX

H   *Herfindahl index* = $\sum_{i=1}^{22}[(\text{PRO}_i - \text{EX}_i)/\sum_{j=1}^{22}(\text{PRO}_j - \text{EX}_j)]^2$

EL   *export demand price elasticity* = $(\text{EX}_t - \text{EX}_{t-1}/\text{EX}_{t-1})/$
     $(\text{PEX}_t - \text{PEX}_{t-1}/\text{PEX}_{t-1})$

RX   *weighted exchange rate* = $\sum_{i=1}^{n}(\text{EX}_i/\sum_{j=1}^{n}\text{EX}_j)\text{RX}_i$

TC   *weighted transportation cost* = $\sum_{i=1}^{n}(\text{EX}_i/\sum_{j=1}^{n}\text{EX}_j)\text{VD}_i$

Data Sources, Indicated by (A)–(E)

CU   capacity utilization rate   (A)

EX   export quantity   (B)

MC   unit production cost   (C)

PEX   export price   (A)

PRO   domestic production quantity   (A)

Table 8B.1   Description of 22 Midstream Petrochemical Industries

Abbreviation	Industry
ABS	ABS resin
AN	Acrylonitrile
BR	Butadiene rubber
CPL	Caprolactam
DOP	Dioctyl phthalate
EG	Ethylene glycol
HDPE	High-density polyethylene
LDPE	Low-density polyethylene
ME	Melamine
ML	Methanol
MMA	Methyl methacrylate acid
PA	Phthalic anlydride
PP	Polypropylene
PPG	Polypropylene glycol
PS	Polystyrene
PTA	Terephthalic acid
PVA	Polyvinyl alcohol
PVC	Polyvinyl chloride
SBR	Styrene-butadiene rubber
SM	Styrene
VAM	Vinyl acetate
VCM	Vinyl chloride

RX   exchange rate   (D)
VD   voyage distance   (E)

(A)   Petrochemical Industry Association of Taiwan, *Petrochemical Indus-tries in Taiwan, Republic of China* (Taipei, 1986–92).
(B)   Ministry of Finance, Department of Statistics, *Monthly Statistics of Exports and Imports, Taiwan Area, R.O.C.* (Taipei, 1986–92).
(C)   Directorate-General of Budget, Accounting and Statistics, Executive Yuan, *Commodity-Price Statistics Monthly in Taiwan Area, R.O.C.* (Taipei, 1986–92).
(D)   Central Bank of China, Economic Research Department, *Financial Statistics Monthly, Taiwan District, R.O.C.* (Taipei, 1986–92).
(E)   Ministry of Communication, Executive Yuan, Taiwan, R.O.C.

References

Athukorala, P. 1991. Exchange rate pass-through: The case of Korean exports of manu-factures. *Economics Letters* 35:79–84.
Athukorala, P., and J. Menon. 1994. Pricing to market behaviour and exchange rate pass-through in Japanese exports. *Economic Journal* 104:271–81.
Brander, J., and P. Krugman. 1983. A reciprocal dumping model of international trade. *Journal of International Economics* 15:313–21.
Clarke, R., and S. W. Davies. 1982. Market structure and price-cost margins. *Economica* 49:277–87.
Cowling, K., and M. Waterson. 1976. Price cost margins and market structure. *Economica* 43:267–74.
Cubbin, J. 1983. Apparent collusion and conjectural variation in differentiated oligop-oly. *International Journal of Industrial Organization* 1:155–63.
Dei, F. 1990. A note on multinational corporations in a model of reciprocal dumping. *Journal of International Economics* 29:161–71.
Dornbusch, R. 1987. Exchange rates and prices. *American Economic Review* 77:93–106.
Feenstra, R. C. 1987. Symmetric pass-through of tariffs and exchange rates under im-perfect competition: An empirical test. NBER Working Paper no. 2453. Cambridge, Mass.: National Bureau of Economic Research.
Fisher, E. 1989. Exchange rate pass-through and the relative concentration of German and Japanese manufacturing industries. *Economics Letters* 131:81–85.
Froot, K., and P. Klemperer. 1989. Exchange rate pass-through when market share mat-ters. *American Economic Review* 79:637–54.
Hooper, P., and C. Mann. 1989. Exchange rate pass-through in the 1980s: The case of U.S. imports of manufactures. *Brookings Papers on Economic Activity*, no. 1:297–329.
Khalizadeh-Shirazi, J. 1974. Market structure and price-cost margins in United King-dom manufacturing industries. *Review of Economics and Statistics* 56:67–76.
Kim, Yoonbai. 1990. Exchange rates and imports prices in the U.S.: A varying-parameter estimation of exchange rate pass-through. *Journal of Business and Eco-nomic Statistics* 8:305–15.
Knetter, M. 1989. Price discrimination by U.S. and German exporters. *American Eco-nomic Review* 79:198–210.

———. 1993. International comparisons of pricing to market behavior. *American Economic Review* 83:473–86.
Krugman, P. R. 1987. Pricing to market when the exchange rate changes. In *Real financial linkages among open economies,* ed. S. Arndt and J. D. Richardson. Cambridge, Mass.: MIT Press.
Liu, Bih-Jane. 1994. Cost externality and exchange rate pass-through: Some evidence from Taiwan. In *Macroeconomic linkage: Savings, exchange rates, and capital flows,* ed. T. Ito and A. O. Krueger, 247–72. Chicago: University of Chicago Press.
Mann, C. 1986. Price, profit margins, and exchange rates. *Federal Reserve Bulletin* 72:366–79.
Marston, R. 1990. Pricing to market in Japanese manufacturing. *Journal of International Economics* 29:217–36.
Menon, J. 1995. Exchange rates and import prices for a small open economy. *Applied Economics* 27:297–301.
Ohno, Kenichi. 1989. Export pricing behavior of manufacturing: A U.S.-Japan comparison. *IMF Staff Papers* 36:550–79.
Shinjo, Koji. 1993. Exchange rate changes and pricing behavior of Japanese firms: A cross-section analysis. *Journal of the Japanese and International Economies* 7: 157–74.
Wu, Chung-Shu. 1995. An investigation of exchange rate pass-through effects on Taiwan import prices. In *Essays on open macroeconomic issues,* ed. Jia-Dong Shea and Chung-Shu Wu, 43–62. Taipei: Academia Sinica, Institute of Economics.

Comment   Kenichi Ohno

Wang and Wu's paper investigates the export-pricing behavior of Taiwan's 22 midstream petrochemical firms. The study is interesting because of its focus on Taiwan as a newly industrialized economy whose role has expanded rapidly in the Asia Pacific region and its use of microeconomic firm-level data. The main finding is that these Taiwanese firms do not exhibit the typical "small country" property of taking international prices as given. Instead, they largely maintain their export prices in NT dollars even when the exchange rate changes. In other words, their exchange rate pass-through is high.

Midstream petrochemical firms are not meant to be representative of Taiwanese exporting firms. Their relatively large size and small number in the home market make them an exception in the Taiwanese industrial landscape, where a large number of small and medium-sized enterprises are the common feature. The lack of export price sensitivity may well be due to this peculiar characteristic of the industry chosen for the study—as Wang and Wu suggest. However, before evaluating the validity of this interpretation—or any other interpretations offered in this paper—several technical issues must be clarified.

Kenichi Ohno is professor of economics at the National Graduate Institute for Policy Studies, Japan.

First, the authors adopt three specifications of pricing behavior for estimation, namely, the export price equation, the markup equation, and the price-cost equation. These are not independent but simply different arrangements of the same variables. While running all equations that have been tried previously is one possible strategy, clearly, a more satisfactory procedure is to begin with a theoretical model that leads to an empirical equation, allowing economic interpretation of the estimated parameters. The present paper does not permit such an interpretation. Nor is there a criterion for choosing among the three specifications when they produce somewhat different results.

Second, the use of the Herfindahl index to measure the degree of domestic monopoly has its limitations, because the number of firms in an industry—or the distribution of their market shares—is not necessarily correlated with the competitive environment of that industry. In the Taiwanese context, the status of contestability (free entry) as well as foreign competition must also be taken into account. Of course, to be fair, this is a broader problem of how to measure the state of competition and is not unique to this paper.

Third, we need more information to interpret the estimated pass-through coefficients. As the authors explain, most petrochemical firms in Taiwan do not export much; they are home market oriented and export only a tiny fraction of their output to a large number of small countries. But what is the market structure like in those foreign countries? If prices there do not follow global trends, due to either import protection or the monopolistic power of Taiwanese exporters, it is easy to understand why the pricing of the Taiwanese firms is not sensitive to the exchange rate. In addition, the possibility of intrafirm trade may be an important factor. If Taiwanese petrochemical products are inputs to Taiwanese subsidiaries abroad, the transfer price may be insensitive to the exchange rate as it does not affect the consolidated profits of the entire industrial group.

Finally, there is an inescapable problem arising from running regressions on only seven annual observations. True, these time series are pooled across 22 firms so there is no apparent lack of degrees of freedom. Even so, what the paper essentially does is find a correlation between the exchange rate and export price movements during seven recent years (1986–92). For such a short period, which can include only a few major turns of the exchange rate, it is very difficult to tell whether the correlation is real or accidental. One suspects that the estimation may not be very robust against alternative sample periods, and this suspicion is vindicated when tables 8.5 and 8.6 are compared. These tables report the estimation results when the sample period is subdivided further into 1986–89 and 1990–92. Many key parameters—including those on marginal cost, exchange rate, and capacity utilization—lose significance from the first period to the second, while others—like transportation cost—become highly significant only in the second period. One would like to have a longer time series, or explore the possibility of using quarterly data, to overcome these weaknesses.

Comment   Y. C. Jao

The Wang-Wu paper is a highly specialized and technical study of the export-pricing behavior of one particular industry, the petrochemical industry, in Taiwan. According to the received theory, developing countries, including newly industrializing countries, are price takers in world markets. Specifically, this behavior implies that exchange rate changes do not affect foreign currency export prices and there should be little or no exchange rate pass-through. With a few notable exceptions, such as OPEC in its heyday, this proposition is generally well founded empirically.

Wang and Wu, however, find that the impact of the exchange rate on the domestic currency export prices, or markup ratio, or price-cost margin, of Taiwan's petrochemical products was very small, ranging from 7 to 19 percent, or in other words, the pass-through effect was remarkably high, ranging from 81 to 97 percent during their sample period. Their results seem to contradict the conventional wisdom.

The authors use a well-specified model to test the pricing behavior of the petrochemical industry, with unit production cost, weighted exchange rate, capacity utilization rate, Herfindahl index, demand elasticity, and transportation cost as the explanatory variables. In general, the estimated coefficients seem to be satisfactory.

The authors explain their results by the following factors: profit volatility, high industrial concentration, small share of exports in total domestic output, and weakness of domestic firms in export markets. Except perhaps for profit volatility, the other factors are reasonable enough. The "market power" factor, in particular, reminds one of the behavior of OPEC, which at the height of its power could exact huge increases in crude oil prices to compensate for the decline of the U.S. dollar.

The obvious question to ask is: how typical is the behavior of Taiwan's petrochemical industry? This issue is not addressed in the paper. An outsider's impression is that the petrochemical industry is most probably a special case, with a pricing strategy unlikely to be typical, even for Taiwan, let alone the whole developing world. Wang and Wu themselves note that the impact of the exchange rate on domestic currency export prices may be expected to increase over time, due to increasing liberalization of trade, foreign competition, and the realization by the export firms concerned of the importance of maintaining export market shares.

Another limitation is the shortness of the sampling period, 1986–92. Some economic variables may change unpredictably. Take the NT dollar–U.S. dollar exchange rate for instance. Between 1983 and 1989, the NT dollar appreciated strongly, with the exchange rate falling from 40.07 to 26.41. Between 1989

Y. C. Jao is professor of economics at the University of Hong Kong and center associate of the Center for Pacific Basin Monetary and Economic Studies, Federal Reserve Bank of San Francisco.

and 1995, the rate was generally stable, fluctuating within a narrow range. Since the Taiwan Strait crisis erupted in July 1995, the NT dollar has shown a mild tendency to depreciate. It is to be hoped that the authors can extend their empirical study as more data become available, in order to take into account the rapidly changing economic environment.

The most significant contribution of Wang and Wu's paper is the demonstration that disaggregative studies of industrial structure can yield richer insights into pricing behavior not otherwise obtainable from highly aggregative studies. However, for reasons already stated, the case of Taiwan's petrochemical industry per se is not enough to upset the general proposition that developing countries, on the whole, are price takers in world markets.

9   Evaluation of Korea's Exchange Rate Policy

Sang-Woo Nam and Se-Jong Kim

9.1   Korea's Exchange Rate Management, 1970–95

9.1.1   Exchange Rate Regimes

Korea maintained a de facto dollar peg regime until the end of the 1970s, although the system, started in 1965, was officially called a unified floating exchange rate system. The exchange rate of the Korean won against the U.S. dollar was fixed until it appreciated considerably in real (effective) terms, seriously deteriorating export competitiveness. There were relatively large nominal devaluations in 1971, 1974, and 1980.

Entering the 1980s, proper management of the exchange rate was considered all the more important for Korea since the government began to expand trade liberalization, phasing out various export subsidies and import protection measures. In early 1980, a new exchange rate system was adopted in which the Korean won was supposed to be pegged to a basket of currencies for major trading partners. The new exchange rate system was designed to maintain a more stable real effective exchange rate (REER) of the Korean won when there are large fluctuations in the exchange rates of major trading partners. The REER is considered the best indicator for assessing the competitiveness of exports in the world market.

However, in practice, Korea's currency basket system did not aim at a rigid peg. In actuality, the authorities did not disclose the weights applied to the currencies of major trading partners, and policy considerations seem to have played an important role in managing the exchange rate. In fact, the International Monetary Fund (IMF) classified the regime as managed floating, and the REER of the won had exhibited sizable fluctuations during the 1980s.

Sang-Woo Nam is professor at the School of International Policy and Management of the Korea Development Institute. Se-Jong Kim is a research associate of the Korea Development Institute.

In March 1990, a new exchange rate system known as the "market average rate" system replaced the former multicurrency basket peg system. Under this system, the basic exchange rate of the Korean won against the U.S. dollar was determined in the market within a specified range around the weighted average interbank rates of the previous day. The rates against other foreign currencies were then determined by the U.S. dollar rate of the currencies in international foreign exchange markets. An important feature of this new system was that it allowed market forces to play a part in determining exchange rates, thereby laying a basis for the market to become more efficient and moving toward a free-floating regime in the future.

The imposition of a limit on daily fluctuations of the exchange rate was designed to avoid exorbitant movements of the rate in the exchange market, which was still shallow and inefficient. However, the range of allowed daily fluctuations had steadily widened in several steps. At the start, the limit, in either direction, was set at 0.4 percent of the weighted average of the interbank rates of the previous day, but it was expanded in several steps to 2.25 percent in December 1995. The government plans to further widen the band of daily fluctuations and ultimately lift the band in accordance with the maturation of the exchange market. There was evidence that the volatility of the daily won-dollar rate had increased in accordance with the continued widening of the band allowed for daily fluctuation under the market average rate system (Kim 1993). This, however, did not mean that the exchange rate had been unstable in the long run. Actually, the REER had apparently been more stable in the 1990s under the market average rate system than in the 1980s.[1]

9.1.2   The Exchange Rate as an Instrument of Macroeconomic Management

In the early 1970s, the Korean won continued to depreciate against the U.S. dollar while the Japanese yen continued to appreciate under a floating exchange rate system introduced in 1971. As a result, the won showed substantial depreciation on a real effective basis, though this depreciation quickly disappeared because of Korea's high inflation rate.

During the latter half of the 1970s, the won remained fixed to the U.S. dollar in spite of Korea's fairly high inflation. Thus the won appreciated on a real effective basis even though the Japanese yen continued to gain strength against the U.S. dollar. Notwithstanding the adoption of the multicurrency basket peg system and a 20 percent devaluation in 1980, followed by a steady nominal depreciation of the won against the U.S. dollar, the won's REER moderately appreciated until 1982. Then the won depreciated relatively steeply on a real effective basis until mid-1986. This trend was due mainly to two factors. First,

---

1. Oum and Cho (1995) report that the standard deviation of the REER (quarterly average) in the 1990s (up to the third quarter of 1995) was 0.025, while it was 0.113 in the 1980s. Their REER is based on data for Korea's 14 major trading partners with time-varying trade weights. Similar results have also been reported by Kim (1992) and Kim (1995).

although Korea's domestic prices showed relative stability, the won's nominal exchange value vis-à-vis the U.S. dollar depreciated continuously through 1986. Second, the strong performance of the Japanese yen against the U.S. currency since 1985 accelerated the effective depreciation of the Korean won.

As Korea's current account registered sizable surpluses (largely with the United States) as of 1986, the Korean won was under immense pressure from the United States to appreciate. The won showed an unprecedented appreciation against the U.S. currency, from an average of 881 won per dollar in 1986 to 671 won in 1989. The won's real effective exchange value also climbed, a result not only of the nominal appreciation but also of the renewed strength of the U.S. dollar. After 1989, Korea's international payments position deteriorated, reversing the upward trend in the won's nominal exchange value vis-à-vis the U.S. dollar to a downward slide. Meanwhile, the exchange value of the Japanese yen against the U.S. currency showed a rising trend from 1991. Consequently, the won depreciated substantially on a real effective basis, reaching in 1993–94 approximately the same level as in 1986–87, despite Korea's relatively higher rate of inflation (see table 9.1).

In real effective terms, the won's exchange rate had by and large maintained a relatively stable trend compared with those of most other currencies, yet it had nonetheless shown considerable fluctuations in one period or another. One major factor in these fluctuations was that the won's exchange rate had been so heavily biased toward the U.S. dollar that changes in the exchange rate between the U.S. currency and the currencies of other major countries, particularly Japan, had not been immediately reflected in the exchange rate of the won. It seems that there is approximately a one-year time lag before a change in the exchange rate between the U.S. dollar and other major currencies even partially affects the value of the won vis-à-vis the U.S. dollar. The decline in the won's REER in both the 1972–73 and the 1986–87 periods was thus largely due to the appreciation of the Japanese yen against the U.S. dollar (see fig. 9.1).

However, an analysis indicates that the differentials in the rates of inflation between Korea and its major trading partners have been relatively quickly reflected in the won's exchange rate against the U.S. dollar. This may very well have been inevitable if Korea's export prices were to remain competitive while its rate of inflation was relatively high. It was also shown that the won's exchange rate against the U.S. dollar was influenced by Korea's domestic macroeconomic conditions as well.

Evidence exists that adjustments of the exchange rate have frequently been aimed at ensuring an adequate level of foreign exchange reserves and correcting imbalances in the current account. For instance, a real depreciation was called for to improve the external balance when concern over the growing external debt heightened in 1985. However, as the current account showed a sizable surplus in the following years with improvements in the external terms of trade, the Korean won underwent substantial appreciation.

Table 9.1   **Trends in Exchange Rates**

Year	Won per U.S. Dollar	Won per 100 Yen	Nominal Effective Exchange Rate[a]	Relative Price[a]	Real Effective Exchange Rate[a]
1970	310.5	86.3	29.1	36.3	80.0
1971	347.1	99.4	33.0	38.4	86.0
1972	392.8	129.6	39.8	42.4	93.7
1973	398.3	146.6	42.6	40.3	105.8
1974	404.4	138.4	42.2	46.6	90.6
1975	484.0	163.1	50.3	54.8	91.9
1976	484.0	163.2	49.5	58.2	85.0
1977	484.0	221.5	55.4	60.4	91.8
1978	484.0	230.0	57.4	65.1	88.2
1979	484.0	220.9	57.6	70.6	81.6
1980	607.4	267.9	72.0	85.5	84.2
1981	681.0	308.8	78.8	96.9	81.3
1982	731.0	293.5	79.6	98.7	80.6
1983	775.7	326.6	84.7	98.6	85.9
1984	805.9	339.3	86.0	97.6	88.1
1985	870.0	364.8	92.2	98.5	93.6
1986	881.4	523.1	110.0	101.7	108.2
1987	822.5	569.2	111.4	102.3	109.0
1988	731.4	571.0	104.3	103.1	101.2
1989	671.4	486.9	92.0	100.6	91.4
1990	707.7	489.1	97.5	101.8	95.8
1991	733.3	544.4	103.3	106.4	97.1
1992	780.7	616.2	113.1	108.5	104.3
1993	802.7	721.9	119.6	110.5	108.2
1994	803.4	786.1	123.7	113.4	109.1

Sources: IMF, *International Financial Statistics* (Washington, D.C., various issues); Bank of Korea.

Note: Calculation of effective exchange rates was based on a trade-weighted currency basket of Korea's four major trading partners: the United States, Japan, Germany, and the United Kingdom. Relative price was calculated using the wholesale price index.

[a]1985–86 = 100.

This tendency to use current account performance as an indicator of the need for exchange rate adjustments seemed to have resulted in notable swings in the REER due to the time lag between a change in the exchange rate and its impact on the current account balance (Kim 1994; Oum and Cho 1995). All other factors being equal, the won's exchange value against the U.S. dollar had also tended to appreciate when the rate of inflation was relatively high, as the government tried to stabilize domestic prices. Finally, there seem to have been attempts to promote exports by depreciating the won during periods of sluggish domestic economic activity (see tables 9.2 and 9.3; see also Nam 1988).

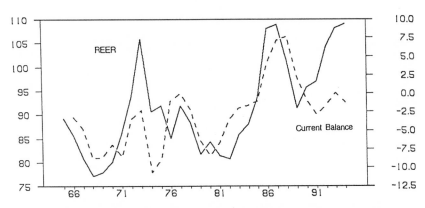

Fig. 9.1   Real effective exchange rate and current balance (percent of GDP)

Table 9.2   Estimation of Nominal Exchange Rate (e), 1968–94

	Dependent Variables	
Explanatory Variable[a]	$\ln e$	$\Delta \ln e$
Constant	−0.58	0.013
$(\Delta)\ln (P_w/P_w^*)$	0.630 (2.60)	0.695 (4.00)
$(\Delta)\ln (P_w/P_w^*)_{-1}$	0.358 (1.56)	0.142 (0.80)
$(\Delta)\ln e^*$		0.008 (0.04)
$(\Delta)\ln e^*_{-1}$	0.589 (3.99)	0.736 (3.65)
$\bar{R}^2$	.969	.588
D.W.	0.55	1.93

[a]Explanatory variables are in differences in logarithms for the second ($\Delta \ln e$) equation.

The Korean government has continuously relaxed its foreign exchange restrictions, and it announced in December 1994 a foreign exchange reform plan that will be implemented in three stages until 1999. While easing restrictions helps the exchange market expand and become more efficient, it exposes the market to greater shocks and potential instability. A particularly serious concern during this transition period is the potentially large inflow of capital resulting from full liberalization.

In order to cope with this situation in a noninflationary way, the Korean won may have to be substantially appreciated. Sterilized intervention in the face of a large capital influx is likely to raise the domestic interest rate, which will further encourage foreign capital inflow. However, nonsterilized intervention in the foreign exchange rate will soon result in real appreciation due to the acceleration of inflation. Actually, in recent years the Korean won appreciated moderately as the net inflow of capital grew much larger than the current account deficit. For the Korean economy, which has a relatively large trade sec-

Table 9.3   Estimation of Real Effective Exchange Rate (REER)

	Dependent Variable: ln REER	
Explanatory Variable	(1)	(2)
Constant	8.09	10.35
$\ln (p_w/p_w^*)$	−0.248 (3.88)	−0.424 (4.97)
$\ln e^*$	−0.571 (3.23)	−0.878 (4.61)
$\Delta\ln y_{-1}$	−0.878 (1.69)	−1.360 (2.81)
$\Delta\ln p_{y-1}$	−0.328 (1.77)	−0.823 (3.38)
CAP/Y	−0.027 (3.51)	−0.029 (4.42)
$(RES/M)_{-1}$	−0.216 (2.86)	−0.197 (2.99)
$(CB/Y)_{-1}$	−0.006 (1.06)	−0.009 (1.84)
ln TOT		−0.568 (2.71)
$\bar{R}^2$	.719	.789
D.W.	1.59	2.39

Note: e, e^* = exchange rate of the won and the currency basket of Korea's major trading partners per U.S. dollar, respectively. p_w, p_w^* = wholesale prices for Korea and Korea's major trading partners, respectively. y, Y = GDP in real and nominal terms, respectively. p_y = GDP deflator. CAP, CB = balance of payments in the capital and current accounts, respectively. RES/M = the ratio of foreign exchange reserves to total commodity imports. TOT = external terms of trade.

tor, a sharp currency appreciation is likely to bring about a recession in the economy as well as growing deficits in the current account.[2]

9.2   Long-Run Behavior of the Exchange Rate

For a country like Korea, where the share of trade in the economy is significant, a two-sector model with tradable and nontradable sectors seems desirable for macroeconomic analysis of the exchange rate. Evidence indicates that relative price movements between tradables and nontradables have been substantial in most countries with a generally rising trend. However, the price ratios have shown differing trends (slopes) among countries, as well as divergences from the trend for individual countries.

The apparent lack of purchasing power parity (PPP) among countries is largely attributable to the existence of nontradables. As noted by Krueger (1983, 67), with the existence of nontradables, PPP would hold only if tradables and nontradables were close substitutes in production, or if trade led to factor price equalization and the technology for producing nontradables were identical across countries.

---

2. There is a claim that Korea's exchange rate management has been asymmetrical, moving closely with the dollar when the Japanese yen is strong and moving closely with the yen when it is weak. To examine this claim, we tried two different variables for e^*, one for the period when it appreciated over the previous year and the other when it depreciated. The coefficients were almost the same, strongly indicating that the claim of asymmetry is ill founded.

For tradables, we may assume that PPP holds at least in terms of rates of change:

$$(1) \qquad \hat{p}_t - \hat{e} = \hat{p}_t^* \quad \text{or} \quad \hat{e} = \hat{p}_t - \hat{p}_t^*,$$

where p_t and p_t^* are the domestic and world prices of tradables, respectively, e is the exchange rate expressed in units of domestic currency per U.S. dollar, and a hat indicates the rate of change. In this form, we may disregard arbitrage and transport costs, as long as these costs constitute a stable portion of the commodity price. If, for example, the currency is not fully depreciated to reflect domestic inflation over that of the world for tradables, the country would face an unsustainable backslide in export competitiveness and a deterioration of the trade balance.

As presented in figure 9.2, the long-run movements of Korea's exchange rate and tradable prices relative to the United States have been very similar, even though a substantial gap persisted in some periods. In the case of Japan, the yen has appreciated much faster than tradable prices have dropped relative to the United States. This divergence may be due to a large exchange rate misalignment at the beginning of the sample period or to the inappropriateness of the price indicator for tradables used in the analysis.[3]

On the other hand, given the internal mobility of resources in the long run, we may expect a roughly similar trend of profitability between tradables and nontradables in the domestic market. Otherwise, resources would shift from the sector for which profits are relatively squeezed to the other sector until profit prospects are more or less equalized between the two. Given that labor cost constitutes the major and fairly stable share of total value added even for tradables, not to mention nontradables, we may state the above equalization condition as follows:

$$(2) \qquad \hat{p}_t - \hat{l}_t = \hat{p}_n - \hat{l}_n,$$

where l_t and l_t and l_n are unit labor costs (wages per unit of production) for tradables and nontradables, respectively.

Using the observation that wage increases are more or less the same in the long run between the tradable and nontradable sectors, the above condition may be rewritten as

3. Manufactured goods were taken as tradables for this purpose. Even though agricultural products can be classified as tradables in many countries, the Korean agricultural market is far from being closely linked with the world market. The agricultural sector, however, is not classified as nontradables either. The fact that the yen appreciated much faster than tradable prices declined compared with the U.S. counterparts seems to indicate that the tradables relevant for analysis of the exchange rate might be a segment of the manufacturing sector with realized or potential comparative advantages.

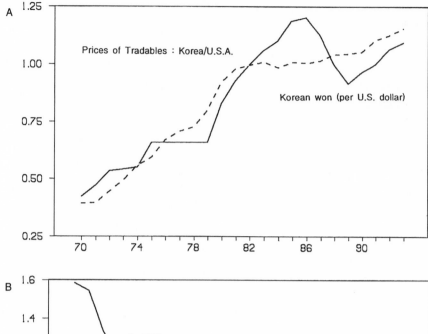

Fig. 9.2   Exchange rate and price of tradables
Note: A, Korea vis-à-vis the United States (1982 = 1.00). B, Japan vis-à-vis the United States (1980 = 1.00).

$$\hat{p}_n - \hat{p}_t = \hat{d}_t - \hat{d}_n,$$

(3)

$$\hat{p}_n^* - \hat{p}_t^* = \hat{d}_t^* - \hat{d}_n^*,$$

where d_t and d_n are labor productivities for tradables and nontradables, respectively, and an asterisk indicates the corresponding variable for the world economy. In the long run, we expect that the price increase for nontradables will be higher than that for tradables to the same extent that labor productivity growth in the tradables sector is faster than that in the nontradables sector.[4]

Figure 9.3 shows that relative prices and the labor productivity gap between tradables and nontradables grew the fastest in Korea and at about the same rate over the 1970–93 period, as equation (3) predicts. For the United States, the relative price of nontradables rose at a slower rate than the gap in labor productivity indicated. This difference may be due to a relatively large increase in nonlabor costs for tradables, which was expected in the sector's extensive restructuring efforts for survival. For Japan, this phenomenon might have been offset by the downward pressure on the price of tradables that resulted from the gradual opening of the domestic market.

Now, the overall inflation rates of the domestic and world economies are given as the weighted average inflation of tradables and nontradables in the respective economies:

(4)
$$\hat{p} = \alpha\hat{p}_t + (1 - \alpha)\hat{p}_n,$$
$$\hat{p}^* = \beta\hat{p}_t^* + (1 - \beta)\hat{p}_n^*,$$

where p and p^* are the composite prices of the domestic and the world economy, respectively, and α and β are the shares of the tradables sector in the domestic and the world economy, respectively.

Using the relationship of equations (3) and (4) in equation (1), we get the following equation for exchange rate change (see Balassa 1964; Hsieh 1982):

(5) $$\hat{e} = (\hat{p} - \hat{p}^*) - [(1 - \alpha)\hat{g}(d) - (1 - \beta)\hat{g}(d^*)],$$

where $\hat{g}(d)$ and $\hat{g}(d^*)$ are the gaps in labor productivity growth between tradables and nontradables for the domestic and the world economy, respectively $(\hat{d}_t - \hat{d}_n$ and $\hat{d}_t^* - \hat{d}_n^*)$. If we ignore the difference in the share of the tradables sector in the domestic and world economies and let the common share for nontradables be ϕ, equation (5) is rewritten as

(6) $$\hat{e} = (\hat{p} - \hat{p}^*) - \phi[\hat{g}(d) - \hat{g}(d^*)].$$

The above equation shows that the exchange rate movement departs from what PPP predicts to the extent that the gap in labor productivity growth

---

4. If we also consider the share of nonlabor cost, eq. (3) may be rewritten as follows:

(3′) $$\hat{p}_n - \hat{p}_t = (\hat{d}_t - \hat{d}_n) + [s_n(\hat{n}_n - \hat{l}_n) - s_t(\hat{n}_t - \hat{l}_t)],$$

where s_t and s_n are the shares of nonlabor cost for tradables and nontradables, respectively, and $\hat{n}_t$ and $\hat{n}_n$ are the increase rates of nonlabor cost for tradables and nontradables, respectively. In eq. (3′), the second term on the right-hand side is most likely negative, since the nonlabor share for tradables is typically larger than that for nontradables $(s_t > s_n)$ and the difference in the increase rate of nonlabor cost between nontradables and tradables is not likely to be larger than that of unit labor cost $(\hat{n}_n - \hat{n}_t < \hat{l}_n - \hat{l}_t)$. In other words, the difference in inflation rates between nontradables and tradables is likely to be a little smaller than the difference in productivity growth between the two sectors. For simplicity of analysis, however, we disregard this point.

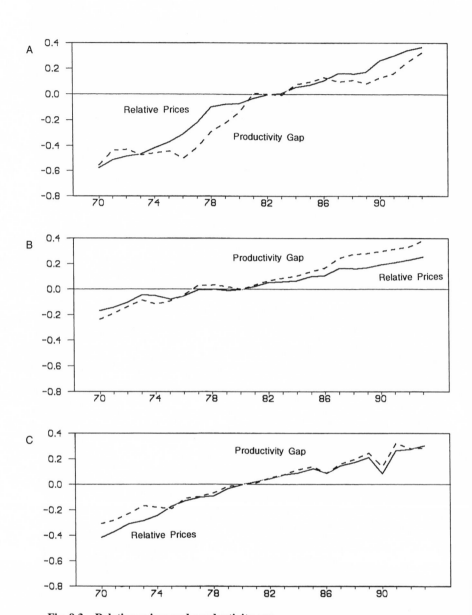

Fig. 9.3   Relative prices and productivity gap

Note: A, Korea (1982 = 1.00). B, United States (1980 = 1.00). C, Japan (1980 = 1.00). Relative prices are ln(prices of nontradables/tradables). Productivity gap is ln(productivity of nontradables/tradables).

between tradables and nontradables for the domestic economy is different from that for the world economy. In the process of rapid catch-up with industrialization efforts, a developing country will generally experience a fairly large gap in labor productivity growth, which tends to appreciate its currency. The degree of appreciation will be greater with a larger or increasing share of the nontradable sector in the economy.

Figure 9.4 shows the movements of labor productivity for tradables and nontradables in Korea, the United States, and Japan. As expected, labor productivity grew much faster in Korea than in the other two countries for both tradables and nontradables, but the growth for tradables was generally faster than that for nontradables after the mid-1970s. Between the United States and Japan, Japan's labor productivity grew faster, but the relative productivity trend between tradables and nontradables was roughly the same for the two countries.

In figure 9.5, the predicted exchange rate on the basis of equation (5) in a logarithmic form is presented together with the actual exchange rate. The equation is clearly a poor predictor of the exchange rate in the short run for both Korea and Japan. In the long run, the won has slightly appreciated given what was expected in light of the differences (between Korea and the United States) in overall inflation and in the productivity gap between tradables and nontradables. This seems to be due mainly to the relative stability, compared to productivity, in the prices of nontradables in the United States. For Japan, the predicted exchange rate is hardly different from that based on relative prices of tradables in figure 9.2.

In the above analysis, the exchange rate is viewed as being determined in the goods market. To the extent that the exchange rate is determined in the broader exchange market where both current and capital transactions are made, long-run exchange rate movements may deviate from predictions based on the above framework. In Korea, however, controls over external capital transactions have been fairly extensive, rigorously matching demand with supply in such a way as to keep capital transactions largely accommodative. Thus ignoring capital flows in the long-run analysis of exchange rate determination should not be too much of a problem for Korea.

9.3   An Econometric Model: The Exchange Rate and Adjustment Mechanisms

9.3.1   The Model

There are well-established alternative approaches explaining the adjustment mechanism through which an exchange rate change affects the trade balance. These approaches are not necessarily mutually inconsistent, but they are largely complementary to one another in understanding the effect of an exchange rate change.

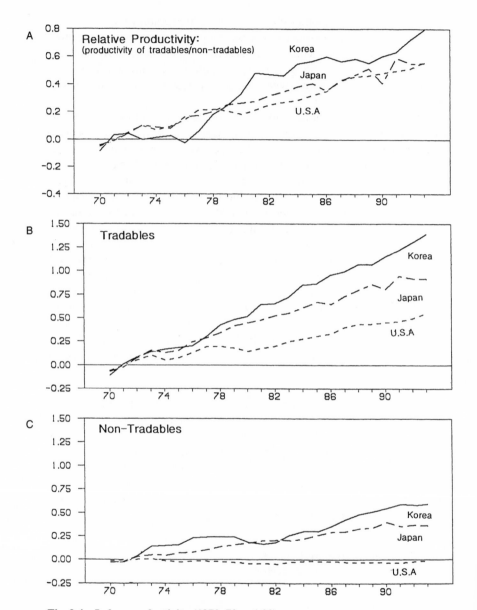

Fig. 9.4 Labor productivity (1970–72 = 1.00)
Note: Productivity figures are in natural logarithms.

A
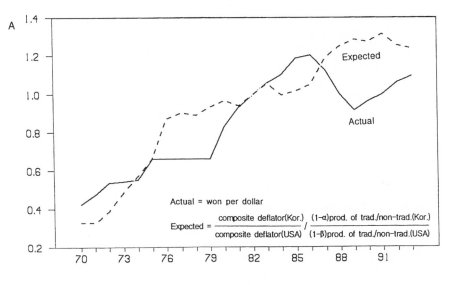

B
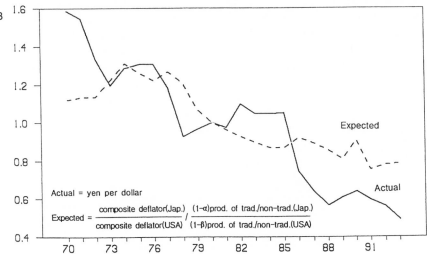

Fig. 9.5   Exchange rate movements: actual versus expected
Note: A, Korean won (1982 = 1.00). B, Japanese yen (1980 = 1.00).

The *elasticities approach* is concerned with how an exchange rate change affects the trade balance by concentrating its attention on price elasticities of exports and imports. While the elasticities approach sees the trade balance directly as the difference between exports and imports, the *absorption approach* pays attention to the trade balance as the difference between aggregate income and expenditure. Unlike the elasticities approach, which is solely concerned with the price effects of an exchange rate change on exports and imports, the focus of the absorption approach is on the effects on income and expenditure (absorption). The immediate impact of an exchange rate change is on absorption, which at a given level of income determines the trade balance.

The *monetary approach* understands the adjustment mechanism of an exchange rate change as a monetary phenomenon. Devaluation raises domestic prices to reduce the real value of the money stock and induces people to cut expenditure below real income to replenish lost real balances. This excess supply of domestic goods is matched by net exports. Deficits in the balance of payments are considered to be a symptom of monetary disequilibrium, which is only transitory and self-correcting without sterilization. If this self-correcting process is to be accelerated, deliberate monetary contraction can be pursued, and devaluation is viewed as a substitute for monetary contraction. This basic monetary argument is based on the assumption of factor price flexibility, which allows an economy to maintain full employment.

The model estimated in this paper combines some features of the approaches sketched above. Export and import functions include both relative prices and income variables. The determination of absorption is an integral part of the model, along the lines of the absorption approach. The model, however, departs from the elasticities and absorption approaches in that it introduces essential dynamics. It does not depend on the critical role of the money stock. Still, as is the case for the monetary model, devaluation leads to a reduction in the real money stock and a change in the interest rate that tends to improve the trade balance by discouraging absorption. Though small, the model incorporates most of the essential dynamics of determining the current account. The complete model including identities is as follows.

Current balance and external debt

$$\mathrm{CB} = x \cdot p_x - m \cdot p_m - i^* \cdot D_{-1} + \mathrm{CB}_0,$$

$$D = D_{-1} - \mathrm{CB} + D_0,$$

$$x = x(\mathrm{WT},\ p_m^*/p_x,\ e_j),$$

$$p_x = p_x(p_w/e,\ p_m,\ \hat{x},\ e_j),$$

$$m = m(y_a,\ x,\ p_m \cdot e/p_w,\ p_x/p_m,\ L_m).$$

Aggregate income

$$y = y_a + (x - m) \cdot \bar{e} - i^* \cdot D \cdot \bar{e}/p_x + y_0,$$

$$y_a = y_a(y,\ \Delta y,\ y_{a-1},\ \Delta m_r,\ r_r).$$

Inflation

$$\hat{p}_w = \hat{p}_w(\hat{p}_m + \hat{e}, \hat{y}, \hat{y}_{ag}, \hat{p}_{w-1}),$$

$$\hat{p}_y = \hat{p}_y(\hat{p}_m + \hat{e}, \hat{y}, \hat{y}_{ag}, \hat{p}_{y-1}).$$

Money and interest rate

$$m_r = M2/p_y,$$

$$r_r = r_r((m_r/y)_{-1}, \hat{y}, \Delta\hat{p}_y).$$

CB	current account balance
CB_0	net balance of invisible trade and unrequited transfers, except for interest payments on gross external debt
D	gross external debt
D_0	residual item in the external debt identity, which includes changes in both foreign asset holdings and the value of nondollar debts outstanding (due to their exchange rate changes against the dollar)
e	exchange rate per U.S. dollar
$\bar{e}$	average exchange rate per dollar in the base year of national income accounts
e_j	exchange rate of the Japanese yen per U.S. dollar
i^*	average interest rate on external debt
L_m	a measure of import liberalization
m	volume of commodity imports
M2	broadly defined money supply
m_r	real money supply (M2)
p_m	unit value of commodity imports in dollars
p_m^*	unit value of world imports in U.S. dollars
p_w	domestic wholesale prices
p_x	unit value of commodity exports in dollars
p_y	GDP deflator
r_r	real interest rate
WT	world trade volume
x	volume of commodity exports
y_0	residual item in the real GDP identity, which includes net services exports (except for interest payments on gross external debt) and statistical discrepancies
y_a	absorption in real terms
y_{ag}	agricultural value added in real terms

In an effort to keep the model as small as possible, the services balance is treated as exogenous except for the interest payment on the gross external debt. Endogenizing external debt and the interest payment is considered important since they constitute essential elements of the dynamics of the model. To the extent that services trade is also affected by relative prices between the domestic and world markets, the model will underestimate the effect of an exchange rate change on the balance of payments.

Exports

The quantity and price of merchandise exports are viewed as being determined by the intersection of their demand and supply curves. For Korea's major exports the number of competitive suppliers is typically limited due to product differentiation or noncompetitive industrial organization, making the price-taker assumption of a small open economy unrealistic. Export demand is determined by foreign income or total world trade volume and the relative export price of the country compared to the rest of the world. The exchange rate affects demand only by changing the export price. To the extent that Korean exports compete closely with Japanese products, movements of the Japanese yen will also affect Korean exports.

Export supply depends mainly on the profit margin captured by the unit value of exports relative to the major costs represented by domestic wholesale prices and the unit value of (intermediate) imports, as well as the production capacity. The growth rate of export volume ($\hat{x}$) is included as a proxy for the export capacity utilization ratio. Moreover, if Korean exports have a particularly competitive relationship with those of Japan, the value of the yen may also affect the pricing of Korean exporters: for example, reducing prices to cut the profit margin as the yen weakens.

Imports

Contrary to the case of exports, Korea may be considered to be "small" as far as imports are concerned, so that the unit value of imports is assumed to be exogenously given. Real imports are a function of real income or output and the cost of imports relative to domestic wholesale prices. Since it is likely that (manufactured) exports are more dependent on imports of intermediate or capital goods than other components of aggregate demand, absorption and exports are entered separately as explanatory variables. Furthermore, import liberalization or external terms of trade (p_x/p_m) may have affected imports if import restrictions were binding or imports were compressed due to unfavorable terms-of-trade movements.

Absorption

Absorption is composed of private consumption and investment and public expenditure. Private consumption may be viewed as depending on permanent income and estimated by current income and lagged consumption. Public expenditure is budgeted on the basis of anticipated aggregate income. To the extent that current or anticipated income is not fully known to consumers or the government, absorption is expected to be negatively affected by changes in income. Finally, explaining private investment as a partial adjustment to the desired capital stock (which may be approximated by current income) and ignoring capital depreciation, investment may be estimated by changes in income and lagged investment. Credit availability and interest rate variables are also included since they will certainly affect absorption by changing the degree of liquidity constraint, profit prospect of investment, or time preference of consumers.

Inflation

How domestic inflation is determined is critical to the dynamics of the whole system. Devaluation is believed to have no lasting effect because inflation accelerates such that the relative price of domestic goods tends to return to the predevaluation level. On the cost side, the major sources of inflation include import prices and labor and other factor costs, and the latter may be estimated as an expectation-augmented Phillips curve. Labor productivity improvement will have a role only to the extent that it is not fully reflected in current wages. Since labor productivity usually moves procyclically the Phillips curve relationship (captured here by the economic growth rate, $\hat{y}$) will be weakened by the offsetting effect of productivity change.

The lagged dependent variable is supposed to be closely related to the expected inflation rate. The growth rate of agricultural production ($\hat{y}_{ag}$) is also introduced, as it is often the major determinant of agricultural prices. The inflation rate in terms of the GDP deflator is added to the model, since wholesale prices are too narrow in their coverage to represent the whole economy. The effect of real money supply on absorption, for instance, should be better captured when the nominal money stock is deflated by the GDP deflator.

Real Interest Rates

The real market interest rate is believed to have a downward trend with the deepening of Korea's financial market. The M2-GDP ratio may serve as a measure of financial deepening. Along this trend, the real interest rate is supposed to fluctuate together with cyclical swings of investment or general economic activity. Furthermore, as inflation accelerates or decelerates the change in the inflation rate may not be fully and immediately reflected in the nominal interest rate. This is so because the market takes only a portion of the change as a shift in inflationary expectations and because the authorities are likely to intervene to stabilize the nominal interest rate.

9.3.2   Estimation Results

Real Exports

The demand elasticity of exports with respect to the world trade volume of manufactured goods estimated to be 2.1 until the late 1980s. The elasticity was estimated as being lowered by 0.01 each year since 1988. The relative export price seems to affect exports with a mean lag of about one year, and the estimated price elasticity is 2.3. The exchange rate of the Japanese yen also turns out to be significant, which strongly indicates that Korean products compete with Japanese products (or those produced in other East Asian countries by Japanese-invested corporations) in a wide range of commodities.

Unit Value of Exports

For a 1 percent increase in domestic wholesale prices or appreciation of the won, the unit value of exports rises by 0.50 percent in the same year, and about 1 percent in the long run. The unit value of imports and the lagged export growth rate (introduced as a proxy for the export capacity utilization rate) also turn out to be significant. A weakening of the Japanese yen by 1 percent is estimated to bring about a decline in Korea's export price by 0.2 percent or so in the short run. The 1973 dummy variable $D(73)$ reflects the prevalent price controls in 1973, which distorted the P_w/e variable.

Real Imports

The income elasticity of imports is estimated at 0.90 for absorption and 0.29 for exports. The impact of the relative price on imports is much smaller than that on exports, with the elasticity estimated at a little less than 0.5 and the mean lag at about six months. None of the other variables such as external terms of trade or measures of import liberalization (average import tariff or import liberalization ratio) seem to have any impact on imports.

Absorption

The long-run elasticity of absorption demand, with respect to income, is estimated at 1.0 with an impact elasticity of 0.38. The variable of change in income (Δy) was excluded since it was not significant and showed signs of multicollinearity with other income variables. The liquidity condition, measured as a change in the real balance of broadly defined money, has a rather strong impact on absorption with some time lag. The real interest rate (corporate bond yield) also turns out to be significant. The dummy variable $D(80.90–91)$ incorporates the recessionary effect of social and political turmoil in the wake of the assassination of President Park, as well as the strong boost of domestic demand (mainly housing construction) in 1990–91 in response to the stagnation of exports (due mainly to a drastic appreciation of the won).

Inflation

The short-run impact and the long-run effect of import cost on wholesale price inflation are estimated at 0.43 and about 0.85, respectively. The Phillips curve relationship (between inflation and recent economic growth) could be identified as well. As for inflation in terms of the GDP deflator, the short-run impact of import cost is much weaker, while the effect of economic growth is much stronger than it is for wholesale prices. The dummy variable $D(73.74)$ is introduced to reflect the wide-ranging price controls (-1) in 1973 particularly and the subsequent easing of controls ($+1$), as they were no longer sustainable due to the oil shock in 1974. The crop situation also turned out to be an important determinant of inflation.

Real Interest Rate

Though statistically not very significant, the real market interest rate turns out to decline with financial deepening and move procyclically. It is also shown that only about half the change in the inflation rate is reflected in the nominal interest rate in the short run. Finally, a dummy variable is introduced to reflect the government's monetary policy stance: a reflationary policy in connection with the 3 August 1972 measure of freezing the curb loan market (-1) and the contrasting policy response to the first and second oil shocks $(-1$ for 1974, $+1$ for 1979).

Estimated Equations (Sample: 1968–94)

1. Real exports

$$\ln x = -4.20 + 2.13 \ln \text{WT} - 0.010 \ t(88) * \ln \text{WT}$$

$$(8.16) \qquad\qquad (3.72)$$

$$+ \ 2.33 \sum_{i=0}^{2} (1/3) \ln(p_m^*/p_x)_{-i} - \ 0.364 \ln e_j,$$

$$(6.82) \qquad\qquad\qquad (2.41)$$

$$\rho = 0.58, \quad \bar{R}^2 = .997, \quad \text{D.W.} = 1.71.$$

2. Unit value of exports

$$\ln p_x = 3.19 + 0.489 \ \ln(p_w/e) + 0.419 \ \Delta \ \ln p_m$$

$$(4.44) \qquad\qquad (6.31)$$

$$+ \ 0.234 \ \Delta \ln x_{-1} - 0.205 \ \Delta \ln e_j + 0.48 \ D(73)$$

$$(2.83) \qquad\qquad (3.39) \qquad\qquad (2.12)$$

$$+ \ 0.525 \ln p_{x-1},$$

$$(4.37)$$

$$\bar{R}^2 = .995, \quad \text{D.W.} = 2.17.$$

3. Real imports

$$\ln m = -0.102 + 0.898 \ln y_a + 0.292 \ln x$$

$$(10.9) \qquad\qquad (6.70)$$

$$- \ 0.471 \ln \sum_{i=0}^{1} (1/2)(p_m \cdot e/p_w)_{-i},$$

$$(3.11)$$

$$\bar{R}^2 = .997, \quad \text{D.W.} = 1.42.$$

4. Real absorption

$$\ln y_a = 0.14 + 0.377 \ln y + 0.613 \ln y_{a=1}$$
$$\quad\quad\quad\quad (4.98) \quad\quad\quad (7.99)$$
$$+ 0.195 \; \Delta \ln m_r - 0.128 \ln(1.0 + r_r)$$
$$(3.01) \quad\quad\quad\quad\quad (1.34)$$
$$+ 0.054 \; D(80.90\text{--}91),$$
$$(4.14)$$
$$\overline{R}^2 = .999, \quad \text{D.W.} \doteq 1.41.$$

5. Inflation: wholesale prices

$$\Delta \ln p_w = -0.014 + 0.434 \; \Delta \ln(p_m \cdot e) + 0.374 \; \Delta \ln y$$
$$(0.90) \quad (11.8) \quad\quad\quad\quad\quad\quad\quad (2.26)$$
$$- 0.388(0.6 \; \Delta \ln y_{ag} + 0.4 \; \Delta \ln y_{ag-1})$$
$$(3.67)$$
$$+ 0.117 \; D(73.74) + 0.476 \; \Delta \ln p_{w-1},$$
$$(7.28) \quad\quad\quad\quad\quad (8.19)$$
$$\overline{R}^2 = .951, \quad \text{D.W.} = 1.63.$$

6. Inflation: GDP deflator

$$\Delta \ln p_y = -0.035 + 0.217 \; \Delta \ln(p_m \cdot e) + 0.656 \; \Delta \ln y$$
$$(1.78) \quad (5.02) \quad\quad\quad\quad\quad\quad\quad (3.43)$$
$$- 0.262 \; \Delta \ln y_{ag} + 0.079 \; D(73.74)$$
$$(3.35) \quad\quad\quad\quad\quad (4.60)$$
$$+ 0.721 \; \Delta \ln p_{y-1},$$
$$(8.87)$$
$$\overline{R}^2 = .884, \quad \text{D.W.} = 2.51$$

7. Real interest rate

$$r_r = -0.041 - 0.030 \ln(m_r/y)_{-2} + 0.182 \ \Delta \ln y_{-1}$$

$$(1.64) \qquad (1.57) \qquad\qquad (1.60)$$

$$- 0.510 \ \Delta \ln(p_y/p_{y-1}) + 0.058 \ D(72.74.79)$$

$$(5.31) \qquad\qquad\qquad (4.84)$$

$$+ 0.838 \ r_{r-1},$$

$$(12.7)$$

$$\overline{R}^2 = .904, \quad \text{D.W.} = 2.05.$$

$t(88)$	time variable since 1988, 1 for 1988, 2 for 1989, . . . ,7 for 1994, 0 otherwise
$D(73)$	1 for 1973, 0 otherwise
$D(80.90–91)$	−1 for 1980, 1 for 1990–91, 0 otherwise
$D(73.74)$	−1 for 1973, 1 for 1974, 0 otherwise
$D(72.74.79)$	−1 for 1972 and 1974, 1 for 1979, 0 otherwise

9.4   Simulation Exercises under Alternative Exchange Rate Regimes

Before undertaking simulation exercises under alternative exchange rate regimes, an assessment of the effects of an exchange rate change is needed in order to check long-run stability and consistency with our expectations. Even though the proposed model has only several structural equations, this task cannot be achieved without running simulations because of the dynamic interactions among variables. To evaluate the long-run dynamics, the simulation exercises start in 1983 and continue to the end of the sample, 1994.[5]

In order to obtain the net effect of devaluation, the results of a simulation with the nominal exchange rate depreciated by 10 percent in 1983 and onward were compared with those of the base simulation. The results of this simulation are presented in figure 9.6. A notable result is that a devaluation quickly raises domestic prices, as much as 80 percent of the devaluation by the fourth year for wholesale prices, and between the fifth and sixth years in the case of the GDP deflator. As a consequence, exporters cannot reduce their unit export value very much (around 2.6 percent during the first two years, which declines to the 1.4 percent level between the fifth and sixth years), which limits export growth in real terms. The effect of a 10 percent nominal devaluation on real exports is the strongest in the third year with 5.5 percent more exports and gradually weakens to 2.8 percent more by the eighth year.

---

5. In order to correct any simultaneous equation biases, two-stage regressions with instrumental variables were used for the simulation exercises. The results, however, were not significantly different from those based on ordinary least squares estimates.

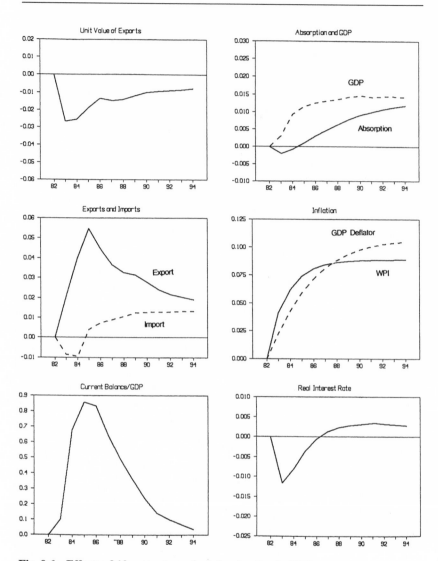

Fig. 9.6   Effects of 10 percent nominal devaluation in 1983

On the other hand, higher prices result in lower real balance of money, which has a negative impact on absorption, while the lower real interest rate during the first several years partially offsets this negative effect. The net effect on absorption is slightly negative from the second to the fourth year of devaluation, before it becomes positive and increases thereafter. The combined effect of the 10 percent nominal devaluation on net exports and absorption leads to a real GDP level that is higher by 0.3 and 1.3 percent by the first and the fourth years, respectively.

Real imports decrease due to higher import costs relative to domestic prices during the first two years after devaluation, but they are positively influenced as the long-run effect on GDP is positive. The effect on the current balance shows a J-curve pattern with little improvement in the short run, followed by the biggest improvement (about 1 percent of GDP) between the third and fourth years and smaller and declining improvements thereafter (around 0.4 percent of GDP between the seventh and eighth years). This pattern results mainly from (1) the time lag between the exchange rate, unit export value, and real exports, (2) continually rising prices that weaken the initial gain in export competitiveness, and (3) the slow reaction of absorption to devaluation-induced income growth, leading to a steady increase in imports.

9.4.1 Fixed Nominal Exchange Rate since 1982

Thanks to its strong anti-inflation policy in the early 1980s, Korea achieved remarkable success in stabilizing prices by 1982. The consumer inflation rate dropped from an annual average of 23 percent during 1979–81 to 7 percent in 1982 and 2.8 percent during 1983–87. As inflation decreased to a level more or less comparable to that of major trading partners, it must have been conceivable to have the Korean won fixed to the U.S. dollar.

Keeping the nominal exchange rate fixed at the 1982 level means that the won was much stronger than it actually was during 1983–87. The average exchange rate in 1986 was more than 20 percent weaker than it was in 1982. On the other hand, during 1989–90, the actual exchange rate was stronger (as much as 8 percent in 1989) than the 1982 rate. The result of this simulation is presented in figure 9.7.[6]

Under this exchange rate regime real exports were 7 to 8 percent lower than actual levels during 1985–87, but 3 to 6 percent higher during 1989–91. The current account balance deteriorated the most in 1987, by 1.7 percent of GDP, while it improved by 1.2 percent in 1990. As for GDP, a 1.8 to 2.0 percent cut occurred during both 1986–87 and 1993–94. Finally, prices in terms of the GDP deflator were lower by about 11 percent during 1986–87 and by 7 percent in 1994.

Overall, there seems to be little evidence that this regime of a fixed nominal exchange rate vis-à-vis the United States is any better than the actual exchange rate management. Since the big swing in the nominal exchange rate that we observed during the sample period is avoided under this regime there are some improvements in the stability of export growth and the current account balance. However, these improvements are offset by a wider range of GDP growth and inflation rates.

---

6. The simulated values in the figure are obtained by adding the net effect (difference between the simulated values and the base simulation results) to the actual values.

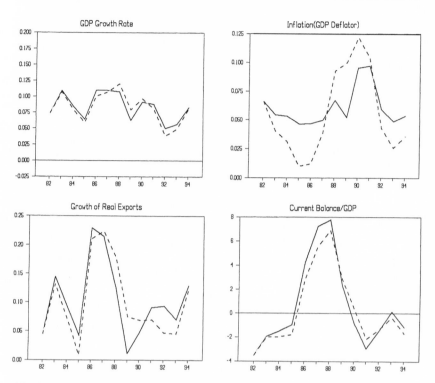

Fig. 9.7   Simulation results: fixed nominal exchange rate against the U.S. dollar since 1982

Note: Actual (*solid line*) and simulated (*dashed line*).

9.4.2   Fixed Real Effective Exchange Rate since 1982

Within the sample period, 1982 (the base year for our simulation exercises) was one of the years when the Korean won was most appreciated. By 1986–87 and again in 1993–94, the won depreciated as much as 35 percent from the 1982 level on a real effective basis. Thus keeping the won's REER at the 1982 level might have meant substantially appreciating the currency. Still, 1982 is used as the base year since our major interest is the evolution of economic profiles rather than absolute performance.

Under the regime of fixed REER, the won's nominal exchange rate per U.S. dollar declined from 731 won in 1982 to 550 won in 1994 (compared with the actual exchange rate of 803 won per dollar). The results presented in figure 9.8 show that real exports are much smaller than the actual volume, particularly during 1987–88 when the difference in exports was about 16 percent and deterioration in the current account balance was as large as 2.0 to 2.8 percent of GDP. Loss in GDP was about 4 percent during 1987–88 and over 5 percent during 1993–94, while the drop in the GDP deflator was 3.8 percent by 1988 and 4.3 percent by 1994.

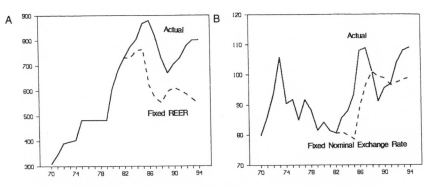

Fig. 9.8   Simulation results: fixed real effective exchange rate since 1982
Note: A, Nominal exchange rate under fixed REER since 1982. B, REER under fixed nominal exchange rate since 1982.

More significant for our present purpose is the path of macroeconomic performance. What is obvious from the simulation results is that export growth and the current account balance are relatively stable under the regime of fixed REER compared with their actual performance. For instance, between 1986 and 1989, the actual increase rate of real exports dropped from 23 to 1 percent, while it declined from 17 to only 9 percent under the fixed REER regime. As a result, the current account surplus, which amounted to 7 to 8 percent of GDP during 1987–88, could be reduced to 4 percent of GDP.

However, the simulation results also show that stability in export growth or reduced imbalance in the current account is sometimes achieved only at the sacrifice of other aspects of macroeconomic performance. As the nominal exchange rate immediately reflects the change in the exchange value of the currency basket, inflation is also likely to be unstable with such large fluctuations in the currency value of major trading partners as observed since the mid-1980s. Likewise, when domestic demand is very weak, as it was in 1992–93, keeping the REER mechanically fixed may not necessarily be rational.

The case of a constant yen-dollar rate. Figure 9.9 indicates that even when the won's REER is maintained constant, the current account surplus remains at about 3 percent of GDP during 1987–88. In order to identify the extent to which these surpluses are due to the strong yen, another simulation was run with both the yen-dollar rate and the won's REER fixed at their 1982 rates. In this case, the won's nominal exchange rate vis-à-vis the dollar was much weaker: 756 won in 1994, compared to 550 won when the actual yen-dollar rates were used.[7] The results presented in figure 9.10 show that the large current account surplus during 1987–88 more or less disappeared in this scenario,

---

7. With the constant yen-dollar rate Japan's prices must have been higher than actual levels, since the yen showed a clear trend of appreciation against the dollar during the sample period. This effect is ignored in our analysis, and to that extent, the simulation represents a slight depreciation of the won on a real effective basis.

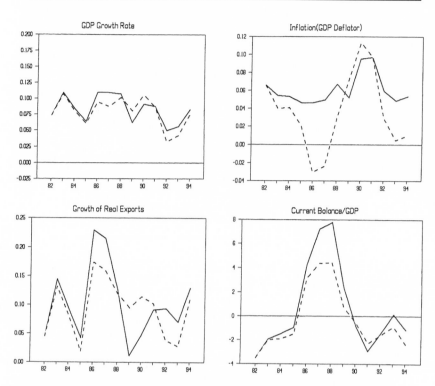

Fig. 9.9   Simulation results: fixed real effective exchange rate since 1982
Note: Actual (*solid line*) and simulated (*dashed line*).

indicating the importance of the yen's exchange rate in determining the competitiveness of Korean exports. One reason why the current account still showed a small surplus may be that the effect of an exchange rate change is somewhat underestimated by treating the services balance as exogenous except for the interest payment on the external debt.

9.5   Conclusion

In Korea, a deficit in the current account is a vice, reflecting weakness in industrial competitiveness. A parallel is found in a firm's capital structure: a low debt-equity ratio is considered good, while we all know that Korean firms could grow rapidly thanks to debt financing. As long as a firm has profitable projects (and the capacity to undertake them) whose expected return is in excess of opportunity (borrowing) cost, it is senseless to increase reserves (not borrow) and forgo the projects.

Despite Korea's high national savings rate, its capital accumulation is inadequate, so investment demand is still strong. It is certainly in Korea's interest to expand investment by borrowing cheaply from abroad rather than seeking a

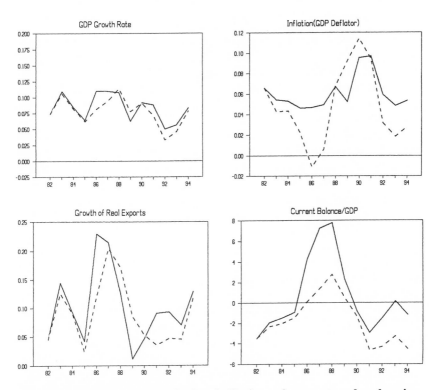

Fig. 9.10   Simulation results: fixed real effective exchange rate and unchanging yen-dollar rate since 1982
Note: Actual (*solid line*) and simulated (*dashed line*).

current account surplus, which accumulates foreign assets whose yield is low. Keeping the currency overly depreciated for the purpose of improving the current account balance has other costs to the economy. Not only is it inflationary, it also disrupts smooth structural adjustments of industries and exports in line with underlying shifts in comparative advantages.

During the period of "three blessings" in 1986–88, Korean firms expanded their capacities in labor-intensive products to exploit the enhanced competitiveness that resulted from the strong Japanese yen. Many of these investments turned out to be bad as their price competitiveness soon worsened with soaring domestic wages, along with the sharp appreciation of the Korean won.[8] The exchange rate policy should have given a signal consistent with underlying changes in comparative advantages so that wasteful investments could have been minimized and industries could have better prepared for the challenge of upgrading the industrial and export structure.

---

8. For one thing, the export share of light manufactured goods, which has shown a steady decreasing trend, rose from 36.9 percent in 1985 to 41.6 percent in 1986–87.

It has also often been suggested that intergenerational equity might be better served in Korea by lowering the savings rate rather than by increasing the (already high) investment rate. However, older generation Korean parents, who have experienced a large improvement in their standards of living during their lifetimes, are likely to be satisfied with the current rate of consumption increase for the younger generation, who will certainly see much smaller economic advancement.

The current account balance is one of the key macroeconomic variables; it shows the extent to which investment exceeds national savings. In macroeconomic management, Korea always has a target for the current account that is considered as serious as that of economic growth or inflation, particularly when it is in deficit. As preceding analyses indicated, the Korean authorities have heavily utilized the exchange rate for the purpose of correcting large imbalances in the current account, as well as securing other macroeconomic objectives.

With essential tasks assigned to the exchange rate one can hardly expect it to be determined or managed according to a rigid rule. A fixed nominal or real exchange rate against the U.S. dollar, for instance, was out of the question because (1) the government wanted neither to subject other macroeconomic policies to the exchange rate nor to lose the exchange rate flexibility that is expected to soften the adjustment to real shocks and (2) it would result in large variations in the effective exchange rate (with Korea's trade share with the United States large but not dominating) when the dollar fluctuates against other major currencies.

If correcting the imbalance in the current account is the major goal of exchange rate policy, a country may peg the (real) value of its currency to a basket of currencies of major trading partners. This is actually what Korea claimed to have done throughout the 1980s, even though the pegging was fairly loose. Any rigid rule of exchange rate changes deprives the economy of an instrument for fine-tuning macroeconomic management while compromising among different policy goals. The results of our counterfactual simulation exercises clearly indicated that a rigid peg to a basket would have brought about larger fluctuations in inflation in exchange for a reduced imbalance in the current account during the latter half of the 1980s. Furthermore, the recession with stagnant absorption during 1992–93 would definitely have been much worse with a rigid basket peg.[9]

For Korea, the trade weights used for forming the basket of currencies may be better if they were replaced by the elasticities that measure the responsiveness of trade to exchange rate changes. Though it may not be easy to come

---

9. If the authorities had actually chosen to keep the REER constant, other policy choices would have to have been different as well. E.g., when inflation dropped sharply due to a large nominal appreciation of the won against the dollar they could have let the repressed prices and fees adjust and repress again when the won depreciated, to make the actual fluctuations of inflation much smaller than the simulation exercises showed.

by reliable elasticities, we have seen in our analyses that Korea's current balance is substantially affected by a change in the value of the Japanese yen vis-à-vis the dollar even with the REER kept unchanged.

This may not be surprising given Korea's export structure, which has closely followed that of Japan with some lag. Currently, Korean exports such as cars, shipbuilding, and semiconductors and other electronics compete with Japanese products all over the world. Since the early 1980s, Korean exports have also been competing with products manufactured in East Asia by Japanese-invested firms whose competitiveness is substantially affected by the value of the yen. As such, the trade weight in the currency basket vastly underrepresents the Japanese yen if the REER is to be a correct reference for the competitiveness of Korean products.

In reality, when the yen fluctuates relative to the dollar, the Korean won has typically remained much closer to the dollar in the short run than keeping the effective exchange rate unchanged would allow. Noting a similar pattern of exchange rate movements in other East Asian newly industrialized countries (NICs), Williamson (1991, 1995) interpreted it as a classic collective action problem caused by the fear of their competitiveness being eroded against the others. He then proposed a joint floating exchange rate system for the East Asian NICs with their currencies pegged to a common basket. Williamson argued that this system would not only make the countries avoid competitive depreciation but also promote trade and financial interdependence among them.

The chance of this scheme's being adopted, however, seems rather low. As Black (1995) points out, these countries, though close competitors in the world market, have their own economic policy problems, unique and significantly different among them. Korea, Black says, is ill advised to have its exchange rate management seriously constrained, as it faces its own program of external capital liberalization and the prospect of reunification, which will require major restructuring of industries. Another problem, as pointed out by Park and Park (1991), is the lack of strong political leadership necessary for bringing the countries to an agreement.

Perhaps a more serious reason for skepticism is the increasingly differential export structure among the East Asian NICs. As these countries, some of them very small in size, move out of traditional labor-intensive exports, they have no other option than specializing in a limited number of industries where they find comparative advantages. Korea faces only limited competition with these countries in the markets for its major export items, such as cars, semiconductors, steel, and shipbuilding. The idea of a common basket peg does not seem to be very appealing to these countries, whose competitive structures have become increasingly divergent.

References

Balassa, Bela. 1964. The purchasing power parity doctrine: A reappraisal. *Journal of Political Economy* 72 (December): 584–96.

Black, Stanley W. 1995. Issues in Korean exchange rate policy: Evaluation and policy implications. Paper presented at KDI Symposium on Prospects of Yen-Dollar Exchange Rates and Korea's Exchange Rate Policy, Korea Development Institute, Seoul, December.

Hsieh, David A. 1982. The determination of the real exchange rate: The productivity approach. *Journal of International Economics* 12:355–62.

Kim, Eui-Jin. 1993. Changes in the variations of the won exchange rate after the market average exchange rate system (in Korean). In *Futures and options economy,* 48–62. Seoul: Korea Futures Association.

Kim, In-June. 1995. A model for the long-run won dollar exchange rate determination using a cointegration test (in Korean). In *On capital market liberalization,* ed. In-June Kim and Joon-Yong Park. Seoul: Bupmunsa.

Kim, Jin-Chun. 1992. Korea's recent foreign exchange rate systems: MCBP vs. MAR system. Report to the Korea Institute for International Economic Policy, Seoul.

Kim, Joon-Kyung. 1994. The effects of the stock market opening on the value of won (in Korean). *Korea Development Review* 16 (fall): 69–96.

Krueger, Anne O. 1983. *Exchange-rate determination.* Cambridge Surveys of Economic Literature. Cambridge: Cambridge University Press.

Nam, Sang-Woo. 1988. The role of exchange rate policy in four East Asian countries. Internal Discussion Paper, Asia Regional Series. Washington, D.C.: World Bank, May.

Oum, Bongsung, and Dongchul Cho. 1995. Korea's exchange rate movements in the 1990s: Evaluation and policy implications. Paper presented at KDI Symposium on Prospects of Yen-Dollar Exchange Rates and Korea's Exchange Rate Policy, Korea Development Institute, Seoul, December.

Park, Yung Chul, and Won-Am Park. 1991. Exchange rate policies for the East Asian newly industrialized countries. In *Exchange rate policies in developing and post-socialist countries,* ed. Emil-Maria Claassen. San Francisco: International Center for Economic Growth.

Strauss, Jack. 1996. The cointegrating relationship between productivity, real exchange rates and purchasing power parity. *Journal of Macroeconomics* 18 (spring): 299–313.

Williamson, John. 1991. Advice on the choice of an exchange rate policy. In *Exchange rate policies in developing and post-socialist countries,* ed. Emil-Maria Claassen. San Francisco: International Center for Economic Growth.

———. 1995. Exchange-rate policies for East Asian countries in a world of fluctuating rates. Paper presented at KDI Symposium on Prospects of Yen-Dollar Exchange Rates and Korea's Exchange Rate Policy, Korea Development Institute, Seoul, December.

Comment   Stanley W. Black

My job as a discussant is difficult because Nam and Kim's paper is a good one that I basically agree with, both in terms of its approach and its conclusions.

Stanley W. Black is the Georges Lurcy Professor of Economics at the University of North Carolina at Chapel Hill.

As a discussant, however, it is my role to criticize, so I offer a few minor criticisms or suggestions.

Section 9.1 of the paper addresses the measurement of the exchange rate and its behavior over time. The choice of currencies of only four industrial countries (the United States, Japan, Germany, the United Kingdom) for the comparison basket to compare the internal and external purchasing power of the won excludes Korea's growing trade with East Asia. As previously shown by Oum and Cho (1995), this can overstate the movement of the real exchange rate. This also appears in comparison between Nam and Kim's figure 9.8*B* and figure 10.3 in my paper (Black, chap. 10 in this volume). The substantial real depreciation of the Chinese currency is omitted, for example. The paper needs to include a discussion of table 9.2 of the single-equation models of the exchange rate. What should we conclude from these results? It would be interesting to test for asymmetry in the adjustment of the won-dollar rate to the yen-dollar rate.

Section 9.2 discusses the long-run trends. Figure 9.2 gives a useful picture of the long-run trends in bilateral real exchange rates versus the U.S. dollar and the Japanese yen, traced to their roots in relative productivity trends in figure 9.3. Section 9.3 develops a structural model. While Nam and Kim's model, based on past Korean exchange rate behavior, is dominated by trade factors, the recent capital account liberalization suggests that capital flows may play a more important role in the future. This is suggested also by the empirical results in the paper by Cho and Koh (chap. 11 in this volume). The estimated results of the model seem quite reasonable to me. I was pleased to see that Nam and Kim's estimated elasticities are quite similar to those estimated 10 years ago by Sung Kwack (1986) and used in my paper. I do wonder whether correction for simultaneous equations bias would lead to any differences.

Section 9.4 offers simulations of the model showing that alternative exchange rate policies such as a fixed nominal or fixed real exchange rate would worsen the behavior of inflation and output. This supports my argument that *flexibility* in the exchange rate is the more important goal for Korea, since the *credibility* of Korean monetary policy has been fairly well established. I note that in a recent paper Oum and Cho (1995) argue that Korean exchange rate policy in the 1990s has approximately stabilized their measure of the real effective exchange rate, while figure 9.8*B* shows that is not the case for Nam and Kim's measure. It is interesting to observe that the simulation with a constant yen-dollar rate removes most but not all of the large current account surpluses of the 1986–88 period. Since the high yen was only one of the "three blessings," it would be interesting to see what effect a constant oil price and constant interest rate would produce.

References

Kwack, Sung Y. 1986. Policy analysis with a macroeconomic model of Korea. *Economic Modeling* 3 (July): 175–96.

Oum, Bong-Sum, and Dong-Chul Cho. 1995. Korea's exchange rate movements in the 1990s: Evaluation and policy implications. *Economic Bulletin* (Republic of Korea) 17 (December): 2–16.

Comment   Leonard K. Cheng

Nam and Kim's paper provides a description of Korea's exchange rate regimes from 1970 to 1995 and analyzes the long-run behavior of the exchange rates of the Korean won, the U.S. dollar, and the Japanese yen by focusing on the role of the productivity gap between tradables and nontradables. It then goes on to estimate an econometric model that captures three different approaches to the balance of trade, namely, the elasticities approach, the absorption approach, and the monetary approach. Finally, the estimated model is used to generate predictions about the effect of two hypothetical exchange rate regimes: (1) a fixed nominal exchange rate since 1982 and (2) a fixed real effective exchange rate since 1982.

I would like to commend the authors for their informative and systematic description of the Korean exchange rate regimes and their interesting results about the deviation of exchange rate movements from changes in relative purchasing power. As for the estimation of the econometric model, I have only one minor query. Since the volume of imports is a function of "absorption," absorption is a function of total output, and output is in turn a function of exports, putting exports as a variable directly in the import demand function implies that exports have a higher import content than output used for domestic absorption (including domestic investment). What is the empirical evidence?

The simulation results obtained from the econometric model suggest that both hypothetical regimes under consideration are inferior to the actual exchange rate regime adopted in Korea. The intuition is that neither fixed exchange rate system has the flexibility to deal with external shocks and changes in comparative advantage.

While Nam and Kim's counterfactual results seem to make good sense, I would suggest that the authors explore alternatives other than the two they have considered. This is not only because it would have been unrealistic for Korea to adopt a fixed exchange rate since 1982 (the United States began to exert pressure on Korea beginning in the mid-1980s to bring about an appreciation of the won) but also because there might be regimes that could perform better than the one actually adopted. With an appropriate multiobjective criterion function for the policymakers (such as a loss function capturing the key policy variables), the authors may even be able to search for an optimal regime, which can be compared with the actual regime.

Leonard K. Cheng is professor of economics at the Hong Kong University of Science and Technology.

It is interesting to note that many Koreans regard "a deficit in the current account as a vice." When many countries are competing for foreign capital (both portfolio investment and foreign direct investment) to benefit their domestic economies, I wonder whether Korea's preoccupation with a current account surplus has much economic justification, because any effective transfer of real resources to Korea must take the form of a current account deficit.

Overall, this is an excellent paper and I have learned a lot from it about Korea's exchange rate policy over the past two and a half decades.

10   Issues in Korean Exchange Rate Policy

Stanley W. Black

10.1   Introduction

As a medium-sized, rapidly industrializing country that has just joined the Organization of Economic Cooperation and Development (OECD), Korea faces a number of unique problems that affect its exchange rate policy. Among these are its asymmetric competitive position vis-à-vis Japan, which is both its major supplier of machine tools and a leading competitor in third markets; the current policy of financial liberalization that goes along with democratic liberalization; and the implications of the potential future unification of the Korean peninsula. The role of Japan as supplier and competitor makes the widely fluctuating yen-dollar exchange rate a key determinant of Korean competitiveness and terms of trade. Financial liberalization is introducing capital flows as a major factor in exchange rate determination. And the impact of German unification on the European Monetary System (EMS) has raised many questions about the potential future effects of Korean unification. This paper will seek to explore these issues.

In the late 1980s, Korean exchange rate policy faced a situation called the "three blessings" or "three lows": low yen-dollar rate, low oil prices, and low world interest rates. The first of these gave Korea an export stimulus, the second reduced the cost of energy imports, and the third lowered the cost of servicing external debt. The major issue at the time was how to prevent this windfall from causing an unsustainable inflationary boom and whether to allow the won to appreciate or to repay external debt.

Stanley W. Black is the Georges Lurcy Professor of Economics at the University of North Carolina at Chapel Hill.

This work is part of the NBER's project on International Capital Flows, which receives support from the Center for International Political Economy. An earlier version was presented at the KDI Symposium on Prospects of Yen-Dollar Exchange Rate and Korea's Exchange Rate Policy, Seoul, 12 December 1995.

In a controversial move, the Korean government adopted a policy to repay much of its external debt, based on the assumption that the "three lows" were a temporary windfall. Balassa and Williamson (1987) argued at the time that appreciation of the won to reduce the external surplus was a more appropriate response, since it would permit additional domestic investment. Cho (1995) has supported this position with simulations indicating a much higher investment path if external debt had not been repaid.

Korea must have lived a charmed life, since until recently the world environment again wore some of the same beneficial aspects, including a low yen-dollar rate, low oil prices, and low interest rates. On the other hand, the low yen-dollar rate was one of a number of factors depressing the Japanese economy, an important market for Korea. Since mid-1995, however, the yen-dollar rate has risen significantly, removing some of the export stimulus. And oil prices have also risen from their lows of late 1995, while long-term interest rates have rebounded from their lows of early 1996. And different from 1988, competition from China and other Asian competitor nations is beginning to raise concerns for Korean policymakers. Financial market liberalization is a new factor affecting both the value of the won and the Korean balance of payments.

This paper will consider the question of the appropriate exchange rate policy for Korea in the face of fluctuations in the yen-dollar rate, increasing competition from lower cost Asian countries, and financial liberalization. Section 10.2 discusses the main exchange rate policy issues for Korea, dealing with external versus internal targets, choice of external comparison basket, and the effects of financial liberalization. Section 10.3 considers the issue of regional currency areas. Section 10.4 discusses Korean unification, and section 10.5 concludes with long-run equilibrium.

10.2   Fundamentals of Exchange Rate Policy

10.2.1   Internal versus External Objectives

The exchange rate defines the external purchasing power of a nation's currency. It is essential that this external purchasing power be consistent in the long run with the currency's internal purchasing power. Maintenance of the purchasing power of the nation's currency is the fundamental responsibility of the central bank or monetary authority. As is well known, there are two approaches to this fundamental problem.

The *internal target* approach consists in the central bank's defining and maintaining a rate of growth of the money supply that is consistent with price stability, defined as a low and stable rate of inflation. The exchange rate is not in this case a target for monetary policy, but simply an instrument that is controlled to ensure consistency between the internal and external purchasing power of the currency. This ensures the competitiveness of domestic exporters in international markets.

The *external target* approach involves setting a fixed exchange rate with a relatively stable currency, usually that of a large trading partner, and using the external price level to anchor domestic prices. In this case monetary policymakers must act to keep domestic interest rates aligned with foreign rates and orient all policy instruments to maintaining the exchange rate. In case domestic inflationary factors cause the exchange rate to become overvalued, devaluation to restore competitiveness is required.

The choice between these two methods of monetary control and exchange rate policy depends on the relative importance of *flexibility* in the exchange rate and *credibility* gained by anchoring the domestic price level to world prices through a fixed exchange rate. This problem has been formalized by Devarajan and Rodrik (1991) in the context of a Barro-Gordon model (1983) of an open economy subject to terms-of-trade shocks. The central bank's credibility is in question because it has an output target that exceeds the level consistent with stable prices. Price and wage setters must choose their behavior before knowing the terms-of-trade shock or the current exchange rate. The central bank has two choices. It may commit itself to a fixed exchange rate, which prevents it from offsetting the terms-of-trade shock *and* from inflating to exploit the prior setting of wages and prices so as to achieve a lower unemployment rate. Or it may adopt a flexible rate to offset terms-of-trade shocks, which then allows it to indulge in inflationary behavior as well.

If the central bank has relatively strong anti-inflation credibility, it will not be tempted to inflate when given the option by flexibility. In this case, the flexible rate option will allow use of the exchange rate to offset terms-of-trade shocks without paying a cost in terms of higher inflation. However, if the central bank's credibility is low, this option is best forgone, in order to avoid the inflationary consequences.

What is the empirical evidence on the choice between pegged and flexible rates? Edwards (1993) has shown that countries with previous experience of low inflation may be able to use a fixed exchange rate to keep their inflation low. But those with high inflation may not be able to gain credibility simply by fixing the exchange rate.

Edwards (1996; chap. 1 in this volume) argues that political instability shortens the time horizon of the authorities and reduces their willingness to undertake necessary devaluations. The second factor makes a peg less attractive, while the first has ambiguous effects. His regressions incorporate political instability (measured as change in government), variability of external shocks, central bank credibility, and ability to sustain a peg with reserves. The findings confirm the importance of the economic and political factors.

It appears that high credibility and high variance of external shocks both contribute to a choice in favor of flexibility, as Deverajan and Rodrik argue. Political instability also contributes to the choice of a flexible rate, suggesting that the unwillingness to devalue may be important.

Considering a different aspect of credibility, countries with independent central banks are found to have better records in controlling inflation than countries with central banks under direct government control (Cukierman, Webb, and Neyapti 1993). But Japan and Korea are both exceptions to these findings, since they have managed to achieve relatively low inflation without requiring their central banks to be formally independent.

The implications of these conclusions for Korea point in the direction of flexibility, it seems to me. One may argue that external shocks coming from the fluctuating yen-dollar rate will remain important. The central bank has established a significant degree of credibility. Governments are more likely to change in the future than they have in the past.

Korea's choices. For Korea, the choice among these options has evolved gradually (see table 10.1). During the Bretton Woods era, the external target approach was the universally chosen option. When floating exchange rates began, Korea continued to peg its exchange rate to the U.S. dollar during much of the 1970s. Since domestic inflation was not under control, occasional devaluations were necessary to keep the external purchasing power of the won in line with its falling internal purchasing power. But when the dollar began its radical appreciation during the 1980s, Korea shifted to a managed basket peg to keep the won from being pulled up with the dollar.

According to Oum and Cho (1995), in the 1980s Korea followed a policy of changing the exchange rate to adjust the current account, which is influenced by the exchange rate with a substantial lag, as in most countries. Since the Korean current account is heavily influenced by fluctuations in the yen-dollar rate, this set up a lagged feedback from the cycle in the yen-dollar rate to the won that caused the current account to fluctuate widely.

As the yen appreciated in the late 1980s after the Plaza Agreement, Korea's surplus grew, leading to appreciation of the won. By 1988 the yen peaked and began to depreciate, while the won kept appreciating as the surplus continued, despite the worsening of the underlying competitive position. Domestic investment increased moderately at first but then took off in an unsustainable boom in 1990–91, as the current account shifted into deficit.

In response to the exaggerated fluctuations of the won, the government in 1990 adopted a new exchange rate policy called the "market average rate" system. The most appropriate description of this shift appears to be from a

Table 10.1   **Korean Exchange Rate Regimes**

Period	Regime	Characteristics
1955–72	Bretton Woods era	Inflation/devaluations
1973–79	Pegged to U.S. dollar	Inflation/devaluations
1980–89	Managed basket peg	Current balance target
1990–97	Market average rate system	Stable real exchange rate

target-based approach, targeting the current balance, to an instrument-based approach, trying to stabilize the real exchange rate. It seems to have approximately achieved stabilization of the real exchange rate, or maintenance of equilibrium between the external and internal values of the won, despite the fact that the won continued to follow the movements of the dollar more closely than the yen. (See Takagi, chap. 7 in this volume, and Frankel and Wei 1994)

During the early 1980s, Korea along with several other dynamic Asian economies took advantage of the sharp reduction of inflation in industrialized countries to bring its own inflation rate under control. As a result, since that time Korea has had the option to use the internal target approach to control the purchasing power of its currency. The liberalization of financial markets that took place in the 1980s has changed the environment in which monetary policy is made in Korea. Despite an inflationary boom period in 1990–91 and continued strong growth of the economy, the Bank of Korea has managed to hold the inflation rate in the neighborhood of 5 to 6 percent per year.

In conjunction with the liberalized financial system, Korea moved in the direction of a market-based exchange rate policy in 1990, allowing market factors to move the won-dollar exchange rate by up to 2.25 percent per day. At the same time, banks and other participants in the market have been allowed to hold foreign currency balances to enable them to create an interbank market for foreign exchange.

10.2.2   Choice of External Relationship

In a multiple-currency world, "the" foreign exchange rate must be defined relative to each trading partner whose currency is used in external transactions. For Korea, the primary trading partners are North America, Japan, Europe, and other Asia. The major currencies involved would thus be the U.S. dollar, Japanese yen, and deutsche mark (as a proxy for other European currencies). Since these exchange rates have fluctuated sharply in recent years, Korea has been forced to accept significant fluctuations in traded goods prices.

The main issue can be illustrated by the following hypothetical example. Assume that Korea exports only to the United States in dollars and imports only from Japan in yen. If $e_¥$ is the won-yen exchange rate and $e_$$ is the won-dollar exchange rate, then export prices are $p_$e_$$ and import prices are $p_¥e_¥$. The terms of trade will then be $p_$e_$/p_¥e_¥ = p_$/p_¥e_{¥/$}$, where $e_{¥/$}$ is the yen-dollar exchange rate. If dollar prices and yen prices remain relatively stable, the terms of trade will fluctuate with the yen-dollar exchange rate, no matter what happens to $e_¥$ or $e_$$. This is the key problem for Korea. Only if the yen-dollar rate follows purchasing power parity will Korea be unaffected by its fluctuations.

If Korea pegs to the dollar, its import prices will then fluctuate with the yen-dollar rate, while export prices are stable. If it pegs to the yen, its export prices will fluctuate with the yen-dollar rate, while import prices are stable.

Choosing a *basket peg* enables Korea to balance its competing interests and minimize the fluctuation of traded goods prices. Define the basket as

$$e_k = e_\$^{\alpha\$} \, e_\yen^{\alpha\yen} \, e_{dm}^{\alpha dm} \, .$$

Then pegging to the basket sets

$$\hat{e}_k = \alpha_\$ \, \hat{e}_\$ + \alpha_\yen \, \hat{e}_\yen + \alpha_{dm} \, \hat{e}_{dm} = 0,$$

where $\alpha_\$$, $\alpha_\yen$, and α_{dm} are the weights applied to the dollar, the yen, and the deutsche mark (or European currency) exchange rates.

The weights are normally chosen to minimize the impact of the resulting fluctuations on the foreign currency value of the balance of trade. Assume that the export and import shares of the dollar, yen, and deutsche mark are w_i and v_i for $i = \$, \yen, dm$. Using the traditional model for exports and imports would put

$$\alpha_i = [\varepsilon(\eta^f - 1)/(\varepsilon + \eta^f)]w_i + v_i\eta,$$

where η and η^f are the domestic and foreign elasticities of demand for imports and ε is the domestic elasticity of supply of exports (assuming ε^f is infinite for a small country). If $\eta^f = 2.5$, $\eta = 0.7$, and $\varepsilon = 2$ for Korea (Kwack 1986), this would give weights approximately equal to the trade shares of the dollar, yen, and mark, or (using 1994 trade shares) 39 percent for the dollar, 36 percent for the yen, 25 percent for the mark.

On the other hand, with $30 billion worth of foreign exchange reserves, Korea may not have to worry about the availability of foreign currency. Weights that would minimize the impact on the domestic currency value of the balance of trade would limit effects on domestic output and employment. In this case, the weights should be

$$\alpha_i = [(1 + \varepsilon)\eta^f/(\varepsilon + \eta^f)]w_i + (1 - \eta)v_i,$$

which would imply weights of 43 percent for the dollar, 32 percent for the yen, and 25 percent for the mark. The larger role for the dollar under the domestic currency criterion reflects the greater importance of dollar markets for domestic currency export receipts, which have a higher elasticity than domestic currency import payments.

What this analysis omits is the impact of competing suppliers in the export market, which for Korea would be Japan and the other Asian industrializing countries, mainly Taiwan and Hong Kong. Including competitors would increase the weight on the yen and add Taiwan and Hong Kong to the basket. For the past 10 years, Hong Kong and Taiwan have both pegged their currencies very closely to the U.S. dollar. So the result would be to add to the weights of both the yen and the dollar in the basket, with perhaps little effect on the overall proportions (see Williamson 1995).

Even if Korea chooses not to peg its currency, the basket represents the appropriate basis for comparison of the movements of the external and domestic purchasing power of the won. Figure 10.1 shows the OECD's measures of

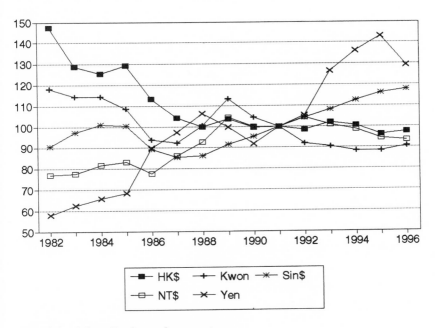

Fig. 10.1   Asian effective exchange rates
Source: OECD, *Economic Outlook,* vol. 58 (Paris, 1997).

nominal effective exchange rates of the won and related currencies. An inverse correlation will be noticed for most of the currencies relative to the movements of the Japanese yen. This reflects the degree to which their dollar pegs, especially during the 1980s, moved their currencies relative to the yen.

Figure 10.2 shows the corresponding real effective exchange rates, including my calculations for the bilateral Chinese yuan-dollar rate. During the 1980s most of the East Asian currencies moved inversely to the yen in real as well as nominal terms. In the 1990s, however, the Hong Kong and Singapore dollars have appreciated more in real terms than the Taiwan dollar, the won, or the yuan, which except for the latter have been relatively stable in real terms.

Figure 10.3 indicates the behavior of the won, in real and nominal terms, along with prices, as measured relative to consumer prices in industrial countries. From the perspective of stability in the real exchange rate, the market average rate system appears to be performing rather well. Put differently, the external value of the won is conforming more closely to its internal value.

10.2.3   Financial Liberalization

In July 1993 the Government of Korea announced a seven-year plan for liberalization of the financial sector of the economy (Park 1993). The major factors include gradually deregulating all interest rates except deposit rates by

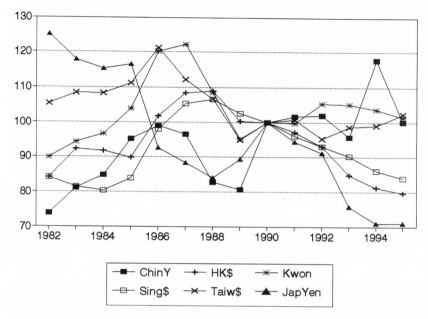

Fig. 10.2 Real effective exchange rates

Sources: OECD, *Economic Outlook*, vol. 58 (Paris, 1997); International Monetary Fund, *International Financial Statistics* (Washington, D.C., various issues); author's calculations.

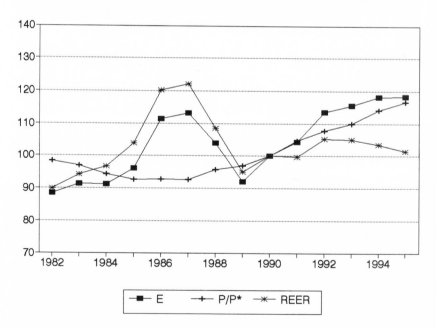

Fig. 10.3 Korea's exchange rate and relative prices

Sources: See fig. 10.2

1997, eliminating government influence over bank lending operations, encouraging the development of competition and new financial instruments, and liberalizing the foreign exchange market and capital flows. The purpose of this program is to use the financial markets to improve the efficiency with which financial resources are channeled to investment. In conjunction with this reform, the "real name" system was implemented in 1993, requiring all accounts to bear the real name of the holder. These major reforms are having important repercussions on the Korean economy and society. The tight network of personal relationships that has characterized the partnership between business and government is being replaced with more impersonal market-based relationships and explicit regulations.

The impact of financial liberalization on the foreign exchange market is significant. Kenen (1993) argues that the primary external effect of a credible liberalization of domestic financial markets in a developing country will be substantial capital inflow, leading to appreciation of the real exchange rate. He treats the existence of capital controls as equivalent to a tax on exporting capital. Liberalization eliminates the tax now and in the future. Thus capital inflow comes in response to the removal of the threat of future taxation of domestic financial assets. If the exchange rate is pegged, such capital inflows will require sterilization of large reserve inflows. If the exchange rate is floating, substantial nominal appreciation will occur.

But appreciation in response to capital inflow is only one possibility. Suppose that the capital controls limit both foreigners who wish to import capital and Koreans who wish to invest abroad. Their removal then leads to substantial portfolio diversification by both foreigners and domestic residents and a sharp increase in both capital inflows and outflows, with little impact on the exchange rate. According to Korean balance-of-payments data, both capital inflows and capital outflows have increased sharply since the liberalization of the financial sector in 1993. In the Korean context, the adoption of the real name system could itself lead to capital outflow. If formerly confidential transactions are now exposed to the authorities, in future such transactions would have to be carried out offshore to remain unknown to the authorities.

In actuality, the real (and nominal) exchange rate of the Korean won has appreciated since the beginning of the 1993–97 liberalization of financial markets. The reasons for this behavior are probably found more in the capital account than in the current account. During the period 1987–89, the influence of the current account on exchange rate policy was so strong that Korea's exchange rate appreciated strongly at the same time that reserves grew sharply and external debt was repaid. Then the external windfall temporarily disappeared with the rise in petroleum prices, interest rates, and the yen value of the dollar during the Gulf War crisis in 1989–90. Strong real wage growth during an inflationary boom provided internal stimulus. Korea's current account quickly turned negative, and the exchange rate depreciated in real terms during the period 1991–93. Thus the capital inflows, far from being a problem for monetary management, were welcome financing for the current account deficit (Folkerts-Landau et al. 1995).

Associated with the program of financial liberalization is a substantial liberalization of the foreign exchange market itself, permitting banks, firms, and individuals to hold foreign currencies more freely and to make transactions more freely (Kim 1994). Also, the permitted daily fluctuation of the won has been gradually increased, moving in the direction of a freely floating system. This does not mean, however, that intervention will be avoided, as foreign exchange reserves have increased by $14.5 billion since July 1993, in response to strong net capital inflows.

10.2.4 Limiting the Rate of Capital Inflow

A range of policies may be considered in the effort to keep capital inflows from overwhelming domestic exchange rate and monetary policies (International Monetary Fund 1995). Keeping the exchange rate flexible will impose some costs on risk-averse investors and thereby limit capital mobility. Taxing the interest earnings of foreign investors will also limit the inflow of capital. Equivalently, the authorities may impose reserve requirements on foreign capital inflows. Intervention in the foreign exchange market will limit the impact of capital inflows on the exchange rate, which if unsterilized will lead to an increase in the domestic money supply. Some amount of sterilized intervention can also be used, at the cost of the interest paid on the bonds issued to soak up the increase in liquidity. Finally, the authorities could simply set limits on the allowed amount of capital inflows of various types. This last tactic, like the taxes and reserve requirements, may be subject to evasion. More seriously, it will create rents and may lead to rent-seeking behavior, bribery, and so on. In summary, the best policy to limit capital inflows will be some judicious combination of all of the above, together with allowing some nonpredictable amount of exchange rate appreciation.

10.3 Should Korea Join a Currency Area?

One solution to some of the problems of exchange rate policy is the formation of a currency bloc. By pegging to a single currency standard, whether that of a large country or of a group of like-minded countries (as in the case of the EMS), a country can reduce the exchange-rate-induced fluctuation in its traded goods prices relative to the members of the bloc. Needless to say, this makes sense only if the partner or partners have stable economies and inflation rates.

For Korea, there are only two choices here, either pegging to a basket including its major markets, such as Japan, the United States, and Europe, or pegging together with a group of competitors, such as Taiwan, Hong Kong, Singapore, Thailand, and Malaysia. The first possibility would essentially require Korea to choose between stability of traded goods prices and the ability to respond to external shocks, as discussed above. While this option could minimize the variability of traded goods prices, it would not eliminate the terms-of-trade fluctuations noted earlier.

The second possibility would require a group of diverse competitors at different levels of development to agree on exchange rate policy and therefore on monetary policy over an extended period of time. It is already clear that these countries face significantly different economic policy problems and have chosen different exchange rate policies in the past. The Hong Kong dollar has been pegged to the U.S. dollar since 1984, while both Taiwan and Singapore have steadily appreciated, Singapore much faster. In addition, Korea's financial liberalization is proceeding on its own schedule, independent of the other Asian industrializing countries.

The feasibility of a currency area also depends on the degree of symmetry of the shocks expected to hit the various member countries. Contemplating the potential members is not reassuring on this score. South Korea will someday have to adjust to reunification with North Korea. Hong Kong is facing reintegration with China and its own entirely different set of structural adjustments. Taiwan continues to face the threat of attempts to reintegrate it into China. Thailand and Malaysia are at different stages in the development process from Korea. Reviewing these issues indicates the advantages of an independent exchange rate policy for Korea, for the foreseeable future.

This does not, however, rule out the usefulness of increased monetary cooperation in East Asia. With growing capital mobility and the potential for external financial shocks to spill over into Asian markets, coordinated strategies for responding to external shocks could be attractive. Coordinated responses to wide fluctuations in the yen-dollar rate could help avoid the extent of fluctuations in real exchange rates that took place in the late 1980s.

10.4 Implications of Korean Unification

When and if Korea reunites, it will face major structural readjustment problems. The example of German unification suggests that such a large real shock may be more easily adjusted to with a flexible rate. While the full implications of reunification are beyond the scope of this paper, it is at least clear that there would be a large demand for new investment to enlarge the capital stock of North Korea, both public and private. Such a large demand shock might also be accompanied by a negative supply shock, if Korea were to follow Germany's example and raise wages in the north without any corresponding increase in productivity. The net excess demand shock would require a contractionary fiscal response. If this were not provided, as it was not in Germany, then tight monetary policy would be needed to prevent inflation. The real interest rate would rise, and the real exchange rate would appreciate at once, then depreciate gradually over time in keeping with uncovered interest rate parity. The size of the net excess demand shock and the implied exchange rate effect could be reduced by more appropriate fiscal policy and wage policy.

10.5 Long-Run Equilibrium

In an economy like Korea, where per capita incomes and real wages are rising strongly over time, one major factor affecting the equilibrium real exchange rate is the rising relative price of nontraded goods, as domestic labor becomes more expensive. Thus the real exchange rate would be expected to appreciate over time as traded goods become relatively cheaper.

The other major factor is the increased attractiveness of Korean real and financial assets, both to foreigners and to Koreans themselves, as rates of return continue to be high and the economy becomes increasingly integrated with the rest of the world. This will also tend to appreciate the real value of the currency, offset to some degree as Korean firms and individuals diversify their asset holdings abroad. Particularly evident here is the drive of Korean *chaebol* to establish overseas operations as part of the process of globalization.

However, structural weaknesses can limit the rate of real appreciation, because of the negative effect it has on the Korean current account. Currently, Korea has been losing market share in the United States to Asian developing countries, offsetting this with sales gains in rapidly growing Asian markets. Among several problems with this process are the increasing tendency of Korean firms to move production to other Asian markets and the continued reliance of Korean firms on imports of Japanese machinery for expansion. Unless Korea can overcome these weaknesses, its ability to resume a healthy path of gradual real appreciation will be in question.

References

Balassa, Bela, and John Williamson. 1987. *Adjusting to success: Balance of payments policy in the East Asian NICs.* Policy Analysis no. 17. Washington, D.C.: Institute for International Economics.

Barro, Robert J., and David B. Gordon. 1983. A positive theory of monetary policy in a natural rate model. *Journal of Political Economy* 91 (August): 589–610.

Cho, Jae Ho. 1995. External debt and policy controversy in Korea. *Southern Economic Journal* 62 (1): 467–80.

Cukierman, Alex, Steven B. Webb, and Bilin Neyapti. 1993. Measuring the independence of central banks and its effect on policy outcomes. *World Bank Economic Review* 6:353–98.

Devarajan, S., and Dani Rodrik. 1991. Do the benefits of flexible exchange rates outweigh their costs? CEPR Working Paper no. 561. London: Centre for Economic Policy Research.

Edwards, Sebastian. 1993. The exchange rate as a nominal anchor. *Weltwirtschaftliches Archiv* 129:1–32.

———. 1996. Exchange rates and the political economy of macroeconomic discipline. *American Economic Review* 86 (2): 159–63.

Folkerts-Landau, David, et al. 1995. Effect of capital flows on the domestic financial sectors in APEC developing countries. In *Capital flows in the APEC region,* ed. Mohsin S. Khan and Carmen M. Reinhart. Occasional Paper no. 122. Washington, D.C.: International Monetary Fund.

Frankel, Jeffrey A., and Shang-Jin Wei. 1994. Yen bloc or dollar bloc? Exchange rate policies of the East Asian economies. In *Macroeconomic linkage: Savings, exchange rates, and capital flows,* ed. Takatoshi Ito and Anne Krueger. Chicago: University of Chicago Press.

International Monetary Fund. 1995. Capital account convertibility: Review of experiences and implications for IMF policies. Occasional Paper no. 131. Washington, D.C.: International Monetary Fund.

Kenen, Peter B. 1993. Financial opening and the exchange rate regime. In *Financial opening: Policy issues and experiences in developing countries,* 237–51. Paris: Organization for Economic Cooperation and Development.

Kim, Young-Soo. 1994. Foreign exchange market in Korea. *Quarterly Review* (Korea Exchange Bank) 28 (3d quarter): 3–13.

Kwack, Sung Y. 1986. Policy analysis with a macroeconomic model of Korea. *Economic Modeling* 3 (July): 175–96.

Oum, Bong-Sum, and Cho, Dong-Chul. 1995. Korea's exchange rate movements in the 1990s: Evaluation and policy implications. *Economic Bulletin* (Republic of Korea) 17 (December): 2–16.

Park, Pyeong Kyu. 1993. Korea's five-year (1993–97) financial reform plan. *Quarterly Review* (Korea Exchange Bank) 27 (2d quarter): 3–15.

Williamson, John. 1995. Exchange rate policies for East Asian countries in a world of fluctuating rates. Paper presented at KDI Symposium on Prospects of Yen-Dollar Exchange Rates and Korea's Exchange Rate Policy, Korea Development Institute, Seoul, December.

Comment   Chong-Hyun Nam

Black has written an excellent paper on the question of appropriate exchange rate policy for Korea. In addressing this delicate subject, he carefully examines the past experience of Korea's exchange rate policy as well as recent developments in its external economic conditions.

My comment will be very brief. Rather than repeating Black's conclusions, with which I agree, I will focus on one issue that I think requires more elaboration. The issue that I want to raise is: how can one detect and measure the existence of misalignment in the exchange rate for a small semiopen economy like Korea? Should we look at movements in the current account balance? Or the overall balance? Or some modified purchasing power parity indexes like the one Black has suggested in his paper?

In the past, up until the late 1970s, the Korean authorities looked more carefully at export performance for detecting a misalignment in exchange rate than at performance in the current account balance per se. They did so because the capital account was under the government's tight control, and thus the current

Chong-Hyun Nam is professor of economics at Korea University and a visiting scholar at the Center for Research on Economic Development and Policy Reform at Stanford University.

account balance was for the most part the intended one at the time. For instance, it was customary for the Korean government to make a long-term investment plan to ensure a desired level of output growth and then calculate the expected shortage in domestic savings. Then the government went out to borrow from abroad to fill the expected domestic savings-investment gap.

In the early 1980s, however, the Korean government began to restrain itself from intervening in resource allocation as well as in financing domestic investments. At the same time, the exchange rate system moved from a virtual peg to the U.S. dollar to a currency basket pegging system, which is classified as managed floating by the IMF's definition. During the 1980s, therefore, determination of the exchange rate was still under the government's discretionary control, and the government looked more carefully at movement in the current account balance in making any judgment on exchange rate misalignment.

But much confusion began to arise starting in the early 1990s, especially with the economy in a transitional period with ongoing capital market liberalization under the so-called market average rate system, which is virtually a floating exchange rate system. Problems arise mainly because both the current account balance and export performance tend to be affected in significant ways by the speed and scope of domestic capital market liberalization for both inbound and outbound flows. Furthermore, export performance can readily affect the economic growth rate, which is a priority concern for policymakers in Korea. Thus the appropriate exchange rate policy has become an inseparable issue from the policy of capital market liberalization in Korea. A major question rests on whether the overshooting effects of capital market liberalization should be and could be contained by government intervention in the exchange market, and if so, whether with sterilization or not? Much study needs to be done on these issues, I believe.

Comment   Baekin Cha

I am glad to have the honor of discussing Black's clear and forthright paper. I should merely like to elaborate on one of his points—the effects of financial liberalization.

Black is very right to tell us that the impact of financial liberalization on the foreign exchange market in Korea will be significant. Among many macroeconomic issues, the financial liberalization has been of the deepest concern to the business sector as well as to policymakers in Korea, and debates have been going on about its possible impacts on the domestic economy. On the one hand, financial liberalization and the likely capital inflow can be a contributing factor to further economic growth through (1) enhancement of international competi-

Baekin Cha is a research fellow at the Korea Institute of Finance.

tiveness of Korean exports resulting from a reduction in business firms' general financial costs and (2) an increase in domestic investment resulting from a fall in domestic interest rates. On the other hand, massive capital inflow may lead to an appreciation of the real exchange rate of the Korean won, which would reduce the competitiveness of Korean exports and worsen current account imbalances. Given the well-known export-oriented characteristic of the Korean economy, such appreciation could easily be channeled to the domestic business cycle in a negative way.

Black is also right to say that appreciation in response to capital inflow is only one possibility. As he points out, if the removal of capital controls leads to equal increases in capital inflow and outflow, there would be little impact on the exchange rate. Although it is true that capital outflow also increased sharply after 1993, it seems doubtful that the magnitude and the trend of capital outflow could counterbalance those of the obviously huge inflow in the future, given the chronic excess demand for funds, the relatively high domestic interest rate, and the degree of current government regulations on investment abroad by domestic residents.

In response to the expected strong net capital inflow, a real policy question will then be whether there should or should not be foreign exchange market intervention, and if there should, what type of intervention will minimize the aforementioned negative impacts.

If the Bank of Korea does not intervene at all in the foreign exchange market, the exchange rate will carry all the burden of adjustment. The positive effect will be easier monetary control, which contributes to price stabilization, but the negative effects will entail appreciation and the resulting lower international competitiveness of Korean exports and current account imbalance.

If the Bank of Korea intervenes, there can be two cases. First, if the bank adopts a sterilized intervention policy by issuing monetary stabilization bonds to absorb the portion of money supply increased by the purchase of foreign exchange, the exchange rate will remain stable and the impact on export competitiveness and the current account balance will be minimized. But this policy will necessarily be accompanied by sterilization costs. For example, at the end of June 1998, the outstanding balance of monetary stabilization bonds was 42.4 trillion won and the interest payment was 2.5 trillion won.

Second, if the Bank of Korea chooses nonsterilized intervention, the positive effects will be a stabilized exchange rate, a reduction in domestic interest rates, and no sterilization cost. But the negative effects will be more difficult management of the domestic money supply and, more important, inflation.

The choice among the above seems the most imminent and important decision that the Korean policymakers must make. While Black's paper is a very useful study covering a wide range of issues related to Korean exchange rate policy, I believe additional benefit could have been gained if it had provided a more detailed opinion regarding the intervention policy issue.

11   Liberalization of Capital Flows in Korea: Big Bang or Gradualism?

Dongchul Cho and Youngsun Koh

11.1 Introduction

Economic liberalization and deregulation has become a general trend in the era of globalization. The Korean economy is no exception to this trend. Despite the miraculous performances under the government-led growth strategy, Korea began to terminate some regulatory policies in the 1980s and accelerated the liberalization process in the 1990s. With respect to external sectors of the economy, the Korean government introduced a market-based exchange rate system in 1990 and began to open the official capital markets in 1992 by partially allowing foreigners to invest directly in Korean stock markets. Since then, the process of capital market deregulation has become irreversible. The only remaining matter seems to be how quickly the liberalization process will, or should, be carried out.

With the current level of interest rate differentials between Korea and developed economies, drastic full-scale liberalization would certainly induce a large amount of capital inflow and appreciate the Korean won. This would affect the price competitiveness of Korean products in international markets, which could bring about significant macroinstability in an economy like Korea's, which relies heavily on external transactions. An urgent question among Korean policymakers is whether there exists any policy combination that could minimize the macroinstability associated with the unavoidable trend of capital market liberalization.

This paper attempts to provide some quantitative, though very crude, assess-

Dongchul Cho and Youngsun Koh are research fellows at the Korea Development Institute.

This work is part of the NBER's project on International Capital Flows, which receives support from the Center for International Political Economy. The authors are grateful for the research assistance of Inchul Kim and for the comments of Chong-Hyun Nam, Koichi Hamada, Anne Krueger, Stanley Black, Andrew Rose, and other conference participants.

ments of several alternative policy choices. In order to perform simulation exercises, we set up a structural macromodel based on neoclassical long-run convergence and Keynesian short-run dynamics. Since the economic environment of the future, particularly in relation to external capital transactions and exchange rate determination, will be completely different from that of the past, there are undoubtedly limitations to what we can learn from past data.[1] For this reason, we employ theoretical relationships rather than only utilizing regression results for some parts of the model.

We do not believe that the exercises performed in this paper can significantly improve general understanding of this rather well-known subject; the simulation results are qualitatively predictable. By applying general theories to the specific data, however, the quantitative results in the paper may help readers to anticipate future dynamic paths of the key macrovariables in the Korean economy. In addition, the paper provides evidence for the convergence of the neoclassical growth model from the Korean data, to which the simulation model anchors.

Section 11.2 reviews recent developments in the exchange rate system and capital market liberalization in Korea as well as the movements of some relevant macrovariables. Section 11.3 briefly explains the econometric macromodel used in this paper, and section 11.4 presents the simulation results. Section 11.5 provides concluding remarks.

11.2   Capital Flows and Related Macrovariables in Korea

11.2.1   Exchange Rate System

With the abandonment of the fixed exchange rate system in 1980, the exchange rate began to float by being pegged to a basket of multiple foreign exchange rates. Nevertheless, the government continued to exercise great discretionary power in the name of "policy considerations," the most important of which seemed to be maintenance of the current account balance.[2]

It was recognized, however, that operation with the exchange rate as an independent policy tool would not be possible since Korea's capital markets would no longer be insulated from the gigantic world capital market. To prepare for the forthcoming capital account liberalization process, the multiple basket peg system was finally replaced, in March 1990, with the "market average rate" system. Under the new system, the exchange rate is determined by demand for and supply of Korean won vis-à-vis foreign exchange, and the government can affect the exchange rate only indirectly through the market. Although the Korean government still appears to be a major player in the exchange market for

1. As a leading example, one can think of Lucas's critique (1976).
2. For details of Korea's exchange rate movements, see Oum and Cho (1995).

the Korean won, its relative market power will certainly diminish as the Korean capital market becomes integrated with the world market.

11.2.2   Capital Market Liberalization to Date

In Korea, capital market liberalization proceeded gradually, taking into account such factors as the current account balance, money supply, and exchange rate. For example, when the current account showed large deficits in the first half of the 1980s (see fig. 11.1), capital outflows were strictly restricted to slow down the pace of foreign debt accumulation. This situation was completely reversed in the latter half of the 1980s. A large current account surplus, reaching 7.8 percent of GDP in 1988, forced the Korean government to decontrol capital outflows. As a result, the net level of foreign debt plunged from 37.7 percent of GDP in 1985 to 1.4 percent in 1989. But the increased capital outflows were insufficient to contain the growth of reserve money (see fig. 11.2). Hence, private credits were restricted, and massive sterilization was conducted through monetary stabilization bonds (MSBs).[3]

However, controls on capital flows became increasingly difficult as the Korean economy got more integrated into the global economy. Foreign investors, as well as domestic companies, constantly demanded greater opening of Korean markets to exploit the big interest differential with overseas markets. To meet their demands to a certain degree, a capital account liberalization plan was finally announced in 1993.[4]

Korean residents now have a great deal of freedom as far as capital outflows are concerned,[5] but considerable restrictions still remain on capital inflows.[6] These restrictions on capital inflows are not expected to be removed in the near future unless the interest rate differential substantially narrows.

11.2.3   Capital Flows and the Interest Rate Differential

Since external capital flows were tightly controlled in Korea, the capital account balance was extremely insensitive to the uncovered interest differential.[7]

3. The outstanding MSBs amounted to 88 percent of reserve money at the end of 1995.

4. This plan was superseded by the foreign exchange reform plan in 1994, which in turn was revised in late 1995. Further liberalization was announced in April 1996. For a survey of Korea's liberalization process, see Park (1992).

5. Individuals, as well as institutional investors, can make unlimited investments in overseas securities. Institutional investors can hold deposits in foreign banks up to $100 million, while lower limits apply to legal entities and individuals. Outward foreign direct investment (FDI) was to be completely liberalized by 1997.

6. The regulations are as follows: nonresidents as a whole can hold up to 20 percent of the outstanding shares of each company, and each nonresident up to 5 percent; bond holding by nonresidents is allowed indirectly through the Korea Trust and Country Fund; direct holding is allowed only for convertible bonds issued by small and medium-sized enterprises; domestic companies can use foreign commercial loans within certain limits only for the import of capital goods and for FDI; delayed payment for imports is currently permitted for up to 120 days.

7. Since futures or forward markets are not yet established in Korea, we could not test covered interest parity.

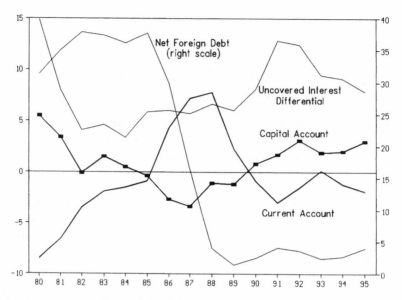

Fig. 11.1   External balances (percent of GDP)

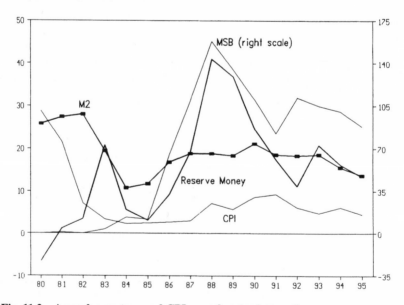

Fig. 11.2   Annual monetary and CPI growth rates (percent)

Table 11.1   **Capital Flows and the Uncovered Interest Rate Differential**

Capital Account Balance	Constant ($\times 10^{-2}$)	$i_t - i_t^f - \log(e_{t+1}/e_t)$ No Time Trend	$t - 1995$	R^2
skb_t	−0.03 (0.13)	0.04 (1.81)		.06
lkb_t	1.26 (2.83)	−0.11 (2.63)		.12
kb_t	1.23 (2.38)	−0.07 (1.47)		.04
skb_t	−0.13 (0.54)	0.09 (2.45)	0.01 (1.69)	.11
lkb_t	0.88 (2.15)	0.09 (1.33)	0.04 (3.76)	.32
kb_t	0.76 (1.63)	0.18 (2.39)	0.04 (4.14)	.29

Notes: skb_t, lkb_t, and kb_t denote short-term, long-term, and total capital account balance (normalized by potential GDP), respectively; and i_t, i_t^f, and e_t denote domestic interest rate (yield rate of three-year corporate bond), foreign interest rate (three-month Eurodollar rate), and won-dollar exchange rate, respectively. The sample period is 1983:1 to 1995:4. Numbers in parentheses are t-statistics. The linear time trend, $t - 1995$, is normalized so that $t = 1995$ yields 0. For further details, see the text.

Using the actual rate of the won-dollar exchange rate depreciation as a proxy variable for the expected rate, $\log(e_{t+1}/e_t)$, table 11.1 shows the results of regressions of the capital account balance (normalized by potential GDP), kb_t, on $i_t - i_t^f - \log(e_{t+1}/e_t)$, where i_t and i_t^f denote the domestic and foreign interest rates at time t, respectively. If capital were perfectly mobile across national borders and there were no uncertainty, this coefficient would in principle approach infinity so that only the exchange rate can, and should, adjust to restore the equilibrium.[8] While the short-term capital account (skb_t) shows a small but significant positive correlation, the long-term capital account (lkb_t) yields a negative correlation.

Although the correlations between the capital account and the uncovered interest rate differential are not strong, it seems clear that the capital account has become more responsive to the interest differential. As a piece of evidence, table 11.1 reports the results of regressions in which a linear time trend is included in the regression coefficient: the time trend appears significant in both skb_t and lkb_t regressions.[9] In particular, the estimates for the kb_t regression

8. Considering the forecast error about e_{t+1} at time t, there must be measurement error in the expected appreciation rate, hence a downward bias in the regression coefficient. Nevertheless, there seems no reason to expect that this bias would change the sign of the coefficient estimate, and the increase in the coefficient estimate over time seems to indicate that capital flows are getting more sensitive to the uncovered interest differential.

9. We also tried several other specifications for the coefficient to test if there is any convexity over time, but the results were not very different from the linear time trend.

imply that the coefficient turned positive in 1991, approximately the same time that the stock market began to open to foreign investors.

11.2.4   Secular Trend of the Interest Rate

The annual yield rate of three-year corporate bonds in Korea is still around 12 percent, which implies an approximately 7 percent real interest rate, given the approximately 5 percent annual inflation rate. Under this circumstance, it is clear that for foreign investors, Korea is an attractive market that has not yet been sufficiently explored. Then the most relevant question to our analysis in this paper is what maintains the high (real) interest rate in Korea and how it will evolve over time.

Figure 11.3 plots three series of interest rates: the official bank loan rate, the yield rate of three-year corporate bonds, and the curb market rate, all of which are converted into real terms by subtracting the actual inflation rate. It is well known that the official interest rates on bank loans and corporate bonds were maintained at levels far below the market rate by severe government controls in Korea until the first half of the 1980s. Although the gap between the official rates and the curb market rate substantially narrowed as a result of the continuous financial deregulations in the 1980s, the curb market rate seemed to be a better measure of the market rate at least until the first half of the 1980s. From figure 11.3, it appears clear that the curb market rate has been in a downward secular trend, from over 20 percent in the early 1970s to around 7 percent in 1995. Using the corporate bond rate, which is widely used as the representative market rate in the 1990s, we can also find a similar downward trend if the sample period is restricted to a recent period, say, 1983–95.

We interpret this downward trend of the real interest rate as evidence for transitional dynamics of the neoclassical growth model. In a stylized neoclassical growth model, employing the Cobb-Douglas production function, $Y_t = A_t K_t^\alpha L_t^{1-\alpha}$, where Y denotes potential output, A level of technology, K capital stock, and L labor supply, the interest rate is equated to the marginal productivity of capital, $\alpha Y_t/K_t$, minus the depreciation rate, δ. In an economy with an initial level of K/L lower than the steady state level, the marginal productivity of capital (hence the interest rate) declines over time to converge to the steady state level (say, the world level of the interest rate).

In order to be convinced that transitional dynamics was a plausible description for the secular trend of the Korean interest rate, we also plotted in figure 11.3 rough estimates of $\alpha Y_t/K_t - \delta$ using $\alpha = 1/3$ and $\delta = 0.066$ per year,[10] which appear to aptly describe the trend of the curb rate. It may be worthwhile to note here that the average growth rate of investment has been far greater

---

10. The estimates of labor income share, $1 - \alpha$, in Korea range from 60 to 70 percent (see table 2 in Hong 1994) and the depreciation rate of capital, δ, is estimated to be 6.6 percent per year by Park (1992).

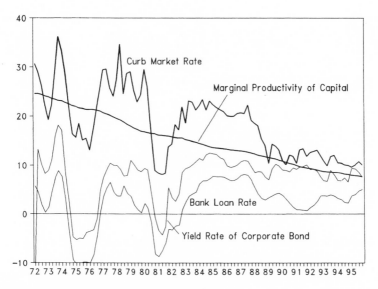

Fig. 11.3   Trend of real interest rate (percent)

than the average growth rate of GDP in Korea since the 1960s.[11] This was the main cause of the declining trend of Y_t/K_t, and it seems unlikely that the trend will suddenly reverse its direction. In order to reflect the downward trend in the long run, therefore, we include $\alpha y_t/K_t - \delta$ in the interest rate specification along with other commonly used variables, such as money supply (see the appendix for details).

11.3   A Brief Description of the Empirical Model

The model we used for the simulations is basically neoclassical in the long run, but Keynesian in the short run (details are in the appendix). That is, all the real variables are determined by the supply side in the long run, which follows the transitional dynamics explained in subsection 11.2.4.[12] In the short run, however, demand shocks do matter as in a typical Keynesian model.[13]

Technically, the way we distinguish long-run from short-run phenomena is by employing error correction types of specifications in which only long-run

11. E.g., the average annual growth rate of investment during the period 1970–95 in Korea was approximately 12 percent, while that of GDP was around 8 percent.

12. See Blanchard and Fischer (1989) for a discussion of dynamic responses of a flexible price model in relation to the capital market opening of an economy with higher interest rates than the world rate. We take this case only as a long-run phenomenon because we assume in our model that prices are sticky in the short run.

13. While the long-run neutrality of money holds in the model, superneutrality does not.

Table 11.2   **Assumptions about Growth Rates of Exogenous Variables (percent)**

Variable	Big Bang(e)	Gradualism(e)	Gradualism(M)
Y_t^f	3.0	3.0	3.0
P_t^f	2.5	2.5	2.5
i_t^f	7.5	7.5	7.5
L_t^*	2.2	2.2	2.2
e_t	–	–	800
$\bar{M}_t$	14.0 (1996–2000)	14.0 (1996–2000)	–
	13.0 (2001–5)	13.0 (2001–5)	–
$\bar{B}_t$	14.0 (1996–2000)	14.0 (1996–2000)	–
	13.0 (2001–5)	13.0 (2001–5)	–

Note: See the appendix for definitions of the variables.

determinants are included in the error-correcting terms. That way, the effects of all the other short-run (say, stationary) disturbances eventually disappear, leaving only the effects of long-run determinants. For example, the interest rate is affected by many factors like money supply in the short run, but it will eventually converge to the sum of the inflation rate and capital productivity. What then becomes important for short-run effects is speeds of convergence toward long-run equilibrium levels, which we let the data determine from the regressions.[14]

We used quarterly data from 1983:1 through 1995:4 for the regressions,[15] although the simulation results will be presented in annual terms. For the future projection, we took the simplest case of the exogenous variables that are presented in table 11.2. Particularly important is the foreign interest rate in real terms, which we assumed to be 4 percent throughout the simulation period.[16]

We are aware of the many limitations of our empirical model in particular as well as of simulation experiments in general. After all, the shortcomings of policy simulations using econometric models have well been recognized since Lucas (1976). Our model is also far from flawless. Perhaps the most important flaw is that it is basically backward looking. For example, the "expected" rate of inflation is simply computed from the past series of the inflation rate, rather than going through the rational expectations of monetary policy reactions. Our

14. In a sense, our model can be viewed as a large vector autoregression system with error-correcting terms. To identify the shocks, we tried to minimize the number of two-way causal relations among contemporary variables. Nevertheless, a few contemporaneous variables remain to cause each other (e.g., consumption and GDP). We did not attempt to correct possible simultaneity bias, hoping that the size of the bias is negligible.

15. The major reason that we restricted the sample period to 1983–95 is to take the longest period in which the corporate bond rate can be used as the representative interest rate.

16. Barro and Sala-i-Martin (1990), e.g., report 3 to 4 percent per year as the acceptable range of the "world real interest rate." We took 4 percent to allow a slight margin for country risk, so that the capital market will be in balance when the real interest rate in Korea reaches 4 percent.

application of forward-looking behavior to determine the exchange rate may then be considered inconsistent with the other parts of the model. Nevertheless, we hope that the following experiments can provide a useful, though rough, quantitative assessment of the effects of capital market liberalization in Korea.

11.4 Simulation Results

11.4.1 Benchmark Case: No Capital Flows

As shown in figure 11.1, Korea has been maintaining a net capital inflow of about 2 percent of GDP since 1992. Therefore, an abrupt shutdown of external capital markets may be interpreted as a regressive "big bang" case. We experimented with this case to see how the model works and to obtain benchmark values of the relevant variables whose dynamic paths will be compared under different regimes.

In this benchmark case, capital cannot flow freely to seek higher returns, and thus interest parity does not hold. Specifically, we let the exchange rate adjust to restore the current account balance by $e_{t+1} = e_t \exp(-\beta \, cb_t)$, where cb_t is the current account balance normalized by potential GDP and the parameter for the adjustment speed, β, was estimated from the data. That is, we assume that capital account transactions are just passively adjusted to support current account transactions. This specification of the exchange rate may be interpreted as a policy reaction function that aims at current account balance using current account performance as a measure of exchange rate misalignment, which appears to fit the Korean data in the 1980s.[17]

Although we will not report the results for this case, we could get a rough idea of the real exchange rate that would be consistent with current account balance (called the purchasing power parity [PPP] rate hereafter). Given the assumptions about all the exogenous variables, this value appears to be around 800 won per dollar in the beginning of 1996. In addition, we could confirm that the real interest rate gradually declines to 4.3 percent in 2005, which is mainly generated by the projection of the secular downward trend in the model (see the appendix for details). It is also confirmed that the rate of CPI inflation converged to around 3 percent under the assumptions for money supply and labor growth rate.

In the following, the discussion will focus on the results of three cases that differ in the speed of capital market liberalization and exchange rate policy. Table 11.3 summarizes the exchange rate dynamics and associated money supply mechanisms for each of the three cases, and figures 11.4A–11.4L report the simulation results.

---

17. In fact, the Korean government appeared to manage the exchange rate aiming at current account balance in the 1980s. See Oum and Cho (1995) for details.

Table 11.3   **Exchange Rate and Money Supply Determination Mechanisms**

Case	Exchange Rate (e_t)	Money Supply (M_t)
Big Bang(e)	$e_{t+1} = e_t \exp(i_t - i_t^f)$	$M_t = \overline{M}_t$ (exogenous)
Gradualism(e)	$e_{t+1} = e_t \exp\{i_t - i_t^f - kb_t/[7.5/(2010 - t)]\}$	$M_t = \overline{M}_t$ (exogenous)
Gradualism(M)	$e_t = 800$	$M_t = \overline{M}_t + 5 (KB_t + CB_t)$

Note: We used 5 as the money multiplier in the M_t specification of gradualism.

11.4.2   Big Bang

We regard as "perfect capital mobility" the case in which uncovered interest parity holds (or the elasticity of kb_t with respect to $i_t - i_t^f - \log(e_{t+1}/e_t)$ is infinity in table 11.1). In this case, the most active role is assigned to capital account transactions concerning the exchange rate determination, and the current account simply responds to exchange rate movements. We assume that this new regime of exchange rate dynamics suddenly replaced the old one at the beginning of 1996. As will be explained below, the only sustainable policy in this case is to let the exchange rate adjust.

Exchange Rate Adjustment

If the government let the exchange rate absorb the interest rate differential in the case of big bang, the exchange rate dynamics can be specified by

$$e_{t+1} = e_t \exp(i_t - i_t^f),$$

while the money supply is controlled by the government. In order to pin e_t down in the simulation, a terminal condition is needed as in other forward-looking dynamic models. We tried several values for the initial e_t and picked the associated dynamic path of e_t that yielded the most consistent results with the path of i_t at the terminal year, 2005. Since i_t almost converges to i_t^f by 2005 (6.5 percent = 4 percent real rate + 2.5 percent inflation rate in this case), the real exchange rate should also converge to the PPP rate that was roughly calculated in the benchmark case.

A typical sticky-price monetary model (Dornbusch 1976, e.g.) would predict the results for this case. The exchange rate initially jumps to appreciate by approximately 15 percent[18] and then gradually depreciates by the interest differential until it converges to the PPP rate around 2005 (fig. 11.4A). The interest rate declines faster than in the benchmark case because of more active

---

18. This estimate of 15 percent is roughly consistent with the result of simple algebra using the interest parity and the long-run trend of the real interest rate without considering feedback effects of all the other variables of the macromodel. From the observation that the real interest rate declines by approximately 0.3 percentage points per year, the cumulative sum of interest differentials can be roughly computed by $\sum_{t=0}^{10} (r_t - r_t^f) = 15$, for $r_t = 7.0 - 0.3t$ and $r_t^f = 4.0$.

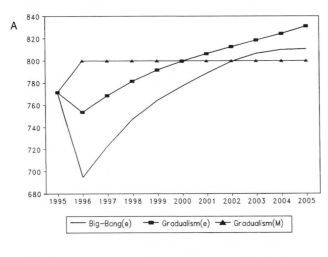

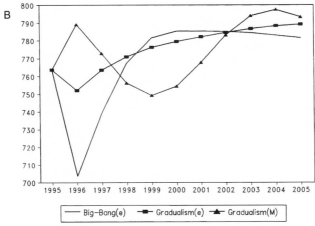

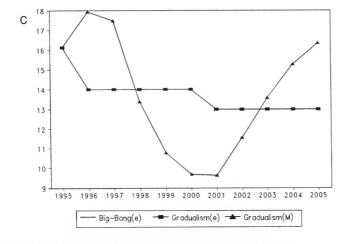

Fig. 11.4   Simulation results: big bang versus gradualism
Note: A, exchange rate (won per dollar). B, real exchange rate (won per dollar in 1990 prices). C, growth rate of money (percent); big bang and gradualism(e) curves coincide.

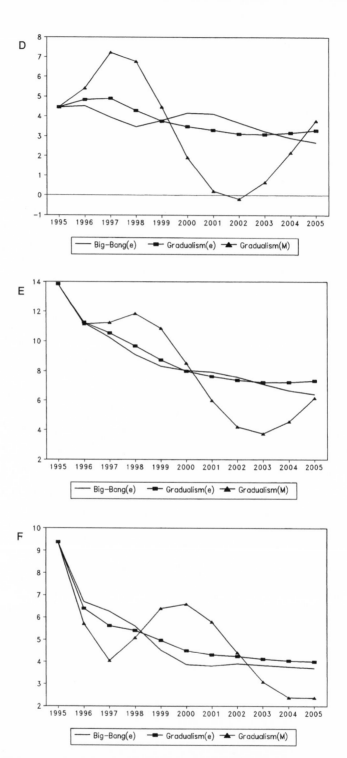

Fig. 11.4   Simulation results: big bang versus gradualism (cont.)

Note: D, rate of CPI inflation (percent). E, nominal interest rate (percent). F, real interest rate (percent).

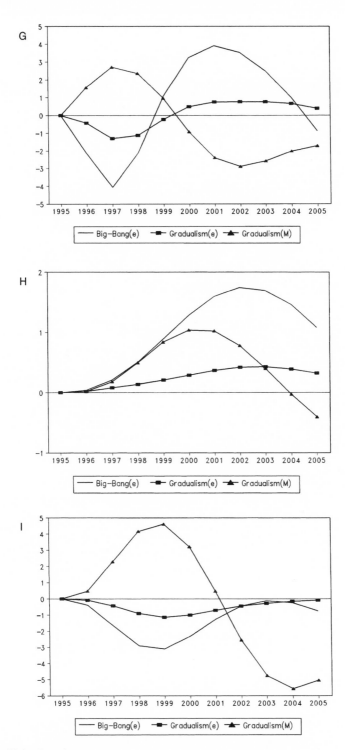

Fig. 11.4 (cont.)
Note: G, GDP, deviation from benchmark (percent). *H*, potential output, deviation from benchmark (percent). *I*, CPI, deviation from benchmark (percent).

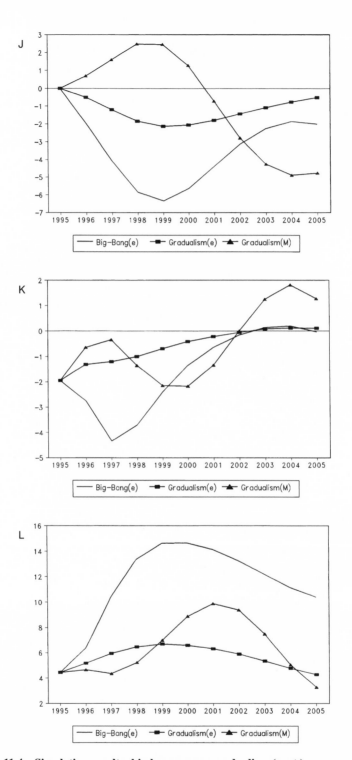

Fig. 11.4   Simulation results: big bang versus gradualism (cont.)

Note: J, PPI, deviation from benchmark (percent). K, ratio of current account balance to GDP (percent). L, ratio of net foreign debt to GDP (percent).

investment[19] and the resulting capital accumulation (fig. 11.4E). Potential output also increases rapidly (fig. 11.4H), but the economy goes through a short-run recession for the first two to three years (fig. 11.4G) due to the contraction of foreign demand that is caused by the exchange rate appreciation. Prices, particularly PPI, which is far more affected by import prices, become very stable (figs. 11.4I and 11.4J). But the current account deficit reaches almost 5 percent of GDP in 1997 (fig. 11.4K) and then approaches balance, rapidly accumulating (net) foreign debt, 15 percent by 1999 (Fig. 11.4L).[20]

Exchange Rate Targeting

Policymakers often fear the rapid accumulation of foreign debt and therefore seek exchange rate stability. To see the effects of this policy, we set the nominal exchange rate at 800 won per dollar, which appears to be approximately consistent with the current account balance at the beginning of 1996. Since interest parity should hold in this big bang case, the only way to support nominal exchange rate stability ($e_{t+1} = e_t$ for all t) is to equate the domestic interest rate with the foreign rate ($i_t = i_t^f$ for all t).[21]

If expansionary monetary policy were used to lower i_t to the level of i_t^f, we could easily confirm unsustainability: the model explodes no later than 1998 with more than 100 percent inflation.[22] The initial monetary expansion to set $i_t = i_t^f$ brings about inflation, hence i_t begins to rise, which requires accelerating monetary expansion to keep $i_t = i_t^f$. If the interest rate gap is not so wide and the gap is expected to narrow soon due to a third factor, then a temporary expansion of the money supply may be a reasonable choice. But Korea's current situation does not seem to be such a case. To save space, we did not report the results of this experiment.

Another, though arguable, way to lower i_t may be to run an extremely large budget surplus.[23] From many regressions of the interest rate on public bonds, however, we only found an extremely small and statistically insignificant elasticity. The interest rate equation in the appendix is the one that yielded the largest elasticity with respect to public bonds. Even with this largest elasticity, a simple calculation shows that the required amount of outstanding bond reduction to equate i_t to i_t^f would be 30 to 50 percent of GDP, or two times larger than the current level of total government expenditure, which would be impossible to achieve.

11.4.3 Gradual Liberalization

The general consensus of the empirical literature seems that while covered interest parity holds, uncovered interest parity does not exactly hold even

---

19. More active investment is mostly induced by the relatively low interest rate.
20. Net foreign debt is simply computed as the accumulation of the current account deficit.
21. The reason that i_t should be equal to i_t^f is that we assumed perfect foresight of investors.
22. The model explodes no matter where the target level of exchange rate is set.
23. How sensible this statement is depends on whether Ricardian equivalence holds.

among the countries maintaining the most liberalized capital markets.[24] Considering this empirical finding, it may be rather reasonable to assume that the elasticity of kb_t with respect to $i_t - i_t^f - \log(e_{t+1}/e_t)$ is finite. Particularly for the case of Korea, in which the capital markets are expected to open gradually, we assume that this elasticity (denoted $f(t)$ below) will be increasing at a gradual pace over time:

$$kb_t = f(t)[i_t - i_t^f - \log(e_{t+1}/e_t)],$$

where $f(t) > 0$ and $f'(t) > 0$ for all t. One can regard the big bang case as the limiting case in which $f(t)$ goes to infinity from the beginning. We have experimented with many specifications of $f(t)$. As can be easily reasoned, the general rule of thumb is that the more rapidly $f(t)$ increases, the closer the results are to the big bang case: the initial appreciation of the exchange rate is larger, or the model is more likely to explode with exchange rate targeting.

In this paper, we only present the results for $f(t) = 7.5/(2010 - t)$, which is one of the most gradual processes we have tried, so gradual that exchange rate targeting does not explode. The rationale of this specification is that (a) the Korean government will completely open capital markets by the year 2010, when the Korean interest rate is expected to be sufficiently close to the world rate ($f(t)$ goes to infinity for $t = 2010$), and (b) $f(1995) = 0.5$ is close to the actual elasticity in 1995.[25]

While this specification is tractable, the most critical question behind this gradual process is how sustainable the gradualism itself would be under the potential threat of speculative attacks. The assumption that capital flows are only partially responsive to the interest rate differential hinges on the presumption that potential speculators are limited in their amount of foreign currency transactions. That is, the big proviso of a successful gradualism appears to be the controllability of the quantity of foreign currency inflows until the interest rate differential narrows, say, by the year 2000.

Exchange Rate Adjustment

This case is basically the same as the case of big bang with exchange rate overshooting, except for the magnitudes. The exchange rate determined by $e_{t+1} = e_t \exp\{i_t - i_t^f - kb_t/[7.5/(2010 - t)]\}$ initially jumps to appreciate to a relatively mild extent and then depreciates over time until it reaches the PPP rate (gradualism(e) in figs. 11.4A and 11.4B). The directions of all the other results are the same as in the big bang case, but the magnitudes are smaller.

Exchange Rate Targeting

Perhaps a more interesting case of gradual liberalization is the one in which the government policy to fix the nominal exchange rate is sustainable. Since

24. This may be due to either the risk-averse behavior of the investors or the "irrational" formulation of the agent's expectations, or something else. See Taylor (1995) for a recent survey.
25. In 1995, kb_t was about 3 percent and the interest differential was about 6 percent.

kb_t is not only finite but rather insensitive to the interest rate differential, the government is given much more room for policy making.

We fixed the exchange rate at 800 won per dollar, as in subsection 11.4.2, and let the central bank accommodate additional money demand to the same extent as the overall balance surplus. Since the level of the exchange rate initially yields approximately the current account balance (gradualism(M) in fig. 11.4K), the money supply expands almost as much as the capital account surplus, which will inevitably generate faster inflation.

This inflation has opposite effects on the subsequent money supply. On the one hand, it raises the nominal interest rate and thus induces more capital inflow, which increases the money supply. On the other hand, the inflation appreciates the real exchange rate and the current account turns to deficit, which decreases the money supply. The relative size of the two effects depends on the specification of $f(t)$, but in the case of very gradual liberalization, $f(t) = 7.5/(2010 - t)$, the latter effect dominates and the money supply declines (fig. 11.4C).[26] The monetary contraction then pushes the economy, which is about to enter a recession in 1999 after the boom generated by the initial monetary expansion, deeper into recession (fig. 11.4G). The deep recession further decreases the rate of inflation (fig. 11.4D), and the nominal interest rate finally drops below the world rate in 2001 (fig. 11.4E), which brings about capital flight from the country, along with current account surplus starting in 2002 (fig. 11.4K). While foreign debt accumulates less than in the big bang case (fig. 11.4L), the potential level of output is smaller (fig. 11.4H) and the economy goes through a similar magnitude of macroinstability in the opposite direction (fig. 11.4G).

Under this gradual liberalization plan and the expected downward trend of the interest rate, sterilized intervention for exchange rate stability appears to be sustainable as well as sensible for macrostability.[27] In order to avoid the initial recession and current account deficit, however, the government should bear the burden of public debt. In other words, the external debt that would otherwise accumulate is replaced by internal debt of the government (incurring higher interest rates). The benefit is gaining macrostability, while the cost is forgoing the opportunity to exploit foreign savings to enhance the potential capacity of the economy.

11.5 Conclusion

We have presented rough estimates of the dynamic paths for important macrovariables under several different liberalization scenarios. Fully admitting the limitations of our experiments, we believe that they can provide more concrete ideas of where the economy will be heading for each case.

---

26. If $f(t)$ is less gradual, the model explodes as in the case of big bang with exchange rate targeting.
27. As mentioned earlier, the effect of government bonds on the interest rate is negligible.

Among very many possible combinations of policies, including the speed of market opening, we are not able to pick an "optimal" one that totally depends on the objective function of policymakers. If the objective is simply to maximize the potential capacity of the economy with price stability, the big bang in conjunction with exchange rate overshooting should be recommended. But in this case, policymakers have to convince people that a sweet boom will arrive after a painful recession for the first couple of years and that the current account will turn into surplus after, say, 10 years.

Perhaps the time horizon here is too long for policymakers, and even when based on economic criteria it is not clear whether maximizing the potential level at the expense of a recession is the best choice. If it is not, a gradual liberalization process can be recommended. A critical justification for gradualism is then the secular downward trend of the interest rate, and the key to a successful gradualism seems to be control over the quantity of foreign currency inflows. In any case, we leave completely unanswered the question: how gradual is "optimal"?

Appendix
The Model

Variables

A	technical level
B	public bond
C^G	government consumption expenditure
C^P	private consumption expenditure
e	exchange rate
I	gross fixed capital formation
KB	capital balance
K	capital stock
L	total labor employed
M	money supply (M2)
MG	imports
MPK	marginal productivity of capital
MPL	marginal productivity of labor
P^c	CPI
P^p	PPI
P^x	unit value index of exports
P^m	unit value index of imports
P^f	foreign WPI
P^o	unit import price of oil
i	interest rate
i^f	foreign interest rate
t	time trend (quarterly)

W	wage
XG	exports
Y	GDP
Y^f	foreign GDP
π	CPI inflation rate
τ	tax rate

An asterisk denotes potential level. Δ denotes first difference.

Identities

Definition of capital stock (annual depreciation rate of 0.066)

$$K_t = (1 - 0.066/4)K_{t-1} + (1/4)(I_t + I_{t-1} + I_{t-2} + I_{t-3})$$

Trend of labor force (annual growth rate of 0.028)

$$L_t = \exp(0.02837 \cdot t/4 - 46.6687)$$

Aggregate production function (capital income share of 1/3)

$$Y_t^* = A_t \cdot K_t^{1/3} \cdot L_t^{2/3}$$

Technology progress rate (annual growth rate of 0.022)

$$A_t = \exp(0.02254 \cdot t/4 - 44.9738)$$

Productivity of labor

$$\text{MPL}_t = (2/3)Y_t^*/L_t$$

Productivity of capital (4 to be annualized)

$$\text{MPK}_t = (4/3)Y_t^*/K_t$$

Trend of capital productivity[28]

$$\text{MPK}_t^* = 0.10 + (4/3)\exp(-0.06447 \cdot t/4 + 125.355)$$

Trend of capital stock[29]

$$K_t^* = [(3/4)A_t/\text{MPK}_t^*]^{3/2} \cdot L_t$$

Trend of consumer price level

$$P_t^* = (M_t/Y_t^*)\exp(-0.03157 \cdot t/4 + 67.0944)$$

---

28. This is obtained by regressing log ($\text{MPK}_t - 0.10$) on t so that MPK_t and the real interest rate converge to 10 percent and 3.4 ($=10.0 - 6.6$) percent, respectively.
29. K_t^* is determined by the exogenous time trend alone.

Definition of the inflation rate

$$\pi_t = \log(P_t^c / P_{t-4}^c)$$

Definition of GDP

$$Y_t = C_t^p + C_t^G + I_t + XG_t - MG_t$$

Regression Equations

$$\Delta \log(C_t^p) = 0.26 \cdot \Delta \log((1 - \tau_t)Y_t) + 0.17 \cdot \Delta \log(M_t / P_t^c)$$
$$\qquad\qquad (8.09) \qquad\qquad\qquad\qquad (1.70)$$
$$\qquad\qquad - 0.09 \cdot [\log(C_{t-1}^p / Y_{t-1})] - 0.06.$$
$$\qquad\qquad\quad (2.23) \qquad\qquad\qquad\qquad (2.27)$$

$$\Delta \log(I_t) = -0.31 \cdot \Delta \log(I_{t-1}) + 0.26 \cdot \Delta \log(XG_t) + 0.29 \cdot kb_t$$
$$\qquad\quad (2.65) \qquad\qquad\qquad (1.98) \qquad\qquad\qquad (1.10)$$
$$\qquad\quad - 0.53 \cdot (i_t - \pi_t - MPK_t) - 0.30 \cdot [\log(K_{t-1}/K_{t-1}^*)] - 0.28,$$
$$\qquad\qquad (1.44) \qquad\qquad\qquad\qquad (1.34) \qquad\qquad\qquad\qquad (7.04)$$

$$\Delta \log(XG_t) = 0.30 \cdot \log(P_{t-2}^f / P_{t-2}^x)$$
$$\qquad\qquad\quad (2.33)$$
$$\qquad\qquad - 0.16 \cdot [\log(XG_{t-1}) - 3.04 \cdot \log(Y_{t-1}^f)] - 0.12.$$
$$\qquad\qquad\quad (2.11) \qquad\qquad\qquad (36.75) \qquad\qquad\qquad (9.73)$$

$$\Delta \log(MG_t) = 0.21 \cdot \Delta \log(I_t) + 0.27 \cdot \Delta \log(I_{t-1})$$
$$\qquad\qquad\quad (1.72) \qquad\qquad\qquad (2.32)$$
$$\qquad\qquad + 0.64 \cdot \Delta \log(C_t^p + C_t^G) + 0.17 \cdot \Delta \log(XG_t)$$
$$\qquad\qquad\quad (0.83) \qquad\qquad\qquad\qquad (1.19)$$
$$\qquad\qquad - 0.24 \cdot \log(e_t \cdot P_t^M / P_t^p) - 0.15 \cdot [\log(MG_{t-1}/XG_{t-1})]$$
$$\qquad\qquad\quad (1.83) \qquad\qquad\qquad\qquad (2.03)$$
$$\qquad\qquad + 1.67.$$
$$\qquad\qquad\quad (1.92)$$

$$i_t = 0.79 \cdot i_{t-1} + 0.02 \cdot \Delta \log(I_t) - 0.12 \cdot \Delta \log(M_{t-1}/P_{t-1}^c)$$

$$\quad (11.51) \qquad (1.51) \qquad\qquad\qquad (1.98)$$

$$\qquad - 0.01 \cdot \log(M_{t-1}/B_{t-1}) + 0.21 \cdot [(\pi_{t-1} + \mathrm{MPK}_{t-1} - 0.066)]$$

$$\qquad (1.31) \qquad\qquad\qquad (3.03)$$

$$\qquad + 0.0002.$$

$$\qquad (0.04)$$

$$\Delta \log(W_t) = -0.34 \cdot \Delta \log(W_{t-1}) + 0.35 \cdot \log(Y_t/Y_t^*)$$

$$\qquad\qquad (2.43) \qquad\qquad\qquad (3.34)$$

$$\qquad - 0.05 \cdot [\log(W_{t-1}/P_{t-1}^c) - \log(\mathrm{MPL}_{t-1})] + 0.36.$$

$$\qquad (1.42) \qquad\qquad\qquad\qquad\qquad\qquad (1.31)$$

$$\Delta \log(P_t^c) = 0.19 \cdot \Delta \log(P_{t-1}^p) + 0.09 \cdot \log(Y_t/Y_t^*)$$

$$\qquad\qquad (1.54) \qquad\qquad\qquad (3.39)$$

$$\qquad - 0.07 \cdot [\log(P_{t-1}^c/P_{t-1}^*)] + 0.02.$$

$$\qquad (1.97) \qquad\qquad\qquad (11.07)$$

$$\Delta \log(P_t^p) = 0.04 \cdot \Delta \log(W_{t-1}/\mathrm{MPL}_{t-1}) + 0.39 \cdot \Delta \log(P_t^c)$$

$$\qquad\qquad (1.82) \qquad\qquad\qquad\qquad (4.01)$$

$$\qquad + 0.12 \cdot \Delta \log(e_t \cdot P_t^M)$$

$$\qquad (4.23)$$

$$\qquad - 0.09 \cdot [\log(P_{t-1}^p) - 0.26 \cdot \log(P_{t-1}^c) - 0.74 \cdot \log(e_{t-1} \cdot P_{t-1}^M)]$$

$$\qquad (2.49) \qquad\qquad\qquad (3.53) \qquad\qquad (13.53)$$

$$\qquad - 0.004.$$

$$\qquad (2.14)$$

$$\Delta \log(P_t^x) = 0.05 \cdot \Delta \log(XG_t) + 0.60 \cdot \Delta \log(P_t^p/e_t)$$

$$\qquad\qquad (2.26) \qquad\qquad\qquad (3.56)$$

$$\qquad - 0.11 \cdot [\log(P_{t-1}^x) - 0.85 \cdot \log(P_{t-1}^p/e_{t-1})] + 0.002.$$

$$\qquad (1.37) \qquad\qquad\qquad (17.61) \qquad\qquad\qquad (0.73)$$

$$\Delta \log(P_t^M) = 0.46 \cdot \Delta \log(P_t^f) + 0.08 \cdot \Delta \log(P_t^o)$$
$$(3.02) \qquad\qquad\qquad (3.43)$$

$$+ \ 0.40 \cdot \Delta \log(P_{t-1}^p / e_{t-1}) - 0.17$$
$$(2.50) \qquad\qquad\qquad (2.18)$$

$$\cdot \ [\log(P_{t-1}^M) - 0.82 \cdot \log(P_{t-1}^f) - 0.18 \cdot \log(P_{t-1}^o)]$$
$$(49.51) \qquad\qquad (10.74)$$

$$- \ 0.001.$$
$$(0.27)$$

Seasonal dummies were included but are not reported. Numbers in parentheses are t-statistics, and variables in brackets are error-correcting terms.

References

Barro, Robert, and Xavier Sala-i-Martin. 1990. World real interest rates. In *NBER macroeconomics annual,* ed. O. J. Blanchard and S. Fischer. Cambridge, Mass.: MIT Press.

Blanchard, Olivier, and Stanley Fischer. 1989. *Lectures on macroeconomics.* Cambridge, Mass.: MIT Press.

Dornbusch, Rudiger. 1976. Expectations and exchange rate dynamics. *Journal of Political Economy* 84 (December): 1161–76.

Hong, Sung-Duk. 1994. An analysis of the factors for the Korean growth: 1963–92 (in Korean). *Korea Development Review* 16 (fall): 147–78.

Lucas, Robert E. 1976. Econometric policy evaluation: A critique. *Carnegie-Rochester Conference Series* 1: 19–46.

Oum, Bong-Sung, and Dong-Chul Cho. 1995. Korea's exchange rate movements in the 1990s: Evaluations and policy implications. Paper presented at KDI Symposium on Prospects of Yen-Dollar Exchange Rates and Korea's Exchange Rate Policy, Korea Development Institute, Seoul, December.

Park, Woo-Kyu. 1992. A research on macro-policy in Korea (in Korean). KDI Research Paper Series, no. 92–01. Seoul: Korea Development Institute.

Taylor, Mark P. 1995. The economics of exchange rate. *Journal of Economic Literature* 33 (March): 13–47.

Comment   Chong-Hyun Nam

I find this paper very interesting. It is not only informative but also very useful, especially for policymakers in Korea.

Chong-Hyun Nam is professor of economics at Korea University and a visiting scholar at the Center for Research on Economic Development and Policy Reform at Stanford University.

As was much discussed in Black's paper (chap. 10 in this volume), a central important issue concerning capital market liberalization policy in Korea is whether there exists a trade-off between the speed of liberalization and the macroeconomic instabilities associated with it. Cho and Koh attempt to provide a quantitative assessment of this issue by simulating the results of alternative policy options, namely, a big bang approach, a gradual approach, and a gradual approach but with exchange rate targeting.

However, they seem to fall short of presenting an explicit model with a detailed discussion, making it difficult to grasp the nature and workings of the model used in the simulations. Nevertheless, Cho and Koh produce some interesting empirical results from their exercises with alternative policy options, although they tend to be modest in making a priority judgment on those policy alternatives, mainly because they do not know the exact objective function of Korea's policymakers.

Though I do not know the exact objective function either, let me try to suggest a set of constraints under which Korea's policymakers might work in ranking the policy alternatives open to them. I believe the first and most important factor for them to consider is the rate of economic growth. As a matter of fact, it has long been considered in Korea that anything less than a 7 percent economic growth rate is a sign of failure of both economic policy and political leadership. I presume that the 7 percent growth rate came from the thought that it provides a kind of bottom line that guarantees full employment with an ever increasing labor participation rate in Korea.

A second factor that policymakers would take seriously is performance in export activities. No doubt, economic and export growth rates are highly correlated, but in Korea any economic growth without corresponding growth in exports is generally believed to be at best transitory and not sustainable, mainly because domestic markets are thought too small to accommodate sustained growth.

A third factor to be considered by policymakers would be the rate of inflation. As Korea becomes more integrated with the world economy, maintaining a stable price level has become more important. I think an upper tolerance limit for the inflation rate is around 5 percent per year at the moment, but it could go lower soon.

A final factor that policymakers would take seriously is the rate of growth in external debt or the rate of accumulation of current account deficits. At the moment, the upper limit of tolerance in the policy-making circle seems to be 2 percent of GNP, implying that net foreign capital inflow should be limited to less than 2 percent of GNP for an any particular year.

Figures 11.4G (GDP growth rate), 11.4I (CPI growth rate), and 11.4K (capital account balance) show that the least cost alternative is a gradual approach with no exchange rate targeting.

But many questions remain as to the way the gradual approach is set up in the paper. A major issue may be that the time horizon for complete liberalization by the year 2010 seems a bit too long from both internal and external points of view. As soon as Korea opens up its bonds markets to foreign investors, the interest rate differential between home and abroad may quickly disappear not only because foreign buying of Korean bonds can be large but also because the interest elasticity with respect to capital account balance could increase significantly as Korea's capital market becomes more efficient with ongoing liberalization. I also wonder whether Korea can delay its liberalization process of capital markets that long, because it embarks on joining the Organization for Economic Cooperation and Development soon.

My final comment is that it would be nice if the authors could make experiments with the model for some more realistic policy packages that reflect, for instance, various levels of liberalization speed, of foreign exchange market intervention, and of sterilization.

Comment   Koichi Hamada

Cho and Koh's paper contains a straightforward, simple experiment to assess the effect of possible "big bang" policies for Korea. The strengths of the paper are that the structure is simple and clearly exposited and that the experiment is easily related to theory. On the other hand, its weakness is that the model is too simple and is abstracted from many relevant factors. Accordingly, the computations from the experiment can only be remotely associated with observable data.

The paper presents an overshooting type of exchange rate determination model. It assumes some kind of short-run structure with price rigidity in connection to the Dornbusch dynamic and also a long-run full employment supply side. The relationship between these two aspects is not an easy problem. The authors do not provide such an explanation that they are related. For example, if the long-run income level is moving, the short-run overshooting process would be different because the money demand function would be shifting as well.

Consider figure 11C.1. Graphically, the jumping path corresponding to the big bang where investors face different interest rates is like the solid line, while the path for the gradual process is something like the dotted arrows.

On the empirical side, we are naturally curious about what is going on in the forward market. If we could obtain any information about forward rates or even their proxies, a discussion of interest rate arbitrage should follow. It would make the artificial discussion of approximation of the forward rate by actual

Koichi Hamada is professor of economics at Yale University.

P (price)

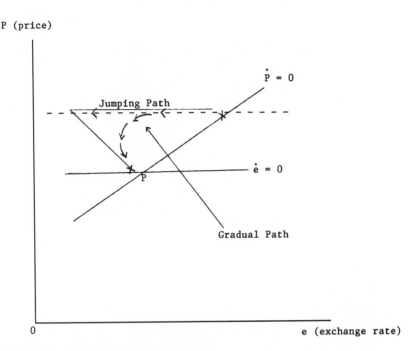

Fig. 11C.1   **The big bang and gradualism**

exchange rates unnecessary. Then the structure of the model and the works of the internal arbitration exchange market would be much clearer. In summary, this paper has the feeling of an isolated theoretical experiment, somewhat aloof from the complexity of real economic situations.[1]

1. In retrospect, after the recent financial turmoil in Korea, I can now understand how drastic and difficult it was for the Korean economy to move from the state where there was no forward market to the state of convertibility, something close to the big bang experiment of this paper.

12 The Foreign Exchange Allocation Policy in Postwar Japan: Its Institutional Framework and Function

Tetsuji Okazaki and Takafumi Korenaga

12.1 Introduction

The Japanese foreign trade regime was substantially different from its present form until the beginning of 1960s. Before 1949 foreign trade was controlled directly by the government, and moreover, there were multiple exchange rates. Although direct control was abolished and a single exchange rate was set as a part of the wide range of policies for transition to a market economy in 1949, a new system to control foreign trade—the foreign exchange allocation system—was introduced. The Japanese government could execute a de facto import quota through this system. This regime continued to operate until trade liberalization progressed under pressure from overseas in the early 1960s.

It is widely admitted that indirect trade control through the foreign exchange allocation system was used as a tool of sectoral industrial policy as well as of macroeconomic policy to maintain the balance of payments. For instance, the official history of the Ministry of International Trade and Industry (MITI et al. 1994) states the following: "It [import control] aimed at effective use of limited foreign currency to promote economic development, and it allowed necessary import goods to be secured, while preventing a rush of imports. Through foreign exchange allocation and approval of imports, MITI could monitor the industries under its jurisdiction and carry out the administrative guidance necessary for their development."

Kosai (1989) also considered foreign exchange control a sectoral policy measure first of all. The foreign exchange allocation system generated rents by creating differences between domestic and foreign prices, and it exerted

Tetsuji Okazaki is associate professor of economics at the University of Tokyo. Takafumi Korenaga is a graduate student of economics at Hitotsubashi University, Tokyo.

The authors thank Takatoshi Ito, Ronald McKinnon, Shinji Takagi, Yoshihiro Yajima, and conference participants for their helpful comments.

substantial economic and political influence. On one hand, rents generated by government intervention have been criticized on the grounds that they cause rent-seeking activities by the private sector, but on the other hand, it has recently been pointed out that rents can be an effective industrial policy measure if appropriate institutional arrangements are provided (Aoki, Murdock, and Okuno-Fujiwara 1996). Taking into account that not a few developing and transforming countries have not liberalized their foreign trade, and that they face serious rent-seeking problems, we can say that the Japanese experience of foreign exchange control has great relevance.

However, little research has investigated the function of foreign exchange allocation from an economic standpoint, although official histories of MITI (MITI et al. 1990) and the Ministry of Finance (MOF 1976) and Inuta (1981), by the author of MOF (1976), describe the details of the institution. Kosai (1989) only mentions import restrictions on dynamos and passenger cars. Both Fukao, Omi, and Eto (1993) and Nakakita (1993) devote only one page to a description of the foreign exchange allocation system. Recently, Takagi (1996) explained the foreign exchange allocation system in detail and also analyzed its function from a macroeconomic standpoint.

Therefore, in this paper we will analyze the institution and the function of foreign exchange allocation in 1950s Japan, focusing on the sectoral and microeconomic aspects. In section 12.2 the foreign exchange allocation system will be explained briefly. In section 12.3 we will analyze its operation and function concerning macroeconomic aspects and allocation by good. In section 12.4 the criteria for allocating foreign exchange to firms will be made clear. In section 12.5 we will analyze the system's operation and function concerning allocation by firm using firm-level data. Section 12.6 concludes the paper.

12.2   Foreign Exchange Budget and Foreign Exchange Allocation System

The Foreign Exchange and Foreign Trade Administration Law (Gaikoku Kawase and Gaikoku Boeki Kanri Ho), enacted in December 1949, provided a new institutional framework for foreign trade, taking the place of direct government control. Article 1 of the law prescribed that its purpose was to develop normal foreign trade and administer foreign exchange and foreign trade, in order to secure balance of payments, stabilization of the currency value, and effective utilization of foreign currency (MOF 1976, 616). It shows that such a microeconomic item as the effective use the foreign currency was originally included in the purposes of the law.

For these purposes the law prescribed the concentration of foreign exchange and the foreign exchange budget system (gaika yosan seido). All foreign currency, precious metals, claimable assets in foreign currency, and foreign currency securities were to be concentrated in the hands of the government, Bank of Japan, or foreign exchange banks. The government would make a foreign exchange budget to efficiently use the concentrated foreign currency (Bank of Tokyo 1960, 2).

The foreign exchange budget system is explained in Bank of Tokyo (1960), Shimada (1960), MOF (1976), Inuta (1981), MITI et al. (1990), and Takagi (1996). We will draw our summary mainly from the outline of the system in Bank of Tokyo (1960). The foreign exchange budget was made starting in January 1950, at first quarterly and later every half-year. It consisted basically of three parts: (1) a summary table, (2) a foreign exchange budget for import goods, and (3) a foreign exchange budget for services, though details of the forms differed each term.[1] In part 1, summary tables of parts 2 and 3, foreign exchange rates, and a projection of the balance of payments were shown.

Part 2 was the core of the foreign exchange budget. It consisted of the budget for foreign exchange allocation system (*gaika wariate sei*) goods (FA goods), the budget for automatic approval system (*jido shonin sei*) goods (AA goods), and the reserve budget.[2] The division between FA goods and AA goods was crucial. The budget for AA goods was allocated in a lump to the AA group of goods, and the import of AA goods was automatically approved as long as the budgeted quantity of AA goods had not been reached. In other words, for AA goods, import was de facto free within the total limit. Accordingly, the liberalization rate of foreign trade was usually defined as the ratio of the AA goods budget to the total budget.

On the other hand, in order to import FA goods, one would apply to the minister of international trade and industry at each dealing ex ante and would receive an allotment of foreign exchange. Moreover, the foreign exchange budget for FA goods was allocated not in a lump but rather to each good, and the minister of international trade and industry would allocate foreign exchange to importers within the limit determined for each FA good. Therefore, for FA goods, the quantity of imports was basically determined by the foreign exchange budget. This means that the government had wide-ranging powers to restrict the quantity of imports.

The foreign exchange budget was decided by the Cabinet Ministers Council (Kakuryo Shingikai), which consisted of the prime minister, the ministers of foreign affairs, finance, agriculture and forestry, international trade and industry, and transportation, and the secretary of the Economic Planning Agency.[3] The draft of the budget for imports and services incidental to imports was made by MITI, and the budget for other services was made by MOF).[4]

In making the budget for imports, MITI used the estimated amount of for-

1. A table of budgeted services receipts was also included before the first half of 1953 (MOF 1976, 278–79).
2. AA goods did not exist at first. There was instead a first come, first served system (*senchaku-jun sei;* MITI et al. 1990, 121).
3. The president of the Bank of Japan participated in the council as an advisory member.
4. The Trade Bureau of the Economic Stabilization Board (Keizai Antei Honbu) made the whole foreign exchange budget until the Economic Stabilization Board was abolished in July 1951 (MITI 1952).

eign exchange that could be spent in each term. That amount was calculated on the basis of projected exports, special procurements by the U.S. Army, balance-of-services trade, and targeted balance of payments. MITI allocated this amount among AA goods and each FA good. The import procedure after the foreign exchange budget was decided continued with (1) import proclamation (*yunyu kohyo*) by MITI, (2) import announcement (*yunyu happyo*) by MITI, (3) foreign exchange allocation by MITI, (4) import approval (*yunyu shonin*) by foreign exchange banks, (5) letter of credit establishment by foreign exchange banks, and (6) import bill settlement by foreign exchange banks. Steps 2 and 3 relate only to FA goods.

By import proclamation, lists of AA and FA goods, currency for settlement, and areas where certain goods were to be shipped were announced. Because import approval by foreign exchange banks was done directly upon import proclamation about AA goods, import proclamation was especially important for such goods.[5] On the other hand, for FA goods, import announcements were done separately for each good based on the import proclamation. The import announcement specified the place where applications for foreign exchange allotment should be handed, time limit for application, applicant's qualifications, the foreign exchange allocation criterion (*gaika shikin wariate kijun*), and so forth. The foreign exchange allocation criteria provided the rules by which foreign exchange was allocated to individual firms, as will be discussed in section 12.4.

According to the import announcement, each firm that wanted to import FA goods handed an application for foreign exchange allocation (*gaika shikin wariate shinseisho*) to MITI. MITI decided on the allocation of foreign exchange to each applicant by reference to the budget and to the foreign exchange allocation criteria. Then, if the minister of international trade and industry decided to allocate the foreign exchange, a foreign exchange allocation certificate (*gaika shikin wariate shomeisho*), valid for four months, was delivered to the applicant (Shimada 1960, 170).

12.3   Movement of the Foreign Exchange Budget and Its Allocation by Good

12.3.1   The Macroeconomy and the Foreign Exchange Budget

The exchange rate of the yen and the trend of the balance of payments for the 1950s and 1960s are summarized in figure 12.1. Japan, which had shifted from a regime of plural exchange rates to a regime of single exchange rate in April 1949, maintained a fixed exchange rate of 360 yen per dollar until August 1971. Change in the real exchange rate measured by export goods should be noted, however. The real exchange rate appreciated rapidly in the early 1950s,

---

5. The import announcement was abolished for FA goods in the latter half of 1959.

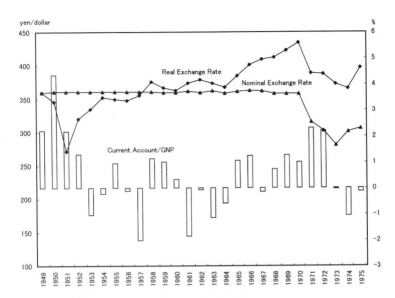

Fig. 12.1   Exchange rates and balance of payments

and it remained above 360 yen per dollar until the end of 1950s. After staying a little lower than 360 yen per dollar for several years, it depreciated rapidly in the latter half of the 1960s. While even in 1949 the yen was said to be overvalued, inflation during the Korean War increased the degree of overvaluation. Until the first half of the 1960s the Japanese economy frequently faced large current account deficits (fig. 12.1), while there remained large latent unemployment. These facts suggest that the rate of 360 yen per dollar was higher than the equilibrium level until the first half of the 1960s. In fact, according to (admittedly fragmentary) data on the black market rate of the yen in the 1950s surveyed by the Bank of Japan, the black market rate was over 400 yen per dollar (fig. 12.2). Overvaluation of the yen formed the macroeconomic background for the adoption of the foreign exchange budget system.

The first column of table 12.1 reports the total foreign exchange budget. The foreign exchange budget tightened from 1954 to the first half of 1955 and then expanded rapidly from the latter half of 1955. It tightened again from the first half of 1957 to 1958, and then a long expansion started in 1959. The background of these changes in the foreign exchange budget scale was as follows.

The purpose of tightening in 1954 was to cope with the current account deficit of 1953 (fig. 12.1). In the foreign exchange budget of 1954, the budget for "nonessential" goods was cut, and a policy of substituting domestic raw materials for imported raw materials was pursued, while the budget for raw materials used in the processing trade and for raw materials whose prices were rising rapidly was expanded (Bank of Tokyo 1960, 215–17). The current account recovered in 1954, and a surplus was expected to continue for the time

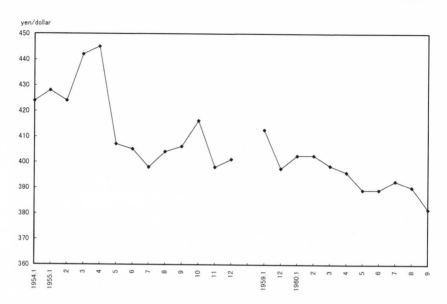

Fig. 12.2   Black market rate of yen
Source: Bank of Japan, Bureau of Foreign Exchange, *Kawase Boeki Geppo* (Monthly bulletin of foreign exchange and trade; Tokyo, various issues).

being. Taking this situation into account, from 1955 to 1956 the government pursued a policy of large foreign exchange budgets in order to support the expansion of exports and production (Bank of Tokyo 1960, 218–23).

However, in early 1957 the balance of payments turned to deficit, and a confrontation over the policy of making the foreign exchange budget took place among the relevant authorities. MITI insisted that large foreign exchange budgets should be continued, coupled with a tightening of fiscal policy, on the grounds that contraction of the budget would cause speculative advances in prices and a decline in exports. On the other hand, MOF and the Bank of Japan stressed the necessity of reducing imports directly by reducing the foreign exchange budget as well as by tightening fiscal policy, because the balance-of-payments deficit was quite serious. Consequently, the foreign exchange budget for imports for the first half of 1957 was set at a level slightly below that of the previous term (Bank of Japan 1957.I-a, 1–4).

In making the foreign exchange budget for the latter half of 1957, MITI and MOF agreed that under the circumstances of a large balance-of-payments deficit, the scale of the budget should be reduced as long as possible. Although there remained disagreement between the two ministries about projected receipts, the foreign exchange budget for the latter half of 1957 was substantially smaller than that of the previous term (Bank of Japan 1957.II-a, 1–5).

The balance of payments turned to surplus in the latter half of 1957, which provided the conditions needed for expanding the foreign exchange budget.

Table 12.1   **Outline of the Foreign Exchange Budget (millions of dollars)**

Year	Total	FA	AA	Reserve	AA/Total (%)
1952	1,242	763	348	131	27.99
	1,501	988	494	19	32.89
1953	1,237	799	300	138	24.26
	1,546	1,250	274	22	17.75
1954	1,100	931	141	27	12.82
	1,090	913	175	1	16.06
1955	1,160	970	190	0	16.38
	1,454	1,218	236	0	16.23
1956	1,765	1,413	352	0	19.94
	2,483	1,969	513	0	20.66
1957	2,236	1,589	497	150	22.23
	1,652	1,242	330	80	19.98
1958	1,628	1,148	330	150	20.27
	1,757	1,161	470	125	26.75
1959	1,941	1,217	630	93	32.46
	2,328	1,581	700	47	30.07
1960	2,624	1,459	1,000	165	38.11
	2,800	1,480	1,150	170	41.07
1961	3,272	1,422	1,850	0	56.54
	3,526	1,526	1,800	200	51.05
1962	3,114	1,264	1,650	200	52.99
	3,154	774	2,380	0	75.46
1963	3,465	796	2,575	94	74.31
	3,815	705	2,860	250	74.97

Sources: Bank of Japan, *Gaikokukawase Binran* (Handbook of foreign exchange; Tokyo, n.d.); Bank of Japan (various dates-a).

However, this time MITI requested the compression of the budget in order to adjust demand and supply in each industry. Although MOF and the Economic Planning Agency insisted that from the standpoint of the long-term economic plan, the foreign exchange budget should be expanded, the foreign exchange budget for the first half of 1958 was even smaller than that for the previous term.[6] As to the foreign exchange budget of the latter half of 1958, the industrial societies requested that the scale be reduced, and it was not expanded substantially (Bank of Japan 1958.I-a, 1–4). After the latter half of 1958, as the Japanese economy entered a large boom with a surplus in the balance of payments, the foreign exchange budget increased until 1961 (Bank of Tokyo 1960, 229–31).

Next, let us consider the allocation of the foreign exchange budget between AA goods and FA goods (table 12.1). The ratio of the AA budget to the total

6. MITI's Bureau of International Trade assumed that it was necessary to expand the foreign exchange budget, projecting a business recovery, but the bureaus in charge of the industries insisted on reducing the foreign exchange budget in order to stimulate recovery (Bank of Japan 1958.I-a, 1–4).

budget (import liberalization ratio) fell below 20 percent in 1953. After a gradual recovery from 1956, it rose rapidly in the early 1960s. From 1953, under the tightening of the total foreign exchange budget, several goods that had been classified as AA goods, such as raw cotton, iron ore, and crude sugar, were converted to FA goods (Inuta 1981, 181). In making the foreign exchange budget for the first half of 1957, the government adopted a policy of increasing the number of AA goods and decided in future not to convert AA goods to FA goods in response to balance-of-payments situations (Bank of Tokyo 1960, 221). Then the recovery of convertibility of European currency at the end of 1958 spurred trade liberalization in Japan. In making the foreign exchange budget for the first half of 1959, the Japanese government decided to promote trade liberalization, and in June 1960 the cabinet agreed on the Liberalization Plan of Trade and Foreign Exchange (Boeki Kawase Jiyuka Keikaku Taiko), which announced that the liberalization ratio would be raised to 80 percent in three years. The rapid increase in the liberalization ratio in the early 1960s was based on this plan.[7]

12.3.2   Allocation of the Foreign Exchange Budget by Good and Generation of Rents

The foreign exchange budget for FA goods was allocated to each good as explained in section 12.2. Table 12.2 shows the composition of the foreign exchange budget by large item. Foods and textiles had the largest weights, but their weights were decreasing. On the other hand, the weights of petroleum, machinery, and raw materials of steel increased. It can be said that changes in the composition of the foreign exchange budget basically reflected changes in the industrial structure. However, examining the changes in detail, we find that there existed various policy factors. Hereafter, we are going to examine allocation of the FA budget by good from the latter half of 1956 to the first half of 1958 (detailed information on the making of the foreign exchange budget is available in unpublished materials from the Bank of Japan). Raw cotton, wool, steel and its raw materials, petroleum, and machinery, which were items with comparatively large budget allocations, will be considered (table 12.3).

Raw Cotton

Allocation of the foreign exchange budget to raw cotton was based on MITI's demand and supply plan for cotton products. Necessary production of cotton products was calculated from estimated demand for cotton products and estimated changes in stocks. And the level of production determined the necessary level of raw cotton imports, which in turn, together with the estimated import price of raw cotton, determined the necessary foreign exchange budget (Bank of Japan 1956.II-b, 113–20). The budget for the latter half of 1956

---

7. On the process of trade liberalization, see Takagi (1996, 20–30).

Table 12.2   Allocation of FA Budget of Foreign Exchange by Good I
(percent of total FA budget)

Good	1953	1954	1955	1956	1957	1958	1959
Foods	31.32	29.01	25.96	16.15	18.35	19.47	14.44
Government monopoly goods	0.98	1.03	1.12	0.67	0.49	0.97	0.87
Lumber	0.00	1.72	0.89	0.79	0.46	0.89	1.77
Materials of daily necessaries	0.57	1.70	2.22	1.57	1.49	1.42	1.49
Textiles	32.72	31.59	29.26	23.81	26.76	27.65	25.40
Materials of fertilizer	1.92	2.23	2.22	1.93	1.34	1.37	1.23
Coal	2.47	2.71	2.93	3.34	4.65	3.47	3.42
Materials of steel	2.16	3.77	8.21	15.88	12.61	4.28	7.43
Nonferrous metals	0.46	1.60	1.71	5.13	3.31	2.29	3.34
Petroleum	5.73	7.44	7.24	6.66	7.26	11.77	10.96
Chemicals	0.55	0.38	0.33	0.44	0.72	0.87	0.98
Medicines	0.60	0.37	0.28	0.17	0.24	0.27	0.27
Machinery	10.45	5.67	7.87	15.45	12.01	11.82	15.91
Other	10.06	10.79	9.77	8.01	10.32	13.46	12.49

Source: Bank of Tokyo (1960).

Table 12.3   Allocation of FA Budget of Foreign Exchange by Good II
(thousands of dollars)

Good	1956 Oct–Mar	1957 Apr–Sept	1957 Oct–Mar	1958 Apr–Sept
Staple foods	186,025	122,034	177,244	142,513
Soybean	48,105	48,000	33,600	40,425
Sugar	65,057	89,706	47,486	54,000
Salt	6,294	5,042	4,942	5,100
Lumber	12,360	6,942	6,000	10,662
Beef tallow	14,330	13,338	10,350	11,000
Hides	8,250	11,150	12,050	11,382
Raw cotton	198,122	216,275	215,300	204,639
Wool	121,000	124,800	141,500	73,500
Pulp for chemical fiber	10,626	14,370	7,010	7,752
Phosphorus ore	10,538	9,123	8,605	6,868
Potash	30,507	20,807	16,330	16,320
Raw materials for steel	159,810	288,503	68,500	57,400
Coal	57,683	82,237	49,363	38,777
Petroleum	104,982	103,616	93,470	141,000
Machinery	146,000	190,000	150,000	123,000

Source: Bank of Japan (1956.II–1958.I-b).

served the interests of the cotton-spinning industry, especially of large enterprises, which had requested a reduction in raw cotton imports in order to support cotton product prices (1956.II-b, 123). Concerning the budget for the first half of 1957, the cotton-spinning industry again requested a reduction in raw cotton imports, but because the margin of the cotton-spinning industry was rather high, MITI did not agree and increased the foreign exchange budget allocation (1957.I-b, 80). However, in the first half of 1957, the actual amount of foreign exchange allotment was far below budget, in order to reduce the output of cotton products, and the import quantity budgeted for the latter half of 1957 was even smaller than that for the latter half of 1956 (1957.II-b, 94–95). Moreover, the budget allocation to raw cotton in the first half of 1958 was curtailed substantially to support production cutbacks under administrative guidance (1958.I-b, 94–95).

Wool

Allocation of the foreign exchange budget to wool was based on MITI's demand and supply plan for wool products. Necessary production of wool products was calculated from estimated demand for wool products and estimated changes in stocks. And the level of production determined the necessary level of wool imports, which in turn, together with the estimated import price of wool, determined the necessary foreign exchange budget (Bank of Japan 1956.II-b, 130–34). Allocation of the foreign exchange budget to wool was expanded from the latter half of 1956 to cope with an increase in domestic demand for wool products. The government aimed at reducing both the domestic price of wool products and the rents generated by the difference between the domestic and import prices of wool (1956.II-b, 136). Also in the first half of 1957, a large amount of the budget was allocated to wool (1957.I-b, 85–86), but the actual amount of foreign exchange allocation was cut in order to reduce the output of wool products. Allocation of the foreign exchange budget to wool in the latter half of 1957 and the first half of 1958 was compressed to support this production reduction (1956.II-b, 105).

Steel and Its Raw Materials

Allocation of the foreign exchange budget to steel and its raw materials (iron ore, scrap iron, and pig iron) was based on MITI's demand and supply plan for steel. To cope with the rapid increase in steel demand due to the expansion of investment, allocation of the foreign exchange budget to steel and its raw materials was increased in the latter half of 1956 and the first half of 1957 (Bank of Japan 1956.II-b, 174–75). Because there was a bottleneck in blast furnace capacity, a large amount of the budget was allocated to scrap, pig iron, steel ingots, and steel products (1957.I-b, 135–39). In the latter half of 1957, allocation of the budget was substantially reduced because of a decrease in steel demand (1957.II-b, 159–61). As the decline in steel prices became serious, production cutbacks of crude steel and some kinds of steel products were started under administrative guidance by MITI in March 1958. Corresponding to this measure, MITI curtailed the production plan for steel of the first half of 1958, and reduced the allocation of the foreign exchange budget to steel and its raw materials (1958.I-b, 133–34).

Petroleum

Allocation of the foreign exchange budget to petroleum was based on MITI's demand and supply plan for petroleum products. Demand levels for heavy oil, volatile oil, kerosene, and light oil, respectively, were estimated, and from these estimates the necessary levels of imports of crude oil and petroleum products were calculated. Under the domestic refinement principle, MITI gave priority to imports of crude oil. However, because demand for heavy oil was especially large in Japan, a substantial amount of the foreign exchange budget was allocated to heavy oil (Bank of Japan 1956.II-b, 208–9). In the first half of 1957, the budget for crude oil and heavy oil was increased because of a serious shortage of water and coal for generating electricity (1957.I-b, 171–72). Moreover, MITI guided petroleum companies to make long-term contracts for chartering tankers to cope with the shortage of tankers caused by the Suez Crisis. For the latter half of 1957, allocation of the foreign exchange budget to petroleum was suppressed because of a projected slowdown in demand growth, which in turn caused a problem of excessive chartering (1957.II-b, 189–91). Then, in the first half of 1958, a large amount of the foreign exchange budget was allocated to petroleum as a countermeasure to the excessive chartering problem (1958.I-b, 159–60).

Machinery

For machinery, foreign exchange allocation according to a demand and supply plan was impossible because of the great variety of machinery. MITI's Bureau of International Trade (Tsusho-kyoku) adjusted the budget claims from each bureau of MITI and each ministry, based on surveys of machinery demand in each industry under their jurisdiction (Bank of Japan 1956.II-b, 220–22). The claims from the bureaus of MITI and other ministries are shown in table 12.4. In the latter half of 1956, large amounts of machinery imports were requested by such sectors as steel, machinery, transportation, and electricity because of rapid investment increases. MITI chose to keep the foreign exchange budget for machinery at almost the same level as the previous term (1957.I-b, 179), thus denying about 10 percent of the demand (table 12.4). Concerning allocation of the foreign exchange budget to machinery, machinery users were inclined to prefer imported machinery on the grounds of high quality, availability of loans at low interest rates from manufacturers, and quick delivery. On the other hand, domestic machinery producers insisted that domestic machinery should be used as much as possible. MITI's goal was to maintain a balance between encouragement of the domestic machinery industry and rationalization of the user industries (1956.II-b, 223–24).

Table 12.4   Claims for Foreign Exchange Budget for Machinery by Ministries and Agencies (thousands of dollars)

Ministry or Agency	1956 Oct–Mar	1957 Apr–Sept	1957 Oct–Mar	1958 Apr–Sept
Total	157,430	288,661	193,529	189,461
(ratio of actual allotment, %)	(92.72)	(65.82)	(77.51)	(64.92)
Bureau of Heavy Industry, MITI	66,382	119,689	54,222	88,202
Bureau of Textile, MITI	22,946	16,780	15,285	10,234
Bureau of Light Industry, MITI	11,159	24,967	19,000	12,939
Bureau of Enterprise, MITI	9,813	10,917	502	18,135
Bureau of Mining, MITI	9,745	11,362	8,968	9,159
Bureau of Public Utility, MITI	7,615	31,886	1,450	3,207
Bureau of Coal, MITI	n.a.	n.a.	2,330	2,329
Ministry of Transportation	n.a.	45,921	15,752	11,493
Ministry of Agriculture and Forestry	5,874	12,041	4,845	6,535
Agency of Defense	5,686	4,999	4,918	2,615
Ministry of Construction	n.a.	2,952	1,951	4,550
Agency of Science and Technology	n.a.	2,357	4,147	1,439
Ministry of Finance	n.a.	n.a.	1,956	500
Ministry of Health and Welfare	n.a.	n.a.	1,000	1,148
Ministry of Education	n.a.	n.a.	1,000	400
Other	18,210	4,790	56,203	16,576

Source: Bank of Japan (1956.II–1958.I-b).

In the first half of 1957, although demand for machinery was still large, MITI denied 34 percent of the claims, expecting investment to be postponed because of constraints on raising funds. In making the foreign exchange budget, MITI's Bureau of Heavy Industry called for a reduction in the budget, while the Bureau of International Trade believed that there was room to increase the budget (1957.I-b, 188–90). This confrontation between the two bureaus reflected the above-mentioned problem of balance.

In the latter half of 1957, MITI denied 22 percent of the claims (table 12.4), on the grounds that the effects of the tight monetary policy would gradually be felt and that investment for rationalization of industries had peaked because of the rapid increase in machine imports in the past two to three years (1957.II-b, 198–99). Moreover, in the first half of 1958, the foreign exchange budget for machinery was reduced to its lowest level since the latter half of 1955. Protection of domestic producers was one reason (1958.I-b, 173–75).

The above discussion shows that in the cases of raw materials, MITI's demand and supply plan for each good was used as a base. It also shows that there were often cases in which allocation of the foreign exchange budget was restrained for purposes of industrial policy. Because restraint of the foreign exchange budget for FA goods constituted a de facto import quota, as stressed in section 12.2, it is probable that for many FA goods rents were generated.

We can roughly measure the scale of rents by subtracting the tariff from the difference between the domestic and import prices of each good. We estimated the scale of rents for 27 goods whose weights were relatively high in the wholesale price statistics (compiled by the Bank of Japan) and whose c.i.f. import prices are available in the customs clearance statistics (compiled by MOF). The results are shown in table 12.5. For 15 of 27 goods, rents were

Table 12.5   **Estimation of Rents (yen)**

Good	Unit	Domestic Price (A)	Import c.i.f. Price (B)	Tariff (C)	B + C (D)	A/D (E)
Staple foods						
Rice	ton	68,767	61,350	0	61,350	1.12
Wheat	ton	52,360	26,350	0	26,350	1.99
Soybean	ton	43,694	43,762	0	43,762	1.00
Other foods						
Refined sugar	ton	132,900	62,995	15,749	78,744	1.69
Flour	ton	44,766	35,857	8,964	44,821	1.00
Crude sugar	ton	59,903	37,671	7,534	45,205	1.33
Textile						
Raw cotton	ton	314,506	295,544	0	295,544	1.06
Wool yarn	ton	2,420,855	1,448,937	144,894	1,593,831	1.52
Wool	ton	1,149,868	614,443	0	614,443	1.87
Fuel						
Coal	ton	7,516	7,159	0	7,159	1.05
Crude oil	kl	6,881	6,359	0	6,359	1.08
Volatile oil	kl	30,928	11,095	0	11,095	2.79
Metal						
Scrap	ton	20,965	17,754	0	17,754	1.18
Steel plate	ton	43,981	39,903	5,985	45,888	0.96
Iron ore	ton	5,726	5,377	0	5,377	1.07
Machinery						
Truck	number	1,015,000	174,190	52,257	226,447	4.48
Car	number	837,430	216,766	86,706	303,472	2.76
Vacuum bulb	number	197	316	47	363	0.54
Materials for construction						
Cedar lumber	m³	11,749	19,766	0	19,766	0.59
Cedar log	m³	8,306	14,169	0	14,169	0.59
Pine lumber	m³	11,225	17,391	0	17,391	0.65
Chemicals						
Salt	ton	3,600	3,839	0	3,839	0.94
Paint	ton	168,112	261,442	39,216	300,658	0.56
Dyestuffs	ton	507,867	2,023,691	505,923	2,529,613	0.20
Other						
Printing paper	ton	64,903	73,704	7,370	81,075	0.80
Pulp for rayon	ton	78,814	71,323	3,566	74,889	1.05
Soybean refuse	ron	42,160	35,368	0	35,368	1.19

Sources: Bank of Japan, *Oroshiuri Bukka Tokei Nenpo* (Statistical yearbook of wholesale prices; Tokyo, 1955); MOF, *Gaikoku Boeki Nenpyo* (Yearbook of international trade; Tokyo, 1955); MOF, *Import Tariffs of Japan* (Tokyo, 1955).

generated. The rents were especially large for automobiles, volatile oil, refined wheat, wool, and flour.[8]

12.4   Criteria for Foreign Exchange Allocation
and Methods of Allocation by Firm

Allocation of foreign exchange to firms meant allocation of the rents generated import restriction. Therefore, there is a substantial possibility that allocation of foreign exchange to firms caused rent-seeking activities in the private sector and corruption of the bureaucracy and political circle. At the same time, however, it might be an effective tool of industrial policy. Concerning the first possibility, some then-bureaucrats of MITI talked in retrospect about the strong political pressures MITI faced with respect to foreign exchange allocation. One of them, who served as chief of the Budget Section (Yosan-ka) of the International Trade Bureau in the 1950s, said that he daily received petitions and requests from Diet members, and that resisting these pressures was one main role of the chief of the Budget Section. Moreover, another then-bureaucrat, who was a vice-chief of the International Trade Bureau in the 1950s, said that several Diet members came regularly to the vice-minister's office to petition about the foreign exchange allocation.[9]

Certain mechanisms to evade such political pressures were prepared in the foreign exchange allocation system, the outline of which was sketched in section 12.2. MITI took the course of reducing the range of its discretion as much as possible concerning the allocation of foreign exchange to each firm, as is discussed in Okazaki and Ishii (1996). The manual of the foreign exchange allocation system, which was written by the authorities at MITI in 1960, states: "Although foreign exchange allocation is prescribed to be at the Minister of International Trade and Industry's discretion in the Foreign Exchange and International Trade Administration Law, it does not imply that the Minister determines the allotment case by case arbitrarily. MITI determines a certain criterion concerning each good, by reference to the purpose of classifying it as an FA good, and allots the foreign exchange mechanically or screens the applications according to the criterion" (Shimada 1960, 158).

It can be said that MITI intended to restrain rent seeking by reducing the room for discretion through the definition of clear allocation criteria an-

---

8. It was widely recognized that the foreign exchange allocation system generated rents. E.g., Amaya, a vice-chief of MITI's Planning Section, states, "The foreign exchange allocation system promoted the accumulation of capital for two reasons, that is, restriction of international competition and giving premiums to firms that were allotted the foreign exchange" (1955, 51–52). And Toshiyuki Miyauchi, a managing director of Itochu Co., criticized the system at the 1959 meeting of the Association of Corporate Executives, "So far the foreign exchange allocation system has been at the center of the industrial policy, but such a distorted situation, in which import premiums exist, is not appropriate when the European currencies have recovered convertibility" (Okazaki et al. 1996, 127).

9. Interview by the Research Institute of Industrial Policy History.

Table 12.6   **Methods and Criteria for Foreign Exchange Allocation by Firm, Latter Half of 1956**

Good	Method[a]	Criterion
Soybean	ATO	Criteria set by the consuming industry based on actual consumption in the first half of 1955, actual allocation in the first half of 1956, and desirable allocation
Sugar	AT	Actual imports in 1955
	ATN	Criteria set by the trade associations of the sugar refining industry based on production capacity, actual production, and per firm rate
Lumber	AT	Actual imports from July 1955 to June 1956
Beef tallow	AT	Actual imports from July 1955 to June 1956
	AC	Actual exports (export link), actual consumption in the latter half of 1955, actual production in 1955, and per firm rate
Hides	AT	Actual imports
	AC	Actual purchases
Raw cotton	AT	Actual exports (export link)
	ATN	Actual exports (export link) and production capacity
Wool	ATN	Actual exports (export link) and production capacity
Pulp for chemical fiber	ATN	Actual exports (export link)
Phosphorus ore	ATO	n.a.
Potash	AT	n.a.
Raw materials of steel	ATN	Actual production and production plan
Coal	ATN	
Crude oil	AC	Actual foreign exchange allotment and actual imports in the past three years
Refined oil	AT	Actual foreign exchange allotment and actual imports in the past three years
Machinery	AC	Individual screening by the Council of Machinery Import Allotment

Source: Bank of Japan (1956.II-b).

[a]ATO, allocation to trading company on order; AT, allocation to trading company; ATN, allocation to trading company on notification; AC, allocation to consuming company.

nounced beforehand. "A certain criterion" in the quotation above is the foreign exchange allocation criterion specified by the import announcement (see section 12.2). The foreign exchange allocation criteria for major goods in the latter half of 1956 are presented in table 12.6. There were four allocation methods: allocation to a trading company (*shosha wariate,* AT), allocation to a consuming company (*juyosha wariate,* AC), allocation to a trading company on order (*hacchusho hosiki shosha wariate,* ATO), and allocation to a trading company on notification (*naijisho hoshiki shosha wariate,* ATN).

The AT method allocated foreign exchange based only on the conditions of trading companies, past import records in many cases; it was used for some sugar imports, lumber, and some beef tallow imports, among others (table 12.6). The underlying view was that past import results showed a company's ability to achieve imports and this method would contribute to long-term import trade relationships (Shimada 1960, 178). Under this method rents were acquired by the trading companies.

In the AC method, foreign exchange was allocated directly to the companies that used the import goods. The ATO method was based on purchase orders put out to trading companies by user companies, and ATN was a kind of ATO in which MITI notified each user company beforehand of the order limit. In the AC, ATN, and ATO methods, the condition of each user company—export record, production capacity, and production—was used as the criterion (table 12.6).[10] Specifically, the use of criteria based on export records like those for raw cotton, wool, and pulp for chemical fiber was called the "export link system" (*yushutsu rinku-sei*). Under the AC, ATN, and ATO methods, rents were acquired by the user companies.

It is notable that in many cases the criteria were based on clear and objective conditions. This fact is the point of the quotation from Shimada (1960) above.[11] It also supports the view of "creating contests" of World Bank (1993). The main point of this view is that the another type of competition—contest-based competition with clear rules, referees, and rewards—works in the East Asian countries, including Japan. In the foreign exchange allocation system, the rents obtained by receiving allocations were attractive rewards for private companies. To obtain more rewards, companies had to win competitions to achieve performance, the rules of which were the allocation criteria. MITI played the role of referee, mechanically and strictly applying the criteria—that is, the rules.

In addition, it is notable that these criteria are thought to have led corporate behavior in specific directions. The cases of export-based and production-capacity-based criteria have special significance. In the former case, rents from foreign exchange allotment are thought to have played the role of an export subsidy. In the latter case, it is thought that investment was promoted by the rents, which functioned as investment subsidies.

These effects were clearly recognized by the people concerned in those days. MITI intentionally used the export link system to promote exports. For instance, Shimada states, "It is an effective export promotion measure" (1960, 179–80). Nishimura (1955), a bureaucrat of MOF, states that the background of the introduction of the export link system to textiles in the early 1950s was a decrease in exports caused by a rise in domestic prices, and that the rapid increase in textile exports in 1953–54 was due mainly to the effects of the export link system. All of the examples of the export link system shown in table 12.6 allocate foreign exchange for raw materials based on the export per-

10. As there was quite a wide variety of machinery, it was impossible to adopt such an objective criterion. Therefore, the Council of Machinery Import Allotment (Yunyu Kikai Wariate Shingikai) under MITI determined an allotment for each application through a screening process referring to industrial policy, trade policy, and social policy. The council consisted of the staffs of the Budget Section and the Import Section of the Bureau of Trade, the sections in charge of machinery industries, and the sections in charge of user industries (Bank of Japan 1956.II-b, 219).

11. It will be tested quantitatively in the next section.

formance of products made with those raw materials. This method was called the "raw materials link system" (*genzairyo rinku-sei*). In addition, foreign exchange for raw materials could be allotted based on the export performance of products that had no input-output relation to those raw materials; this was called the "deficit-covering link system" (*shukketsu hosho rinku-sei;* Nishimura 1955).

The deficit-covering link system was applied to the exports of ships, production plants, whale oil, raw silk, and canned food, among others, in 1953–54 (*Ekonomisto* 33, no. 7 [1955]: 17–21). The companies that exported those goods were allotted foreign exchange to import crude sugar. They acquired a de facto export subsidy by selling the crude sugar to sugar-refining companies at the higher domestic price. The shipbuilding industry especially enjoyed the benefits of this system. It enabled shipbuilders to cut export prices and consequently spurred the first export boom of ships in 1953–54. The deficit-covering link system was strongly criticized by the International Monetary Fund's research mission in 1954, and it was abolished in 1955. The criticism from overseas suggests that this system had large export promotion effects.

In contrast, the criteria based on production capacity were not intended to promote investment but to level the capacity utilization ratio. However, it was recognized that they had the effect of investment promotion. A bureaucrat at MITI wrote in a 1956 article, "The companies invested aiming at an increase in the amount of the import quota, because the method of foreign exchange allocation is based on the amount of equipment" (Hiramatsu 1956). Moreover, the *Oriental Economist* commented, "The overinvestment in such industries as textiles, sugar refining, and milling is mainly due to the raw materials allotment policy of the government based on equipment capacity" (*Toyo Keizai Shinpo* 2604 [1953]: 15).

12.5   A Quantitative Analysis of Foreign Exchange Allocation by Firm: The Wool-Spinning Industry

12.5.1   A Brief History of the Wool-Spinning Industry

The Japanese wool-spinning industry contracted substantially during World War II. Although its equipment was reconstructed in accordance with the equipment restoration plan approved by the occupation authority in 1948, raw material imports were a crucial constraint on the recovery of the industry (Textile Society of Japan 1958, 310–13). Imports of wool were very low for a few years after the war because imports of raw materials in general were under strict constraint and priority was given to raw cotton among the textile materials. It was not until 1949, when the trade agreement was concluded between sterling area nations, that wool imports got back on track (Wool Spinning Association of Japan 1987, 92).

Meanwhile, wool imports were shifted to private trade from state trade at the beginning of 1950. Simultaneously, MITI announced "detailed criteria of allotment of the foreign exchange for wool import from January to March 1950" (*Showa 25-nen 1–3-gatu yomo yunyu shikin wariate saimoku*), the substance of which was that the total foreign exchange budget for wool ($9,613,000) would be divided into two parts: one for domestic demand (70 percent) and the other for export (30 percent). The former was allocated according to the production capacity of each firm, while the latter was allocated according to the export record of each firm (Wool Spinning Association of Japan 1987, 94, appendix 24–25). It is notable that both export records and production capacity were already in use as criteria.

In July 1950 an important revision in the method of allocation was introduced. In the method adopted in January 1950, the amounts of foreign exchange for export and domestic demand, respectively, were set beforehand; however, after July 1950, foreign exchange was preferentially allocated according to export records, with the remaining part allotted by considering production capacity for domestic demand (MITI 1950).[12] The method after July 1950 is generally called the export link system of wool (Textile Society of Japan 1958, 321).

The method of allocation was revised frequently after that. In particular, important revisions were made in August 1953 and April 1955. Before August 1953 foreign exchange was allocated ex post in accordance with past export records; after August 1953 it was allotted ex ante according to the export plan of each firm and was adjusted subsequently in line with actual exports. At the same time another system, "achievement rewards" (*suiko hosho*), was introduced; it was related to the above revisions in order to increase export incentives.[13] Under this system, additional foreign exchange was allocated to each firm according to the achievement ratio of its export plan. The revision in April 1955 was needed to cope with problems caused by the 1953 revision. The method adopted in 1953 greatly stimulated exports. It was criticized by foreign countries and gave rise to a shortage of wool in the domestic market. Therefore, in April 1955, export incentives were reduced by abolishing the achievement rewards and decreasing the ratio of foreign exchange allocation to exports of each firm (Textile Society of Japan 1958, 325–26).

These methods and actual allocation were determined by the Hemp and Wool Section (Mamo-ka) until fiscal year 1955 and by the Silk, Wool and Chemical Fiber Section (Kinu Ke Kasen-ka) thereafter, both of MITI's Bureau of Textile. We found an almost complete collection of original documents concerning the foreign exchange allocation for wool imports made by those sections of MITI. Moreover, in those materials firm-level records of exports and production capacity are also available. Hereafter, we will quantify the foreign exchange allocation method at the firm level and then analyze the effects of the method.

12. The ratio of the amount of foreign exchange allotment to the amount of exports differed according to the kind of the product.
13. For details, see Wool Spinning Association of Japan (1987, 104–6, appendix 58–63).

Table 12.7   **Determination of Foreign Exchange Allocation for Wool Imports by Firm**

Fiscal Year	Export Performance (α)	Production Capacity (β)	Adjusted R^2	Sample Size (number of firms)
1953 Oct–Mar	2.017 (8.814)	11,603 (16.045)	.997	21
1954 Apr–Sept	0.954 (8.986)	5,165 (4.807)	.987	45
Oct–Mar	1.324 (4.175)	4,997 (1.388)	.947	47
1955 Apr–Sept	1.732 (28.481)	4,484 (10.860)	.998	47
Oct–Mar	1.275 (15.543)	13,533 (13.958)	.996	55
1956 Apr–Sept	0.319 (2.119)	23,449 (13.182)	.967	50
Oct–Mar	1.487 (12.585)	28,759 (18.522)	.993	54
1957 Apr–Sept	1.186 (17.297)	5,208 (5.658)	.988	54
Oct–Mar	1.066 (10.352)	16,702 (11.691)	.984	51
1958 Apr–Sept	0.989 (16.461)	8,043 (13.237)	.985	44
Oct–Mar	0.738 (29.118)	9,078 (35.950)	.991	64
1959 Apr–Sept	1.134 (25.606)	381 (4.777)	.933	63
Oct–Mar	0.914 (16.456)	18,039 (28.553)	.989	50
1960 Apr–Sept	0.561 (14.034)	15,148 (24.350)	.977	45
Oct–Mar	0.691 (21.758)	7,904 (29.200)	.985	59

Note: Numbers in parentheses are *t*-values.

12.5.2   The Rule of Foreign Exchange Allocation and Measurement of Marginal Rent

First, we regress the amount of foreign exchange (in yen) allocated to each firm on the firm's amount of actual exports (in yen) for the previous term and equipment capacity (in physical units) using cross-sectional data in order to examine how foreign exchange allocation was linked to these variables (table 12.7). The sample firms are those with available data concerning foreign exchange allotment, exports, and production capacity.[14] The data are taken from the original documents at MITI.

The coefficients of both the export (α) and the equipment capacity (β) variables show how much foreign exchange is additionally allocated given growth in the exports and increase in the equipment capacity of each firm. As indicated by the high adjusted R^2, the foreign exchange allocation to each firm is explained fully by its export performance and equipment capacity. This implies that foreign exchange was allocated to each firm according to the clear and objective rules discussed in the previous section. Moreover, it is notable that the movement of the coefficient α reflects the above-mentioned revision of the

14. In regard to the foreign exchange allocation to production capacity, production capacity in each firm was counted by mule-conversion unit (*mule-kanzan sui*) before the latter half of 1954 but by real unit (*jitsu sui*) after the first half of 1955 (Wool Spinning Association of Japan 1987, 107–8). In the regression we use the unit actually adopted during each term.

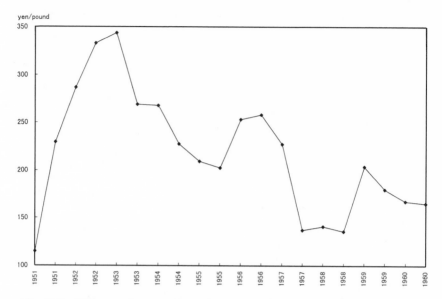

yen/pound

Fig. 12.3   Difference between domestic and import prices of wool

allocation method; that is, the rise in α from the first half of 1953 to the first half of 1955 roughly corresponds to the introduction of the new distribution method in August 1953. The method itself increases the allocation of foreign exchange to exports on a per yen basis.

Besides the coefficient α, the difference between the domestic and foreign prices of wool affects the size of the incentive to export as well as investment under the foreign exchange allotment system. We take the domestic price of wool (P_d^w) from the wholesale price statistics of the Bank of Japan and its import price (P_i^w) from the customs clearance statistics of MOF. The difference between them is illustrated in figure 12.3, and this price difference $(P_d^w - P_i^w)$ denotes the size of the rents per pound of wool imported. This premium on imported wool is at least about 17 percent of its import price. If we denote the export price of wool products by P_e^y, the allocation of the rents per pound of wool yarn exported is

$$\alpha \cdot P_e^y \cdot (P_d^w - P_i^w)/P_i^w \ (= \ R_1).$$

Similarly, the allocation of the rents per unit of spinning equipment is

$$\beta \cdot (P_d^w - P_i^w)/P_i^w \ (= \ R_2)$$

with the physical units adjusted.

Figures 12.4 and 12.5 illustrate R_1 and the growth rate of wool yarn exports and R_2 and the increase in wool-spinning equipment, respectively. The data on exports and investment are taken from the customs clearance statistics of MOF and the *Monthly Statistical Bulletin of Textile Industry* (Sen'i Tokei Geppo) of

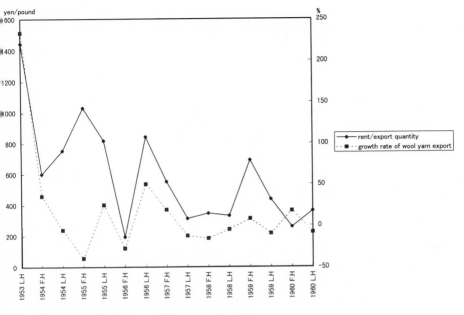

Fig. 12.4   Rents (R_1) and exports of wool yarn

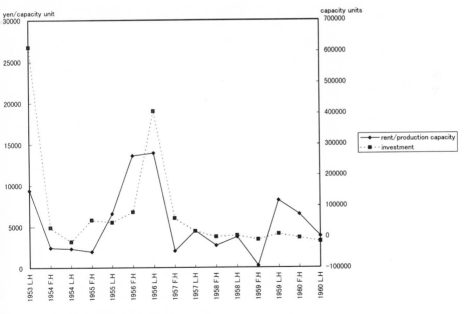

Fig. 12.5   Rents (R_2) and investment

MITI. The rise in the growth rate of exports in 1952–53 and the equipment increase in 1956 suggest a relation between the size of rents and exports and a relation between the size of rents and investment.

12.5.3   Estimation of Export Function

To test the former relation, we estimate a simple export function for wool yarn. In addition to R_1, other factors affecting the flow of exports must also be taken into account. Price and income variables, which are usually incorporated into an export function, are taken as ratios of foreign to domestic in this case because, in those days, the Japanese domestic market for wool products was blocked; that is, the foreign and domestic markets were separated. We also take the U.S. market as the foreign market because the United States had the largest share in Japan's exports of wool yarn in most of the periods under study.[15] In addition to the above factors, the effects of other export promotion policies must be also considered. Here, we take into account only the financial export subsidy offered by the export advance bill system (*yushutsu maegashi tegata seido*), one of the systems of export priority financing in Japan. The reason is that a great amount of subsidies from that system flowed into trading companies, and into producers, if at all, *through* trading companies, and many major trading companies assumed important roles in exporting textile products in particular (Taisa 1989, 211–2).[16]

To summarize, the dependent variable is export volume of wool yarn, and the independent variables are as follows: R_1, the relative export price of wool yarn (P_d^y/P_e^y); the ratio of U.S. GNP to Japanese GNP (NI_u/NI_j); and the rate of financial export subsidy by the advance bill system (sub). All the variables but the subsidy rate are transformed into the form of growth rates. The domestic price of wool yarn (P_d^y) is based on the wholesale price statistics of the Bank of Japan, and the export price (P_e^y) is available from the customs clearance statistics of MOF. GNP of the United States is quoted from U.S. Department of Commerce (1986) and converted to yen at the official exchange rate ($\$1 = ¥360$). GNP of Japan is obtained from Economic Planning Agency (1965). With regard to the financial export subsidy, the subsidy rate is applied; it is the difference between the discount rate on Bank of Japan most favored commercial bills and that on Bank of Japan most favored export advance bills, both offered by commercial banks. Those data come from issues of the *Economic Statistics Monthly* (Bank of Japan).

---

15. The choice of the United States as foreign market is in part due to the availability of data. Though the major destinations of wool yarn exports in those days were the United States and some Asian countries, biannual data on national income for the latter countries are not available to us. Moreover, since a large share of exports to those Asian countries were via Hong Kong, it is impossible to construct an appropriate mixture of foreign income variables.

16. In regard to export promotion, it is generally acknowledged that the Japanese government had various export promotion policy tools other than foreign exchange allocation (Itoh and Kiyono 1988). But there is also much difficulty in using sectoral and biannual data on those policy variables. Further research in this direction would be of interest.

Table 12.8   **Estimation of Export Function**

Method	R_1	P_e^y/P_d^y	NI_u/NI_j	sub	Constant	Adjusted R^2	D.W.
Ordinary least	1.422***	1.982	−13.708	450.89	−964.73*	.355	1.542
squares	(3.014)	(0.335)	(−0.887)	(0.563)	(−1.492)		

Note: Numbers in parentheses are *t*-values.

*Significant at the 10 percent level.
**Significant at the 5 percent level.
***Significant at the 1 percent level.

The results are displayed in table 12.8. The estimating method adopted is ordinary least squares.[17] The coefficient of R_1 is positive and statistically significant, as expected, while the coefficients of relative price and relative income are insignificant. For the financial export subsidy, the sign of the coefficient is positive but statistically insignificant.[18] These results imply that the movement of wool yarn exports was basically determined by the size of allotted rents, not by the fundamental variables and not by the advance bill policy.[19]

12.5.4 Estimation of Investment Function

The investment effect of the allocation method based on production capacity cannot be tested simply by adding R_2 to the usual independent variables of the investment function—profit rate and interest rate—since the size of rents affects the profit rate itself. Therefore, we first adjust the profit rate by extracting the value of rents due to R_2 from the profit itself, and then we regress investment on the adjusted profit rate, the interest rate, and R_2.

We assume the business profits plus depreciation expenses and the total assets of the wool-spinning industry in Mitsubishi Economic Research Institute (various years) to be profits and total assets.[20] If we denote by K^y equipment capacity, the value of rents due to R_2 is $R_2 \cdot K^y$. The adjusted profit rate is obtained by extracting $R_2 \cdot K^y$ from profits and dividing the residual by total assets.

Next, we regress investment on the adjusted profit rate (π), R_2, and the inter-

17. The only second-order serial correlation of residuals is found in ordinary least squares estimation, partly because of using biannual data. The following results do not change even when we assume those serial correlations by the Pagan (1974) method. It should be noted, however, that in this estimation, by using a poor income variable, the income effect is not well captured, thus some reservation must be shown in interpreting the results.

18. Other formulas for the policy variables by that system, e.g., the total value of the subsidies, were also tested, but the results are similar.

19. We also estimated an export function for wool fabrics. The result is quite similar to the one above, except the significance of the size of rents, R_1, is a bit weaker. The difference in the incentives of rents to those wool product exports is probably due to the fact that foreign exchange was allocated basically to wool-spinning firms, not to wool-weaving firms.

20. Selection of sample firms is based on the availability of both financial data and export and equipment capacity data at the firm level. Then we aggregate these data in each term.

Table 12.9   Estimation of Investment Function

Method	π	R^2	i	Constant	Adjusted R^2	D.W.
Ordinary least	70.036***	105.66***	−179.49	407.63	.690	1.925
squares	(4.041)	(4.940)	(−1.351)	(0.688)		
Pagan (1974)	71.885***	107.94***	−174.23	374.21	.701	2.042
	(4.234)	(5.304)	(−1.350)	(0.662)		

Note: Numbers in parentheses are *t*-values.
***Significant at the 1 percent level.

est rate (i). The dependent variable is the increase in wool-spinning equipment. We assume financial costs over the total liability with interest of the wool-spinning industry to be i (Bank of Japan, various dates-c).[21]

The results are exhibited in table 12.9. We display two estimation results: ordinary least squares and Pagan's (1974) nonlinear least squares.[22] The results are quite similar. The coefficient of R_2 is positive and statistically significant at the 1 percent level, while that of π is significant at the 5 percent level. The coefficients of the other variables are less significant statistically. It is notable that R_2 is of greater significance than π in the investment decision, in a statistical sense. This suggests that the effect of investment promotion was larger because the allotment of rents was linked to equipment capacity.

12.6   Concluding Remarks

The foreign exchange allocation system functioned as one of the basic frameworks of the Japanese economy until trade liberalization progressed in the first half of the 1960s. Most imports were subject to de facto control by the government through this system, and MITI used the system as a tool of industrial policy. Consequently, for many important goods, substantial rents were generated. It is notable that the existence of rents, their danger, and their utility were clearly recognized by the people concerned. Therefore, MITI set clear and objective allocation criteria and committed to these criteria by announcing them publicly in order to restrain rent-seeking activities. This method caused competition for the allocation of rents among private enterprises. As criteria, export performance and production capacity were often adopted. The former was intentionally adopted as an export promotion measure, and its effect was quantitatively confirmed in the case of the wool-spinning industry. The latter had the effect of promoting investment not only by pushing up the profit rate

21. When we take the user cost of capital as the cost variable, the main results do not change.
22. The only second-order serial correlation of residuals is found in ordinary least squares estimation to some degree, which is statistically significant at the 20 percent significance level in the LM test proposed by Breusch and Pagan (1980). We apply Pagan's (1974) method by assuming that serial correlation. While the correlation is partly due to using six-month data, researchers have often found strong serial correlation of residuals in estimating investment functions.

but also by linking the allocation of rents with equipment capacity. In short, the foreign exchange allocation system in postwar Japan promoted exports and investment by stimulating competition to acquire rents.

To the above conclusions of this paper, certain qualifications should be added. First, the fact that the Japanese foreign exchange allocation system promoted exports and investment while restraining rent-seeking activities does not directly imply that the Japanese policy regime was the best and should be transmitted to present-day developing and transforming countries. The Japanese policy selection was made under historical conditions in which devaluation of the nominal exchange rate was difficult, there existed an effective bureaucracy and supporting private trade associations (Okazaki 1996), and so forth. Also we cannot deny that there were problems in the Japanese system. Unproductive rent-seeking activities did exist even in Japan, and as mentioned above, additional incentive to invest created excess capacity. Moreover, the export link system had the effect of increasing the welfare of export companies and overseas consumers at the expense of domestic consumers.[23]

References

Amaya, Naohiro. 1955. Boeki jiyuka, kokansei kaifuku to wagakuni no tachiba (Standpoint of Japan concerning trade liberalization and recovery of convertibility). *Gaikoku Kawase* 129:15–19.

Aoki, Masahiko, Kevin Murdock, and Masahiro Okuno-Fujiwara. 1996. Beyond the *East Asian Miracle:* Introducing the market-enhancing view. In *The role of government in East Asian economic development: Comparative institutional analysis,* ed. Masahiko Aoki, Hyung-Ki Kim, and Masahiro Okuno-Fujiwara. Oxford: Oxford University Press.

Bank of Japan. Bureau of Foreign Exchange. Various dates-a. *Gaikoku kawase yosan no gaiyo* (Abstract of the foreign exchange budget). Tokyo: Bank of Japan. Unpublished. (In text citations, 1957.I-a, e.g., means "first half of 1957," 1957.II-a means "second half of 1957")

———. Various dates-b. *Yosan hensei jijo* (Making the foreign exchange budget). Tokyo: Bank of Japan. Unpublished. (In text citations, 1956.I-b, e.g., means "first half of 1956," 1956.II-b means "second half of 1956")

———. Research and Statistics Department. Various dates-c. *Shuyo kigyo keiei bunseki* (Financial statements of principal enterprises). Tokyo: Bank of Japan.

Bank of Tokyo. 1960. *Gaika yosan seido no kaisetsu* (A commentary on the foreign exchange budget system). Tokyo: Bank of Tokyo.

Breusch, Trevor, and Adrian Pagan. 1980. The Lagrange multiplier test and its applica-

23. Muto (1960), the chief of MOF's Section of Foreign Exchange, states that the allotment system and permission system diverted industries from making true business efforts to petitioning government offices, and that it spoiled industries by protecting them from international competition. Nishimura (1955) points out that the deficit-covering link system for sugar caused a national loss by reducing export prices of machinery, and that the loss was imposed on domestic consumers through a rise in the sugar price.

tions to model specification in econometrics. *Review of Economic Studies* 47: 239–53.

Economic Planning Agency. 1965. *Kokumin shotoku hakusho* (White paper on national income). Tokyo: Economic Planning Agency.

Fukao, Mitsuhiro, Masao Omi, and Kimihiro Eto. 1993. Tan'itsu kawase reto no saiyo to boeki min'eika (Adoption of a single exchange rate and privatization of trade). In *Sengo nihon no keizai kaikaku: Seifu to shijo* (Economic reform in postwar Japan: Government and the market), ed. Yutaka Kosai and Juro Teranishi. Tokyo: University of Tokyo Press.

Hiramatsu, Morihiko. 1956. Boeki jiyuka to shuyo sangyo no doko (Trade liberalization and the major industries). *Gaikoku Kawase* 140:9–12.

Inuta, Akira. 1981. Waga kuni sengo no gaikoku kawase kanri to gaishi kisei (Control of the foreign exchange and foreign capital in postwar Japan). *Keizai Ronshu* (Toyo University) 7 (1,2): 155–200.

Itoh, Motoshige, and Kazuharu Kiyono. 1988. The tax system and the fiscal investment and loan program. In *Industrial policy of Japan,* ed. Ryutaro Komiya, Masahiro Okuno-Fujiwara, and Kotaro Suzumura, 121–53. New York: Academic.

Kosai, Yutaka. 1989. Kodo seicho-ki no keizai seisaku (Economic policies during the high growth period). In *Kodo seicho* (High economic growth), ed. Yasukichi Yasuba and Takenori Inoki. Tokyo: Iwanami Shoten.

Ministry of Finance (MOF), 1976. *Showa zaisei shi: Shusen kara kowa made* (Financial history of Showa era: From the end of the war to the peace), vol. 15. Tokyo: Toyo Keizai Shinposha.

Ministry of International Trade and Industry (MITI). 1952. Bureau of International Trade. Foreign Exchange Section. Tsusho kyoku no shin kiko to sono gyomu (The new organization of the Bureau of International Trade and its duties). *Gaikoku Kawase* 56:3–5.

———. Bureau of Textile. 1950. Yomo seihin yushutsu rinku seido yoryo (Outline of wool products export link system). *Yomo* (Wool) 3 (May–June): 3–4.

Ministry of International Trade and Industry (MITI) and Research Institute of International Trade and Industry, eds. 1990. *Tsusho sangyo seisaku shi* (History of the industrial policy), vol. 6. Tokyo: Research Institute of International Trade and Industry.

———. 1994. *Tsusho sangyo seisaku shi* (History of the industrial policy), vol. 1. Tokyo: Research Institute of International Trade and Industry.

Mitsubishi Economic Research Institute. Various years. *Honpo jigyo seiseki bunseki* (Analysis of business conditions of principal Japanese companies). Tokyo: Mitsubishi Economic Research Institute.

Muto, Kenjiro. 1960. Jiyuka no tachiokure wo torimodose (Recover the delay of the trade liberalization). *Toyo Keizai Shinpo* 2924:30–32.

Nakakita, Akira. 1993. Boeki to shihon no jiyuka seisaku (Liberalization of trade and capital). In *Sengo nihon no keizai kaikaku: Seifu to shijo* (Economic reform in postwar Japan: Government and the market), ed. Yutaka Kosai and Juro Teranishi. Tokyo: University of Tokyo Press.

Nishimura, Keisuke. 1955. Tokushu boeki hoshiki ni tsuite: Sono kaiko to tenbo (On the special trade methods: Its past and future). *Gaikoku Kawase* 120:8–11.

Okazaki, Tetsuji. 1996. The government-firm relationship in postwar Japanese economic recovery: Resolving coordination failure by coordination in industrial rationalization. In *The role of government in East Asian economic development: Comparative institutional analysis,* ed. Masahiko Aoki, Hyung-Ki Kim, and Masahiro Okuno-Fujiwara. Oxford: Oxford University Press.

Okazaki, Tetsuji, and Susumu Ishii. 1996. Industrial policy in postwar Japan: Its role and institutional basis. *Acta Asiatica* 71:48–67.

Okazaki, Tetsuji, Shinji Sugayama, Tamotsu Nishizawa, and Seiichiro Yonekura. 1996. *Sengo nihon keizai to keizai doyukai* (The postwar Japanese economy and the Association of Corporate Executives). Tokyo: Iwanami Shoten.

Pagan, Adrian. 1974. A generalized approach to the treatment of autocorrelation. *Australian Economic Papers* 13:267–80.

Shimada, Yoshihito, ed. 1960. *Boeki kawase kanri ho* (The Foreign Exchange and Foreign Trade Administration Law). Tokyo: Yuhikaku.

Taisa, Masayuki. 1989. *Sangyo boeki shinko to kin'yu seisaku: Nihon ginko yugu tegata seido no kenkyu* (Promotions to industry and trade, and financial policy: A study of the system of priority financing by Bank of Japan). Tokyo: Toyo Keizai Shinposha.

Takagi, Shinji. 1996. The Japanese system of foreign exchange and trade control, 1950–1964. New York: Columbia Business School. Working paper.

Textile Society of Japan. 1958. *Nihon sen'i sangyo shi, Soron-hen* (A history of the Japanese textile industry, volume of a general history). Tokyo: Textile Society of Japan.

U.S. Department of Commerce. 1986. *National income and product accounts of the United States, 1929–82*. Washington, D.C.: U.S. Department of Commerce.

Wool Spinning Association of Japan. 1987. *Nihon yomo sangyo ryakushi* (A brief history of the Japanese wool-spinning industry). Tokyo: Wool Spinning Association of Japan.

World Bank. 1993. *The East Asian miracle: Economic growth and public policy*. New York: Oxford University Press.

Comment   Ronald I. McKinnon

This careful study of a little-known part of Japanese history throws light on an important issue in development economics. To what extent can high growth in East Asian economies be attributed to astute government interventions in the early stages of economic development? In particular, was detailed foreign exchange allocation by an incorruptible MITI in the 1950s to early 1960s essential to Japan's successful development as a great industrial exporter in the postwar period?

The complex exchange allocation system, with different lists and eligibility criteria that Okazaki and Korenaga so carefully describe, was not instituted as part of a grand economic plan to spur economic development. Rather, it was an accidental outcome of the great inflation, macroeconomic instability, and (incipient) capital flight that Japan suffered in the late 1940s. In the successful Dodge stabilization of 1949, unifying the currency at 360 yen per dollar became the critically important nominal anchor for the Japanese price level. However valuable as a monetary anchor, the 360 yen rate was (perhaps accidentally) somewhat overvalued. Despite strict controls on capital account, shortages of foreign exchange persisted through the early and middle 1950s. Many key product prices—such as that for basic steel—were substantially

Ronald I. McKinnon is professor of economics at Stanford University.

above those prevailing on world markets. As late as 1957, there was speculation that the yen might be devalued—which increased pressure for (covert) capital flight. Because it was not easy to make a distinction between current and capital account transactions, foreign exchange allocation, according to officially specified import lists, became a necessity.

According to Okazaki and Korenaga's analysis, MITI distinguished an automatic approval (AA) list of imports permitted on a first come, first served basis. But subject to an overall foreign exchange budgetary limitation, there was also an FA list requiring detailed bureaucratic processing of each item. Liberalization took the form of letting the AA list grow in size relative to the FA list until more or less complete liberalization occurred in the early 1960s. After 1952, a decade or more of deflationary pressure was necessary to allow the Japanese economy to "grow into" the exchange rate of 360 yen per dollar so that exchange controls on current account could be relaxed in the 1960s.

In the 1950s, however, economic rents from foreign exchange allocation were substantial, and who received them was (is) a matter of great interest to development economists. Despite the possibilities for moral hazard in the situation, Okazaki and Korenaga show that MITI's licensing procedures were insulated from political pressure on the one hand and corruption on the other—a feat that most developing countries would envy. More positively, they indicate two dominant criteria for allocating the rents: (1) inputs for exporters based on past or prospective export performance and (2) inputs to support underutilized investment capacity or new investment in certain areas—presumably including tradable goods.

If the yen was indeed overvalued, then this is precisely the allocation of rents one would want to compensate for that overvaluation. That is, the overvaluation tends to make exporting look unduly unprofitable and also tends to depress investment—particularly in tradables. Thus, to a substantial extent, MITI's allocation of economic rents pushed resource allocation in the Japanese economy closer to what would have occurred if the real exchange rate in the 1950s had been correctly valued! By using foreign exchange allocations to promote exports on the one hand and investment on the other, MITI was simply compensating for the yen's overvaluation.

No doubt that MITI was reasonably clever, as well as incorruptible, in following this rent allocation strategy. However, developing economies would hardly be advised to maintain overvalued currencies as a matter of deliberate policy in order to put their industry ministries in the position of allocating licenses for scarce foreign exchange over the whole range of industrial and consumer imports. The result is much more likely to be serious decline in the efficiency of the economy as rent seeking and corruption become rampant. This was documented in gory detail by Bhagwati (1978) and Krueger (1978) and further analyzed in McKinnon (1993).

For successful economic development, the first-best strategy is to operate with a properly valued real exchange rate and to dispense with the elaborate rent allocations that MITI so successfully undertook. In 1949, Japan faced very special circumstances when a major inflation and multiple exchange rate regime had to be overcome with a stabilization program that was, to some extent, externally imposed, that is, the Dodge plan. The fact that MITI's bureaucracy did very well in helping overcome the effects of currency overvaluation, which lasted almost a decade, is a tribute to Japan's civil service. Nevertheless, this is a second-best approach compared to maintaining an equilibrium exchange rate: Okazaki and Korenaga document some of its distortions by, for example, firms installing excess capacity because of the licensing procedures. The lesson for other developing countries is clear enough. In the 1950s, MITI's astute allocation of import licenses helped to overcome much of the allocative distortion from an overvalued yen. However, currency overvaluation itself, while sometimes unavoidable, is not generally a desirable policy for promoting economic development.

References

Bhagwati, Jagdish. 1978. *Anatomy and consequences of exchange control regimes.* Foreign Trade Regimes and Economic Development, vol. 11. Cambridge, Mass.: Ballinger.
Krueger, Anne O. 1978. *Liberalization attempts and consequences.* Foreign Trade Regimes and Economic Development, vol. 10. Cambridge, Mass.: Ballinger.
McKinnon, Ronald I. 1993. *The order of economic liberalization: Financial control in the transition to a market economy,* 2d ed. Baltimore: Johns Hopkins University Press.

Comment   Shinji Takagi

I recently prepared a paper on substantially the same topic, namely, the Japanese system of foreign exchange and trade control in the 1950s and early 1960s (see Takagi 1997). Fortunately, however, my paper and Okazaki and Korenaga's differ significantly in emphasis and purpose. While I emphasized how the system was used as a macroeconomic tool and was liberalized over time, the authors here emphasize how the system was used as a tool of industrial policy in allocating foreign exchange to different sectors of the economy.

With my previous exposure to the topic, I must first point out that the system of foreign exchange allocation in Japan that Okazaki and Korenaga talk about was never invariant throughout the period. Because regulations and institutional arrangements changed frequently, and many of these changes were unimportant for the purpose of this study, it is indeed proper that the authors consider only the essential features of the system. The only problem, however,

Shinji Takagi is professor of economics at the University of Osaka.

comes from the fact that an intermediate category of goods was introduced into the import-licensing system in November 1959. The treatment of this group of goods, namely, those under the automatic fund allocation (AFA) system, should be made explicit in their discussions.

It is also important to note that the Japanese system of foreign exchange and trade control was never introduced as a tool of industrial policy. It may well be true that the Japanese authorities came to use the system as such. However, the system was introduced as a response to a perceived need, namely, the need to cope with the economic reality of the immediate post–World War II era in which the currencies of most major countries remained inconvertible. Given the inconvertibility of most major currencies, including sterling, the Japanese authorities had to devise and maintain a system under which foreign exchange earnings in sterling, for example, could somehow be allocated to finance imports from the sterling area.

Another important factor in the introduction and the operation of the system was the fact that Japan was a war-torn country with little production capacity for exports. It also took Japan years to establish normal commercial relationships with many of the world's leading economies. With the beginning of economic recovery and growth in the middle of the 1950s, Japan's independence and subsequent entry in the International Monetary Fund and General Agreement on Tariffs and Trade, and the restoration of convertibility for most European currencies in December 1958, however, the situation changed drastically. In the late 1950s, for example, the foreign exchange budget was routinely replenished when the ceiling was reached. It is thus not clear to what extent the import quotas or the foreign exchange allocation rules were binding in the latter part of the author's sample period. In this context, it is striking that the estimated rents (in table 12.5) do not seem large.

At least for the earlier period, the control procedures may have been binding, and there were probably potential rents to be exploited. An important contribution of Okazaki and Korenaga's has been to demonstrate quantitatively that the Japanese bureaucrats devised and then fairly strictly followed a foreign exchange allocation rule based on export performance and production capacity. This is an important discovery, and it throws new light on the never-ending debate about the role of the bureaucracy in the remarkable recovery and growth of the Japanese economy in the 1950s. Opinions differ as to the contribution of industrial policy and the bureaucracy in that process. Even the effectiveness of the allocation rule in promoting exports and investment can be questioned. Thanks to Okazaki and Korenaga's work, however, one thing seems clear: the bureaucracy was not excessively corrupt in the implementation of that policy.

Reference

Takagi, Shinji. 1997. Japan's restrictive system of trade and payments: Operation, effectiveness, and liberalization, 1950–1964. Working Paper 97/111. Washington, D.C.: International Monetary Fund.

13 The Syndrome of the Ever-Higher Yen, 1971–1995: American Mercantile Pressure on Japanese Monetary Policy

Ronald I. McKinnon, Kenichi Ohno, and Kazuko Shirono

As defined by *Webster's Tenth New Collegiate Dictionary,* a *syndrome* is 1: a group of signs and symptoms that occur together and characterize a particular abnormality; and, 2: a set of concurrent things (as emotions or actions) that usually form an identifiable pattern.

From 1971, when the yen-dollar rate was 360, through April 1995, when the rate briefly touched 80 (fig. 13.1), the interactions of the American and Japanese governments in their conduct of commercial, exchange rate, and monetary policies resulted in what we call "the syndrome of the ever-higher yen." Our model of this syndrome is unusual because it links "real" considerations—that is, commercial policies, including threats of a trade war—with the monetary determination of the yen-dollar exchange rate and price levels in the two countries.

We hypothesize that the yen continually appreciated against the U.S. dollar because the Japanese and American governments were caught in a mutual policy trap. Since the late 1960s, the United States faced continual erosion of its worldwide market share in manufactures—often losing ground to Japanese competitors—in one market after another. This erosion was exacerbated by a fall in the American savings rate that led to large current account deficits in the early 1980s and subsequently. Although high-saving Japan began to run correspondingly large current account surpluses, it still used "invisible" regulatory restraints to protect some of its more backward sectors in industry, agriculture, and services. This appearance of unfair trading by Japan infuriated

Ronald I. McKinnon is professor of economics at Stanford University. Kenichi Ohno is professor of economics at the National Graduate Institute for Policy Studies, Japan. Kazuko Shirono is a graduate student of economics at the University of Tokyo.

Thanks to Takatoshi Ito for helpful comments, and to the discussants and conference participants.

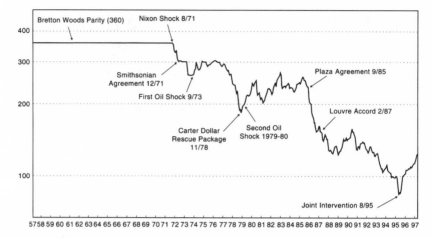

Fig. 13.1   Nominal yen-dollar exchange rate (semilog scale)
Source: International Monetary Fund (IMF 1997).

American businesspeople and government officials and led to numerous trade disputes. Repeated American threats of a trade war caused the yen to ratchet up in 1971–73, 1977–78, 1985–87, and 1993–mid-1995 (fig. 13.1). While ameliorating commercial tensions by temporarily making Japanese industry less competitive, these great appreciations imposed relative deflation on Japan without correcting the trade imbalance between the two countries.

Why, asymmetrically, should continual yen appreciation against the dollar be a forcing variable in determining the Japanese price level but not the American one? Because of the United States' large size and history as the center country in the world payments system, the U.S. Federal Reserve System (Fed) independently determines American monetary policy—sometimes with high price inflation as in the 1970s, but also with greater price stability after the early 1980s (fig. 13.2).

In contrast, Japanese monetary policy has not been independently determined. When American mercantile pressure—arising out of continual trade disputes—drove the yen up episodically, the Bank of Japan (BoJ) was reluctant to enter the foreign exchange market, or adjust domestic monetary policy, strongly enough to drive the yen back down and thus antagonize the Americans further. Although often resisting yen appreciation in the short run, the BoJ allowed the Japanese economy to deflate relative to the American economy in the longer run—and thus validated the yen's increase. In effect, the BoJ was forced to follow a dependent monetary policy that after 1985 led to absolute deflation and to serious macroeconomic disturbances in Japan: the now famous *endaka fukyos* (high-yen recessions) in 1986–87 and more severely in 1992–95. Figure 13.2 shows the Japanese wholesale price index (WPI) rising more slowly than the American index after 1975 and then falling absolutely from

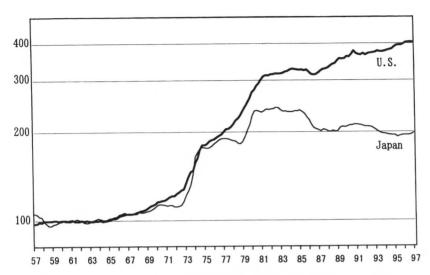

Fig. 13.2   WPI price level of tradable goods (semilog scale, 1960: 1 = 100)
Note: Each graph is taken from line 63 of IMF (1997). In March 1978, the U.S. WPI was reorganized as the U.S. PPI.

1985 through 1995—when the yen remained seriously overvalued by the purchasing power parity (PPP) criterion.

These contractions in the Japanese economy then led to a fall in imports such that the Japanese trade surplus with the United States (and rest of the world) widened. Concerned with the increase in its trade deficit, the American government applied more mercantile pressure on Japan to do something about it—including pressure for further yen appreciation! And so the cycle continued—thus reinforcing the syndrome.

In effect, the U.S. government initiated mercantile actions—whose consequences it did (does) not fully understand—that promoted the syndrome. Nevertheless, the Japanese government was very slow to learn how its own reactions supported or validated the yen's continual appreciation. It tolerated relative deflation in the Japanese price level and only reluctantly liberalized its protected sectors. Thus the two countries were trapped in a mutual interaction that generated political discord and undermined economic efficiency in both.

Fortunately, in April 1995 officials at the U.S. Treasury finally realized that further deflation and exchange rate overvaluation might cause a serious macroeconomic breakdown in Japan with a slump in investment and a major banking crisis. They relaxed commercial pressure on Japan, and the BoJ worked with the Fed to depreciate the yen and reexpand the Japanese economy from mid-1995 to mid-1997 (McKinnon and Ohno 1997, chap. 11). The consequent dramatic fall in the yen, from 80 yen per dollar in April 1995 to close to PPP at 125 yen per dollar by May 1997 (fig. 13.3), effected an easing of Japanese monetary policy and a modest economic recovery. (Unfortunately, Japan's sharp tax increase in April 1997 aborted this recovery.)

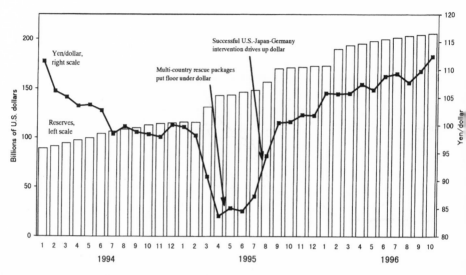

Fig. 13.3   Yen-dollar exchange rate and Japanese foreign exchange reserves, 1994–96
Source: IMF (1997).

Although this remarkable fall in the yen confirms our mercantile pressure theory of the yen-dollar exchange rate, we do not yet know whether this remission from the syndrome from mid-1995 to mid-1997 is temporary or permanent. Mercantile pressure from the United States to appreciate the yen, with deflationary repercussions in Japan, could well up again.

Thus this paper focuses on how the syndrome worked up to early 1995. In section 13.1 we describe the origins of American mercantile concerns and episodic pressures resulting in yen appreciations after 1970. In section 13.2 we use more recent data from 1985 to early 1995 to design an econometric test to show how yen appreciation was a "forcing" variable for determining commodity price deflation in Japan, and how this was sometimes resisted, but not fully offset, by the Japanese monetary authorities.

The problem posed by the ever-higher yen for financial adjustment between the two countries has many facets. These include labor market and wage adjustment, trade imbalances and capital transfers, the speed of induced prices changes, asset bubbles, and the generation of business cycles in both countries. In particular, by 1978 the expectation that the yen would go ever higher became firmly embedded in nominal interest rates: yields on yen bonds were driven down so that they have averaged about 4 percentage points less than those on dollar bonds ever since. All of these, as well as other related issues are covered in McKinnon and Ohno's (1997) book *Dollar and Yen: Resolving Economic Conflict between Japan and the United States.* In this paper, we focus more narrowly on the mercantile origins of the upward pressure on the yen, and its implications for relative and absolute price deflation in Japan.

13.1   Mercantile Pressure on the Yen-Dollar Exchange Rate

When President Nixon closed the gold window in August 1971, he also imposed a tariff surcharge on imports of manufactured goods and demanded that trading partners in Europe and Japan appreciate the dollar value of their currencies. They all formally appreciated by 10 to 20 percent (the yen by 17 percent) in the famous, but temporary, Smithsonian Accord of December 1971—at which time Nixon removed the surcharge.

We hypothesize that after 1971 the United States pursued a similar policy—but one increasingly narrowly focused on Japan—of coupling protectionist threats with demands, implicit or explicit, for yen appreciation. (The major exceptions were the strong dollar policy of the first Reagan administration from 1981 to 1984 and the fall of the yen after April 1995.) Figure 13.4 shows that the yen's 250 percent appreciation against the dollar from 1970 to 1994 was the greatest among the currencies of U.S. trading partners.

No matter how much the dollar fell (fig. 13.1), at least some U.S. government officials typically saw further room for yen appreciation. Since the Nixon shock in 1971, various secretaries of the treasury—notably Blumenthal in 1977, Baker in 1985–87, and Bentsen in 1993—have suggested that the dollar was too high against the yen and in each of these cases the dollar subsequently fell. These attempts to "talk" the dollar down were accompanied by intense trade negotiations aimed at forcing the Japanese to open or share this or that market.

But talk is cheap. Why should it force the yen up over the long term? Although the exchange rate is a forward-looking asset price, the (forward) "fundamentals" are difficult to define, let alone model by foreign exchange traders

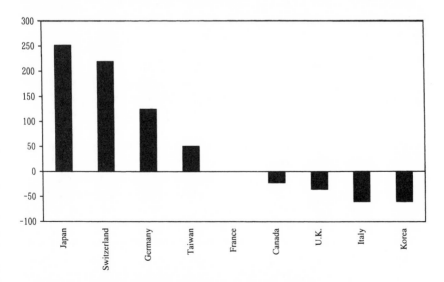

Fig. 13.4   Nominal appreciation against the dollar, 1970–94
Sources: IMF (1997) and Bank of Japan, *Economic Statistics Monthly* (Tokyo, various issues).

or econometricians. Thus, under certain circumstances, talk on exchange rates by treasury secretaries, and the commercial disputes themselves, can affect peoples' perceptions of future relative monetary policies in the two countries. The anxiety that Japanese investors feel about continually adding to their portfolios of dollar assets is then heightened, and actual or incipient portfolio readjustment then causes the yen-dollar rate to fall.

More precisely, we identify two concerns that have induced American governments to pressure, sometimes only implicitly, Japan to appreciate its currency:

1. The perception, since the late 1960s, by individual business interests in the United States that Japan was an "unfair" international competitor. Let us call these microeconomic concerns *commercial pressure.*

2. Deteriorating U.S. current account balances, beginning in the late 1970s but burgeoning in the 1980s and 1990s: the counterpart of Japan's current surpluses. Conventional academic wisdom held that this called for dollar devaluation or yen appreciation. Let us call this macroeconomic concern *academic pressure.*

The exchange markets perceive that sudden yen appreciation reduces the competitiveness of Japanese exporters worldwide against their American counterparts in the short run and thus will temporarily relieve commercial pressure on the exchange rate. The markets also perceive that many (academic) economists and policymakers believe that yen appreciation will reduce the American trade deficit in the future. So when it does appreciate, academic pressure will also temporarily slacken. Thus, in times of intense American concern over the U.S. trade position, market makers find a consensus for driving the yen-dollar rate down (the yen up) to alleviate that concern. Although commercial pressure and academic pressure on the yen-dollar rate are hardly independent of one another, let us discuss each in turn.

13.1.1   Commercial Pressure

Why should commercial tension be (have been) more intense between Japan and the United States than between other pairs of industrial countries? Since the early 1950s, productivity and output growth in Japanese manufacturing industries was much higher than in their more mature American counterparts. And this growth was highly uneven: more explosive in Japanese industries such as electrical machinery, automobiles, and consumer electronics than in others. The overall Japanese economy, now the world's second largest, grew rapidly: total Japanese exports were only about one-quarter of the American level in 1964 but had risen to well over three-quarters by 1995. Thus, whether the exchange rate was fixed or floating, or trade imbalances were present or absent, and no matter how assiduously each country's diplomats had sought political harmony, a serious problem of mutual economic adjustment would still exist.

But adjustment was also complicated by unfortunate trends in the political economy of each country. On the Japanese side, the government operated too long under the principle of "developmental authoritarianism," or more simply what Murukami (1992) calls "developmentalism," for promoting the industrial sector—well past the point when such action might have been needed to support recovery from wartime devastation. For the next several decades, the government targeted—although not always successfully or accurately—particular industries to be internationally competitive. To prevent the domestic distribution of income from being unduly skewed by such favoritism, the government then used a complex regulatory apparatus to cosset or shield many other "disadvantaged" industries—often outside the manufacturing sector—from the rigors of international and domestic competition (McKinnon and Ohno 1997, chap. 2).

To foreigners trying to sell in Japan, the concerted regulatory power of the various ministries, often operating through industry-wide trade associations of domestic Japanese business firms, appeared to be a formidable barrier, and a possible shield for collusive behavior in other international markets. Whence the proliferation of books on Japan as an "unfair" international competitor. Upscale in this genre, Laura Tyson—President Clinton's principal economic advisor from 1993 to 1996—published the book *Who's Bashing Whom? Trade Conflict in High-Technology Industries.* After several chapters documenting extreme regulatory hurdles facing American producers of semiconductors, cellular telephones, supercomputers, and other high-technology goods trying to sell in the Japanese market—and the intense political confrontations arising out of these disputes—Tyson concludes: "The[se] cases of U.S.-Japan trade competition . . . provide compelling historical evidence of the persistence of structural and policy impediments to the Japanese market. Although formal protection has been phased out, primarily in response to American *gaiatsu* (pressure), the peculiar features of Japanese capitalism impede access to foreign suppliers to shape competition to the advantage of their Japanese rivals" (1992, 266).

Similarly, in a more extensive review of industry studies covering Japanese manufacturing, primary products, and services in their book *Reconcilable Differences? United States–Japan Economic Conflict,* C. Fred Bergsten and Marcus Noland conclude:

> In Japan there is scant evidence of significant tariffs and quotas outside of agriculture. Nevertheless, it is widely believed that the Japanese market is effectively closed to manufactured imports. The methods of import control include discriminatory networks of affiliated firms (*keiretsu*); administrative guidance on the part of government officials to intimidate importers; misuse of customs procedures and product standards, testing, and certification procedures to discourage imports; incomplete enforcement of patent and trademark rights; government procurement procedures that advantage domestic suppliers; and restrictions on the distribution channels for imported products, to name a few. (1993, 72)

But airport newsstands sport plenty of downscale versions of how Japan Inc. was conspiring to undermine the American economy through collusive trading practices. Although in the 1990s Japan has liberalized many of its more restrictive regulatory barriers to foreigners selling in the Japanese market—such as the opening of large-scale discount retailers (Organization for Economic Cooperation and Development 1995)—the idea of an overly intrusive Japanese bureaucracy persists in the minds of foreign protagonists in trade disputes.

American concern with commercial pressure from its faster growing political allies goes back a long way. As early as 1956, the United States put pressure on Japan to impose a "voluntary" export restraint (VER) on Japanese cotton textiles entering the American economy. In 1966, a number of European countries and Japan were persuaded to impose a VER on steel exports to the United States, which spread to specialty steels in the 1970s. In 1968, U.S. television producers filed antidumping suits against Japanese producers—and the U.S. government imposed substantial antidumping duties on imports of Japanese televisions in 1971. In the late 1960s, severe measures to protect all manufacturing industries were introduced in the U.S. Congress. These ultimately failed but nevertheless put pressure on the American government to "do something" to help American manufacturing industries (Baldwin 1988).

As long as the Bretton Woods system of par values for exchange rates was firmly in place and the U.S. current account showed a surplus—as was generally the case in the 1950s and 1960s—the dollar's exchange rate was insulated from protectionist pressure. This was a great strength of the par value system (McKinnon 1996). However, this pressure intensified when inflation in the United States increased after 1968: U.S. wholesale prices began drifting upward relative to those in Germany and Japan. President Nixon responded by devaluing the dollar in August 1971.

But this one-time dollar depreciation did not end the protectionist pressure. In the late 1970s, the U.S. government introduced trigger prices on steel imports, which, when VERs expired, were (and are) associated with a variety of antidumping suits filed by American steel companies against foreign steel producers in general, and against Japanese producers in particular, throughout the 1980s into the 1990s. The American government increasingly focused on Japan as it made its way up the ladder from simple to more complex industrial goods. Voluntary restraints on Japanese exports to the American market proliferated: televisions beginning in the 1970s, machine tools in the 1970s and 1980s, and automobiles in the 1980s.

The U.S. government made it increasingly easy for American firms to prove allegations of "dumping" against foreigners, particularly those with appreciating currencies. The procedures used by the U.S. Department of Commerce in evaluating "fair" foreign prices for selling in the U.S. market became increasingly arbitrary with incredible bookkeeping (discovery) costs imposed on foreign firms victimized by antidumping suits—whether successful or not. The standards for determining material injury to American producers became ever weaker (Krueger 1995).

Before the mid-1980s, government-to-government negotiations to relax commercial pressure on the United States took the form of ad hoc VERs. These were certainly outside the spirit of the General Agreement on Tariffs and Trade (GATT) but were not inconsistent with any of its specific articles. Similarly, private antidumping suits were potentially consistent with the antidumping articles of the GATT.

By the late 1980s, however, the retreat of international communism as an organized economic and military threat to the United States made it even more difficult for the American president to suppress domestic protectionist interests, which had always been heavily represented in Congress. By 1988, aggressive unilateralism outside the rules of the GATT had become firmly institutionalized in American trade law under what is now popularly called "Super 301." In her book *American Trade Policy: A Tragedy in the Making,* Anne Krueger suggests that

> the Omnibus Trade and Competitiveness Act of 1988 extended Section 301 of the Trade Act of 1974 to broaden considerably the scope of the unfair trade procedures and took it well beyond procedures that are consistent with the GATT in principle. In particular, Congress instructed the USTR [U.S. Trade Representative] to take an inventory of other countries' unfair trading practices . . . in a report to Congress by the end of May each year. . . . The 1988 trade act also instructed the USTR to take retaliatory action against imports from the named country (or countries) in the event that the USTR could not negotiate for the removal of the named practices. (1995, 64)

Without requiring reciprocity by the United States, Section 301 cleared the way for the USTR to demand unilaterally that other countries take action to open their national markets to American goods if the USTR believed that "structural impediments" existed (Ito 1992, 376). One result was to demand specific shares in foreign markets through so-called voluntary import expansions. The first was negotiated in 1986 in semiconductors to assure foreign producers (imagined to be mainly American) 20 percent of the Japanese market, with riders for keeping Japanese prices sufficiently high that American producers could compete more easily at home and in third markets. There have been recriminations and subsequent renegotiations into the 1990s over whether or not the Japanese were violating these riders (Itoh 1994).

Krueger notes that Super 301 was not renewed by the Bush administration when it expired at the end of 1990. But she also notes that

> by the winter of 1994, however, bilateral trading relations with Japan had deteriorated under the Clinton Administration's pressure for "quantitative targets." In March 1994, President Clinton reinstituted Super 301 by executive decree. He insisted that the bilateral trade balance with Japan, and even the magnitude of Japanese imports of individual items, were legitimate subjects for bilateral bargaining. He threatened retaliation (presumably punitive tariffs) if Japan did not address to the satisfaction of the United States, the "unfair trading practice" of a large bilateral trade imbalance. (1995, 67)

This reinstituted Super 301 was the basis for acrimonious discussions in the first four months of 1995 on opening Japanese markets to American automobiles and components when the yen ratcheted up sharply from 100 to 80 yen per dollar (fig. 13.3).

3.1.2   The Great Relaxation of Commercial Pressure, 1995–96

Only in April 1995 did the American government finally realize that something had gone terribly wrong with its commercial and exchange rate policies toward Japan. At 80 yen per dollar, the greatly overvalued yen (PPP was closer to 125 yen per dollar; McKinnon and Ohno 1997) threatened a collapse in the Japanese financial system, and a much deeper depression than the *endaka fukyo* the Japanese economy was already suffering from in 1993–95.

So what was the American response? On the commercial side, U.S. officials abandoned further significant pressure on Japan. The dispute over automobile components was settled quietly in July 1995 with no fixed numerical targets, and with Japan promising only to simplify bureaucratic restraints on importing while encouraging dealers to stock a wider range of foreign vehicles and parts. Afterward, new potential flashpoints for invoking Super 301 against Japan were ignored for at least a year. Most important, because of its great symbolism, the long-simmering dispute between Eastman Kodak and Fujifilm over Kodak's alleged inability to market its film in Japan (because of Fuji's alleged monopolization of the Japanese market) was defused by finally sending it to the World Trade Organization after the American government pointedly decided *not* to invoke Super 301:

> In May of last year [1995], Kodak officials were brimming with confidence when their new Chairman, Mr. George Fisher, announced that the company had filed a complaint against Japan's Fuji with the U.S. Trade Representative. . . .
>   A year after the filing, the world's two photographic giants—having spent untold millions on lawyers, lobbyists, and public relations—have fought each other to a standstill. Yesterday the U.S. Trade Representative's office announced not threats or sanctions in the usual U.S. government fashion, but a decision to take Kodak's complaints to a multilateral forum—the World Trade Organization. (*Financial Times,* 14 June 1996)

For Japan's partial recovery in 1996 into early 1997 from the mid-1995 crisis, this relaxation of American commercial pressure was necessary—but not itself sufficient to reexpand the economy. In mid-1995, no formal commercial compact ensured that the United States would tolerate a fall in the yen toward PPP over the coming year. We show that concerted joint interventions by the BoJ and the Fed in summer 1995 were also needed to drive the yen-dollar rate to 100 by the end of the year (McKinnon and Ohno 1997). This signaled to the markets that the American government would not complain if the yen depreciated further. Thus the BoJ could successfully reflate, with the yen further depreciating to about 108 per dollar in summer 1996 and to 125 per dollar in early 1997 (fig. 13.3), to promote Japan's modest economic recovery.

3.1.3   Academic Pressure: The Trade Balance
Approach to the Exchange Rate

In addition to the political influence wielded by individual American companies, pressure to appreciate the yen from 1971 to mid-1995 was also partly conceptual or "academic." It arose out of a particular interpretation of economic theory. Most economists espouse an exchange rate doctrine based on the elasticities model of the balance of trade. They convinced American policymakers that devaluing the dollar would, in itself, reduce the U.S. trade or current account deficit—and that exchange rate changes can be treated as a rather clean and acceptable instrument of economic policy. And because Japan has had the biggest current account surpluses—until 1994, about the same size as the U.S. deficit (fig. 13.5)—the yen-dollar rate becomes the focal point of attempts by the American government to reduce the trade deficit by talking the yen up.

But when applied to mature industrial economies that are financially open and would otherwise be stable, this elasticities approach for correcting a trade imbalance is misplaced (Komiya 1994). The persistent overall current account surplus of Japan, and the overall deficit of the United States, reflects Japan's saving surplus on the one hand, and abnormally low saving by the United States on the other. Exchange rate changes, arising out of perceived changes in (future) national monetary policies, cannot systematically affect these national

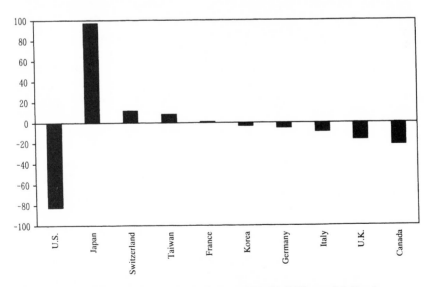

Fig. 13.5   Average current account balance, 1990–94 (billions of dollars)
Sources: See fig. 13.4.

saving-investment balances (McKinnon and Ohno 1997). Instead, as interdependence grows, changes in nominal exchange rates begin to affect the domestic economy through multiple channels, and the presumption that devaluation improves the trade balance becomes tenuous.

True, devaluation immediately makes domestic products cheaper than foreign products. This *relative price effect* certainly works to improve the trade balance—as the elasticities approach would have it—as long as the Marshall-Lerner elasticities condition holds. (We assume throughout that this condition is satisfied.) But in a highly open industrial economy, there are several other effects that may partly or completely offset the favorable relative price effect.

The first is the *reverse absorption effect:* devaluation tends to stimulate part of domestic spending—particularly investment by tradable industries—and worsens the trade balance. Conversely, appreciation dampens domestic investment, causes recession, and perpetuates a trade surplus—*endaka fukyo,* in Japan. As Kawai (1994) shows, when the adverse effect of exchange movement on macroactivity is present, the impact of real devaluation on the trade balance cannot be theoretically ascertained. In their empirical work, Miyagawa and Tokui (1994) estimate that a 1 percent real effective appreciation of the yen reduces domestic investment by about 0.7 to 0.9 percent of the total capital stock—although there is a partial offset through a reduction of imported material prices.

Second, there is the *pass-through effect.* If the home currency is kept substantially undervalued (overvalued), in view of the law of one price, imported inflation (deflation) will arise through commodity arbitrage, which dilutes and eventually eliminates the initial international price gap in tradable goods. In the long run, the price advantage of domestic industries will disappear, and the real exchange rate is unaffected by manipulation of the nominal exchange rate. That is, there is mean reversion toward PPP.

Third, and closely related to the pass-through effect, an engineered depreciation of the dollar against the yen is typically validated ex post, involuntarily or even imperceptibly, by the *Bank of Japan's tightening its long-term monetary policy* relative to that of the United States. Historically, the BoJ accepts a higher yen (which is assumed, in American minds, to reduce Japan's surplus) so as to placate the U.S. Congress and trade officials. This subtle deflationary bias imposed on Japan's monetary policy will, sooner or later, reduce absorption (i.e., domestic spending) in Japan relative to what it would have been without such monetary adjustment. This tends to keep Japan's production above its spending, thus perpetuating its current account surplus which the cheaper dollar was originally supposed to eliminate, and also speeds mean reversion to PPP.

Fourth, the *J-curve effect* is known to increase the trade gap at least temporarily, before the quantities of exports and imports have had time to respond to the change in the relative price. The adverse effect lasts all the longer if the country starts with the position of a substantial trade gap. In the very long run,

Kawai (1994) suggests that the trade balance would return to the original level so that the curve is an elongated S rather than a J.

Fifth, a continued overvaluation of the yen prompts an exodus of Japanese manufacturing bases to China and Southeast Asia, that is, the *hollowing-out phenomenon.* This increases Japanese exports of capital and intermediate goods in order to build and operate new factories in these countries. Over time, the country origins of "Japanese" brand products will shift from Japan to the rest of Asia, with probably only a minor impact on the global trade balance of the United States.

But there is much opposition to this idea that the elasticities approach to the trade balance does not work for financially open, mature industrial economies like Japan and the United States. For example, using data since the late 1970s, Cline (1995) shows a remarkable correlation of the Japan-U.S. bilateral trade gap with the real yen-dollar rate lagged two years. Ito (1992) also finds a similar lagged correlation of 12 to 24 months. Bergsten and Noland (1993) invoke Cline's diagram to make the same point. In figure 13.6, we have replicated this diagram with our own data extended to include earlier years. Following Cline, the bilateral trade balance (T) is defined in percent of total bilateral trade; that is,

$$(1) \qquad\qquad T = \frac{X - M}{X + M},$$

where X is Japan's exports to the United States and M is Japan's imports from the United States. Here the real exchange rate is defined as the relative price of tradables between the two countries (deflated by bilateral wholesale prices).

We immediately notice that the cyclical movements of the bilateral trade balance and the real yen-dollar rate are, if the best-fitting lag structure is cho-

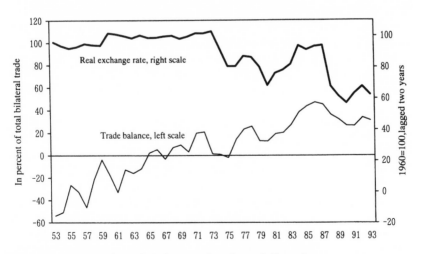

Fig. 13.6   Japan-U.S. trade balance and real yen-dollar rate

sen, highly synchronized during the floating rate years. But this two-year lag need not reflect delayed relative price effects as the elasticities approach would have it. Instead, fluctuations in national income and absorption, also associated with exchange rate changes, could be responsible.

To illustrate this last point, consider the Japanese experience from 1993 to 1996 with income fluctuations. In 1993 to mid-1995, when the yen was high and rising and domestic prices falling, this inadvertent "tight money" situation caused the Japanese economy to slump and its current account surplus to balloon as the demand for (net) imports fell. But with the relaxation of American commercial pressure allowing the BoJ to reflate the economy with incidental yen depreciation beginning in mid-1995 (fig. 13.3), Japan's current account surplus fell dramatically in 1996 as its recovering economy sucked in imports. However, a naive econometrician, wedded to the elasticities approach with a two-year lag, would attribute the 1996 decline in Japan's current surplus to the delayed relative price effects from yen overvaluation in 1994! For example, in explaining the sharp fall in the Japanese trade surplus in 1996, "Fred Bergsten, director of the Institute for International Economics, a private Group, says that 'the main reason the Japanese trade surplus is down is because of the sharp rise of the dollar against the yen in 1993 and 1994.' He adds that it takes about two years for these currency changes, which made Japanese goods more expensive in the U.S., to influence the trade figures" (*Asian Wall Street Journal,* 21 August 1996, 1).

From the perspective of the elasticities model based on relative price effects that so influences Bergsten, this correlation between Japan's overall trade surplus and the lagged yen-dollar rate is spurious. Rather than price effects, it is fluctuations in Japanese income and absorption from changes in monetary policy forced by fluctuations in the yen-dollar rate (see section 13.2 below) that dominate fluctuations in the trade surplus. Even so, over the whole half-cycle (about two years) from depression to recovery, the impact of the exchange rate on Japan's *cumulative* current surplus is ambiguous.

More fundamentally, figure 13.6 also uncovers two further facts that are not favorable to Bergsten's and Cline's interpretation: (i) apart from cyclical movements, the long-term declining trend in the real exchange rate has no explanatory power over the rising structural surplus of Japan vis-à-vis the United States; perhaps more important, (ii) in earlier years of the Bretton Woods fixed-rate dollar standard, movements in the trade balance occurred without any perceptible changes in the real exchange rate. Clearly, there exists a persistent upward trend in the bilateral trade balance over the past 40 years (at least to mid-1995) spanning two different international monetary regimes. All this points to the strong possibility that changes in the trade balance need not be triggered by movements in the real exchange rate. Independently of the real exchange rate, the structural trade balance can shift smoothly with changes in national saving-investment balances when capital markets are integrated (McKinnon 1996, chap. 4).

In general, exchange appreciation by a financially open economy does not alter its cumulative trade balance in any predictable way. Thus it is not surprising that from 1971 to mid-1995, academic pressure to appreciate the yen against the dollar failed to "correct" the bilateral trade imbalance between the two countries. However, we suggest that American mercantile pressure (academic and commercial pressure together) did succeed in (i) appreciating the yen after 1971 and (ii) forcing relative deflation on Japan after the early 1970s. This led to serious macroeconomic instability in Japan after 1985.

13.2   A Causality Analysis of Yen Appreciation and Japanese Monetary Policy

Suppose that price inflation in American tradable goods was given exogenously. Can we then demonstrate empirically our proposition that the yen-dollar exchange rate was indeed the forcing variable "causing" the relative price deflation in Japan? (The alternative interpretation is that under floating exchange rates after 1971, the BoJ freely determined Japanese monetary policy and the Japanese price level according to domestic economic conditions. In this more traditional view, the yen-dollar rate would then adjust passively to be consistent with the independently chosen Japanese monetary policy.)

Consider first the question of causality in long-term PPP. The concept of purchasing power parity was originally proposed by Gustav Cassel in the early twentieth century. According to his formulation, the exchange rate is determined by the ratio of the "purchasing powers" of two national currencies. The purchasing power of a currency in turn is determined by the inverse of the price of a typical goods basket. Thus the PPP exchange rate (E^{PPP}) is shown by the following equation:

(2) $$E^{\mathrm{PPP}} = P/P^*,$$

where P is the price level in the home country and P^* is the price level in the foreign country. Suppose Japan is the home country and the United States is the foreign country, and (for example) let the price of a certain goods basket be 100,000 yen in Japan and $1,000 in the United States. Then the PPP yen-dollar exchange rate for this basket is 100 (= 100,000/1,000). According to the original interpretation of PPP by Cassel, an increase in the Japanese price level would proportionally depreciate the yen against the dollar, and an increase in the American price level would proportionately depreciate the dollar against the yen.

It is important to distinguish tradable goods from nontradable goods when we discuss PPP. For tradable goods, PPP holds in the long run—aside from temporary deviations and when transportation costs, tariffs, and other frictional factors are taken into account. Because industrially diversified economies, like Japan and the United States, each produce thousands of similar goods and are not specialized in a few products, persistent shifts in their overall

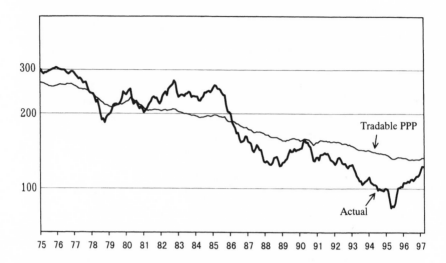

Fig. 13.7   Actual and PPP yen-dollar exchange rates (semilog scale)
Note: Tradable PPP is based on the price survey of manufactured goods conducted by the Research Institute for International Price Mechanism (in 1993). For the fourth quarter of 1992, its estimate of the tradable PPP yen-dollar exchange rate was 150.5. This benchmark has been updated and backdated using the Japanese overall WPI and the U.S. PPI.

terms of trade are unimportant. Thus, in the long run, commodity arbitrage will align their average price *levels*—as represented by *P* and *P**—internationally. In contrast and by definition, such commodity arbitrage does not occur over non-tradable goods and services. Therefore, internationally divergent movements of nontradable prices do not necessarily indicate goods market disequilibrium. In what follows, we focus on the PPP relationship among tradable goods.

Under floating exchange rates since the early 1970s, *short-term* PPP seldom holds. Frequent exchange rate bubbles and overshooting keep the actual exchange rate mostly away from the PPP level. For the yen-dollar exchange rate, the short-term violation and the long-term validity of PPP are depicted in figure 13.7. (See McKinnon and Ohno 1997 for alternative methods of computing PPP rates.) During the past two decades, both the actual and PPP yen-dollar exchange rates had declining trends (fig. 13.7) reflecting the long-term yen appreciation against the dollar and the relative fall in the Japanese price level. In the short run, however, deviations occur because the actual exchange rate changes much more rapidly than the PPP rate, whose movement depends on the more slowly evolving national price levels.

13.2.1   Three Hypotheses

Although many studies on the validity of long-term PPP exist, how to investigate the mechanism by which such a relationship holds between major currencies has not been fully established. Generally speaking, the causality between two endogenous variables, such as the exchange rate and the relative price—that is, the ratio of relative price levels $P/P*$—is mutual. The empirical observation of long-term PPP only demonstrates correlation; it does not prove causality. Understanding the dominant causality, which is unlikely to be unilateral, requires another set of empirical inquiries.

Following Cassel, the traditional interpretation of PPP presupposes that the main causality runs from prices to the exchange rate: autonomous changes in domestic price levels induce proportional changes in the exchange rate. The assumption of such one-way causality is still widely accepted. Dornbusch (1988) defines the concept of PPP thus: "Purchasing power parity (PPP) is a theory of exchange rate determination. It asserts (in the most common form) that the exchange rate change between two currencies over any period of time is determined by the change between two countries' relative price levels." Also, in an empirical study of PPP in the 1970s, Frenkel (1981) estimates a traditional PPP equation with the exchange rate as the dependent variable and the relative price as the independent variable.

However, the exchange rate may also cause the movement of relative national price levels. In this case, the PPP relationship becomes an equation determining domestic prices. If the home currency *accidentally* appreciates, independent of the fundamentals, the residents will find that imported goods are now cheaper—and this will exert downward pressure on the domestic price level. Causality is reversed from the previous case: the exchange rate movement is causal to the changes in the fundamentals. For instance, empirical studies by Helkie and Hooper (1988) and Ohno (1990) treat the exchange rate as an explanatory variable that determines domestic prices. In addition, practically all contributions to the literature of exchange rate pass-through treat the exchange rate as an exogenous shock.

Because the exchange rate is an asset price dominated by expectations, it could also *anticipate* future changes in the fundamental variables and move first. Then true causality runs from Japanese monetary policy to the yen-dollar rate—although the time sequence is reversed from the traditional Cassel case.

In sum, there are three alternative and mutually exclusive interpretations of the fact that the nominal exchange rate and relative national price levels move in the same direction in the long run:

Hypothesis 1. The exchange rate is an "adjusting variable" that passively accommodates changes in the fundamentals (prices, monetary policy, etc.). In this case, the flexibility of the exchange rate—despite short-term volatility—contributes to economic adjustment in the medium to long run. Causality runs from the fundamentals to the exchange rate.

Hypothesis 2. The exchange rate is a "forward-looking variable" that anticipates future autonomous changes in the fundamentals. In this case, the true causality is from the fundamentals to the exchange rate, but the movement of the exchange rate precedes the fundamentals in the observed time-series sequence.

Hypothesis 3. The exchange rate is a "forcing variable" that produces changes in relative national price levels, monetary policies, and so forth. In this case, the exchange rate is causal in the true as well as the time-series sense. These changes in the fundamentals would not occur without the initial change in the exchange rate.

Under the maintained assumption that the U.S. price level is independently determined by the Fed, hypothesis 3 corresponds to our basic proposition that the appreciating yen caused the Japanese price level (rate of relative price deflation) and the BoJ's long-run monetary policy.

13.2.2 An Economic Model of Domestic and External Shocks to the Japanese Price Level

In this section, we first model the causal relationship between the yen-dollar rate and Japanese prices (hypothesis 1 vs. hypotheses 2 and 3) theoretically by positing an economic structure unique to the problem at hand—unlike the popular Granger and Sims tests or vector autoregression methodology. We then test this economic model empirically by looking at the price behavior of Japanese manufactured goods. We ask the question: when general inflation or deflation occurs, did domestic prices or internationally exposed prices change first? By comparing the prices of similar goods destined for home or foreign markets, we can show whether recent Japanese inflation—or, more often, deflation—is homemade or externally imposed.

The model can be construed to describe either the entire economy or individual industries. Like us, Marston (1991) also uses Japanese sectoral data to see how yen appreciations affect the relative price structure—namely, how Japanese firms set their export price relative to the same good's domestic price. Marston defines this exchange-rate-induced price discrimination as the "pricing to market" effect. While his and our studies have similar data sets, Marston begins his investigation by assuming causation from the exchange rate to prices. In contrast, our aim is to test for the direction of causality itself.

All goods are assumed to be tradable, differing only in degree. All variables are in logarithms and refer to the manufacturing sector of the Japanese economy.

Let the *average* (i.e., domestic sales and exports combined) price level be

$$(3) \qquad P = \theta P_D + (1 - \theta)P_X,$$

where P_D is the domestic sales price, P_X is the external price (export or import price, depending on whether the good is mostly exported or imported), and θ is the share of domestic sales in total sales. Assuming for simplicity that PPP always holds for the external price, we have

$$(4) \qquad P_X = E + P_X^*,$$

where E is the nominal exchange rate (domestic currency per foreign currency). P_X^* is the foreign (dollar) price, which is assumed—or controlled—to be given.

We assume that the interaction of domestic aggregate demand and aggregate supply determines the domestic price as in the standard macroeconomic model. Thus the domestic price can be written in a reduced form,

$$(5) \qquad P_D = P_D(\alpha, \ \gamma),$$

where α and γ are various shift parameters of the aggregate demand and supply functions, respectively. For example, α includes fiscal and monetary policies and autonomous changes in consumption and investment; γ includes productivity shocks, wage push, and so forth.

In this simplified framework, let us consider whether domestic price changes are driven mainly by domestic shocks or by exchange rate shocks. Two cases are examined below: (i) price changes precede exchange rate changes as in hypothesis 1; (ii) exchange rate changes precede price changes as in hypotheses 2 and 3. In distinguishing these two cases, we confine our empirical analysis to the period from 1985 to early 1995—when yen appreciation and Japanese price deflation were most severe.

Case (i): $P \rightarrow E$

In this case, representing hypothesis 1, an initial shift in the domestic parameter (either α or γ) lowers the domestic price. Subsequently, the exchange rate gradually adjusts to reflect the new relative price between home and abroad: the change in P precedes the change in E. This exchange rate dynamics can be described as follows:

$$(6) \qquad \dot{E} = \lambda(P - E), \qquad \lambda > 0,$$

where $P - E$ is the deviation from tradable PPP and λ is the adjustment speed. (Recall that the foreign price is assumed to be fixed throughout.) Suppose, for instance, that monetary tightening causes absorption (total domestic spending) to contract. This will lower P_D according to equation (5). Since P_D is part of P (eq. [3]), P also declines. This creates a temporary deviation from PPP ($P - E < 0$), prompting E to passively and gradually adjust to the new relative price between home and abroad. P_X also moves in tandem with E, because of equation (4).

The entire sequence can be summarized as

$$(\alpha, \ \gamma) \rightarrow P_D\downarrow \ \rightarrow P\downarrow \ \Rightarrow E\downarrow \ \rightarrow P_X\downarrow,$$

where $\rightarrow$ indicates an immediate effect and $\Rightarrow$ a lagged effect. Figure 13.8 depicts the movement of each variable after a domestic shock induced domestic price deflation. Note that the average price level (P) and the internal relative

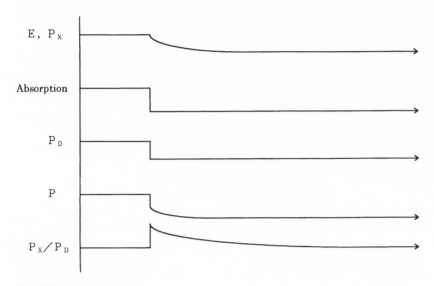

Fig. 13.8 *P* precedes *E*

price (P_X/P_D) move in opposite directions—that is, they are negatively correlated.

Case (ii): $E \rightarrow P$

In this case, representing hypotheses 2 or 3, the exchange rate first appreciates independent of the current fundamentals, lowering P_X according to equation (4). Since the reduction in P is proportionally not as large as the appreciation of E, this creates an overvaluation of the home currency $(P - E > 0)$.
Assuming Japan to be the home country, the yen's overvaluation leads to *endaka fukyo* (high yen-induced recession) and the hollowing-out of domestic
industries, both of which reduce absorption (especially investment)

$$(7) \qquad \dot{A} = -\mu(P - E), \qquad \mu > 0,$$

where A is absorption. As A declines, P_D also falls due to equation (5)—currency overvaluation is part of the demand shift parameter α.

The causal sequence can be summed up as follows:

$$E\downarrow \;\rightarrow\; P_X\downarrow \;\rightarrow\; P\downarrow \;\Rightarrow\; A\downarrow \;\rightarrow\; P_D\downarrow.$$

This is consistent with hypothesis 3. Solid lines in figure 13.9 describe the
changes in the key variables after an exogenous exchange rate shock. At the
time of the shock, the movements of the average price level (P) and the internal
relative price (P_X/P_D) are positively correlated—unlike case (i).

Alternatively, if hypothesis 2 is true when the exchange rate appreciates, the
key variables behave according to the dotted lines in figure 13.9. In this case,

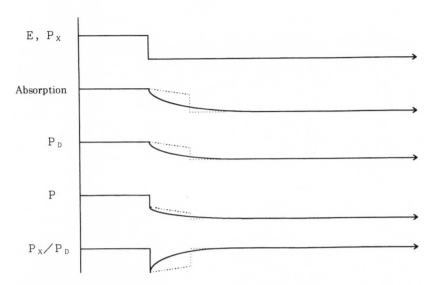

Fig. 13.9 *E precedes P*

the exchange rate changes in anticipation of the future downward jumps in A and P_D. P_X immediately declines proportionally to the appreciation, but the domestic price does not change very much until the fundamentals actually change later. (However, from the initial overvaluation, absorption and P_D begin to adjust downward slowly.) In this case also, the average price level and the internal relative price are positively correlated.

The Dornbusch overshooting model is perhaps the most famous of the exchange rate as a forward-looking variable. However, the assumptions of our model differ from Dornbusch's. Most important, prices are sticky in his model, but prices in immediately affected markets are assumed to be flexible in ours. In other markets, however, the dynamics of our model allow for a lagged response of the exchange rate to the relative price as in equation (6), or for a slow change in absorption due to exchange rate overvaluation as in equation (7). The assumption that prices in directly affected markets can change fairly fast is not inconsistent with Japanese data. A large movement of the yen-dollar exchange rate is passed through—albeit incompletely—to yen export or import prices rather quickly.

13.2.3   Data Analysis

Using our economic model, we can distinguish hypothesis 1 from hypotheses 2 and 3 by examining the correlation between the average price level (P) and the ratio of the export price relative to the domestic price in the same product category (P_X/P_D).

In order to remove global price drift, the Japanese "average" price level, including both domestic and export goods as in equation (3), is deflated by the

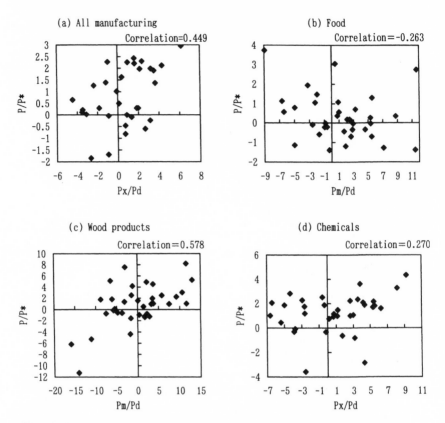

Fig. 13.10   Correlation between price movements and internal relative price
Note: A, all manufacturing; B, food; C, wood products; D, chemicals

U.S. producer price index for the corresponding industry. Thus the corrected P, now really P/P*, measures Japanese inflation relative to U.S. inflation. If P/P* and P_X/P_D are negatively correlated, hypothesis 1 is accepted. If they are positively correlated, we accept hypothesis 2 or 3.

The WPI for the entire manufacturing industry, as well as WPIs for seven two-digit-level industries (food, wood products, chemicals, general machinery, electrical machinery, transport machinery, and precision machinery) are examined. Selection of individual industries is dictated by the comparability of Japanese and U.S. price indexes.

The domestic price data are taken from the BoJ's "domestic wholesale price index." For the external price, the BoJ's "export price index" is used. Because imports are greater than exports for food and wood products, we use instead the BoJ's "import price index" for these industries.

To capture causality between the yen-dollar rate and Japanese prices when deflationary pressure on Japan was greatest, that is, after the Plaza Agreement,

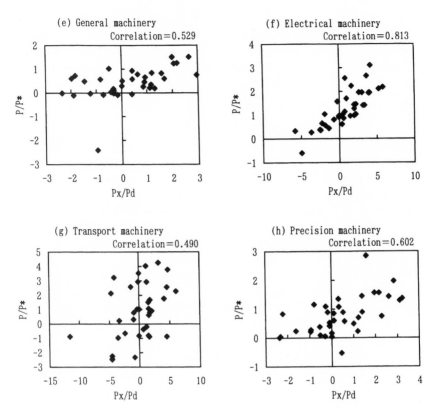

Fig. 13.10   (cont.)

Note: E, general machinery; F, electrical machinery; G, transport machinery; H, precision machinery.

the sample period is 1985:4–1994:4. Observations are based on quarterly rates of price change, from the last month of the previous quarter to that of the current quarter. Figure 13.10 plots P/P^* against P_X/P_D for all these time-series observations and also displays the overall correlation coefficient between the two within each product category.

Figure 13.10A shows the plot for the whole of the Japanese manufacturing industry, while figures 13.10B through 13.10H show those for individual industries. For all industries except food and chemicals, the correlation between P/P^* and P_X/P_D is positive and statistically significant at the 5 percent level (the critical value is ±0.35). In particular, electrical machinery—a key export industry of Japan—carries a high positive correlation coefficient of 0.813. For all of manufacturing together, this correlation is 0.449 and statistically significant.

These results confirm the existence of positive correlation between the Japanese price level and its internal relative price (with a few exceptions)—and thus support hypotheses 2 and 3. In the decade before 1995, a large part of Japanese price instability originated in externally exposed prices, and major inflations and deflations rarely began with domestic price changes. Thus we can safely reject hypothesis 1.

13.2.4   Distinguishing Hypothesis 2 from Hypothesis 3: The Monetary Reaction of the Bank of Japan

But is the true causation from anticipated domestic prices (as determined by future fundamentals such as monetary policy) to the exchange rate, as under hypothesis 2, or from the exchange rate to future prices, as under hypothesis 3? In other words, is the yen-dollar rate an "anticipatory" variable or a "forcing" one for determining macroeconomic conditions in Japan?

To answer this question, we focus on the monetary policy of the BoJ as the key fundamental variable. While there are other fundamentals (fiscal policy, current account balance, product innovation, demand shift, etc.), it is not unreasonable to single out the BoJ's monetary policy because (i) it is widely recognized that monetary policy is one of the most important determinants of the exchange rate and aggregate demand, (ii) monetary policy is more flexibly implemented than fiscal policy, and (iii) changes in the monetary stance of the BoJ can be measured—albeit imperfectly.

Monetary policy is part of α (the shift parameter in the aggregate demand function) represented in equation (5) above. If the exchange rate moves in anticipation of a future change in monetary policy, the subsequent change in monetary policy must be consistent with the initial exchange rate movement. For example, if the market expects a monetary tightening by the BoJ and therefore appreciates the yen, and assuming that expectations are on average correct, we should see an actual tightening. When the policy is later implemented, interest rates will rise and prices will fall. These reinforce and validate the initial exchange rate appreciation.

In contrast, if the exchange rate is an exogenous shock that truly causes undesirable price variation, the subsequent monetary policy should tend to offset the exchange rate impact on the macroeconomy. In this case, the exchange rate is the cause and monetary policy the effect.

We propose to distinguish hypothesis 2 from hypothesis 3 by observing the typical monetary policy reaction immediately after a large change in the yen-dollar exchange rate. More specifically, we will first investigate informally the policy intentions of the BoJ when it changes the official discount rate. Second, we will statistically estimate the monetary reaction function of the BoJ to see whether its policy tends to validate or offset the yen's preceding movement.

The existing literature (Yoshino and Yoshimura 1995) shows that the BoJ's principal policy instrument is the manipulation of short-term interest rates, changes in the official discount rate, and guidance of the call money rate, rather

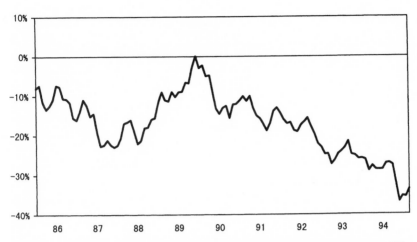

Fig. 13.11   Real exchange rate (deviation of yen-dollar rate from tradable PPP)

than high-powered money. Nor, according to Takatoshi Ito (1992, 132), did the BoJ aim in practice to control systematically any monetary aggregate as an intermediate target—even the "official" target of growth in M2 + CD. Our study also accepts that changes in short-term interest rates are the best representation of the BoJ's policy intentions and examines their correlation with the exchange rate.

Figure 13.7 plots the actual and PPP yen-dollar exchange rates since 1975, while figure 13.11 displays the divergence between these two exchange rates since October 1985. The decade 1985–94 can be divided into three distinct periods: the first period, beginning in the spring of 1985, in which the yen appreciated sharply above PPP and continued appreciating into 1988; the second period of moderate yen depreciation from 1989 to a brief return to PPP by mid-1990; and the third period of prolonged yen appreciation from 1990 through 1994, taking the yen even further above PPP—until the joint interventions of May–August 1995 finally reversed this trend (fig. 13.3).

Over the same decade, the BoJ's policy toward the discount rate and the call rate was correlated with these large movements in the yen-dollar exchange rate. Between 1986 and 1995, the discount rate was changed 19 times. The call rate was also guided to trace the changes in the discount rate—as can be seen in figure 13.12. The discount rate was lowered in steps from 1986 to early 1987 then kept constant at a low level until mid-1989 (it was maintained at 2.5 percent for 27 months), followed by rapid increases up to the summer of 1990. After that, a long period of discount rate reduction ensued.

Comparing figures 13.11 and 13.12, yen appreciation and the falling discount rate roughly coincide, as do yen depreciation and the rising discount rate. Moreover, turning points in the real exchange rate precede those in short-term

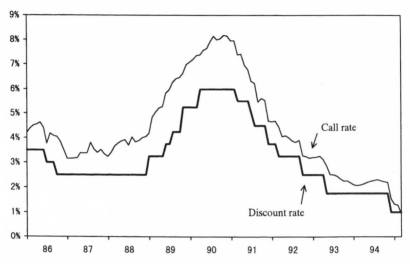

Fig. 13.12   Discount rate and call rate

interest rates by a few months to a year. We conclude from these figures that, since the Plaza Agreement, the BoJ conducted interest rate policy to offset, rather than validate, movements in the yen-dollar rate. It has attempted to slow down or reverse sharp movements in the yen, and to alleviate the deflationary impact of yen appreciation on the macroeconomy.

The BoJ's concern over exchange rate shocks is also documented by its official statements when the discount rate was changed—see table 13.1. During the period of yen appreciation in 1986–87, the BoJ sought to counter the high yen and weak domestic business conditions. Increased interest rates in 1989–90 were designed to prevent inflation caused by the now lower yen. (This monetary tightening in the late 1980s was also intended to end the domestic asset bubble, which was the delayed consequence of the BoJ's trying to dampen the yen's appreciation in the mid-1980s and the first *endaka fukyo;* Ueda 1992.) Subsequently, discount rate reductions, which took the entire interest rate structure to historically low levels by 1994, were designed to stimulate a domestic economy reeling from the bursting of the asset bubble and the second *endaka fukyo.*

We conclude that the BoJ regards the movement of the yen-dollar rate as an exogenous shock to the Japanese economy and reacts to stop its trend or to ameliorate its more extreme effects—but without succeeding in preventing them altogether. These results support hypothesis 3: that yen appreciation was a forcing variable in causing price deflation in Japan. Indeed, it is hard to believe hypothesis 2: that the BoJ intended to allow the WPI to fall from 1985 to 1995 (fig. 13.2) and that the exchange rate was just anticipating this deflationary policy.

Table 13.1   **Changes in the Discount Rate**

Date	New Rate (%)	Reason(s) for Change
30 Jan 1986	4.50	To stimulate domestic demand
7 Mar 1986	4	To counter yen appreciation, stimulate domestic economy
19 Apr 1986	3.50	To counter yen appreciation, participate in global monetary coordination
1 Nov 1986	3	To counter yen appreciation, stimulate domestic economy
21 Feb 1987	2.50	To counter yen appreciation, stimulate domestic economy
31 May 1989	3.25	To check inflation in advance
11 Oct 1989	3.75	To check inflation caused by yen depreciation in advance
25 Dec 1989	4.25	To check inflation in advance
20 Mar 1990	5.25	To check inflation in advance, calm financial and security markets
30 Aug 1990	6	To check inflation in advance
1 July 1991	5.50	To stimulate domestic economy
14 Nov 1991	5	To prevent recession
31 Dec 1991	4.50	To stimulate domestic economy
1 Apr 1992	3.75	To stimulate domestic economy
27 July 1992	3.25	To stimulate domestic economy
4 Feb 1993	2.50	To stimulate domestic economy
21 Sept 1993	1.75	To stimulate domestic economy
14 Apr 1995	1	To stimulate domestic economy, counter yen appreciation
8 Sept 1995	0.50	To stimulate domestic economy, promote yen depreciation and stock market recovery

Source: Japan Economic Journal (various issues).

13.2.5   Estimating the Bank of Japan's Reaction Function

But to confirm our intuition, we need a more precise statistical technique for showing how the BoJ reacts to, and tries to offset, what it regards as exogenous shocks in the yen-dollar rate. We shall directly estimate the policy reaction function of the BoJ to test whether it guides short-term interest rates to offset exchange rate movements.

The policy reaction function, estimated by Yoshino and Yoshimura (1995), shows that the BoJ responded *both* to domestic business conditions and to the exchange rate. Ueda (1992, 1995) even accuses the BoJ of overreacting to the current account surpluses and yen appreciations of the early 1970s and the mid-1980s by creating the excessive domestic liquidity that ignited domestic inflation and the asset bubble.

Let us estimate the BoJ's policy reaction function with a slightly different specification than Yoshino and Yoshimura's. Let the monetary policy reaction function be

(8) $i_t^s = \beta_0 + \beta_1 i_{t-1}^s + \beta_2 \pi_{t-1} + \beta_3 y_{t-1} + \beta_4 s_{t-1} + \eta_t,$

where i^s is the call rate, π is the inflation rate, y is the output gap, s is the real exchange rate, and η is the error term. The output gap is the deviation of the index of industrial production from its log-linear trend. The real exchange rate is measured as the deviation of the actual exchange rate from PPP—as shown in figure 13.11. An increase in s indicates yen depreciation against the dollar, and vice versa.

Monthly data are used, and all explanatory variables are lagged one month in equation (8). Alternatively, if two-month lags are taken for the explanatory variables (except the lagged call rate itself), we have

$$(9) \qquad i_t^s = \delta_0 + \delta_1 i_{t-1}^s + \delta_2 \pi_{t-2} + \delta_3 y_{t-2} + \delta_4 s_{t-2} + v_t.$$

The explanatory variables are lagged because of the delays in recognition and action associated with interest rate policy. These lags reflect the time required for the BoJ to collect the data needed to initiate an action, and they are perhaps a month or two in duration. Although inflation and business statistics are officially announced after two months or so, the BoJ usually has earlier access to preliminary data. As to the real exchange rate, the nominal exchange rate is known without delay, but the prices with which to deflate it also come with lags. Technically, these lags also enable us to lessen the simultaneous equation bias in the estimation of any policy reaction function.

For price data, the WPI and the CPI, up to $t - 1$ or $t - 2$, are used as alternatives. We posit that the BoJ does not react to a temporary blip but does react to a sustained movement in the price level. How many months constitute a "sustained" period cannot be determined a priori. Experimentation showed that monthly price variation contains too much noise, while a twelve-month movement would be too long because the BoJ reacts sooner. Somewhat arbitrarily, we choose the cumulative change over either three-month or six-month intervals to be the "sustained" price movement to which the BoJ reacts. For example, in equation (8), π_{t-1} is the cumulative price change from four months before to one month before, or from seven months before to one month before. Tables 13.2 and 13.3 report the results of estimating equations (8) and (9), respectively, by the method of ordinary least squares.

In table 13.2, where the explanatory variables are lagged one month, parameters in all specifications carry the correct signs (they should all be positive) regardless of whether the WPI or CPI is used. In response to inflation, a business boom, or yen depreciation, the BoJ raises the short-term interest rate—and vice versa. Although the coefficients of the inflation indexes are statistically insignificant at the 5 percent level, the output coefficient is generally significant—except under specifications 1 and 2 where the WPI, but not the real exchange rate, is included.

The outstanding feature of table 13.2 is that the real exchange rate induces a positive and significant policy reaction in all cases. The importance of the real exchange rate is also revealed in Durbin's h statistics. Without inclusion of the real exchange rate, h is significant at the 5 percent level (exceeding 1.96) and points to the possibility of misspecification or a missing variable. The adjusted R^2 also improves slightly when the real exchange rate is included.

Table 13.2   Policy Reaction Function of the Bank of Japan: Explanatory Variables Lagged One Month

Variable	Using WPI Inflation				Using CPI Inflation			
	(1)	(2)	(3)	(4)	(5)	(6)	(7)	(8)
Constant	0.00086	0.00075	0.00954	0.00937	0.00134	0.00131	0.00997	0.00997
	[0.86]	[0.74]	[3.94]	[3.93]	[1.40]	[1.37]	[4.51]	[4.50]
Call rate (−1)	0.997	0.981	0.848	0.854	0.955	0.950	0.835	0.830
	[42.9]	[41.2]	[21.6]	[21.7]	[47.3]	[46.1]	[24.6]	[24.4]
Inflation (−1) 3-month moving average	0.0579		0.0230		0.0605		0.0520	
	[1.91]		[0.77]		[1.61]		[1.49]	
Inflation (−1) 6-month moving average		0.0387		0.0110		0.0705		0.0611
		[1.95]		[1.03]		[1.56]		[1.45]
Output gap (−1)	0.0081	0.0049	0.0319	0.0290	0.0156	0.1350	0.0345	0.0328
	[1.03]	[0.54]	[3.32]	[2.79]	[2.53]	[2.05]	[4.75]	[4.30]
Real exchange rate (−1)			0.0199	0.0198			0.0206	0.0207
			[3.90]	[3.95]			[4.27]	[4.27]
$\bar{R}^2$	.976	.976	.978	.978	.975	.975	.979	.979
S.E.	0.00297	0.00297	0.00280	0.00279	0.00298	0.00299	0.00278	0.00278
h	1.872	1.878	1.546	1.490	2.249	2.116	1.600	1.426

Note: Dependent variable is call rate. Sample period is October 1985 to July 1995 ($n = 118$). Numbers in brackets are t-statistics.

A possible reason for the insignificance of the inflation indexes in table 13.2 is that the real exchange rate already provides the information needed to forecast future price movements. Thus the actual (lagged) price data become superfluous. This interpretation is consistent with hypothesis 3, which states that exchange rate shocks are the primary cause of (future) domestic inflation.

Table 13.3 extends the lags on the explanatory variables (except on the call rate itself) to two months as in equation (9). Here, all parameters also carry the correct signs—except for the output gap in specification 2, which is insignificant. Inflation now seems to be more significant. However, in the BoJ's reaction function, the main story again is the importance of the yen-dollar rate's deviations from PPP. Not only is the real exchange rate highly significant when measured by its t-statistics, but the adjusted R^2 and Durbin's h both improve—and the effects of the output gap become more positive—when the exchange rate is included.

Like the results found by Yoshino and Yoshimura (1995) and Ueda (1992, 1995), our results for the 1985–94 period also show that the BoJ reacts systematically to the exchange rate, as well as to domestic output and inflation. In the short run, movements in the yen-dollar rate are not accommodated but instead are partially counteracted.

How then does our statistical study differ from these earlier ones? We consider these reactions of the BoJ *together with* with our finding of positive correlation between P and P_X/P_D. Together, these confirm the validity of our hypothesis 3.

13.3   Conclusion

The second part of this paper presented a series of new causality tests for price movements and exchange rate fluctuations based on Japanese monetary and price data since the Plaza Agreement. We discovered that exchange rate movements precede changes in relative national price levels, and that any initial movement of the exchange rate not only anticipates the BoJ's long-run policy but actually causes it. True, in the short run, the BoJ reacts by adjusting its call money rate to resist these exchange rate movements. But this resistance was insufficient to prevent a long-term downward trend in Japanese prices relative to those in the United States, with a parallel downward drift in the PPP value of the yen-dollar exchange rate, at least through 1995.

We showed that, on net balance, flexibility in the yen-dollar exchange rate should not be considered an automatic stabilizer. Quite the contrary. The erratically appreciating yen has been an independent (or exogenous) source of disturbance—and imposed undue deflation on the Japanese economy in the past 10 years.

The first part of the paper offered an explanation of why the yen rose in such a puzzling fashion since 1971—despite some resistance from the BoJ in the short run, particularly in the past decade. Mercantile pressure from the United

Table 13.3   Policy Reaction Function of the Bank of Japan: Explanatory Variables Lagged Two Months (except call rate)

	Using WPI Inflation				Using CPI Inflation			
	(1)	(2)	(3)	(4)	(5)	(6)	(7)	(8)
Constant	0.00044	0.00040	0.00867	0.00887	0.00114	0.00104	0.0102	0.00991
	[0.44]	[0.40]	[3.49]	[3.60]	[1.17]	[1.08]	[4.36]	[4.30]
Call rate (−1)	0.989	0.991	0.863	0.862	0.960	0.948	0.827	0.820
	[43.47]	[42.20]	[21.06]	[21.03]	[46.25]	[45.15]	[22.37]	[22.41]
Inflation (−2) 3-month moving average	0.0812		0.0546		0.0634		0.0638	
	[2.75]		[1.88]		[1.67]		[1.80]	
Inflation (−2) 6-month moving average		0.0485		0.0342		0.117		0.112
		[2.51]		[1.83]		[2.61]		[2.66]
Output gap (−2)	0.0017	−0.0009	0.0261	0.0245	0.0130	0.0087	0.0357	0.0312
	[0.22]	[−0.097]	[2.60]	[2.28]	[2.07]	[1.33]	[4.48]	[3.84]
Real exchange rate (−2)			0.0182	0.0188			0.0207	0.0203
			[3.58]	[3.74]			[4.20]	[4.18]
$\bar{R}^2$	.976	.976	.978	.978	.975	.976	.978	.979
S.E.	0.00295	0.00297	0.00281	0.00281	0.00301	0.00296	0.00282	0.00277
h	1.932	1.975	1.789	1.818	2.238	2.364	1.885	1.954

Note: Dependent variable is call rate. Sample period is October 1985 to July 1995 ($n = 118$). Numbers in brackets are t-statistics.

States, consisting of commercial pressure from individual American companies affected by Japanese competitors and academic pressure to devalue the dollar (appreciate the yen) to "correct" American trade deficits, created a climate where the yen would increase episodically. Caught up in this syndrome at least up through early 1995, the Japanese authorities were too inhibited by this mercantile pressure, that is, by threats of trade war, to act—or be able to act—decisively to stop the yen's appreciation. And thus Japan suffered *endaka fukyo*.

Only the American government's sudden relaxation of mercantile pressure in spring and summer 1995, the suspension of trade hostilities combined with joint action by the Fed and BoJ to drive the yen back down that signaled to the markets that the American government would now tolerate a lower value for the yen, allowed the yen to depreciate and the Japanese economy to recover somewhat in 1996. And this relaxation of commercial pressure (no new trade disputes) has continued through 1998. (The downturn in Japan's economy in 1997–98 was triggered by the April 1997 tax increase.) But whether this remission from the syndrome of the ever-higher yen is temporary or permanent remains to be seen.

References

Baldwin, Robert E. 1988. *Trade policy in a changing world economy.* Chicago: University of Chicago Press.

Bergsten, C. Fred, and Marcus Noland. 1993. *Reconcilable differences: United States–Japan economic conflict.* Washington, D.C.: Institute for International Economics, June.

Cline, William R. 1995. *Predicting external imbalances for the United States and Japan.* Policy Analyses in International Economics, no. 41. Washington, D.C.: Institute for International Economics, September.

Dornbusch, Rudiger. 1988. *Exchange rates and inflation.* Cambridge, Mass.: MIT Press.

Frenkel, Jacob. 1981. The collapse of purchasing power parity during the 1970s. *European Economic Review* 16:145–65.

Helkie, William L., and Peter Hooper. 1988. An empirical analysis of the external deficit, 1980–86. In *External deficits and the dollar: The pit and the pendulum,* ed. R. Bryant, G. Holtham, and P. Hooper. Washington, D.C.: Brookings Institution.

International Monetary Fund (IMF). 1997. *International financial statistics.* Washington, D.C.: International Monetary Fund, March. CD-ROM.

Ito, Takatoshi. 1992. *The Japanese economy.* Cambridge, Mass.: MIT Press.

Itoh, Motoshige (with the Ministry of International Trade and Industry). 1994. *Misperceptions of the trade surplus: What is wrong with the Japanese economy?* (in Japanese). Tokyo: Toyo Keizai Shinposha.

Kawai, Masahiro. 1994. *International finance* (in Japanese). Tokyo: Tokyo University Press.

Komiya, Ryutaro. 1994. *Economics of trade surpluses and deficits, absurdity of Japan-U.S. friction* (in Japanese). Tokyo: Toyo Keizai Shinposha.

Krueger, Anne. 1995. *American trade policy: A tragedy in the making.* Washington, D.C.: AEI Press.
Marston, Richard. 1991. Pricing behavior in Japanese and U.S. manufacturing. In *Trade with Japan: Has the door opened wider?* ed. P. Krugman. Chicago: University of Chicago Press.
McKinnon, Ronald I. 1996. *The rules of the game: International money and exchange rates.* Cambridge, Mass.: MIT Press.
McKinnon, Ronald I., and Kenichi Ohno. 1997. *Dollar and yen: Resolving economic conflict between the United States and Japan.* Cambridge, Mass.: MIT Press.
Miyagawa, Tsutomu, and Joji Tokui. 1994. *Economics of yen appreciation: Changing international competitiveness and the problem of current account surplus* (in Japanese). Tokyo: Toyo Keizai Shinposha.
Murakami, Yasusuke. 1992. *Anti-classical political economy* (in Japanese), 2 vols. Tokyo: Chuo Koronsha.
Ohno, Kenichi. 1990. Estimating yen/dollar and mark/dollar purchasing power parities. *IMF Staff Papers* 37:700–25.
Organization for Economic Cooperation and Development. 1995. *Japan.* OECD Economic Surveys. Paris: Organization for Economic Cooperation and Development.
Tyson, Laura D'Andrea. 1992. *Who's bashing whom? Trade conflict in high technology industries.* Washington, D.C.: Institute for International Economics, November.
Ueda, Kazuo. 1992. *Monetary policy under balance-of-payments disequilibrium* (in Japanese). Tokyo: Toyo Keizai Shinposha.
———. 1995. Japanese monetary policy: Rules or discretion? Part II. Paper presented at Bank of Japan's seventh international conference, Tokyo, 26–27 October.
Yoshino, Naoyuki, and Masaharu Yoshimura. 1995. The exogeneity test of monetary policy: Instrumental targets and money supply (in Japanese). Tokyo: Bank of Japan, Monetary Research Institute.

Comment   Kazuo Ueda

The paper addresses basically two issues: long-run movements in the yen and the Japanese current account, on one hand, and the current *endaka fukyo* (recession as a result of yen appreciation) on the other. I will concentrate on McKinnon, Ohno, and Shirono's analysis of the first issue in the following. I believe that the explanation of the 1991–93 recession requires a more complete treatment of the bad loan problem than do the authors.

The basic logic of the paper runs as follows: The Japanese current account has been mainly determined by long-run trends in U.S.-Japanese savings but has been largely independent of real exchange rate movements. In periods of large Japanese current account surpluses the United States adopted a policy of "talking down" the dollar. This has had strong effects on the yen-dollar rate, but not on the Japanese current account. The appreciation of the yen, after the fact, has been validated by the tight monetary policy of the Bank of Japan.

Kazuo Ueda is a member of the policy board of the Bank of Japan.

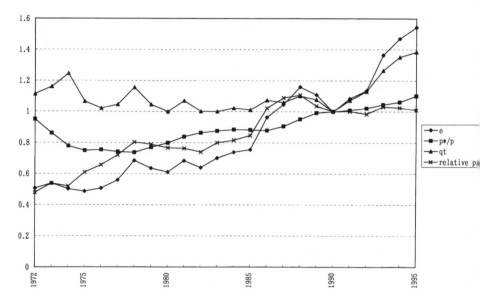

Fig. 13C.1   Determinants of yen movements

I agree with some of these assertions, but not with all of them. Here is why. Let us note the convenient identity:

$$e = (p^*/p)(q_T)[(p_T^*/p^*)/(p_T/p)],$$

where e, p, p_T, and q_T are the nominal effective yen, CPI, export unit value, and real effective yen, respectively, measured in export unit value. Asterisks indicate weighted averages of foreign variables, with the weights being the same as those used in the calculation of the effective exchange rates. Simply put, the equation decomposes the movements in yen into monetary factors, real yen in terms of traded goods, and the Balassa-Samuelson effect.

Figure 13C.1 shows the decomposition.[1] It reveals a number of interesting things about the yen during the past two decades. First, the most important determinant of the yen appreciation has been the Balassa-Samuelson effect. Between 1972 and 1990, the yen appreciated by 68.5 percent (in log difference terms), of which only 5.5 percent is explained by monetary factors, −11 percent by movements in real yen, and 74 percent by the Balassa-Samuelson term. Figure 13C.2 shows that the majority of the Balassa-Samuelson effect took

1. The nominal and real effective rates are from the IMF's *International Financial Statistics*, with some of the 1995 data being rough estimates by myself. The real rate using the CPI does not exist before 1977. For 1972–77, it was identified with the bilateral U.S.-Japan real rate. The equation holds as an identity in this estimation because the foreign relative price between traded and nontraded goods has been calculated from the values of other variables using the equation.

Fig. 13C.2   Traded versus nontraded goods price movements

place in Japan. Hence, the major determinant of the yen appreciation up to 1990 was the productivity improvement in the Japanese traded goods industries. There could have been instances when the "talking down the dollar" policy of the United States worked, but this does not seem to have been the major reason for the yen appreciation.

Interestingly, the real effective rate was almost constant between 1972 and 1990. Hence, I agree with the authors that exchange rate movements were not a major determinant of the long-run trend in the current account.

Since 1990, the nominal effective yen has appreciated by 43 percent, of which 32 percent is explained by the appreciation of the real effective rate. The contribution of other factors is small. Thus the appreciation of the yen since 1990 may have been different in nature than that in previous periods. Therefore, I disagree with the paper's presumption that the appreciation since 1990 has been created by the same mechanism as before.

Another strong assertion of the paper is that in most cases the appreciation of the yen was "supported" by subsequent monetary tightening by the Bank of Japan. This is hard to agree with. First, as shown above, the relative monetary policy movements as reflected in relative CPI movements have not been a major determinant of the yen.

Second, as I have argued elsewhere (Ueda 1996), the Bank of Japan has consistently responded with monetary expansion to strong appreciation of the yen. Figure 13C.3 shows periods of loose monetary policy, identified by the

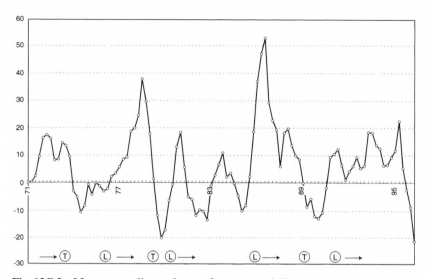

Fig. 13C.3   Monetary policy and rate of yen appreciation
Note: Circled *L*s with rightward arrows indicate periods of loose monetary policy. Circled *T*s indicate the start of periods of tight monetary policy.

Bank of Japan's discount rate changes (indicated by circled *L*'s and rightward arrows; a circled *T* indicates the start of a period of tight monetary policy). All four periods of monetary expansion during the past 25 years coincided with yen appreciation (upward movements in the graph). It is rather difficult to find a causal link between yen appreciation and "tight" monetary policy.

Reference

Ueda, K. 1996. Japanese monetary policy: Rules or discretion, Part II. IMES Discussion Paper no. 96-E-16. Tokyo: Bank of Japan.

14 Testing for the Fundamental Determinants of the Long-Run Real Exchange Rate: The Case of Taiwan

Hsiu-Ling Wu

14.1 Introduction

The real exchange rate between two countries' currencies has been recognized as a key measure of the prices of foreign goods relative to domestic goods in those countries. Since the real exchange rate reveals the relative competitiveness of exported goods from the two economies, it is desirable to characterize the behavior of the real exchange rate and test for its fundamental determinants.

The behavior of the real exchange rate is intimately related to the behavior of deviations from purchasing power parity (PPP). According to PPP theory, nominal exchange rates adjust to offset changes in relative prices, so the real exchange rate should remain at a constant value. However, there is widespread agreement that substantial deviations from PPP have occurred since the abandonment of the Bretton Woods system.[1] That is, there is no equilibrium value to which the real exchange rate tends to return. In empirical tests, many authors indeed cannot reject the hypothesis that real exchange rates follow a random walk process (see, e.g., Frenkel 1981; Hakkio 1986; Mark 1990). Thus changes in the real exchange rate are considered permanent. Some kinds of real disturbances are believed to upset the relationship between the nominal exchange

Hsiu-Ling Wu is an associate research fellow of the Chung-Hua Institution for Economic Research.

The author thanks Yueh-Fang Ho for research assistance and Nancy Zigmund for editorial improvements.

1. There are two versions of PPP theory, absolute PPP and relative PPP. Absolute PPP theory, which relies on the law of one price, states that the general level of prices, when converted to a common currency, will be the same in every country ($P = EP^*$). Absolute PPP holds only if two price levels are computed in the same way as weighted tradable prices in a competitive world market with no transportation costs or trade barriers. Therefore, absolute PPP can hardly be expected to hold in the real world. Relative PPP theory says that the rate of change in the nominal exchange rate is equal to the domestic inflation rate minus the foreign inflation rate. The validity of relative PPP is often tested by implementing the regression analysis of $\ln P = \ln E + \ln P^* + e$.

rate and relative price levels as postulated by PPP so that the behavior of real exchange rates is found to be inconsistent with PPP.

To assess the fundamental factors determining the behavior of the real exchange rate, a number of studies have considered productivity differentials between the nontraded and traded sectors of economies as a prime cause of permanent changes in the real exchange rate. According to Balassa (1964), if productivity in the domestic traded goods sector grows more rapidly than productivity in the nontraded goods sector, under the assumption of equalization in wages across sectors, the relative price between traded and nontraded goods has to fall. Since the prices of traded goods are equalized between countries through international arbitrage, the general price level will rise at home. It follows that the real exchange rate will appreciate. Hsieh's (1982) work uses time-series data for Germany and Japan versus their respective major trading partners to study the relationship between movements in real exchange rates and productivity growth differentials in the traded and nontraded sectors. His study has provided strong evidence supporting the idea that productivity differentials are useful in explaining the movements in real exchange rates.

Marston (1987) investigated the effects of productivity growth differentials between the United States and Japan on alternative real exchange rates between the yen and dollar. Since real exchange rates based on alternative price series can diverge when there are shifts in supply factors within a country, Marston considered different expressions of real exchange rates to evaluate the relative competitiveness of the two economies. For instance, from 1973 to 1983 the yen appreciated in terms of the GDP deflator by 0.3 percent, while the real exchange rate expressed in terms of the GDP deflator for traded goods alone depreciated 26.7 percent. This result suggests that real exchange rates based on different price indexes may lead to very different conclusions. Thus it is desirable to find out what can account for the divergence between two real exchange rate series. According to Marston, the differential movement between any two real exchange rates results from relative unit labor cost changes in traded sectors at home and in the foreign country and unit labor cost changes in traded sectors of each country relative to the nontraded sectors. Since sectoral wage trends are similar in the United States and Japan, it is relative productivity movements in traded and nontraded sectors that explain the difference of movements in real exchange rates.

In the real world, it is observed that during the 1973–1983 period, productivity growth in the Japanese traded sector was 73.2 percent greater than in the nontraded sector, and productivity in the U.S. traded sector grew only 13.2 percent faster than in its nontraded sector. The markedly higher productivity growth differential together with the lack of any substantial decline in nominal wages in the United States, therefore, reduced the relative competitiveness of U.S. exports.

The empirical purpose of this article is to investigate the factors that determine long-run movements of the real exchange rate of the New Taiwan (NT) dollar against the U.S. dollar. Recent developments in time-series analysis have provided new ways of analyzing the long-run relationships for our purpose. In particular, the theory of cointegration provides a means of establishing whether a long-run relationship exists between economic variables. Since testing for cointegration among economic variables seems to have become a standard method of assessing the empirical support for the equilibrium of economic behavior, we wish to test the behavior of the real exchange rate by applying the principle of cointegration. This paper is not limited to a test of the theory of PPP. It will also test for the role of the fundamental factor—productivity— that has been identified in several papers as determining movements in real exchange rates.

The organization of the article is as follows. In section 14.2 I give an introduction to the evolution of exchange rate management in Taiwan. In section 14.3 the movements of real exchange rates, nominal exchange rates, and relative price levels are briefly discussed. In section 14.4 analysis using cointegration approaches is discussed. Section 14.5 tests for the long-run properties of real exchange rate movements. In section 14.6 I evaluate the effects of changes in nominal exchange rates and in foreign and domestic price levels on the real exchange rate. In section 14.7 I look into the relationship between real exchange rate change and relative productivity growth of traded and nontraded sectors. Section 14.8 summarizes the overall findings of the paper.

14.2 The Evolution of Exchange Rate Management in Taiwan

Before January 1979, the NT dollar was tied to the U.S. dollar. This was primarily because the United States was Taiwan's most important trading partner and most Taiwanese international contracts were denominated in U.S. dollars. The pegging system helped reduce exporters' uncertainties in international trade. However, the system had some drawbacks. It was commonly recognized that the domestic economy would become more vulnerable to external disturbances. For instance, Taiwanese exports would be less competitive in the U.S. market as the U.S. dollar soared against other currencies.

With the promulgation of the revised Foreign Exchange Regulation, a foreign exchange market was established on 1 February 1979, and a managed floating rate system was introduced in Taiwan. When the new exchange rate system was adopted, the exchange rate of the NT dollar against the U.S. dollar was at first fixed by an ad hoc committee comprising five representatives from five appointed banks[2] and one representative from the central bank. From

---

2. They are the Bank of Taiwan, the International Commercial Bank of China, the First Commercial Bank of Taiwan, the Chang-Hwa Commercial Bank of Taiwan, and the Hwa-nan Commercial Bank.

March 1980, the central bank delegated the other members of the committee to fix the daily spot and forward exchange rates. The ad hoc committee took into account the demand and supply of foreign exchange as well as the real effective exchange rate index of the NT dollar when fixing the spot rate of the NT dollar against the U.S. dollar.[3]

After trial and error, the mechanism for exchange rate determination evolved in 1982 into a form that was based on the weighted average rate of interbank transactions in U.S. dollars on the previous business day.[4] Daily fluctuations of the interbank rate have only been allowed to float within a 2.25 percent range from the weighted average rates on all interbank currency exchange transactions, which were established daily by the five representatives from the ad hoc committee. To maintain an orderly foreign exchange market, the central bank also intervened on many occasions by buying and selling the U.S. dollar in the interbank market.

As was widely noticed, because of the huge trade surplus and the considerable influx of private short-term capital, the supply of foreign exchange far exceeded the demand in Taiwan during the mid-1980s. As a result, the exchange rate of the NT dollar against the U.S. dollar appreciated steadily from 1986 to 1989. The NT dollar appreciated against the U.S. dollar by 12.25 percent over 1986, 24.34 percent over 1987, 1.35 percent over 1988, and 7.13 percent over 1989. During this period, the central bank's intervention in the foreign exchange rate involved direct buying and selling of foreign exchange in the interbank market to stabilize wide fluctuations in the value of the NT dollar that otherwise have would occurred, since officials at the central bank believe that the exchange rate should be adjusted in a smooth way rather than in substantial one-shot appreciations. This intervention, however, has two additional effects. First, it raises the level of foreign exchange reserves. Second, it generates an expansionary effect on the local money supply. Hence, the central bank has introduced a series of measures to liberalize foreign exchange controls since 1986 to address the external disequilibrium. It has also applied other policies, such as increasing reserve requirements for savings deposits and issuing bonds and treasury bills to banks to limit credit expansion.

In addition to liberalizing Taiwanese capital controls, the central bank also changed the foreign exchange rate trading system in 1989 to accelerate economic liberalization and internationalization in Taiwan. The bank abolished the former system, which used the weighted average rate of interbank transac-

3. E.g., the devaluation of the NT dollar against the U.S. dollar by 4.63 percent in August 1981 was to make up for the loss of competitiveness resulting from real effective overvaluation since the U.S. dollar was strengthening against other currencies.

4. Taiwan has mechanisms for managing exchange rates in both the interbank and customer-bank foreign exchange markets. The interbank market consists of foreign exchange transactions between banks. Customer-bank transactions refer to individuals changing currency with a designated foreign exchange bank. It is the interbank market that has played a pivotal role in setting exchange rates.

tions as the central rate on the next business day and had set limits on daily fluctuations. According to the central bank, after some additional modifications are made, the structure of the foreign exchange market in Taiwan will be more complete and concrete, since its operating methods will be similar to those prevailing in developed countries. This should make the exchange rate for the NT dollar more flexible, and it will reflect its actual value in the market.

14.3   The Movements of the Real Exchange Rate

Exchange rate changes can be measured in nominal or real terms. A measure in real terms against one currency provides a better measure of relative competitiveness than do measures in nominal terms. Consider the real exchange rate (R) defined in terms of nominal exchange rate (E) adjusted for relative price levels (P^*/P), that is, $R = EP^*/P$. In our case, the nominal exchange rate is defined as the NT dollar price of U.S.$1, so that an increase in E indicates a depreciation of the NT dollar; the asterisk denotes the foreign (U.S.) economy. A rise in real exchange rate (i.e., a real depreciation of the NT dollar) corresponds to a fall in the purchasing power of domestic currency for foreign products. This change in relative purchasing power occurs because the NT dollar prices of U.S. products rise relative to those of Taiwanese products.

Figure 14.1 shows the fluctuations of the nominal exchange rate, relative price level, and real exchange rate between 1985 and 1995. The nominal exchange rate appreciated by 34.35 percent from 1985 to 1989. This was matched by a 22.16 percent real appreciation during the same period. Thus it seems that both nominal exchange rate appreciation and inflation differentials between domestic and foreign countries were responsible for changes in real exchange rates, though the real exchange rate movements were mainly caused by the nominal appreciation of the NT dollar during the 1985–89 period. The upward movements of the relative price level offset some effects of the nominal appreciation of the NT dollar against the U.S. dollar, so that the magnitude of real appreciation was smaller than that of the nominal exchange rates.

As shown in figure 14.1, the nominal exchange rate started to fluctuate in a more stable range between NT$27.5/U.S.$1 and NT$25.5/U.S.$1 since 1989. During the same period, fluctuations of the real exchange rate were also not as volatile as in the 1985–89 period. However, during the period 1989–95, it appeared that real exchange rate movements were dominated more by inflation differentials between Taiwan and the United States than by nominal exchange rate changes. Hence, in the following sections I will evaluate aspects of real exchange rate behavior by analyzing (1) the extent to which real exchange rates revert, in the long run, to PPP, (2) the persistent effect of a nominal exchange rate and domestic and foreign price level adjustment on the real exchange rate, and (3) the equilibrium relationship between the real exchange rate and differentials of productivity growth between traded and nontraded goods.

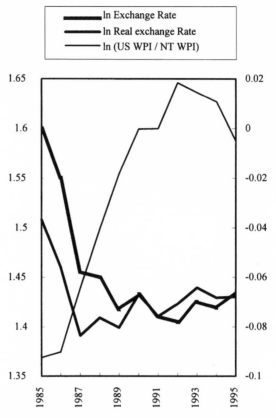

Fig. 14.1 Nominal exchange rate, real exchange rate, and relative price level between U.S. and NT dollars

14.4 Vector Autoregressive Modeling and the Cointegration Approach

This section discusses the cointegration approach, which provides not only an estimation methodology but also explicit procedures for testing a long-run relationship among variables that is suggested by economic theory.

According to the Granger representation theorem, if a $p \times 1$ vector, X_t, generated by $(1 - L)X_t = d + c(L)e_t$, is cointegrated, then there exists a vector autoregression (VAR), an error correction, as well as a moving average representation of X_t (see Engle and Granger 1987). A set of variables, X_t, that is cointegrated indicates the existence of long-run equilibrium relationships among economic variables. That is, though each series may be nonstationary, there may exist stationary linear combinations of the variables. The basic idea is that individual economic time-series variables wander considerably, but certain linear combinations of the series do not move too far apart from each other. In economic terms, there is a long-run relationship among the variables.

The most common test for cointegration is the two-step procedure of Engle and Granger (1987), which performs the tests in a univariate setup. The first step is to fit the cointegrating regression, which is the ordinary least squares estimation of the static model. Second, a unit root test is conducted on the estimated residuals. To test for cointegration is just to test for the presence of a unit root in the residuals of the cointegrating regression. If the null of a unit root is rejected, then the null of no cointegration is also rejected. However, the long-run parameter of the cointegrating vector estimated from this approach can be severely biased in finite samples. An improved procedure for testing for cointegration, allowing for more than one cointegration vector, is suggested in Johansen (1988) and Johansen and Juselius (1990).

Following Johansen and Juselius (1990), let the p variables under scrutiny follow a vector autoregression of order k (VAR(k)) as below:

$$X_t = \mu + \Pi_1 X_{t-1} + \cdots + \Pi_k X_{t-k} + \varepsilon_t, \qquad t = 1, \ldots, T,$$

where $\varepsilon_1, \ldots, \varepsilon_t$ are innovations of this process and are assumed to be drawn from a p-dimensional i.i.d. Gaussian distribution with covariance Γ and X_{-k+1}, $\ldots, X_0$ are fixed. Let Δ represent the first-difference operator. The equation can be reparameterized into the equivalent form presented below:

$$\Delta X_t = \mu + \Pi X_{t-k} + \sum_{i=1}^{k-1} I_i \Delta X_{t-i} + \varepsilon_t, \qquad t = 1, 2, 3, \ldots,$$

where

$$I_t = -I + \sum_{j=1}^{i} \Pi_j, \qquad i = 1, \ldots, k-1, \quad \Pi = I + \sum_{j=1}^{k} \Pi_j.$$

The coefficient matrix Π contains information about the long-run relationship among the variables. Since ε_t is stationary, the number of ranks for matrix Π determines how many linear combinations of X_t are stationary. If $0 < \text{rank} (\Pi) = r < p$, there exist r cointegrating vectors that make the linear combinations of X_t stationary. In that case, Π can be factored as $\alpha\beta'$, with α and β being matrices. β is a cointegrating vector that has the property that $\beta' X_t$ is stationary even though X_t itself is nonstationary; α then contains the adjustment parameters.

Based on the unrestricted estimation that is parameterized in terms of level and differences, Johansen (1988) proposed likelihood ratio statistics for testing the number of cointegrating vectors. First, we must solve for the eigenvalues of

$$|\lambda S_{kk} - S_{k0} S_{00}^{-1} S_{0k}| = 0,$$

where S_{00} is the moment matrix of the residuals from the ordinary least squares regression of ΔX_t on $\Delta X_{t-1}, \ldots, \Delta X_{t-k+1}$; S_{kk} is the residual moment matrix from the ordinary least squares regression of ΔX_{t-k} on $\Delta X_{t-1}, \ldots, \Delta X_{t-k+1}$; and S_{0k} is the cross-product moment matrix. The cointegrating vector, β, is solved out as the eigenvectors associated with the r largest statistically significant eigenvalues are derived using two test statistics, "maximum eigenvalue statistics" and "trace statistics." The first statistic tests the hypothesis that there are $r = s$ cointegrating vectors against the alternative of $r = s + 1$ by calculating the maximum likelihood test statistics as $-T\ln(1 - \lambda_{s+1})$, where T is the sample size and λ_{s+1} is an estimated eigenvalue. The second statistic tests the hypothesis that there exist at most r cointegrating vectors. It is performed by calculating so-called trace statistics:

$$-T\sum_{i=r+1}^{P} \ln(1 - \lambda_i),$$

where $\lambda_{r+1}, \ldots, \lambda_p$ are the estimated $p - r$ smallest eigenvalues. Given the number of cointegrating relations, with or without a linear trend, the data can also be analyzed by another reduced rank regression by calculating the test statistics

$$-T\sum_{i=r+1}^{P} \ln[(1 - \lambda_i^*)/(1 - \lambda_i)],$$

where λ_i^* are eigenvalues obtained from cointegration analysis assuming there is no linear trend.

14.5   Real Exchange Rate in the Long Run

In this section, I investigate the behavior of the real exchange rate with cointegration methods to see whether its long-run movement is consistent with the implications of PPP theory. The relative PPP theory asserts that the rate of change in the nominal exchange rate is equal to the domestic inflation rate minus the foreign inflation rate. This implies that when the nominal exchange rate goes up or down, relative price levels will adjust continuously in order to keep the real exchange rate close to its long-run equilibrium level. The equation for the relative PPP theory may be rearranged to produce an expression for the change in the real exchange rate, so that the real exchange rate change should equal zero.

To investigate whether there are deviations of the real exchange rate away from its equilibrium value, I test for cointegration relations among changes in nominal exchange rates and domestic and foreign price levels without imposing any proportionality and symmetry restrictions, instead of checking the stochastic process of the real exchange rate series by a unit root test.[5] I do this because of the suggestion of Cheung and Lai (1993) that measurement errors in price variables would cause violations of the symmetry restrictions of the

---

5. If the real exchange rate series is stationary, i.e., the series contains no unit root, then it tends to fluctuate around the mean in the long run. Nonstationary series, however, wander widely and rarely return to an earlier value. Thus real exchange rates change, and this change quantifies deviations from PPP.

absolute PPP theory and thus cause us to erroneously accept the hypothesis of a nonstationary real exchange rate.[6]

The estimating model for such a version may be empirically formulated as:

$$\ln E = a_0 + a_1 \ln P + a_2 \ln P^* + u,$$

where E denotes the bilateral nominal exchange rate, P is the domestic price level, P^* stands for the foreign price level, and u is the error term. Testing for a cointegrated relationship among a set of variables is done in two steps. The first step is to verify the order of integration of the variables. Second, cointegration tests are conducted on variables with compatible properties. The stochastic properties of variables can be investigated by applying the augmented Dickey-Fuller (ADF) test. The hypothesis that the variable X_t is an $I(1)$ series is tested by conducting a regression on the following equation:

$$\Delta X_t = \mu + \beta t + \alpha X_{t-1} + \sum_{i=1}^{P} K_i \Delta X_{t-i} + \varepsilon_t,$$

where X_t stands for variables appearing in the equation; p is the number of lags chosen to ensure that the estimated residuals, ε, are approximately white noise; μ is the constant term; and t is a time trend (see Dickey and Fuller 1979; Dickey 1981). If we cannot reject the hypothesis that X_t is a unit root process, then the unit root test is applied to ΔX_t. X_t is an $I(1)$ series only when ΔX_t is not a unit root process.

Monthly observations from January 1981 through September 1995 were used for the empirical study. The nominal exchange rate series, which are monthly average rates, are collected from *Financial Statistics Monthly (Taiwan District)* published by the Central Bank of Taiwan. The relevant price indexes for Taiwan are also from *Financial Statistics Monthly,* whereas the U.S. data are from the *International Financial Statistics* tape from the International Monetary Fund.

The results of the unit root test are reported in table 14.1. The autoregressive lag lengths are chosen to be shortest for the residuals from the regression, which the Box-Ljung Q-statistic suggests are white noise. As shown in table 14.1, the null hypothesis of a nonstationary exchange rate cannot be rejected for the log levels of all the variables. The unit root tests of the first difference of the logarithms of the variables lead us to reject the unit root null hypothesis at the 95 percent significance level, since the ADF statistics are significantly negative. In summary, the tests indicate that the variables of nominal exchange

---

6. Since observed price series are imperfect proxies for theoretical price variables, some measurement errors exist. These measurement errors can be associated with international differences in consumption patterns, variations in product quality, and differences between listed and transaction prices. If symmetry and proportionality conditions are not consistent with the data, the imposition of these conditions can bias PPP tests on real exchange rates toward finding nonstationarity. In such a case, a finding of a nonstationary real exchange rate can indicate a violation of the symmetry or proportionality restrictions and still be consistent with PPP theory.

Table 14.1   **Unit Root Tests for Nominal Exchange Rate and Price Levels**

	Variables				
	ln E	ln WPI	ln WPI*	ln CPI	ln CPI*
Level	−0.93941	−1.6104	−0.00234	1.4516	−1.6834
First difference	−3.747	−4.0775	−5.937	−7.0238	−5.1668

Note: The critical value at the 95 percent significance level is −3.45 for $N = 100$ (Fuller 1976, 373).

Table 14.2   **Johansen Maximum Likelihood Procedure: Cointegration Likelihood Ratio Test Based on Maximal Eigenvalue of the Stochastic Matrix**

Null	Alternative	Statistic	95% Critical Value
(ln E, WPI, WPI*)			
$r = 0$	$r = 1$	18.2347	21.0740
$r \leq 1$	$r = 2$	6.4360	14.9000
$r \leq 2$	$r = 3$	4.2808	8.1760
(ln E, CPI, CPI*)			
$r = 0$	$r = 1$	18.5323	21.0740
$r \leq 1$	$r = 2$	11.4005	14.9000
$r \leq 2$	$r = 3$	5.4206	8.1760

rates and domestic and foreign price levels are compatibly integrated of order one and these variables are suitable for the cointegration test.

To test for the cointegration relationship, the Johansen approach to the cointegration test was performed in the VAR framework. In order to avoid any bias of the regression result by measurement errors, the cointegrating regression was considered without imposition of symmetry and proportionality restrictions. Table 14.2 reports the values of the Johansen test statistics, indicating that changes in nominal bilateral exchange rates are not cointegrated with those in domestic and foreign price levels, when either the WPI or CPI is used. The results appear to suggest that the simple notion of the PPP relationship did not hold for the real exchange rate between the Taiwanese and U.S. currencies during the period under review. This implies that the nominal bilateral exchange rate for the NT dollar vis-à-vis the U.S. dollar and the corresponding price levels drifted away from each other following shocks to the Taiwanese economy. More generally, this indicates that movements in real exchange rates can be regarded as permanent and the real exchange rate should not be expected to return to the equilibrium PPP value.

14.6   Impulse Response Analysis

Our inability to reject the null hypothesis of a cointegration relationship between the nominal exchange rate and foreign and domestic price levels implies that shocks to the real exchange rate are so persistent that it does not return to the long-run value, as PPP theory predicts. Because real exchange rates are constructed by nominal exchange rates and relative price levels, the variability in real exchange rates can be dominated by either nominal exchange rates or relative price level changes. In this section, we investigate the extent to which the nominal exchange rate and foreign and domestic price level changes affect the real exchange rate through an analysis of their impulse response functions.

For this purpose, we estimated an unrestricted VAR consisting of the first difference in the logarithms of the nominal exchange rate and domestic and foreign price levels:

$$A(L)X_t = \mu_t,$$

where

$$X_t = (\Delta P_t,\ \Delta E_t,\ \Delta P_t^*),\quad A(L) = \sum_{j=0}^{k} A_j L^j,\quad A_0 = I.$$

Akaike's information criterion was employed to select the lag length of the VAR system. Inverting $A(L)$, we get the moving average representation $X_t = A(L)^{-1}\mu_t$. To evaluate the dynamic response of the variables in X_t to an innovation in ΔP_t, ΔE_t, and ΔP_t^*, μ_t is orthogonalized by means of a Choleski factorization of Ω. Let $\varepsilon_t = B\mu_t$, with B chosen to be a lower triangular matrix such that $B\Omega B' = I$. I is a diagonal matrix. Thus we can write $X_t = C(L)\varepsilon_t$, where

$$C(L) = A(L)^{-1}B(L)^{-1} = \begin{bmatrix} C_{11}(L) & C_{12}(L) & C_{13}(L) \\ C_{21}(L) & C_{22}(L) & C_{23}(L) \\ C_{31}(L) & C_{32}(L) & C_{33}(L) \end{bmatrix}.$$

The changes in P, E, and P^* responding to a unit shock to P are given by $C_{11}(L)$, $C_{21}(L)$, and $C_{31}(L)$, respectively. Similarly, the changes in P, E, and P^* responding to innovations in E and P^* are presented by $C_{12}(L)$, $C_{22}(L)$, and $C_{32}(L)$ and $C_{13}(L)$, $C_{23}(L)$, and $C_{33}(L)$. Therefore, the implied changes in R following shocks to P, E, and P^* are $(-C_{11} + C_{21} + C_{31})$, $(-C_{12} + C_{22} + C_{32})$, and $(-C_{13} + C_{23} + C_{33})$, respectively. Notice that if PPP theory held, $(-C_{12} + C_{22} + C_{32}) + (-C_{13} + C_{23} + C_{33}) - (-C_{11} + C_{21} + C_{31})$ would be identically zero.

Table 14.3 shows the cumulative impulse response functions of ΔP, ΔE, and ΔP^*, together with the implied impulse response function for ΔR.[7] From this

---

7. The price level considered here is based on the WPI.

Table 14.3   **Cumulative Impulse Response Changes**

$$\Delta P_t = C_{11}(L)\varepsilon_t^p + C_{12}(L)\varepsilon_t^E + C_{13}(L)\varepsilon_t^{p^*}$$
$$\Delta E_t = C_{21}(L)\varepsilon_t^p + C_{22}(L)\varepsilon_t^E + C_{23}(L)\varepsilon_t^{p^*}$$
$$\Delta P_t^* = C_{31}(L)\varepsilon_t^p + C_{32}(L)\varepsilon_t^E + C_{33}(L)\varepsilon_t^{p^*}$$

$$\begin{bmatrix} C_{11} & C_{12} & C_{13} \\ C_{21} & C_{22} & C_{23} \\ C_{31} & C_{32} & C_{33} \end{bmatrix} = \begin{bmatrix} 1.7726 & 0.09293 & 0.005026 \\ 0.12405 & 1.09206 & -0.4756 \\ 0.5096 & -0.1907 & 1.431 \end{bmatrix}$$

$$\Delta R_t = -1.13\varepsilon_t^p + 0.804\varepsilon_t^E + 0.9513\varepsilon_t^{p^*}$$

table it is seen that a unit of innovation in the domestic price level generally leads to a 1.77 percent increase in the domestic price level. Relatively small changes in the domestic price level follow shocks in the nominal exchange rate and the foreign price level. A unit innovation in the nominal exchange rate is followed by an approximately 1.09 percent increase in the nominal exchange rate. One percent shocks in domestic and foreign price levels lead, respectively, to a 0.12 percent increase and a 0.475 percent decrease in the value of the nominal exchange rate. A unit shock to the foreign price level causes a greater change in foreign prices than do innovations in the domestic price level and the nominal exchange rate. In table 14.3, we also report the change in the real exchange rate following unit innovations in ΔP, ΔE, and ΔP^*. This cumulative change is near minus one for a shock to the domestic price level and one for a shock to the foreign price level. The estimates indicate that each unit change in the domestic and foreign price levels is followed by a unit increase in the real exchange rate. The cumulative change of innovations in the nominal exchange rate of 0.804 percent suggests that a 1 percentage point change in the nominal exchange rate will induce a 0.804 percent change in the real exchange rate.

In summary, there is again no evidence to support the idea that there is a long-run relationship between the nominal exchange rate and relative price levels, as postulated by PPP theory. Innovations in nominal exchange rate changes are followed by permanent changes in the real exchange rate. It also appears that innovations in domestic and foreign price levels lead to permanent changes in the real exchange rate.

14.7   Real Exchange Rate Movements and Productivity Growth

The earlier analysis suggests that there is no systematic tendency for the real exchange rate to revert to a constant equilibrium level after a shock. Permanent shifts in the real exchange rate can result from permanent changes in the nominal exchange rate and in domestic and foreign price levels. In this section, a popular model of real exchange rate determination proposed by Balassa (1964) is called upon to attest to the validation of the observations. The Balassa proposition suggests that when productivity advances more rapidly in a country's traded goods sector than in its nontraded sector, that is, when real shocks cause permanent changes in the price of traded goods relative to nontraded goods, the relative price levels between the home and the foreign country are subject to change. Hence, the underlying equilibrium real exchange rate is also subject to change. However, this is not the whole story, in our view. As the nominal exchange rate changes, relative labor unit costs would change when both domestic and foreign labor cost are computed in the same currency. In such a way, nominal exchange rate changes induce differences between the two countries in the growth rates of unit labor costs and then cause the real exchange rate to change. In the following section, we will investigate the movement of real exchange rates based on the model of productivity differentials. First, we briefly present the basic model used to explain long-run changes in the real exchange rate.

Following Hsieh (1982), let P and P^* denote the domestic and foreign price indexes, which are defined as the weighted averages of the prices in the traded and nontraded goods sectors:

$$P = (P_t)^{1-\alpha}(P_n)^{\alpha}, \quad P^* = (P_t^*)^{1-\beta}(P_n^*)^{\beta},$$

where α and β are constant weights between zero and unity. Then the real exchange rate can be expressed as

(1)
$$\frac{EP^*}{P} = E\left(\frac{P_n^*}{P_t^*}\right)^{\beta}\left(\frac{P_n}{P_t}\right)^{-\alpha}\left(\frac{P_t^*}{P_t}\right).$$

Assuming constant returns to scale and a fixed supply of labor at home and abroad, with labor being the only factor of production, and free mobility of labor between sectors, the same nominal wage W will prevail in both sectors. Let A_t and A_n denote the average productivities of labor in the traded and nontraded goods sectors, respectively. Perfect competition among producers in both sectors ensures that prices equal average production cost:

(2)
$$P_t = W/A_t, \quad P_n = W/A_n$$
$$P_t^* = W^*/A_t^*, \quad P_n^* = W^*/A_n^*$$

Substituting equation (2) into equation (1), one obtains

(3)
$$R = E\left(\frac{A_n^*}{A_t^*}\right)^{-\beta}\left(\frac{A_n}{A_t}\right)^{\alpha}\left(\frac{W^*/A_t^*}{W/A_t}\right).$$

Expressing equation (3) in logarithms, one obtains

(4) $\ln R = \alpha(\ln A_n - \ln A_t) - \beta(\ln A_n^* - \ln A_t^*) + \ln E$

$+ \ln(W^*/A_t^*) - \ln(W/A_t).$

The theory outlined above suggests that the behavior of the real exchange rate could reflect productivity growth. The first term on the right-hand side of equation (4) is the difference in growth rates of labor productivity between the domestic nontraded and traded sectors. The second term is the difference between the two foreign sectors. The third term can be considered the difference in the growth rates of unit labor cost between the two countries.

Hsieh's (1982) work uses time-series data to estimate equation (4) in order to find supporting evidence for the idea that productivity differentials between sectors can explain the behavior of the real exchange rate series. However, as there is a consensus among researchers that many economic time series have no tendency to return to an equilibrium value, we have little confidence that equation (4) provides a good approximation of the relationship among variables without a formal test of the nature of the data set. If a unit root exists in any one of the series, the statistical interpretation and properties of the least squares estimates for the model may not be valid. Thus we will consider the time-series behavior of each series individually and then investigate the possibility of a long-run equilibrium among the series.

As discussed, equation (4) provides a framework for the analysis of the real exchange rate. As far as the variables used in the model are concerned, the traded sector is manufacturing industries. Labor productivity in manufacturing is calculated by dividing the real output of manufacturing by the number of employees and work hours. The nontraded sector then is defined as the service sector only. The labor productivity of this sector is computed in a similar way by dividing the real output of the service sector by the number of workers in that sector and average work hours. The data on real output in manufacturing and services in Taiwan are obtained from the NIAQ data bank. The data on number of workers, average work hours, and wage rates are taken from the WAGE data bank. For the United States, real output information is collected from the US data bank, and the remaining elements are taken from the NIPA data bank. All these data banks are accessible in the AREMOS/UNIX economic database system maintained by the Education Ministry of Taiwan.

First, we consider the stochastic properties of the series of differences in productivity changes between the traded sectors and nontraded sectors at home and abroad, and the differences in unit labor cost changes. According to the ADF test statistic, for all the series examined, the hypothesis of a unit root could not be rejected at the 95 percent significance level. Unit root tests were applied also to the first-differenced series, and the $I(1)$ null hypothesis could be rejected for all the series, as shown in table 14.4. These findings suggest that the levels of series are $I(1)$. The Johansen cointegration approach is next performed in the VAR framework. First, different values of the lag length $k = 1, \ldots, 8$ are considered. In most cases, a lag of $k = 4$ is required to remove serial correlation in the residuals. The test for a linear trend in the nonstationary part of the process is performed by

$$-T \sum_{i=r+1}^{P} \ln[(1 - \lambda_i^*) / (1 - \lambda_i)],$$

where λ_i^* are eigenvalues obtained from cointegration analysis assuming no trend. Since a linear trend is confirmed, we proceed with the Johansen proce-

Table 14.4   **Unit Root Test for Variable Series in Equation (4)**

	Variables			
	$\ln R$	$\ln A_n - \ln A_t$	$\ln A_n^* - A_t^*$	$\ln E + \ln(W^*/A_t^*) - \ln(W/A)$
Level	-1.233	-1.868	-0.398	-0.586
First difference	-6.92	-9.80	-11.53	-6.80

Note: Real exchange rates are denominated in WPI.

Table 14.5   **Johansen Maximum Likelihood Procedure**

Null	Alternative	Statistic	95% Critical Value
Cointegration Likelihood Ratio Test Based on Maximal Eigenvalue of the Stochastic Matrix			
$r = 0$	$r = 1$	57.3693	27.0670
$r \leq 1$	$r = 2$	20.1958	20.9670
$r \leq 2$	$r = 3$	5.1362	14.0690
$r \leq 3$	$r = 4$	.8724E-3	3.7620
Cointegration Likelihood Ratio Test Based on Trace of the Stochastic Matrix			
$r = 0$	$r \geq 1$	82.7022	47.2100
$r \leq 1$	$r \geq 2$	25.3329	29.6800
$r \leq 2$	$r \geq 3$	5.1371	15.4100
$r \leq 3$	$r = 4$	.8724E-3	3.7620

dure. Table 14.5 reports the values of the Johansen test statistic for the numbers of cointegrating vectors. In the case under consideration, the hypothesis of no cointegrating vector ($r = 0$) can be rejected at the 95 percent level, indicating that the series in X_t are cointegrated, as suggested by the model. The (normalized) estimates of the equilibrium relation are given by (1, 1.16, -1.01, 0.53506). The average speed of adjustment toward the estimated equilibrium state, α, is found to be (-0.00292, -0.19305, 0.3146, -0.4048). In our case, the coefficients are significantly differently from zero with the correct signs. The results show that improvements in the productivity of the nontraded sector at home lead to long-run depreciation of the real exchange rate, a result that is the same as the Balassa (1964) analysis. Conversely, faster productivity growth in the nontraded sector abroad results in an appreciation of the real exchange rate. Furthermore, differences in unit labor cost will also cause the real exchange rate to rise.

It should be noted that a fundamental model-building point is the assumption of perfect competition. Under this assumption, prices are set equal to the marginal cost, and the prices of traded goods do not violate the law of one price. Since models of international trade have increasingly emphasized how traded goods prices are affected by market structures that deviate from perfect competition, we would also like to relax this assumption and see how the equilibrium relationship changes.

Relaxing the assumption of perfect competition in traded goods sectors only, we can see that the firms will then set a price at which marginal revenue equals marginal cost. The prices of traded goods at home and abroad represent some markup over unit cost:

$$P_t = (W/A_t)(1 + m), \qquad P_t^* = (W^*/A_t^*)(1 + m^*),$$

where m and m^* are domestic and foreign profit margins over costs. Profit margins vary because of characteristics of the market structure and changes in the macroeconomic environments. Plugging the new price equations for traded goods into the real exchange rate expression and taking logarithms, we obtain

(5) $$\ln R = (1 - \beta)\ln(1 + m^*) - (1 - \alpha)\ln(1 + m)$$

$$+ \alpha(\ln A_n - \ln A_t) - \beta(\ln A_n^* - \ln A_t^*)$$

$$+ [\ln E + \ln(W^*/A_t^*) - \ln(W/A_t)].$$

Equation (5) can be interpreted as saying that, as before, real exchange rate changes depend on relative changes in productivity between nontraded and traded sectors at home and abroad and on the difference between foreign and domestic changes in unit labor cost. At the same time, since marginal revenue is computed by taking profit margins into account, differences in profit margins are also linked to the real exchange rate. This relationship can be justified simply because the markup is an important measure of the competitiveness of producers.

To model markup differences in our empirical setting, we consider a time-specific effect estimation. Since markup differences are unobservable and might vary as demand and cost conditions change, we assume that the differences between markups change over time. Thus, if the links among real exchange rates, productivity differentials between the nontraded and traded sectors of the two countries, and differences in unit labor cost between the countries are close in the long run, the time-specific effect coefficients measure the changes in profit margin differential. As suggested in Greene (1993, chap. 6), the time-specific effect can be estimated by introducing dummy variables. We assume that profit margins are adjusted once every year and then estimate the model above including an additional 14 dummy variables.[8]

The estimates of the time effect are shown in table 14.6. These figures suggest that the movements of markup differentials increase as the real exchange rate changes. That is, in the short run, allowing for imperfect competition,

---

8. Our data span 15 years. Fourteen dummy variables were introduced since one of the time effects must be dropped to avoid multicollinearity.

Table 14.6   **Estimates of Time-Specific Effect**

Q_T	
0.40	(0.0683)
0.47	(0.0713)
0.53	(0.0736)
0.51	(0.0766)
0.71	(0.0766)
0.92	(0.0765)
1.11	(0.0814)
1.36	(0.0846)
1.52	(0.0902)
1.57	(0.0968)
1.78	(0.1090)
1.85	(0.1250)
1.94	(0.1340)
2.08	(0.1450)

Note: Numbers in parentheses are standard errors.
Equation: $\ln R_T = Q_T + \alpha(\ln A_n - \ln A_t)_T - \beta(\ln A_n^* - \ln A_t^*)_T + [\ln E + \ln (W^*/A_t^*) - \ln (W/A_t)]_T$

adjustments of markups also have something to do with real exchange rate changes.

14.8   Conclusion

In this paper, we set about analyzing the behavior of the real exchange rate. We found that the PPP relationship does not hold in the long run. Analyses of impulse response functions also suggest that changes in the nominal exchange rate and domestic and foreign price levels result in permanent changes in the real exchange rate. The empirical tests of the productivity differential model strongly support the hypothesis that it is differential productivity growth between traded and nontraded goods that leads to the observed changes in real exchange rates. Thus, if the productivity differential between the nontraded and traded sectors increases in Taiwan, the real exchange rate will depreciate. Similarly, if the productivity differential between the nontraded and traded sectors in the United States increases, the real exchange rate will decline, implying an appreciation. In addition, real exchange rates are influenced by differences in unit labor costs between the countries. In the short run, since firms in traded sectors can price to market, changes in markup differentials over traded goods prices will also have something to do with real exchange rate movements.

The lack of PPP is attributable to several factors. One of them, emphasized in this paper, is that price differentials may reflect productivity differences. Figure 14.2 shows the movements of labor productivity for the traded and nontraded sectors in Taiwan and the United States. As shown, Taiwan's labor productivity grew faster than that of the United States in both sectors. However,

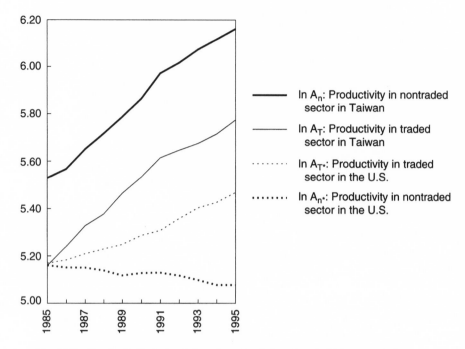

Fig. 14.2   Productivity in traded and nontraded sectors in Taiwan and the United States

far from expectations, the growth of Taiwan's labor productivity in the nontraded sector is faster than that in its traded sector. This yields a depreciation on average when the real exchange rate is denominated in WPI during the period under review.

According to our model, the growth rate of unit labor cost in the traded sectors of the two countries could also account for real exchange rate movements. Figure 14.3 shows the unit labor cost changes in the traded sectors in Taiwan and the United States. Obviously, the diagram exhibits a distinct divergence as the unit labor cost in Taiwan gets higher and higher and that in the United States declines. The differences in the growth of labor unit cost explain, to some extent, movements in the real exchange rate of the NT dollar relative to the U.S. dollar.

If we decompose changes in the real exchange rate of the NT dollar relative to the U.S. dollar, both changes in the nominal exchange rate and changes in relative price levels are responsible for changes in the real exchange rate. Differences in labor productivity growth induce price differentials so that real exchange rates are pushed upward. On the other hand, since relative wage growth in Taiwan is also increasing as the nominal exchange rate appreciates, the upward pressure on the real exchange rate is offset by wage growth movement. This yields a depreciation on average. Since the nominal exchange rate

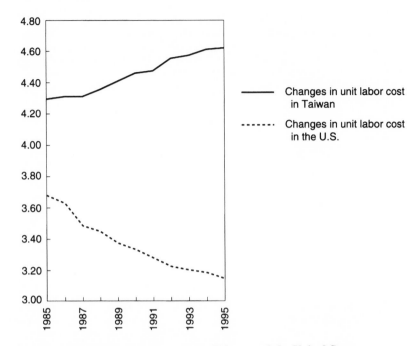

Fig. 14.3   Changes in unit labor cost in Taiwan and the United States

and domestic and foreign price levels all appear to have an effect on the real exchange rate, this implies some degree of predictability of real exchange rates.

References

Balassa, B. 1964. The purchasing power parity doctrine: A reappraisal. *Journal of Political Economy* 72:584–96.

Cheung, Y. W., and K. Lai. 1993. Long-run purchasing power parity during the recent float. *Journal of International Economics* 34:181–92.

Dickey, D. A. 1981. The likelihood ratio statistics for autoregressive time series with a unit root.*Econometrica* 49:1057–72.

Dickey, D. A., and W. A. Fuller. 1979. Distribution of the estimators for an autoregressive time series with unit root. *Journal of the American Statistical Association* 74: 427–31.

Engle, R., and C. Granger. 1987. Cointegration and error correction: Representation, estimation, and testing. *Econometrica* 55:251–76.

Frenkel, J. A. 1981. The collapse of purchasing power parities during the 1970s. *European Economic Review* 16:145–65.

Fuller, W. A. 1976. *Introduction to statistical time series.* New York: Wiley.

Greene, W. H. 1993. *Econometric analysis.* New York: Macmillan.

Hakkio, C. C. 1986. Does the exchange rates follow a random walk? A Monte Carlo study of four tests for a random walk. *Journal of International Money and Finance* 5:211–29.

Hsieh, D. A. 1982. The determination of the real exchange rate: The productivity approach. *Journal of International Economics* 12:355–62.

Johansen, S. 1988. Statistical analysis of cointegration factors. *Journal of Economic Dynamics and Control* 12:231–54.

Johansen, S., and K. Juselius. 1990. Maximum likelihood estimation and inference on cointegration—With applications to the demand for money. *Oxford Bulletin of Economics and Statistics* 52:169–210.

Mark, N. 1990. Real and nominal exchange rates in the long run: An empirical investigation. *Journal of International Economics* 28:115–36.

Marston, R. 1987. Real exchange rates and productivity growth in the United States and Japan. In *Real-financial linkages among open economies: An overview,* ed. Sven W. Arndt and J. David Richardson. Cambridge, Mass.: MIT Press.

Comment   Chi-Wa Yuen

The objective of Wu's paper is to investigate empirically the factors that determined the long-run movements of the real exchange rate between the NT dollar and the U.S. dollar over the period from January 1981 to September 1995. Using cointegration techniques, she tests (1) an implication of PPP that the equilibrium real exchange rate is time invariant[1] and (2) the Balassa-Samuelson hypothesis that differential productivity growth between the traded and nontraded goods sectors across countries is an important determinant of real exchange rate movements.

Two main results emerge from this study: (1) The nominal exchange rate is not cointegrated with relative (domestic and foreign) price levels, implying persistent deviations of the real exchange rate from its constant long-run PPP value. Innovations in the nominal exchange rate, the domestic price level, and the foreign price level each result in permanent changes in the real exchange rate. (2) Observed changes in the real exchange rate can be explained by differential productivity growth between the traded and nontraded goods sectors. In other words, the paper rejects PPP and provides support for the Balassa-Samuelson hypothesis as an explanation of divergence from PPP.

Chi-Wa Yuen is associate professor of economics and finance at the University of Hong Kong.

1. The relative version of PPP implies that the rate of change of the nominal exchange rate (defined as domestic currency units of foreign currency) is equal to the excess of the domestic inflation rate over and above its foreign counterpart, i.e., $\Delta E/E = \Delta P/P - \Delta P^*/P^*$. Restated in terms of the real exchange rate R (defined as EP^*/P), it also implies that $\Delta R/R = 0$. This was examined in the earlier literature by testing the hypothesis that $a_0 = 0$ and $a_1 = -a_2 = 1$ in either one of the following regressions: (i) $\ln E = a_0 + a_1 \ln P + a_2 \ln P^* + u$ (*absolute* version); or (ii) $\Delta \ln E = a_0 + a_1 \Delta \ln P + a_2 \Delta \ln P^* + v$ (*relative* version). (The former is well known to be more restrictive than the latter.) Alternatively, one can test PPP either by directly comparing the actual exchange rates with those implied by PPP (i.e., P/P^*) or by checking the law of one price for individual tradable commodities (e.g., the *Economist*'s Big Mac index).

In fact, there are a number of familiar reasons why, a priori, we should not expect PPP to hold exactly. First, international trade is not perfectly free in the way described in textbooks, due to (a) transportation costs and trade barriers, (b) slow price and wage adjustments in goods and labor markets (especially since these markets are less integrated internationally than capital markets), and (c) the practice of discriminatory pricing under imperfect competition. Second, statistical or measurement problems exist: (a) Price differentials may reflect productivity or quality differences. (b) There is no internationally standardized basket of goods; in constructing price indexes, different weights are attached by different countries to the same good because consumption patterns differ from country to country. (c) Price indexes contain nontraded goods components, which should be excluded from tests of PPP (as PPP, based on arbitrage in international commodity markets, should hold only for traded goods).

Wu has made an effort to address some of these problems—for example, productivity differentials, WPI versus CPI, and profit margin or markup. She is especially concerned about the Balassa-Samuelson hypothesis that under differential productivity growth and wage equalization across traded and nontraded goods sectors and international equalization of prices of traded goods, higher growth in the traded goods sector at home will lead to a fall in the relative price between traded and nontraded goods, followed by a rise in the domestic price level, and ultimately a depreciation of the real exchange rate. The empirical support she finds for this hypothesis implies that the long-run divergence from PPP can be explained by differences in productivity growth between Taiwan and the United States. In addition, she finds that real exchange rate movements can be explained in part by differences in unit labor cost and adjustments of markup differentials on traded goods prices under imperfect competition in the short run.

The existing evidence on PPP is in general sensitive to the choice of time period, countries, and price index. Despite the mixed results, it is widely accepted that PPP holds better for countries with closer geographical proximity and trade linkages, for traded goods than for nontraded goods, and for the long run than for the short and medium runs. But contrary to PPP, nominal exchange rates show more volatility than the corresponding relative national price levels. It would therefore be informative to provide a more systematic comparison of the behavior of the NT dollar–U.S. dollar exchange rate with some of these general patterns.

The evidence from studies based on cointegration methods has also been mixed. But it has commonly been found that cointegration tests fail more easily under floating (rather than fixed) rate regimes, and more frequently when CPIs—which have a higher nontraded goods component—(rather than WPIs) are used as price indexes. Regarding the latter, the qualitative results in this paper do not depend much on the choice of price index. Regarding the former, as the NT dollar was pegged to the U.S. dollar prior to August 1981, the sample in this study contains data from both the fixed and floating rate periods. It is not clear why the author does not drop the relatively short (with respect to the data series) fixed rate period from her study, especially since the behavior of exchange rates can in principle be very different under the two regimes. Given the predominance of floating rate data in this paper, however, her results can be viewed as largely consistent with those from previous studies.

Bearing in mind that exchange rates and price levels are both endogenous variables determined by some other exogenous variables, one should realize that PPP is not really a *theory* of exchange rate determination. Rather, it simply suggests a *relation* among these variables that should be satisfied in equilibrium. Like the quantity theory of money, I tend to believe that PPP must hold as a long-run proposition ceteris paribus (i.e., holding constant the PPP-divergent factors mentioned above). Whatever negative evidence we may find must reflect limitations in the data or the empirical methodology. If one is willing to take such a strong view, it becomes immaterial whether the data we have support or reject PPP. What is more interesting economically is to be able to understand the quantitative significance of the various economic factors (relative money supplies and demands, volume of trade and size of capital movements, etc.) that are candidate determinants of the exchange rates. For instance, what are the distinct patterns in the movement of the NT dollar–U.S. dollar exchange rate that differentiate it from other bilateral exchange rates? What is the nature of the shocks that are responsible for the observed movement (transitory or permanent, real or monetary, aggregate or idiosyncratic, anticipated or unanticipated)? In what way is the nature of these shocks related to the institutional features in Taiwan? These are questions that I, as a participant in this "regional" conference (with an aim to understanding better the peculiarities of an Asian country like Taiwan), would most like to see addressed.

Comment   Ponciano S. Intal, Jr.

In this paper, Wu sets out to evaluate the movement of the real exchange rate of Taiwan vis-à-vis the United States during the 1980s using currently popular analytical techniques like cointegration analysis. She shows that PPP does not hold for the case of Taiwan vis-à-vis the United States. Most important, Wu tested the productivity differential model of real exchange rate movements. She concludes that "it is differential productivity growth between traded and the nontraded goods that leads to the observed changes in real exchange rates" between Taiwan and the United States.

I would like to commend Wu for her meticulous analysis. I have only a few

Ponciano S. Intal, Jr., is president of the Philippine Institute for Development Studies, a government research institution. He was formerly a deputy director-general of the National Economic and Development Authority, the Philippines' economic planning agency.

comments, centering on the use of data, the need to explain the real appreciation of the NT dollar using the CPI series, the empirical test of PPP theory, and the applicability of the analysis to developing country comparisons.

Use of Data

The paper states that using the WPI series, the NT dollar depreciated in real terms relative to the U.S. dollar during the 1980s. However, using the CPI series, the NT dollar appreciated in real terms vis-à-vis the U.S. dollar during the same period. The paper also states that U.S. productivity grew faster in the traded sector than in the nontraded sector relative to Taiwan during the period.

Given that U.S. productivity grew faster in the traded sector than in the nontraded sector relative to Taiwan, the productivity differential model of the real exchange rate (eq. [4]) suggests that the NT dollar would depreciate in real terms vis-à-vis the U.S. dollar. This is consistent with the real exchange rate series using the WPI but not with that using the CPI instead. It appears that the paper uses the WPI series in its analysis of the relationship between the real exchange rate and the differential in productivity changes.

I think the use of the WPI series instead of the CPI series in the analysis stands on shaky grounds. WPIs are generally heavily weighted by tradable goods, while CPIs include more nontraded goods and services. Considering that the real exchange rate is underpinned by the relative price of tradables to nontradables and considering that the paper uses the productivity of the service sector as the indicator of the productivity of the nontraded sector, I think it is only logical that it is the CPI series that should have been used in the analysis, rather than the WPI series.

Explaining the Real Appreciation of NT Dollar

Given that it is the real exchange rate using the CPI series that is the more appropriate real exchange rate to use in the analysis, then the paper would have to explain why the real exchange rate appreciated when the productivity differential model implies otherwise. This seems to suggest that there are other factors that help determine the long-run real exchange rate in addition to productivity differentials and labor cost differentials. In effect, the author may have to resort to a more complex model of real exchange rate determination (see, e.g., Edwards 1989) in order to explain the movement of the NT dollar in real terms vis-à-vis the U.S. dollar.

An alternative although rather pedestrian way to explain the real appreciation of the NT dollar is to decompose the determinants of the nominal exchange rate and of relative prices. The appreciation of the nominal NT dollar during the 1980s appears to stem from Taiwan's high saving rate and balance-of-payments surplus combined with the deregulation of Taiwan's capital account and foreign exchange market, especially after the Plaza Accord. The rise in inflationary pressure in Taiwan vis-à-vis foreign competitors can be explained using the so-called Scandinavian model of inflation whereby the balance-of-payments surplus becomes increasingly difficult to sterilize and the sharp rise in the growth of the tradable sector pushes wages and nontradable prices upward significantly.

Empirical Test of the PPP Theory

It is not surprising that the cointegration test used in the paper shows that relative PPP does not hold for the case of the NT dollar in real terms. Virtually all empirical analyses end up with the same result as long as the hypothesis is that the long-run real exchange rate is constant. This particular hypothesis requires stringent assumptions about the behavior of the real sector.

However, in view of the recent modeling efforts on the determination of the real exchange rate (see, e.g., Edwards 1989), I wonder whether the formulation of empirical tests of PPP should not be modified accordingly. Specifically, Edwards (1989) shows that the equilibrium real exchange rate need not be a constant value; rather it is a path of values satisfying simultaneous equilibrium conditions for both the external and internal sectors of an economy, given equilibrium values of other variables affecting the real exchange rate (e.g., world prices, technology, tariffs). Basically, PPP implies that monetary shocks do not have permanent real exchange rate effects. Given this, it seems that the appropriate test of "dynamic" PPP is whether there are deviations of the real exchange rate from its equilibrium path. Unfortunately, the "vector of equilibrium values" of the real exchange rate cannot be not defined exogenously; rather, it is endogenously determined within a specific model of real exchange rate determination. This may mean that the usual tests of PPP (i.e., comparison of price changes or test of deviations of the real exchange rate from zero) may have to give way to "full model" tests that take into consideration the effects of the other determinants on the equilibrium real exchange rate.

Real Exchange Rate and Productivity Differentials in Developing Countries

Some simple comparisons of real exchange rates and average labor productivity indexes among developing countries in Southeast Asia and China during the 1980s suggest that the productivity differential model of real exchange rates does not apply to developing countries. Table 14C.1 presents indexes of real exchange rates and labor productivity in selected countries. Notice that Indonesia and China registered the most significant and successful real exchange rate depreciations among the developing countries in Asia (and possibly the world) during the 1980s. Notice also that Indonesia (and most likely China also) registered significant increases in labor productivity, especially in the tradable sector (proxied by the manufacturing sector) relative to the rest of the economy. In contrast, the Philippine peso depreciated far less than the Indonesian rupiah and Chinese renminbi; moreover, the productivity improvements in the Philippine manufacturing sector were also meager.

In effect, the Philippine peso appreciated in real terms vis-à-vis the Indone-

Table 14C.1   **Indexes of Real Effective Exchange Rates and Average Labor Productivity (1975 = 100)**

Country	1980	1985	1990
China, People's Republic			
Exchange rate	116	195	215
Labor productivity			
Overall[a]	122	166	203[b]
Manufacturing[a]	n.a.	n.a.	n.a.[b]
Indonesia			
Exchange rate	141	162	239
Labor productivity			
Overall	126	131	140
Manufacturing	156	195	227
Malaysia			
Exchange rate	125	109	129
Labor productivity			
Overall	125	138	163
Manufacturing	104	117	161
Philippines			
Exchange rate	99	101	112
Labor productivity			
Overall	120	96	104
Manufacturing	122	107	119
Singapore			
Exchange rate	111	103	101
Labor productivity			
Overall	116	147	187
Manufacturing	114	136	189
Thailand			
Exchange rate	109	113	115
Labor productivity			
Overall	118	136	167[b]
Manufacturing	121	131	165[b]

Sources: Intal (1992a) for real effective exchange rates; Intal (1992b) for average labor productivity indexes.

Note: An increase in the value of the real effective exchange rate index means an exchange rate depreciation.

[a]Base year is 1976.

[b]1989.

sian rupiah or the Chinese renminbi. This result is in sharp contrast to the implications of the productivity differential model of real exchange rates. The key reason for this is that simple real exchange rate equations like equation (4) in the paper embody stringent explicit or implicit assumptions about the nature of factor and commodity markets, especially factor market flexibility and factor mobility, low or no tariffs and nontariff barriers, and full employment. In most cases, developing countries do not meet these conditions.

More important, in the case of successful reforming economies like Indonesia and China during the 1980s, the real exchange rate was not determined in any way by productivity differentials. Rather, real exchange rate changes were major policy decisions made in concert with other major structural reforms related to the opening up of the economy and greater deregulation of economic activities. The end result is higher productivity growth in the economy, especially in the tradable sector, and a higher economic growth rate. Thus, in this particular instance, the real exchange rate became the determinant of the change in productivity in the tradable sector and the whole economy, instead of the other way around as the productivity differential model indicates.

References

Edwards, S. 1989. *Real exchange rates, devaluation and adjustment: Exchange rate policy in developing countries.* Cambridge, Mass.: MIT Press.
Intal, P. 1992a. Real exchange rates, price competitiveness, and structural adjustment in Asian and Pacific economies. *Asian Development Review* 10 (2): 86–123.
Intal, P. 1992b. International competitiveness. Unpublished paper.

15   Hong Kong's Currency Board and Changing Monetary Regimes

Yum K. Kwan and Francis T. Lui

15.1 Introduction

A currency board, first introduced in the British colony of Mauritius in 1849, is a rule-based monetary institution that is rather different from a central bank. Although there are variations, a typical currency board has two essential characteristics. First, the board has the obligation to exchange on demand local currency for some major international currency, which is often called the reserve currency, and vice versa, at a fixed exchange rate stipulated in the legislation. Second, local currency is issued based on at least 100 percent reserve of securities denominated mainly in the reserve currency.

Since the nineteenth century, dozens of currency boards had been established in British colonies and other places, often in response to monetary or exchange rate disturbances.[1] However, when these colonies became independent nations after World War II, most decided to replace the currency board with a central bank. Very few currency boards survive today. Some people may be inclined to believe that this form of monetary institution has already lost its practical importance. This judgment is premature. Recently, Argentina and Estonia have enacted laws to establish currency boards, which have also been

Yum K. Kwan is associate professor of economics at the City University of Hong Kong. Francis T. Lui is director of the Center for Economic Development, Hong Kong University of Science and Technology.

This work is part of the NBER's project on International Capital Flows, which receives support from the Center for International Political Economy. The authors are grateful to the Center for International Political Economy and the Center for Economic Development for the support of this project. A direct allocation grant from the Hong Kong University of Science and Technology is appreciated. Constructive comments by Barry Eichengreen, Zhaoyong Zhang, and other conference participants have significantly helped the authors in the revision of this paper. Any opinions expressed here are those of the authors and not those of the institutions providing support.

1. For more detailed discussion of the history of currency boards, see Schwartz (1993) and Hanke and Schuler (1994). See also Walters and Hanke (1992).

recommended for Russia, Bulgaria, and other nations in Eastern Europe (see Hanke, Jonung, and Schuler 1993). The currency crisis of Mexico in 1995 has further stimulated people to consider the system seriously. If this renewed interest could be sustained and these countries were to adopt currency boards eventually, then as Schwartz (1993) has commented, "a watershed would have been reached in the annals of political economy."

Do the potential benefits of currency boards outweigh their costs in these countries? Some of the theoretical advantages and disadvantages of currency boards are well known.[2] For example, convertibility of currency is guaranteed and there is little or no uncertainty about the exchange rate. On the other hand, in times of domestic liquidity crisis, a currency board arrangement cannot act as a lender of last resort. In theory, its reserve currency can only be used to buy local currency or foreign securities. It would be a violation of its basic principle if the reserve were to be used to purchase the assets of a domestic bank suffering from a run.[3] Moreover, since a currency board is a rule-based arrangement, active discretionary monetary policies are precluded. Whether this macroeconomic self-discipline is regarded as an advantage, however, is more controversial.

To assess the viability of adopting currency boards as monetary institutions, we should not satisfy ourselves with theoretical discussions alone. Since they have been in existence for almost one and a half centuries, a more fruitful approach is to analyze rigorously the empirical data generated from actual experience. This literature is generally lacking. In this paper, we shall analyze the macroeconomic implications of a currency board regime using Hong Kong data and methods developed by Blanchard and Quah (1989) and Bayoumi and Eichengreen (1993, 1994). The viability of the regime is also discussed.

In section 15.2 we shall briefly discuss the historical background of Hong Kong's currency board and argue why its experience provides us with a unique natural experiment to evaluate some aspects of the system. In section 15.3 we shall outline the structural vector autoregressive model implemented in this paper. Section 15.4 presents the quantitative results and their interpretations. Section 15.5 summarizes some general properties and implications about currency boards that we have learned from the Hong Kong experience.

---

2. Williamson (1995) provides a useful summary of the advantages and disadvantages of currency boards.

3. The currency board of Hong Kong is an exception to this rule. There is no formal legislation prohibiting the board from using its foreign exchange to purchase domestic assets, although the board has so far refrained from doing so in a significant way. See the balance sheet in table 15.7. One interpretation is that the legislature provides an "escape clause" under which the board can act as a lender of last resort during financial crises. As long as the escape clause is only invoked in truly exceptional and justifiable situations, it will not jeopardize the credibility of the currency board. See Persson and Tabellini (1990) for an illustration and discussion of escape clause models. See also n. 13 below.

15.2   Historical Background of Hong Kong's Currency Board

The currency system of Hong Kong, following that of China, was based on the silver standard in the nineteenth and early part of the twentieth centuries.[4] In 1934, the United States decided to buy silver at a very high fixed rate, and that led to large outflows of silver from Hong Kong and China. As a result, both governments abandoned the silver standard. In December 1935, Hong Kong enacted the Currency Ordinance, later renamed the Exchange Fund Ordinance, and purchased all privately held silver coins. At the same time, the note-issuing banks, which were private enterprises, had to deposit their silver reserves with the newly created Exchange Fund and received certificates of indebtedness (CIs) in return. The Exchange Fund sold the silver in the London market for sterling. From then on, if an authorized bank wanted to issue more notes, it was obligated to purchase more CIs from the Exchange Fund with sterling at a fixed rate of HK$16 per pound. The Exchange Fund would also buy the CIs from the banks if the latter decided to decrease the money supply. Thus the monetary system had all the features of a currency board, with the exception that legal tenders were issued by authorized private banks rather than directly by the board.

The peg to sterling lasted for more than three decades, despite four years of interruption during World War II. In 1967, because of devaluation of sterling, the HK$16 peg could no longer be sustained. In July 1972 further pressure from the devaluation of sterling forced the eventual abolition of the link between sterling and the HK dollar. The latter was pegged to the U.S. dollar at a rate within an intervention band. This also did not last long. Again devaluation of the U.S. dollar and an inflow of capital to Hong Kong led to the decision to free-float the HK dollar against the U.S. dollar. The currency board system was no longer operating.

Under the free-floating system from 1974 to 1983, authorized banks still had to purchase CIs, which at this time were denominated in HK dollars, from the Exchange Fund if they wanted to issue more notes. The fund maintained an account with these banks. The payment for the CIs was simply a transfer of credit from the banks to the account of the Exchange Fund. Starting from May 1979, the note-issuing banks were required to maintain 100 percent liquid asset cover against the fund's short-term deposits. This cover did not imply that the Exchange Fund could effectively limit the creation of money because the banks could borrow foreign currency to obtain the liquid assets. Money growth in this period was higher and more volatile than before. In 1978, the government also decided to transfer the accumulated HK dollar fiscal surplus to the Exchange Fund, which has since then become the government's de facto savings account.

---

4. For more details on the historical development of the monetary regime in Hong Kong, see Greenwood (1995), Nugee (1995), and Schwartz (1993).

During the initial phase of the free-floating period, the HK dollar was very strong. However, from 1977 onward, it was subject to considerable downward pressure. The trade deficit was growing. Money supply, M2, increased at the rate of almost 25 percent a year, mainly because of even faster growth in bank credit. The start of Sino-British negotiations over the future of Hong Kong in 1982 led to a series of financial crises: stock market crash, real estate price collapse, runs on small banks, and rapid depreciation of the HK dollar. On 17 October 1983, the government decided to abolish the interest-withholding tax on HK dollar deposits and, more important, to go back to the currency board system. The exchange rate was fixed at U.S.$1 = HK$7.8. Banks issuing notes had to purchase CIs with U.S. dollars at this rate from the Exchange Fund. The reserves accumulated were invested mainly in interest-bearing U.S. government securities. Table 15.1 summarizes the historical evolution of Hong Kong's monetary institutions.

Several new changes to the currency board system of Hong Kong, now popularly known as the "linked exchange rate system," were introduced. In 1988, the Exchange Fund established new "accounting arrangements," which in effect empowered it to conduct open market operations. Legislative changes also allowed the government more flexibility in manipulating interest rates. Since March 1990, the fund was permitted to issue several kinds of "Exchange Fund bills," which were similar to short-term Treasury bills. In 1992, a sort of discount window was opened to provide liquidity to banks. The Hong Kong Monetary Authority (HKMA) was established in December 1992 to take over the power of the Exchange Fund Office and the Commissioner of Banking. The HKMA has since been active in adjusting interbank liquidity in response to changes in demand conditions.

Several remarks should be made here. First, the monetary institution in Hong Kong has not been a static system. In less than half a century, it has evolved from the silver standard, to a currency board with sterling being the reserve currency, then to a free-floating regime, and finally back to a currency board with a U.S. dollar link. More recently, as Schwartz (1993) has observed, there has been some "dilution" of the features that distinguish a currency board. Given historical hindsight, one can hardly believe that the present system will last forever, despite persistent assurances by the Hong Kong government that the linked exchange rate is there to stay permanently. This view is supported by the observation that historically no fixed exchange rate could be sustained for a very long period.[5] This motivates us to simulate in section 15.4.4 the conditions under which the Hong Kong currency board may collapse.

Second, from 1974 to now, Hong Kong has used two polar cases of mon-

---

5. Eichengreen (1994) casts doubt on the future of any pegged exchange rate regime in the twenty-first century. He predicts that only the two extremes of flexible exchange rate and monetary unification will survive.

Table 15.1   **Exchange Rate Regime for the Hong Kong Dollar**

Date	Exchange Rate Regime	Reference Rate
Until 4 Nov 1935	Silver standard	
6 Dec 1935	Pegged to sterling	£1 = HK$16
23 Nov 1967		£1 = HK$14.55
6 July 1972	Fixed to U.S. dollar with ±2.25% intervention	U.S.$1 = HK$5.65
14 Feb 1973	band around a central rate	U.S.$1 = HK$5.085
25 Nov 1974	Free float	
17 Oct 1983	Pegged to U.S. dollar	U.S.$1 = HK$7.80

Source: Nugee (1995).

etary systems, namely, free floating (1974–83) and currency board (1983–present). There have been no other economic institutional changes of a comparable order of magnitude. The government still follows the "positive noninterventionism" policy formulated more than two decades ago. It has been persistently keeping the size of the government small and leaving small budgetary surpluses in most fiscal years. It has also refrained from using fiscal policy as a fine-tuning tool. The legal system has remained intact, and Hong Kong's economic freedom has always been rated at the highest level by international agencies. These similarities between the two periods provide us with a relatively homogeneous setting in which to conduct a natural controlled experiment to compare the implications of the two systems.

Third, while structural homogeneity is needed for a controlled experiment on the one hand, sufficiently rich data variation is necessary for statistical purposes on the other. If the economic conditions of the two periods had remained perfectly stable, the data would hardly contain enough information for inferring the macroeconomic performance of the two systems. We need to observe how the two regimes respond to external shocks. Indeed, Hong Kong as a small open economy is extremely sensitive to external shocks, which may overshadow the "treatment effect" of a currency board system. Fortunately, by adopting the approach in Blanchard and Quah (1989), it is possible to isolate the supply and demand shocks during the two periods. Counterfactual simulations can be performed to identify the effects of the change in monetary regime.

Fourth, Hong Kong has gone through a number of major economic shocks from 1974 to now. This period covers the time span of several business cycles. There have also been big swings in real estate and stock markets. The quarterly data available are reasonably rich in variations that allow us to make meaningful inferences.

Last, the economic health and significant financial strength of Hong Kong provide an almost ideal situation to test the vulnerability of a currency board system when it is confronted with a crisis. At the end of 1996, foreign currency assets in the Exchange Fund amounted to U.S.$69.55 billion, the world's seventh largest reserve. The ratio of foreign currency assets in the Exchange Fund to currency in circulation was almost six. The value of the government's accumulated fiscal reserve was also substantial. In fact, it was contributing 27 percent of the Exchange Fund (see HKMA 1997). If simulations show that Hong Kong's currency board will face a crisis when it is subject to shocks of specified magnitude, it is hard to imagine that the currency board in a country with poorer economic health can survive in the same scenario.

15.3   Empirical Model

In this section, we discuss a framework that will be used to compare the macroeconomic performances of the flexible and linked exchange rate regimes when they are subject to exogenous shocks. To properly take into account the heterogeneity induced by these shocks, we adopt Blanchard and Quah's (1989) approach to identify them explicitly.

Our empirical framework is the structural vector autoregression (VAR) model initiated by Blanchard and Watson (1986), Sims (1986), and Bernanke (1986). Following Blanchard and Quah (1989) and Bayoumi and Eichengreen (1993, 1994), we formulate a bivariate model in output growth and inflation rate to identify two series of structural shocks: (1) those that have only transitory effects on the output level and (2) those that have permanent effects on the output level. Shocks of the first type are interpreted as demand shocks originating from innovations in the components of aggregate demand, while the second type are supply shocks originating from innovations in productivity and other factors that affect aggregate supply. This distinction is crucial for solving the identification problem discussed below. We now briefly describe the model and refer the reader to the above references and the surveys in Giannini (1992) and Watson (1994) for details.

Let $X_t = (\Delta y_t, \Delta p_t)'$, where y_t and p_t denote the logarithms of output and price level, respectively. X_t is assumed to be covariance stationary and have a moving average representation of the form

$$(1) \qquad X_t - \mu = B_0 e_t + B_1 e_{t-1} + B_2 e_{t-2} + \cdots \equiv B(L)e_t,$$

where $e_t = (e_{dt}, e_{st})'$ is a bivariate series of serially uncorrelated shocks with zero mean and covariance matrix Ω, $B(L) = B_0 + B_1 L + B_2 L^2 + \cdots$ is shorthand notation for the matrix polynomial in backshift operator L, and μ is the mean of X_t. Equation (1) is taken to be structural in that e_{dt} and e_{st} have behavioral interpretations as the demand shock and supply shock, respectively. The coefficient matrices in $B(L)$ capture the propagation mechanism of the dynamic system. In particular, the (i, j) element of B_k is the kth-step impulse response of the ith endogenous variable with respect to a one unit increase in the jth shock.

Equation (1) is not directly estimated. We proceed in the following steps. First, we estimate a VAR in X_t:

(2) $$A(L)(X_t - \mu) = u_t,$$

where $\{u_t\}$ is a bivariate series of serially uncorrelated errors with zero mean and covariance matrix Σ and $A(L)$ is a matrix polynomial in L. Second, we invert the estimated autoregressive polynomial in equation (2) to obtain the Wold moving average representation, which is the reduced form of equation (1):

(3) $$X_t - \mu = u_t + C_1 u_{t-1} + C_2 u_{t-2} + \cdots \equiv C(L)u_t.$$

Again, $C(L) = I + C_1 L + C_2 L^2 + \cdots$ is shorthand for the matrix polynomial as stated. In our implementation the reduced form VAR is estimated with six lags and the Wold representation in equation (3) is expanded up to 200 lags, which is more than adequate. Given estimates of the reduced form parameters $C(L)$ and Σ and the reduced form residuals u_t, is it possible to recover the structural parameters $B(L)$ and Ω and the structural residuals e_t? This is a classical identification problem in simultaneous equations models, and the answer is yes provided that enough a priori restrictions have been placed on the structural parameters. By comparing equations (1) and (3) it can be checked that the structural and reduced forms are related by the following relationships:

(4) $$B_0 e_t = u_t, \quad \text{for all } t,$$

(5) $$B_j = C_j B_0, \quad j = 0, 1, 2, \ldots,$$

(6) $$B_0 \Omega B_0' = \Sigma.$$

Equations (4) and (5) imply that the structural form in equation (1) can be recovered from the reduced form in equation (3) once B_0 is determined. Thus the identification problem boils down to imposing sufficiently many restrictions so that B_0 can be solved from equation (6).

In our bivariate system, there are seven structural parameters in B_0 and Ω, but only three reduced form parameters in Σ; we thus need four restrictions to just-identify the structural model. The first three restrictions come from assuming Ω to be the identity matrix. The zero-covariance restriction dictates that the two structural shocks are uncorrelated, implying that any cross-equation interaction of the two shocks on the dependent variables is captured by the lag structure in $B(L)$. The two unit-variance restrictions imply that B_0 is identified up to multiples of the two standard deviations. Thus B_j has the interpretation of being the jth-step impulse response with respect to a one standard deviation innovation in the structural shocks. The last restriction comes from Blanchard and Quah's (1989) idea of restricting the long-run multiplier. Since demand shocks are assumed to have no permanent effects on output level, this translates into the restriction that the long-run multiplier (i.e., the sum of impulse responses) of demand shocks on output growth must be zero; that is,

(7) $$B_{11}(1) \equiv B_{11,0} + B_{11,1} + B_{11,2} + \cdots = 0,$$

where $B_{11}(1)$ and $B_{11,j}$ are the upper left-hand corners of $B(1)$ and B_j, respectively.

To see how equation (7) can be translated into a restriction on B_0, let J be the lower triangular Cholesky factor of Σ and notice that equation (6) can be written as (after assuming $\Omega = I$)

$$(8) \qquad B_0 B_0' = \Sigma = JJ'.$$

Thus B_0 can be determined from J up to an orthogonal transformation S; that is,

$$(9) \qquad B_0 = JS, \qquad SS' = I.$$

Orthogonality implies that S (up to one column sign change) must be of the form

$$(10) \qquad S = \begin{bmatrix} a & \sqrt{1 - a^2} \\ \sqrt{1 - a^2} & -a \end{bmatrix}.$$

Equations (5) and (9) imply

$$(11) \qquad B(1) = C(1)B_0 = HS, \qquad H = C(1)J.$$

Equation (7) then implies a restriction

$$(12) \qquad H_{11}a + H_{12}\sqrt{1 - a^2} = 0,$$

which determines a and hence S. Once S is found, B_0 can be determined by equation (9). Given B_0, the structural parameters and the structural shocks can then be recovered from the reduced form via equations (4) and (5).

The output and price data are quarterly Hong Kong real per capita GDP (in 1990 prices) and the corresponding GDP deflator from 1975:1 to 1995:3, taken from various issues of *Estimates of Gross Domestic Product* and *Hong Kong Monthly Digest of Statistics,* published by the Hong Kong government.[6] Both output and price series exhibit strong seasonality, and they are deseasonalized before use by a spectral method by Sims (1974) and implemented in Doan (1992, sec. 11.7). The full sample is divided into two halves corresponding to the two exchange rate regimes: the free-floating period straddles 1975:1–83:3 and the currency board period covers 1983:4–95:3.

15.4   Results and Interpretations

In this section, we present the empirical results and interpret them. In particular, we use these results to compare the macroeconomic performance of the free-floating and currency board regimes from several perspectives.

---

6. Hong Kong Census and Statistics Department (1995, various issues-b). Quarterly population figures are obtained by log-linearly interpolating the annual data.

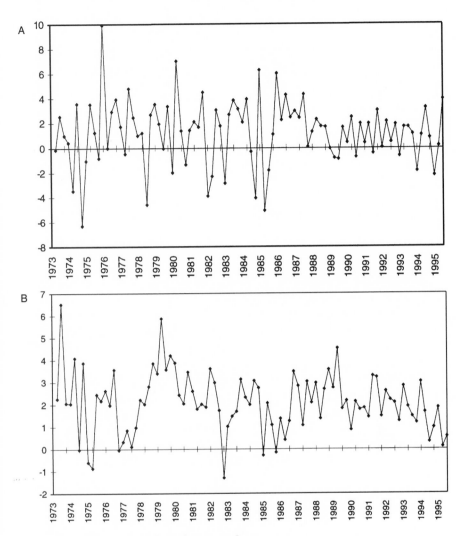

Fig. 15.1   Macroeconomic performance data
Note: A, per capita real GDP growth rate (percent). B, inflation rate (percent).

15.4.1   Institutional Effect or Environmental Effect?

Figure 15.1 displays the data for the full sample period, covering both the free-floating and currency board regimes. It can be seen that both inflation and output growth are somewhat more stable during the currency board years than in the free-floating years. More precisely, the standard deviations of output growth rates during the free-floating and currency board years are 2.94 and 2.23, respectively, and those of the inflation rates are 1.55 and 1.05, respectively.

Table 15.2   Summary Statistics of Vector Autoregression Estimation

Statistic	VAR 1: (Free Floating)		VAR 2: Currency Board	
	Output Growth Rate	Inflation Rate	Output Growth Rate	Inflation Rate
R^2	0.35	0.53	0.35	0.43
D.W.	1.7	1.58	2.01	1.97
Ljung-Box Q	[0.42]	[0.88]	[0.86]	[0.12]
Overall significance[a]	[0.01]		[0.001]	
Data range	1975:1–83:3		1983:4–95:3	

Note: Numbers in brackets are *p*-values.

[a]Reports the *p*-value of a likelihood ratio test for the null hypothesis that all regressors in the system (except the constant terms) are zero.

What is behind the observed reduction in volatility in both output growth rates and inflation rates? Some believe that this simply reflects a more congenial international environment during the 1980s than in the 1970s. On the other hand, advocates of fixed exchange rates and currency boards, including the Hong Kong government, sometimes argue that this is due to the inherent superiority of the linked exchange rate regime over the free-floating system (e.g., see Sheng 1995). Granted that both arguments are reasonable and neither can be rejected a priori, it is then necessary to disentangle the "institutional effect" from the "environmental effect." In our structural VAR model, the structural parameters B_j play the role of institution, and the structural shocks u_t represent the external environment. By estimating two separate structural models for the two exchange rate regimes, we obtain two sets of structural parameters representing two institutions and two sets of shocks representing two different external environments. We show below that both the parameters and the shocks have changed.

Table 15.2 reports the summary statistics of the estimations for equation (1) in section 15.3 under the free-floating and currency board regimes. It can be seen that they are statistically significant at the 0.01 and 0.001 levels, respectively. The estimated parameters for the structural equation (1) are different across the two regimes. This is evident from a likelihood ratio version of the Chow test, which rejects the null hypotheses of no structural change at the 5 percent level.[7] The result supports the Lucas critique. We need to use a different set of structural parameters to capture the institutional effect due to a change in the monetary regime. It is assumed, however, that these parameters are invariant under exogenous shocks.

Figure 15.2 presents the quarterly demand and supply shocks (1975–95) that

---

7. The likelihood ratio statistic LR $= -2(\ln L_0 - \ln L_1 - \ln L_2) = -2(699.76 - 291.85 - 428.66) = 41.5$ rejects the null hypothesis of no structural change at the 5 percent level according to a chi-squared distribution with 26 degrees of freedom. The terms $\ln L_0$, $\ln L_1$, and $\ln L_2$ are the log likelihood values of the VARs estimated by using the full sample (1975:1–95:3), the free-floating period (1975:1–83:3), and the currency board period (1983:4–95:3), respectively.

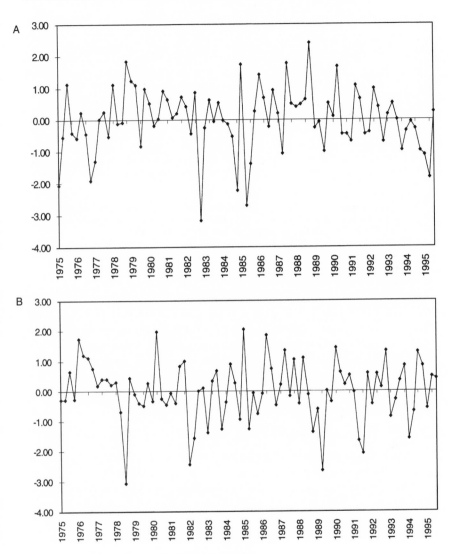

Fig. 15.2   Demand (A) and supply (B) shocks

are identified by using the econometric framework in section 15.3. Table 15.3 reports summary statistics for the shocks. By the skewness and kurtosis tests, one can observe that both types of shocks during the free-floating period exhibit substantial nonnormality, which can be attributed to a few large negative shocks. The skewness of the shocks can be clearly discerned from their empirical distributions, depicted in figure 15.3.[8] Shocks during the currency board

---

8. The empirical distribution is obtained by matching the first four sample moments with a Gram-Charlier expansion. See Johnson and Kotz (1970, 15–20).

Table 15.3   **Characteristics of Structural Disturbances**

Characteristic	Demand Shocks		Supply Shocks	
	Free Floating	Currency Board	Free Floating	Currency Board
Skewness	−1.01 [0.003]	−0.18 [0.57]	−0.91 [0.008]	−0.31 [0.34]
Kurtosis	4.50 [0.03]	3.47 [0.38]	4.69 [0.01]	2.91 [0.95]
Maximum	1.84	2.40	1.97	2.04
Minimum	−3.17	−2.69	−3.06	−2.64

Notes: Skewness $(b_1^{1/2}) = m_3/m_2^{3/2}$ and kurtosis $(b_2) = m_4/m_2^2$, m_k is the kth sample moment around the mean. Numbers in brackets are p-values for testing either population skewness = 0 (symmetry) or kurtosis = 3 (normal shape).

For testing symmetry, Fisher's test statistic $\xi = x (1 + 3/n + 91/4n^2) − (3/2n)(1 − 111/2n)$ $(x^3 − 3x) − (33/8n^2)(x^5 − 10x^3 + 15x)$ is approximately distributed as $N(0,1)$ under the null hypothesis, where $x = b_1^{1/2}(n − 1)/[6(n − 2)]^{1/2}$ and n is the sample size. The approximate normality is very accurate even in a small sample, see Kendall and Stuart (1958, 298).

For testing kurtosis = 3, the test statistic $z = y[(n − 1)(n − 2)(n − 3)/24n(n + 1)]^{1/2}$ is approximately distributed as $N(0,1)$ under the null hypothesis, where $y = [n^2/(n − 1)(n − 2)(n −3)]$ $[(n + 1)m_4 − 3(n − 1)m_2^2]/s^4$ and s is the sample standard deviation (with divisor $n − 1$). See Kendall and Stuart (1958, 305–6).

period, on the contrary, show no strong evidence against normality, as is clear from the skewness and kurtosis tests and their empirical distributions.

This indicates that the two exchange rate regimes are subject to exogenous shocks of different characteristics. Simply comparing the macroeconomic performance in the two periods without properly controlling for the environmental effect can be misleading. This forces us to use better methods.

15.4.2   Variance Decomposition and Impulse Response Functions

The relative importance of demand and supply shocks changes dramatically across the two exchange rate regimes. This is demonstrated by the results on variance decomposition of the shocks and the estimated values of the impulse responses.

Table 15.4 shows the percentages of variance in output growth rate and inflation that can be explained by the demand shocks in the last n quarters, where n is the number in the extreme left-hand column. The percentages explained by the supply shocks are given by 100 minus the table entries. Table 15.5 is similar to table 15.4 but shows the variance in output level and price level explained. As can be readily seen, during the free-floating regime, demand shocks explain little of the variations in output growth and level, but a substantial fraction of inflation or price movements.[9] On the other hand, supply shocks can account for most of the output changes, but little of the price fluctuations.

---

9. The values in the "output level" columns of table 15.5 decline when n becomes larger. This is because the variance of output level explained by demand shocks must converge to zero in the long run. Readers are reminded that in section 15.3, we have built in the identifying restriction that demand shocks have no long-term effects on output level.

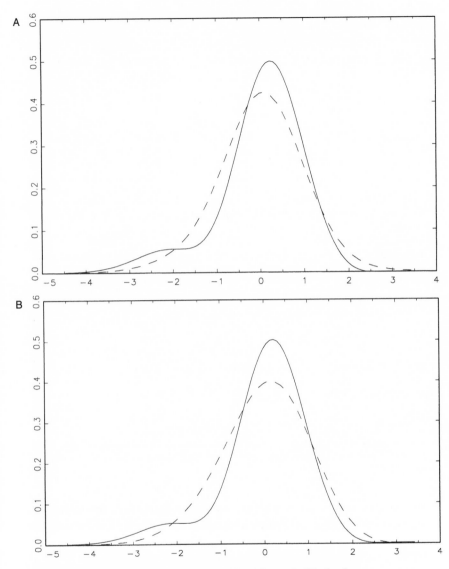

Fig. 15.3   Density functions of demand (A) and supply (B) shocks
Note: Free-floating period (*solid line*) and currency board period (*dashed line*).

In the currency board regime, the results are different. Demand shocks can explain much of the variations in the output and price series, at least in the short run. The movements explained by the supply shocks are also substantial.

The dynamic impulse responses of output and price with respect to demand shocks are consistent with the variance decomposition results above. In figure 15.4, the impulse responses, or cumulative effects of demand shocks on output

Table 15.4   **Percentage of Forecast Error Variance Explained by Demand Shocks**

	Output Growth Rate		Inflation Rate	
Quarter	Free Floating	Currency Board	Free Floating	Currency Board
1	0.66	67.16	96.57	16.71
4	9.62	57.71	86.40	37.79
8	9.25	62.61	82.38	37.52
12	9.63	63.65	82.05	38.78
16	9.76	62.70	81.83	39.10
20	9.75	62.78	81.83	39.21
24	9.76	62.80	81.79	39.27
28	9.77	62.81	81.79	39.28
32	9.77	62.81	81.79	39.29

Note: The corresponding percentages explained by supply shocks are given by 100 minus the table entries.

Table 15.5   **Percentage of Forecast Error Variance Explained by Demand Shocks**

	Output Level		Price Level	
Quarter	Free Floating	Currency Board	Free Floating	Currency Board
1	0.002	80.44	99.94	8.28
4	0.124	73.51	99.99	74.38
8	0.050	33.06	99.87	86.20
12	0.024	16.18	99.45	84.55
16	0.013	9.21	99.20	83.16
20	0.008	5.65	99.12	83.45
24	0.005	3.79	99.00	83.37
28	0.004	2.72	98.88	83.09
32	0.003	2.03	98.80	83.02

Note: The corresponding percentages explained by supply shocks are given by 100 minus the table entries.

and price during the last n quarters, are plotted against n.[10] The response of output is both smaller and shorter in duration under the flexible exchange regime. On the other hand, the response of price level under the currency board regime is smaller than that under the free-floating system.

Figure 15.5, depicts the impulse responses of output and price to supply shocks, respectively. The effects of supply shocks on price level across the two regimes are negative, a result consistent with simple economics. The impact of supply shocks on price level in the currency board regime appears to be bigger than that under the free-floating regime. Supply shocks, however, have smaller effects on output during the currency board years. These results are also consistent with the patterns in variance decomposition.

---

10. The magnitude of the demand shock in each period is one standard deviation.

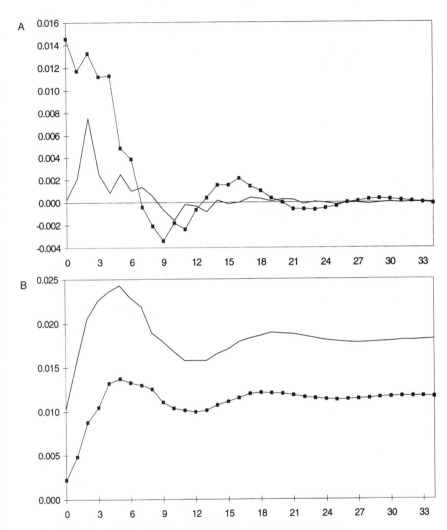

Fig. 15.4   Response to demand shocks: output (*A*) and price (*B*)
Note: Free-floating period (*plain line*) and currency board period (*boxed line*).

What can we draw from the variance decomposition and impulse response exercises? In fact, the results can be interpreted in a convenient way. The aggregate supply curve during the free-floating years is very steep. It flattens in the subsequent period. The aggregate demand curve, on the other hand, has a relatively flat slope under the free-floating regime. It steepens in the currency board years. These changes in the slope explain why the Chow test detects a structural shift in the model.

Why has the aggregate supply curve, or more properly, the short-run supply curve, flattened over time? Bayoumi and Eichengreen (1994) discovered a sim-

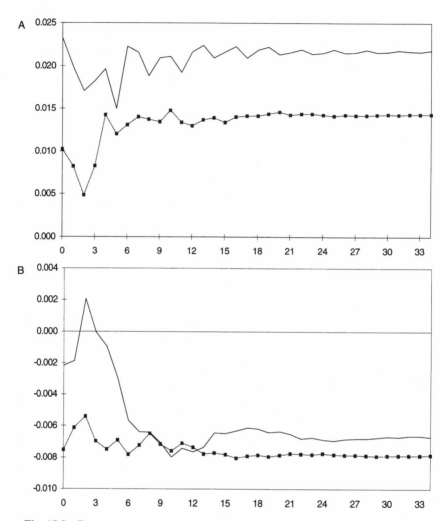

Fig. 15.5   Response to supply shocks: output (A) and price (B)
Note: Free-floating period (*plain line*) and currency board period (*boxed line*).

ilar pattern for the industrial countries over the past hundred years. The explanation does not necessarily lie in the adoption of a currency board. After all, during part of the sample period studied by Bayoumi and Eichengreen, countries were moving from fixed exchange to free floating, while Hong Kong was heading in the opposite direction. The flattening of the short-run aggregate supply curve indicates that there are more nominal rigidities. Probably the latter are due to increases in labor legislation and union influences in Hong Kong since the 1980s.[11]

11. A number of laws on labor protection have been introduced since the 1980s. These range from long-service payment, severance compensation, leaves for pregnant female workers, etc.

The steepening of the aggregate demand curve under the currency board can be usefully analyzed by a simple textbook model (Sachs and Larrain 1993, chaps. 13 and 14). In a fixed exchange rate regime, an increase in the domestic price will hurt exports and increase imports. The underlying *IS* curve of the economy will shift to the left. Since a small open economy has to face a given world interest rate, the *LM* curve will have to adjust endogenously so that it intersects the *IS* curve at the level equal to the world interest rate. The decline in output due to the increase in price, and hence the slope of the aggregate demand curve, is therefore completely determined by the magnitude of the movement of the *IS* curve. In the case of a free-floating regime, an increase in price causes the *LM* curve to move to the left. The changes in the exchange rate and price will then lead to an adjustment of the *IS* curve so that it intersects the *LM* curve at an interest rate equal to the prevailing world interest rate. This time the slope of the aggregate demand curve depends on how responsive the *LM* curve is to an increase in price. In general, the slope of the aggregate demand curve under a currency board can be either steeper or flatter than that under a free-floating system, depending on the relative responsiveness of the *IS* and *LM* curves to a change in price level. It appears that the *IS* curve in Hong Kong is not as sensitive to price change as the *LM* curve. Thus the aggregate demand curve is steeper under the currency board regime.[12]

We can draw the following conclusions from the results above. Output in Hong Kong under a currency board seems to be less susceptible to supply shocks, which are usually not induced by government short-term policies. However, demand shocks do cause greater short-term volatility in output under the currency board system. If a government with a currency board is able to discipline itself to pursue a stable and predictable fiscal policy, the volatility of the economy may be lower than that under a free-floating system. An explanation of why Hong Kong's economy has been less volatile after the adoption of the linked exchange rate is that stable fiscal policy has always been the philosophy of the financial branch of its government.

15.4.3   Counterfactual Simulations

As discussed in subsection 15.4.1, the two periods under consideration are subject to shocks with different properties. One way to compare the performance of the two regimes is to consider the following two cases:

Case 1. What would have happened to the economy if the currency board system were adopted from 1975 to 1983?

Case 2. What would have happened to the economy if the free-floating system were adopted from 1983 to 1995?

To answer the question in case 1, we apply the demand and supply shocks of 1975–83 to equation (1) estimated for the currency board regime and com-

---

12. It can be shown by a simple calibrated model that the *IS* curve in Hong Kong is not as responsive to price change as the *LM* curve.

Table 15.6   Counterfactual Simulations

Case	Output Growth Rate (%)		Inflation Rate (%)	
	Mean	Standard Deviation	Mean	Standard Deviation
Case 1: 1975–83				
Actual (free floating)	1.54	2.94	2.07	1.55
Simulated (currency board)	1.27	2.46	1.82	1.21
Case 2: 1983–95				
Actual (currency board)	1.22	2.23	1.94	1.05
Simulated (free floating)	1.51	2.79	2.13	1.36

pare the simulated results with the actual time path. To answer the question in case 2, we do the simulations in a similar way, but this time we apply the shocks of 1983–95 to equation (1) for the free-floating regime. The approach is based on the assumption that the supply and demand shocks identified in the estimation procedure of section 15.3 are invariant under change in exchange rate regime. This exogeneity assumption makes a lot of sense for Hong Kong. In this small open economy whose external sector is much larger than its GDP, most supply and demand shocks are external. The government has been following the same stable fiscal policy throughout the two periods under consideration. Moreover, there is no central bank in Hong Kong to determine the money supply, which is largely rule based in both regimes and automatically adjusts to external shocks. Thus there is no a priori reason to believe that the supply and demand shocks are regime dependent.

The counterfactual exercise amounts to replacing the structural residual e_t in equation (1) with a hypothetical residual e_t^* and then simulating a new data path X_t^*, given structural parameters μ and $B(L)$. For example, in case 1, e_t, μ, and $B(L)$ are the residual and structural parameters for the free-floating regime, while e_t^* is taken to be the residual for the currency board regime. In practice, however, the moving average representation in equation (1) is difficult to work with. We instead perform the simulation by equation (2) with a reduced form residual u_t^* constructed from e_t^* via equation (4). It is straightforward to check that our two-step procedure is equivalent to a direct simulation of equation (1).

Summaries of these counterfactual simulations are presented in table 15.6. The results show that if the currency board system were adopted in the first period, the average growth rate would have declined, but inflation would have gone down also. Since the standard deviations are also lower, we can say that both output growth and inflation would have been more stable. The patterns for the second period are similar. The cost of a currency board system is lower output growth. However, there are also benefits. The inflation rate decreases, and the economy is less volatile. The trade-off is transparent when the comparison is in terms of levels (rather than growth rates) as depicted in figures 15.6 and 15.7.

The counterfactual simulations disentangle the effects of regime shift and

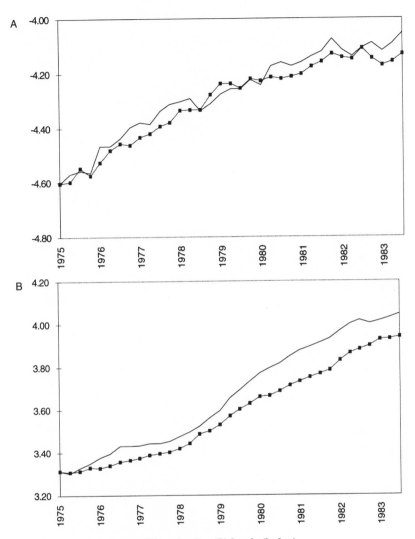

Fig. 15.6   Case 1: output (*A*) and price (*B*) levels (in log)
Note: Actual (free floating; *plain line*) and simulated (currency board; *boxed line*).

changes in the external environment. As an example, consider the reduction in output growth volatility when the monetary system changes from free floating to currency board. The standard deviation of output growth rates goes down from 2.94 to 2.33, a roughly 32 percent reduction in volatility. From simulation case 1, we see that if the currency board system were adopted in the environment of the 1970s, output volatility would have declined to 2.46, a 20 percent reduction from 2.94. This implies that 62.5 percent of the reduction in output volatility that we actually observe from the data is due to the adoption of the

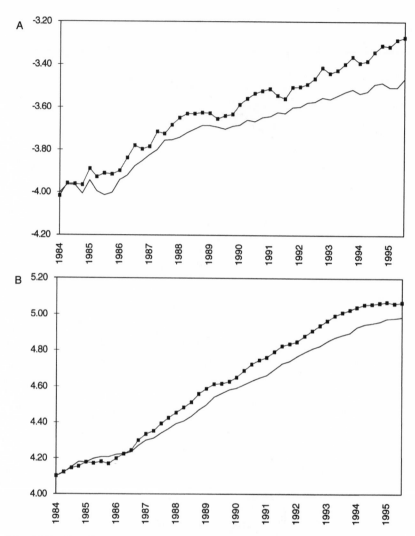

Fig. 15.7   Case 2: output (A) and price (B) levels (in log)
Note: Actual (currency board; *plain line*) and simulated (free floating; *boxed line*).

currency board, while the remaining 37.5 percent is due to a more tranquil external environment in the 1980s. Similarly, the marginal effect of the currency board on inflation volatility is to reduce it from 1.55 to 1.21, or about 28 percent. The observed reduction, however, is from 1.55 to 1.05, or a decline of 48 percent. One can then make the following decomposition. The difference in external environment during the 1970s and 1980s accounts for 42 percent of the reduction in inflation volatility, while the change in the monetary regime explains the remaining 58 percent of the reduction.

15.4.4   Currency and Banking Crises

The Hong Kong government has been vehemently claiming that the Exchange Fund is financially strong and the linked exchange rate will be defended. As can be seen from the balance sheet of the fund in table 15.7, Hong Kong indeed owns one of the largest foreign reserves in the world. Does it mean that the HK$7.8 link is immune to crisis? In theory, because of the 100 percent backup, a crisis would not occur even if people exchanged all the currency for foreign assets. However, one should note that at the end of 1996, total M3 equaled HK$2,586 billion, more than five times the foreign currency assets in the fund. Of this M3, 41.2 percent is in bank deposits denominated in foreign money (see HKMA 1997). Suppose people decide to change the portfolio of M3 by exchanging HK dollar deposits for foreign money. If the change is big enough, the banking sector must sell its domestic assets for foreign money to avoid bank runs. It is not clear whether the fund is willing to buy these domestic assets. However, the Exchange Fund Ordinance does allow the financial secretary the flexibility to do so even though Hong Kong's monetary institution is a currency board.[13] Suppose the Exchange Fund will indeed provide the foreign liquidity to avoid bank runs. If people decide to increase their foreign exchange holdings from 41.2 to 47.9 percent of M3, the accumulated earnings in the balance sheet of the fund will disappear. If the foreign deposits ratio goes up further to 53.5 percent, the entire fiscal reserve will also be used up.[14]

These rather simplistic calculations tell us that a run on the HK dollar could occur even when the change in people's portfolio holdings is not exceptionally big. We do not have an estimate of portfolio holdings as a function of other variables. However, one can reasonably speculate that the confidence in the HK dollar will suffer significantly and the link will face a crisis if the fiscal reserve is completely used up.

The amount of fiscal reserve is affected by shocks to the economy. Since the Hong Kong government has been following a reasonably stable fiscal policy, we focus our attention here on supply shocks. How big are the supply shocks if the fiscal reserve is to be eliminated? This can be answered by making use of the empirical estimates in this paper.

The long-run impulse response of the logarithm of $y(t)$ with respect to a supply shock of one standard deviation is 0.0143. This means that a one-

---

13. The Exchange Fund Ordinance, Section 3(2), states, "The Fund, or any part of it, may be held in Hong Kong currency or in foreign exchange or in gold or in silver or may be invested by the Financial Secretary in such securities or other assets as he, after having consulted the Exchange Fund Advisory Committee, considers appropriate" (HKMA 1994, 51). See also n. 3 above.

14. After 1 July 1997, the money accumulated in the Land Fund will be handed over to the Hong Kong Special Administrative Region Government. This fund, which amounts to roughly HK$120 billion, is generally regarded as part of the fiscal reserves of Hong Kong. Thus the financial strength backing up the Hong Kong dollar could be further enhanced. China also promises to use its own foreign reserves to support the HK dollar in case of emergency.

Table 15.7   Exchange Fund Balance Sheet (millions of HK dollars)

	1989	1990	1991	1992	1993	1994	1995	1996
Assets								
Foreign currency assets	149,152	192,323	225,333	274,948	335,499	384,359	428,547	493,802
HK dollar assets	9,625	3,874	10,788	12,546	12,987	24,126	32,187	40,715
Total	158,777	196,197	236,121	287,494	348,486	408,485	460,734	534,517
Liabilities								
Certificates of indebtedness	37,191	40,791	46,410	58,130	68,801	74,301	77,600	82,480
Fiscal reserve account	52,546	63,226	69,802	96,145	115,683	131,240	125,916	145,898
Coins in circulation	2,012	2,003	2,299	2,559	2,604	3,372	3,597	4,164
Exchange Fund bills and notes	0	6,671	13,624	19,324	25,157	46,140	53,125	83,509
Balance of banking system	978	480	500	1,480	1,385	2,208	1,762	474
Other liabilities	1,603	391	4,834	3,220	7,314	22,614	38,600	45,130
Total	94,330	113,562	137,469	180,858	220,944	279,875	300,600	361,655
Accumulated earnings	64,447	82,635	98,652	106,636	137,542	128,610	160,134	172,862

Sources: HKMA (1994, 1995, 1997).

Table 15.8   **Postshock Output Level (percent of preshock output)**

Duration (quarters)	Size of Negative Supply Shock (in standard deviations)			
	1	2	3	4
1	98.6	97.1	95.7	94.3
2	97.2	94.4	91.6	88.9
3	95.8	91.7	87.7	83.8
4	94.4	89.0	83.9	79.0
5	93.1	86.5	80.3	74.5
6	91.7	84.0	76.9	70.2
7	90.4	81.6	73.6	66.2
8	89.1	79.3	70.4	62.4

standard-deviation shock will reduce output permanently by 1.43 percent, other things being equal. Thus we can calculate the postshock output level $y(t)^*$ by the formula

$$y(t)^* = (1 - 0.0143x)y(t)$$

for a supply shock of x standard deviations. Similarly, for K periods of negative supply shocks, each of size x, the postshock output level should be

$$y(t)^* = (1 - 0.0143x)^K y(t).$$

In table 15.8, we calculate the percentages, $100(y(t)^*/y(t))$, for $x = 1, 2, 3, 4$ and $K = 1, 2, \ldots, 8$. From data for 1985–94, the average ratios of total government expenditure and revenue to GDP are 16 and 16.8 percent, respectively (see Hong Kong Census and Statistics Department, various issues-a). We assume that the revenue ratio is fixed. Postshock revenue is

$$0.168y(t)^* = [0.168(1 - 0.0143x)^K]y(t).$$

Thus the effect of the supply shock on revenue is equivalent to a "tax cut," with the new effective tax rate being the term inside the brackets above. The effect is shown in table 15.9. From GDP data, we can infer that each percentage point decline in the revenue-output ratio will reduce revenue by HK$12 billion. Making use of table 15.8, one can come up with results in different scenarios. For example, if there are negative three-standard-deviation supply shocks lasting for two years, the loss in revenue every year will be approximately HK$51.6 billion. It only takes about three years for the fiscal reserve to be completely depleted if political pressures prohibit the government from reducing its expenditures accordingly. Since major historical changes in Hong Kong's future are upcoming, large negative supply shocks or perhaps even significant structural shifts in the transition period cannot be ruled out. The stability of the currency board system in the future has yet to be tested.

Currency crises can lead to bank runs. But bank runs can occur for other

Table 15.9   Postshock Effective Revenue-Output Ratio (percent)

Duration (quarters)	Size of Negative Supply Shock (in standard deviations)			
	1	2	3	4
1	16.6	16.3	16.1	15.8
2	16.3	15.9	15.4	14.9
3	16.1	15.4	14.7	14.1
4	15.9	15.0	14.1	13.3
5	15.6	14.5	13.5	12.5
6	15.4	14.1	12.9	11.8
7	15.2	13.7	12.4	11.1
8	15.0	13.3	11.8	10.5

reasons too. Since the typical currency board does not provide a lender of last resort, bank runs are often regarded as the Achilles' heel of the system. Indeed, banking crises did occur in Hong Kong a number of times, all during the currency board years. The government and the banking system resorted to several ways to deal with them.

In 1994 there were 180 licensed banks in Hong Kong, 16 of which were owned mostly by local shareholders (HKMA 1994, 90–91). Government policies toward runs on local banks and foreign banks seemed to be different. The government did not attempt to support Citibank in 1991 when rumors caused a short-lived run, nor did it try to rescue the Bank of Credit and Commerce International's Hong Kong branch before its collapse in the same year. However, it moved to take over two small local banks in the mid-1960s and three more in the period 1982–86. It also provided some emergency funds to support five banks in the same period, four of which were later acquired by others. The note-issuing banks also played an important role in cushioning the shocks from the runs. They supported one bank in 1961 and three in 1965–66, and took over three more in the same period. Thus, in the 1960s, the government relied mainly on the financially strong note-issuing banks to either lend to or take over troubled local banks. In more recent years, the government seemed to have resorted to the Exchange Fund for playing the role of lender of last resort.[15] This is another reason to say that some of the features of a currency board have been diluted in Hong Kong.

15.5   What Can We Learn from Hong Kong's Experience?

The performance of the currency board in Hong Kong has not been bad so far. Although it may have lowered output growth, inflation has also gone down.

15. See Jao (1991, chap. 13) and Ho, Scott, and Wong (1991, chap. 1) for more details about banking crises in Hong Kong.

In fact, the more revealing results from the counterfactual exercises concern stability. When both regimes are subject to the same exogenous shocks, output and prices are less volatile under a currency board.

The stability result is not general. Simulations on impulse responses show that output is less sensitive to supply shocks under a currency board than under a free-floating regime. On the other hand, demand shocks can cause stronger short-term volatility in output in a currency board system. The relative stability in output in Hong Kong to a large extent must have come from the government's self-discipline in fiscal policy, which is based on two rules: maintaining a balanced budget or small surplus and keeping government size small. Other countries without a stable rule-based fiscal policy may not succeed in reducing output volatility even if they have currency boards.[16]

The fiscal restraint affects not only output stability but also the credibility of the exchange rate system. A weakness of the currency board system is that people may doubt the determination and capability of the government to maintain perfect convertibility at the specified rate. The conservative fiscal policy has been instrumental in creating surpluses in almost every budgetary year. Without the significant fiscal reserve, confidence in the HK dollar may suffer. In recent years, since the Exchange Fund has been acting as if it could be a lender of last resort, its financial strength, which is partly supported by a large fiscal reserve, is all the more important. Perhaps one reason why fiscal policy in Hong Kong is coordinated with its monetary system is that the financial secretary has the authority to control both.

Despite the financial strength of the Exchange Fund, the HK dollar has occasionally been subject to considerable speculative pressure. For example, in mid-January 1995, the HK dollar depreciated 0.4 percent briefly. On all such occasions, the speculations have been effectively countered (HKMA 1995). Given the excellent track record, do people have enough confidence in the HK dollar? As mentioned in subsection 15.4.4, 46.2 percent of M3 is in deposits denominated in foreign currency. This large portion is an indication that people only have limited confidence in the future of the HK dollar, in spite of all the assurance the government has provided.

Should other countries adopt the currency board system? The above analysis indicates that the decent performance in Hong Kong has been due to a combination of favorable factors, and yet, the possibility of monetary collapse cannot be ruled out. It is doubtful that many countries have equal or better conditions.

---

16. The financial secretary of Hong Kong articulated his commitment to noninterventionist rule-based fiscal policy by referring to a story in Greek mythology. The half-bird, half-woman Sirens sang so beautifully that all sailors who heard them would dive into the sea and try to swim to them, only to drown and die at their feet. He said that he would tie himself to the mast of the ship when he heard them singing. See Tsang (1995).

References

Bayoumi, T., and B. Eichengreen. 1993. Shocking aspects of European monetary integration. In *Adjustment and growth in the European Monetary Union,* ed. F. Torres and F. Giavazzi. Cambridge: Cambridge University Press.

———. 1994. Macroeconomic adjustment under Bretton Woods and the post–Bretton Woods float: An impulse response analysis. *Economic Journal* 104 (July): 813–27.

Bernanke, B. 1986. Alternative explanations of the money-income correlation. *Carnegie-Rochester Conference Series on Public Policy* 25:49–99.

Blanchard, O. J., and D. Quah. 1989. The dynamic effects of aggregate demand and supply disturbances. *American Economic Review* 79 (September): 655–73.

Blanchard, O. J., and M. Watson. 1986. Are business cycles all alike? In *The American business cycle: Continuity and change,* ed. R. Gordon. Chicago: University of Chicago Press.

Doan, T. A. 1992. *RATS user's manual version 4.* Evanston, Ill.: Estima.

Eichengreen, B. 1994. *International monetary arrangements for the 21st century.* Washington, D.C.: Brookings Institution.

Giannini, C. 1992. *Topics in structural VAR econometrics.* Berlin: Springer.

Greenwood, J. 1995. The debate on the optimum monetary system. *Asian Monetary Monitor* 19 (March–April): 1–5.

Hanke, S. H., L. Jonung, and K. Schuler. 1993. *Russian currency and finance: A currency board approach to reform.* London: Routledge.

Hanke, S. H., and K. Schuler. 1994. *Currency boards for developing countries.* San Francisco: Institute for Contemporary Studies Press.

Ho, R. Y. K., R. H. Scott, and K. A. Wong. 1991. *The Hong Kong financial system.* Hong Kong: Oxford University Press.

Hong Kong Census and Statistics Department. 1995. *Estimates of gross domestic product 1961 to 1995.* Hong Kong: Government Printer.

———. Various issues-a. *Hong Kong annual digest of statistics.* Hong Kong: Government Printer.

———. Various issues-b. *Hong Kong monthly digest of statistics.* Hong Kong: Government Printer.

Hong Kong Monetary Authority. 1994, 1995. *Annual report.* Hong Kong: Hong Kong Monetary Authority, Press and Publications Section.

———. 1997. *Monthly statistical bulletin,* April issue. Hong Kong: Hong Kong Monetary Authority, Press and Publications Section.

Jao, Y. C. 1991. *Hong Kong's financial system towards the future* (in Chinese). Hong Kong: Joint Publishing (H.K.) Company.

Johnson, N. L., and S. Kotz. 1970. *Distributions in statistics—Continuous univariate distribution,* vol. 1. New York: Wiley.

Kendall, M. G., and A. Stuart. 1958. *The advanced theory of statistics,* vol. 1. London: Griffin.

Nugee, J. 1995. A brief history of the exchange fund. In *Money and banking in Hong Kong.* Hong Kong: Hong Kong Monetary Authority.

Persson, T., and G. Tabellini. 1990. *Macroeconomic policy, credibility and politics.* Chur, Switzerland: Harwood.

Sachs, J. D., and F. Larrain. 1993. *Macroeconomics in the global economy.* New York: Harvester Wheatsheaf.

Schwartz, A. J. 1993. Currency boards: Their past, present and possible future role. *Carnegie-Rochester Conference Series on Public Policy* 39:147–87.

Sheng, A. 1995. The linked exchange rate system: Review and prospects. *Hong Kong Monetary Authority Quarterly Bulletin,* no. 3 (May): 54–61.

Sims, C. 1974. Seasonality in regression. *Journal of the American Statistical Association* 69:618–26.

———. 1986. Are forecasting models usable for policy analysis? *Federal Reserve Bank of Minneapolis Quarterly Review* 10 (winter): 2–16.

Tsang, D. 1995. Looking downwards from Olympus (in Chinese). *Ming Pao,* 23 October.

Walters, A. A., and S. Hanke. 1992. Currency boards. In *The new Palgrave dictionary of money and finance,* ed. P. Newman, M. Milgate, and J. Eatwell. London: Macmillan.

Watson, M. 1994. Vector autoregression and cointegration. In *Handbook of econometrics,* vol. 4, ed. R. F. Engle and D. L. McFadden. Amsterdam: Elsevier.

Williamson, J. 1995. *What role for currency boards?* Washington, D.C.: Institute for International Economics.

Comment   Barry Eichengreen

Currency boards are at one end of the spectrum between monetary policy credibility and monetary policy flexibility. They maximize the commitment to stable policy at the expense of all ability to tailor monetary conditions to macroeconomic and financial circumstances. Governments that attach a high shadow price to credibility are attracted to this option. For example, at the beginning of the 1990s, Argentine policymakers, burdened by their country's succession of failed battles with inflation and prepared to take drastic steps to establish their anti-inflationary credibility, resorted to a currency board. Estonia, Lithuania, and eventually Bulgaria were attracted to the arrangement by the special monetary difficulties of the transition to the market and, in the first two cases, of proximity to an unstable Russia.

Whether their examples should be emulated by other countries is a contested issue. Although currency boards were advocated for Russia following the dissolution of the Soviet Union and for Mexico following its financial meltdown in 1995, in both cases there was also resistance to the proposal, and policymakers ultimately shunned the arrangement on the grounds that they could not afford the sacrifice of policy flexibility it entailed.[1]

Unfortunately, systematic empirical analysis of these issues is difficult. While all countries are special, the circumstances of those that have opted for currency boards tend to be so unusual as to render hazardous all attempts at generalization. Most modern currency boards are so recent or short-lived that there exist only a very few years of time-series data on their operation, affording little opportunity for systematic econometric work.

Here is where the case of Hong Kong's currency board comes in. Hong

Barry Eichengreen is the John L. Simpson Professor of Economics and Political Science at the University of California, Berkeley, and a research associate of the National Bureau of Economic Research.

1. Prominent advocates of currency boards in these contexts are Hanke, Jonung, and Schuler (1993).

Kong operated a currency board vis-à-vis sterling from 1935 through the early 1970s, at which point the instability of sterling led it to sever that link. It then floated until 1983, when the turbulence associated with negotiations with China over the colony's future led to a confidence crisis, to which the government responded by reestablishing the currency board, this time with a peg to the U.S. dollar. Thus the last two decades divide into a pair of 10-year periods, one of floating and one featuring a currency board, over which the comparative performance of alternative monetary arrangements can be analyzed and compared.[2]

A logical starting point is to compare price, output, and interest rate behavior under the two regimes. But because global economic conditions also differ across periods, and a small, dependent economy like Hong Kong is especially sensitive to the external environment, such comparisons tell us little about the performance of Hong Kong's monetary arrangements narrowly defined. To address this problem, Kwan and Lui utilize a variant of the structural vector autoregression methodology of Blanchard and Quah, distinguishing macroeconomic disturbances, which they attribute to the global environment, from subsequent adjustments, which they interpret in terms of the structure of the Hong Kong economy.

The disturbances identified by their structural VAR approach are intuitively plausible and readily interpretable in terms of historical events. For example, there is a large permanent shock (a "negative supply disturbance") around the time of OPEC II. The 1983 crisis provoked by the negotiations with China shows up as a negative shock with both temporary and permanent components. The "tequila effect" in early 1995 shows up as a negative temporary shock. The presumption that temporary shocks should raise prices while permanent shocks should reduce them is not imposed in estimation but is supported by the results, consistent with the authors' interpretation of permanent and temporary disturbances in terms of aggregate supply and aggregate demand shocks, respectively.[3]

Still, one can question whether these estimates are in fact useful for distinguishing the effects of global economic shocks from the operation of Hong Kong's monetary regime. Domestic policy, and not just the external environment, is a source of shocks; and prominent among the potential sources of

2. Admittedly, Hong Kong's experience is special as well. Its currency board is permitted to engage in open market operations, and since 1992 a sort of discount window has been opened to provide liquidity to the banks. Neither feature is typical of currency boards. Moreover, Hong Kong's Exchange Fund holds massive excess foreign currency reserves, including the cumulated fiscal surpluses of the government. (A third of the Exchange Fund's foreign assets come from this source.) Together, these facts blunt the trade-off that typically exists between a currency board arrangement and lender-of-last-resort operations. I would have liked to see the authors discuss how distinctive they consider Hong Kong's currency board arrangements, and how far they think the lessons of its experience can be generalized.

3. Note that this restriction is not imposed in estimation. It is a feature of the Bayoumi and Eichengreen (1993) implementation of the structural VAR approach, but not of the original Blanchard-Quah formulation, specified in terms of output and unemployment.

domestic disturbances is monetary policy, especially in the 1973–82 period when the Hong Kong dollar was floating. For this reason the attribution of shocks to external factors and responses to internal factors is unlikely to be strictly correct.[4]

Other authors have attempted to distinguish demand shocks of internal and external origin by estimating larger dimension systems identified by the imposition of additional long-run restrictions (see, e.g., Erkel-Rousse and Melitz 1995). The identifying restrictions required to render this exercise feasible are somewhat arbitrary, and cautious econometricians may be reluctant to impose them. Nonetheless, it is difficult to pass judgment on the operation of Hong Kong's currency board in the absence of such an analysis.

The authors interpret their impulse response functions in terms of the Mundell-Fleming model. This is a peculiar choice, since Mundell considered the behavior of output and interest rates, taking prices as fixed, while the authors' empirical analysis focuses on output and prices without considering interest rates. It would be more straightforward and informative to describe the results in terms of the textbook aggregate-supply–aggregate-demand model—that is, in terms of output and prices themselves. From this perspective, the authors' findings make intuitive sense. They suggest that supply shocks have had a smaller impact effect on prices and a larger impact effect on output in the currency board years. This of course is just what one would expect: shifts in the aggregate supply curve trace out the slope of the aggregate demand curve, and under fixed rates the latter will be very flat in price-output space, domestic prices being tied to foreign prices. Demand shocks, on the other hand, have larger short-run output effects in the currency board years than under a floating system. Since shifts in the aggregate demand curve trace out the short-run aggregate supply curve, the results suggest that the latter has become flatter over time, reflecting the growth of nominal rigidities.[5] This interpretation is consistent with recent commentary bemoaning the declining flexibility of Hong Kong's labor market.

An implication is that Hong Kong's decision to eliminate exchange rate

---

4. In fact, the authors are not entirely consistent in their attribution of shocks to the external environment and responses to policy. At one point they note that supply shocks are less prevalent in the currency board years and identify this as one of the advantages of a currency board. It is peculiar to identify supply shocks with government policy, however, especially insofar as they emanate from the monetary sector, in which case their effects should only be temporary. What they are likely to be picking up, obviously, is the effect of the two OPEC oil shocks and the commodity price boom of 1974–75—a more turbulent global economic environment prior to the reestablishment of the currency board, in other words.

5. Interestingly, this is precisely what Tam Bayoumi and I (Bayoumi and Eichengreen 1996) found on the supply side when estimating the same model using annual data for the industrial countries spanning the past hundred years: short-run aggregate curves grow flatter over time, as if nominal rigidities grow more important. But we also found that aggregate demand curves grew steeper, as more and more countries moved in the direction of greater exchange rate flexibility to facilitate the use of demand management policies to offset the effects of supply disturbances, which increasingly affect output as the short-run aggregate supply curve grows flatter.

flexibility (in terms of the U.S. dollar) may have had significant costs in terms of the sacrifice of monetary autonomy. As disturbances have come to increasingly affect output rather than prices, the government has acquired a growing incentive to use monetary policy to offset the effects of shocks, something for which greater exchange rate flexibility is required. Indeed, many other countries have moved in the direction of greater flexibility, as predicted.[6] Meanwhile, Hong Kong has moved the opposite way, with the government tying its hands precisely as the value of policy flexibility has grown. The implication is that Hong Kong has paid a price for its monetary policy credibility.

Next, Kwan and Lui challenge the view that Hong Kong's currency board is immune from attack because international reserves are five times the monetary base. As the authors note, although reserves are five times the base, M3 is five times reserves. (Here is one indication of Hong Kong's importance as a financial center: bank deposits are 25 times as large as currency in circulation!) It is entirely possible for a shift out of bank deposits, or even a relatively modest shift from HK dollar to U.S. dollar deposits, to deplete the Exchange Fund of reserves and cause the collapse of the currency peg.

Whether investors have an incentive to run on the Exchange Fund's reserves by shifting out of domestic currency deposits in favor of U.S. dollar deposits depends on the monetary policy they expect to be pursued in the aftermath of the event. If they think that policy will be more inflationary than before, they have an incentive to attack. This could be the case if they anticipate that the Chinese government will under certain circumstances compel the Hong Kong authorities to run more expansionary policies now that the colony has been returned to their jurisdiction. It could happen if an attack itself heightens the suspicions of the Chinese authorities about the advisability of the currency board arrangement and leads them to plump for a more expansionary policy.[7]

Thus only if the authorities can credibly commit to continuing to run the same monetary policies as the United States will Hong Kong's currency board be immune from attack. Given the questions that inevitably surround Beijing's policies toward Hong Kong, this is anything but certain. Just as Argentina's currency board was no guarantee of exchange rate and monetary stability when the tequila effect was felt in early 1995 (and the dilemma of having to chose between the stability of the exchange rate and the stability of the banking system was obviated only by the injection of $8 billion of assistance from the IMF), the existence of a currency board will be no guarantee of monetary stability.

All of the above was written in mid-1996 as a comment on the authors' conference draft and, in fairness to Kwan and Lui, left largely unchanged. But a commentator reading page proofs two years later cannot resist adding a few

---

6. As late as 1984 only a quarter of International Monetary Fund (IMF) member countries had gone over to floating rates. But by the end of 1994 the proportion operating systems of managed and independent floating rates had risen to more than 50 percent.

7. This last-mentioned situation is modeled by Obstfeld (1986).

thoughts suggested by the Asian economic and financial crisis. For one thing, those events have considerably accelerated the transition to greater exchange rate flexibility in the region, a transition that, I argued above, is an inevitable consequence of the multilateralization of trade and the rise in international capital mobility. For another, events in Asia have fanned the controversy over the merits of currency boards. In particular, academics and policymakers are deeply split over the advisability of a currency board for a country like Indonesia in the throes of an economic, financial, and political crisis. My own reading of the debate is that a currency board is appropriate only under the most exceptional economic and financial circumstances, as emphasized above, but also only when there exists broad-based political support for moving to one extreme on the trade-off between policy credibility and policy flexibility. Indonesia is not such a case. On the other hand, Hong Kong, where a return to managed money would raise uncomfortable questions about who is ultimately responsible for the management, qualifies on all these grounds. Finally, the events of 1997–98, which included a series of increasingly fierce attacks against the HK dollar by hedge funds and others, confirm that a currency board is no guarantee of insulation against speculative attacks.

References

Bayoumi, Tamim, and Barry Eichengreen. 1993. Shocking aspects of European monetary unification. In *Adjustment and growth in the European Monetary Union,* ed. Francisco Torres and Francesco Giavazzi, 193–240. Cambridge: Cambridge University Press.
———. 1996. The stability of the gold standard and the evolution of the international monetary system. In *Modern perspectives on the classical gold standard,* ed. Tamim Bayoumi, Mark Taylor, and Barry Eichengreen, 165–88. Cambridge: Cambridge University Press.
Erkel-Rousse, H., and J. Melitz. 1995. New empirical evidence on the costs of European monetary union. INSEE Working Paper no. 9516. Paris: Institut National de la Statistique et des Études Économiques.
Hanke, Steve H., Lars Jonung, and Kurt Schuler. 1993. *Russian currency and finance: A currency board approach to reform.* London: Routledge.
Obstfeld, Maurice. 1986. Rational and self-fulfilling balance-of-payments crises. *American Economic Review* 76:72–81.

Comment   Zhaoyong Zhang

It is a great pleasure for me to read and comment on Kwan and Lui's paper on Hong Kong's currency board and changing monetary regimes. In this paper,

Zhaoyong Zhang is a lecturer in the Department of Economics and Statistics at the National University of Singapore.

the authors attempt to assess the viability of adopting currency boards as the monetary institution by analyzing the macroeconomic implications of a currency board regime using Hong Kong data. They show that a currency board is less responsive to supply shocks but more to demand shocks than a floating rate system. The viability of the current exchange rate regime in Hong Kong relies on a stable fiscal policy.

It has widely been recognized that exchange rate policy plays a key role in determining economic performance in developing countries. While in principle exchange rates could be left to be determined by free market forces based on fundamentals, this has hardly been seen in the less developed economies in the past few decades. Most developing countries, especially the small and medium-sized countries, made a return in the 1980s to fixed exchange rates after the abandonment of the Bretton Woods system in the 1970s as a cornerstone of their monetary disinflation programs. This has raised some interesting issues concerning the selection of exchange rate regime. Kwan and Lui's paper thus draws a useful lesson from a study of Hong Kong's experience, enhancing our understanding of currency boards and the selection of exchange rate regime.

In less than half a century, the exchange rate regime in Hong Kong has evolved from the silver standard (since the last century till 1935), to a currency board with sterling being the reserve currency (1935–73), then to a floating system (1974–83), and finally back to a currency board with a U.S. dollar link since 1983. An interesting question associated with the evolution of the exchange rate regime will be how long the current system can last. In other words, what will be the future exchange rate regime in Hong Kong? Kwan and Lui have conducted some simulation exercises and conclude that a stable fiscal policy is the key to preventing the current exchange rate system from experiencing a crisis. Hong Kong's success in sustaining a pegged rate under a currency board arrangement depends on its specific conditions: it is small, open, and well integrated with the world economy, with a high degree of wage-price flexibility in which nominal magnitudes can adjust readily to exogenous shocks. But one has to recognize that a policy regime appropriate for ending high inflation may well be inappropriate for long-run economic management (see Sachs 1996). Examples are the 1992–93 European Exchange Rate Mechanism (ERM) crises and the 1994 Mexican peso crisis. Moreover, the effect of Hong Kong's return to China after 1997 on the credibility of the current system and on the confidence of people in Hong Kong's future prosperity cannot be undervalued.

The experience of some transition economies in Eastern Europe indicates that a pegged exchange rate is much more efficient at stabilizing the economy than a floating rate. Estonia stabilized with a pegged exchange rate under a currency board arrangement, while Latvia initially relied on a floating exchange rate. As a matter of fact, both countries succeeded in ending high inflation, but Latvia experienced a much deeper, longer recession, suffering from excessively high real interest rates and less confidence in the stability of the currency (Sachs 1996). Offsetting this observation, the simulation results from Kwan and Lui show that output growth under a currency board system is lower than under floating rates. Returning to the transition economies, it has been observed that in Estonia GDP in 1993, 1994, and 1995 grew −7, 6, and 6 percent, respectively, while Latvia's GDP growth rates for the same years were −15, 2, and 1 percent (see Sachs 1996). In fact, it is difficult from figures 15.4 and 15.5 in Kwan and Lui's paper to infer whether one exchange rate regime is superior to the other.

It seems that the eventual abolition of the first currency board system in the early 1970s was mainly caused by exogenous shocks such as the devaluation of sterling and the U.S. dollar, a large inflow of foreign capital to Hong Kong, and so on. This raises a question concerning the "permanency" of the current currency board system. If similar shocks happen again, could the current exchange rate regime be sustained even given the conditions described by Kwan and Lui? This issue deserves discussion in addition to the study of the viability of the regime.

Other concerns are related to generalizing the experience of Hong Kong in adopting the currency board system, drawing lessons and policy implications for countries adopting the currency board system, examining critically under what circumstances a "permanent" pegged rate is appropriate, and so on.

References

Frankel, Jeffrey A. 1995. Monetary regime choices for a semi-open country. In *Capital controls, exchange rates and monetary policy in the world economy*, ed. S. Edwards. New York: Cambridge University Press.

Sachs, Jeffrey. 1996. Economic transition and the exchange-rate regime. *American Economic Review* 86 (2): 147–52.

Contributors

Stanley W. Black
Department of Economics
Gardner Hall CB #3305
University of North Carolina
Chapel Hill, NC 27599

Baekin Cha
Korea Institute of Finance
6th floor, KFB Building
4-1, 1-Ga, Myong-Dong, Chung-Gu
Seoul 100-021
Korea

Leonard Cheng
Hong Kong University of Science and
    Technology
Department of Economics
School of Business and Management
Clear Water Bay, Kowloon
Hong Kong

Dongchul Cho
Korea Development Institute
POB 113
Chongnyang, Seoul
Korea

Sebastian Edwards
Anderson Graduate School of Business
University of California, Los Angeles
110 Westwood Plaza
Los Angeles, CA 90095

Barry Eichengreen
Department of Economics
549 Evans Hall #3880
University of California, Berkeley
Berkeley, CA 94720

K. C. Fung
Department of Economics
Social Sciences 1
University of California, Santa Cruz
Santa Cruz, CA 95064

Koichi Hamada
Economic Growth Center
Yale University
27 Hillhouse Avenue
New Haven, CT 06520

Ponciano Intal, Jr.
Philippine Institute for Development
    Studies
NEDA sa Makati Building
106 Amorsolo Street
Legaspi Village, Makati City
Philippines

Peter Isard
International Monetary Fund
700 19th Street NW
Washington, DC 20431

Takatoshi Ito
Institute of Economic Research
Hitotsubashi University
Naka 2-1, Kunitachi
Tokyo 186-8603
Japan

Y. C. Jao
University of Hong Kong
School of Economics and Finance
Pokfulum Road
Hong Kong

Se-jong Kim
440 Sutack-dong, Kurij
Kyonggi
Korea

Youngsun Koh
Korea Development Institute
POB 113
Chongnyang, Seoul
Korea

Takafumi Korenaga
Department of Economics
Hitotsubashi University
2-1, Naka, Kunitachi-shi
Tokyo 186-0004
Japan

Anne O. Krueger
Department of Economics
Stanford University
Stanford, CA 94305

Yum K. Kwan
Department of Economics and Finance
City University of Hong Kong
Tat Chee Avenue, Kowloon
Hong Kong

Kenneth S. Lin
National Taiwan University
Department of Economics
21, Hsu-Chou Road
Taipei 10020
Taiwan

Francis T. Lui
Center for Economic Development
Hong Kong University of Science and
  Technology
Clear Water Bay, Kowloon
Hong Kong

Ronald I. McKinnon
Department of Economics
Landau Economics Bldg.
Stanford University
Stanford, CA 94305

Gian Maria Milesi-Ferretti
Research Department
International Monetary Fund
Room IS 12-1266
700 19th Street NW
Washington, DC 20431

Chong-Hyun Nam
Department of Economics
Korea University
1, 5-Ga, Anam-dong, Sungbuk-ku
Seoul, 136-701
Korea

Sang-Woo Nam
P.O. Box 184, Chongnyang
207-43 Chongnyangri-dong
Dongdaemun-gu
Seoul 130-012
Korea

Kenichi Ohno
National Graduate Institute for Policy
  Studies
Saitama University
Urawa, Saitama 338
Japan

Tetsuji Okazaki
Faculty of Economics
University of Tokyo
7-3-1 Hongo
Bunkyo-Ku, Tokyo 113
Japan

Assaf Razin
Department of Economics
Littauer Center, Room 109
Harvard University
Cambridge, MA 02138

Andrew K. Rose
Haas School of Business Administration
University of California, Berkeley
Berkeley, CA 94720

Jeffrey D. Sachs
Harvard Institute for International
    Development
One Eliot Street
Cambridge, MA 02138

Kazuko Shirono
Graduate School of Economics
University of Tokyo
Bunkyoku, Tokyo 113
Japan

Yun-Wing Sung
Department of Economics
Chinese University of Hong Kong
Shatin
Hong Kong

Steven Symansky
Department of Fiscal Affairs
International Monetary Fund
IS 3-800
700 19th Street NW
Washington, DC 20431

Shinji Takagi
Faculty of Economics
Osaka University
1-7 Machikaneyama Toyonaka
Osaka 560
Japan

Kazuo Ueda
Member of the Policy Board
Bank of Japan
C.P.O. Box 203
Tokyo 100-8630
Japan

Kuo-Liang Wang
Department of Economics
National Cheng-Chi University
Mucha, Taipei, Taiwan
Republic of China

Chung-Shu Wu
Institute of Economics
Academia Sinica
Nankang, Taipei, Taiwan
Republic of China

Hsiu-Ling Wu
Chung-Hua Institution for Economic
    Research
No. 75 Chang-Hsing Street
Taipei, Taiwan, 106
Republic of China

Chi-Wa Yuen
School of Economics and Finance
University of Hong Kong
Pokfulam Road
Hong Kong

Zhaoyong Zhang
Department of Economics and Statistics
National University of Singapore
10 Kent Ridge Crescent
Singapore 119260

Author Index

Subject Index